BREAKING GROUND

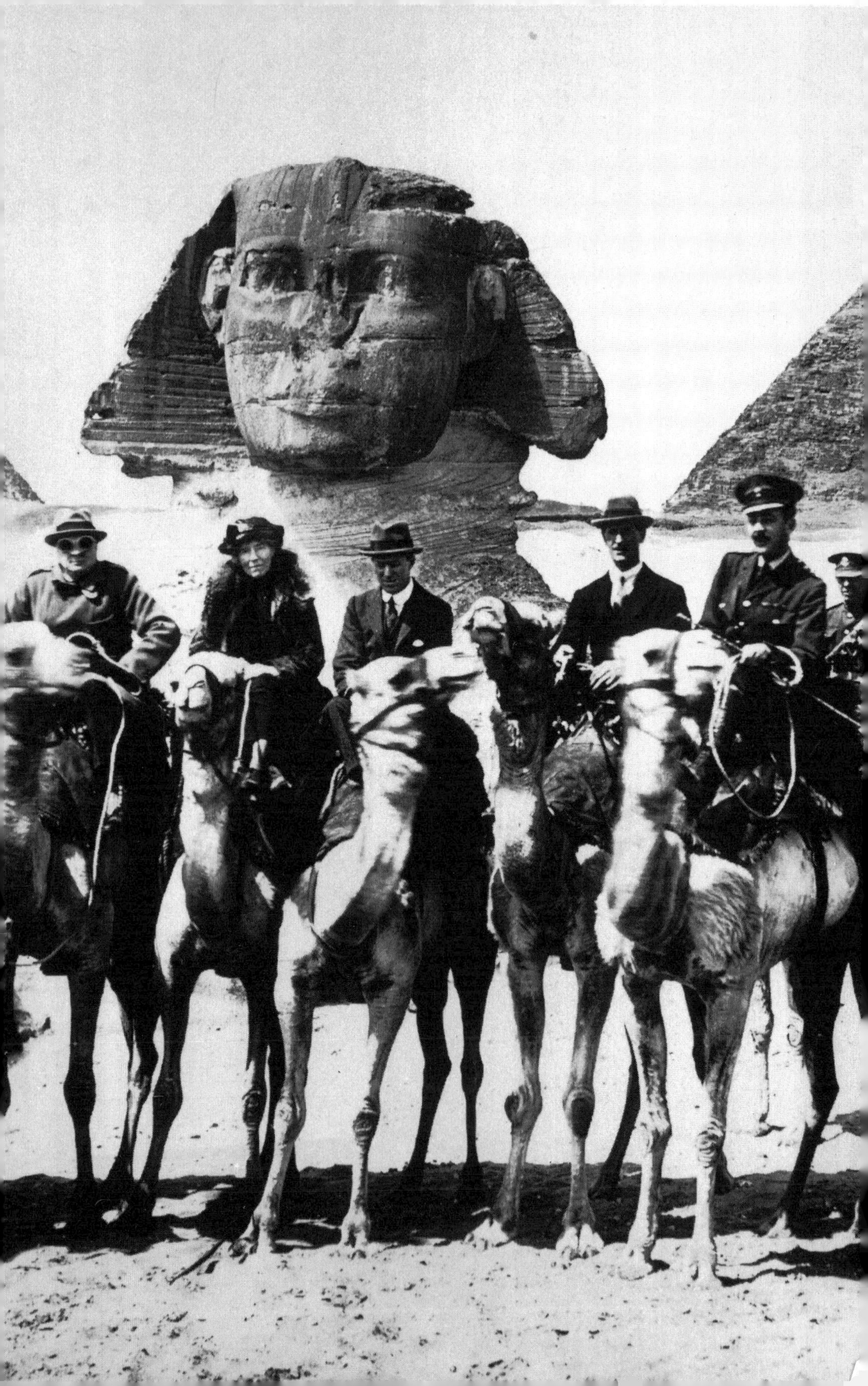

BREAKING GROUND

Pioneering Women Archaeologists

Getzel M. Cohen and
Martha Sharp Joukowsky,
Editors

THE UNIVERSITY OF MICHIGAN PRESS
Ann Arbor

In Memoriam
Elizabeth Gwyn Caskey

First paperback edition 2006

Published in the United States of America by
The University of Michigan Press
Manufactured in the United States of America
⊗ Printed on acid-free paper

2009 2008 2007 2006 6 5 4 3

A CIP catalog record for this book is available from the British Library.

Library of Congress Cataloging-in-Publication Data

Breaking ground : pioneering women archaeologists / Getzel M. Cohen and Martha Sharp Joukowsky, editors.
p. cm.
Includes bibliographical references and index.
ISBN 0-472-11372-0 (alk. paper)
1. Women archaeologists—Biography. I. Cohen, Getzel M. II. Joukowsky, Martha.
CC110.B74 2004
930.1'092'2—dc22 2003023590

ISBN 0-472-03174-0 (pbk. : alk. paper)
ISBN 978-0-472-03174-0 (pbk. : alk. paper)
ISBN 978-0-472-11372-9 (cloth)
ISBN 978-0-472-02536-7 (electronic)

Preface

THE MODERN SCIENCE OF ARCHAEOLOGY did not originate as a science. In the eighteenth and early nineteenth centuries archaeology was essentially treasure hunting.[1] Wealthy Europeans or their agents went out to Mediterranean lands and the Middle East in order to collect museum pieces and send them back home. Others made voyages of exploration to find biblical sites and in the process often collected artifacts as well. Among these travelers to the Middle East, incidentally, were a number of extraordinary women who may be seen as important predecessors of the first generation of pioneer women archaeologists. Generally, these European travelers—male and female—had no real interest in systematic excavation. Their objective was either exploration or the acquisition of antiquities.

One may see examples of this European desire for antiquities throughout the Mediterranean and the Middle East. Thus, in 1784 the Comte de Choiseul-Gouffier wrote to L. F. S. Fauvel, his agent in Athens, "Take everything you can. Do not neglect any opportunity for looting all that is lootable in Athens and the environs. Spare neither the living nor the dead."[2] Seventeen years later, in 1801, the Turkish government gave Lord Elgin permission to remove the sculptures from the Athenian acropolis and ship them to England. Napoleon's expedition to Egypt 1798 "marked the beginning of a process of investigation and discovery in which the military authorities, scholars and art thieves of Europe would combine in unholy alliance to uncover the evidence of past civilizations."[3]

Farther east, in the first two decades of the nineteenth century, Claudius James Rich, an agent of the East India Company in Baghdad, visited sites in

Mesopotamia and wrote about them. He also collected antiquities that were subsequently sold to the British Museum. His activity was sufficiently well known to attract the attention of Lord Byron, who wrote in *Don Juan,*

> Claudius Rich, Esquire, some bricks has got
> And written lately two memoirs upon't.

In Egypt, according to Kent Weeks,

> Egyptologists, most of them philologists by training, considered archaeological data merely footnotes to the story told by the written word. Archaeology's goal, it was argued, should simply be to find more texts. Archaeological context was ignored, and objects were saved only if they were deserving of display in the museums. Excavators felt perfectly justified in plowing through sites . . . saving only inscribed objects and pieces of aesthetic appeal and tossing the rest into the Nile. It was an exciting time: excavators plundered tombs, dynamited tombs, committed piracy and shot their competitors in order to assemble great collections.[4]

In the second half of the nineteenth century this "exciting time" gave way to more sedate pursuits! Archaeology began to change from the search for treasure to the systematic excavation and study of ancient sites and of the objects, both big and small, found there. Thus, in 1860 Giuseppe Fiorelli took over the excavation at Pompeii and began to record the results of his digging. In the last quarter of the nineteenth century Heinrich Schliemann (for all his brutal excavation techniques) and Wilhelm Dörpfeld kept accurate records of their fieldwork at Troy, recorded debris layers and published timely and scholarly reports of their work. In Egypt and then in Palestine W. M. Flinders-Petrie was one of the first archaeologists to dig carefully, record his results, and provide contextual analysis. Among other things, he also developed techniques for the sequential dating of pottery.

Modern, systematic archaeology began its existence as a new discipline, usually subordinated to another field. Classical archaeology, for example, was subordinate to philology within the field of classical studies. Egyptian archaeology had to emerge from under the wing of philologically oriented Egyptologists. And Near Eastern archaeology owed much of its rise to the European fascination with the Bible.

Of course, as a new discipline, not yet fully integrated into university curricula and conducted far off from university campuses, archaeology offered women unique professional opportunities. Some of the pioneering women archaeologists did not have university appointments; many had (some) independent means. But the same can be said, incidentally, of male archaeologists of this time. Schliemann and Arthur Evans, for example, were both quite wealthy. And Schliemann did not have a regular university position.

In her introduction Margaret Root distinguishes two generations of early female archaeologists: those born from around the middle of the nineteenth century to about 1890 and those born between 1890 and 1940. This distinction is a useful one because, among other things, it calls attention to the fact that the earliest women archaeologists were becoming active in the field just when modern archaeology—as we know it—was beginning to emerge. As Root's introduction and the various biographies make clear, archaeology opened up new opportunities but also presented new challenges for women. Thus, the first woman archaeologist (chronologically) in this book, Jane Dieulafoy, excavated the palace of Xerxes at Susa with her husband Marcel in 1884–86. This was, in fact, the first great European archaeological expedition at Susa. And Esther Van Deman, working in Italy in the first part of the twentieth century, became a pioneer in the field of Roman construction techniques by focusing on objects as small as bricks. She was also one of the first archaeologists to exploit the potential of photography.

This, very briefly, is the background to the growth and development of archaeology in the late nineteenth and twentieth centuries. It is also the background to the exploits and accomplishments of the women whose lives are profiled in this book. Their lives may serve as models both for those interested in gender studies and for the history of archaeology; in fact, they were pioneers both as women and as archaeologists.

Breaking Ground presents twelve fascinating women whose contributions to the development and progress of Old World archaeology—in an area ranging from Italy to Mesopotamia—have been immeasurable. Our purpose is to examine the lives of these pioneer archaeologists in the early days of the discipline, tracing their path from education in the classics to travel and exploration and ultimately international recognition in the field. In this volume the reader will share in the adventures of these women pioneers. It is our hope that the courage, individualism, and professional achievement of each of them will encourage a broader appreciation of their legacy to archaeology.

The range of the contributors adds significantly to the breadth of the work. In some cases the bond between biographer and subject is close, the biographer having studied or worked with the archaeologist. The writer is therefore able to bring firsthand recollections to the biography. In other cases, the biographers are familiar with the body of work of the subject, but do not have firsthand knowledge. These biographers did extensive research, using primary sources such as archival materials and field notebooks. In one case the biographer is the granddaughter of her subject and herself an archaeologist, bringing to her essay an intriguing blend of family stories and professional scholarship.

We are honored that the authors accepted our invitation to write their respective biographies. Publishing the lives of these outstanding women assures that their voices will continue to be heard. These essays ask as many questions as they answer. To each of these pioneer's achievements there are caveats, but we suspect that a long list of successors will wonder with respect and admiration how these women did it at all. The success of the volume is due to the authors who entered fully into the spirit of the research, generously sharing ideas and information about their subjects.

It is a pleasure to acknowledge the contribution of Margaret Cool Root. In her introductory essay, Professor Root places these archaeologists in a larger historical and social context. Sheila Cohen showed rare dedication in editing these manuscripts; we are most grateful, too, to Susan Heuck Allen, Julia Asher-Greve, William Dever, Michelle Hobart, Mary Hollinshead, Barbara Lesko, and Peg Lourie for their assistance. We are also happy to acknowledge the Joukowsky Family Foundation, the Cotsen Family Foundation, and the Louise Taft Semple Fund for their generous financial support. Additional pioneering women biographies can be found at http://www.brown.edu/Research/Breaking_Ground/

NOTES

1. In general see I. Morris, ed., *Classical Greece: Ancient Histories and Modern Archaeologies* (Cambridge, 1994), 8–47; B. M. Fagan, ed., *Oxford Companion to Archaeology* (Oxford, 1996), s.v. "History of Archaeology"; E. M. Meyers, ed., *Oxford Encyclopedia of Archaeology in the Near East* (Oxford, 1997), s.v. "History of the Field"; and the extensive literature cited in each of these.

2. Qtd. in W. St. Clair, *That Greece Might Still Be Free* (Oxford, 1972), 58; see also C. P. Bracken, *Antiquities Acquired* (Newton Abbot, 1975), 17; R. Eisner, *Travelers to an Antique Land* (Ann Arbor, 1991), 80–81; Morris, *Classical Greece,* 24.

3. H. V. F. Winstone, *Uncovering the Ancient World* (New York, 1986), 25.

4. *Oxford Encyclopedia of Archaeology in the Near East,* s.v. "History of the Field: Archaeology in Egypt."

Contents

Contents

Introduction

WOMEN OF THE FIELD, DEFINING THE GENDERED EXPERIENCE

Margaret Cool Root

Who Are These Women?

THE BIOGRAPHIES ASSEMBLED HERE characterize aspects of the professional and personal lives of selected women archaeologists of the pioneering era, primarily though not exclusively women from Great Britain, Canada, and the United States. Their dates of birth range from the middle of the nineteenth century to the early years of the twentieth century. In my introductory comments I shall approach these lives as representing two overlapping conceptual generations: the first encompassing people born from around the middle of the nineteenth century to about 1890; the second encompassing those born between about 1890 and 1910.

The first-generation female pioneers of scientific archaeology emerge out of the depths of Victorian ideologies about the subordinate position of women. It will be essential to understand them collectively as women within the restrictive framework of a very specific social setting. Beyond that, each of these remarkable women was, of course, a distinct individual who must ultimately be understood on her own terms as an intellect and as a human being.

The second generation (born between about 1890 and 1910) frames people who saw their twenty-first birthdays before World War I (and the ensuing social and political shifts) as well as those who did not turn twenty-one until the Great Depression. This latter profound event had, in its own way, radically altered the lives of the upper- and middle-class families who were the breeders of women archaeologists at this time. Yet the cumulative cohort of this second (and two-part) generation has a certain symbolic cohesiveness of paradox. Women born around 1890 reached their twenty-first birthdays when women's suffrage was still in the future. Those born in 1910 or a few years earlier reached maturity in an era during which suffrage was a nascent but still bitterly contested reality. In both cases, the young and aggressively patriarchal academic establishments into which these women now had to fit were perhaps more hostile in some ways to the success of women in archaeology than was the Victorian milieu of the first generation (in which archaeology itself still lay outside the bounds and conformities of conventional academe).

The group of biographies published here does not pretend to be exhaustive. It focuses on a representative set of exemplary women who were great pioneers particularly of field archaeology. Fairly, I think it can be said, that despite inevitable selectivity, this volume contains a richly informative cross-section of those women who worked in Old World archaeology during its pioneer phase.

The project does, by design, lean heavily on the notion of archaeology as site survey and excavation, but it also embraces some figures whose primary scholarly contribution came in interpreting the material record once revealed through excavation. Others included here mainly contributed to the sphere of education in archaeology rather than to pathbreaking discoveries and publications. In gathering together a diverse range of lives representing various types of impact in the field, this project happily avoids the pitfall of many great-man biographies. All too often the great-man biographical narrative lionizes a small number of individuals at the expense of a much larger contextualizing experience, intellectual and political history, and supporting cast of characters.

The Agenda

The biographies presented here are not written according to any particular mandate of gender politics. *Breaking Ground* is not an explicitly feminist project in which the contributing biographers were identified according to their qualifications as feminist or gender theorists. Depending upon the types of sources available, the idiosyncratic pattern of the life of the given subject, and the particular mind-set of each author, the biographies vary in amount of personal detail, in interpretive text and subtext, and so on. Over all, the book has a documentary spirit, with the authorial voices emerging out of the substantive arenas of the field itself. That having been said, I hasten to suggest, however, that an interpretive biography of any female—even of the present day—must be political in the expansive sense of the term (viewing a life captured within spheres of competing social framings of power, collective social memory, and individual ambition). In particular, it seems quite simply impossible to contemplate the notion of an interpretive biography of a Victorian woman that is not political in that expansive sense. The very fact that a collection of biographies specifically of the pioneer women of the field has remained so emphatically not done until now, despite the great interest in biographical and historical accounts of archaeology in general over the last several decades, is itself a reflection of a social-political reality. An important book edited by Margarita Díaz-Andreu and Marie Louise Stig Sørensen focuses on the post-pioneer phase. It explores with historiographical acumen the careers of a cohort of women archaeologists only partly overlapping the group discussed here.[1]

As with the selection of biographers for *Breaking Ground,* the invitation to write this introduction came without the stipulation of any predetermined intellectual stance in relation to the project. In keeping with the mainly documentary goal of the endeavor, then, my own aim here is to engage the issues as I see them primarily from a social-historical angle—not in terms of theoretical abstractions about the gendered experience and not as a rostrum from which to polemicize. Neither shall I attempt, however, to pose as a neutral discussant, for this would be specious and would in fact detract from the importance of this volume. Some of the material we are faced with here comes very close to home for me and is deeply disturbing for reasons both historical and personal. One thing hits me with tremendous force. Despite (or could it be because of?) all the best credentials and opportunities in a Bryn Mawr education in archaeology and a coming of age as a feminist and part-time peace activist in the consciousness-raising late 1960s, I was sadly ill-informed about and even indifferent to the personal histories (as women in a man's world) of most of the people chronicled in these volumes. I have no memory of relating historically on any empathetic level to the beleaguered lives of the female pioneers, so laced with painful ambiguities and wrenching subtexts. My privileged academic environment seemed to presuppose institutional professional success for a talented and committed woman. The expectation of success carried with it pronounced, if now unspoken, pressures to do even better than male peers in order to achieve something of a claim to rewards. But still, the expectation was unconditional. It did not seem a matter of option. Many nascent female archaeologists like myself spent a great deal of time on social-political problems and anxieties of the later 1960s and early 1970s (including issues of women's rights) that were mapped out large, bold, and crisis-ridden. Yet perhaps paradoxically there may have been a tendency (at least on my part) to avert introspection from an all too recent legacy of thwarted or muted enterprise directly attributable to the gender politics rampant in institutional archaeology. Perhaps such introspection on this particular issue was too close to home, too threatening in its temporal and personal proximity to an exhilarating activist present that seemed to demand so much fearless forward momentum on so many fronts. It is only now, really, having achieved some critical distance on personal nuances of my own professional history as a woman of the field and as a woman with a certain personal history of my own, that I am seduced to ponder the persisting poignancy of these biographies as well as my generation's link to them.

The introductory remarks that follow attempt to provide some background that will unify features of the varied biographical record, cast certain issues in historical or social-political terms as I see them, and suggest some interpretive avenues opened up by this collection of narratives. I take as my core material, but do not limit myself to, the biographies assembled here.

The Sounds of Silence

Why create an anthology of biographies of women archaeologists of the pioneering era? One answer to this question is simple: Few women archaeologists have until quite recently made it onto the pages of synthetic histories of early archaeology. This tends to be the case even for the very small number of individual women archaeologists who have received book-length biographical treatment. Thus the positioning of these lives within a collective narrative remains by and large still to be accomplished in a systematic, analytical, and serious way. Moreover, as it becomes ever clearer that women's participation was on various levels profoundly significant to the emerging field of scientific archaeology, this project addresses a critical gap in our understanding of the history of the pioneering moments of the modern era of archaeological endeavor broadly speaking. It is not "just" a book about muted women. It is a book about the field as well. That said, this book does attempt to offset the traditional erasure of women's roles in narratives of the field. In order to explain the importance of this task I shall offer observations on a few well-known and influential publications that will, I hope, make the point. My commentary on the problem of erasure is designed to be used interactively with the actual biographies of the specific women archaeologists we have been able to include in our project, since these essays clarify the distinctive contributions of so many scholars about whom little or nothing has been said in synthetic publications.

It has only been very gradually that the feminist movement of the 1960s and 1970s (and the revisions of disciplinary canons in academe that it inspired) has had demonstrable effect in encouraging the active evaluation of women archaeologists in discussions of the field.[2] And not all historians of archaeology have even yet bought into the less patriarchal program energetically. Up through the 1970s, few histories of archaeology or biographical compendiums highlighted any women at all. Many went to some lengths to avoid reference even to the most obviously significant of them. Archaeologists and others reading about the discipline in synthetic overviews before the last couple of decades of the twentieth century have had precious little inducement to ponder the complex role models of women in the field. From the small number of examples analyzed here, we can appreciate the tension in publications of the seventies between those that began to consider any specific women seriously and those that persisted either in total erasure or at best in a trivializing reference.

Dawson and Uphill's 1972 *Who Was Who in Egyptology* aimed to capture all players on the Egyptological scene from 1500 onward who were no longer living when the second edition went to press in 1969.[3] Two distinguished women Egyptologists, Hilda Petrie and Gertrude Caton-Thompson, were not even listed although they fit the date-of-death criterion. John Wilson's 1964 *Signs and Wonders upon Pharaoh* was specifically subtitled *A History of American Egyptology*.[4] What a pity that the American Egyptologist Elizabeth Riefstahl (1889–1986) was not at least mentioned here. Although she had not yet died (and thus technically fell outside Wilson's dead-before-dealt-with parameters for critical assessment), she would have been close to seventy-five when *Signs and Wonders* went to press. She was surely ripe at least for a note of recognition within the small field of *American* Egyptologists! Riefstahl's absence from this good and popular account of American Egyptology was a special pity because she was to live for over twenty more years. In terms of the generational positioning of her accomplishments in the field, she belonged in an account bracketed at mid–twentieth century. Her longevity was, I am convinced, not the real reason she was ignored in *Signs and Wonders*. Had she been a male member of the

Egyptological community, she probably would have fared differently. Although Wilson actually cataloged an extensive international range of Egyptologists in addition to the American ones who were the focus of his book, he (like Dawson and Uphill) also studiously ignored several key British women: Margaret Murray, Gertrude Caton-Thompson (whose biographies we offer in this volume) as well as Hilda Petrie and Grace Crowfoot. Despite the lack of a cataloged biosketch for Caton-Thompson, Wilson did mention her (p. 170). Thus there can be no possibility that he was simply unaware of her work. Rather, he knew about her but chose not to integrate her into his listing of record. By contrast, Michael Hoffman, publishing *Egypt before the Pharaohs* in 1979, extolled Caton-Thompson's enlightened and rigorous field method, giving her long-overdue acknowledgment.[5]

Wilson depended heavily for his biographical catalog in *Signs and Wonders* on the first edition of Dawson and Uphill's *Who Was Who in Egyptology*.[6] We have already seen that Caton-Thompson remained absent even from the greatly expanded and updated *second* edition of that work. Thus we have here a good example of the way one omission in a scholarship that defined canonicity perpetuated future omissions. The result (even if it was not in every case consciously disdainful of women's contributions) was the repeated erasure of women from the scholarly apparatus that formed the core history of the profession available to emerging players up through the academic generation of the 1960s and 1970s.

In his expansive 1975 interpretive survey of the history of archaeology worldwide, Glyn Daniel referred to women of the pioneering and later generations occasionally; but the pattern was spotty.[7] For all its considerable merits in other respects, this book was seriously inadequate in its representation of the significant contributions of women. To start with, Daniel ignored the role of female pilgrims and then early travelers and travel writers in the emergence first of interest in exploration, ethnography, artifact analysis, and excavation and subsequently in the scientific evolution and documentation of these facets of the archaeological enterprise.[8] Only recently has feminist scholarship richly contextualized this important aspect of the backdrop of women's roles in the preacademic history of the field;[9] but basic information on the early women travelers and writers has been common currency for a long time. As Daniel progressed through the chronology, in a book that lay some emphasis upon the social and institutional historiography of the field, he lightly dismissed Amelia Edwards (1831–92). This dynamic traveler and prolific writer was instrumental in the creation of the Egyptian Exploration Fund, in the promotion of fieldwork in Egypt, in the support of the brilliant career of Sir Flinders Petrie, and ultimately in the creation of the first professorship in Egyptian archaeology as opposed to language study (held first by Petrie himself).[10] Yet Daniel alluded to her only secondarily, as an appendage to a masculine narrative, simply noting that Petrie "wrote to Miss Edwards, the secretary of the Fund."[11] Happily, Daniel's dismissal of Edwards can be contrasted with Brian Fagan's strong statement of her significance in a book that appeared in the same year:

> Amelia Edwards took up the cudgel on behalf of scientific archaeology in an incredible burst of literary productivity . . . arguing that the only solution to the orgy of destruction that called itself archaeology was systematic recording of monuments and proper scientific excavations. Amelia Edwards was so concerned that she stopped writing fiction altogether and concentrated on Egyptology to the exclusion of all other topics.[12]

The contrast between the approaches of Daniel and Fagan reminds us that the problem has not simply been a reflection of ponderous evolution of a patriarchal discipline's navel gazing. Differing personal perspectives by these male authors have played a part in the contested siting and tone of women's place within the disciplinary narrative. Interestingly, Daniel does not mention Hilda Petrie, Sir Flinders's wife and archaeological collaborator. More surprisingly, he mutes the contribution of the famous Near Eastern archaeological pioneer, Gertrude Bell (about whom there will be more to say later). She is not even indexed. Despite this remarkable oversight, she is in fact mentioned once in the text.[13] The reference, however, is limited to a passing comment on her role in the creation of the Iraq Antiquities Department and the Iraq Museum. She is not considered as an early archaeologist at all. Compare the more generous appraisals by Seton Lloyd and Max Mallowan.[14] One might argue that the more focused Near Eastern subject matter and professional investment of Lloyd and Mallowan would have made it well-nigh impossible for either of these authors to ignore Bell's archaeological projects completely. Yet the pattern of erasure of women in Egyptology publications suggests an ever-present potential for silencing even in field-specific works and even of the high-profile women.[15]

Glyn Daniel's record of citing—much less problematizing—the contributions of the pioneering women archaeologists in the history of the field represents the weak end of the spectrum. Even when he moved up into the fairly recent past, he tended to avoid analytical discussion of key women. In his brief comments on Kathleen Kenyon, Daniel praised her "re-excavation" of Jericho, which "revealed the great importance of this remarkable site."[16] But he neglected this natural opportunity here to say anything (positive or negative) about her controversial field method,[17] even though field method is a topic of great interest to Daniel and one that threads through his entire book.

In sum, the trivializing or total erasure of women's contributions from the pioneering era on into the "scientific" era has occurred in a wide range of publications. The problem is surely symptomatic of the traditional and essentially patriarchal mind-set of our culture—at least as much as it may reflect the particular sexual politics of an individual chronicler. The examples I have used to illustrate the problem, I hope, are powerful precisely because the publications they are drawn from are significant and influential representatives of their genres.

Are There Great Women Archaeologists?

Some readers might protest (at least privately) that few women have tended to be recorded on the pages of the history of greatness in archaeology because few women were great. This is a dicey and to a certain extent circular issue. If the history is written by people representing or at least operating compliantly within a tradition that validates erasure, how will we expect to judge the possibility of greatness? If we do not even hear of the silenced women, how will we ever be in a position to reckon with them?

We are familiar with this basic dilemma in the discourse of new canon formation in literary history and in art history: If the works of women creators (or those of members of ethnic minorities) are not legitimized by inclusion, by anthologizing, they will not be assessed; they will not be contextualized. The same is true for scholarly product. The worst curse is the curse of erasure. Acknowledgment—even in the form of hostile criticism—is vastly preferable. The citation patterns along gender lines in certain arenas of archaeology have been analyzed recently, suggesting that, at least in segments of the discipline where studies have been attempted, the pervasive muting of women's scholarship is only very gradually ceasing.[18]

A major issue we must deal with particularly regarding the pioneer women archaeologists involves the very fact that the pioneer era in the history of archaeology was the Victorian age, with its notorious harnessing of women to a crippling intellectual, sexual, and economic dependency on men. Later in this essay we shall consider in some detail specific implications of this factor for the history of women in the field. For now, suffice to acknowledge that the stage was set for a history based on the heroic great man or "cowboy" model of archaeological visionary and adventurer. The synthetic histories of the field have for the most part been written by these men, and they are for the most part about men, often cast quite explicitly as heroes and adventurers. Women do not have a natural place in these masculine narratives born of the Victorian mind-set.

In this context the characterization of Hilda Petrie by her husband, the great Flinders Petrie, is interesting. This wife-collaborator worked as an archaeologist in the field and as an archaeological illustrator, was largely responsible for the administration of Petrie's campaigns, excavated on her own, and facilitated (probably to a degree we shall never know) the legendarily prolific output of the famous man. Petrie's autobiographical *Seventy Years in Archaeology* is dedicated "To My Wife on whose toil most of my work has depended." In one passage he describes Mrs. Petrie's role with words that might perhaps qualify as effusive in comparison with his offhand and patronizing attitude elsewhere in the same memoirs toward the other people who worked with him:

> This book is not a personal record, except as regards work. I will only say that it was entirely due to my wife that the resources of the British School were raised, to enable work to be carried on by me and our students; much of the facsimile drawing and plans were hers, and latterly the chief management, and paying, of hundreds of workmen.[19]

Decent as this acknowledgment may be—and devoted to his wife as we gather Petrie to have been within the parameters of Victorianism—the subtext here is nonetheless essentially belittling.[20] Hilda Petrie is presented as the dutiful toiler enabling the work of the great man to flourish. Even more blatant examples of the muted female mate in archaeology abound, to be sure.[21] Among others, Kenneth Hudson alludes to these issues of the gendered social history of the archaeological product specifically with reference to Tessa Wheeler, first wife of the famous, charismatic, and notoriously womanizing Sir Mortimer Wheeler.[22] Tessa Wheeler's hard work in the trenches furthering Sir Mortimer's career while he pursued heroic equestrian explorations in the surrounding countryside caused bitter controversy.[23]

The husband-wife story is always complicated. Readings of any specific relationship will vary depending upon access to nuanced information and the perspective adopted toward such information as exists. Margaret Drower has, for instance, a much more positive take than I have on the message of Petrie's autobiography dedication to Hilda as toiler.[24] Whatever the case in this specific situation, a great deal of unacknowledged collaborative and independent work on the archaeological pursuits attributed to the great man was probably often contributed by the wife. This is an important dynamic to consider in any retrospective attempt to understand the significance of a wife and woman of the field.

Heroic narratives of archaeology, of course, have also suppressed the contributions of female coworkers who are not the wives of the male principals. It is poignant, for instance, to see that Flinders Petrie refers in only one line of his *Seventy Years of Archaeology* to the contribution of his protégée, the distinguished archaeologist Margaret Murray: "Miss Murray, my colleague, came to help with the Osireion."[25] The disjuncture between Petrie's casually demeaning allusion to this woman professional and Murray's own memoirs recounting aspects of her position relative to Petrie's commanding fame are evocative. In her autobiography, Murray describes her programmatic activities in Egyptological instruction at University College London.[26] Although Petrie had the glory and the professorship, Murray held the fort administratively and did the hands-on instruction in the discipline. And because Petrie's incessant excavation schedule severely curtailed hers, she was simply unable to dig in Egypt while employed as a teacher at UCL.

To be fair, the heroes of the field sometimes muted the contributions of male collaborators as well. But even here there is a subtext about women's lot. A classic example seems to be the plight of Arthur Mace, a cousin of Flinders Petrie and a largely unacknowledged participant in Howard Carter's discovery and publication of the tomb of Tutankhamun.[27] Notably, Mace, who was at best of marginal interest to Flinders Petrie,[28] himself marginalized Mrs. Petrie in his personal correspondence. He was leery of her bluestocking aura and disparaged her motives as an archaeologist.[29] This suggests that, in the sometimes megalomaniacal egocentric shadow of a giant such as Petrie, lesser male archaeologists might often assert a jealous hostility toward the female members of the team. Thus the pioneer woman in the field could be insidiously disparaged both by the great man leader and by the subordinate male archaeologist wishing to enhance his own stature and self-esteem at her expense.

One final note on Hilda Petrie. She is not indexed in the insightful account of early Egyptology by Brian Fagan, who devotes many pages to Flinders Petrie's seminal role and extraordinary record of publication. In this context, Fagan includes a photo of the Petries with a caption referring to Mrs. Petrie as "his wife (in helmet at left)."[30] There is something particularly sad about this image and its text. For here is Hilda Petrie in full excavation gear that radically rejects British standards of decorum, standing staunchly in the desert. She is a transposed Victorian woman, wife, and mother, but she is also an archaeologist. Yet despite her helmet and dusty trousers (which might be viewed as signs of her own heroic status as an aggressively displaced female in an age of severe social restriction) she has no name and no independent product. This erasure of the woman is most troubling perhaps because it seems at once to mute the woman and also to inscribe uneasy ambiguity upon her representation. Why are we not told her name? Presumably space was a limiting factor. What, then, are we meant to make of the fact that her helmet (rather than her name and archaeological role) is singled out when only a few words had to suffice to explain the presence and identity of this person? Is the reference to the helmet meant obliquely to allude in a positive spirit to her archaeological activities? Or is it intended negatively to suggest an affectation? Or is the reference simply a reflection of the conventionally trivializing tendency our society has to describe women by what they wear rather than who they are?

Fagan's book also raises another issue about the silencing of women. Although not even referring to Hilda Petrie except obliquely, as we have seen, Fagan does index and mention Sarah Belzoni (d. 1870), wife of Giovanni Belzoni, numerous times. He does not actually problematize her activities in relation to Belzoni's archaeological explorations, publications, and exhibitions in the theoretical and historiographical context of the important theme of *The Rape of the Nile.* (Sarah Belzoni was, for instance, the acknowledged author of part of Belzoni's influential *Narratives of the Operations and Recent Discoveries within the Pyramids* [1820].) Yet Fagan does feature her as a figure of some significance. Interesting as Mrs. Belzoni was, she was not an archaeological collaborator of her husband to the massive extent and with the same impact on the evolving nature of modern Egyptological inquiry as was Hilda Petrie. Thus the unevenness of the treatment of these two wives of the field becomes puzzling.

The point here is to address some of the gendered messages embedded in histories of women in the field rather broadly even when written by astute commentators. This comparison between the relative weight given by Fagan to Mrs. Petrie versus Mrs. Belzoni exemplifies the fact that in many influential histories of the field a haphazard quality persists regarding the decision about which women to represent as individuals of any substance and which to ignore. A result of this phenomenon is that we have yet to arrive at a core list (however short) of women who are acknowledged repeatedly and then evaluated as players in the history of the field.

Having, I hope, answered the first-level aspect of the question "Why Women?" I shall proceed now to discuss some of the issues that emerge in the posing of this ostensibly simple question.

Women's Roles

In archaeology, work in the dirt tends to be considered heroic, whereas analysis and interpretation of the actual material record once exhumed tends to be considered humdrum labor—a repetitive domestic chore of academic ordering. As such it has traditionally been assigned to women.

The majority of pioneering women of the field certainly did tend to publish catalogs of finds for the excavations they worked on rather than the sweeping (heroic) characterizations of the sites. Cogent discussions of the sexual politics of the field particularly among feminist archaeologists of prehistory and the New World have examined this important issue in rigorous and compelling fashion.[31] These studies highlight the insidiousness of the multiple factors that have predetermined (even into the present) many women's activities in the profession. I am in full sympathy with the argumentation and thrust of this discourse except in one sense: the sense in which the active ingredient in the dialectic may seem to disparage as kitchen-work the artifactual analysis typically assigned to women rather than to disparage the system that has severely limited the options for and ranges of legitimacy of women in the field. Heroic stature in archaeology does not have to be defined by the patriarchal standard of the hero or cowboy model. To suggest (without careful modulation) that it is only through unfettered access to a capacity to conform to this patriarchal standard that one can achieve due recognition in archaeology is to play unintentionally into the hands of a mind-set that perpetuates the erasure of the legacy of the pioneer women. Let me try to explain what I mean here.

It is true that women were (and frequently still are) most often assigned the find-analysis tasks for publication, and men were and still are usually the ones to whom large-scale and/or theoretical endeavors are assigned because of stereotyping about the proper spheres and mentalities of women and men. Nevertheless, the work of numerous pioneer women—first in artifactual or detail analysis and then in the synthetic studies of iconography, stylistic valence, cultural transmission, social history, and economics emerging out of these systematic and close readings—has been truly pathbreaking. The cutting-edge nature of many of these explorations can be appreciated as all the more exciting because the projects yielding them may frequently have been considered at the time of their suggestion or assignment to represent the contained, safe, meticulous, essentially domestic work suitable for a mere woman. Whatever the parameters that may have defined initial ventures by women into these areas, in many cases their results have been the stuff that has really shifted the field from treasure hunt to historical endeavor and then from tabulation of dry chronologies to exploration of the workings of social systems. I think particularly of Grace Crowfoot with the study of textiles, for instance; and later of Virginia Grace with the development of the study of stamped amphora handles; Edith Eccles in the study of Aegean seals; Cleo Fitch in the study of lamps; Dorothy Thompson in the study of terra-cotta figurines. Elizabeth Douglas Van Buren (d. 1961) was a truly remarkable scholar whose work first on architectural terra-cottas of ancient Greece and Italy in the early years of the twentieth century (under her maiden name) and subsequently on an extraordinary range of iconographical studies relating to the textual and material records of the ancient Near East charted entire areas of inquiry.[32]

It is an unintended, but no less unfortunate, disservice to denigrate this type of archaeological achievement because it has been tainted by association with the limitations imposed by society upon the female sex—in effect a form of double prejudice. Far better to acknowledge and deplore the factors that have led to the channeling of many women's efforts into certain areas of research and scholarly production and then to dignify their work with energetic critical assessment.

In this context, it is important to note that even in the area of publishing interpretive studies based on artifact assemblages, women of the pioneer generations ran into difficulty. Margaret Murray recounts repeated refusal by the male establishment to publish her manuscripts on the "unpleasant subjects" of ancient Egypt (i.e., on women and social conditions) simply because she was a woman and women should not know of such things—whereas men could and did publish on these topics.[33] Against the backdrop of this type of struggle for voice, the remarkable contributions of the pioneers begin to stand out in increasingly high relief.

Despite what may have happened to them in the assignment of material for publication, many of the pioneer women were, in fact, actively engaged in the trenches. Some exercised considerable creative initiative in the determination of excavation sites and in the designing of field strategy. This is all the more impressive given that the challenges for women in the field came from several directions simultaneously. A common stereotype suggests that the biggest challenge a pioneer-generation woman had to face on site was that posed by the male chauvinism of local workers incapable of accepting the authority of a female trench master. But the challenges posed by the male chauvinism of the heroic excavation director were frequently and demonstrably much worse. The supposed problem of native male workers' presumed difficulty in accepting the authority of a female excavation director was one rationale used by the archaeological establishment for avoiding the placement of women in directorial positions; but the excuse seems to have been a ruse. Egyptologist Marjory V. Seton-Williams (b. 1910), for instance, describes her failure to get the post of professor of Western Asiatic Archaeology at the Institute of Archaeology (replacing Sir Max Mallowan). Professor Emery, on the interview panel, asked her if she had ever "had any difficulty controlling [her] men in the Middle East as surely they would never take orders from a woman." Seton-Williams reports that she assured Emery that this had never posed a problem for her; but she learned later that Emery never even allowed women on his excavations as underlings—much less was he apt to vote a woman into a position of leadership in the field.[34] The laden query about female difficulties regulating native male workers masked an entrenched set of social views that were not about to be altered by Mary Seton-Williams's confident assurances born of experience.

Women were in fact able to negotiate in these arenas effectively as professionals. They did not even need to be particularly masculine in affect in order to be authoritative. But it was extremely rare for a woman to get the chance to demonstrate this by actually leading an excavation on her own. Sometimes the opportunity to do so seems to have emerged as an antagonistic rather than a supportive gesture. Hetty Goldman (1881–1972) recounts the situation at the American School of Classical Studies in Athens, where the tone was so hostile to women excavators that she perceived that she had been allowed to excavate at Halae only because the school wanted to get her as far from Athens as possible.[35] Seton-Williams interprets her invitation in the early 1960s to lead an expedition at Tell el-Fara'in in Egypt as a ruthless maneuver in which she was "used as a catspaw by one of the warring factions" of the excavations committee of the Egyptian Exploration Society.[36]

In addition to battling a host of assumptions perpetuated by the male establishment about their handicaps in this regard, women were also faced with other forms of discrimination that increased the odds of their failure as excavators. Margaret Murray recounts with candor the fact that Petrie offered her no instruction before sending her into the field for the first time at Abydos (whereas he spent considerable effort training the male students). One can only speculate that women may also have been marginalized in favor of the male excavation participants when it came to the all-important discussions and theorizings back at base camp. Sending her out to the excavation site armed with no instruction on substantive technique or on protocols for labor management, Petrie brutally tested Murray's capacity to exert authority over her workers, evidently expecting her to fail.[37]

Many stories could be told of more recent (and sometimes subtle) disparities in treatment between women and men on excavations.[38] Certainly some more recent women excavation directors have been just as biased toward men (and against all, or at least certain "types" of, women) as were the male heroes of the pioneer era. This tendency mirrors the ranges of biases that have been explored up to the present in classroom treatment (by female as well as male teachers) of girls and women versus boys and men. Once again, we must, however, be struck by the explicitness of obstacles so often encountered by the women of the field in the nineteenth and early twentieth centuries.

Again—Sounds of Silence

Although a significant number of pioneer-era women were hands-on dirt archaeologists, their "masculine" role in the archaeological endeavor has routinely been downplayed. Harriet Boyd Hawes's turn-of-the-century discovery of the Minoan town of Gournia and her subsequent excavation and publication of it offer a painful example.[39] Sometimes full credit for the discovery of this important Bronze Age site is given to Richard Seager, a gentleman collector-excavator who only joined her team two years into the project and did not collude in this corruption of the facts.[40] In other instances, the discovery of Gournia and the launching of its excavation program have been described only slightly more palatably as a joint venture with Seager.[41] All in all, it is eminently understandable that Harriet Boyd Hawes energetically supported the Women's Archive project championed by Eleanor Roosevelt before World War II, having learned, as she put it, "how easily women's acts are ascribed to men or completely wiped out."[42]

A Look at the Seamy Side

A more complex response to my initial rhetorical question, "Why Women?" suggests a range of issues about the history and historiography of scientific archaeology as well as about the social history of modern Western civilization itself in the nineteenth and early twentieth centuries. By looking at the finished side of a garment, one can appreciate the grand scheme of its design and the intended display of the production effort—but only from a limited perspective. It is by examining the seamy side that one learns how a garment is really put together, what its frailties are, what shortcuts were taken with resources or technique, and where the most attention to structural detail was lavished.

In the history of the archaeological pioneers, the lives of the women of the field provide glimpses of the seamy side of an emergent science. It has been possible to write male-oriented histories of archaeology that inscribe the charisma and genius of selected great men onto the development of a tradition without delving into issues of social and intellectual history—much less into extensive detail on the inner lives of these individuals. Some recent work has begun to seriously contextualize the archaeological heroes socially and politically.[43] But these efforts still tend to assume that the male experience is the normative one and therefore not in need of introspective analysis. By contrast, it would be impossible to create an adequate history of archaeology that systematically weaves the pioneering women into its fabric *without* addressing issues of the intimate history and personal identity of the protagonists. This is in large part because their social displacement had to be extraordinary in order for them to become players in the field. Their intellectual contributions cannot fully be reckoned with except against the backdrop of their individual responses to Victorian society. Similarly, their contributions cannot be fully gleaned without appreciation of the challenges these women faced simply in order to be there at all, to be heard at all.

Certainly, intellectual inquiry about the ancient past that was pursued in an environment of colonialism, of oppression, of sexual anxiety, and eventually of raw discord on the issue of personal and sexual freedom will have been colored to some extent by the social context of the period in which this inquiry occurred. Thus, we may even hazard a guess that the biographies assembled in *Breaking Ground* and the questions they raise (which would not normally be raised through a heroic biography of one of the male pioneers) will someday be valuable in an intellectual reassessment of the historiography of classical and Near Eastern archaeology.

The Victorian Backdrop

Archaeology, as we have noted, began to emerge as a field of systematic scientific endeavor during the nineteenth century. Building upon strategies and interests already emerging in the preceding century, this was a period of aggressive mercantile and military development and expansion in the Middle East, particularly by Britain. The hegemonic mentality of the nineteenth century, popularly encapsulated with respect to the British endeavor in the code word *Victorian,* suggests (along with numerous other features of the culture of the time) a whole notional system of imperialism and its social effects. This hegemonic vision explicitly encouraged the advancement in Europe and North America of Old World archaeology.[44]

In ideological terms, the retrieval of the material past of lands under the colonial or imperial control of Western European lands or within their aspirational sight lines was one way that these theaters of hegemony were staked out by the West. This process was literal (in the sense of the large-scale expatriation of antiquities to Western museums and collections); and it was spiritual in the sense of the complexly overlaid interpretations of the past that were inspired by an era of seminal scholarship predicated largely on a colonialist ideology.

More practically, the mercantile-imperial adventures of the eighteenth and nineteenth centuries created European infrastructures in the Greater Mediterranean that encouraged and facilitated antiquarian exploration. Most dominant (male) personalities in the early archaeological adventure were in some way attached to trading, military, and diplomatic endeavors in ancient lands. Furthermore, the elaborate infrastructures of empire created a new context in the Greater Mediterranean for travel and ethnographic observation even by Western women. Heretofore, exotic travel by women had been linked closely with pilgrimage to Christian holy sites. Now it became open to a remarkable cadre of women travelers who often wrote impressive, subtly observant narratives of their encounters with the lands, ruins, and people of the East.[45] Such women are an important part of the backdrop for the first pioneer generation of women archaeologists.

Paradoxically this imperialist age, with its opening of new frontiers far away, simultaneously worked to increase male anxiety at home about the roles and sexuality of upper- and middle-class women. The hegemonic Western order created notions of expansive horizon for men while it inversely created a brick wall for women. Indeed, one striking aspect of the Victorian era was its extremely restrictive notions of the roles of middle- and upper-class women. This restrictive mentality became a secondary ideology of the imperial age that effectively subjugated women intellectually, sexually, and economically.

Multiple pressures from multiple "scientific" perspectives hammered home the notion that Victorian middle- and upper-class women were destined for a passive, exclusively reproductive, role. Ethnographic studies among "primitive peoples" coupled with social spins on Darwinian evolutionary theory were co-opted to support an ideology that "protected" the top socioeconomic strata of the female sex. Within the imperialist social order, a theory of eugenics stipulated that procreation by the middle and upper classes was the only viable mission in a woman's life. For a woman to reject procreation deliberately (e.g., through refusal to marry) or to put the procreative mission at risk through untoward behavior (such as a "heroic" loner mission in the archaeological field) was tantamount to treason against the imperialist enterprise.[46]

Insidiously, the propaganda of the eugenics campaign portrayed its position as sympathetic to feminism. Motherhood was characterized as work. For the upper and middle classes, motherhood was the only work suitable for a woman. (The desperately beleaguered members of the Western female underclasses are not the protagonists of the social drama about women and archaeology that we are describing here; they are the sorry supporting characters of an even darker world of exploitation.) Such propaganda established a critical barrier against the possibility of exploring a vocation outside the home. Even worse, it polarized married childbearing women and unmarried childless women.[47] Ironically, for the women of the socioeconomic classes concerned here, the work of motherhood was itself restricted almost exclusively to procreation and social maintenance, since retainers were employed for the myriad activities that today would usually be considered the sphere of mothers who focus their work effort in the home.

One activity that was said to put women's procreative capacity at risk was education. Intellectual pursuits (even the reading of newspapers) were said, quite literally, to lead to the desexualization, denaturing, and sterilization of the female. Beyond that, dominant ideology also promoted the more general notion that any pursuit that broke the established sex boundary was sure to provoke dire illness in the upper- or middle-class woman.

As a backdrop against which to appreciate the first generation of women whose biographies are assembled in our volume, I recommend Charlotte Perkins Gilman's chilling short story "The Yellow Wallpaper" (1892). Drawn from Gilman's personal experience, the tale describes the psychological unraveling of a young American woman whose purported illness (apparently a postpartum depression) was treated professionally in the manner mandated by nineteenth-century gender ideology: She was forced to "rest" month after month—deprived even of the stimulus of reading or writing—effectively imprisoned in a chamber in which the faded yellow wallpaper took on a bizarre metaphorical life of its own.[48]

Any woman of this era who ventured into the archaeological field was clearly a radical nonconformist. The personal histories and motivating forces leading to such nonconformities were, however, highly individual. Some of the pioneer women were feminists or at least had connections to feminists and to the suffrage movement. The mother of Hilda Petrie's good friend in childhood was Dame Millicent Fawcett, a leader of the suffrage movement. As an adult, Hilda Petrie maintained a close friendship with Miss Lina Eckenstein, a medievalist with feminist intellectual interests and author of *Women under Monasticism.* (Eckenstein served as registrar for the Petrie excavation at Abydos.) Margaret Murray's mother had wanted to become a physician but of course had been thwarted in this unseemly ambition. Murray herself was an earnest feminist, whose scholarly interests ranged to specific issues of the social history of women in ancient Egypt and whose wry autobiographical candor about the life of a woman pioneer reveals a politicized attitude.[49] Gertrude Caton-Thompson was also involved in the suffrage movement beginning around 1910. Mary Hamilton Swindler was intensely concerned with issues of women in education.

An interesting contrast is Gertrude Bell. A few women pioneers in archaeology and ethnography successfully constructed masculine-like identities for themselves in the field or at least represented themselves as constructed on the heroic male model.[50] Bell is one example. Not coincidentally, she became the most widely known Victorian female figure in the field and remains the most consistently cited (if not always problematized) of the women pioneers in synthetic histories of archaeology. Most interestingly, Bell was passionate in her rejection of the tenets of feminism and women's suffrage (a founding member, in fact, of the Anti-Suffrage League); and she was an equally passionate imperialist.[51] Her outstanding work in the formation of the Iraq Antiquities Department and the Iraq Museum are textured—but not diminished—by understanding that these activities were on one level part of the performance of colonialist power within a theater of British diplomatic strategy and factionalized indigenous response.

It is poignant, given Bell's political stances and what we know of the Victorian discourse around women and eugenics, to contemplate how she may have felt about her reluctant spinsterhood. She must have been deeply conflicted in her personal nonconformity to expectations of women as propagated by the hegemonic culture within which she had publicly subsumed herself. Bell's position in the Middle East was that of an ex-patriot single Englishwoman who was heavily invested in the political intrigues of the colonial experience and able to inspire unique loyalties among certain groups of men in her adopted sphere. In this, she was, on a superficial level, dangerously similar to Lady Hester Stanhope (1776–1839). Stanhope was a niece of Prime Minister William Pitt and a somewhat bizarre social renegade: a "fallen woman," at once self-absorbed and consumed by notions of her rightful position at dead center of Middle Eastern power politics.[52] Her sexual, political, and even "archaeological" escapades in the Middle East were notorious and must have created a dreaded stereotype of the lost female soul living among and forging unfathomable political loyalties with exotic sheiks.

Gertrude Bell, who had certainly not renounced sexuality although she remained childless and unmarried, must have had aggressively to defy the potential for comparison to the social notoriety and open sexual improprieties of Lady Hester Stanhope earlier in the century. And it can be said that in this, as in the professional reputation she cultivated, Bell emerges as the flip side of the Stanhope specter. Her "masculine" strength of character in the practice of deep Middle Eastern political involvements seems the reverse of Stanhope's chaotically, flamboyantly "feminine," lifestyle. Furthermore, Bell's championing of the cause of desperately needed protocols in the legitimate recording, division, and safeguarding of archaeological finds might (in Bell's worldview) have reclaimed some virtue lost through the wanton, destructive "femininity" practiced by Lady Hester. The Lady Hester image was one to avoid at all costs; but for an attractive single Victorian woman like Bell to manage this as rather a loner in the field—successfully treading the very fine line between heroic nonconformity and reclusive craziness—was a significant achievement within the strictures of nineteenth-century society.[53]

In sum, the conflicts inherent in the gendered experience of Gertrude Bell resolved themselves through active rejection of the "female" antiparadigm and embrace of a degendered (or even masculinized) paradigm. Her physical (even libidinous) energy was definitely of heroic proportions, yet it seems sometimes to have come perilously close to a death wish (as with the most daring of her mountain-climbing exploits). At the end, she did apparently induce her own death through an overdose of sleeping tablets. It is interesting that so much of Bell's energy was channeled in her later years into essentially politicized aspects of the archaeological cause, despite her precocious and quite brilliant accomplishments earlier on in field investigation and in the study of oriental languages. In this channeling she effectively tested the limits of what a woman could do at that time—perhaps she tested these limits so fiercely and thus taxed her identity as a woman so severely that she depleted her supply of self. In the last year of her life, she expressed a desire to return to the "comfortable arena of archaeology and history and to take only an onlooker's interest in the contest over actual affairs."[54] One glimpses through this woman archaeology pioneer a life permeated with shades of personal disappointment and occasionally desperate frustration as she walked her own self-constructed tightrope above the gendered constraints of Victorianism.

Hilda Petrie had a very different relation to Victorianism. A feminist in her sympathies, she was also a mother of two as well as the wife of a complex and dominating archaeological hero (as we have already discussed). She must have been conscious of the unresolvable tensions between being an adequate normative mother and wife on the one hand and avoiding erasure as a woman of the field in the shadow of her husband on the other. Thus her life layered outward fulfillment of certain societally imposed expectations with experiences and self-expectations that radically departed from the Victorian norm. In this case, I remain curious about how she related to her motherhood. The Petrie children did not accompany their parents to Egypt; and Mrs. Petrie was away from them (even during their babyhood) for months at a stretch. In the winter of 1908, when she had to leave the field and return to England because of the birth of her second child (Ann), she seems to have been extremely resentful of the trivialities of the domestic sphere and the frustrations of dealing with her son's misbehavior—wanting more than anything to be back in Egypt, with young John and his infant sister left in competent English hands. Flinders Petrie answered her letters with assurances of love and appeals to her womanly duty as a mother. He concluded one missive: "Keep a brave heart, as you have my second self—John—with you to make a brighter and better boy than his father."[55] This is perhaps telling about the Petries as an archaeological couple and about how Mrs. Petrie came to terms with her situation. All aspects of Hilda Petrie's charges as a woman were essentially filtered, it seems, through the professional and personal needs of her husband, so that even her maternal duties were translated ultimately into a notion of how they would reflect on and serve the legacy of Flinders Petrie.

Who, we ask again in a deeper way now, were these first-generation women of the field? How did they negotiate the kaleidoscopic nonconformities that drew each of them as individuals out into the physical and intellectual adventures and social ambiguities of archaeology? There is no way to provide a universally applicable answer to this question, of course. But one wonderful anecdote says a great deal about this negotiation. In her autobiography Margaret Murray describes a special moment at Abydos. News of a disturbance at the Osireion prompted Hilda Petrie, Lina Eckenstein, and Margaret Murray herself to go out into the night from the base camp to investigate the possibility of a nocturnal vandal. Murray does not belabor any notion of their bravery. Rather, she describes with some glee the utter shock with which the retired architect, Mr. Stannus, witnessed the spectacle of three women cavorting in the moonlight:

> [We] joined hands and danced with a great variety of fancy steps all the way from the camp to the dig . . . Poor Mr. Stannus, he had always been accustomed to the Victorian man's idea of what a lady should be, a delicate fragile being who would scream at the sight of a mouse.[56]

The vision of these Victorian women in the Egyptian desert, loosed temporarily from the confines of society at home and more fleetingly even from the patriarchal strictures of excavation routine, is a real delight. The moment has the ring of life-filled, aggressive exuberance—even a subconsciously clandestine mapping and appropriation of the camp terrain with a totally unexpected female marker.

Toward the Second Generation

Archaeology liberated the first generation of women pioneers from the worst aspects of Victorian life at home. No matter what the details of individual circumstances with respect to men, and no matter what private anxieties with respect to their social displacement, at the very least these women were escaping the horrors of Gilman's "Yellow Wallpaper." It is important to acknowledge also that a man like Petrie (egocentric as he was) did incorporate liberated women into his teams. In doing so, he was himself stepping outside the bounds of a Victorian patriarchal propriety that seems to have had a particular stranglehold on Egyptology; and he was to some extent establishing a platform for women like Margaret Murray to cry out against its gender ideology.

The discipline of archaeology was so young in the mid–nineteenth century that it was not as burdened (as some other areas of study were) with its own traditions, rigid expectations, and social barriers. In this sense, it was more open to women (just as it was more open to eccentric men) than were other intellectual arenas. Another factor contributing to a certain openness is perhaps less universally appreciated. Around the middle of the nineteenth century social pressures from an unexpected source began to weaken the ideological barriers against the substantive education of middle-class women as potential wage earners. Specifically, in Great Britain, the 1851 census revealed that the empire was causing such a serious drain on the male population at home that one-third of British women would not find a husband.[57] In the United States, the lure of the western frontier created a similar problem. On both sides of the Atlantic this was a burgeoning crisis, since middle-class women were not trained for any economically productive work, and those who did not marry usually became burdensome appendages to the family. Thus, as so often happens, women came to be treated more liberally because of neither a moral insight nor a dawning realization that they are as competent as men—but, rather, because of the economic exigencies of the still-patriarchal culture.

In any event, the revelations of the mid-nineteenth-century census ultimately helped make the case for increased educational opportunities for women. Archaeology came onto the scene at the right moment for a two-staged female coup. First, its beginnings were late enough so that, although it unfolded in the restrictive Victorian milieu, it was at least unencumbered by some of the traditions that inhibited more established disciplines from welcoming women.[58] Second, it had already laid the groundwork for some gender inclusiveness (however limited, as we have seen) as education began opening up to women and producing a new generation of women trained in substantive areas.

There is an irony here, alas—one that had a great impact on the generation that should have reaped the fruits of the pioneer women's achievements. As archaeology matured and became institutionalized over the years, it became increasingly hostage to the same sorts of conservatisms that were rampant in older fields such as classics. The practice of archaeology in the academy felt the pressure increasingly to avoid the stigma of antiestablishment eccentricity (such as the promoting of females in leadership positions), particularly because archaeological fieldwork depended so much on fund-raising and other forms of public and private social support.

This context sheds light on an episode in London in 1910 concerning Margaret Murray. For all her feminism, her nonconformities, and her jibes at the repressed Mr. Stannus at Abydos described earlier, Murray deployed a hard-line social conservatism in dealing with the extramarital love affair between her young woman assistant and the Coptic specialist Walter Crum, working in the Department of Egyptology. Judging by letters between Murray (in London) and Petrie (in Egypt), Murray was at least as adamant as Petrie about the necessity of dismissing both of them and effectively ostracizing them from the academy forever, since Crum would not renounce his love and his wife refused to divorce him.[59] It was considered essential to preserve impeccable decorum for the sake of the young discipline of archaeology.

A Price of Conservatism

The first-generation women of the field took part in the structuring of archaeology as a discipline. The efforts of several archaeologists (such as Caroline Morris Galt and Mary Hamilton Swindler) as well as the efforts of numerous women in other specializations contributed to the advancement of educational opportunities for their sex. Eventually this work created a different backdrop for the women archaeologists of the second generation.

Advances in the acceptance of women into the academy were, however, made at a heavy price. Repeatedly, as I have already hinted, women felt the need to suppress elements of their political stance on societal conventions in order to avoid compromising the goal of education for women. Thus, for instance, Emily Davies gave up her work for suffrage because she feared that it would prove a barrier to her foundation of Girton College, Cambridge. In many female institutions, young women had to adhere with impeccable attention to two sets of standards. First, they had to be more ladylike than any normal paragon of female Victorian virtue in order to avoid legitimizing the notion that the taint of education would inevitably lead to the defeminization, the utter denaturing of women. Second, they had to perform more brilliantly than men at the same intellectual tasks in order to demonstrate that they had the same brainpower as men. The first class at Bryn Mawr College in 1889 pledged an oath promising to uphold this double protocol.[60]

The exotic eastern pantaloons defiantly maintained by Jane Dieulafoy in the 1880s after her return to Paris from her archaeological explorations at Susa in Persia (as collaborator with her husband, the engineer Marcel-Auguste Dieulafoy) certainly raised eyebrows and set her apart as a romantic and eccentric figure in Paris.[61] Her masculinized oriental affectations would have been a serious professional handicap if she had hoped to gain social reentry in the role of a female student (rather than a writer-journalist–salon personality) in the context of the institution-oriented priorities of the second generation of pioneers.[62] This is especially so in the buttoned-up arenas of Great Britain and North America. For the second-generation pioneers, the political stakes had become too high, the realization too clear that political gains remained unstable, to allow for exuberant flourishes and symbols at home—or for moonlit dances by women in the field.

Similarly the difficulties second-generation women faced on excavations were perhaps on some levels more challenging than those encountered by their predecessors in the earlier years. As archaeology became more professionalized, new social mechanisms of discrimination took root. Professionalism typically carries with it the perceived need to cultivate and maintain a level of status (e.g., by creating and promoting a mystique of exclusive expertise through restricted access to professional membership). The same types of phenomena observed by Duffin for the medical profession as it closed ranks in the second half of the nineteenth century can be tracked somewhat later in the field of archaeology.[63]

The notion that the mixing of the sexes on excavations would be detrimental is particularly remarkable. One is struck by the narrowing social mentality in some expeditions. Looking back, the field experienced by the first generation of pioneers (in the second half of the nineteenth century) seems in comparison yeasty and generous, populated as it often was by men and women who were (blessedly) social misfits of the Victorian era. The field as experienced by the women of the second pioneer generation had developed institutionalized proprieties that redeployed many of the Victorianisms that the first generation had to some extent evaded. All this is to challenge the comfortable idea that with the passage of time issues for early women of the field resolved themselves through some irresistible process of social maturation, some inexorable march along a continuum toward real parity of opportunity and acknowledgment.

At this juncture I feel a certain social pressure (generated not from any source except my own feminine [?] desire to keep a party light) to suggest that at last the field is neutral, that a level ground has finally been reached between the exotic nonconformist (if socially anxiety ridden) days of the early pioneers and the oddly neoconservatist days of the early-twentieth-century field. But, with the lives of the second generation of pioneers now marked out here for the record, will there indeed be no need for special synthetic compendiums of the biographies of later women archaeologists? I leave this as an open question to the reader. From here we move logically to a conclusion that is at once backward-looking, contemporary, and forward-looking.

Writing about Lives

Any biographical project is fraught with layers of subjectivity—perhaps even more layers of subjectivity than is the scientific pursuit of archaeology or any other field of data collection and interpretation.[64] The whole notion of scientific objectivity and its exaltation as a desired and achievable result of inquiry is itself, after all, arguably a reflection of the male hegemonic discourse. As Lorraine Code has noted:

> The ideal notions of the autonomous reasoner—the dislocated, disinterested observer—and the epistemologies they inform are artifacts of a small, privileged group of educated, usually prosperous, white men. Their circumstances allow them to believe that they are materially nowhere or everywhere, even effectively autonomous, and to imagine that they are nowhere and everywhere, even as they occupy an unmarked position of privilege. Moreover, the ideals of rationality and objectivity that have guided and inspired theorists of knowledge throughout the history of western philosophy have been constructed through processes of suppressing the attributes and experiences commonly associated with femaleness and underclass social status: emotion, connection, practicality, sensitivity, idiosyncrasy. These systematic excisions of "otherness" attest to a presumed—and willed—belief in the stability of a social order that the presumers have good reasons to believe that they can ensure, because they occupy the positions that determine the norms of conduct and inquiry.[65]

The erasure to which pioneer women of the field fell victim makes it difficult or impossible even to assemble the complete professional oeuvre for some of them. It is far more difficult to fathom the complexities of their psychological situations, their personal visions either of their own work or of the larger contextual arena in which they labored.

Recent studies of female autobiography have problematized many issues at stake in attempting to sift narratives in order to separate individuality from culturally inscribed expectation.[66] Carolyn Heilbrun notes with great analytical astuteness that autobiographies by women such as our first-generation pioneers, born in the mid–nineteenth century, have a narrative flatness that belies their exciting lives:

> Above all, in the lives of Victorian and post-Victorian women, the public and private life cannot be linked as in the male narrative.

> These women are therefore unable to write exemplary lives; they do not dare to offer themselves as models, but only as exceptions chosen by destiny or chance.[67]

Gertrude Bell confirms Heilbrun's thesis. Bell certainly considered herself to be more or less unique among women;[68] and in this sense she did not, could not, link herself with a collective vision of potential liberation for women as a group, as a class. Her antisuffrage activism was but one public manifestation of a much deeper and complex gender detachment.

Heilbrun continues, suggesting that "the unspoken law that women who 'make it' must not identify themselves as women, or dare to annoy men by their self-identification as women, serves to erase from the record these women's love and support of one another."[69] I would add that this factor tends to erase from the record whatever private reflections these women may have had about the nature of their personal experiences and the ways in which they may have seen their femaleness bearing upon their work.

The autobiographical travelogue writings of Amelia Edwards present an instructive example of self-ambiguities resolved through the deployment of a hegemonic voice that at once masculinized her authorial observations and distanced her from the women who participated in her journeys. As Melman astutely remarks, Edwards consistently "referred to herself in the de-gendered, impersonal 'the author' (but to her female travel companions in the diminutive 'Lady' or 'the Bride')."[70]

Margaret Murray's autobiography, for all its apparent anecdotal candor and for all the freedom that may be thought to be earned by living a hundred years, is still quite cautious in its direct social commentary. It is not a critically introspective self-analysis and self-assessment but rather a series of reminiscences that leave the reader to infer any politicized context. It remains a very special memoir, however, because it speaks definitely in a female voice, it offers glimpses of comradely solidarities of women in the field, and it gently implies the legitimacy of reflexive memoirs about the life specifically of a woman of the field.

The privilege of self-reflexive writing in scholarship has tended to be a gender-specific one. In her introduction to *Women Writing Culture,* Ruth Behar signals a double standard still operative in ethnographic discourse today: Women writing self-reflexively are condemned as emotional and pejoratively female; men's work that is packed with heroic navel-gazing is considered good exposition simply because it conforms to the established hegemonic code of authorial voicing and pseudo-objectivity.[71] This gendered hierarchy in scholarly writing also operates in archaeological circles—even today; but it was much more explicitly evident in the era of our woman pioneers. It predetermines the nature of the documentary legacy left by the pioneering women and adds to the need for subtle textual analysis of the sometimes cryptic voices of nineteenth-century female scholarship, letter writing, and autobiography in order to reach some core of the real person, mind, and intellectual agenda.

Is There a Female Archaeology?

The very project of our volume whispers the possibility of something specific we might hope to learn from understanding the lives and work of women archaeologists—something different from what we might expect to learn from the lives and work of men. Leaving aside the negative channeling of womanly endeavors in the field as discussed earlier, are there positive ways of seeing issues and performing intellectual tasks embedded in the archaeological enterprise that particularly exploit approaches that might be characterized as female? Many readers here in the first decade of the twenty-first century will cringe from this rhetorical question as a "politically incorrect" postulate that serves only to revive and reinforce stereotypes of the male hegemonic discourse. Yet some feminist thinkers have recently been reassessing this question.[72] In contemporary ethnographic practice, for instance, some attention is being focused on the important potentials of the reflexive female voice as a critical filter of experience encountered in the field.[73] It is now being recognized, furthermore, that early Western women travelers in the Orient (who were the direct ancestors of our women archaeological pioneers) probed in their writing nuances of Middle Eastern cultures that their male counterparts were not (could not be?) receptive to. As Melman poses it:

> Could women, conventionally identified in the Christian west as the "other within," develop their own notion of the "other without," of peoples, or races or—for that matter—classes outside a dominant culture?[74]

And did these Western women (again in Melman's words) "develop a separate, feminine experience?"

Is it possible for us to apply this model of querying to Old World archaeology—to the study of ancient cultures? Suggested one rave review of Gertrude Bell's *The Desert and the Sown* in the *Times Literary Supplement* (1907) almost a century ago:

> Women perhaps make the best travelers, for when they have the true wanderer's spirit they are more enduring and, strange to say, more indifferent to hardship and discomfort than men. They are unquestionably more observant of details and quicker to receive impressions. Their sympathies are more alert, and they get into touch with strangers more readily.[75]

Although dated in its formulations, this generous encomium neither trivializes the concept of a female heroic by encasing it in a discursive framework of domestic (wifely) toil nor praises Bell for a transcendent masculinity of achievement. We could perhaps refine a set of questions hinted at by these somewhat naively offered notions of special female capacity for investigation in the field. There may indeed be factors of the "female experience" that are radically different from the hegemonic privilege of "objectivity" ascribed to the male. By the same token, all sorts of class and status definitions, issues of identity, and self-perceptions may affect any scholar's interpretation of the archaeological record.

Hopefully, future projects will make use of the invitation offered by *Breaking Ground* further to explore what the contributions of women archaeologists really have been. Ultimately, we will be in a far better position than we currently are to evaluate such concerns substantively. When we are able to do so, we will be better equipped to review and interpret the history of the field in every way. As Cheryl Claassen hints in the introduction to her edited volume *Women in Archaeology,* important information about the archaeological record, and equally important analytical perspectives on that record, have gone largely ignored simply because the producers of the work have been women.[76]

They were pioneering women of the field. They were conflicted and complicated pioneering women. They were pioneering women whose lives, ambitions, and accomplishments must beckon us down crisscrossing paths of enhanced awareness of a collective history of archaeology.

NOTES

1. *Excavating Women: A History of Women in European Archaeology* (London and New York: Routledge, 1998). The studies assembled in this volume deal with European women working in the archaeology of Europe and Scandinavia, with less coverage therefore of women working in the Near East and Egypt. American scholars are not included. I had already written "Women of the Field" before

Excavating Women was available to me, but its analytical scope is complementary to many of the issues I foreground here with reference to the particulars of the Victorian era. It is a pleasure to be able to acknowledge its significance and relevance even at a late stage.

2. For classical archaeology one important example of new work triumphing over the traditional erasure of women's contributions is found in Stephen L. Dyson's *Ancient Marbles to American Shores: Classical Archaeology in the United States* (Philadelphia: University of Pennsylvania Press, 1998).

3. Warren R. Dawson and Eric P. Uphill, *Who Was Who in Egyptology,* 2d ed. (London: Egypt Exploration Society, 1972). This publication has now appeared in a third edition to which I have not yet had access.

4. John A. Wilson, *Signs and Wonders upon Pharaoh: A History of American Egyptology* (Chicago: University of Chicago Press, 1964).

5. Michael Hoffman, *Egypt before the Pharaohs: The Prehistoric Foundations of Egyptian Civilization* (New York: Alfred A. Knopf, 1979), 138–39.

6. Wilson, *Signs and Wonders,* ix–x.

7. Glyn Daniel, *A Hundred and Fifty Years of Archaeology* (London: Duckworth Press, 1975).

8. For example, Daniel, *Hundred and Fifty Years,* 16–25 and 68–77.

9. For example, Billie Melman, *Women's Orients: English Women and the Middle East, 1718–1918: Sexuality, Religion, and Work* (Ann Arbor: University of Michigan Press, 1992).

10. Joan Rees, *Amelia Edwards: Traveller, Novelist, and Egyptologist* (London: Rubicon Press, 1998).

11. Daniel, *Hundred and Fifty Years,* 135.

12. Brian M. Fagan, *The Rape of the Nile: Tomb Robbers, Tourists, and Archaeologists in Egypt* (New York: Charles Scribner's Sons, 1975), 322.

13. Daniel, *Hundred and Fifty Years,* 205.

14. Seton Lloyd, *Foundations in the Dust: The Story of Mesopotamian Exploration* (London: Thames and Hudson, 1980); Max Mallowan, *Mallowan's Memoirs* (New York: Dodd, Mead, 1977).

15. In *The Road to El-Aguzein* (London: Kegan Paul International, 1988), 23, Marjory Seton-Williams remarks that Mortimer and Tessa Wheeler convinced her to study prehistory rather than Egyptology in the 1930s because as a woman she could not hope to get a job in Egyptology. Was there an especially patriarchal mindset among Egyptologists in this era—even more pervasive and intimidating than what existed in other subfields of Old World archaeology?

16. Daniel, *Hundred and Fifty Years,* 332.

17. See Dever in this volume and Philip J. King, *American Archaeology in the Mideast: A History of the American Schools of Oriental Research* (Philadelphia: American Schools of Oriental Research, 1983).

18. Mary Beaudry and Jacquelyn White, "Women in Historical Archaeology," in *Women in Archaeology,* ed. Cheryl Claassen (Philadelphia: University of Pennsylvania Press, 1994), 138–58. See also Anabel Ford, "Women in Mesoamerican Archaeology: Why Are the Best Men Winning?" in Claassen, *Women in Archaeology,* 159–72.

19. Flinders Petrie, *Seventy Years in Archaeology* (New York: Greenwood Press, 1932), 176.

20. See Margaret S. Drower, *Flinders Petrie: A Life in Archaeology* (London: Victor Gollancz, 1985).

21. For candid discussions see Barbara Tedlock, "Works and Wives: On the Sexual Division of Textual Labor," in *Women Writing Culture,* ed. Ruth Behar and Deborah A. Gordon (Berkeley and Los Angeles: University of California Press, 1992), 267–73; and Lori D. Hager, "Sex and Gender in Paleoanthropology," in *Women in Human Evolution,* ed. Lori D. Hager (London: Routledge, 1997), 18–19, on Mary Leakey and Louis Leakey.

22. Kenneth Hudson, *A Social History of Archaeology: The British Experience* (London: Macmillan, 1981), 1, 107–8.

23. Jacquetta Hawkes, *Mortimer Wheeler: Adventurer in Archaeology* (London: Weidenfeld and Nicolson, 1982), 149, 153, 156–59.

24. Drower, *Flinders Petrie,* 434.

25. Petrie, *Seventy Years in Archaeology,* 199.

26. Margaret Murray, *My First Hundred Years* (London: William Kimber, 1963), 103.

27. Christopher C. Lee, *The Grand Piano Came by Camel: Arthur C. Mace, the Neglected Egyptologist* (Edinburgh: Mainstream, 1992).

28. As per passing references in Petrie, *Seventy Years in Archaeology.*

29. Lee, *Grand Piano,* 32 and 42–43.

30. Fagan, *Rape of the Nile,* 354.

31. Joan Gero, "Socio-Politics of Archaeology and the Woman-at-Home Ideology," *American Antiquity* 50 (1985): 342–50. See also Dimitra Kokkinidou and Marianna Nikolaidou, "A Sexist Present, a Human-less Past: Museum Archaeology in Greece," in *Gender and Material Culture in Archaeological Perspective,* ed. Moira Donald and Linda Hurcombe (London: Macmillan, 2000), 33–55.

32. See Edith Porada, "Necrology," *American Journal of Archaeology* 67 (1963): 83–84.

33. Murray, *My First Hundred Years,* 97–98.

34. Seton-Williams, *Road to El-Aguzein,* 121.

35. See Mellink and Quinn in this volume.

36. Seton-Williams, *Road to El-Aguzein,* 125.

37. Murray, *My First Hundred Years,* 118–19.

38. In published form, see, for example, Tracy Sweely, "Male Hunting Camp or Female Processing Station: An Evolution within a Discipline," in Claassen, *Women in Archaeology,* 173–81. It would be interesting to assemble anecdotal recollections of women who emerged in the field in the 1960s and 1970s. I suspect many of the stories would be quite revealing of the perpetuation of difficulties up through this period predating a somewhat more enforced code of at least superficial political correctness in these matters.

39. Diane L. Bolger, "Ladies of the Expedition: Harriet Boyd Hawes and Edith Hall in Mediterranean Archaeology," in Claassen, *Women in Archaeology,* 41–50.

40. Mary Allsebrook, *Born to Rebel: The Life of Harriet Boyd Hawes* (Oxford: Oxbow Books, 1992), 230.

41. Daniel, *Hundred and Fifty Years,* 193. See now Marshall J. Becker and Philip P. Betancourt, *Richard Barry Seager: Pioneer Archaeologist and Proper Gentleman* (Philadelphia: University of Pennsylvania Museum, 1997) for a contextualization of Seager's role.

42. Allsebrook, *Born to Rebel,* 230.

43. See, e.g., Ann C. Gunter, ed., *The Construction of the Ancient Near East,* Culture and History 11 (Copenhagen: Academic Press, 1992), 8, with several references, as well as assembled articles.

44. On the ancient Near East see Jerrold S. Cooper, "From Mosul to Manila: Early Approaches to Funding Ancient Near Eastern Studies Research in the United States," in Gunter, *Construction,* 133–34; on ancient Greece, see Richard Jenkyns, *The Victorians and Ancient Greece* (Oxford: Basil Blackwell, 1980). Lynn Meskell has brought together several relevant articles in her edited volume, *Archaeology Under Fire: Nationalism, Politics and Heritage in the Eastern Mediterranean and Middle East* (London and New York: Routledge, 1998).

45. Melman, *Women's Orients;* Mary Louise Pratt, *Imperial Eyes: Travel Writing and Transculturation* (London: Routledge, 1992); Anne M. Lockwood, "Voyagers out of the Harem Within: British Women Travel Writers in the Middle East," Ph.D. diss., University of North Carolina, Chapel Hill, 1997.

46. Lorna Duffin, "Prisoners of Progress: Women and Evolution," in *The Nineteenth-Century Woman: Her Cultural and Physical World,* ed. Sara Delamont and Lorna Duffin (London: Croom Helm; New York: Barnes and Noble, 1978), 57–91.

47. Duffin, "Prisoners of Progress"; Dea Birkett, *Spinsters Abroad: Victorian Lady Explorers* (Oxford: Oxford University Press, 1989).

48. Denise D. Knight, *"The Yellow Wall-paper" and Selected Stories of Charlotte Perkins Gilman* (Newark: University of Delaware Press, 1994).

49. Murray, *My First Hundred Years.*

50. Carolyn G. Heilbrun, "Non-autobiographies of 'Privileged' Women: England and America," in *Life/Lines: Theorizing Women's Autobiography,* ed. Bella Brodzki and Celeste Schenck (Ithaca: Cornell University Press, 1988), 62–76; Tedlock, "Works and Wives," 274.

51. Gertrude Bell has been the subject of numerous biographical monographs. See, for example, H. V. F. Winstone, *Gertrude Bell* (London: Jonathan Cape, 1978); Susan Goodman, *Gertrude Bell* (Leamington Spa: Berg, 1985); Janet Wallach, *Desert Queen: The Extraordinary Life of Gertrude Bell: Adventurer, Adviser to Kings, Ally of Lawrence of Arabia* (New York: Nan A. Talese/Doubleday, 1995).

52. Joan Haslip, *Lady Hester Stanhope: A Biography* (London: Cassell, 1934); Ian Bruce, ed., *The Nun of Lebanon: The Love Affair of Lady Hester Stanhope and Michael Bruce. Their Newly Discovered Letters* (London: Collins, 1951).

53. Lockwood, "Voyagers," 71–107, gives a different and more sympathetic perspective on Lady Hester Stanhope. It does not delve into the issue of Gertrude Bell's probable reaction to the Stanhope mystique, nor does it purport to address the notion of Stanhope as an "archaeologist."

54. Letter from Bell quoted in Goodman, *Gertrude Bell,* 112.

55. Drower, *Flinders Petrie,* 315–17.

56. Murray, *My First Hundred Years,* 116.

57. Sara Delamont, "The Contradictions in Ladies' Education," in Delamont and Duffin, *The Nineteenth-Century Woman,* 139.

58. Melman, *Women's Orients,* 254–55.

59. Drower, *Flinders Petrie,* 312.

60. Delamont, "Contradictions in Ladies' Education," 145 and 156.

61. For a brief account of Jane Dieulafoy at Susa, see remarks in Elizabeth Carter, "A History of Excavation at Susa: Personalities and Archaeological Methodologies," in *The Royal City of Susa,* ed. Prudence O. Harper, Joan Aruz, and Françoise Tallon (New York: Metropolitan Museum of Art, 1992), 16–24 and photograph p. 21. Anick Coudart places Dieulafoy in a larger historiographic context particularly informative to our project: "Archaeology of French Women and French Women in Archaeology," in *Excavating Women,* 68–85.

62. Specifically relevant to our discussion here on Jane Dieulafoy's reentry into Parisian intellectual society after Susa is Eve and Jean Gran-Aymerich's *Jane Dieulafoy: Une vie d'homme* (Paris: Perrin, 1991).

63. Lorna Duffin, "The Conspicuous Consumptive: Woman as an Invalid," in Delamont and Duffin, *The Nineteenth-Century Woman,* 28.

64. Articles in Meskell, *Archaeology under Fire,* offer by implication diverse glimpses of macro-issues at stake in any attempt to place individual biography within the context of a supposedly objective scientific realm of Old World archaeology.

65. Lorraine Code, *Rhetorical Spaces: Essays on Gendered Locations* (New York: Routledge, 1995), 31.

66. See discussions, with much background, in Brodzki and Schenck, *Life/Lines.*

67. Heilbrun, "Non-autobiographies of 'Privileged' Women," 70.

68. Wallach, *Desert Queen,* 82.

69. Heilbrun, "Non-autobiographies of 'Privileged' Women," 70.

70. Melman, *Women's Orients,* 5.

71. Ruth Behar, "Introduction: Out of Exile," in Behar and Gordon, *Women Writing Culture.*

72. See Joan Gero and Margaret W. Conkey, eds., *Engendering Archaeology: Women and Prehistory* (Oxford: Basil Blackwell, 1991).

73. For example, Ruth Behar, *Translated Woman: Crossing the Border with Esperanza's Story* (Boston: Beacon Press, 1993).

74. Melman, *Women's Orients,* 1–2.

75. Quoted in Wallach, *Desert Queen,* 79–80.

76. Claassen, *Women in Archaeology,* 1–2.

Jane Dieulafoy
(1851–1916)

Eve Gran-Aymerich

(Translated by Alexandra L. Lesk Blomerus and Paul M. Blomerus)

JANE DIEULAFOY WAS BORN at the dawn of the Second Empire and died in May 1916, just as the battle of Verdun was raging. A contemporary of George Sand, Marie d'Agoult, and Colette, she was among those who heralded the arrival of the modern woman. While these women were accomplished as writers, artists, or philosophers, Jane Dieulafoy gained notoriety by venturing into a domain where no French woman before her had ever dared to tread: archaeological exploration. In Persia, she became an explorer and field archaeologist at a time when archaeology was a nascent science still in the process of being defined. She opened to French women a career in which they had not previously been represented at all. She remained loyal to her chosen vocation until the end of her life, devoting her last efforts to excavating the Hassan Mosque.[1]

Like all nineteenth-century women who wanted equality with men, Jane Dieulafoy provoked sarcasm and scandal. But she did not have to endure the terrible loneliness that was so often the price for claiming this recognition. Instead she was "the beloved companion" of Marcel Dieulafoy, the husband with whom she had a partnership founded on mutual understanding, respect, and reciprocal admiration. We, like her contemporaries, cannot separate those "who were as one." Whether in Paris or on the tells of Susa, they shared the same experiences and were united by the same passion for archaeology, art, and the Orient.[2]

Childhood in Paris and Toulouse

Jane Magre Dieulafoy was born in Toulouse on June 29, 1851, at 8 rue Jouxtaigues, in the old quarter of the Dalbade, in the heart of the old city, on the bank of the Garonne River. Her father died very soon after Jane's birth. She was the youngest of six children. The eldest, a brother, had been accidentally killed as a young man during a trip to Spain. Jane, her mother, and her four sisters developed a strong family cohesion that lasted throughout their lives.

Jane had a happy childhood, shared between Toulouse and the family's properties Terride and Langlade, where she lost herself in the pleasures of country life, already demonstrating the great vitality that impelled her on the battlefield and in the discovery of a far distant country. But after 1862 her mother chose to entrust her education to the Sisters of the Convent of the Assumption in Auteuil. This decision, which forced the little girl to live in Paris, far from her mother and beloved sisters, may seem surprising but no doubt can be explained by the exceptional intellectual qualities that Jane showed very early. Her mother, whose love for her youngest daughter never faltered, must have wanted for Jane more than the traditional education that she could give her. Indeed, at the Convent of the Assumption Jane was able to develop her talent for drawing and painting. Her mother's wish for an education that would nurture Jane's gifts seems to have been fulfilled by the sisters of the Auteuil convent. There, Jane learned several modern languages and acquired a good knowledge of Greek and Latin texts. She does not seem to have suffered greatly under the convent routine and harbored no grudge against those who imposed the cloister and its strict rules on her. She was very fond of her teachers. After the success of the first expedition in Persia, she sent them a copy of her first book, inscribed to her "old teachers" and to Marie-Eugénie de Jésus, the mother superior of the convent. The letter she sent them upon her return on August 9, 1889, makes it clear that, in Persia, Jane behaved no differently from the adolescent who had stood up to their iron rule. She showed the same courage, determination, and enterprising spirit. In any case, far from thwarting the young girl's strong personality, the pedagogy of the Sisters of the Assumption contributed to her balanced and harmonious development.

To judge the girl by the woman she became, Jane never felt irresistibly drawn to household chores or home management. Nothing repelled her more than the gloomy toils of a housewife and the thought of devoting her whole life to a boring routine. She little resembled other middle-class provincial girls. Small, slender, and blond, Jane lacked neither grace nor charm. But, with a face always crinkled in a smile, she clearly indicated that she did not care a great deal about her physical attractiveness. She adopted toward herself, others, and life in general, an attitude at once affectionate and mocking. Yet she was not at all bitter or withdrawn; on the contrary, she always wanted to get to the bottom of things before others did. She had a tremendously vibrant intelligence, devoid of affectation yet full of humor, simplicity, and generosity. From their first conversation, Marcel no doubt succumbed to her charm, which everyone acquainted with Jane recognized.

When the Dieulafoys met in late 1869 or early 1870, Marcel had just returned from Algeria. Also born in Toulouse, in 1844, he belonged to the same bourgeois merchant class as Jane, and their families were certainly acquainted.[3] In 1863, Marcel had been admitted to the École Polytechnique and two years later attended the École des Ponts et Chaussées, where he became a brilliant engineer specializing in railways. He was then sent to Aumale in Algeria to help develop that country by building roads and railways. During his youth and early professional life, as in his later discovery of Persia or assignment in Morocco, he maintained his faith in European civilization and in the progress he thought it could bring. But his interests were divided between study and meditation, on the one hand, and adventure and the unknown, on the other. Marcel was a man of action who wanted to change the world, but in Algeria the Orient began to exert its lifelong power over him.

From their first meeting Jane was impressed by this tall, elegant young man with good manners and a face still tanned by the hot Algerian sun, a man who exuded at once a firm determination and a deep gentleness. She was only nineteen years old and had just left the convent. Despite her misgivings about the kind of marriage she saw around her and her determination not to submit to the authority of a spouse, Jane quickly accepted his marriage proposal, and May 11, 1870, marks the beginning of their forty-six-year companionship. When they were united "for better or worse," they agreed on a way of life. Their relationship was founded on their acknowledgment of equality in difference. Jane gave up neither her identity nor her independence, while Marcel respected and admired her precisely for what distinguished her from other women. In 1870 he was employed by the Midi Railways and was determined in his free time to nurture his passionate curiosity about art and archaeology. To their cultural itinerary he added the discovery of the great countries of Europe—their opulence, monuments, and museums. He was most interested in the origin of religious architecture and the Western military, which he thought he had found in Muslim countries.

Jane enthusiastically supported his projects, which promised the life of which she had always dreamed. Yet her desire for adventure, her fondness for risk and action were soon to be satisfied in a most unexpected way: only three months after their marriage, war was declared against Prussia, and the Dieulafoys entered the struggle.

Married Life and the War

Marcel was not drafted, as his professional responsibilities exempted him from military service. But on September 2, 1870, news arrived at Toulouse of the catastrophic events near Sedan: the flagging French forces were at the mercy of the Prussians. The Republic had organized as a "government of national defense" under Léon Gambetta and Jules Favre. But the Prussian armies had reached the very walls of Paris, where the siege continued until the end of January 1871. The government was forced to retreat to the provinces, and in early October Gambetta left the capital for Tours. There he organized the Army of the Loire, which he placed under the command of General Chanzy. Marcel was eager to play his part for his country, and in October he requested assignment to the engineering corps. Enlisted as a captain, he was given command of the troops based at Nevers.

Jane did not hesitate for an instant: she could not imagine staying in Toulouse when the man with whom she was determined to share every experience was going to risk his life. She donned a soldier's overcoat and joined Marcel on the Loire, but because the army would not accept women except as canteen workers or in disguise, she finally chose to wear the gray shirt and trousers of a *franc-tireur* (sharpshooter) and to participate in every mission.

Her love for Marcel propelled her, as well as her concern to defend her country at all costs. Whatever she did, Jane's determination must have been strong enough to convince Marcel to allow her to take such great risks. Did he surrender to Jane's sense, despite her youth, of patriotic duty? No doubt, she could not resist the vocation of "woman warrior," as her companions liked to call her. Certainly, Jane never condoned the war whose horrors she came to know. But perhaps her participation allowed her to fulfill some of her aspirations. In experiencing the same hardships as the men, did she not demonstrate that women could have the qualities usually attributed to men? Additionally, war allowed her to put on the masculine clothing that she would eventually wear exclusively as a symbol of equality with men.[4]

During the terrible winter of 1870–71, Jane fully assumed her chosen responsibilities. With Marcel and his men she spent nights in the snow and cold as well as sharing their interminable journeys on horseback. In these dramatic circumstances, the soldiers rose to the occasion, and acts of heroism became a daily occurrence. Jane, however, was especially remarkable for her audacity and composure, which were acclaimed by General Barrail during the course of an inspection visit at the Nevers encampment. The cross of the Legion of Honor, which Jane would receive upon her return from the expedition in Persia, recognized as much the soldier of 1870 as the intrepid explorer and archaeologist she became.

Nonetheless, despite the soldiers' determination, the provincial armies proved to be powerless to break through the Prussian lines and liberate Paris. Crushed by the siege and the terrible winter, the capital was forced to surrender on January 28, 1871. At the end of their strength and hope, with an enduring bitterness in their hearts, the Dieulafoys made their way back to Toulouse, where daily life gradually resumed its normal rhythm.

Actually, the young couple did not embark on a normal conjugal life until the end of the winter of 1871. Upon his return to Toulouse, Marcel was assigned to the municipal maintenance service. In this capacity he had charge of municipal buildings and historic monuments and conceived some very large projects for his city. The Dieulafoys moved into a large apartment at number 63, rue d'Alsace-Lorraine (in the early 1970s the apartment still preserved the Dieulafoys' decor; and the collection of Persian faience that they assembled could still be admired there). Like Marcel, Jane again put on civilian clothes and probably gave up her masculine clothing during this period in Toulouse. Indeed, it is difficult to imagine that she would dare to wear a coat and trousers when Marcel had to tend to important municipal matters. Such a practice would have shocked the sensibilities of the citizens of the city.

Starting in 1874, Marcel, who retained his burning interest in architecture and archaeology, became architect of historic monuments under Eugène Viollet-le-Duc, Napoleon III's architect. He thus had many occasions to discuss with Viollet-le-Duc his ideas about the origins of Western architecture. These exchanges inspired him to go to the Orient and verify the intuitions he had in Algeria. Having returned from the ordeal of war, the Dieulafoys now sought to realize the dreams they had forged at the beginning of their marriage. They set out on the path to the Orient together.

They left France each year, for many years, on journeys of discovery to Egypt and Morocco. In the 1870s the archaeological riches of Egypt were being brought out of the desert by Auguste Mariette, who was well known in Paris for the Egyptian temple he reconstructed for the 1867 World Exposition.[5] The Dieulafoys probably sought him out to guide them through Saqqarah. But the Dieulafoys also visited the countries of northern and southern Europe: England, Belgium, Austria, Italy, and Spain. If Jane kept a journal on these first travels, no trace of it remains. She apparently did not feel the need to record her experiences for posterity.

Meanwhile, Marcel maintained his deepening conviction that the Orient held the secret to medieval Western architecture. He began to think that he should dedicate himself entirely to resolving this question. In 1879, with Jane's concurrence, he decided to take a leave from his post at the Midi Railways and to move decisively, along with his wife, into an archaeological career.

The Exploration of Persia

During the 1880s the Dieulafoys discovered Persia, traveling from Tabriz to Tehran, Esfahan, and Shiraz. They also undertook to excavate the ruins of Susa. For Jane Persia would be a place of self-fulfillment, for in the Orient she became a writer and archaeologist. The notes she took on places they passed through—whether on horseback or in camps, caravansaries, or mud huts—gave rise to the travelogues published in the review *Le Tour du Monde* followed by the report of the excavations at Susa. In the 1890s she began publishing historical novels in which the heroes conjured up by Jane's vivid imagination walked in the ruined palaces where Darius, Artaxerxes Mnemon, and Parysatis had lived and breathed.[6]

As for Marcel, he was preoccupied by the question of the beginnings of Gothic art in twelfth-century Europe. He discussed this subject intensely with Viollet-le-Duc, who suggested in his *Dictionnaire raisonné de l'architecture française du XIe au XVIe siècle* that the Crusades and Eastern architecture were the origin of the "Gothic revolution."[7] In defense of this thesis, Marcel Dieulafoy supplied his observations from his time in Morocco, Egypt, and Spain. Marcel's experience and his passionate interest in the origins of European Gothic art gave his "patron" the idea of sending him to Persia to examine oriental monuments of the Sasanid period and verify their hypothesis.

Before he could depart on this expedition, Marcel had to go to Paris to gather the necessary supplies and organize the expedition. While he was there, Viollet-le-Duc introduced him to Louis de Ronchaud, the secretary general of the Ministry of Fine Arts. De Ronchaud obtained leave for Marcel from the Midi Railways and, once he became director of the National Museums, put all his influence and energy behind Dieulafoy's endeavors.[8]

For many decades, the Orient had fascinated Europeans. Orientalism became the mode that Byron, Lamartine, Victor Hugo, and George Sand fostered in their writing. In politics the Orient, and in particular Persia, was the stake in European rivalries. France and Great Britain fought for preeminence in the countries of the Levant. The British and the Russians each tried to subjugate Persia, which remained independent. The French thought they could play an intermediary role and in so doing opened up an enormous market for their products. After a fruitless attempt by Napoleon I to curb the progress of Britain in Asia, France had no presence in Persia for thirty years. Then, in 1840, Louis-Philippe sent a diplomatic delegation headed by M. de Sercey to obtain the same commercial advantages enjoyed by the Russians and the British.

From the commercial point of view, the 1840 diplomatic attempt ended in failure, but it had other interests as well: among the delegation were the painter Eugène Flandin and the architect Pascal Coste, who had come to study art and archaeology. Left alone after the diplomats departed, Flandin and Coste explored the whole country—from Tabriz to Tehran, from Azerbaijan all the way to the province of Fars, from there to the Zagros Mountains, and then to the banks of the Tigris. They uncovered ruins and inscriptions, established iconographic documentation of excellent quality, and spent two months at Persepolis, where they made some preliminary soundings, excavated several relief[9] sculptures, and recorded architectural details useful for restoring the monuments.[10] Thus the results of the diplomatic mission yielded a scientific element, which proved very important for knowledge about ancient Persia. Only Susa remained closed to them, as it had been until then to all Europeans, with the exception of the Englishman H. C. Rawlinson, the future consul general of Baghdad. Rawlinson was able to enter Susa behind an army of two thousand men sent by the shah to put down the fierce Bakhtyaris tribesmen. He would later make a substantial contribution with his work on cuneiform inscriptions.[11]

During those same years, 1841 and 1842, while Flandin and Coste were absorbed in uncovering monuments, bas-reliefs, and inscriptions, a young Englishman, Austen Henry Layard, would visit the site of ancient Susa and the tomb of Daniel. Welcomed by the Bakhtyari chief in his residence of Kala Tul, this avid traveler and adventurer succeeded where the two Frenchmen had failed. Afterward, Layard returned to Turkey and visited the British ambassador, reporting to him a wealth of information on this region, which was still completely closed to European trade.[12] In the service of the British ambassador to Constantinople, Layard would begin to excavate the site of Nineveh in 1845.[13] At Susa, another Englishman, Kenneth Loftus, succeeded Layard in 1850–53. He led a brief excavation campaign, after which he participated in demarcating the borders.[14]

When the Dieulafoys left on their first expedition to Persia, they did not yet know that they would excavate at Susa. But they set out for the Orient motivated by the same curiosity as many scholars of their day. Jane proved to be more than a courageous and devoted companion. She called herself Marcel's collaborator (*collaborateur*), deliberately using the masculine form: "a [female] collaborator would have been a great annoyance," she said.[15]

The Dieulafoys dedicated the year 1880 to preparing for their departure. To reach Persia, they decided to pass through the Caucasus and the large city of Tauris, taking the northern route. On a cold February morning in 1881, they left Paris for Marseilles. There, they embarked on the *Ava,* a large freighter bound for Constantinople, then on a Russian boat to Poti on the eastern coast of the Black Sea. The trek across the Caucasus took ten days, during which the snow and cold were excruciating. Finally, having arrived at the border of the shah's empire, they crossed the Araxes on a ferry, and, via Azerbaijan, reached Tauris. From there, they explored Persia on horseback (in fourteen months, they would travel six thousand kilometers) photographing and documenting all the monuments, bridges, dikes, and mosques that they encountered along the way, whether in towns or the desert, from Tauris to Tehran, from Esfahan to Shiraz.

In order to reach the Susa region the Dieulafoys had to detour past Baghdad and Amarah in Turkish territory, as Bakhtyari terrain remained closed to them. Most often, they joined up with caravans, but their situation was quite precarious because they traveled as individuals without official escort. To those around them the Dieulafoys appeared to be two unassuming *faranguis,* two Westerners, two Christians, left to their own devices. On many occasions, only their weapons protected them from aggression and the hostility of the indigenous population. Although, unlike Layard, the Dieulafoys did not adopt native dress, Jane did travel in disguise: more often than not, she dressed like a man to travel more easily through regions where the presence of a woman without a veil and on horseback would only have provoked disgust and hostility. She, of course, wore trousers and sturdy boots, and she always carried a rifle on her shoulder and a whip in her hand. The weapons were not just for show; on many occasions she made use of them. En route, she further changed her appearance when she shaved her blond hair, which had been infested by lice. And she fooled everyone, from robbers on the highways to the shah himself, who did not want to believe her when she revealed her actual gender.

In Tehran, when the shah received the Dieulafoys, he addressed them in French. At first he took Jane for a young man and then, when he knew her gender, had difficulty imagining that she had been able to travel all the way to Tehran on horseback. The shah doubted that she would be able to carry out the planned expedition. Among members of the royal family, Zellé Sultan, the shah's son who administered the southern provinces, gave the Dieulafoys the warmest welcome. He facilitated their contacts with provincial governors, guaranteed them some protection, and, when they were about to begin the Susa excavations, assured them of his support and helped iron out numerous difficulties. This enlightened prince wanted to see his country develop and proved to be very open to Western ideas.

The Dieulafoys kept moving in Persia, making only brief stops in the large cities. They had neither the time nor the occasion to mingle extensively with the local people, remaining Western observers and rationalists. Like all travelers of this time, they confronted innumerable dangers—crossing an immense country in the grip of anarchy, insecurity, and a relentless climate, which exposed them to terrible fever.

During this journey of exploration, Jane kept a journal and took notes on all aspects of the territory they passed through, but neither she nor Marcel forgot the object of their expedition: the study of Persian monuments. Everywhere they went, despite fatigue and disease, they documented and photographed every building worthy of interest. Strenuous work led both of them to the limits of their reserves.

The last part of the journey that led the Dieulafoys to Susa would be the most difficult and the most eventful. Access to the Susa region was reputedly very difficult, as ferocious warriors defended the pass through the Bakhtyaris Mountains. The warriors who inhabited them were in constant rebellion against the shah. In order to reach Susa, the Dieulafoys had to get to Basra and Baghdad. An agonizing journey took them across deserts and swamps as far as Dezful. Finally, they climbed the tumulus that dominated the Kerkheh plain. They had discovered Susa and the tell of the royal palace; and, under the brambles, the bases of several columns exposed some thirty years before by Colonel Williams and Kenneth Loftus.

But concerned about not being able to return to Shushtar because of the rising waters, the Dieulafoys decided to leave again just a few short days after their arrival at Susa. Climatic conditions were indeed catastrophic, and torrential rains prevented them from visiting or recording monuments as they had before. Fever plagued both of them and left them debilitated. They returned to Marseilles via the Indian Ocean, the Red Sea, and the Suez Canal.

Altogether, the success of this enterprise can be attributed to the Dieulafoys' exceptional relationship. Jane was certainly not an ordinary woman, and she had to have had an extraordinary temperament to overcome fatigue, disease, and innumerable dangers. She never took the man's position, but, by surpassing what was considered "feminine" during this period, she earned a deserved equality with men. But Jane did not play the part of a heroine: she had known discouragement, fatigue, and even, sometimes, despair. She had been ashamed of her shaven head, which, despite her efforts, continued to be infested with lice, and of her ragged and filthy clothing. But her passionate curiosity and eagerness to observe and analyze a totally alien world allayed any regrets or homesickness as well as the suffering that usually results from two long years of exile.

The Return to Paris

Upon returning to Paris at the end of 1882, Jane reopened her travel journals to polish the account she had promised to *Le Tour du Monde.* Marcel worked on the first volumes of his *Art antique de la Perse,* which focused on the Achaemenids, Parthians, and Sasanids. Both were launching careers as writers of travel and archaeology.

Persia had transformed Jane Dieulafoy, the creative spirit awakened within her. Stimulated by the wealth of her experiences, she set out enthusiastically to write and eventually publish her writing. From this time on "the writing demon" never left her. Long after this trip, images would live on in her until they surfaced in her novels. "I think, therefore I live,"[16] she wrote during one long month when her strength, sapped by the fever that had never left her from Susa to Basra, prevented her from writing. Everything interested her, not only history and archaeology but also politics and economics. She became ethnographer, sociologist, journalist, and, finally a novelist.

Photography was another component of the Persian exploration. In

1881–82, the Dieulafoys' documentary task was greatly facilitated by the availability of photographic equipment. Art and archaeology had benefited greatly from an instrument that could faithfully reproduce monuments, sculptures, and inscriptions, considerably reducing if not eliminating the role of individual interpretation that is inevitable when a painter or architect depicts these remains. Indeed, those pursuing scholarly research such as art historians, archaeologists, and epigraphers could turn to photographic documents with almost total confidence. Thus, the most important part of the Dieulafoys' baggage was the photographic materials, the camera itself and its lens, the glass plates in leather boxes, and the chemicals.

The camera was not only an excellent ambassador, opening doors and allowing them to obtain permits and protection, but it also revealed the countryside, the people, and the monuments more than the fullest description could. Even today, the photographs have undeniable historical value, since the look of the sites and towns she captured has changed over time. All they saw was recorded in plans and measured as well as photographed. The plates were developed whenever they stopped.

As scientific interest in this first expedition was considerable, the remarkably precise photographic plates of the monuments of ancient and Muslim Persia were scrutinized with avid curiosity and studied with minute attention. The work of the Dieulafoys was monumental, and the discoveries they made at Persepolis and Pasargade have been considered among the best of the nineteenth century. Jane Dieulafoy's splendid photographs would eventually illustrate Marcel's five-volume *L'Art antique de la Perse.*

The photographic plates occupied a very prominent place in Jane's publication of their travel in Persia as well. The richness, interest, and beauty of the plates along with Jane's literary talent, vivacious style, and gift of observation helped make her travelogue a great success when it was serialized in *Le Tour du Monde* from 1883 to 1886.

The Dieulafoys received equal attention in the response to their first published works. From the moment that the first two volumes of *L'Art antique de la Perse* appeared, the exceptional quality of Jane's photographs elicited an outstanding reception. And Marcel's new and original ideas on the architecture of ancient Persia caused a sensation, although they also inspired controversy.[17] Additionally, Jane's serialization of the journey published from 1883 in *Le Tour du Monde* was immediately successful. Her rich and vibrant portrait of this little-known country attracted the curiosity of a public greatly intrigued by the Orient and by adventurous journeys in lands where the way of life was so different from their own. The Dieulafoy name was already gaining a certain cachet in well-to-do Parisian circles.

As time passed, instead of fading, their Persian memories remained vivid. The tells of Susa haunted the nightly dreams of Marcel, who envisioned the citadel and the Achaemenid palace uncovered and restored. So the Dieulafoys conceived the idea of a second expedition that would take them back to Susa to excavate the immense city. They submitted this proposal to de Ronchaud, who had become director of the National Museums, and he responded enthusiastically. French excavations at Susa could complete the Department of Oriental Antiquities collection, which, created in 1881 and directed by Léon Heuzey, combined finds from the excavations of Paul-Emile Botta at Nineveh and Khorsabad[18] with those of Ernest de Sarzec at Tello, ancient Lagash.[19]

However, the proposal for the Susa project met with bureaucratic resistance, probably because Marcel was not an archaeologist by training or because it was difficult to convince politicians that it would be advantageous for France to acquire an excavation site in Persia. Indeed, at this time, French policy on oriental archaeology singularly lacked coherence and consistency. But de Ronchaud, an intimate friend of President Jules Grévy, used all his influence to advance the Susa project. In addition, from 1882 to 1884 Jules Ferry was able to win over his fellow members of the government and sway public opinion on colonial politics. He encouraged the Dieulafoys' Persian project as an opportunity for France to stake out a position in Persia, which offered large markets for French industry.

Eventually de Ronchaud gained official approval and assembled a sum of thirty thousand francs drawn from museum budgets, to which the Ministry of Public Education added ten thousand francs.[20] For this expedition the Dieulafoys needed to assemble a proper team, so they called upon Charles Babin, a civil engineer, as well as Félix Houssaye, a naturalist and student of the École normale supérieure.

Thanks to de Ronchaud and upon the personal intervention of Doctor Tholozan, the shah's personal physician, they obtained royal authorization to dig at Susa. The shah had several reservations concerning objects the archaeologists would discover. Valuable pieces in gold or silver were to be the property of the Persian government, but the French could exchange them for their equivalent weight in bullion.

The Campaign in Susa

In mid-December 1884, the four team members left Paris for Toulon, taking the maritime route in order to reach Susa as quickly as possible. After calling at the port of Philippeville in Algeria, they reached Aden via the Suez

Canal and the Red Sea; then, hugging the coast of Persia, they arrived at Bandor-e-Busher in early February 1885 after a voyage of a month and a half. They journeyed through the Susa region in a caravan to Dezful and, when they finally once again caught sight of Susa, it seemed that "the winters had passed without changing a crevice" in the tells. The team set up their camp on the north tumulus, and Jane already had the feeling that they were "the heirs of the Salamis conquerors."[21]

As the days went by, a routine developed. Camp amenities were basic and did not fare well in bad weather. In February and March it often rained all day so ceaselessly and violently that it was impossible to leave the tents. When it was not raining and the work progressed, physical activity and the exhilaration of the discoveries made them forget their lack of basic comforts, shortages, physical suffering, and isolation. The total solidarity and absolute focus of the four companions in misery permitted them to keep working. Jane was companion and collaborator to the three men, with whom she worked on an equal footing, but she was also a "mother figure," lavishing attention and lifting spirits in order to make daily life endurable.

Once the team had settled on the tells of Susa, the problem arose of how to explore the site. Where to begin? Before the French expedition, Kenneth Loftus and Colonel Williams had overseen a preliminary exploration of the site during which they had uncovered the bases of six monumental columns and one of the sculpted bulls that had served as their capitals. On three square pedestals in the center of the room, they found trilingual inscriptions in cuneiform. The text came from Artaxerxes Mnemon, who conquered the Greeks at Cunaxa and restored the palace begun by Darius, son of Hystaspes. The British archaeologists had noted the evident traces of Greek influence at Susa and recognized, on the base of a column, a Greek inscription that closely resembled the epitaph of one of Alexander the Great's generals and permitted the identification of Shush with the Susa of the Greeks. The French team chose to explore three tells simultaneously—that of the apadana, or throne room, the citadel, and finally the tumulus from which rose the private residence of the "King of Kings."

The beginning of the first campaign was problematic due to the machinations of the *mirza* Abdoul Raïm, who had been sent by the governor of Dezful to oversee the French and who held fanatical Muslim views. The team managed to recruit workers, whose number rose to as many as three hundred but varied depending on the nature of the work. The archaeologists' first task was to create good morale among these men of such different temperament and customs. They succeeded rather well thanks to the confidence and respect that they inspired. The rules were clear and always scrupulously observed. Yet, while peace and security were assured within the camp, it was subject to attacks from outside. Night was the favored time for robbery attempts, and certain tribes tried to drive away the workers in order to take their places. Only the armed intervention of an opposing tribal chief restored order.

The workday started at 5:30 A.M. when the workers lined up to receive tools from the storeroom and set out for the excavation. A half-hour break allowed the workers to eat a meal of barley cakes, and then work continued until 4:00 P.M. Tasks and responsibilities were equally divided among the team of directors. Jane supervised the trenches and scrupulously kept up her excavation journal, where she registered every object and structure that was found.

Before digging into the soil of the tumuli, the team performed a survey of the area, but according to Jane, "the *kalchè* layer is a closed book that is very difficult to start deciphering."[22] This was why they chose an area already explored by the Loftus team and continued to excavate the apadana. They found a sufficient number of fragments of addorsed bulls to be able to reconstruct a model of the gigantic animals that once crowned the columns. The question of how to transport these heavy items would not be resolved until the end of the second campaign.

Although Loftus had not gone below what he had believed to be a layer of virgin clay, Marcel Dieulafoy observed that this was in fact collapsed mud brick walls, which he decided to investigate. His wisdom would be rewarded by the extraordinary discovery of the Lion Frieze and the monumental entrance to the palace. In fact, many pieces of faience glazed brick were found. They were concentrated at a point where the paving of the palace could not be excavated because it disappeared under a compact mass (four meters wide and seventy centimeters high, penetrating more than fifty centimeters into the paving) which had been crushed under the weight. The frieze that they discovered was complete in height (seventy-two centimeters), but its length could not be determined because it was lost in the wall of the trench.

Marcel probed the part of the debris that was buried under the earth and extracted from it a fragment decorated with the profile of a wild animal with a white muzzle and yellow nostrils. They had just discovered the Lion Frieze! The team was overjoyed at having discovered such a compensation for the hardships and difficulties of so many months. The elation of the four archaeologists is understandable, as the friezes from Susa were the first examples found in Persia. Excavators at Persepolis had never paid much attention to the enameled brick debris scattered over the site.

Jane Dieulafoy set about extracting the bricks. The work was all the more laborious and delicate because she had to "oversee the extraction of each brick, record its relative and absolute position, draw it in situ, and give it a find number, as well as helping with its transportation and arrival in storage," as Marcel explained. All these measures were of course necessary for the ultimate restoration of the frieze. With a team of fifty men, Jane extracted pieces of the frieze along its whole length. The conservation of these faience sherds was painstaking: "each block, sometimes broken into seven or eight pieces, was cleaned of dirt with the point of a knife, drawn on graph paper, placed in a basket with a find number under it, and then taken back to camp."[23] During this first campaign, the work conducted on the citadel remained fruitless, and the earth was practically sterile through a depth of four meters.

In May 1885 weather conditions obliged them to quit working. So the Dieulafoys decided to return to Paris to arrange for transporting the crates containing the glazed faience bricks of the Lion Frieze. Babin and Houssaye returned to Tehran, where they stayed until the second campaign. The precious crates did not reach Paris at the same time as the Dieulafoys because the Turkish authorities held them at Basra under the pretext of clearing customs.

The Dieulafoys arrived in Marseilles on July 1, 1885, then reembarked in October without waiting for the shah's authorization, which would guarantee their protection and grant them permission to excavate until April 1886. They hastened to Busher, where they had asked Babin and Houssaye to rejoin them. At Basra, the War Ministry had put a gunboat at their disposal. This managed to convince the Turkish customs officials to return the confiscated crates containing the Lion Frieze. The crates were loaded aboard an English ship that took them as far as Port Said, where a freighter took them on the last leg of the journey. Thus, whatever happened to their discoverers, the famous lions arrived at the Louvre, where they inspired awe in the Parisian public.

The road to Susa was fraught with innumerable dangers, but at the moment when their destination appeared before them just across the Karkheh, the expedition was beset by its most serious peril and Jane demonstrated her extraordinary character. They had to cross the river on rafts. The Dieulafoys climbed aboard theirs with two heavy trunks, but when the craft threatened to sink, Marcel jumped back onto the bank while Jane continued on across the river. She landed and found herself alone, loaded down by too many weapons and separated from her husband by a river three hundred meters wide. Suddenly, the vegetation shook, and eight nomads jumped out menacingly. Jane did not have time to think. She loaded her revolvers and, gripping one in each hand, she exclaimed in her loudest voice: "I have fourteen bullets to use on you; go and fetch six of your friends!" Taken aback, the men stopped at a respectful distance. For thirty minutes, Jane had to keep them at bay and, despite her fear, summoned the strength of character to prevent them from attacking.

When the party finally reached Susa, they resumed their old routine. Fortunately, living conditions were considerably improved by the construction of the first "Susa House," a modest structure built of mud bricks gathered from the upper layers of the site. This house was the predecessor of the veritable fortress that would be erected by Jacques de Morgan—whose towers still rise proudly above the plain today.

In December 1885, as the team resumed excavating at Susa, they had to adapt to a radical change of perspective. Whereas during the first season they had explored the whole site (thinking that they had all the time in the world), they now had to take into account the very short time allotted to the project (four months); the modesty of the budget (five thousand francs); and the new exigencies of the French state, which did not seem to want to invest in Susa. The state was no longer concerned with enriching its national collections by gathering beautiful pieces from the Susan palace. Marcel Dieulafoy felt compelled to give up his work on the citadel and to concentrate his efforts on the Achaemenid tumulus. The plan of action thus called for reconstructing the outer defensive wall and defensive works; then exposing Artaxerxes' palace; searching for the location of the grand staircase whose ramp Jane Dieulafoy had discovered; and extending the excavations in the area of the Lion Frieze.

The Achaemenid palace received the most attention. Eighty diggers or pick-men were put to work to uncover the east wing of the structure that surrounded the rectangular courtyard lying between the throne room and the pylons. The new trenches cut through a "swelling" of earth between the pylons and the apadana. The work in this area proved to be deceptive. One morning when they were preparing to suspend work there, a workman ran up brandishing a faience sherd that was white as snow. On one of its faces appeared, in high relief, a hemisphere in beautiful yellow enamel dotted with blue, green, and white stars in a cluster. It was a masterpiece of ceramics. Jane examined it a number of times and finally discerned "the shoulder of a human figure, dressed in a cloak of splendid colors."[24] The trench, having become so promising, was taken down to the level of the gravel foundations of the apadana. It was noted with surprise that the floor tiling was missing and that across the bed of gravel lay sections of earthen walls with foundations in a lower level. They removed these walls and discovered "an enormous mass loaded with magnificent enameled bricks"[25] supported by a carefully constructed brick wall. The Palace of Darius, destroyed by fire in the time of Xerxes and buried eighty years later under a layer of gravel, had been discovered.

The daily harvest of enameled bricks began. They were able to reconstruct "two life-size warrior figures," part of a scene showing archers in profile, walking, with spears in hand and each with a bow and quiver over his shoulder. The famous "Frieze of the Immortals" had been discovered. Jane returned to her Herodotus and reread his description of the royal guard, in the list of troops passing the Hellespont under the eyes of Xerxes. On the warriors of the bricks from Susa could be recognized the distinctive elements of the ten thousand "Immortals"—the wreath, the gold jewelry, and the silver pomegranate that tipped the spear. In the parade of these men, "beautiful in line, beautiful in form, beautiful in color,"[26] Jane saw ceramic work of extraordinary quality, in which she traced Greek influences. However, she stressed the differences from Hellenic style: "The artistic formulas, borrowed from afar by the Achaemenids, were fixed in religious molds the day they were acquired."[27] From that moment the Dieulafoys suspected a phenomenon that modern historians call "acculturation": in the fifth century Greeks and Persians had exchanged cultural models, which each then adopted and modified.

From the first instant of discovery until the last piece of enameled brick was extricated, Jane Dieulafoy remained at the center of the action. She could not leave the trench for fear that "the gold mine" might dry up. In the evening she would be so exhausted that she could not enter in her little journal the daily work, finds, and events. Digging in the trench of the archers continued up until the end of the excavation. Little by little, gaps in the frieze were filled in. A trilingual inscription discovered on one of the bricks revealed the name of King Darius and that of Otanes, chief conjurer against the magician Smerdis and loyal companion of Darius I, who ruled from 521 to 485 B.C. and built the apadana. The hypothesis that Marcel had put forward based on the stratigraphy of the site was thus confirmed: the "Frieze of the Immortals" did indeed come from the Palace of Darius, son of Hystaspes. Achaemenid art of the first dynasties had come to light, and, according to Marcel himself, "it seemed a quality that no one could have imagined."

The excavation of the apadana continued. The east and west colonnades were exposed, as well as some new column bases adjacent to those discovered the preceding year, and the body and head of one of the bulls that formed the capitals. Although he had had to give up exploring the site as a whole, Marcel was still determined to continue clearing the outside of the perimeter wall and resolved to reerect one of the monumental gates that connected the royal household to the city. While the Dieulafoys devoted themselves to the Achaemenid tumulus, Babin drew up a rigorously exact map of the site.[28]

Despite difficulties, the excavations were very fruitful: not only had the archaeologists been able, at least in part, to satisfy the rigorous scientific requirements that they followed while excavating the fortifications and studying the architecture; they had also brought to light some objects of great interest. In fact, the Lion Frieze and the one containing the archer figures were extraordinary examples of Achaemenid ceramic art that had been previously overlooked. The marble bulls were magnificent testimony to the Achaemenid sculpture of Susa.

Before the end of the work season, one nagging problem remained to be solved: that of transporting all these archaeological relics, which were destined to enrich the galleries of the Louvre Museum. Moreover, in order to take with them all the objects discovered, they had first to obtain permission from the governor, who was to divide the archaeological material. After a long and bitter negotiation, permission was granted when it was revealed that the governor's master, Prince Zellé Sultan, demanded something in return: he would not authorize the "export of the crates unless the French government promised to grant him the sash of the Legion of Honor."[29] Marcel promised to make known in France "the prince's noble conduct," and thus all the objects discovered at Susa were acquired. The archaeological finds reached Busher after a long and difficult journey. The four archaeologists boarded the *Sané,* a ship put at their disposal by the War Ministry and, exhausted but relieved to have succeeded, returned to Marseilles.

Life in Paris

From Marseilles, the Dieulafoys traveled to Paris. They left behind four hundred crates, which were carried in six cars of the Paris-Lyon-Marseilles railway. The development of the railway allowed more than forty-five tons of objects and archaeological monuments to be quickly and easily transported right to the heart of Paris.

It took the Dieulafoys several months to rid themselves of the bouts of fever that still wracked them and to return to their hard work. But in Persia Jane had taken an irreversible step: at Susa, she had shared the work equally with her three companions; she had confronted the same dangers, and, like Marcel, she had become a "true archaeologist." She had taken full responsibility for an area of the excavation, supervising in particular the delicate extraction of the enamel frieze, the crowning object of the expedition. Moreover, her diary of the first trip to Persia revealed her to be a true writer. She was a journalist (a forerunner of today's leading reporters) as well as a storyteller of subtle charm who often rose to philosophical reflection. She definitively left behind the restricted sphere of middle-class culture. When she declared herself to be her husband's [masculine] collaborator, Jane voluntarily affirmed her membership in the male world of action, adventure, and responsibility. She had already adopted male dress out of necessity, and this became the sign of what she wanted to be: a soldier of war, an explorer in Persia, and an archaeologist at Susa.

But what would become of her in Paris? Jane quickly developed a response to this question: she definitively renounced feminine attire, kept her hair short, and adopted stylish trousers, a severely buttoned white percale shirt, and a frock coat that showed to advantage her slender adolescent figure. After having known the ease, comfort, and freedom of men's trousers, Jane could not give them up in Paris without losing the way of life that she had invented for herself. This decision appears to have had a ceremonial beginning. Among the Dieulafoy archival material may be found two photographs taken the same day. One shows Jane, with hair cut very short, dressed in women's clothes, and the other shows her in the masculine garments that she never, thereafter, gave up and that made her famous.[30]

Moreover, the Persian adventure was not over. It continued in the Louvre, where they had to set up the Susa finds. On their return to Paris, the Dieulafoys met with Louis de Ronchaud (now director of the National Museums), as well as Léon Heuzey and Edmond Pottier (who were both responsible for the Department of Oriental Antiquities at the Louvre), in order to design the layout of the rooms where the friezes and the monumental capital would be placed. The four hundred crates had been placed in the cellar of the museum, and nothing yet had been unpacked. Léon Heuzey thus assessed the importance of the discoveries by examining the watercolors that the Dieulafoys had made of the friezes. This important Hellenist, who had been among the first to place archaeology on the same footing as philology at the French School at Athens, very early in his career, had cast his eye toward the western part of Asia. He had inaugurated the Department of Oriental Antiquities in 1881, becoming its first curator.[31] Not surprisingly, Heuzey enthusiastically received the relics from Susa that the Dieulafoys had brought back with such great difficulty. His department previously had had no objects that could testify to the splendor of

Achaemenid culture. Now no other collection in Europe could rival the Louvre, graced by the two friezes and the monumental capital. The Susan monuments took their place in the two large rooms on the first floor overlooking Saint-Germain-l'Auxerrois, but the enameled bricks had first to be cleaned and conserved—a task that consumed months of effort before the opening of the Dieulafoy Rooms on October 20, 1886.

During the whole summer of 1886, the Dieulafoys were at the center of Parisian life, with the spotlights trained on them. Scientific reviews as well as the mainstream press devoted long tributes to their expedition. The *American Journal of Archaeology* published an article by Ernest Babelon, keeper of the Cabinet des Médailles, and *L'Illustration* gave the expedition a double-page spread featuring portraits of the Dieulafoys. An article in *Le Temps* paid warm homage to all the members of the expedition but expressed particular admiration for Jane, "one of our most distinguished and courageous explorer-travelers."

On July 9, Marcel presented a paper to the Académie des Inscriptions et Belles-lettres, which rewarded his efforts by electing him to their membership in 1895. As for Jane, she received the cross of the Legion of Honor during the opening ceremony for the Achaemenid rooms in the Louvre. This decoration was no small achievement, for since the creation of the order only thirty-seven women had received it. The Legion of Honor recognized Jane Dieulafoy for the courage and exceptional valor she had displayed in Persia, but it also paid homage to the woman who had fought in the *francs-tireurs* uniform in 1870.

Jane Dieulafoy's decoration was widely publicized, and the public flocked to the Louvre to see the monuments brought back from Susa. The great museum had rarely known such crowds of people. The Department of Oriental Antiquities was now the richest in Europe, and the two rooms dedicated to Susa were the jewel in the crown. There on display was the column topped by its capital, the Lion Frieze, and the Archer Frieze, with the small objects behind glass.

In 1891 a third room completed the display of Achaemenid antiquities. There, Marcel Dieulafoy constructed a scale model of the apadana of Artaxerxes. Painstakingly rigorous and exact in his reconstruction of the monument, Marcel roughed out the framework using the recessed beam fittings that he had examined so carefully while the whole was still in situ at Susa. The columns topped by the addorsed bulls incorporated the beams that supported the roof; the Lion Frieze, with its short frontal dimension, concealed the thickness of the ceiling; while the archers followed at the top of the brick walls that enclosed the room on three sides. The apadana currently in the Louvre is the third version since the one executed by Marcel Dieulafoy. Although only an approximation, this reconstruction provides a gripping image of the ancient reality and helps give museum-goers an immediate sense of Achaemenid architecture, as well as the splendor and solemnity but also the delicacy and refinement of this civilization.

The pedagogical concern that guided the work on the apadana in the Louvre also emerged in the Dieulafoys' participation in the World Exposition of 1889. This exposition extolled not only the Republic, which was celebrating the centenary of the Revolution, but also the achievements of industry: the Eiffel Tower and the extraordinary "Hall of Machines," the culmination of a half century's effort, glorified the prowess of engineers and heralded the twentieth century. But it was "the retrospective exhibition of work" that gave significance to all the rest: these marvels of technological advancement could only be understood as the product of a laborious transformation, a gradual progress toward the dawn of reason. Thus men of science and the future such as Eiffel, Contamin, and Dutert were honored in the same fashion as the archaeologists Heuzey, de Sarzec, and Dieulafoy. For his part, Marcel Dieulafoy reconstructed the two archers from the famous frieze and had a "lovely reconstruction" of the apadana of Artaxerxes at Susa located at the pavilion of public works. Of special interest was his demonstration of how he thought a capstan and pulley would have been used in fifth century B.C. The shah visited Paris that year and through his visits to the exposition and the Louvre, he was able to see and appreciate the work accomplished at Susa by the Dieulafoys.

The success of their Persian expedition only served to reinforce the Dieulafoys' desire to resume their work at Susa. But negotiations to continue the excavations, begun with the Persian authorities in 1886, were stagnating. The Dieulafoys remained in Paris, where Marcel joined the administrative office of the Midi Railways. He thus resumed a professional career that could assure him the necessary income and still leave him enough time and freedom to concentrate on archaeology. He continued to publish the final volumes of *L'Art antique de la Perse* and prepared *L'Acropole de Suse,* which appeared in 1897. In the meantime, Jane edited the journal of the excavations at Susa, which had been serialized in *Le Tour du Monde* and would be published by Hachette in 1888, one year after *La Perse, la Chaldée et la Susiane,* the account of their first expedition.

The tells of Susa needed further excavation, and the Dieulafoys would have been the first to admit that they had barely scratched the surface. For lack of time and money, they had not been able to dig down to the earliest levels. In order to judge the results fairly, it is important to remember the conditions under which they worked. The Dieulafoys had been the first French people to explore Susa and had paved the way for the French Archaeological Delegation in Persia, which Jacques de Morgan was appointed to direct in 1897.[32] The expeditions of 1884–86 took place under strict constraints of time imposed by the shah and a very modest budget, which had not allowed them to undertake a full exploration of the site. In spite of this, the scientific world was unanimous in recognizing the merits of the work done by this first team of archaeologists. Even the English, rivals of the French in archaeology as in politics in this part of the world, paid homage to the Dieulafoys in September 1886 in a series of articles underscoring the importance of their discoveries. Hence, in 1887, when the great A. H. Layard, excavator of Nineveh and Babylon, recounted his 1842 visit to Susa, he recalled the French excavations that he had read about in the account by Jane Dieulafoy, "the accomplished, courageous and enterprising wife of the explorer."[33] He noted, in the most complimentary terms, how much he had gained from reading it, expressing above all his great admiration for the remarkable photographs.

Nevertheless, despite the Dieulafoys' desire to continue their work and the willingness of the French government to support this venture, they faced stronger and stronger opposition to their return from the Persian authorities. Negotiations bogged down, yet it was essential to find a solution, for the English, who for some time had shown an interest in Susa, now went on the offensive. In January 1887, scarcely six months after the French expedition had returned, rumors had already begun circulating that English archaeologists had asked permission to excavate at Susa. Then came reports that the British Museum had sent Mr. and Mrs. Bent to Persia; with the shah's authorization and after an archaeological exploration of the Susa region, they had begun working at Takht-i-Suleiman in order to determine the location of Ecbatana.

What was at stake here was acknowledging France's exclusive rights to the excavations at Susa. An agreement was struck with representatives of the British government that Susa would be left to the French while the English were to explore Takht-i-Suleiman. It was not, however, the Dieulafoys who would continue the work they had begun in Persia. The death of de Ronchaud in 1887 and the resignation of President Grévy the same year deprived them of their support in Paris, while in Tehran, the diplomatic envoy, M. de Balloy, did not favor them. In November 1889 a representative of public education, Jacques de Morgan, landed in Persia and, after traveling around the country during 1889–91, was entrusted with the directorship of the French Archaeological Delegation in Persia. He followed in the footsteps of the Dieulafoys on the tells of Susa and would reveal the city's extraordinary antiquity. Deeply embittered, the first explorers of Susa regarded him as a usurper and harbored a deep grudge against him. If Marcel suffered a terrible rage at being excluded from the site that he had wanted to probe right to its foundations, Jane too endured the wrenching loss. A wound had been opened that, although cauterized by reason, would never completely heal. Jane would always cherish this part of Asia.

For the Dieulafoys, Persia was relegated to the land of faraway dreams and paradise lost. Now that she had to resign herself to life in the Paris of her century, Jane sought "a way to pass the days and to ease the burden," as she put it to a journalist in 1905. Writing, like traveling, was her reason for living, the elixir that permitted her to escape the everyday drudgery, the boredom that ate away at bourgeois housewives who were reduced to domestic chores. In order to be fully in the world, Jane had to write.

The expedition to Persia and the excavation of Susa had given birth to two documentary works, founded in the observation of a world quite foreign to that of the readers of the *Tour du Monde.* Jane had taken her place among the great travelers and explorers who, through their accounts, stimulated a taste for faraway countries and helped develop literary exoticism. With actual travel no longer possible, and modern Persia now inaccessible, Jane rediscovered her country of choice by plunging into its past. Spurred on by the resounding success of her two travelogues about Persia, she tackled the literature of the imagination, embarking upon a new adventure in her literary career.

Although the Dieulafoys would never again lay eyes on Persia, it remained vividly alive in Jane's memory.[34] She brought the Achaemenid capital back to life with her first historical novel, *Parysatis,* dedicated to the queen of that name. It appeared in 1890 and fulfilled her desire for fame, receiving the commendation of the Académie française. Against the grandiose backdrop of the citadel and palace of Susa, she detailed the queen's every movement, "fueled by terrible passions . . . pitilessly wrenching the hearts of all those close to her and sacrificing them to the glory of the monarchy." She took extreme care in reconstructing the setting, and the archaeology (enriched by extracts from the texts and brought to life by her imagination) allowed Jane Dieulafoy to take us back in time, to resuscitate in flesh and thought actors who had disappeared from history. Her book became an opera, set to music by Camille Saint-Saëns, and was successfully mounted in the Roman arena of Béziers in 1902.

Thanks to the expeditions in Persia, the Dieulafoys became important personalities in the scholarly and social landscape of Paris. While Jane was making her mark as an author, Marcel had been elected to the Académie des Inscriptions et Belles-lettres in 1895. Their salon, first on rue Guénégaud near the Institut de France, then on the rue Chardin on Passy hill, was among the best attended and pleasantest in Paris. Scholars, poets, artists, painters, and musicians (the majority members of the *Institut*) participated in the theatrical matinees they hosted. The Dieulafoy salon—very much like that of Juliette Adam, of the countess de Luynes, or of the poet José-Maria de Hérédia—should be ranked among the antechambers of academia. Before the outbreak of World War I, which would return her with Marcel to the shores of a familiar Orient, Jane earned a most respected place in Parisian society. The salon in rue Chardin was among the most fashionable places in the capital, and Jane contributed actively to the blossoming and recognition of women's literature in France.

At the beginning of the twentieth century, the question that George Sand had dared to pose in 1863 continued to be raised: "Why no women in the Académie?" In 1894, the issue of women's candidacy at the Institut de France was reopened as a subject for heated debate.[35] *La Gazette de France* constructed a fictional scenario in which Madame Dieulafoy aspired to a seat on the Académie des Inscriptions et Belles-lettres. Not long after, Jane appeared high on the list of forty women who, in the eyes of the readers of the review *Femina,* should become part of a French women's academy. The public found the ostracism of female writers unjust, and so the idea of a specifically feminine academy gradually emerged, created in the image of the Académie Goncourt (begun in 1903). At the initiative of the director of *La Vie Heureuse,* a prize that bore the name Femina was launched, and a prize committee was formed. The publisher Hachette, which numbered Jane among its successful authors, donated the five thousand francs for the prize from its budget. Alongside Juliette Adam, Madame Alphonse Daudet, and the journalist Séverine, Jane Dieulafoy played a vital role in establishing this prize, which continues to this day in the Prix Femina.

Another Orient

Having explored the Orient in Africa and Asia, traveling throughout it and immersing themselves in it as in an invigorating sea, the Dieulafoys could not give up the enriching experience of these journeys. And yet, once enchanted by the Persian Orient, which had become their "second homeland," they could now no longer even get a foot in the door. Jacques de Morgan had maneuvered so adroitly that they had been ousted from Susa altogether.

Then another "Orient" on France's southern borders—Spain and Portugal—attracted their attention in 1888. Until 1914 they returned there twenty-three times on trips that took them off the beaten track to discover all the Iberian provinces and their art, still almost completely unknown in France. Together, and always associated in their discoveries, they visited churches, cathedrals, and modest chapels, palaces, museums—all the while drawing up an inventory of Spanish and Portuguese architecture, paintings, and sculpture. Hence Marcel dedicated a work to *La Statuaire polychrome en Espagne* (Paris, 1908) and presented, in the condensed form of a volume for the collection *Ars una, species mille,* a synthetic vision of *L'Art en Espagne et au Portugal* (Paris, 1913). For her part, Jane presented the Spanish provinces in two essays, *Aragon et Valence* (Paris, 1900) and *Castille et Andalousie* (Paris, 1908), and consecrated a last work to *Isabelle la Grande* (Paris, 1920).

At the very end of the century, the Dieulafoys took their career in a new direction: that of Hispanic studies. From Persia to Spain the link is less tenuous than it might at first seem; indeed, Marcel had not forgotten his initial theory about the oriental influence on medieval art in the West, for which he had first sought confirmation in Persia. His work on Spain and Portugal opens with a chapter dedicated to "Persian Art under the Sassanides" and a second in which he draws a parallel between "the church and the mosque." After having followed the trail back to Persia and its origins, the Dieulafoys were following it back again as far as Spain, which during eight centuries of partial Muslim domination had become the crucible where Muslim and Christian cultures met and then melded.

Perhaps, for the Dieulafoys, the travels in Spain were a way to allay their previous disappointments and an attempt to escape the anguishes of the threat of war. History, archaeology, and the study of fine arts were a refuge from the appalling vision of a Europe on the brink of self-destruction. Jane, the soldier of 1870, could see that war was imminent and used all her energy and influence to get women incorporated into the army administration. In April 1913, she presented a proposal to the minister of war that sought to make up the deficit of soldiers in the army by freeing up those in the auxiliary services to join combat units and putting women in the places thus left vacant. Despite the support of a large number of women and a positive reception in the press, including British newspapers, Jane's proposal was greeted by an embarrassed and polite silence. Women remained in the place that was considered their destiny, the home.

In August 1914 war was declared, and the Dieulafoys did not hesitate a moment. They once again joined the struggle against the enemy whom they had confronted in 1870. Their oriental dream seemed to fade to nothing. Yet when Marcel requested reenlistment in the engineering corps, it was to Morocco that he was posted. Jane accompanied him. Would Morocco at last give them the chance they had been waiting for since 1889 to fuse the two civilizations to which they were equally attached?

On September 10, 1914, they embarked at Bordeaux for Morocco. Upon arriving in Rabat, they received a very cold reception from General Lyautey, the *résident général.* He thought Jane had ignored the order for women not to accompany their husbands, which had been laid out in a dispatch sent to Paris that never reached Marcel. In spite of these initial difficulties, relations between Jane and the *résident général* rapidly improved. Her enterprising spirit and energy, her knowledge of war, and her unlimited devotion to her cause earned the officer's admiration.

At Rabat, Marcel was in charge of the engineering corps and, in particular, the construction of the Fez-Maknes railway, which would open at the end of their tour of duty; he also drew up plans for the hospitals in these two towns. Jane saw to the smooth operation of the ambulance service and ministered to the wounded in the clinic. Meanwhile, being in the neighborhood of the "tower of Hassan," the demon of archaeological discovery continued to possess them. Forty years earlier, on one of their North African expeditions, they had visited the ruins of this famous Hassan Mosque, the largest in the Muslim world, of which the majestic and unfinished tower was the only vestige still visible. Now that they were in Rabat for several months, perhaps for several years, they could plan to excavate the monument.

The Dieulafoys immediately submitted their proposal to General Lyautey, who quickly approved it because it dovetailed with his policy on Moroccan antiquities. Indeed, a Historical Monuments Service had already been established to carry out a systematic restoration and oversee the preservation of ancient native cities. Remarkable administrator and politician that he was, Lyautey thought that, in order to win the Moroccans over to France, he had not only to launch the country toward the future and furnish it with a modern infrastructure but also to embrace its identity by uncovering its past and restoring these testaments to its history. The excavation of the Hassan Mosque would give Moroccans new proof of France's sincere interest in their civilization and religion.

On October 1, 1914, tents were pitched on the site, and work commenced. Marcel, monopolized by his military business and the engineering corps, could not devote himself entirely to the excavation of the mosque, so it was Jane who directed the work. In his account of 1920, Marcel emphasized the magnitude of his debt to his "beloved partner" and insisted that she be credited with the greater portion of this work.[36]

And, in fact, Jane dedicated all her mornings to the mosque, deciding, in consultation with Marcel, which areas to excavate and firmly leading a considerable troop of prisoners of war, who were often difficult and almost always insolent. One morning in February 1915, when the layout of the monument had already begun to emerge, a German noncommissioned officer, "who spoke French like a Parisian," came to find Jane to tell her how much he would like to participate in the excavation. After this engaging introduction, he added that he was actively encouraging his men in their work, so that, after the German victory, his country would find the work already done. Jane felt that this was so audacious she took cruel revenge: she had the noncommissioned officer who was so interested in archaeology sent to work on a site, but it was a road construction site!

The tension that pervaded the ruins of the mosque was amplified by political events in France and Morocco that could have encouraged the Moroccans to join the "holy war" against the "infidels."[37] In this context of disorder, one can imagine the courage and force of character it must have taken for this woman, who was over sixty and already wracked by illness, to succeed in directing the excavation and exploration of the Hassan Mosque. The general's interest in the excavation never flagged; moreover, this interest was confirmed when a host of Moroccan dignitaries came to the site. Si Bouchaïd Doukkali, the sultan's minister of justice, helped to interpret a succession of rooms that Jane had just discovered and which formed the madrasa of the mosque, a type of hostel for students. Sultan Mouley Youssef himself visited the excavation and could appreciate the work accomplished and the spirit in which it had been conducted. The mosque was partially restored to its former splendor; the columns that defined its outlines were reerected, and the tower of Hassan once again became a minaret.

A similarly prestigious site that had come to General Lyautey's attention was the Roman city at Volubilis, which he wanted to have explored. The success of the excavation at the Hassan Mosque encouraged him in this project, and he asked the Dieulafoys to lend their expertise. They came to the site and sketched a plan of the work that would need to be done. The privilege of undertaking this work would not, however, fall to them because each day Jane, suffering from the amoebic dysentery that would eventually kill her, felt her strength waning. She was a victim of the lack of cleanliness and hygiene at the local clinic, and in April 1915 her very serious condition necessitated her return to France, where they hoped that a sojourn at Pompertuzat would permit her to regain her strength. Jane's condition did indeed improve at Pompertuzat, but neither Marcel nor she could imagine her withdrawing from the national effort at the height of the war and abandoning all that they had begun in Morocco. After a few weeks' recovery, they left France and returned to Rabat.

However, not long after their arrival, Jane again experienced the same symptoms; until October, she made use of her increasingly rare periods of remission to resume her work at the clinic and with the ambulance service. This active woman could not renounce the rule that she lived by: always she had to make herself useful and work toward the collective good. In taking over the clinic and in the ambulance service, just as when she had fought on the Loire front in 1870–71, Jane proved the place that women could occupy in war. The dramatic time in Morocco had seen the two principal axes that oriented this exceptional life come together: war and archaeology.

In the autumn of 1915 Jane Dieulafoy's condition suddenly took a turn for the worse, and return to France was inevitable. For a second and last time, the Dieulafoys boarded a ship bound for Bordeaux. At Langlade, their home in Toulouse, they passed the autumn and winter in the anguished hope of seeing signs of improvement that never came. Exhausted by the illness, Jane died in Marcel's arms on May 25, 1916. With her final words she asked about the fate of France at Verdun, where for more than four months tens of thousands of men had been perishing.

Conclusion

Jane Dieulafoy was undoubtedly a pioneer in the history of archaeology. When she and her husband first undertook the Susan excavations, field archaeology was still underdeveloped. The French consuls in Iraq had begun the exploration of the Near East but had never assigned a single excavation to a "specialist" who was free from all other professional constraints and entirely dedicated to archaeological work. In this era, archaeology was still conceived as a science that claimed the attention of two categories of people: the "scholar" who attended to the study of the sites and monuments; and the "man in the field" who recovered the objects. This was, for example, how the roles were divided between Léon Heuzey, curator of the Department of Oriental Antiquities at the Louvre, and the French consul at Basra, Ernest de Sarzec, who explored the Tello-Lagash site. Marcel and Jane Dieulafoy were not professional archaeologists in the modern sense of the word (as they had not received formal training). However, they were among the first representatives of a new generation of archaeological players. Dedicated both to the exploration of a site, as well as to the study and publication of their discoveries, in this couple the scholar and the field archaeologist were fused.

As a couple, equality seems to have been taken for granted and was established at the outset of their marriage. But Jane's decision to participate as a combatant in the Franco-Prussian War of 1870–71, causing an abrupt passage into the world of men, transformed their marriage into an unusual partnership where all experiences were shared. And yet she appeared in the public eye, despite everything, as Marcel's assistant although Marcel himself affirmed that, without her, he would never have been able to face the innumerable dangers he encountered and that Jane accomplished all the tasks of a real archaeologist at Susa. Despite Marcel's efforts on her behalf this public perception persisted.

Jane, understandably, could not resign herself to occupying the secondary role the public assumed she had. That is why, on her return from Persia, Jane Dieulafoy started writing, dedicating herself to travel narratives as documentaries, historical essays, novels, and even journalism. She very quickly realized that she would achieve social recognition of her status as a "woman equal to a man" only as a writer. The narrative of her Persian experiences as explorer and archaeologist set her among the extraordinary women who distinguished themselves by their well-known "masculine" qualities: their courage and endurance; their intelligence and initiative. It was a career that would assure her complete autonomy and give her a position among female intellectuals who, at this time, were still exposed to male sarcasm and were styled as "bluestockings."[38]

In a society that was quick to reject women who distanced themselves from the dominant model, Jane Dieulafoy deliberately sacrificed feminine attributes. Her fate demonstrates the contradictions of a society faced with radical transformations, one of which was the status of women. It is not the least of the paradoxes of a world about to enter the twentieth century, that Jane Dieulafoy, whose actions in life caused scandal and notoriety, was crowned with success as well: respected in political, academic, and artistic circles, she occupied an important place in the social and cultural world of her day. She had proved her archaeological skills in the excavation of the Hassan Mosque as well as on the tells of Susa. It is perhaps this image of a woman archaeologist, confronted by the hardships of work in the field and assuming the reins of leadership, that leaves the most lasting impression. Although she had to struggle for equality along with nineteenth-century feminists, her manner of practicing archaeology as a career gave her all the characteristics of a modern woman.

Although the Dieulafoys developed autonomous careers as writers within their unity as a couple—Marcel published scientific analyses, while Jane entered the literary world—they claimed recognition for their joint archaeological work. Their two excavations at Susa were the first great European archaeological expeditions organized in Persia, beginning a long era of French excavation in Iran that lasted through the 1970s. Acknowledging these collective accomplishments, the Achaemenid rooms of the Louvre Museum were named after both Monsieur and Madame Dieulafoy.

WORKS BY JANE DIEULAFOY
A SELECTED BIBLIOGRAPHY

Books, Monographs, Articles, and Lectures

La Perse, la Chaldée, la Susiane, relation de voyage. Paris: Hachette, 1887. 2d ed., Paris: Éditions Phébus, 1989.

A Suse, journal des fouilles, 1884–1886. Paris: Hachette, 1888. 2d ed., Paris: Éditions Phébus, 1989.

Aragon et Valence. Paris: Hachette, 1901.

"Ce que l'on dit de nous." *Le Figaro,* December 6, 1903, and continuing daily.

Castille et Andalousie. Paris: Hachette, 1908.

Isabelle la Grande. Paris: Hachette, 1920.

Marcel Dieulafoy, coauthor. *Le Théâtre dans l'intimité.* Paris, 1900.

Lectures at l'Université des Annales et la Société française des fouilles archéologiques

"Eschyle-Les Perses. Conférence faite à d'Odéon le 9 novembre 1893." *Revue Bleue,* 610–18. Paris, 1896.

"L'Espagne au temps des rois catholiques." In *Comoedia,* l'févier 1908. Paris.

"L'évolution religieuse de l'Espagne au XVIe s." *Conférences faites au musée Guimet.* Paris, 1909.

———, trans. *L'Épouse parfaite* by Luis de Leon, Paris, 1906.

Fiction

Parysatis. Paris, 1890.

Volontaire 1791–1793. Paris: Colin, 1892.

Rose d'Hatra et *L'oracle.* Paris: Colin, 1893.

Frère Pélage. Paris, 1894.

Déchéance. Paris, 1897.

Works by Marcel Dieulafoy with Jane Dieulafoy as Contributor

L'Art antique de la Perse: Achéménides, Parthes, Sassanides. 5 vols. Photographs by Jane Dieulafoy. Paris: Librairie centrale d'architecture, 1884–89.

Les origines de l'architecture du Moyen Âge et ses rapports avec l'architecture perse. Paris: Société centrale des architectes, 1887.

L'Acropole de Suse, d'après les fouilles en 1884, 1885, 1886. Paris: Hachette, 1893.

"Les Antiquités de Suse découvertes et rapportées par la mission Dieulafoy, 1884–1886." *Catalogue du musée du Louvre.* Paris, 1893.

Reflets de l'Orient sur le théâtre de Calderon. Paris, CRAI (Comptes rendus de l'Académie des Inscriptions et belles-lettres) 1900.

La Statuaire polychrome en Espagne. Paris: Hachette, 1908.

L'Art de l'Espagne et du Portugal. Encyclopédie de l'art universel Ars una, species mille. Paris: Hachette, 1913.

La Mosquée d'Hassan à Rabat. Paris, 1920.

Suggested Readings about Jane Dieulafoy

Desplantes, F. *Une exploratrice, Madame Jane Dieulafoy.* Rouen, 1889.

Darmesteter, J. "Parysatis et le roman historique." *Revue bleue* (1890).

Pottier, E. *Notice biographique de Jane parue en introduction à Isabelle la Grande.* Paris, Hachette, 1920.

Gran-Aymerich, È., and J. Gran-Aymerich. "Jane Dieulafoy. *Les grands archéologues," Archéologia* 189 (April 1984): 77–81.

———. *Jane Dieulafoy, une vie d'homme.* Paris: Perrin, 1991.

Gran-Aymerich, È. *Naissance de l'archéologie moderne. 1798–1945.* Paris: CNRS Éditions, 1998.

———. "Archéologie et politique française en Iran convergences et contradictions. Des missions Dieulafoy à la Délégation archéologique française en Iran (1881–1947)." *Journal asiatique* 287 (1999–1): 357–74.

Gran, Aymerich, È. *Dictionnaire biographique d'archéologie, 1798–1965.* Paris: CNRS Éditions, 2001.

Chevalier, N. *La Recherche archeologique française au Moyen-Orient, 1842–1947.* Paris: Editions Recherches sur les civilisations, 2002.

NOTES

The biography of Jane Dieulafoy and her intellectual odyssey may be reconstructed not only from her published works but also from the very important personal archives that are preserved in the Library of the Institute of France. The documents include the correspondence addressed to Jane and Marcel Dieulafoy by important persons in the political and cultural world of their day. Moreover, there are many unedited works of Jane Dieulafoy in these archives: commentaries on the daily press and the political events; notes prepared for conferences; projects not realized; personal journals inspired by the experience of the war, travels in Spain and the stay in

Morocco during the World War I. Other important references include E. Pottier, "Les antiquités de Suse rapportées par la mission Dieulafoy," *Gazette des Beaux Arts*, 1886; F. Desplantes, *Une exploratrice, Madame Jane Dieulafoy* (Rouen, 1889); C. Diehl, "Discours prononcé aux funérailles de Marcel Dieulafoy, le 28 février 1920" (CRAI, 1920); R. Cagnat, *Notice sur la vie et les travaux de Marcel Dieulafoy, lue le 18 novembre 1921* (Académie des inscriptions et belles-lettres, 1921); È. Gran-Aymerich and J. Gran-Aymerich, "Jane Dieulafoy, Les grands archéologues," *Archéologia* 189 (April 1984): 77–81; È. Gran-Aymerich and J. Gran-Aymerich, *Jane Dieulafoy, une vie d'homme* (Paris: Perrin, 1991); and È. Gran-Aymerich, "Archéologie et politique française en Iran convergences et contradictions. Des missions Dieulafoy à la Délégation archéologique française en Iran (1881–1947)," *Journal asiatique* 287 (1999): 357–74.

1. Jane Dieulafoy published the account of their journey to Persia first in the review *Le Tour du Monde*, then in a volume with the great Parisian publisher Hachette. For their work in Susa, see Jane Dieulafoy's account in the volume *A Suse, journal des fouilles, 1884–1886* (Paris, Hachette, 1888).

2. See Marcel's *L'Art antique de la Perse: Achéménides, Parthes, Sassanides*, 5 vols. (Paris, 1884) and *L'Acropole de Suse, d'après les fouilles en 1884, 1885, 1886, sous les auspices du musée du Louvre* (Paris: Hachette, 1893).

3. Both the Magre and Dieulafoy families were deeply rooted in Toulouse and the surrounding region. They belonged to a merchant middle class that, for many generations, had linked its destiny to that of Toulouse and played an active part in its administration. Each of their ancestors who had left Toulouse had returned. Like them, Marcel, his brother George, and Jane went up to Paris, where they felt perfectly at home, but remained loyal to their hometown.

4. George Sand is known to have worn men's clothes for convenience, particularly when traveling. During Jane's time, another woman obtained official permission from Napoleon III to wear men's clothes: Rosa Bonheur, the celebrated painter of animals, found trousers more comfortable for visiting the slaughterhouses where she found her "models."

5. Since 1850 and his celebrated discovery of the Serapeum at Memphis, Auguste Mariette had dedicated himself to safeguarding Egyptian antiquities and defending the interests of French archaeology along the banks of the Nile. He enjoyed an impressive success for his temple reconstruction on the Champ-de-Mars in Paris.

6. Her first historical novel, *Parysatis* (Paris, 1890), was set at Susa and brought back to life the terrible queen of Darius II, who, having failed in her attempt to place Cyrus, her favorite son, on the throne, waged a merciless war against Atarxerxes, who had defeated his brother. This novel was awarded a prize by the Académie française.

7. Until 1868 Viollet-le-Duc had maintained the French origin of this great movement, but the work of Viscount Melchior de Vogüé in Palestine—particularly in central Syria, where he studied civil and religious architecture of the first through seventh centuries—had revealed characteristics of Gothic architecture in certain fourth-century churches. Viollet-le-Duc therefore reconsidered his earlier opinion: see entry for "arch" in his *Dictionnaire raisonné de l'architecture française du XIe au XVIe siècle* (Paris, 1858–68).

8. Louis de Ronchaud (1816–87), a friend of the poet Lamartine, had traveled through Greece on foot and developed a boundless admiration for Greek antiquity. After becoming administrator of the Louvre Museum in 1881, he founded the École du Louvre the following year.

9. See E. N. Flandin and P. Coste, *Voyage en Perse, entrepris par ordre de M. le ministre des Affaires étrangères, d'après les instructions dressées par l'Institut,* 4 vols. (Paris, 1843–54).

10. Further undertakings included making squeezes of inscriptions and sculptures and drawing plans. Their work, published in 1844 with the backing of the French government, was remarkable for its exceptional illustrations—engravings made from their drawings and watercolors. See Flandin and Coste, *Voyage en Perse.*

11. As a political agent for the British government in Baghdad, H. C. Rawlinson (1810–95) recovered, under very dangerous conditions, the trilingual inscriptions of Behistun, thus supplying one of the principal keys for deciphering cuneiform writing.

12. Because Layard arrived at Constantinople exactly when England was preparing to mediate between Turkey and Persia in their boundary dispute, he was officially assigned to help craft an accord between the two countries.

13. See M. T. Larsen, *The Conquest of Assyria* (London: Routledge, 1996).

14. See S. Lloyd, *Foundations in the Dust: The Story of Mesopotamian Exploration* (London: Oxford University Press, 1980).

15. Dieulafoy, *La Perse.*

16. Ibid.

17. Marcel's documentation, for Persepolis in particular, far surpassed that gathered in 1874 by the Stolze and Andreas expedition.

18. See É. Fontan, ed., *De Khorsabad à Paris: La découverte des Assyriens* (Paris: Réunion des musées nationaux, 1994).

19. Ernest de Sarzec (1837–1901), French consul at Bosra, was one in a series of consuls archaeologists to the Near East, of whom the first was Paul-Émile Botta. Léon Heuzey (1831–1922), Hellenist director of a celebrated archaeological expedition in Macedonia, guaranteed the study and scientific publication of de Sarzec's excavations at Tello.

20. This sum was modest compared to the 130,000 francs accorded annually to the French delegation in Persia, directed by Jacques de Morgan beginning in 1897.

21. Dieulafoy, *A Suse.*

22. Ibid.

23. Ibid.

24. Ibid.

25. Ibid.

26. Ibid.

27. Ibid.

28. Babin's work was of such high quality that Jacques de Morgan and Roman Ghirshman would use it on later expeditions.

29. Dieulafoy, *A Suse.*

30. The two photographs are in an album of photographs of Jane, collected by

Marcel, among the few archival documents still preserved at the Dieulafoy townhouse, rue Chardin in Passy.

31. The Department of Oriental Antiquities was created on the occasion when the Louvre acquired objects recovered from Tello, including the famous statues of the *patesi* Gudea.

32. Jacques de Morgan (1857–1924), a mining engineer and geological prehistorian, had completed an important expedition in Persia in 1889–91 for the Ministry of Public Instruction and had directed the Egyptian Antiquities Service from 1892 to 1896; there he had accomplished remarkable work on Egyptian prehistory at Negada.

33. Henry Layard, *Early Adventures in Persia, Susiana, and Babylonia* (London, 1887).

34. Years later in the May 1914 preface to an account of a trip made by Louis Watelin (a collaborator of de Morgan who later became one of his enemies) she could still evoke the place and the experience with as much intensity as if she were still there.

35. In a notable way, Jane had conquered this bastion of antifeminism, where it was unthinkable to admit a woman. In 1921 when Marcel died, her name was read out in conjunction with that of her husband in Marcel's funerary eulogy.

36. *La Mosquée d'Hassan à Rabat* (Paris, 1920).

37. In particular the sorry Khenifra affair ended in the loss of a whole French colony and thirty-three officers.

38. In one instance, it would have been better if she had abstained from writing. Jane Dieulafoy was held responsible for the failure of the negotiations with the shah of Persia for the continuation of archeological work at Susa—she did not know how to hold back her pen and dared to express her feelings regarding the political and social state of Persia and the way its sovereign ruled.

Esther B. Van Deman

(1862–1937)

Katherine Welch

ONE HUNDRED YEARS AGO a number of gifted women made the then unorthodox decision to become classical archaeologists. Among this group was an American woman, Esther Boise Van Deman. Esther Van Deman was the first woman to earn an international reputation in Roman archaeology. She was the first Fellow in Latin at Bryn Mawr College, one of the first women admitted to graduate study at the University of Michigan, where she received an M.A. in 1892, and the first woman to earn a Ph.D. in Latin at the University of Chicago in 1898. As a Carnegie Fellow beginning in 1906, Van Deman was the third woman to obtain a fellowship in the American School of Classical Studies in Rome. She went on to establish herself as the first American woman archaeologist in Italy and to win wide acclaim for her pioneering work in the field of Roman construction techniques. Her work on Roman aqueducts is still one of the fundamental contributions to the history of Roman architecture.

In addition to her scholarly accomplishments, she taught herself the art of photography in order to illustrate her publications and lectures. Many of her photographs are archaeological and thus "scientific" in nature. However, many are also keenly artistic and evocative and, deservedly, have been the subject of exhibitions in the United States and Italy. This very private woman had striking abilities both as a scholar and as a photographer, and although she reveals little about herself personally in surviving records, her spheres of achievement reveal a woman of uncommon stature.

Early Life and Education

Esther Van Deman was born on October 1, 1862, on a prosperous farm owned by her father, Joseph, in South Salem, Ohio. Her family had settled there because her grandfather, a Virginian, had served in the Revolutionary War; after the war he received a tract of land in the territory north of the Ohio River that Virginia distributed to its veterans. The Van Demans were of German descent, and Van Deman's mother, Martha Millspaugh, was of Scottish Presbyterian origin.[1] Van Deman was fortunate to have received a solid education in her childhood at the South Salem Academy, and her strong sense of independence and ability to strike out on her own probably go back to her childhood in this pioneer community.[2] As an adult she was "an attractive young woman with blue eyes, fair skin, and light hair . . . she was engaged to be married at three different times, but in each case found herself finally unwilling to surrender her complete independence."[3]

In the late 1870s the Van Deman family left Ohio to move to Kansas, where another daughter was living. Elizabeth, the older sister of Esther Van Deman, had married a man named Magoffin and settled in the small rural town of Sterling in the center of the state. The Magoffins had a son, Ralph Van Deman Magoffin, who eventually pursued a career in archaeology, most probably inspired by his aunt. He taught classical history and archaeology at Johns Hopkins until 1923 and then taught at New York University from 1923 until his retirement in 1939. He was an active member of the Archaeological Institute of America, eventually becoming president of the organization for ten years.[4] The seeds of his career may perhaps be traced back to the strong bond of affection that had developed between him and his aunt in the 1870s and 1880s, when they shared a home in the lonely prairie town of Sterling, Kansas.[5] There was an adult relationship between the two, as we have a photograph dating to 1906–7 of Magoffin in Rome, taken by Esther Van Deman, examining a Latin inscription.[6] He also credits his aunt with some of the photographs in his publications, indicating long contact between the two.

Esther Van Deman began her college education when she was already in her twenties, as was common at the time. She attended the College of Emporia, an institution founded by Presbyterians in 1883 and located about one hundred miles east of Sterling. She spent two years at this college (1884–86), where she followed the Philosophical Course, which consisted of studying Latin, German, English, Mathematics, and Bible.[7] In 1886, at the age of twenty-four, Van Deman passed the entrance examinations for the University of Michigan, and she went there the following year.[8] At Michigan, she studied with Professor Francis W. Kelsey, under whose guidance she began research on the cult of the Vestal Virgins. The results of this research were eventually made public when she delivered a paper, "The Duties of the Vestals," at a conference that Kelsey organized in 1895.

Van Deman received her Bachelor of Arts degree in Latin in 1891. The following year she remained at the University of Michigan, earning her Master of Arts degree, also in Latin. After receiving her Master of Art's degree, Van Deman moved to Pennsylvania, where she spent a year (1892–93) as the first Fellow in Latin at Bryn Mawr College. She then taught for three years at two different schools: first she served as a Latin instructor at Wellesley College (1893–95) and then taught the subject at the Bryn Mawr School in Baltimore (1895–96). We do not know why Van Deman left Wellesley for Baltimore. In fact, her departures from all of her jobs are cloudy, but it is possible that she made this move to be closer to her sister's family, the Magoffins, who were residing in Washington, D.C., at the time.

Almost immediately (in 1896), however, she decided to enroll in the Ph.D. program at the University of Chicago. The University of Chicago must have been an exciting opportunity for Van Deman. It was a new university with an outstanding faculty, located in a big city in the Midwest, where Van Deman was most at home. Indeed, she always thought of herself as a midwesterner, and seems not to have been generally enamored of the "Eastern Establishment." The University of Chicago may also have appealed to her because it was less confining than the small all-female institutions where Van Deman had previously worked. At Bryn Mawr and Wellesley at the time, she would have lived in dormitories with women undergraduates. At Chicago she could live independently in a room rented in the community, as she had done in Ann Arbor when she was at the University of Michigan.[9] Her doctoral thesis was titled "The Cult of Vesta Publica and the Vestal Virgins" (the work was never published), and in 1898 she became the first woman to earn a Ph.D. in Latin from the University of

Chicago. Subsequently, she took a position as associate professor of Latin at Mount Holyoke College.

Life in Rome

In 1901, already at age thirty-nine, Van Deman went to Rome as a student in the American School of Classical Studies, with the goal of gathering more information about the cult of Vesta. Her mentor Kelsey was the Annual Professor of the School during that same year.[10] At the time Van Deman would have been one of approximately ten to fifteen women in the School. Indeed, the School of Classical Studies had included women students and visiting scholars from its very first year (1895–96).[11] It was this first trip to Rome that changed the direction of her career toward archaeology and away from a conventional academic future teaching Latin in the United States.[12] While pursuing her studies in history and philology, she became absorbed in a cosmopolitan, international world at a time when the city was in full expansion as the new capital of Italy. The archaeological atmosphere must have been electric, and Van Deman was exposed on a daily basis to it as she observed the excavations and material remains of the Atrium Vestae for her research.

The Forum Romanum was then being excavated by the architect Giacomo Boni; and the excavations on the Esquiline and all over Rome undertaken due to the demand for new housing in and around the city had recently and breathlessly been recorded by Rudolfo Lanciani.[13] Van Deman's acquaintance with such dynamic individuals as Boni, Christian Hülsen (vice director of the Deutsches Archäologisches Institut in Rome), and Thomas Ashby (director of the British School at Rome from 1906 to 1925) eventually drew her more toward archaeology and away from philological pursuits. She decided to embrace the study of building materials and techniques and the dating of Roman walls.[14]

Van Deman remained in Rome as a student until 1903. She then returned to the United States to become associate professor of Latin and Archaeology at the Woman's College of Baltimore (later renamed Goucher College). However, she was back in Rome in summer 1905 and then, in 1906, won a prestigious fellowship from the Carnegie Institution that allowed her to study at the School of Classical Studies in Rome from 1906 to 1909. She was in fact only the third woman to have the honor of being a Fellow of the School, having been preceded by Mabel Douglas Reid (1900–1901) and Susan Helen Ballou (1904–6).[15] Much of Van Deman's surviving correspondence with Kelsey centers around her concern about obtaining funding to work in Rome. Unlike most of the women involved in archaeology at the time, Van Deman was not a wealthy woman. Her winning of the Carnegie Fellowship, therefore, was a pivotal event that allowed her a three-year stay in Rome to conduct research without financial anxiety. This lengthy stay seems to have influenced her subsequent determination to remain in Rome and not return to the United States to teach. In fact, from this point Van Deman spent most of the rest of her life in Italy.

During her fellowship years Van Deman traveled extensively in Italy and Germany, and in 1913 she visited North Africa—traveling by mule with an Arab guide (a truly courageous journey). These trips, which had the goal of examining and documenting the walls of Roman buildings, are spectacularly documented in Van Deman's photographs.

After her fellowship expired, from 1910 on she continued to be supported financially by the Carnegie Institution of Washington as a Research Associate. She also became the first woman to lead the celebrated "walks" through Rome sponsored by the School of Classical Studies.[16] She returned to the United States for brief periods for the purpose of lecturing and had one lengthy stay of five years (1917–22) for health reasons. More specifically, in 1917 she seems to have experienced a "nervous collapse" that sent her back home to a sanatorium. We do not know why, but it has been suggested that the collapse was due to the strains of her work.[17]

In Rome, from 1902 to 1903 and from 1906 to 1917, Van Deman lived at the Pensione Girardet at Piazza Esquilino, an enterprise that catered to American and English women. This *pensione* was within walking distance of the German Archaeological Institute, then centrally located on the Capitoline Hill. At the German Archaeological Institute, with its excellent library and renowned lecture series, Van Deman had the opportunity for intense intellectual contact with major figures in the field of classical archaeology. When she returned to Rome in 1922, she rented a room in what became known as "Pensione Fersen" (an establishment run by the Fersens and de Daehns, political refugees from the 1917 upheavals in Russia), which for many years served as an informal residential annex to the American Academy in Rome. It is said that Van Deman boldly knocked on the door and insisted that the Fersens take her on as a paying guest; thus began the tradition of the "Pensione Fersen." The space was conveniently located directly across from the American Academy on the Janiculum hill in the Villa Sforza Cesarini (a villa belonging to a family that was a branch of the Torlonias).[18] It was in this cosmopolitan, international community that Van Deman lived for the rest of her life. This housing arrangement also afforded her close contact with the architects and artists of the Academy. In fact, it was shortly after she moved here that she wrote a work on the Neronian Sacra Via, illustrated by the architect G. Clay. While it is possible that discussions with artists at the Academy had some influence on her photographic work, most of her photography actually predates the year 1922, indicating that she was largely self-taught.

Van Deman's joy at being allowed to stay in Rome, as a Research Associate—to continue her work on Roman construction and prove herself as a scholar, rather than having to return to the United States to resume a conventional career teaching Latin—is reflected in a letter to Louise Fitz Randolph, a former colleague at Mount Holyoke:

> It is now over and the big step is taken—I've said I wish to stay *always* and show him [Jesse Benedict Carter, director of the School of Classical Studies] all the work and my methods. Now it rests with him to say what is to be my future here. I think I have no warmer friend anywhere, and he speaks of me as a father of his "newest baby"—as a remarkable & promising specimen and one he believes in.[19]

Van Deman is self-consciously wistful in another excerpt from the same letter when she says, "I feel that I shall never swing in a hammock under a nice old apple tree in America again."[20]

Van Deman's gladness to be in Rome was also tempered by her impatience and annoyance with the American Academy's conventional preoccupation with social graces and appearances.

> All runs well here—only I'm too busy to think & see no relief soon. It is overwhelming the amount of things which pile up. The last is the news of a swell reception for our & the artists' school next Christmas night by the Ambassador—who dined with us Thanksgiving—and I've no hat & dress ready & no hour to find one. We have a lunch for the Carters next Tuesday—& a lot of such trials when one is busy.[21]

And, indeed, feminine social pressures may have beset her as she endeavored to achieve recognition from the male scholars in her field. At one point, the wife of the School's director insisted that Van Deman buy a presentable new hat and gloves for a tea.[22]

Sometimes Van Deman evidently felt patronized by her male colleagues, as is clear from her letters. When she discovered the Sacra Via of Nero's time, above the Atrium Vestae, she wrote:

> I'm likely to publish it all at once & let the Rostra wait; for the latter cannot be done by anyone else,—while the new [Sacra] Via is clear as day when you've got the key (and someone may steal it from me). The Sacra Via—or the new via taking its place in importance, at least—the *Nova Via* & the *Clivus Sacer* are all one continuous structure, as shown by the concrete foundations. It is rather a good thing, I expect, and I'm mainly glad it is a *woman* who settled what Hülsen, Boni, Ashby and Vaglieri give up or misunderstand. All but Hülsen patronize women habitually—hence my pleasure.[23]

In the end she chose to engage in a long collaboration with Thomas Ashby, one of the men mentioned in her letter as "patronizing," although her collaboration with Ashby had hardly begun at the time she wrote this letter. She presumably thought differently about him later, as their correspondence and the acknowledgment of her expertise in his book on aqueducts suggest (see below).

At first, Van Deman was part of a circle of intellectuals in Rome that included relatively few women.[24] At the time women archaeologists from America usually went to the American School of Classical Studies in Athens. One female colleague of Van Deman's in Rome was the English Eugénie Strong, a historian of Roman art who arrived at the British School in 1909 (when Van Deman's work was already well along, however) and who in 1907 had published her *Roman Sculpture from Augustus to Constantine.* Other women active in the field of classical archaeology during the first decades of the twentieth century also tended to concern themselves with Greek art: notably, Gisela Richter and Margarete Bieber in Greek sculpture; and Mary Hamilton Swindler in ancient painting. These women were all considerably younger than Van Deman, but their interest in sculpture and painting helps to put into perspective Van Deman's decision to take up the study of Roman construction, a highly technical, "gritty," and unconventional choice of subject for a woman. Karin Einaudi speculates that this may have been a provocative move; Van Deman may have wished to prove that women could also engage in such "nonfeminine" topics as Roman building materials and techniques.[25] She had, by way of example, Harriet Boyd, who in 1901 published an excavation at Gournia on Crete that she herself had directed, something that was recognized as unprecedented in contemporary newspaper accounts.[26]

Surprisingly, considering that she was an American woman, Van Deman managed to secure from Giacomo Boni, director of the Forum Romanum excavations, permission to study and publish the remains of the Atrium Vestae, which he had excavated. As K. Geffcken has suggested:

> What had probably been, in origin, a topic interesting to her as a woman became a subject of bricks and construction, which she studied with the evidence of her fine photographs and without any romanticizing of the location.[27]

Esther Van Deman's legacy today is not altogether positive, perhaps partly because of the problems of dating in her work on the Atrium Vestae, but also possibly because of the single-mindedness with which she pursued her work on aqueducts and Roman construction. She was evidently a driven woman and does not seem to have cultivated traits perceived as desirably feminine (according to contemporary expectations) perhaps because she felt they would hamper her success in the field. A confidential communication to the Carnegie Institution of Washington, which relied on information from Francis Kelsey, remarked on her "inadequate sense of humor" and, especially, on her excessive "conscientiousness in accumulating details." The forceful and uncompromising nature of her character reveals itself especially early on in her career. In a 1901 letter to Kelsey, written when he was Annual Professor of the American School of Classical Studies in Rome, she complained of hearing that Kelsey had excluded women from attending Christian Hülsen's lectures at the German Archaeological Institute and threatened in her upcoming trip to Rome to conduct her work outside the Classical School altogether because of this situation.[28] Van Deman's sense of entitlement may be connected to other experiences in her life. It is worth considering Van Deman's early years in a pioneering community in Kansas, a state which was relatively advanced in women's rights; it had its first woman mayor, for example, as early as 1887.[29]

Roman Construction Techniques

Once Van Deman made her decision to study Roman construction, specifically concrete and wall-facing techniques, most of her energy was devoted to this pursuit, and it is for this work that she is recognized as a pioneer. Among classicists around the American Academy in Rome, Esther Van Deman was famous not only as someone who could tell the age of a wall by looking at it but also, allegedly, as "the only archaeologist in Rome who could date a brick by the taste of the mortar."[30] While there is no good evidence that Van Deman ever tasted Roman mortar for dating purposes, it is not out of the question, given her search for empirical methods for dating Roman walls. Indeed, field archaeologists at various sites today claim to be able to differentiate types of pottery, for example local versus imported versions of the same ware, by tasting the break surfaces of potsherds. Van Deman's single-minded devotion to her craft is suggested by an anecdote based on a friend's observations. It seems that as she was packing to leave Rome for a lecture tour in the United States, this friend saw her tucking concrete samples into the folds of a new dress (which, naturally, she had purchased only reluctantly).[31]

Van Deman's work on Roman construction, though flawed in many of its conclusions, was both important and influential in its time. Indeed, Van Deman was the first scholar to think about Roman architecture in terms of masonry and chronology. Because her ideas were based on a great deal of hard work and close observation of the ancient remains, they provided the foundation for the broad, general chronology for Roman buildings established by later scholars.

Esther Van Deman also spent much of her time wandering in the Roman Campagna documenting aqueducts. These investigations resulted in a monumental work *The Building of Roman Aqueducts* (1934), which is, even today, a basic text in the discipline of Roman archaeology. She never published the handbook of Roman construction on which she worked so hard throughout her professional life; however, a version of it was published posthumously by her colleague, Marion Elizabeth Blake, who had inherited Van Deman's notes. (Van Deman's fastening on the modest Blake as her scholarly executrix may have initially been more a burden than a boon for Blake, who was diverted by it from her life's work on mosaics, but she handled the responsibility nobly.)[32]

Blake first met Van Deman at Mount Holyoke College when she, as a student, heard the archaeologist lecture on the subject of Roman construction. She had further contact with her at the American Academy in Rome. Devoted to her and to the work she had done, Blake used Van Deman's notes to publish *Roman Construction from the Prehistoric Period to Augustus* in 1947. This book was almost exclusively based on Van Deman's research, and Van Deman had taken nearly all the photographic illustrations in the book. Blake's indebtedness to her late colleague is acknowledged in the introduction to the book:

> Dr. Esther Boise Van Deman is well known by reputation to all classical archaeologists. After the appearance of her preliminary presentation of her methods of dating concrete monuments, few scholars ventured to publish any article involving a knowledge of Roman construction without paying due respect to her opinion. She gave so freely of her unpublished information that many may feel that there is little new in the present volume, in which are embedded the results of her years of study. It is to be hoped, however, that those who have missed her kindly guidance will welcome such aid as it can give to their research problems. Dr. Van Deman will also be recalled by hundreds who heard her lecture on her sabbatical trips to America, but she will be remembered most vividly by those whose privilege it was to see the Forum and Palatine under her aegis. Such expeditions invariably either began or ended in the Atrium Vestae so that she could point out the very spot where she first noticed that a doorway had been blocked in ancient times by bricks of a different size, color, and texture from those in the rest of the wall. My own acquaintance with Dr. Van Deman began when, as a freshman at Mt. Holyoke College, I heard her lecture and became fascinated that anyone could tell the age of an ancient wall just by looking at it. When in 1924 my chance came to go to the American Academy, there I found Dr. Van Deman awaiting me, eager to bestow upon me as much of her vast store of information as I could absorb.[33]

Blake, in writing the book, was concerned primarily with the presentation, in descriptive and photographic form, of buildings that are securely dated (by inscriptions, literary sources, and brickstamps). For this reason, the book did not generate as much controversy as publications by Van Deman, who had tried to develop and then present a scientific system for dating concrete buildings purely on the basis of the appearance and size of their brickwork facings and concrete matrices.

Later Blake published *Roman Construction from Tiberius to the Flavians* (1968). Blake's work Roman *Construction in Italy from Nerva through the Antonines* (1973) was edited and completed posthumously by Doris Taylor Bishop. A bundle of notes for a fourth volume, which would have covered the Severans through Constantine, was given to the library of the American Academy in Rome on Bishop's death by her husband. It is now housed in the Photographic Archive and is still often consulted by scholars. Throughout Blake's work, she continues to refer to Van Deman and her theories, even into her discussion of buildings of the fourth century A.D.[34] This three-generation undertaking by women archaeologists is still fundamental reading for students of Roman architecture.[35]

The models available to Van Deman at the time she undertook work on Roman construction were Giacomo Boni's excavations in the Forum, which had been improvised for lack of any accepted model of stratigraphic technique at the time. There was also Heinrich Jordan and Christian Hülsen's important multivolume work *Topographie der Stadt Rom im Altertum,* but this for the most part concerned identifying and dating buildings by means of textual sources rather than by masonry techniques.[36] As far as Roman construction was concerned, the only existing technical study was J. Durm's *Die Baukunst der Römer,* which was concerned less with dating than with outlining how different categories of Roman building were constructed as well as decorated.[37]

With these works in mind and with the support of her mentor Francis W. Kelsey, Van Deman decided to embark on a major investigation of the features of Roman construction. Her goal was to isolate the norms that characterized building construction and wall-facing techniques in different periods of Roman history from Republic to Empire. In her two articles published in 1912 in the *American Journal of Archaeology,* Van Deman outlined the methodology she had developed in order to categorize the materials and types of mortar used in Roman walls, with the goal of being able to date buildings on empirical, technical grounds.[38] The methodology, which was revised by Giuseppe Lugli and others, we now know is incapable of yielding the intricate scientific results that Van Deman tried to garner. But in broad outline, it works for buildings within the city of Rome and in Latium.

The basic method of the study of Roman brickwork, initiated by Van Deman and still used today, consists of close observation and description of the bricks and mortar, particularly with regard to size and composition.[39] Van Deman's system also called for dating ancient monuments by a combination of external evidence (literary passages, dedicatory inscriptions) with internal evidence—that is, the relation of the building or portion of a building to the building above or below it, as well as to those adjoining it on the same level. Accordingly, she assigned six phases to the Atrium Vestae: (1) Republican (2) First imperial Atrium: Nero (3) Second imperial Atrium: Flavian emperors, particularly Domitian (4) Third period: Hadrian

(5) Fourth period: Antonines, probably Lucilla (6) Fifth period: Severans, probably Julia Domna.

She also considered as internal evidence the harmony, or absence thereof, in the general plan of the building itself; the structural unity of the monument and uniformity or diversity of its materials and methods of construction; and the character of the materials. Van Deman outlines this method in the introduction to her monograph *Atrium Vestae,* which was the definitive text on the monument until the American Academy in Rome's excavations began in the area in 1987.[40]

> A careful examination was made of the building as a whole, as well as of the individual walls of the various parts; in this examination special consideration was given to the following points:
>
> 1. The comparative level of the individual walls in each part and the relation, with respect to level, between the various parts.
> 2. The unity, in the several parts, in architectural plan and in structure, the latter as shown especially by continuity in brickwork and concrete.
> 3. The superimposition of walls of one type upon those of another.
> 4. The methods of construction, that is, the thickness of the individual walls and the occurrence and frequency, in them, of bonding-courses composed of large square bricks, the *tegulae bipedales* of Vitruvius; and where it could be ascertained the depth of the concrete foundations and the width of the courses of brick and the layers of mortar.
> 5. The character of the materials employed, as shown by the size, color, and composition of the bricks and by the color and composition of the mortar.
>
> For the determination of the specific periods to which the various parts of the Atrium belong, a comparative study was made, especially with regard to the methods of construction and the materials employed, of all the buildings in and near Rome to which a certain date can be assigned. To this evidence was added that afforded by the literature and coins. The number of brickstamps accessible to me was not sufficient to warrant their use as evidence, except in a very limited sense.

Van Deman has been harshly criticized for her mistrust of the evidence for dating provided by brickstamps and for her refusal to take into account the brickstamps from the Atrium Vestae. These indicate that Van Deman's third imperial Atrium Vestae phase (which she had assigned to the Hadrianic period on the basis of her dating system) was in fact Trajanic.[41] This criticism is unfair for a number of reasons.[42] First of all, Van Deman dated the different phases of the Atrium Vestae on the basis of the criteria outlined above as well as her knowledge of the cult of the Vestals, specifically which emperors were most associated with the cult:

> The number of coins of the time of Hadrian which refer to the cult, as well as the well-known activity of that ruler in building, lead to the assumption that the enlargement of the Atrium is to be ascribed to him rather than to any other of the post-Flavian emperors.[43]

Mainly, though, she dated her third imperial Atrium Vestae to the Hadrianic period because of the appearance of the brickwork:

> The construction of the walls of the groups both on the east and on the south is of the distinctive type which may be recognized everywhere as that of Hadrian.[44]

Van Deman may subsequently have become less convinced of the distinctiveness of Hadrianic brickwork. It should be noted that the above statement was written three years before she published her two seminal articles on Roman construction in *American Journal of Archaeology.* In one of these she acknowledged that Trajanic and Hadrianic brickwork are often similar in appearance.[45] How much of a role brickstamps played in Van Deman's dating of the different phases of the Atrium Vestae is not entirely clear. She had been suspicious of the evidence from brickstamps, since in her view bricks could be reused or kept in storage for a time after their production.[46] Previous work on the Atrium Vestae had yielded a sizable number of brickstamps, seventy-four of which had been published in 1884 by H. Dressel (*Corpus Inscriptionum Latinarum* XV.I) and must therefore have been known to Van Deman. Notably, however, most of these brickstamps had been published as Hadrianic.[47] Therefore, if Van Deman took these brickstamps into account, she would have been perfectly justified in considering them further evidence for the Hadrianic dating of her third imperial phase of the building.

Eventually, H. Bloch's *Bolli Laterizi* (Rome, 1947) demonstrated that the great majority of brickstamps in the Atrium Vestae are in fact Trajanic, not Hadrianic, in date. Bloch differentiated the Trajanic from Hadrianic brickstamps through detailed comparison with brickstamps in securely dated Trajanic buildings, such as the Baths of Trajan, the Markets of Trajan, and the renovated Forum of Caesar. Recent excavations in the area of the Atrium Vestae have corroborated this dating.[48]

Bloch's work had first appeared as a series of three articles in the *Bulletino della Commissione archeologica comunale di Roma,* beginning in 1936 (the year before Van Deman died).[49] He was certainly conducting his research in Rome shortly before Van Deman's death, but it is not clear how well, or even whether, she knew his work.[50] Moreover, Van Deman wrote and published her book on the Atrium Vestae before her long-term collaboration with Thomas Ashby had begun. Ashby certainly knew and appreciated the value of brickstamps for dating Roman buildings, and he even seems to have anticipated a number of Bloch's conclusions, as Ashby's notes indicate.[51] And in 1924 he donated his own extensive collection of brickstamps to the American Academy in Rome, so Van Deman would have had the opportunity to study them if she wished to do so.[52] Though she is justifiably censured for her dismissal of the value of brickstamps for dating and her refusal even to discuss the many brickstamps in the Atrium Vestae and the problem of their chronology, she should be given the credit she deserves—she was after all a specialist in Roman masonry, not in brickstamps. In 1909, the year her monograph was published, she did not yet have the benefit of Bloch's work. Indeed, her work preceded Bloch's by a quarter of a century. She may have decided that the issue of the brickstamps in the Atrium Vestae was too complicated to try to resolve and, therefore, that the evidence provided by brickstamps was not to be trusted.

The crux of the difficulty with Van Deman's work on the Atrium Vestae was that she dated her third imperial Atrium Vestae to the Hadrianic period because she thought that the brickwork looked Hadrianic, as opposed to Trajanic. But in reality it is often difficult to make such a precise distinction. There are two main problems with studying Roman concrete by means of visual analysis and measurements of the sizes of bricks and mortar bands, as Van Deman did.[53] The first is that most Roman concrete comes down to us in a weathered state. This means that no color or matrix of concrete will necessarily be uniform for an individual building or for different buildings of a given period. It is not possible, therefore, with complete confidence to use a photograph of a Roman wall with a known date to identify a wall sample with no accompanying dating information. Description and measurements of bricks and their interstices provide useful information, but they suggest tendencies in chronology rather than absolutes. The second and more important problem with studying ancient concrete and wall facings is that in a given period bricks were not always the same size and were not always laid regularly. Brick dimensions and bands of mortar can exhibit variability in different buildings during a single period and even in the same building. Van Deman's system had more limited usefulness than she had hoped; in reality it can only distinguish among broadly different types of brickwork. The fact that Van Deman never published her handbook on construction may suggest her increasing awareness of the limitations of her system.

Giuseppe Lugli, Lanciani's successor as professor of Roman archaeology at the University of Rome, was certainly aware of these limitations when he published his own book on Roman construction (the book that eventually superseded Van Deman's work as the classic reference for dating Roman concrete walls).[54] Even Lugli, in writing it, relied to a great extent on Van Deman's fundamental groundwork. But he revised Van Deman's intricate system of dating of Roman walls to specific imperial dynasties.[55] Like Van Deman, Lugli wrote comprehensive descriptions, recording the dimensions and colors of bricks and mortar bands. But for each masonry sample he measured the height of five courses of bricks together with five mortar bands, which he called a *modulo*. His system of *moduli* combined with his descriptions of masonry types of different periods works well in a broad way; for example, it can be used to differentiate Trajanic and Severan brickwork. But even its effectiveness is now considered to be limited, since Trajanic brickwork, which is the most regular of Roman brickwork, does not always follow expected patterns. With masonry of periods other than the Trajanic the variation can be considerable.[56]

Despite its methodological shortcomings, Van Deman's monograph on the imperial Atrium Vestae (1909) was a milestone in the study of Roman architecture. The pictures and colored phase plans are models of graphic illustration and set the standard for subsequent such publications.[57] Indeed, Van Deman played a large part in establishing the high level of close observation and graphic presentation that is expected today in the analysis and publication of individual Roman buildings. L. Ball has noted that she did establish the correct relative chronology of the different phases of the Atrium Vestae. If she had proposed broad dates to those phases, as Lugli did later, her dating could not have been faulted, and her work on the Atrium Vestae would now have a more positive legacy.[58] As Christian Hülsen wrote presciently (in July 1909) in the introduction to her monograph:

> The House of the Vestals has presented, since its excavation, many problems of great interest to the student of Roman topography and

> Roman architecture. Professor Van Deman undertakes this task with great energy and with an accurate knowledge of the situation. The House of the Vestals is taken up in her monograph not as an isolated problem, but in connection with a thorough and extensive study of Roman brickwork. As a result of these studies the author has been able to reconstruct the history of the Atrium Vestae in the first and second centuries AD. For the history of the republican building also, the remains of which are deeply buried under the imperial Atrium and are sketched for the first time in Professor Van Deman's work, valuable suggestions are given. Although some of the author's statements may be subject to criticism and even corrected by later researchers, her work marks a decided advance in the investigation of one of the most interesting monuments of the Roman Forum, and is besides a valuable contribution to the history of the architecture of the Romans and to our knowledge of their methods of construction.[59]

Van Deman's publications on Roman construction and the Atrium Vestae should be given their due as truly pioneering works in establishing the methodological foundation for the dating and publication of individual Roman buildings.[60]

Aqueducts

Van Deman's magisterial study *The Building of Roman Aqueducts* was the product of many years of fieldwork during which she and Thomas Ashby energetically followed the courses of the aqueducts around Rome, isolated their sources, and established their building histories.[61] It is notable that Van Deman did this work from the age of sixty-three to her late sixties, indicating that she possessed a remarkable degree of physical vigor. Her book contained painstaking descriptions of the aqueduct remains in the city of Rome and in the countryside. It also addressed the structural development of the aqueducts and their construction methods. Ashby's study *The Aqueducts of Ancient Rome* (Oxford, 1935), published posthumously, traced the course of the aqueducts outside the city of Rome.[62] The two books thus self-consciously complemented each other—Ashby's more archaeological and illustrated with copious plans; Van Deman's more technical and illustrated with many of her own crisp, evocative photographs. The work on aqueducts of these two scholars continues to be influential and, indeed, will never be eclipsed because so much of the physical evidence that they documented has disappeared as a result of Rome's expansion into the Campagna after World War II.[63]

In their collaboration, Van Deman and Ashby visited all of the extant remains of aqueducts in and around Rome, visiting ruins along cliffs, gorges, valleys, fields (both cultivated and wild), and in farmhouses.[64] Most of their fieldwork was conducted from 1924 (shortly before Ashby was forcibly retired from his position as director of the British School) to 1931, when Ashby died.[65] Using Frontinus's *On Aqueducts,* they located the sources of the four great aqueducts (the Claudia, Marcia, Anio Novus, and Anio Vetus) in the upper parts of the Anio River valley, at springs and lakes near Subiaco, Mandela, and Vicovaro. The aqueducts followed the course of the Anio River from their sources to a point just south of Tivoli, where they turned south to Gallicano (where the Aqua Marcia crosses a gorge at the famous Ponte Lupo). The two then followed the course of the aqueducts to the west, where the conduits tunnel through the hills and cross the ravines of the Roman Campagna and then come together at a point south of the Capannelle racetrack (near Cine Città), six miles from Rome. From here the aqueducts proceed on the picturesque, well-preserved arches to the Porta Maggiore (the ancient Porta Praenestina), where they were distributed to reservoirs and then fed the city by means of pipes.

In order to distinguish one aqueduct from another Van Deman and Ashby used several criteria: construction materials, quality of workmanship, mineral deposits, and directness of course. The actual length of the four different aqueducts varied from forty-three to sixty-two miles. Since only about a third of these aqueducts' courses was carried on arches—the rest ran beneath the ground—the work of distinguishing the aqueducts from one another was notably difficult. In the Gallicano-Capannelle stretch, for example, much of the length of the channels had disappeared because of erosion or plowing. Here Van Deman and Ashby had to follow the courses of the aqueducts by tracing the bits of calcium carbonate that mark the position of the ancient downshafts for cleaning the aqueduct channels.[66]

This kind of work required a high degree of dedication, and Van Deman evidently showed no lack of it during her many years of work on this project. In the introduction to his book on aqueducts, Ashby writes:

> In elucidating the chronology and construction of the aqueducts, and especially of the various bridges by which they cross the branch valleys of the Anio and the deep ravines between Gericomio and Pallavicina, I have relied upon the dating established by Dr. Esther B.

> Van Deman's work, *The Building of the Roman Aqueducts.* How much the present work owes to her will be gathered partly from the frequency with which her name is cited; but long days of study together in the field and at home constitute a debt which ordinary forms of acknowledgment cannot properly express.[67]

A 1932 cartoon shows Van Deman and Ashby working in the Roman Campagna.[68] Interestingly, it shows Ashby expounding and Van Deman taking dictation. The surviving correspondence between the two scholars suggests that this was not the way that the two actually worked but rather the way that the public naturally assumed they worked.

A letter written by Ashby on Christmas Day 1927 reveals the collaborative and businesslike relationship that existed between the two scholars. The letter was written in preparation for a trip to follow the course of the aqueduct Claudia-Anio Novus from Tor Fiscale to the emergence of the channels in the vicinity of Le Capannelle. It demonstrates the intricacy of the method and the numbering system that Ashby and Van Deman used to identify and follow the courses of the different lines of aqueduct.

> *Dear Miss Van Deman,*
>
> *. . . All right—you do your trip first. Then we were (to) join in, I thought, from the Tor Fiscale (or thereabouts) to the opera Don Bosco (the place where the priests are) to look at the last bit of Claudian arches—,*[sic] *nearer Rome than where we stopped last time: but you had better do Capannelle first.*
>
> *I should leave new bits of aqueduct out of the main bits anyhow, and stick to Frontinus. We really can't be sure if the Marcia is within 200 paces to the left of the 38th mile of the Sublacensis and the Claudia within 300, the Cl. must be 100 paces further down (towards Rome) than the Marcia.—Then there's Albudinus to reckon with, also.*
>
> *[No.] 111. I found this in a field of artichokes near (SE from) the pool*-, which seems to be the concrete top of the underground conduit—can't get in now. Also there's some further S.E. again—in the drive on the western edge just E. of the Marrana, and at the turn of the drive.*
>
> *[No.] 112. There is I think (I didn't put it down) a tiny bit just N.W. of the piscina (which is 50 m. E. of the Villa Berton). But there's a big bit 120 m. N.W. of the villa in the pine avenue (about 60*

m. in length) of the Cl. and A.N. (cf. Not. Scav. 1887, 558) this must be your [nos.] 113–114—but the stables are further on, really. You don't see much but the top of the Claudia except in the ditch. Then there's an interval of 150 m.

Then the road turns down (I think, by the Chapel) to Capannelle station. On your right you see the specus [no.] 115 of Claudia with concrete sides and a stone top slab; and this carries on along the back of the racing stables for a length of some 200 m., till you get to the crossroads from the Appia Nova to the Tuscolana (Sette Bassi)—and this must be your [no.] 116. I was all over it last month alone.

Yours as ever, T. Ashby.

**Which please look at to see if the E. wall isn't 2 periods as I say.*[69]

Written without any concession to Christmas sentimentality, the letter reflects Ashby's respect for Van Deman's opinion. In addition, the letter is relatively formal in tone (no first names are used) and suggests a relationship of respectful distance between the correspondents.[70] It also reveals that Van Deman did much of the aqueduct tracking alone, unaccompanied by her collaborator (Ashby was not free to go on such trips frequently until after his dismissal as director of the British School in Rome in 1925).

Van Deman's single-mindedness in pursuing aqueducts certainly contributed to her image as a legendary "character" at the Academy. Frank Brown, director of the American Academy from 1965 to 1969, "recollected an endless walk [with Van Deman and others] to the Ponte Lupo where he was left somewhat behind, carrying photographic equipment and picnic baskets."[71] (Brown, according to some who knew him, disliked Van Deman and is said to have referred to her as a "man-woman.") Van Deman was allegedly known around the American Academy as "Aqueduct Annie," and one doubts that this term was wholly affectionate.[72] Nina Longobardi, an Academy librarian who knew her near the end of her life, remembered Van Deman as a lonely woman in need of company.[73] It is difficult to know today what exactly prompted impressions such as these.

Articles

It is worth noting that Van Deman's writing style changed over the course of the three decades. Her early articles on the Vestal statues, the Rostra, and the Porticus of Gaius and Lucius are quite dry and factual, even grave in tone. Her later articles, however, contain unexpected rhetorical and humorous flourishes. This was perhaps connected with a diminished need to prove herself after she had become established and respected (years of exposure to the work of European colleagues may also have played a role). Compare the excerpts from the introduction to her monograph on the Atrium Vestae of 1909 (quoted above) with the following quotations from publications in the *American Journal of Archaeology* in 1923 and 1924:

> Through its long halls [Caligula] passed from one scene of wild revelry to another, and in one of the narrow, covered passages of this older "Palatium" [the Domus Tiberiana] lurked the assassins at whose hands he met his death.[74]
>
> Out of the ruins [of the Sacra Via destroyed in the fire of A.D. 64] there arose, phoenixlike, a more splendid group of structures at a new level and with a new orientation, the general plan of which is still clear, though the walls themselves are much broken and, in certain parts, destroyed by the following centuries of restoration. With its buried walls and vanished streets, the old-time character of the region also disappeared and the thronging quarter of the people was replaced by stately arcades and spacious halls forming but an architectural link between the Augustan Forum below and the oriental splendors of the entrance court of the great palace above, with the golden statue of its builder towering over it all.[75]
>
> [In the Flavian period] new streets cut into pieces the unwieldy mass of the Golden House and the homes of the populace sprang up amid the ruins throughout the whole city. As a part of the great policy of restitution to the people of their stolen rights and possessions, the district of the Sacra Via, as will be shown at a later time, was given back to the people in a new form, its old-time character as a region of barter and trade again restored and the magnificent arcades and halls transformed into the great warehouses for the people, the *horrea piperataria et Vespasiani. Sic transit gloria Mundi.*[76]

After having made the decision to specialize in the field of Roman construction, Van Deman published two important articles in 1912 in the *American Journal of Archaeology* concerning the chronology of Roman brick-faced walls. These articles laid out the basic tenets of her system for dating Roman walls, which she hoped to use in expanded form in her handbook on Roman construction. However, while Esther Van Deman is best remembered for her articles on construction, as well as her work on aqueducts and her monograph on the Atrium Vestae, she covered many other subjects in her numerous articles, many of the ideas in which were highly original and are still accepted today. Though Italian scholars regularly cite her, these articles are undervalued in American scholarly circles today and, therefore, deserve some detailed comment here.

Although her dissertation was never published, she did publish two articles in 1908 related to her dissertation subject. One, on the Vestal inscriptions, appeared in the *American Journal of Philology;* and a paper on the statues of the Vestals was published in the *American Journal of Archaeology*. The article on the statues of the Vestals, "The Value of the Vestal Statues as Originals," was Van Deman's only foray into sculptural studies. It demonstrated for the first time that the portrait statues of the Vestal Virgins (recognizable by their distinctive headdress) found in and around the Atrium Vestae use statue formats of the classical period, such as the so-called "Large and Small Herculaneum Woman" types and the "Artemisia" type. The article is useful in its exposition of the different hairstyles and attributes used by the Vestals, although none of them should be considered "special badges of office" since none are used consistently and none are exclusive to the Vestals. Keeping in mind that it is general practice for Roman portrait statues to combine realistic portrait heads with "ideal" body types, the article, including the conclusion, seems now somewhat naive in its insistence that, because the statue bodies comprise Greek types, the statues should not be classified as "portrait statues."[77]

She also wrote a series of important and influential articles for the *American Journal of Archaeology,* the *Journal of Roman Studies,* and the *Memoirs of the American Academy in Rome,* concerning monuments in and near the Roman Forum.[78] Of these articles, "The Porticus of Gaius and Lucius," published in 1913, and "The Sacra Via of Nero," published in 1925, are particularly noteworthy.

"The Sacra Via of Nero" identified for the first time the remains of the stretch of the Via Sacra constructed by Nero as part of the massive urban building campaign associated with his Domus Aurea of A.D. 64. This incarnation of the Sacra Via had previously been thought to date to the time of Constantine. The Neronian Sacra Via, which proved to be lined by covered porticoes and probably to be flanked on both sides by vast porticoes, is important as a particularly early example of the colonnaded street, an architectural type that became ubiquitous during the High Empire. Through stratigraphic analysis of the scarps left by Boni (who had cleared the Sacra Via down to its Augustan level) Van Deman was able to show that Nero and subsequently Hadrian had raised the level of the older Sacra Via. She also demonstrated that the expanded Neronian Sacra Via led to a colonnaded plaza on the Velia with the colossal statue of Nero as Helios as its focus. Van Deman's arguments were strongly opposed by Ferdinando Castagnoli, but recent work in the area has corroborated her Neronian dating of the porticoed Sacra Via.[79] This recent work does call into question Van Deman's reconstruction of the elevation of the arcaded porticoes lining the street (the remains with which she was working are actually a product of a Flavian rebuilding of the original Neronian colonnaded street) and her chronological connection of the foundations of the porticoes with those of other adjacent buildings, such as the Atrium Vestae. It has also been pointed out that Van Deman's reconstruction of a great Neronian, warehouselike porticus on either side of the Neronian Sacra Via is purely speculative, since the extant remains are wholly Flavian in date.[80]

The article on the Porticus of Gaius and Lucius demonstrated for the first time that the portico adjoining the front of the Basilica Paulli (also known in the literature as the Basilica Aemilia and Basilica Fulvia) on the north side of the Forum Romanum was in fact a separate and discreet monument dedicated to Augustus's grandsons and intended heirs, Gaius and Lucius Caesar. Van Deman made this identification on the basis of a monumental building inscription containing a dedication to Lucius Caesar, grandson of Augustus and designated heir to the throne, along with his older brother Gaius. The inscription was discovered near the southeast sector of the Basilica, where it can still be seen. Van Deman associated this inscription with a passage in Suetonius (Aug. 29.4) that mentions a "Porticus Gaii et Lucii" and one in Cassius Dio (56.27.5) that mentions a "Stoa Iulia"; she postulated that the structure eventually became known as the Porticus Iulia; Stoa Iulia would then be a Greek translation of this later name. These arguments are still generally accepted.[81]

For all her articles on monuments, Van Deman made detailed and thorough investigations. One example was her examination of the remains of a ruin adjacent to the so-called Domus Tiberiana at the northwest corner of the Palatine hill near the Temple of Castor and Pollux on the far side of the Clivus Victoriae. Boni, who excavated them in 1900–1901, had associated these with the "House of Caligula," known from a passage in Suetonius (Gaius 22):

> A part of the palace he built out as far as the Forum, making the temple of Castor and Pollux its vestibule.[82]

The ruins that Van Deman analyzed consisted of a marble-lined pool containing a fragment of a marble slab inscribed with the name Germanicus—part of Caligula's official name.[83] She generated a plan of the area showing a peristyle with a pool in the center. Recent excavations conducted by H. Hurst (1983–89) have partly changed our view of the residence. The building was actually an elaborate version of a conventional Roman house, with both a peristyle and an atrium that was probably taken over from a house (or houses) of the republican period. Hurst argues that the pool area cannot have exactly matched Van Deman's reconstruction, which includes elements that have now been reassigned to the atrium area of the complex. Pottery, lamps, and brickstamps recovered in these new excavations, however, indicate that the structure was post-Augustan and pre-Flavian, thus bolstering the probability of Van Deman's dating of the peristyle and pool to the time of Caligula. Her suggestion that this complex included a ramp leading from the Forum to the Palatine, subsequently rebuilt by Domitian and incorporating a stretch of the earlier wall of the Caligulan era, is still generally accepted.[84]

In her article on the Sullan Forum, Van Deman focused on some bits of tufa paving beneath the Augustan paving level (which is the level down to which Boni excavated the Forum) as a repaving of the Forum in the time of Sulla, for which there is some literary evidence (Festus 416 L). This idea, which many scholars still accept, received some support from excavations near the Curia Julia in the 1960s.[85] C. F. Giuliani and P. Verduchi have argued, however, that a distinct travertine paving level located above the tufa paving discussed by Van Deman and below the Augustan level is in fact the paving of the age of Sulla and that Van Deman's tufa remains belong to earlier, pre-Sullan structures.[86] Associated with this travertine paving level (which Giuliani and Verduchi argue is Sullan in date but which other scholars, including the present author, still believe is Caesarian) is a notable and vast network of underground chambers, probably used for the gladiatorial shows that took place in the Forum.[87] The jury is still out on what exactly constitutes the paving of the Sullan Forum; future excavations may be able to resolve the issue. In this article Van Deman also showed that the arcade at the back of the Rostra Augusti made of concrete faced with *opus incertum* did not belong to the Caesarian rostra, as Boni had thought, but functioned as a viaduct supporting an extension of the Clivus Capitolinus.[88] Van Deman dated the structure to the time of Sulla on the basis of its wall-facing technique (which she called "opus quasi reticulatum"). Coarelli has since argued, however, on the basis of literary evidence as well as the wall-facing technique (which he identifies as *opus incertum* [Vitruvius 2.8.1]) that it is nearly one hundred years earlier in date.[89]

Van Deman's article "The So-Called Flavian Rostra" dealt with the Rostra Augusti located on the west side of the Roman Forum. This monument, still a tourist attraction today, consists of two parts: a rectangular structure facing the Forum and—right behind it—a platform in the shape of a hemicycle with steps leading up to it from the west. Otto Richter, who had excavated the monument, argued that the hemicycle was a separate and earlier structure, probably the Rostra of Julius Caesar (attested by Cassius Dio 43.49.1). Van Deman proposed, however, that the two structures were in fact contemporary, and both Augustan, on the basis of their nearly identical wall technique and type of concrete. She further maintained, on the basis of a close examination of the color and matrix of the concrete in the different parts of the monument, that part of the concrete core of the hemicycle was in fact a remnant of the Caesarian Rostra. She also argued that the hemicycle had been built onto and over this remnant during the Augustan period, together with the rectangular structure facing the Forum. These arguments have not been accepted for two reasons.[90] There exists a coin of 45 B.C. that shows a curved platform decorated with beaks of ships; this probably represents the Rostra of Julius Caesar and is good evidence that the hemicycle is to be identified as such.[91] More importantly, there is persuasive archaeological evidence that the hemicycle is earlier than the rectangular platform. A low wall just in front of the hemicycle and integral to it is cut by the foundation of the rectangular platform (that is, the Rostra Augusti)—a fact noted by Richter and not noticed (or ignored) by Van Deman. Here we have a good example of the limitations of Van Deman's system of dating Roman walls by visual determination.

Van Deman's Art of Photography

Esther Van Deman taught herself the art of photography in order to illustrate her publications and to provide the raw material for her projected handbook of Roman construction. However, one is not able to find, in her writing, any expression of interest in this skill. Nevertheless, she proved to be a superb photographer.[92] Recognized as such, her work has been the subject of public exhibitions over the years. A major one was held in 1991 at the American Academy in Rome; it then traveled to the Kelsey Museum of the University of Michigan (Van Deman's alma mater) and then later was hung in the New York offices of the American Academy in Rome.[93] The latest exhibition "Esther Boise Van Deman: An Archaeologist's Eye, Images from the Photographic Archive, American Academy in Rome," was held in New York City in January 2002.[94] Her skill is praised in this description in the *New York Times:*

> Two Van Deman studies of light and shadow, showing a succession of stone arches, highlight her sophisticated understanding of how a camera can be coaxed into registering more than the naked eye when natural light weaves in and out of semienclosed dark spaces.[95]

The images in Van Deman's photographic archive were all taken between 1898 and the early 1930s. Her method of gathering data was to record on catalog cards her measurements and observations about the walls and buildings that she examined. All of her photographs are carefully numbered and annotated.[96] Although her intent was to gather archaeological data, the striking quality of Van Deman's photographs of the Campagna indicates a perfectionism and a passion for this work. Capturing the composition of the concrete matrix, the texture of the brickwork, the details of the architectural carving, and the degree of finish of the wall surface in a single shot of a monument is very difficult and requires superb photographic skills. It can only be done at a certain time of day when the light is just right. Van Deman must have returned repeatedly to the many monuments scattered about the hills, valleys, and gorges of the Roman countryside in order to obtain such good images.

Van Deman's "study" archive, which she bequeathed to the American Academy (along with the collection of lantern slides, which she used to illustrate her lectures), consists of more than twenty-seven hundred negatives, which have been carefully studied and analyzed by Karin Einaudi.[97] The subject matter includes not only the documentation of masonry construction and Roman aqueducts for which Van Deman is well known but also images of her trips to Europe and North Africa and views of many of the lesser-known ancient monuments in the city of Rome. As John D'Arms wrote:

> Van Deman amassed her photographic archive at a time when Rome was rebuilding itself as the new capital of Italy, when its past was being unearthed at an unprecedented pace, and when many photographers strove to record the fugitive presence of the ancient Roman past.[98]

Van Deman's extensive photographs of the people and landscapes in the Roman Campagna must have been stimulated by the general awareness at the time that life there was soon to change irrevocably. Such awareness is illustrated by Van Deman's collaborator Thomas Ashby in the introduction to his Roman Campagna book:

> Now, the city is spreading rapidly on every side beyond the walls: and, except for the quarter along the Via Appia and on the Aventine and Caelian, we have already lost most of the picturesqueness of the narrow lanes shut in by high walls, of the vineyards and gardens still within the city, of churches half-forgotten which seemed in their peaceful repose so far from the bustle and noise of the town. Whatever the necessities of modern life may be . . . there is no doubt that the mediaeval feeling, which, to many lovers of Rome, was not the least of its attractions, is disappearing fast. That this is in large measure inevitable, and that similar processes occur elsewhere, is true: but Rome occupies a unique position. It is not, and perhaps never will become, a manufacturing or commercial city, or a business centre of the first rank: it is as the seat of Government even more than as a resort of foreign residents and tourists that it has grown to its present size, and is still growing, faster perhaps than any city in the world—and yet the supply of houses is still unequal to the demand. The Campagna Romana thus remains almost unspoilt, and there is no city which one can so quickly and easily leave behind as Rome . . . The greater part of the Campagna is pasture-land, and that which is under cultivation is very largely cornland, so that the population at any time of year is extremely small in proportion to the area, while in summer it is reduced to a minimum. This state of things, which has gone on so long, will not continue very much longer, and signs of change are everywhere apparent.[99]

Van Deman's photographs, alone, document many monuments that have now disappeared, and much that is now covered over by housing and factories can only be seen through the images in her archive. Additionally, her photographs are of significant scholarly value not only because they document Roman walls and excavations that would otherwise be unknown, but also because, at an anthropological level, they record a way of life in the Roman Campagna that was visibly disappearing in Van Deman's time and now no longer exists. While Van Deman's professional writings give little or no information about the circumstances in which she worked, her photographic archive provides a "fugitive and sometimes surprising insight into her private milieu and, for all, it tells us what Europe was like in the eyes of an American at the turn of the century."[100]

Einaudi was the first to notice that Van Deman was a keen observer of peasant women. She was a photographer with a good eye for portraits, and as a result her portrait photographs are often of striking poignancy and quality. The portrait of Anna Salviati in her vineyard, for example, shows the towering figure of the woman, hands on hips, chin tilted up, wearing a playful smile on a face framed by a profusion of grapes on the vine. This stylization cannot have been unself-conscious on the part of either the subject or the photographer. Van Deman's attitude toward these peasants whose images she recorded may be gleaned from a statement in the preface to her book on aqueducts. Along with Thomas Ashby, Rudolfo Lanciani, and the American Academy in Rome she acknowledges "the kind hospitality and helpful guidance of the humbler dwellers on the wide stretches of the Campagna and among the faraway hills and lonely valleys which remain a treasured memory."[101]

It is interesting to consider why Van Deman took so many moving photographs of Italian peasant women and their families. Perhaps she permitted a "gentler" side of her personality to emerge when she was outside of the competitive archaeological circles of Rome.[102] It might also be conjectured that Van Deman was interested in what she did not have—marriage, children, domestic obligations, the things that would have been normal for a woman of her time. Could she have had a farmwoman's natural feeling of kinship for *contadine*? But how can we know if she thought in these terms? Another possibility is that, as anyone who has done fieldwork in the Italian countryside knows, when Van Deman did her archaeological research she was forced to intrude on people's homes and farmland. Taking photographs of those who lived on the grounds where the ruins were located was an obvious way not only of being polite but of gaining access to the material she wished to study. And Van Deman was such a skilled and meticulous photographer that she naturally took pride in executing her portrait photographs as carefully as she did her archaeological pictures.

Notably, in the sections of the Van Deman archive that deal with Italy there are proportionally many more photographs of women than of men. But in the part of the archive that deals with North Africa, there are fewer portraits in general (presumably because of the Muslim prohibition against images), and there are more photographs of men than there are of women. One may surmise that, in Italy, Van Deman was relatively comfortable in the procedures required to gain access to her material (she knew the culture and could speak the Italian language), but in North Africa she required French- and Arabic-speaking male guides and protectors. She was, therefore, much in the company of men and naturally took many more pictures of men. Women were not in evidence among the Roman ruins in North Africa. It may be the case, then, that Van Deman's captivating photographs of peasants in the Roman Campagna, mainly peasant women, were taken more for opportunistic reasons than necessarily from any female identification. Nonetheless portraiture seems to have held a particular personal interest for Van Deman. She took a number of spirited self-portraits that showed the same care and stylization apparent in the portraits of the men and women she encountered in her archaeological work.[103] Through her artistry in this medium she expressed herself in a different way than in her writing.[104]

It is to be hoped that the whole of Van Deman's valuable photographic corpus will soon be published, as T. Ashby's has been.[105] Today, the complete collection may only be studied in the Photographic Archive at the American Academy in Rome.[106]

Van Deman as Mentor and Teacher

During the years Esther Van Deman lived in Rome she returned to America on a number of lecture tours, which enhanced her scholarly stature. She took pride in this aspect of her life, though the publicity seemed to make her uncomfortable. Anxious about future employment, in 1908 she wrote to Randolph at Mount Holyoke:

> Thank you for the Yale notice. I hear I'm getting liberal advertising. I need it for my future in America but I dislike that sort of thing. I often wish I'd never left the common life of teaching.[107]

In 1926 Van Deman was appointed Carnegie Research Professor of Roman Archaeology of the University of Michigan. This position came with a good salary and did not necessitate a return to the United States to teach. She elected to continue residing in Rome and in 1931 she retired on her Carnegie pension.

In the series of teaching appointments Van Deman held before making the permanent move to Rome in 1909 (at Wellesley College, Mount Holyoke College, and the Women's College of Baltimore) she does not seem to have been particularly happy. One biographer has suggested that it was due to the restrictive atmosphere of women's colleges during that time and perhaps also because she had difficulty working under women supervisors and had a tendency to hold grudges.[108] M. E. Blake stated that "she enjoyed teaching but chafed at the restrictions imposed by convention on college teachers. Too outspoken for her own good, she was constantly at odds with the administrators."[109] A colleague at Mount Holyoke was more analytical:

> Her teaching has been eminently successful, but it seems to me that she will never enjoy work in a college for women nor in fact anywhere that "residence" is required unless it should be in Utopia where people have no nerves and feelings. She has a very unusual executive ability and a restless energy which forces her to plan continually for other people and in a position where she had entire charge of her department she would be much more likely to enjoy her work.[110]

In a recommendation to the University of Chicago Graduate School in 1896, Francis W. Kelsey, her mentor, praised her as "a woman of high ideals, of comprehensive grasp as well as faithfulness to detail." However, Van Deman could be abrasive, for example, in a scathing missive she sent to Kelsey when she needed letters of recommendation from the presidents of Wellesley and Bryn Mawr:

> I am puzzled by a failure to get any answer from Mrs. Irvine [president of Wellesley] after three weeks' waiting and two letters. I fear both were lost, or else I shall imagine her worse than woman*ish* in her neglect of business duties. President Thomas [M. Cary Thomas of Bryn Mawr] was less neglectful, and she delayed because she always does—perchance to increase one's sense of her dignity.[111]

To be evenhanded, in her years in Rome, her intolerance was not just reserved for women. Several letters reveal Van Deman's irritation with Italian bureaucrats as she went about arranging for casts of Roman antiquities to be made and sent to Mt. Holyoke College.[112] For example, on December 16, 1907, she wrote of trying to obtain a cast of one of the vestal statues in the Museo Nazionale Romano:

> I am sorry not to find more small casts, but we cannot do much better. Let me know as quickly as possible, for it means always several

> visits to find these people in the mood for business. I am not an ardent lover of them in business matters. I am glad to say the Director of the Terme is to be sent to Naples, for I wished to box his ears, when I saw him, for his half-insolence & delays.[113]

In another letter Van Deman remarks:

> I've learned a lot about casts wrestling with these men. I confess now that it has been rather a nerve trying ordeal at times . . . I see that one is at their mercy, if one . . . is not here to watch them. My angry Director cooled down and begged my pardon in a rarely sweet temper and we shook hands on our reconciliation . . . The other one was a scamp & no gentleman.[114]

Despite a good deal of difficulty dealing with her women superiors (as well as in her business dealings with men) she was supportive of junior women scholars such as Marion Blake and Lily Ross Taylor and helpful to contemporaries such as Gertrude Bell.[115] Marion Blake, who first encountered Van Deman as a student at Mt. Holyoke, became a much-appreciated colleague who eventually was honored as the beneficiary of her scholarly papers. When Gertrude Bell left Rome for the Dalmatian coast, she expressed gratitude for Van Deman's notes on construction that would aid her examination of the Roman ruins there.

> My dear Miss van Demen [*sic*], I must begin a letter to you this peaceful afternoon while I journey between the snowy mountains of Dalmatia a.[*sic*] the wonderful rocky islands . . . I have been studying the papers you gave me. I don't know how to thank you enough for the trouble you took in writing them for me, nor how to admire enough the knowledge you have gained.[116]

When Van Deman liked a person she could be warmly affectionate. This is apparent, for example, in her correspondence to Louise Fitz Randolph, her former colleague at Mount Holyoke. Concerned with the business of copying and shipping casts for the college, they are, nevertheless, affectionate and familiar in tone. The letters are often signed "with much love, yours as ever," and the request "to give my love to all our Pearsons people."[117]

In the same series of letters, she reveals a generosity to fellow Americans in Rome. In one case it was monetary:

> I've been tying up my money badly by helping an American over a hard place, but another friend turned up later, so I have less anxiety about her.[118]

In another instance, it was medical:

> On our return to Roma from Naples, I had the sad experience of helping nurse a cholera case—a poor American lady who died in torture, after one day.[119]

It is fortunate that at least these few letters have been preserved. Esther Van Deman, in personal terms, is an elusive figure. What she admired most in a person is perhaps best exemplified by her characterization of Eugénie Strong: "I like Mrs. S. very much . . . She is simple and sensible."[120]

Fascism

No biography written about Esther Van Deman would be complete without mentioning her devotion to fascism. When Esther Van Deman died, A. M. Colini, writing her obituary for the Italian publication *Bullettino Comunale,* suggested that Van Deman was caught up not only in the archaeological fervor in Rome in the first decades of the twentieth century, but also in the political ardor of Italy in the years preceding World War II:

> Van Deman was not only Roman but also Italian by choice and a great admirer of the renovation work of Fascism. And this devotion to our Fatherland was demonstrated in a particularly difficult political moment, that of the war of Abissinia. When she found herself giving a series of lectures in America, she asked to be able to add to her subject ten minutes in which to speak of Italy; and before her departure she offered her most precious gold to the Monteverde chapter of the Fascist party. [Another obituary of Van Deman states that the gold given by her to the Fascio was her engagement ring.][121]

Van Deman's attitude was common among foreign academics living in Rome at the time and may have been connected with the general atmosphere of excitement as so many ancient structures began to emerge in the Fascist-sponsored excavations. Of Van Deman's politics, Marion Blake wrote: "Like many Americans who resided in Italy in the confused years following World War I, she conceived an ardent admiration for Mussolini, from which she never wavered."[122] It is possible that her single-mindedness for her work prompted her sympathies in this direction. On the other hand, the fact that she bequeathed her engagement ring (which she had presumably been harboring since her youthful Kansas days) to the Fascist party perhaps suggests a predilection beyond mere opportunity.

Conclusion

On May 3, 1937, at the age of seventy-four, Esther Van Deman died and was buried in the Protestant Cemetery in Rome. She bequeathed her photographs, as well as some ancient coins, vases, and other small objects to the American Academy in Rome and another part of her small but interesting collection of antiquities to the Kelsey Museum in Michigan, where it can still be seen today.[123] Though she is now universally recognized as a phenomenon in the history of the study of Roman architecture, in her own lifetime Van Deman and her contributions seem to have been better appreciated in Italy than in the United States (a natural occurrence since she lived in Italy and after 1906 was known in the United States mainly from her lecture tours). This is suggested by two obituaries—one American, the other Italian—written to commemorate her. Van Deman's obituary in the *American Journal of Archaeology* acknowledges her as a "pioneer in the study of Roman building materials and an authority on the chronology of brick construction" but is fairly pedestrian in its outline of her accomplishments. It lists her degrees, fellowships, and publications and mentions that she "delivered many lectures before Societies of the Archaeological Institute of America, and American Universities. During 1924–1925, she was Charles Eliot Norton Lecturer for the Archaeological Institute."[124]

Compare this rather clipped summary of Van Deman's career with the spirited obituaries found in Italian journals, for example one in the *Bullettino Comunale* written by A. M. Colini, a Fascist archaeological team member and director of the Soprintendenza Archeologica di Roma. This notice includes a lengthy account and analysis of Van Deman's scholarly contributions. Her identification of the Neronian Sacra Via is rightly termed "brilliant." Colini wryly notes that anyone who did not know Van Deman would marvel at her ability to penetrate remote and primitive areas of the Roman Campagna and tirelessly track down the remains of various Roman aqueducts. He expresses astonishment that she, as a foreigner, obtained permission to document and photograph the excavations by the Ministry of the Interior on the Viminal Hill.[125] Normally such activities were denied to foreigners, but Van Deman, Colini notes, "carried away by her passion," seemed to have the tenacity to penetrate almost any institutional circle.[126]

While her work on various monuments in and around the Roman Forum, published as a series of articles in the *American Journal of Archaeology,* the *Journal of Roman Studies,* and the *Memoirs of the American Academy in Rome,* has been influential, Van Deman's theories concerning an empirical formula for the precise dating of Roman walls are no longer accepted in their entirety. She was a pioneer in archaeology, it is true, but it is in the sphere of her photographic documentation of a disappearing Campagna (both its ancient ruins and its inhabitants), a precious archival record, that Van Deman's most lasting contribution will perhaps be found. She succeeded in making permanent relics of ancient Rome that would otherwise have been ephemeral and beyond recovery today. Her photographic skill and artistry, combined with an archaeologist's training, continues to be recognized many decades later.

WORKS BY ESTHER B. VAN DEMAN
A SELECTED BIBLIOGRAPHY

Books, Monographs, and Articles

"The Cult of Vesta Publica and the Vestal Virgins." Ph.D. diss., University of Chicago, 1898.

"The Value of the Vestal Statues as Originals." *American Journal of Archaeology* 12 (1908): 324–42.

"Notes on a Few Vestal Inscriptions." *American Journal of Philology* 29 (1908): 172–78.

The Atrium Vestae. Washington, D.C., 1909.

"The So-called Flavian Rostra." *American Journal of Archaeology* 13 (1909): 170–78.

"Methods of Determining the Date of Roman Concrete Monuments." *American Journal of Archaeology* 16 (1912): 230–51, 387–432.

"The Porticus of Gaius et Lucius." *American Journal of Archaeology* 17 (1913): 14–28.

"The Sullan Forum." *Journal of Roman Studies* 12 (1922): 1–31.

"The Neronian Sacra Via." *American Journal of Archaeology* 27 (1923): 383–424.

"The House of Caligula." *American Journal of Archaeology* 28 (1924): 368–98.

"The Sacra Via of Nero." *Memoirs of the American Academy in Rome* 5 (1925): 115–26. (With drawings by G. Clay.)

The Building of the Roman Aqueducts. Washington, D.C., 1934.

Blake, M. *Ancient Roman Construction in Italy from the Prehistoric Period to Augustus.* Publication based mainly on Van Deman's notes. Washington, D.C., 1947.

Photography Catalog

Einaudi, Karin, ed. *Esther B. Van Deman: Images from the Archive of an American Archaeologist in Italy at the Turn of the Century*. Rome, 1991.

Suggested Readings about Esther B. Van Deman

Blake, M. E. *Dictionary of American Biography*. Vol. 22, suppl. 2. New York, 1958.

Einaudi, K. *Fotografia archeologica 1865–1914*. Rome: de Luca, 1978.

———. "Esther Van Deman: Un archeologa americana." In *L'Archeologia in Roma Capitale tra Sterro e Scavo,* 41–47. Rome, 1983.

———. "Esther Van Deman, collaborazione e corrispondenza con Thomas Ashby." In *Il trionfo dell' acqua,* 21–34. Rome, 1992.

Meritt, L. Shoe. *Notable American Women, 1607–1950: A Biographical Dictionary.* Vol. 3. Cambridge, Mass., 1971.

Selected Archival Material

Letters by and about Esther Van Deman are preserved in the Kelsey Museum at the University of Michigan. Another part of her professional correspondence is housed at the Mount Holyoke archive. The majority of the latter concern arranging for a series of casts to be made in Italy and sent to Mount Holyoke College.

A bundle of notes by M. Blake (for a projected fourth volume on Roman construction), based on Van Deman's notes, was given to the library of the American Academy in Rome and is now housed in the Photographic Archive.

NOTES

I owe a great debt of gratitude to Katherine A. Geffcken and Karin Einaudi, whose excellent and comprehensive essays in the exhibition catalogue, *Esther B. Van Deman: Images from the Archive of an American Archaeologist in Italy at the Turn of the Century,* ed. Karin Einaudi (Rome, 1991), inspired me to want to write about Esther Van Deman. Geffcken's essay "Esther B. Van Deman, a Profile" and Einaudi's essay "An Archaeologist's Archive" have together served as the major sources for the biographical information contained in this chapter. I have also relied extensively on verbal and written communications with Geffcken and Einaudi; as well as on K. Einaudi, *Fotografia archeologica 1865–1914* (Rome, 1978); K. Bull-Simonsen Einaudi, "Esther Boise Van Deman: Un archeologa americana," in *L'Archeologia in Roma Capitale tra Sterro e Scavo* (Rome, 1983), 41–47; and K. Einaudi, "Esther Van Deman, collaborazione e corrispondenza con Thomas Ashby," in *Il trionfo dell' acqua* (Rome, 1992), 21–34. Also useful were the biographies of Van Deman by M. E. Blake (*Dictionary of American Biography,* vol. 22, suppl. 2 [New York, 1958], 676–77) and L. Shoe Meritt (*Notable American Women 1607–1950: A Biographical Dictionary,* vol. 3 [Cambridge, Mass., 1971], 507–8). I am also grateful for the help of James C. Anderson Jr., James Packer, Russell T. Scott, and especially Joanne Spurza for sharing with me her expertise on the Atrium Vestae. Van Deman's professional correspondence, part of which is housed at the University of Michigan and part at Mount Holyoke, as well as two obituaries written for her, help convey some idea of her character. Much of her correspondence in the Mount Holyoke archive concerns the arranging for a series of casts to be made in Italy and sent to Mount Holyoke College. Letters by and about Van Deman preserved in the Kelsey Museum at the University of Michigan are another important source of archival information. These have been studied by K. Geffcken and yield further insight into Van Deman's personality. Finally I would like to thank Geffcken for reading and critiquing several drafts of this biography.

1. Blake, "Van Deman," 676.

2. K. A. Geffcken, "Profile," (Rome, 1991), 8.

3. Blake, "Van Deman," 676; cf. Meritt, "Van Deman," 507. The chronology of the engagements is unknown.

4. Ralph Van Deman Magoffin (1874–1942) received a B.A. at the University of Michigan in 1902 and after a year as Fellow of the American School of Classical Studies in Rome (1906–7) entered Johns Hopkins and was awarded a Ph.D. in 1908. His dissertation on the history of Praeneste (1908) was important enough to be reprinted in 1978: *A Study of the Topography and Municipal History of Praeneste* (Baltimore, 1908), reprinted in *Studi su Praeneste,* ed. F. Coarelli (Perugia, 1978), 47–101. He also wrote popularizing books such as *The Lure and Lore of Archaeology* (Baltimore, 1930). He was recorder of the Archaeological Institute of America for seven years and its president for ten years (1921–31), expanding the organization to more than fifty local societies and a larger membership than it had ever had. At Rome and during his travels in Greece he acquired a number of antiquities (Etruscan vases, Greek coins, Roman sculpture, and Greek and south Italian vases), which he brought first to Johns Hopkins and then to New York University, where they still form the bulk of the study collection in the Department of Classics. This information on Ralph Van Deman Magoffin was given to me by Dr. Larissa Bonfante.

5. Geffcken, "Profile," 8.

6. Einaudi, *Fotografia archeologica,* 17, fig. 6.

7. Geffcken, "Profile," 9.

8. The University of Michigan had been admitting women undergraduates since 1870; see R. Bordin, *Women at Michigan: The "Dangerous Experiment," 1870's to the Present* (Ann Arbor, 1999), 7 ff.

9. I thank K. A. Geffcken for this information.

10. Lucia Valentine and Alan Valentine, *The American Academy in Rome, 1894–1969* (Charlottesville, Va., 1973) 178.

11. The American Academy in Rome was founded as the American School of Architecture. In 1897 the name was changed to American Academy in Rome, reflecting the inclusion of painters and sculptors. In 1912 the American Academy in Rome and the American School of Classical Studies at Rome merged. The original AAR became the School of Fine Arts, and the ASCSR the School of Classical Studies. The name American Academy in Rome was retained for the overall institution, housed in the new Janiculum building in 1914.

12. Einaudi, *Images from the Archive,* 15.

13. Ibid. R. Lanciani, *Storia degli scavi di Roma e notizie intorno le collezioni romane di antichità* (Rome, 1902; rpt. Rome, 1993); *Forma Urbis Romae* (Rome, 1893–1901; rpt. Rome, 1988). See *L'Archeologia in Roma Capitale tra sterro e scavo* (Rome, 1983).

14. In 1906 Van Deman began plans for a handbook based on these studies; however, it was never published. Einaudi, *Images from the Archive,* 16.

15. See *American Academy in Rome: Celebrating a Century* (New York, 1995), ed. W. A. Linker and J. Max. Incidentally, Valentine and Valentine (*American Academy,* 50) write that Van Deman was the first Fellow in the School of Classical Studies. This is incorrect. I thank K. A. Geffcken for this information.

16. Van Deman began to lead these "walks" in 1907. They were designed to allow members of the community to examine and study the antiquities of Rome and environs under expert guidance and they remain an ongoing tradition at the American Academy in Rome.

17. Meritt, "Van Deman," 508; Blake, "Van Deman," 677.

18. The Villa Sforza Cesarini is located behind the seventeenth-century "Fontanone" of Pope Paul V. The owners of the villa, who sympathized with the regimes of the "old order" and eventually showed their support for fascism, allowed the émigrés to rent living accommodations at the villa. Olga Fersen always insisted that the establishment was not a *pensione* in the strict sense but a home for paying guests.

19. Letter of August 17, 1911, Van Deman correspondence, Mt. Holyoke College Archives.

20. Ibid.

21. Letter to Randolph, December 16, 1907, Van Deman correspondence, Mt. Holyoke College Archives.

22. A recollection by Lily Ross Taylor, Valentine and Valentine, *American Academy,* 50–51.

23. Letter to Randolph, April 2, 1908, Van Deman correspondence, Mt. Holyoke College Archives.

24. Bordin, *Women at Michigan,* 1–6.

25. Einaudi, *Images from the Archive,* 17.

26. Richter Sherman, *Women as Interpreters of the Visual Arts, 1820–1979* (Westport, 1981), 32–33.

27. Geffcken, "Profile," 13.

28. Geffcken, "Profile," 10. In the 1901 letter to Kelsey she wrote: "Of course you must have had reasons . . . If I feared such actions next year, I should ask about remaining outside the school wholly . . . I am so sorry to have our U. of M. seem to be drawing such a line, for it is so true to us women always."

29. Geffcken, "Profile," 9.

30. P. MacKendrick, *The Mute Stones Speak: The Story of Archeology in Italy* (New York, 1976), 320.

31. Geffcken, "Profile," 13.

32. A thought suggested to me by K. A. Geffcken.

33. M. Blake, *Ancient Roman Construction in Italy from the Prehistoric Period to Augustus* (Washington, D.C., 1947), v.

34. I am grateful to James C. Anderson for this information.

35. Richter Sherman, *Visual Arts* 34; Einaudi, *Fotografia archeologica*, 14–15.

36. Heinrich Jordan and Christian Hülsen, *Topographie der Stadt Rom im Alterthum* (Berlin, 1871–1907).

37. J. Durm, *Die Baukunst der Etrusker* Die Baukunstder Römer (Stuttgart, 1905).

38. Einaudi, *Images from the Archive*, 15–16.

39. The methodology was not entirely new. John Henry Parker (who was the first to use actual photographs instead of drawings to illustrate archaeological material) wrote in the 1870s: "No artist ever thinks of shewing [sic] the thickness of the mortar between the joints of stones or the thickness of bricks, yet on these two points the date of a building often hangs." J. H. Parker, *The Archaeology of Rome* (Oxford, 1878), pt. 6, p. vi; see P. J. Holliday, *The Fascination with the Past: John Henry Parker's Photographs of Rome* (San Bernardino, 1991), 10.

40. Van Deman, *Atrium Vestae* (1909), 3–4. Also see R. T. Scott, "Atrium Vestae," in E. M. Steinby, ed., *Lexicon Topographicum Urbis Romae*, vol. 1 (Rome, 1993): 138–42; R. T. Scott, "Excavations in the Area Sacra of Vesta, 1987–89," in *Eius Virtutis Studiosi: Classical and Postclassical Studies in Memory of F. E. Brown* (Washington, D.C., 1993), 160–81; R. T. Scott, "Regia/Vesta 1987," *Archaeologia Laziale* 9 (1988): 18–26; R. T. Scott, "Lavori e ricerche nell'area sacra di Vesta 1990–1991," *Archaeologia Laziale* 11, 2 (1993): 11–12; R. T. Scott et al., "Vesta 1996," *Memoirs of the American Academy in Rome* 42 (1997): 249–54.

41. H. Bloch, *I Bolli Laterizi e la storia edilizia romana* (Rome, 1947), 67–85.

42. The following analysis of Van Deman's work on the Atrium Vestae is based on information supplied to me by J. Spurza.

43. Van Deman, *Atrium Vestae*, 7.

44. Ibid., 33.

45. Esther Van Demen, "Methods of Determining the Date of Roman Concrete Monuments," *American Journal of Archaeology* 16 (1912): 417–18.

46. Van Deman, *Atrium Vestae*, 1 n. 9, 4 n. 1.

47. Trajanic and Hadrianic are difficult to distinguish because many of the names of the brick makers and supervisors, which appear on the stamps, are the same in the two reigns. The confusion has been alleviated to a great extent by the work of Eva Margareta Steinby, "I bolli laterizi e i critici tecnici nella datazione delle cortine laterizie romane. Esame su un gruppo di edifici dei primi anni di Adriano," *Miscelánea Arquelógica II* (Barcelona, 1974), 389–405, esp. 389–96. I am grateful to J. C. Anderson for this information.

48. Scott, *Atrium Vestae*, 138–42.

49. *Bullettino della Commissione archeologica Comunale di Roma* 64 (1936): 141–225; 65 (1937): 83–187; 66 (1938): 61–221.

50. A Jewish refugee from Germany, Bloch was not affiliated with any of the foreign academies at the time but was taking degrees at the University of Rome.

51. J. C. Anderson, *The Thomas Ashby Collection of Brickstamps in the American Academy in Rome* (London, 1991), 10 n. 35, 12–16.

52. Ibid.

53. The following information is supplied from L. F. Ball, "A Reappraisal of Nero's *Domus Aurea*," *Journal of Roman Archaelogy* suppl. 11 (1994): esp. 234–41 ("Appendix I *Modus Operandi*").

54. G. Lugli, *La tecnica edilizia romana* vols. 1 and 2 (Rome, 1957).

55. Lugli, *La tecnica edilizia romana.* Lugli designed his catalog to suggest absolute dates but on a comparatively broad scale (e.g., "IV period"). (Claudio, Nerone, Vespasiano: 41–79 d.Cr.)

56. Ball, "Reappraisal," 235.

57. As noted by J. Spurza.

58. Ball, "Reappraisal," 241 n. 140.

59. Van Deman, *Atrium Vestae,* introduction.

60. Lugli, *La tecnica edilizia romana,* 13. For other comments on the method of Van Deman, see Steinby, "I bolli laterizi"; Einaudi, "Esther Boise Van Deman."

61. Van Deman, *The Building of Roman Aqueducts* (Washington, D.C., 1934).

62. T. Ashby, *The Aqueducts of Ancient Rome* (Oxford, 1935).

63. H. B. Evans, *Water Distribution in Ancient Rome: The Evidence of Frontinus* (Ann Arbor, 1994), 1; Anderson, *Brickstamps,* 6–7, with n. 11 (documentation of Ashby's written concern for the decimation of the Campagna's ancient remains).

64. The following discussion of their work is based on the useful summary by MacKendrick, *The Mute Stones Speak,* 317–20.

65. Ashby's death in England in 1931, an apparent suicide, must have been a terrible blow to the elderly Van Deman. On Ashby see Richard Hodges, *Visions of Rome: Thomas Ashby, Archaeologist* (London, 2000).

66. MacKendrick, *The Mute Stones Speak,* 319–20.

67. Ashby, *Aqueducts of Ancient Rome,* x.

68. Einaudi, *Images from the Archive,* 23, fig. 45.

69. Einaudi, "Collaborazione e corrispondenza." Einaudi calls attention to the lack of sentimentality, considering it was written on Christmas Day. *Trionfo dell' Acqua.* Gli antichi acquedotti di Roma (Rome, 1992).

70. Ibid., 25.

71. Einaudi, *Images from the Archive,* 23.

72. Contra Valentine and Valentine, *American Academy,* 89, who do not give their source for this nickname. It is interesting to note that, to this day, Esther Van Deman arouses debate and criticism—sometimes verging on the personal—of a very negative kind among scholars in the field.

73. Prior to Ashby's death in 1931, he and Van Deman had been working together on aqueducts intensively for the last six years. K. Geffcken provided me with this information based on her conversations with Nina Longobardi, long-time librarian of the American Academy in Rome.

74. "The House of Caligula," *American Journal of Archaeology* 28 (1924): 396.

75. "The Neronian Sacra Via," *American Journal of Archaeology* 27 (1923): 403.

76. Ibid., 423–24.

77. The conclusion states that, because of their use of Greek body types, the statues "as original Vestal statues lose all importance, and, apart from their portrait heads, can have no bearing upon questions concerning the priesthood." Van Deman, "The Value of the Vestal Statues as Originals," *American Journal of Archaeology* 12 (1908): 341.

78. The articles are "The So-called Flavian Rostra" (1909), "The Porticus of Gaius and Lucius" (1913), "The Sullan Forum" (1922), "The Neronian Sacra Via"

(1923), "The Sacra Via of Nero" (1925), and "The House of Caligula" (1924). Also note Van Deman's contributions to the study of Roman topography—somewhat undervalued in English-speaking scholarly circles—but frequently cited in the Italian literature.

79. F. Castagnoli, "Note sulla topografia del Palatino e del Foro Romano," *Archeologia Classica* 16 (1964): 173–99, esp. 195–99.

80. For full bibliography, see M. Medri, "Suet., *Nero,* 31.1: Elementi e proposte per la recostruzione del progetto della Domus Aurea," in *Meta Sudans,* ed. C. Panella, vol. 1 (Rome, 1996), 168–72, esp. n. 19 and fig. 156. See also R. T. Scott, "Foro Romano. Area Sacra di Vesta" *Bolletino di Archeologia* 19–21 (1993): 88–55.

81. F. Coarelli, *Foro Romano, vol. 2. Periodo Repubblicano e Augusteo* (Rome, 1985), 175; D. Palombi, "Porticus Gai et Luci," in *Lexicon Topographicum Urbis Romae,* ed. E. M. Steinby, vol. 4 (Rome, 1999), 122–23.

82. cf. Cassius Dio 59.28.5, who says much the same thing.

83. This was actually an unstratified find and had probably been reused, a fact not mentioned by Van Deman.

84. H. Hurst, "Domus Gai," in *Lexicon Topographicum Urbis Romae,* ed. E. M. Steinby, vol. 2 (Rome, 1995), 106–8.

85. Coarelli, *Foro Romano vol. 2,* 134–35, 198, 218; N. Lamboglia, "Prime conclusioni sugli scavi nel Foro di Cesare dietro la Curia (1960–1970)," *Cuardernos de Trabajo de la Escuela espanola de historia y arquelogía en Rome* 14 (1980): 123–34.

86. C. F. Giuliani and P. Verduchi, *L'area centrale del Foro Romano* (Florence, 1987), 53–66; N. Purcell, "Forum Romanum (The Republican Period)," in Steinby, *Lexicon Topographicum Urbis Romae* 2:325–35, esp. 331.

87. G. Carettoni, "Le gallerie ipogee del Foro Romano e I ludi gladiatorii forensi," *Bullettino della Commissione archeologica Comunale di Roma* 76 (1956–58): 23–44.

88. G. Boni, *Notizie degli Scavi di Antichità* (1900): 627–34.

89. Coarelli, *Foro Romano,* 154; F. Coarelli, "Public Building in Rome between the Second Punic War and Sulla," *Papers of the British School of Rome* 45 (1977): 1–19, esp. 14.

90. For a full discussion see Coarelli, *Foro Romano,* 2:233–57; also P. Verduchi, "Rostra Augusti," in Steinby, *Lexicon Topographicum Urbis Romae,* 4:214–17.

91. Coarelli, *Foro Romano,* 243, fig. 46.

92. M. Loke, "Studying Ancient Ruins with the Eye of a Poet," *New York Times,* December 28, 2001.

93. The 1991 exhibition was curated by Karin Einaudi, then director of the Fototeca Unione (which houses Van Deman's photographic archive) of the American Academy in Rome. In an earlier exhibition, held in 1979, some of Van Deman's photographs were displayed and published along with others in this period and earlier. Einaudi, *Fotografia Archeologica.*

94. The 2002 exhibition was held at the City University of New York in the Graduate Center Art Gallery.

95. Loke, "Studying Ancient Ruins," 1.

96. Einaudi, *Images from the Archive,* 18.

97. Einaudi, *Fotografia archeologica;* Einaudi, *Images from the Archive.*

98. Einaudi, *Fotografia archeologica,* preface, 3.

99. T. Ashby, *The Roman Campagna in Classical Times* (London, 1927), 19–20.

100. Einaudi, *Images from the Archive,* 14.

101. Van Deman, *The Building of the Roman Aqueducts,* preface.

102. Einaudi, *Images from the Archive,* 21.

103. Einaudi, *Images from the Archive,* fig. 1 (self-portrait: "working in her study"); fig. 14 (self-portrait: "contemplating a view in the Swiss Alps"). Einaudi, *Fotografia archeologica,* 13 (self-portrait: "on board ship wearing the captain's hat").

104. A description of a 1914 portrait illustrates this point:

> But her best self-portrait . . . doesn't have her in it. Instead, in the middle of some ruins she placed her umbrella, a folding ruler, a thermos, a leather camera case and other personal items on the remnant of a thick brick wall, which faced a massive dark structure atop neat rows of rough-hewn rocks. (Loke, "Studying Ancient Ruins")

105. Ashby took large numbers of photographs of the countryside around Rome, which complement those taken by Van Deman: *Thomas Ashby; Un archeologo fotografa la campagna romana tra '800 e '900,* BSR Archive, vol. 1 (Rome, 1986); *Archeologia a Roma nelle fotografie di Thomas Ashby, 1891–1930,* BSR Archive, vol. 2 (Naples, 1989); *Il Lazio di Thomas Ashby,* BSR Archive, vol. 4 (Rome, 1994).

106. A complete list of Van Deman's photographs is included in the on-line (Unione Romana Biblioteche Scientifiche) catalog of the holdings of the library consortium in Rome. The photographic holdings of the Fototeca Unione, housed at the Academy, have been published in microfiche form (cf. K. Einaudi, ed., *Ancient Roman Architecture: Photographic Archive on Microfiche,* vols. 1 and 2 [Fototeca Unione, American Academy in Rome: distributed by the University of Chicago Press, 1982]) but the Van Deman photographic archive could not be included in this publication because it was a specific entity with separate ownership.

107. Letter of March 6, 1908: Van Deman correspondence, Mt. Holyoke College Archives.

108. Geffcken, "Profile," 10.

109. Blake, "Van Deman," 676; Meritt, "Van Deman," 507.

110. Written by Mary Gilmore Williams (another Michigan alumna teaching at Mount Holyoke) to Kelsey: Geffcken, "Profile," 10–11.

111. Geffcken, "Profile," 10.

112. The copies of antiquities for the purpose of research and display were for the Roman Room, Dwight Hall at Mount Holyoke College. Van Deman spent a number of years (mainly 1907 to 1911) occupied with this service to the college.

113. Letter to Randolph Van Deman correspondence, Mt. Holyoke College Archives.

114. Letter to Randolph, April 2, 1908, Mt. Holyoke College Archives.

115. Geffcken, "Profile," 11.

116. K. Geffcken, "Esther Van Deman and Gertrude Bell (1910)," in *Esther B. Van Deman,* ed. Einaudi (Rome, 1991), 24–27.

117. Van Deman correspondence, Mt. Holyoke College Archives.

118. Letter of January 31, 1908, Mt. Holyoke College Archives.

119. Letter of August 17, 1911, Mt. Holyoke College Archives.

120. Letter to Randolph, April 2, 1908, Mt. Holyoke College, Archives.

121. Translation from the original Italian: *Bullettino della Commissione archeolgica comunale di Roma* 66 (1938): 323–24. Obituary of Van Deman by Maria Barosso in *L'Urbe* 2, no. 5 (1937): 43–44.

122. Blake, "Van Deman," 677.

123. Walter F. Snyder, "Ancient Coins Bequeathed by Esther Boise Van Deman to the American Academy in Rome,"*Memoirs of the American Academy in Rome* 15 (1938) 21–22; W. T. Avery, F. Blank, and C. G. Starr, "Vases Bequeathed by Esther Boise Van Deman to the American Academy in Rome," *Memoirs of the American Academy in Rome* 17 (1940) 57–65; *Bulletin. University of Michigan Museums of Art and Archaeology* 13 (2000–2001): 32ff. The subject of Van Deman as collector will be covered in the publication of the American Academy's study collection of antiquities (in preparation).

124. Obituary of Van Deman in *American Journal of Archaeology* 41 (1937): 315–16.

125. The photographs that Van Deman took, incidentally, are staggering in their demonstration of the enormous scale and depth of the trenches.

126. A. M. Colini, *Bulletino Comunale* 66 (1938): 323–24. See also Barosso's obituary.

Margaret Alice Murray

(1863–1963)

Margaret S. Drower

AS A SUBJECT FOR ACADEMIC STUDY, archaeology is comparatively new, in spite of the awakening interest in antiquity in the nineteenth century. Field archaeology was not regarded as a suitable subject for the universities of the Western world until the last decade of the nineteenth century, though Egyptian hieroglyphs and Babylonian cuneiform were taught, with Latin and Greek, at two of the older universities, in Paris, and Berlin. It was a woman novelist and traveler, Amelia Blanford Edwards, who founded, in London, the first academic chair of Egyptology. Her intention was to nominate to it the field archaeologist W. M. Flinders Petrie, whose work she admired. He did receive the post, but as he had no philological training, he delegated most of the teaching in his department to one of his first students—and so it came about that Margaret Murray, during the forty years between 1896 and 1936, prepared two generations of Egyptologists for their careers in the field.[1]

The Early Years

Margaret Alice Murray was born in Calcutta, on July 13, 1863. Her father was James G. Murray, an English businessman, whose family had a long connection with the East India Company. As a child she had heard eyewitness accounts of the Indian Mutiny, the siege of Lucknow, and the massacre of Cawnpore. She had vivid memories of her youth in India, although in 1870 she and her sister Mary were brought to England by way of the Red Sea and then by train to Alexandria, where they embarked again, as the Suez Canal was not quite finished. Their parents returned to India without them, leaving them with their grandmother, and an aunt and an uncle who was the vicar of Lambourn on the Berkshire Downs.

Details of Margaret Murray's family history and early life are vividly remembered in her autobiography, written in her hundredth year.[2] She greatly admired her mother, whose early ambition to be a doctor had been frustrated, but who had worked indefatigably in her youth for organizations that (in the early nineteenth century) were being started in Bristol and London for the relief of poverty. That admirable woman had devoted much of her life to visiting Indian women imprisoned in the zenanas, but she was not a missionary and did not believe in proselytizing. With a woman friend, Murray's mother had started a charity called the "Friend in Need," destined to give the homebound Indian woman gainful employment. Her two children were taught at home the basic subjects of arithmetic, geography, and history and had tutors in music, drawing, French, and German.

In England, Murray attributed her early interest in archaeology to the kindly influence of her Uncle John, something of an antiquary, whose knowledge of the surroundings of Lambourn (rich in earthworks and standing stones), as well as interest in church architecture and local antiquities, stimulated the child's imagination. A French governess was entrusted with the education of the two sisters, but, in 1873, their mother came home and took them for a time to Bonn, Germany. Bonn was then a quiet university town, where the children soon became fluent in German, an accomplishment that was to serve Murray well in future years. In 1877 the family settled in London, and the girls went to school at the Crystal Palace in Sydenham. By a curious coincidence, Monsieur Mariette, their French teacher, was a brother of the great Egyptologist Auguste Mariette. Might he have first raised Margaret Murray's curiosity about Egypt?

In 1880, the family returned to Calcutta, and for the next seven years India was again Murray's home. At the age of twenty, in the face of considerable parental opposition, she decided to train as a volunteer nurse in the General Hospital at Calcutta. To mark her social difference from the other nurses, she was called a "lady probationer." At twenty-one she found herself in charge of the whole establishment during an epidemic. The medical knowledge and confidence that she gained at this time, she later said, served her well in an excavation camp. When she finally returned to England in 1886, she inquired about further hospital training but was rejected on the grounds that she was too short (she was, in fact, less than five feet tall).

Returning to live with her Uncle John, now rector of Rugby, and her grandmother, Murray became a district visitor in a parish of railway workers, an experience that yielded a fund of amusing anecdotes. For recreation she joined a wood-carving class and acquired a skill that, as she later said, stood her in good stead when she came to study techniques of ancient craftsmanship, in particular that of relief sculpture. Both she and her sister taught in the Sunday school, and she discovered a natural love of teaching.[3] Mary soon married and settled again in India. On a visit to India, when Murray was helping with her sister's new baby, she and Mary read in the overseas edition of *The Times* that classes in Egyptology were to be given at University College London. In the previous term, through a bequest by the novelist Amelia Edwards, the College had acquired its first chair of Egyptology. The first Edwards Professor, W. M. Flinders Petrie, was to spend the winter excavating in Egypt. Classes in hieroglyphs would be taught by assistants during his absence. It was her sister, Murray always said, who insisted that she must attend these classes as soon as she returned to England: "I cannot go but you must."

Early Career

Because University College London accepted students regardless of gender or religious preference, Margaret Murray could, in January 1894, become a pupil. The class, conducted by Francis Griffith (Petrie's assistant and erstwhile student), was held in the Edwards Library, which was presided over by James Walker. It held a small museum of antiquities collected by Amelia Edwards and supplemented by Petrie's own purchases and annual discoveries. Petrie himself was in Egypt, excavating at Coptos. There were twenty women in the class and several elderly men. Griffith, though a brilliant linguist, was not a gifted teacher, and his pupils, desperately copying one translation after another from the blackboard, found his grammatical explanations difficult to follow. Murray had the sense to work between classes with Adolf Erman's *Egyptian Grammar,* written in German. She remarked, "we were all floundering in the sea of grammar; but I was beginning to swim."

Returning in the early summer, Petrie was quick to notice the ability of this small, determined young person. Finding that Murray excelled in facsimile drawing, he set her the task of reproducing some of the reliefs he had found in the ruins of the Twelfth Dynasty temple at Coptos on slabs of limestone, some of which he had brought back.[4] One of the finest depicted King Sesostris I at his jubilee, striding out in front of the ithyphallic god of fertility, Min. This relief she was spared the embarrassment of having to draw—it was shown in photograph only, with a label concealing the god's offending member. She was also required to reproduce in facsimile most of the inscriptions in hieroglyphic, Latin, Greek, and Coptic, of which he had brought back paper squeezes. Her work was so accurate and her line so sure that she was thenceforward to act as the professor's chief illustrator. The volumes that came out year after year almost always contained examples of her skill as a copyist—doubly valuable since photographic illustrations were expensive and little used in archaeological publications.

Next, Petrie encouraged Murray to venture on her first piece of research. He suggested that she trace the descent of property in the Old Kingdom. Dismayed, Murray asked how she should do this. He showed that by using large tomes in the library (such as Richard Lepsius's *Denkmäler aus Ägypten und Äthiopien* and Auguste Mariette's *Les mastabas de l'Ancien Empire)* she could find the lists of farm names in the reproductions of reliefs of Old Kingdom tombs and apply the information in her research. In these reliefs, each tomb owner was followed by a procession of servants, and when the farm changed hands, another owner's name would be substituted. She collected about 450 names from different tombs, and Petrie then showed her how to put the article together and how to submit it for publication. It appeared in *Publications of the Society of Biblical Literature,* the only English periodical at that time concerned with matters archaeological.[5] It was published under her name: "Miss Margaret Murray," causing her great pride and bringing her to the attention of many in what was still a very select field of scholarship.

In November 1895 Petrie went out to Egypt again. This time he took with him two of his women students, Miss Paget and Miss Pirie. They were to copy reliefs in Old Kingdom tombs at Saqqara and later join him in Western Thebes, where he was to excavate an area of mortuary temples. Murray must have been longing to go to Egypt herself, but Petrie had other ideas for her. In the following winter Francis Griffith married and left London for Manchester. Henceforward, James Walker would teach the advanced class in hieroglyphs and Murray would be entrusted with the beginners. This arrangement worked very well. Her students declared her an excellent teacher, and she was appointed as junior lecturer in 1898. In the following year she was established as a lecturer on a salary of forty pounds a year. She was certainly gratified by this unexpected launch into a professional career, for she enjoyed teaching and realized she had a gift for explaining complex grammatical points to beginners. However, she can have heard with only mixed feelings that, in the summer of 1897, Petrie had decided to marry Hilda Urlin, a pretty girl she had seen in the Egyptology department the previous autumn making facsimile copies under his guidance. It was Hilda who now would accompany Petrie to Egypt every winter and act as field assistant in his future endeavors.

Egypt at Last

Murray's first and only opportunity to dig in Egypt came in the winter of 1902, when Petrie asked her to be a member of his team excavating at Abydos, near Baliana. There he had been finding tombs of First Dynasty kings in the desert at Umm el-Qa'ab. There was a mysterious structure he wanted to investigate: preliminary soundings the previous year in the area behind the great temple of Sethos I had established that a large stone building lay buried beneath the sand. It appeared to be funerary in character; and the upper part of the long sloping passage with painted scenes from the Book of Gates seemed to lead down to a subterranean hall. Petrie needed someone who could decipher the texts. Neither he nor his helpers could do so. Besides his wife, there were other women in the camp that winter: Miss Hansard, who was an artist, and Lina Eckenstein, a medievalist friend, both helped with the drawing and recording of finds in the camp. Margaret Murray and Hilda Petrie, he decided, were to undertake the new excavation. While the preliminary clearance was in progress, Murray busied herself in copying the hieratic, demotic, and Coptic graffiti in the temple (there were many, for it had been used as a nunnery in Christian times).

On the first day of work, Petrie set his new recruit a test. His wife, he said, was indisposed, so she would have to take the men across to the site herself. The workmen refused to take the commands of this tiny woman seriously and began to disperse in confusion, but she promptly marched them back to camp, letting them know that she was very angry and that they would lose a day's pay. After that she had no difficulty with the workmen. It was not an easy excavation. The underground building was deeply buried in loose sand, and, on windy days, sand and loose stones would cascade down on the excavators. As she later wrote:

> The Roman filling [was] so loose that there were continual rivulets of sand running down the sides, and a high wind would bring down half a ton of sand and stones in one fall . . . To sit in a deep pit under an irregular but continuous fire of small stones, with the chance of a big stone coming down too, is an experience more amusing to look back upon than to endure.[6]

The building proved to be a large underground hall of red granite blocks sculptured with funerary texts bearing the name of Sethos I. Defeated by seepage water and the sheer size of the monument, the excavators were forced to abandon the task of excavation (the clearance was only finally achieved in 1930 by Henri Frankfort with the aid of a large steam pump). But Margaret Murray's careful facsimiles of the texts were published as a volume under her own name, with a long and important commentary on the worship of Osiris.[7]

That winter, in spite of its discomforts (and life in a Petrie camp was a somewhat Spartan experience), must have been one of the happiest of Murray's life. She enjoyed the routine of camp life, as well as the encounters with the villagers and the little Coptic community. She often superintended, with evident relish, the evening "clinic," when the workmen and basket-boys came to the camp to have their small injuries dressed and ask for medicine for stomach complaints and sore eyes. But she was not asked to go out with Petrie again. Instead, the following winter he invited her to go to Saqqara to copy the relief sculpture in several Old Kingdom mastabas (tombs) along with two other women, Miss Hansard and Miss Jessie Mothersole. They lived in a small house belonging to the Antiquities Service on the edge of the desert. Mariette had already copied some of these tombs, but not very accurately. They were so full of detail, Petrie obviously felt they deserved more thorough recording. His old foreman, or *reis,* was still alive and could instruct his son Khalifa which mastabas to reopen. Several were of great importance, especially that of Ptahhotep and Akhethotep, which is still kept open for visitors as one of the finest and most interesting in the whole necropolis. The drawings, traced outlines with a heavier line on the right-hand side to hint at relief sculpture, were published in Petrie's *Egyptian Research Account* series with his usual promptness.

Appointment to University College London

Murray was never again able to go to Egypt to work. During the school year she was needed to teach at the college; in the summer it was far too hot to dig in Egypt; and by late summer most of the sites in the Nile valley were submerged under the inundation. James Walker still taught the advanced Egyptian language course, but Murray now taught not only the elementary language students, but other subjects that were gradually added to the curriculum: history, religion, arts and crafts of the ancient Egyptians. She also taught the last stage of the language, Coptic, as a necessary adjunct to the understanding of the earlier language. She had learned by watching Griffith's mistakes as a teacher. Realizing that most of her students were unfamiliar with linguistics and found it hard to follow Erman's grammar while they struggled with German and its unfamiliar script, she devised a simplified grammar of ancient Egyptian, suitable for beginners, and later added an elementary grammar of Coptic. "I am not a linguist," she said, "but I am a teacher of language, and I think I can safely say that any student who began his study of Egyptian with me had never anything to unlearn even if he became a linguist."[8] Raymond Faulkner dedicated his valuable *Concise Dictionary of Middle Egyptian* "to Margaret Murray, who first taught me Ancient Egyptian, in gratitude and affection."

Murray's rank in the college, at first, was junior lecturer. In 1921 she became a lecturer, in 1922 senior lecturer, and assistant professor in 1924 when she was sixty-two years old. It was slow promotion. But, in 1931, she was awarded an honorary doctorate, a surprising tribute for those days and all the more remarkable because she had never, as she said, passed an examination in her life. Her students clubbed together to purchase her doctoral robes, which she could not herself have afforded to buy. Then, in 1932, she was made an honorary fellow of the college, a distinction rarely given to a woman. (University College London waited until 1949 to elect its first woman professor.)

At first Murray could only come to London for two days a week, for her father had died in 1891 and she was nursing her paralyzed mother. Much of the preparation for her classes was done by her mother's bedside (a fact she does not mention in her autobiography). She was for many years on the Refectory Committee, concerned with the provision of nutritious and affordable lunches for the students, and later served as secretary to the Board of Studies in Anthropology and as a member of the Professorial Board. She also played a tactful part in reconciling the (at times) frosty relationship between Petrie and his anthropologist colleagues.

Breaking Ground

Professional Activities before the First World War

During the winter months Murray shouldered a heavy load of teaching in all three terms of the semester, including evening classes twice a week. In the summer she helped the Petries mount and catalog their current finds for summer exhibition in the college and assisted them in showing the public around. Thus, it was generally in the later summer of the long vacation that she could get away from London. She usually attended the August meetings of the British Association for the Advancement of Science (Petrie was often chairman of the Archaeological Section), and she was several times invited to visit museums in other cities in Britain to advise them on their Egyptian collections. At the invitation of the Society of Antiquaries for Scotland, she wrote a catalog of the Egyptian objects in their museum and was rewarded by being elected a fellow (F.S.A. Scot.). She performed the same service for the National Museum of Antiquities in Edinburgh, producing a booklet illustrated by a few photographs and her own careful drawings. In Dublin she made a comprehensive catalog of the Dublin National Museum scarabs and other Egyptian antiquities and was asked back in 1910 to write another, and she was responsible for the Egyptian section of the catalog of the Ashmolean Museum in Oxford, first drafted by Francis Griffith and published in 1900.

In 1910 Murray was invited by the trustees of the Manchester Museum to write an illustrated catalog of a remarkable tomb group that Petrie had found at Deir Rifeh in Upper Egypt in 1907 and presented to the museum. In her introduction to this small book, *The Tomb of the Two Brothers,* she felt it necessary to justify the excavation and the dismantling of graves in general. Quoting Petrie, she explained: "The printed description distributed in all the libraries of the world will last far longer than the objects themselves. To leave important remains without any diffused record is a crime only exceeded by that of their destruction." Murray superintended the opening of the two painted coffins from the tomb. And on May 6, 1908, with an audience of five hundred (including museum officials and members of the Manchester Egyptian Association) she performed, with the aid of John Cameron, what was probably the first public unrolling of a mummy by a woman. The operation took an hour and a half. The catalog includes a detailed description of the order in which the bandages were removed; Cameron's anatomical report; and an account by another expert on the clothes employed by the embalmers. "At the close of the ceremony members of the audience who wished to have a piece of the mummy wrappings as a memento were invited by the Chairman of the meeting to leave their names and addresses."

An excellent observer, Murray wrote in her autobiography about cataloging the Ashmolean collection:

> I subjected to careful examination with a powerful lens any bead the material of which I could not recognize at once . . . In a small string of beads from a grave of the First Dynasty at Abydos the largest bead was perhaps three eighths of an inch long, oval in shape, dark blue in colour and highly polished; it was labelled lapis lazuli. A minute fracture invisible except under the lens showed the fracture to be glass. As glass of that period was unknown, I had to have corroboration of my discovery. I therefore took the bead to Sir Henry Miers, the well-known mineralogist, who by the fracture and its specific gravity proved that the bead was glass and not lapis lazuli.[9]

Activism

Though a passionate feminist, Margaret Murray was not a militant suffragist. Perhaps her diminutive height deterred her from taking part in the more violent demonstrations. But she was a member of the Women's Social and Political Union, led by Emmeline Pankhurst, and was among those who walked in the first procession of protest to the Houses of Parliament in 1907. It was thanks to Mrs. Amos, the wife of Judge Amos, Petrie's friend in Cairo, that she first became interested in the suffrage movement. An active member herself, Mrs. Amos had stayed with the Petries in their camp at Abydos in 1903, and Murray had been fired with enthusiasm by her forthright views. In 1913, she advocated before the British Association for the Advancement of Science meeting that women, as well as men, receive training in anthropology before the government sent them out with their husbands to administer colonial territories. Anthropology, she was told by several of the men present, "is not a subject for women." In 1914 she was already becoming known to the public. Her photograph appeared in the *Illustrated London News* under the heading, "The Ideal Excavator." The author coupled Murray's name with that of two other academic women in an article entitled "The Women's Progress."[10]

In the college, she was staunch in support of women students and a firm advocate for their well-being. University College had been the first academic institution in England to allow women to study for degrees. As early as the 1860s, women had been allowed to attend lectures, though special provision had to be made for them and they had been segregated from the male students. Later, they were allowed to sit in the same lecture hall, and in 1878 they were admitted to degrees on the same footing as men were. Egyptology was first made a university subject here, and when Murray entered the college in the 1890s, twenty of the seventy-two women students were studying it.

College Hall, the first hall of residence for students, was opened in 1882, and a lady superintendent of women students was appointed. This "superintendent" was later to be known as the "Tutor to Women Students." Murray was a firm friend of the first superintendent, Miss Morrison, and, after her death, of her successor, Miss Winifred Smith. Similarly, she believed that women members of the academic staff were treated as second-class citizens and was instrumental in ensuring that their common room, small and stuffy compared with that of the men, was exchanged for a more comfortable sitting room. When a larger and better common room was found in which women members of the academic staff could relax and drink their coffee after lunch, it was given the name "Margaret Murray Room." In the course of time, after she left the college, the doors of the common room were opened to men, but it was designated a quiet reading room for the academic staff. Eventually, with the expansion of the college, it was converted into an administrative office and, unfortunately, Murray's name was removed from the door.

Work during World War I

Upon the outbreak of World War I, Egyptology classes ceased. Hoping that her nursing experience would qualify her for hospital work, Murray went to St. Malo in Brittany to help in a hospital staffed by English doctors. But her health broke down after a year and she was sent home. Convalescing in Glastonbury, she became interested in the local tradition of the Holy Grail. She wrote a paper linking the legend with ancient Egyptian mythology, claiming that many of the place-names that survived in the legend were located in the Egyptian delta—a suggestion that met with little acceptance.

Murray's work on the Holy Grail tradition was one of several articles published during the war in Petrie's new journal, *Ancient Egypt,* to which she was to be a constant contributor in the years to come. Petrie himself was the editor, and besides contributing an article himself to each number, he wrote most of the book reviews. He could not, however, read German, and the task of reviewing all German books and periodicals fell to Murray.

She continued to do this for many years, until 1919, when Georgina Aitken, one of Petrie's old students, took over the German reviews. Murray seldom failed to produce at least one article for each number of the journal. When Petrie left England for Palestine, most of the responsibility for editing the journal and seeing it through the press fell to her also. Later, in 1933, she was named joint editor.

Murray gave a course of lectures in Manchester during World War I, replacing T. E. Peet, who was absent on military duty. She also became deeply involved in the Serbian cause. Specifically, she was one of the first and most active members of a committee formed by Elsie Inglis, founder of the Scottish Women's Hospitals, to bring young Serbian girls to England to train as doctors. Later known as the Yugoslav Medical Women's Scholarship Fund, the organization persisted after the war, and, for the rest of her life, Murray continued to take an interest in every young Serbian woman who came over on a scholarship to train in London.

Folklore, Witchcraft, and Postwar Responsibilities

It was during World War I that Margaret Murray first began her research into witchcraft, the subject that, perhaps more than any other, made her known to the general public. Ancient religion was a subject that had always drawn her particular interest. She was much influenced by the writings of the anthropologist Sir James Frazer, whose monumental volumes of *The Golden Bough: A Study of Comparative Religion* came out in the early years of the twentieth century and ran to a number of editions. Another influence was that of her friend and colleague, Charles Gabriel Seligman, author of studies of tribal customs and beliefs in the Nilotic Sudan.

During World War I and the 1920s, Murray turned her attention to the study of medieval witchcraft. Reading extensively on the subject in English, French, German, and Flemish, she also consulted unpublished records of the trials of witches among the *Edinburgh Justiciary Records* and in the *Guernsey Graaffe.* She formulated the theory that the medieval witch cult was based on actual ritual practices: that these represented the remains of an ancient pagan religion that was displaced by Christianity but survived, in England at least, until the eighteenth century. Her first book on this subject, *The Witch Cult in Western Europe* (1921), had, for a time, a considerable influence. As a result, she was asked to contribute the article "Witchcraft" to the fourteenth edition of the *Encyclopedia Britannica.*

A more popular book, *The God of the Witches,* appeared in 1933. The old religion, she maintained, gradually retreated to the remoter parts of the country. Priests drawn from the peasant class were outwardly Christian but carried on the old pagan rites. Her frank account of the orgiastic rituals practiced in the witches' covens caused some raised eyebrows even among her colleagues, and she received some unpleasant anonymous letters. Anthropology was still considered a subject unsuitable for women. Some reviewers dismissed her theory, one calling it "vapid balderdash,"[11] a verdict less rudely endorsed by Hugh R. Trevor-Roper[12] and more recently by Robin Briggs, who writes:

> The fundamental defect of the Murrayite approach is its literal-mindedness, which includes a refusal to accept that fantasy is a genuine experience. Any attempt to explain the stories in purely realistic terms can only lead to a gross distortion of their meanings and a complete misunderstanding of the way they were produced.[13]

Recent editions of the *Encyclopedia Britannica* refer to her "now discredited theory," but Elizabeth Bacon's article in the latest *Encyclopedia Americana* appears to accept Murray's thesis without citing her books in the bibliography.

Another theory of Margaret Murray's, which even at the time of its publication received yet less credence from historians, was her belief that "a fundamental dogma of the pre-Christian religion of Europe" survived into medieval times. This dogma, she argued, involved a divine victim, the sacrifice of the chieftain or king, originally the tribal chief in person and later a substitute. She claimed that at least four notable murders in historic times, those of William Rufus, Thomas à Becket, Joan of Arc, and Gilles de Rais, were explicable as manifestations of this survival from pagan times. Undeterred by the critics, Murray maintained her belief in the divine victim until late in her life.

She herself was far too down-to-earth to be superstitious and ridiculed the "absurd stories" of the occult properties of such ancient Egyptian phenomena as unlucky mummies and "the curse of the Pharaohs." But she believed in telepathy and ghostly apparitions in modern times, which she took to be a form of atmospheric photography: a "striking of light rays in some special combination of the elements of the atmosphere." She was known occasionally to have cast a spell in jest—she was said once to have made a waxen image of the kaiser during World War I and melted it—"and you see, we won." A colleague in the Institute of Archaeology who knew her well wrote after her death:

> A woman of courage, a happy explorer, her amusing and strong personality made a marked impact on all who studied with her. When she contemplated her enemies her bright blue eyes flashed in dangerous indignation and she was ready if only in jest to practice magic in order to remove from office a colleague of whose appointment she disapproved. Indeed, on one occasion she cast a spell on an intended victim in a saucepan at the Institute of Archaeology in the presence of two reputable witnesses, and achieved her aim with conspicuous success. The subject immediately fell ill, and was promoted to some higher and more suitable office.[14]

Since James Walker had died in 1914, the entire running of the Department of Egyptology had devolved on Murray for most of each year, with Petrie teaching a class or two before he left for Egypt in November. She was also an indispensable member of the executive committee set up by Petrie to conduct the affairs of the British School in England during his absence. Besides day classes, Murray taught in the evening school and gave courses outside the college. Sometimes there were classes in the British Museum, followed by "a demonstration in the Egyptian Galleries" (the fee, one guinea for a course of six). Sometimes there were Oxford Extension lectures for extramural students. While Petrie was in Egypt, Murray was also custodian of the Petrie Museum and had the pleasant duty of showing visitors around the collection. When, in 1927, Queen Mary came to the college, Murray, as the senior woman member of the academic staff, was one of those who escorted her round the cases. The queen subsequently presented the museum with some beads and a wooden statuette from her own collection (unfortunately, the figure turned out to be a fake).[15] The vice-chancellor of the university, the duke of Athlone, came on another occasion with his wife Princess Alice, who showed a genuine interest in what Murray showed her and came again unofficially. A friendship sprang up between the two women that lasted the rest of their lives.

Fieldwork in the 1920s and 1930s

After the war Margaret Murray longed to return to Egypt to excavate, but she realized that it was out of the question. Instead, she took advantage of the long summer vacation to work in the islands of the Mediterranean. Her first choice was the island of Malta. In 1921 Dr. Themistocles (later Sir Themistocles) Zammit, the head of the local Antiquities Service and director of the Malta Museum, invited her to investigate two prehistoric sites (under threat from the proposed construction of an aerodrome) in the extreme south of the island. The first yielded no finds, though there were signs that megalithic structures had existed there.

Then she was given the important megalithic site of Borg en Nadur, on a triangular promontory in the Bay of Marsaxlokk, near St. George's Bay, where the great stone structures had already been partially investigated. Between 1922 and 1925, Murray conducted four seasons of excavation there. She was assisted by a number of people: Dr. Edith Guest, her friend from the medical faculty of the college, who undertook the photography and identification of the bones; Francis Turville-Petre, who later achieved fame as the finder of the Galilee skull; and, in the first season, Gertrude Caton-Thompson, her friend and former student, who had been asked by Zammit to investigate the prehistoric levels of the cave at Ghar Dhalam nearby. Accommodation proved a problem since the island was not yet a tourist resort and local inns were far from comfortable. In the end they settled into a clean hotel in Valetta, eight miles away. This arrangement required catching a tram at 5 A.M. and then a carozza, or motorbus, a far-from-comfortable form of transport. But Borg en Nadur was a site that amply rewarded their discomfort. The Neolithic temple lay on the landward side of a huge Bronze Age wall. In it Bronze Age pottery of a type new to Malta was found. In the later settlement, of about the fourteenth century B.C., there was plentiful evidence of domestic activity: here food had been cooked and flour ground. There was a great deal of pottery, some very large jars and rectangular pottery basins with internal divisions. The Borg en Nadur culture, as it is now called, is thought to have come from Sicily, where numerous parallels have been found.[16]

Murray's work at this site was followed by a more general study of the prehistoric pottery of Malta. Working in the National Museum in Valetta, with the help of Harris Colt and Theresa Strickland (later to become Mrs. Harris Colt), she compiled a corpus of the Bronze Age pottery of Malta (1934). In particular, she studied the finds from the remarkable temple at Tarxien where, as she demonstrated, the division between Neolithic and Bronze Age can be clearly shown. She also compiled a list of "Egyptian Objects Found in Malta." She learned enough Maltese to converse with her workmen and made a number of Maltese friends. She published a small volume of Maltese folktales in English, based on the original version by Father Magri, S.J., and her friend Liza Galea. Her version of the stories reads easily, and her footnotes show that she had absorbed much of the local folklore.

In the summer of 1931, at the suggestion of her friend Louis Clarke, director of the Cambridge Museum of Archaeology and Ethnology, Murray investigated megalithic remains on Minorca at the museum's expense. The project was initially inspired by Edith Guest, who had visited the island on holiday one summer and been struck by the remarkable megalithic remains and the little that appeared to be known about them. Quite different from the Neolithic temples of Malta, they are of three types. The most striking is the *taula,* a long slab set upright and crowned by a smaller horizontal slab, the whole surrounded by a half-moon of stones. The *talayot,* of which there are about three hundred examples on the island, is a squat circular tower with a flat top, possibly a fortified farmhouse; and the *naveta* is a low mound shaped like an upturned boat, probably used as an ossuary. Murray's party excavated two taulas; the one at Trepuco, near the capital Mahon, is one of the largest on the island. The other, Sa Torreta on the east coast, was smaller and more overgrown.

In the first season, 1931, Murray was assisted by Edith Guest, Hilda Campion, one of the Egyptology students, Balakrishnan Nayar of Madras, and another student named John Vernon. Little was known about the megaliths of Minorca, but one or two of the local inhabitants expressed an interest and came out from Mahon to watch the work and help. The party was comfortably lodged throughout its stay in the home of the German consul and his wife. But the excavation was not an easy one. The site had first to be cleared, for it had been used over the centuries as a rubbish dump. Bone, shells, and potsherds were evidence of Bronze Age occupation. Some of the pottery was handmade. Later wares could be compared with Villanovan of the eleventh and tenth centuries B.C. and with Iberian painted pottery.

The excavators concluded that the taulas are the earliest monuments on the island, dating to the Bronze Age; the navetas, they concluded, are also Bronze Age. With the advent of the Iron Age, the holy places were deserted, and the sacred precinct became a rubbish dump. At Sa Torreta, eight miles south of Mahon, the taula was much smaller than the one at Trepuco; the galleries surrounding it, Murray surmised, could have been dwelling places for priests or perhaps workhouses or storehouses. In the naveta, Bronze Age pottery was found, and the bones of more than fifty individuals, without a single complete skeleton. These must have been reburials in some secondary rite after the preliminary interment. John Cameron of Cambridge, who reported on the skeletal material, found one skull that had been subjected to a trepanning operation—the first authentic example known from the islands of the Mediterranean.

Murray also dug in England, heading a team of volunteers in the summer of 1925 to excavate a site called "Homestead Moat in Whomerle Wood," southeast of Stevenage in the county of Hertfordshire. All that seems to have been found here were "mediaeval relics such as an earthenware vase and some ironwork, possibly of twelfth century date."[17] Was she perhaps looking for evidence of the practice of witchcraft? There appears to be no trace of a publication of her excavation results, and her motive must remain obscure. The dig is not mentioned in her autobiography.

Travels

In the annual entry for Murray in *Who's Who?* she always listed "travel" under the heading "recreation." She loved traveling and would have liked more opportunity to see the world, but she lacked both the time and the means. Her salary was always small and the revenue from most of her books meager, though her contributions to Hammerton's *Wonders of the Past* and her book *The Splendour That Was Egypt* brought her some money, and the latter eventually proved a bestseller.

She was once able to return to Upper Egypt. In the late summer of 1920 she stayed as the guest of a Coptic family in the village of Naqada, north of Dendera, the scene of one of Petrie's most important excavations, where there was a flourishing Coptic community. Here she was able to witness the domestic rituals of the village, two of which she was convinced were survivals from Pharaonic times. One was Nawruz, the festival of the High Nile, when family groups congregate at midnight on the banks of the river to celebrate the height of the flood. The other was a remarkable ceremony performed on her behalf by the priests when she was bitten by a dog in the village. At one part of the service, seven small boys pretended to be dogs and bite her. She would thus, she was assured, be protected from the risk of rabies. She gives a vivid description of both these rituals in her autobiography.[18]

In later life, when the pressure of teaching lessened, Murray made several adventurous trips. One (which she does not mention in her autobiography) was to South Africa, where she went in July 1929 with her friend Mrs. Benson, who came straight from Petrie's dig in Palestine to join her in Johannesburg. Here they attended the meeting of the British Association for the Advancement of Science, whose theme was the prehistory of southern Africa. Together they visited Kimberley with the other delegates, exploring gravel beds and visiting a diamond mine. In the lecture hall at

Johannesburg, Murray listened proudly to her former student, Gertrude Caton-Thompson, lecturing on the results of her epoch-making excavations at Zimbabwe and to the lively discussion that followed.[19]

In the early 1930s, Murray traveled during a summer vacation as a tourist to Russia, visiting museums in Leningrad, Moscow, Kharkov, and Kiev. During one winter break she was invited by the Society of University Women to lecture on witchcraft in Finland, and in 1935 at the age of seventy-two she undertook a strenuous lecture tour at Christmas time to Norway, Sweden, Finland, and Estonia. She was delayed by pack ice on the way home.

Legacy

Margaret Murray's excavations in Malta and Minorca made a valuable contribution to the prehistory of Europe, but it is as a teacher of Egyptology that she will be chiefly remembered. In Rosalind Janssen's book, *The First Hundred Years,* published in 1992 for the centenary of the Edwards chair of Egyptology at University College London, one or two of her old students recorded their reminiscences of Murray as a teacher. All agreed on the pleasure and informality of her classes.[20] Tuition was given in the Edwards Library at the end of the long gallery where Petrie's museum cases held the crowded display of his years of excavation and discovery in Egypt. The students (seldom more than four or five, sometimes fewer) sat around a large table. The teaching was informal, with Murray often embarking on a long digression, for instance, on the pagan origin of witchcraft or her memories of purdah in India. In her lectures on Egyptian history and religion she would digress into her own unorthodox and sometimes highly fanciful theories, but she provided an excellent grounding in both subjects. She did not lecture with lantern slides, but in talking of art and architecture she would take the trouble to haul down from the library shelves the heavy German volumes of reproductions of temple reliefs and tomb paintings. One class, which she called "The Origin of Signs," was an opportunity to talk about all aspects of ancient Egyptian civilization. She used colored facsimiles of painted hieroglyphs from tomb and temple inscriptions as a peg from which to hang a discussion of the functions of the different tools and implements depicted; the methods used in cooking and brewing; the elements of architecture, house design, clothing, boat-building; and so on. Sometimes she would reminisce about her experiences in Egypt, and occasionally she would pass around a box of chocolates.

A number of other subjects were studied by Murray's diploma students: elementary mineralogy and geology, a course largely devoted to the identification of the various stones found in Egypt (taught by a professor in the geology department); ethnology and anthropology (a series of formal lectures by C. G. Seligman, an authority on the Nilotic tribes of the Sudan); elementary surveying (for which students mapped the front quadrangle of the college with the aid of an alidade and leveled up and down the portico steps); and the elements of skeletal anatomy, in which students learned to measure the cephalic index of skulls and to recognize immaturity in bones (taught by a doctor from the medical school with the aid of a skeleton kept in the department). Students were encouraged to attend a class at the Institute of Archaeology on the use of the camera for archaeological recording. A short course in Aegean pottery, given by the professor of classical archaeology, taught them to recognize and date Minoan and Mycenaean wares and sherds.

Those who completed the two-year course were equipped to be useful assistants in the field. They were required to pass an examination and, if successful, were awarded the college diploma in Egyptology. Many went out with the professor the following winter. Some, such as Ernest Mackay, Randall MacIver, and Gertrude Caton-Thompson, after their apprenticeship with the professor, went on to direct their own excavations or to become inspectors of antiquities. Others, like Rex Engelbach and Guy Brunton, were appointed to posts as directors in Cairo's Museum of Antiquities.

Murray's *Splendour That Was Egypt* distills much of what she taught her students during the informal lectures given around a table in the Edwards Library.[21] It contains a number of her highly individual theories (some now disproved) and some outdated spellings of royal names. It is also marred by her adoption of Petrie's by-then outmoded chronology, which added an entire Sothic cycle to the history of ancient Egypt and thus placed the beginning of the First Dynasty at 4777 B.C. (instead of the more generally accepted approximation of 3100 B.C.). Her chapter about Petrie, too, must be read with reservations. She clearly idolized him and presented him as the inventor of modern archaeological method—true only in the sense that he first applied careful techniques of excavation being developed in Europe to sites and monuments in Egypt, hitherto subjected only to the plunder of treasure seekers. One or two of her pet theories also appear in this book. For instance, she states that the new popularity of certain jewel stones during the Twelfth Dynasty shows the coming into Egypt of a fair race:

> Dark stones, such as hematite, garnet and green jasper were worn, while pale amethyst, which is only tolerable in color when worn on a fair skin, was much in vogue.[22]

Murray's highly personal reaction to the official art of the Twelfth Dynasty recalls another subjective interpretation from her history classes:

> Of the private life of Senusert III nothing is known, but the portraits of him in later life are so tragic in expression that it would seem that some terrible misfortune and unhappiness had overtaken him. His public career was a series of brilliant successes, therefore the tragedy which must have befallen him could have been only in his private capacity as a man.[23]

An important section of *The Splendour That Was Egypt* deals with the position of women, a subject in which Murray was particularly interested. According to her, women in Egypt "enjoyed a peculiar position from the fact that all landed property descended in the female line from mother to daughter." A husband enjoyed the property as long as his wife was alive, "but on her death her daughter and the daughter's husband came into possession." Similarly she maintained that "Pharaoh safeguarded himself from abdication by marrying every heiress without any regard to sovereignty, so that if the chief heiress died he was already married to the next in succession and thus retained the sovereignty." In appendices to the book, Murray traced the complicated genealogies (without references) that she claimed proved her point, and she also drew parallels of matrilineal descent in the families of David and Solomon and of Julius Caesar. The theory of matrilineal descent in Egypt had now been discredited.[24]

More Fieldwork

In the summer of 1933, W. M. Flinders Petrie had at last retired from University College at the age of eighty. Murray may have expected to succeed him in the Edwards chair of Egyptology, but she was herself seventy years old, and it was decided to appoint someone younger. The choice fell on a scholar from the British Museum, Stephen Glanville, an excellent language man who also had experience excavating in Egypt. Murray retired two summers later in a mood of acute disappointment. In her autobiography she remembers how she descended the steep staircase from the Egyptology department for the last time in tears, "as from a prison-house, full of bitterness and frustration." Her feelings may, perhaps, be understood, though Glanville treated her with the utmost tact and consideration during the two years when she still taught some of the classes in the department.

In the summer of 1935, her last in the college, Murray received a distress call from the Petries, who now lived in Jerusalem. The professor, who had been excavating a huge Bronze Age mound, Tell el-Ajjul south of Gaza, was in difficulties with the Palestinian Department of Antiquities. All archaeologists in the field were required to make lists of all objects found. It was necessary to submit these lists to the Department of Antiquities before decisions were made about the objects, what would be kept for the Palestine Museum and what the excavator might take as his share. This list was something that Petrie had always insisted on making himself, but the museum authorities in Jerusalem (who disapproved of Petrie's work for a number of reasons) had this year refused to accept his closely written sheets of paper, maintaining that they were incomprehensible and must be redone. There was nothing for it but to make a new list.

Able to take a sabbatical term before her retirement, Murray went out to Jerusalem by way of Cairo and then directly to Tell el-Ajjul, where she stayed alone in the excavation house with only the Bedouin guard for company. It was exceptionally hot, even for Palestine in midsummer, and cataloging the pottery in a storeroom with a corrugated iron roof was decidedly onerous. The list, rewritten in her clear round hand, took twelve days to complete. When she sent it to the authorities in Jerusalem, she added a polite note saying that she was returning the revised lists and, "as they were written in words of one syllable she hoped they would prove satisfactory."[25] She next took the opportunity to explore Jerusalem and the surrounding countryside and also visited Petra in neighboring Jordan.

The following spring, in March and April 1937, Murray embarked on a small dig of her own at Petra, an enterprise that, curiously, she mentions only briefly in her autobiography. This remarkable site, which was already much visited and greatly admired by tourists, had seen very little archaeological investigation. The "rose-red city," carved out of the rock in the eastern slopes of the Wadi Arabah south of the Dead Sea, had been an Edomite stronghold; a prosperous caravan city; the capital of the Nabataeans until its capture by Trajan in A.D. 106. Murray had been especially attracted by the handsome painted pottery, a thin fine ware lavishly decorated with plant designs in red paint, sherds of which lay about on the site. The cliffs were honeycombed with cave dwellings. Jack Ellis and Judge Saunders, both of whom had been helping the Petries at their new dig in Sinai, Shaikh

Zoweyd, during the previous winter, came as her assistants. They recruited a team of untrained Bedouin from the locality. (Gertrude Caton-Thompson, who was visiting Palestine that spring, mentions in her autobiography seeing "a small witch" approaching.[26] It was, of course, Miss Murray.)

The work was concentrated in the caves of one particular valley, part of which had been a street of rock habitations. Six or seven workers were assigned to each cave. At that time, very little scientific investigation had been carried out in the area. Murray's careful drawings of the small finds included pottery, both plain and painted, and one important find was made: a life-sized mold for casting a metal head, perhaps of a queen of Petra. Her publication provided the nucleus of a corpus of Nabataean pottery in the Petrie style.

Murray subsequently wrote a most readable guide for visitors to Petra, with photographs taken by Richmond Brown, Petrie's erstwhile photographer and assistant. It contains chapters on the flora and fauna of the valley; a chapter on the monuments; two on the history of the city; and others on the religion of the Nabataeans, manners and customs, and trade. Perhaps the most interesting chapter is her account of her personal experience as an excavator:

> Every excavation, no matter where it is, is always somewhat of an adventure. There is generally the problem of the weather, which if not propitious may hold up the whole expedition for days on end. The paid workmen are often excessively difficult: the "know-all" who begins to teach you your own job before he had been a week at it or the fool who ruins your well-laid plan of work by not listening to even the clearest orders are only equalled by the too-eager youngster who is just as disastrous to the work. Of course, there are many good workers, but often the best men, like the best cooks, have uncertain tempers. Perhaps the unpaid workers are the greatest problem of all, the people who think it will be "so thrilling" to excavate, and have visions of themselves figuring in all the newspapers as making the find of the season in the shape of vast treasure of gold and jewels like another Aladdin's cave. Such people little realize the number of days that one had to spend in biting winds or in burning sunshine watching the workmen, who may toil all day and find nothing. And when a find does occur, there is all the business of recording; its position and level must be marked on the plan, a rapid

> description must be entered in the notebook, and later on the object must be drawn and photographed. You are lucky if it has not to be cleaned as well. A small and unimportant find of several objects lying together may take the excavator several hours to record properly, and if the find is at all spectacular, such as gold, the recording is a business to shudder at.
>
> If excavating in safe and comfortable England can be regarded as an adventure (which it certainly is) it is even more adventurous in foreign parts. But I have always found that the more adventurous the work, the more uncomfortable is the life, till now to my mind adventure is synonymous with discomfort. Sandstorms, scorpions and snakes can make life definitely unhappy in some parts of the Near East. At Petra we were spared the sandstorms, but we had howling gales and floods; scorpions we saw many times, but the snakes had not yet begun to show as the weather was still too cold for them. On the other hand, the flowers were not affected by the winds and they were a perpetual joy, and the birds were delightful to watch. There are generally compensations even for the discomforts of the weather.[27]

Petrie's work in Sinai (where he was in Egyptian territory and the museum authorities, under their director Rex Engelbach, one of his old students, were willing to approve his application to dig) was now finished, and he longed to go back to Tell el-Ajjul, where he was conscious of work uncompleted. Suspecting rightly that he would be refused if he applied to dig under his own direction, he named Margaret Murray and Ernest Mackay (another old pupil of his) as joint permit holders.[28] The permit was granted and the dig proceeded, ostensibly under new auspices, but, in fact, under Petrie's direction. At eighty-five he was still able to climb the high mound with his picked band of helpers from England while his wife, as always, ran the camp; and Murray spent much of her time drawing and making up pottery lists. This was the last season at Ajjul. Later that year the camp was raided by bandits, who smashed and burned what they could not carry away. After they broke camp, Murray never saw Petrie again; in 1942, at the age of eighty-nine, he died in Jerusalem.

An Active Retirement

In 1937 Murray went to Cambridge to live in a small cottage facing the large open space called Parker's Piece. Here she stayed during World War

II, rendering service by giving lectures that proved popular to alleviate the boredom of men and women in isolated army camps manning searchlights and antiaircraft guns. She embarked on a new line of research on the history of Cambridge town under the Tudors and Stuarts, using the town records preserved in the Guildhall and in Downing College; in the parish records of fourteen churches in the diocese; and in Ely Cathedral. The history was never published; it contained, she told me with some glee, evidence of the recurrent feud between town and gown in Cambridge.

After the war Murray returned to London and was often to be seen in the new Department of Egyptology (the Edwards Library and the museum had both been destroyed by enemy action in 1942, though most of the books and nearly all the museum objects had been moved before the war started and were housed in temporary accommodation). When Stephen Glanville left the college in 1946 to occupy a chair of Egyptology at Cambridge, Murray attempted to interfere in the appointment of his successor, writing a strong letter to the provost of the college to protest against the choice of a philologist rather than an archaeologist as the next Edwards professor. Her own choice would have been Bryan Emery, whose admirable excavations in the area of the First Dynasty royal tombs at Saqqara she had had an opportunity to visit as she passed through Cairo on her way to Jerusalem. In spite of her protest, an eminent Czech Egyptologist-philologist, Jaroslav Cerny, was chosen. For a time she came little to the college, but in 1953, when Cerny left London to take up a teaching post in Oxford, to her delight Emery was appointed to the Edwards chair. Thenceforward, Murray came frequently to the college again and continued to borrow books from the library for the rest of her life. In 1953 the college celebrated Petrie's centenary.[29] As might have been expected, both Lady Petrie, who at seventy-two was tall and gaunt, and Margaret Murray, smaller than ever at ninety, played prominent roles in the celebrations and in the dinner that followed, at which many old students sat down with their former teacher.

Murray was now living in a bed-sitting room in Endsleigh Street, close to the college and almost next door to the Institute of Archaeology, where she could take the elevator one floor up to the library. Most days she would walk to the British Museum to consult books in the spacious reading room of the British Library. She would lunch in nearby Holborn in an Express Dairy café, which she would declare was the one frequented by Karl Marx when he, too, was reading in the British Library. Twice a week she would climb the stairs of the City Literary Institute to teach Egyptian history and Egyptian religion to classes of adult education students. She continued to teach there until she was ninety-three years old, despite the retirement age of sixty-five for lecturers at the institute. The reason given for the exceptional bending of the rules was her reputation as an inspiring teacher. She offered, according to the authorities, "a unique learning opportunity to students that was not able to be provided by another tutor." When she finally did retire, she nominated one of her former students, Veronica Seton-Williams, as her successor in these evening classes.

From 1952 to 1954 Murray was president of the Folklore Society. In her 1954 presidential address, titled "England as a Field for Folklore Research," she pointed out that, whereas the Scottish, Irish, and Welsh were interested in their respective cultures, the English went abroad to look for folklore, neglecting the wealth still untouched in their own country.

About this time, Murray began to find it too difficult to manage on her own, and she moved to a home in North Finchley where she could be looked after by a retired couple, both of whom were trained nurses. She suffered from arthritis but still managed to come to University College by taxi from time to time to read in the Edwards Library. She would lunch in the refectory and meet Bryan Emery in the academic staff common room afterwards. She enjoyed an occasional outing: sometimes one of her old students would call for her in a car and take her out.

She made friends easily with children, who were delighted (if a little awed) to see her. My own little girls were amused to be addressed, as a term of endearment, as "old lady." Who, they wondered, was the old lady? For the small son of Dr. Violet MacDermot, whose husband occasionally fetched Murray by car to their home in Blackheath for lunch, she never failed to bring a "treasure," which had to be put in a special box—a piece of lapis lazuli, perhaps, or a Roman lamp. Until the end of her life she continued to take an interest in the young doctors who came over on scholarships from Yugoslavia. When they left London, she would give each of them, as a parting gift, a piece of English china, which, as she used to say, she had been "in the habit of picking up at country fairs."

Eventually Murray was forced to admit that she would be better off in hospital; she moved to the Queen Victoria Hospital at Welwyn, north of London. As Violet MacDermot put it, "She used to have an audience of doctors and nurses listening to her stories. I remember once going to see her and she was surrounded with excavation publications, rather large books to read in bed, and she said, "What is so interesting is that there is always something new round the corner waiting to be discovered!"

During this time Murray was writing two books, both of which were published in her hundredth year. One, *The Genesis of Religion,* emphasized the role of women as custodians of tradition. The first deities, she argued, were female rather than male. Pregnancy, rather than birth, was the most important factor in primitive religion. Before the role of the father was understood, maternal love was "an indication of a Mysterious Power, unseen but overruling." Her last book, her autobiography challengingly titled *My First Hundred Years,* came out in the summer of 1963. It was widely reviewed in the daily press, and Leonard Cottrell interviewed her on the radio.[30] She was, she told him, planning another book on early religion:

> I am particularly interested in Dr. Leakey's new finds in Tanganyika of sub-human remains, probably half a million years old. This new find . . . shows that there was some sort of ritual already in the minds of the people, and if there is a ritual it means that the feeling towards that great Power we call God was quite well established.

On July 13, 1963, a party of her doctors, friends, and former students gathered at Ayot St. Lawrence (once the home of Bernard Shaw) not far from the hospital, to celebrate her hundredth birthday. Two days later a party was given for her in University College. She was brought by her doctor in his car.[31] Protesting at first that she had no hat to wear, she had been fitted with a modish toque by Aage Tharup, the queen's own hat designer, who had come out to the hospital to try it. Some thirty of her old colleagues and students were present: Bryan Emery, the Edwards Professor, made a short speech of welcome, and she cut her birthday cake, decorated by the college chef with hieroglyphs denoting year 100: life, prosperity, and health. She was presented with an illuminated copy of the resolution passed by the Professorial Board of the College at their last meeting, recording "the high honour which, through her renowned scholarship, she has brought to the College where she taught for so many years." Dr. Murray talked to each of the guests in turn and finally, waving and smiling, left in her car for the hospital.

That was to be her last view of the college that for seventy years had been her world; but she was still planning a new piece of research. "The shelf is not a comfortable place," she said, "and I have no wish to be on it." She still borrowed books from the library, and in October she wrote to Emery asking his opinion of Quibell's dating of certain archaic structures at Hierakonpolis; she wished to develop an idea of her own about the identity of King Scorpion. He wrote her a long and considered reply. She died on November 13, just four months after her hundredth birthday.

Looking back over her long life, Margaret Murray felt a sense of privilege to have lived in so stirring an age of progress:

> When I look back to the beginnings of archaeology and remember how little was known, how few people were interested, and how inadequate and almost childish the investigations were, and then contrast those conditions with the conditions at the present day, with departments and Professors of archaeology in the universities of every country, with great national museums in even the smallest country, archaeological societies totaling tens of thousands of members and showing world-wide interest in the subject, I feel I am indeed privileged in having seen and being permitted to know and work with some of the great men who opened up, the pioneers who led the way into a new and hitherto unheard-of investigation into the history of man.
>
> On looking back across the years, I can see that I have lived through one of the most momentous periods of that miracle of world history, the advance of man. I have seen the coming of the use of electricity in sound and vision, the discovery of the X-ray and the germ theory of disease, the motorisation of all vehicular traffic, the invention of the aeroplane, the discovery of atomic power. The material world in which we live now is a very different place from the world of my youth.[32]

In the library of the Institute of Archaeology in University College London, a bronze bust of Margaret Murray sits between those of two other archaeologists who were prominent in the college, Sir Mortimer Wheeler and Gordon Childe. All three are by the same artist. Murray's was obtained by subscription from a number of her past students. A painted portrait, by her old student Winifred Brunton, fittingly hangs in the Petrie Museum. It is not the museum that she knew, the long gallery on the top floor at the end of which she used to teach. The exhibits are far better mounted and the lighting is better; but in between the glass cases—the familiar sculptured stones and the pottery and beads—she would feel at home still, and the numbers of students who now study in the museum and read in the Edwards Library would astonish her. Egyptology is now a first-degree subject, taken by many young enthusiasts who do not necessarily hope to make archaeology their career but who are fired, as she was a hundred years ago, by the splendor that was Egypt.

WORKS BY MARGARET ALICE MURRAY
A SELECTED BIBLIOGRAPHY

Books, Monographs, and Articles

"The Descent of Property in the Early Periods of Egyptian History." *Proceedings of the Society of Biblical Archaeology* 17 (1895): 240–45.

"The Stela of Dua-er-neheh." *Proceedings of the Society of Biblical Archaeology* 19 (1897): 77 and plate.

"Scarabs in the Dublin Museum." *Proceedings of the Royal Irish Academy* (1902): 31–38.

"Egyptian Antiquities." Science Museum, Dublin, 1902, ix, 40.

"Egyptian Antiquities." Science Museum, Dublin, 1903, vii, 66.

"Guide to the Collections of Egyptian Antiquities." Edinburgh Museum of Science and Art, 1903.

The Osireion at Abydos. Publications of the Egyptian Research Account, no. 9. London, 1904.

Elementary Egyptian Grammar. 1905. 5th ed., London, 1932.

Saqqara Mastabas Part I–II. Egyptian Research Account, 1905–37. London.

"The Astrological Character of the Egyptian Magical Wands." *Proceedings of the Society of Biblical Archaeology* 28 (1906): 33–43.

"St. Menas of Alexandria." *Proceedings of the Society of Biblical Archaeology* 29 (1907): 25–30, 51–60.

"Ptolemaic Clay-Sealings." *Zeitschrift für aegyptische Sprache und Altertumskunde* 44 (1907): 62–70.

"On the Title smr w ‘ ti." *Liverpool Annals of Archaeology and Anthropology* 1 (1908): 23–24.

"The Coffin of Ta-aath in the Brassey Institute at Hastings." *Proceedings of the Society of Biblical Archaeology* 30 (1908): 20–24.

"Priesthoods of Women in Egypt." *Transactions of the Third International Congress for the History of Religions,* vol. 1 (1908), 220–24.

"Index of Names and Titles of the Old Kingdom." *British School of Archaeology Studies,* vol. 1. London, 1908.

The Tomb of Two Brothers. Manchester Museum Publications 68. 1910.

"'General Guide to the Art Collections, Part III.' Egyptian Antiquities." National Museum of Science and Art, Dublin, 1910.

"Figure Vases in Egypt" and "An Egyptian Hippocampus." In *Historical Studies,* edited by E. R. Knobel, W. W. Midgley, I. G. Milne, M. A. Murray, and W. M. F. Petrie, 39–46. London: British School of Archaeology in Egypt, 1911.

C. G. Seligman, coauthor. "Note on the 'Sa' Sign." *Man* 11 (1911): 113–17.

C. G. Seligman, coauthor. "Note upon an Early Egyptian Standard." *Man* 11 (1911): 165–71.

Elementary Coptic (Sahidic) Grammar. 1911. 2d ed., London, 1927.

Ancient Egyptian Legends. Wisdom of the East Series. London, 1913.

"The Cult of the Drowned in Egypt." *Zeitschrift für aegyptische Sprache und Altertumskunde* 51 (1914): 127–35.

"Evidence for the Custom of Killing the King in Ancient Egypt." *Man* 14 (1914): 17–23.

"The Coptic Stela of Apa Teleme." *Ancient Egypt* 1 (1914): 156–58.

"Royal Marriages and Matrilineal Descent." *Journal of the Royal Anthropological Institute* 45 (1915): 307–25.

"The Egyptian Elements in the Grail Romance." *Ancient Egypt* 3 (1916): 1–14, 54–69.

"The Temple of Ramses II at Abydos." *Ancient Egypt* 3 (1916): 121–38.

"Egypt and the Holy Grail." *Journal of the Manchester Egyptian and Oriental Society* (1916–17): 15–16.

"Some Pendant Amulets." *Ancient Egypt* 4 (1917): 49–56.

"Some Fresh Inscriptions (from Sir Frederick Cook's Collection at Richmond)." *Ancient Egypt* 4 (1917): 62–68.

"The Statue of Nefer-Sma-Aa." *Ancient Egypt* 4 (1917): 146–48.

"Sculpture of Ptolemy I." *Ancient Egypt* 4 (1917): 167–68.

"The 'Devil' of North Berwick." *Scottish Historical Review* 15 (1918): 310–21.

"The First Mace-head of Hierakonpolis." *Ancient Egypt* 5 (1920): 15–17.

"The Ceremony of Anba Tarabo." *Ancient Egypt* 6 (1921): 110–14.

"Origin of Some Signs." *Ancient Egypt* 6 (1921): 35–38.

"Nawruz, or the Coptic New Year." *Ancient Egypt* 6 (1921): 79–81.

"The Stele of the Artist." *Ancient Egypt* 6 (1921): 27–35.

"Knots." *Ancient Egypt* 6 (1922): 14–19.

"General Results of the Season's Excavations in Egypt." *Man* 23 (1923): 106.

"Stone Implements from Borg en Nad." *Man* 23 (1923): 65–66.

Sir W. M. Flinders Petrie and G. Brunton, coauthors. *Lahun II: The Pyramid.* Egypt 33. London: British School of Archaeology, 1923.

Cambridge Excavations in Malta. 3 vols. 1923–29.

"Maqrizi's Name of the Pharaohs." *Ancient Egypt* 9 (1924): 51–54.

"The Derivation of the Name Thebes." *Ancient Egypt* 9 (1924): 55.

"Bronze Age Pottery from Minorca." *Man* 24 (1924): 140–41.

"Royal Inheritance in the XIXth Dynasty." *Ancient Egypt* 10 (1925): 100–104.

"The Coptic Inscriptions." In *Tombs of the Courtiers,* by W. M. F. Petrie, 24–25. London, 1925.

"Egyptian Finger-Counting Rhymes." *Folklore* 36 (1925): 186–87.

"The Costume of the Early Kings." *Ancient Egypt* 12 (1927): 33–40.

"Notes on Some Genealogies of the Middle Kingdom." *Ancient Egypt* 12 (1927): 45–51.

"A Coptic Ostrakon." *Ancient Egypt* 12 (1927): 97.

"The Dying God." *Ancient Egypt* 13 (1928): 8–11.

"A Statue of Kheper-ka-Ra." *Ancient Egypt* 13 (1928): 8–11, 105–9.

"Egyptian Objects Found in Malta." *Ancient Egypt* 13 (1928): 45–51.

"The Cart-ruts of Malta." *Man* 28 (1928): 21–22.

"The Cerastes in Royal Names." *Ancient Egypt* 14 (1929): 18–21.

"The Sign obt." *Ancient Egypt* 14 (1929): 43–45.

Egyptian Sculpture. London, 1930.

"A Pharaoh of the Old Kingdom." *Ancient Egypt* 15 (1930): 8–10.
"Queen Meryt-amon." *Ancient Egypt* 15 (1930): 55.
"The Bundle of Life." *Ancient Egypt* 15 (1930): 65–73.
Egyptian Temples. London, 1931.
"An Early Sed-festival." *Ancient Egypt* 17 (1932): 70–72.
"The Sign . . . ntr F." In *Studies Presented to F. Ll. Griffith*, 312–15. London, 1932.
Cambridge Excavations in Minorca. 3 vols. 1932–38.
Dorothy Pilcher, coauthor. *A Coptic Reading Book with Glossary, for the Use of Beginners*. London, with Murray, 1933.
"The Pharaoh's Third Title." *Ancient Egypt and the East* 18 (1933): 26–28.
"China and Egypt." *Ancient Egypt and the East* 18 (1933): 39–42.
"Rhymes and Rain-Charms." *Ancient Egypt and the East* 18 (1933): 45–48.
"Ritual Masking." In Mélanges Maspero, *Memoires de l'Institut français d'archéologie orientale*, 251–55. Cairo, 1934.
"The God Ash." *Ancient Egypt and the East* 19 (1934): 63–64.
"Queen Tety-Shery (Mother of King Seqenen-Ra, XVIIth Dynasty)." *Ancient Egypt and the East* 19 (1934): 115–17.
"Sacred Stones in Ancient Malta." *Ancient Egypt and the East* 19 (1934): 28–31.
Corpus of the Bronze Age Pottery of Malta. London, 1934.
"Coptic Painted Pottery." *Ancient Egypt and the East* 20 (1935): 1–15.
"Sir Temistocle Zammit." *Ancient Egypt and the East* 20 (1935): 125–26.
"James Leslie Starkey." *Man* 38 (1938): 42–43.
Petra, the Rock City of Edom. London, 1939.
J. C. Ellis, coauthor. *A Street in Petra*. Egypt 62. London: British School of Archaeology, 1940.
"William Matthew Flinders Petrie." *Religions* 41 (1942): 21–24.
"The Serpent Hieroglyph." *Journal of Egyptian Archaeology* 34 (1948): 117–18.
The Splendour That Was Egypt. London, 1949. Revised edition, 1963.
"Some Canaanite Scarabs." *Palestine Exploration Quarterly* (1949): 92–99.
Egyptian Religious Poetry. Wisdom of the East series. London, 1949.
"The Inscriptions." In *Seven Memphite Tomb Chapels*, by H. F. Petrie. Egypt 65. London: British School of Archaeology, 1952.
W. M. F. Petrie et al., coauthors. *City of the Shepherd Kings and Gaza V*. Egypt 64. London: British School of Archaeology, 1952.
"The Scarabs." In *Lachish III . . . the Iron Age*, by Olga Tufnell. 2 vols. London, 1953.
Additional notes and text to *Ceremonial Slate Palettes*, by W. M. F. Petrie. London, 1953.
"Cranial Deformation in Ancient Egypt?" *Man* 54 (1954): 56.
"Ex Africa semper aliquid. . . ." *Man* 54 (1954): 36.
"Indians in Africa." *Man* 56 (1956): 160–61.
"Egypt and Africa." *Man* 61 (1961): 25–26.
"First Steps in Archaeology." *Antiquity* 35 (1961): 1211–13.
The Genesis of Religion. London, 1963.
My First Hundred Years. London, 1963.

Folklore and Witchcraft

"Organizations of Witches in Great Britain." *Folklore* 23 (1917): 228–58.
"Child-Sacrifice among European Witches." *Man* 18 (1918): 60–62.
"Divination by Witches' Familiars." *Man* 18 (1918): 81–84.
"Witches' Familiars in England." *Man* 18 (1918): 101–4.
"The Devil's Mark." *Man* 18 (1918): 148–53.
"Witches' Transformations into Animals." *Man* 18 (1918): 188–89.
"Witches' Fertility Rites." *Man* 19 (1919): 55–58.
"The Devil's Officers and the Witches' Covens." *Man* 19 (1919): 137–40.
"Witches and the Number Thirteen." *Folklore* 31 (1920): 204–9.
The Witch-Cult in Western Europe: A Study in Anthropology. Oxford, 1921. Reprint, 1962.
"The Witch-Cult in Palaeolithic Times." *Man* 22 (1922): 3.
"The Sheela - na - gig at Oaksey (North Wiltshire)." *Man* 23 (1923): 140–41.
"Fertility Figures [at Hexham]." *Man* 29 (1929): 133–34.
"Witchcraft." *Encyclopaedia Britannica.* 14th ed., 1929, 686–68.
The God of the Witches. London, 1930. 2d ed., London, 1962.
"The Horned God." *Man* 32 (1932): 237–38.
L. Galea, coauthor. *Maltese Folktales*. Malta, 1932.
"Witchcraft and Its Suppression." In *Universal History of the World,* ed. by J. A. Hammerton, (1933) 5:3253–63.
"Female Fertility Figures." *Journal of the Royal Anthropological Institute* 64 (1934): 93–100.
"A Sheela-na-gif Figure at South Tawton." *Man* 36 (1936): 184.
"A Witch-Glove from Wiltshire." *Man* 38 (1938): 97.
"The Meaning of the Cowrie-Shell." *Man* 39 (1939): 167, 40.
"The Cowrie Shell in Formosa." *Man* 40 (1940): 15.
"The Meaning of the Cowrie-Shell." *Man* 40 (1940): 160, 176.
"Cowries Representing Eyes (New Guinea)." *Man* 42 (1942): 144.
"The Divine King in Northumbria." *Folklore* 53 (1942): 214–15.
"The Yale Ox." *Man* 44 (1944): 87–89.
"A Male Witch and His Familiar (a Cat)." *Folklore* 63 (1952): 227.
"The Puck Fair of Killorgen." *Folklore* 64 (1953): 351–54.
The Divine King in England: A Study in Anthropology. London, 1954.
"England as a Field for Folklore Research." Presidential address to the Folklore Society. *Folklore* 65 (1954): 1–9.
"Folklore in History." Presidential address to the Folklore Society. *Folklore* 66 (1955): 257–66.
"The Inkpool." *Folklore* 66 (1955): 204–13.
"Ancient and Modern Ritual Dances in the Near East." *Folklore* 66 (1955): 401–9.
"A Mediaeval Stone Mould and Leaden Clamp." *Folklore* 66 (1955): 412–13.
"The Divine King in England." *Atti dell' VIII Congresso internazionale di storia delle religioni.* 1955 (1956): 378–80.

Reviews

Early Records of Travel, by D. Paton. *Ancient Egypt* 3 (1916): 81.

Notes on the Story of Sinuhe, by A. H. Gardiner. *Ancient Egypt* 3 (1916): 181–82.

Egyptian Records of Travel in Western Asia Vol. II, by D. Paton. *Ancient Egypt* 4 (1917): 173.

Das Alte Aegypten, by A. Wiedemann. in *Man* (April 1922): 61.

Introduction à l'étude des Hieroglyphes, by H. Sottas and E. Drioton; *Les Textes des Pyramides Egyptiennes* (1923), by L. Speleer; and *Coptica* (1922), by W. E. Crum and H. I. Bell. *Ancient Egypt* 10 (1924): 23, 56, 117.

The Nile and Egyptian Civilization, by A. Moret. *Man* 23 (1923): 162.

The Phonetics of Arabic, by W. H. T. Gardner; *Ort der Herkunft und Zweck der Zusammenstellung der Grossen Papyrus Harris (Aegyptus 7:1–40),* by V. Struve; and *Imhotep,* by L. B. Hurry. *Ancient Egypt* 11 (1926): 94, 122–23, 126.

Fishing from the Earliest Times, by W. Radcliffe; *Bemerkungen zur Schiefertafel von Hierakonpolis,* by L. Keimer; *Egyptian Grammar* (1927), by Alan H. Gardiner; *Akephalos, der Kopflose Gott,* by K. Preiserdanz; *Ancient Cities of Iraq: A Practical Handbook,* by D. Mackay. *Ancient Egypt* 12 (1927): 26–27, 63, 100–101, 103–4, 105.

La Magie dans l'Égypte antique, by F. Lexa; and *Les statues vivantes,* by Weynants Ronday. *Man* 27 (1927): 57, 238.

Grundzüge der aegyptischen Vorgeschichte, by A. Scharff. *Man* 28 (1928): 123.

Egyptian Grammar, by A. H. Gardiner. *Man* 28 (1928): 212–13.

Dramatische Texte zu altaegyptischen Mysterienspielen II, by K. Sethe. *Ancient Egypt* 14 (1929): 50–51.

Imhotep, by J. B. Hurry; *The Most Ancient East,* by V. Gordon Childe; and *Witchcraft in Old and New England,* by G. L. Kittredge. *Man* 29 (1929): 76, 91–92, 197–98.

"Probleme der aegyptischen Vorgeschichte," in *Archiv für Orientforschung* 5 (1929), by L. Von Bissing; and *The Plural and the Dual in Old Egyptian* (1929), by R. O. Faulkner. *Ancient Egypt* 14 (1929): 62–63, 118–19.

Witchhunting and Witch Trials, by C. L'Estrange Owen. *Man* 30 (1930): 38–39.

An Introduction to Egyptian Religion, by A. W. Shorter; and *The Tomb of Ken-Amun at Thebes* by N. de Garis Davies. *Ancient Egypt* 16 (1931): 111–12.

The Tomb of Meryet-Amun at Thebes by H. E. Winlock and *The Tomb of Nefer-hotep at Thebes,* by N. de Garis Davies. *Ancient Egypt* 18 (1933): 117–18, 122–23.

Voodoos and Obeahs: Phases of West Indian Witchcraft, by J. J. Williams, S. J.; and *Witchcraft and Demonism,* by G. l'Estrange Owen. *Man* 34 (1934): 15, 57.

The Script of Harappa and Mohenjo-daro, by G. R. Hunter; *Egypt and Negro Africa,* by C. G. Seligman; *The Dawn of Conscience,* by J. H. Breasted; and *A Short History of Egypt,* by A. Weigall. *Ancient Egypt* 19 (1934): 56–58, 122.

The Bucheum, by Sir Robert Mond and Oliver Myers. *The Indas Civilisation* by Ernest MacKay; *Palestine and Israel,* by F. Petrie. *Ancient Egypt* 20 (1935): 59–60, 63, 111–12. Obituaries of C. H. Corbett, 124, James Edward Quibell, Sir Temistocle Zammit 125–6.

Ancient Egyptian Dances, by I. Lexova; and *The Cemeteries of Armant,* by R. Mond and O. H. Myers. *Man* 38 (1938): 15, 30.
Ancient Egyptian Religion, by J. Cerny. *Man* 54 (1954): 57.
The Cultures of Prehistoric Egypt, by E. Baumgärtel. *Man* 56 (1956): 160–61.
The Panchatantra, by A. W. Ryder. *Folklore* 67 (1956): 118–20.
Crime in Bedfordshire, by E. Curtis. *Folklore* 68 (1957): 445–46.
When Egypt Ruled the East, by G. Steindorff and K. Seele. *Man* 58 (1958): 136.
The Divine Kingship in Ghana and Ancient Egypt, by Eva Meyerowitz. *Man* 60 (1960): 183–84.

Selected Archival Material

There are letters from Margaret Murray, in her last years, in the archives of the Petrie Museum in University College, London; and some of her lecture notes, handwritten on long slips of paper, are preserved in the archives of the college.

An incomplete bibliography of Margaret Murray's writings, compiled by Wilfred Bonser and A. J. Arkell, appeared in *Folklore* 72 (September 1961).

NOTES

1. See M. S. Drower, *Flinders Petrie: A Life in Archaeology* (London: Gollancz, 1985), chap. 9.
2. M. A. Murray, *My First Hundred Years* (London: Kimber, 1963).
3. Murray, *My First Hundred Years,* 90.
4. W. M. F. Petrie, *Koptos* (London: B. Quaritch, 1896).
5. "The Descent of Property in the Early Periods of Egyptian History," *Publications of the Society of Biblical Literature* 17 (1895).
6. Murray, *My First Hundred Years,* 119.
7. *The Osireion at Abydos* (London: B. Quaritch, 1904), 2.
8. Murray, *My First Hundred Years,* 95–96.
9. Murray, *My First Hundred Years,* 192.
10. *Illustrated London News,* April 18, 1914.
11. Cecil H. L. Ewen, *Some Witchcraft Criticisms* (London: published by the author, 1939).
12. H. Trevor-Roper, *The European Witch-Craze of the Sixteenth and Seventeenth Centuries* (Harmondsworth: Penguin, 1969).
13. Robin Briggs, *Witches and Neighbours: The Social and Cultural Contact of European Witchcraft* (London: Harper Collins, 1996), 37.
14. Max Mallowan in the *Dictionary of National Biography* (1961–70), 778.
15. Rosalind Janssen, *The First Hundred Years: Egyptology at University College London, 1892–1992* (London: University College, 1992), 21.
16. J. D. Evans, *Malta* (London: Thames and Hudson, 1963), 184f.
17. *Transactions of the Hertfordshire Archaeological Society* 7 (1925): 183.
18. Murray, *My First Hundred Years,* 143–47.

19. G. Caton-Thompson, *Mixed Memoirs* (Gateshead: Paradigm Press, 1983), 125.

20. Among those who studied Egyptology at University College under Margaret Murray's tuition may be noted the following: Mary Brodrick, Myrtle Broome, Hellmut Brunner, Guy and Winifred Brunton, Gertrude Caton-Thompson, Walter Crum, Rex Engelbach, R. O. Faulkner, Henri Frankfort, Battiscombe Gunn, Kosaku Hamada, Gerald Harding, A. G. K. Hayter, Sir Laurence Kirwan, Violet Mac Dermot, D. Randall MacIver, Ernest Mackay, Rosalind Paget, Emily Paterson, Annie Pirie (Mrs. Quibell), Rev. J. M. Plumley, J. E. Quibell, Günter Rudnitzky, Veronica Seton-Williams, Alan Shorter, R. W. Sloley, Sidney Smith, J. L. Starkey, Sir Herbert Thompson, Olga Tufnell, G. A. Wainwright, and Shemuel Yeiven. This list (which does not pretend to be comprehensive) contains the names of students who went on to make their name in some branch of Egyptology, whether as archaeologists or philologists. For more information on them, see *Who Was Who in Egyptology,* 3d ed., ed. Maurice Bierbrier (London: Egypt Exploration Society, 1995).

21. Margaret A. Murray, *The Splendour That Was Egypt,* rev. ed. (London: Sidgwick and Jackson, 1963), 21.

22. Ibid., 23; also Murray, *My First Hundred Years,* 194–95.

23. Murray, *Splendour That Was Egypt,* 24.

24. See e. g. Gay Robins, "The God's Wife of Amun in the Eighteenth Dynasty of Egypt," in *Images of Women in Antiquity,* ed. Averil Cameron and Amelie Kuhrt (London, Routledge, 1993), 65–78.

25. Murray, *My First Hundred Years,* 139.

26. Caton-Thompson, *Mixed Memoirs,* 176.

27. M. A. Murray, *Petra, the Rock City of Edom* (London: Blackie and Sons [1939]).

28. Drower, *Flinders Petrie,* 409ff.

29. Janssen, *The First Hundred Years,* 64ff.

30. *Times of London,* November 9, 1963; reviewed by Jacquetta Hawkes in *Antiquity* 37 (1963): 311ff.; see also "Dr. Margaret Murray: A Long Life's Work for Egyptology," *New Scientist* 12, no. 261 (1961): 423–24.

31. R. M. Janssen and Jac. J. Janssen, "A Centenarian Egyptologist," in *Getting Old in Ancient Egypt* (London: Rubicon Press, 1996), 143–50.

32. Murray, *My First Hundred Years,* 198–99, 203.

Gertrude L. Bell

(1868–1926)

Julia M. Asher-Greve

"IT WAS ONLY WHEN SHE DIED suddenly in the summer of 1926, and *The Times* thought the event worthy of a leading article, that the public at large awoke to the fact that it had lost perhaps the greatest woman of her generation . . . Yet since the publication of her *Letters* in 1927, her story has become an epic. Indeed it threatens to become a legend."[1] Bell's life and work have been the subject of political, social, cultural, anthropological, archaeological, and gender studies.[2] It is, however, her involvement in Near Eastern politics, adventurous travels, and explorations in the Orient[3] that excite this interest, while her archaeological work has, unfortunately, not received the same attention. It is my privilege to present Gertrude Bell as one of the pioneer women of archaeology, giving her work in the field the full merit it deserves.

A Woman Larger Than Life

Bell's personality, talents, and way of life elicited responses ranging from high admiration to derogation.[4] She was labeled an eccentric who made herself at home in the desert by carrying china, silver, and Parisian clothes; a romantic and amateur who overcame disappointment in love with travel, archaeology, and, later, politics; an orientalist-agent and arch-imperialist.[5] Her vitality, energy, and enthusiasm, as well as her capacity for hard work, were truly remarkable.[6] Max Mallowan, Leonard Woolley's young assistant when he first met Bell, remembered her defending the rights of the Iraq Museum "like a tigress"; he was also impressed with her intellect and profound interest in archaeology, recalling her striking appearance, delicate features, and elegant dress.[7] The German archaeologist Walter Andrae, admired her ease with languages, assuming that it resulted from the good family connections that allowed her to travel widely.[8] Leonard Woolley, not always pleased by Bell, wrote a highly complimentary appreciation, published posthumously as part of his review of *The Letters of Gertrude Bell.*[9] These portraits may be partial because Andrae and Woolley, conventional men caught in patriarchal ideology, viewed Bell as an exceptional woman but not as a colleague. Recurring references to her family wealth and connections, couture clothes, eccentricities, or alleged intelligence activities often served to cast doubt upon her sincerity, emphasizing her gender and thus her outsider status.

Descriptions by Virginia Woolf and her friend Vita Sackville-West reflect the range of reactions to Bell's personality. Virginia Woolf felt intimidated:

> Miss Bell has a very long nose: she is like an Aberdeen terrier; she is a masterful woman, has everyone under her thumb, and makes you feel a little inefficient. Still, she is extremely kind, and asks so and so to meet you, and you are very grateful to her.[10]

Sackville-West, whose impressions are the last written during Bell's lifetime, visited her in Baghdad after an arduous journey and admired her vigor:

> I had known her first in Constantinople, where she had arrived straight out of the desert, with all the evening dresses and cutlery and napery that she insisted on taking with her on her wanderings; and then in England; but here she was in her right place, in Iraq, in her

> own house, with her office in the city, and her white pony in a corner of the garden, and her Arab servants, and her English books and her Babylonian shards on the mantelpiece, and her long thin nose, and her irrepressible vitality. I felt all my loneliness and despair lifted from me in seconds . . . and I would like to see her museum, wouldn't I? did I know she was Director of Antiquities in Iraq? wasn't that a joke? and would I like to come to tea with the king? . . . [She was] poring out information: the state of Iraq, the excavations at Ur, the need for a decent museum, what new books had come out? what was happening in England? The doctors had told her she ought not to go through another summer in Baghdad, but what should she do in England, eating her heart for Iraq? Next year, perhaps . . . but I couldn't say she looked ill, could I? I could, and did. She laughed and brushed that aside . . . Then jumping up—for all her movements were quick and impatient . . .
>
> She was a wonderful hostess, and I felt that her personality held together and made a centre for all those exiled Englishmen whose other common bond was their service for Iraq. They all seemed to be informed by the same spirit of constructive enthusiasm; but I could not help feeling that their mission there would have been more in the nature of drudgery than of zeal, but for the radiant ardour of Gertrude Bell. Whatever subject she touched she lit up; such vitality was irresistible.[11]

Of the archaeologists who knew Bell, David G. Hogarth and Salomon Reinach wrote quite laudatory obituaries.[12] Hogarth, who had known her since she was a student at Oxford, described her career as unique:

> No other woman of recent time has combined her qualities—her taste for arduous and dangerous adventure with her scientific interest and knowledge, her competence in archaeology and art, her distinguished literary gift, her sympathy for all sorts and conditions of men, her political insight and appreciation of human values, her masculine vigour, hard common sense and practical efficiency—all tempered by feminine charm and a most romantic spirit.[13]

Apart from her books and articles, several volumes of private letters have been published, and most biographers have researched her unpublished diaries, letters, and notes.[14] There are also reminiscences by her stepmother, her sister Elsa Richmond, friends, and colleagues.[15] But despite this plethora of information, biographers have provided little insight into her character, and Bell remains an enigmatic, complex, and occasionally contradictory personality.[16]

Background and Education

Gertrude Bell's family and education provided the foundation for an unusual life and unique career. She was born Gertrude Margaret Lowthian Bell on July 14, 1868, at Washington Hall, near Newcastle upon Tyne, in northeast England.[17] Her grandfather, Sir (Isaac) Lowthian Bell (1816–1904), made baronet in 1886, was a distinguished scientist, Fellow of the Royal Society, author of several books, mayor of Newcastle, Liberal member of Parliament, innovative industrialist, and one of the wealthiest men in Britain.[18] He studied physics, chemistry, and metallurgy in Denmark, France, Germany, and Edinburgh, traveled widely, and loved intellectual debate.[19] Gertrude Bell is said to have inherited not merely her grandfather's money but also his brilliant mind, adventurousness, curiosity, exuberance, and love of nature. Her father, Sir (Thomas) Hugh Bell (1844–1931), eldest son of five children, studied science in Germany and France. As energetic and curious as his father, he managed the Bell factories, promoted Liberal politics, public education, and health, lectured extensively, and was a passionate traveler.[20] His first wife, Maria (Mary) Shield, Gertrude Bell's mother, died in 1871 after giving birth to Gertrude's brother Maurice.[21]

Gertrude Bell grew up in Red Barns, a seaside mansion near the town of Middlesborough in north Yorkshire. Her father's house had been built by Philip Webb, who had previously collaborated with William Morris and Edward Burne-Jones on Lowthian Bell's Rounton Grange, where Bell spent much of her childhood. In Rounton Grange, which became her favorite home when her parents moved there after her grandfather's death in 1904, she did nearly all her writing and created a beautiful rock garden.[22] Employing Britain's most avant-garde architect and designers testified to the family's progressive tastes, and the revolutionary nature of Red Barns may have inspired Bell's early interest in architecture. The family also kept a home in London Belgrave, a meeting place for the political, intellectual, literary, and artistic elite—a social and intellectual environment described as "high culture" and "intellectual aristocracy."[23]

In the five years between her mother's death and her father's remarriage in 1876, Gertrude Bell and her father developed a close bond that lasted throughout her life. She remained her father's daughter, often traveling with him and missing him when he was not with her. He became her most important role model; she consulted him on political issues and frequently quoted his opinions as authoritative. The bond was so strong that Gertrude wished to die before her father.[24] This wish was granted since Hugh Bell did survive his daughter. Speaking at her memorial at the Royal Geographic Society on April 4, 1927, he said, "I think there never were father and daughter who stood in such intimate relations as she and I did to one another."[25]

In addition to her indulging and loving father, Bell's stepmother had an important influence on her education.[26] Reared in Paris with Charles Dickens and Henry James as regular guests of her parents, Florence Olliffe was a sophisticated, multilingual woman equally comfortable in literary, artistic, and upper-class circles. She also wrote several books, successful plays, numerous articles, and an opera.[27] Gertrude Bell unhesitatingly accepted Florence as a mother, and they developed a warm relationship.[28] Cultured and elegant, Florence Bell suggested books for her stepdaughter to read and advised her on her wardrobe, but she also criticized Gertrude's writing style and insisted on good manners—a constant topic of dispute between them.[29] Florence's pride in her stepdaughter is evident in her commentaries interspersed in Bell's published letters.[30]

Bell was a high-spirited, strong-willed, courageous, and adventurous child who taxed the patience of her governesses. She loved the country and riding, preferring the company of her brother and male cousins, with whom she could climb on trees, rocks, or the roof of the greenhouse.[31] While spending much time at the home of her favorite cousin, Horace Marshall, she came into early contact with the ancient world through her uncle, Thomas Marshall, a classical scholar.[32] A voracious reader, who at eleven read history and Classics authors, she implored her mother, "Only books please for my presents from you and Papa."[33] Ready comprehension conferred the confidence that she could learn anything. Until age fifteen governesses taught her at home.

Aware of Bell's exceptional intelligence, her parents sent her in 1884 to Queen's College in London, one of the few exclusive schools for young women. This was a rather enlightened decision by her parents, not only because few upper-class girls went to school but especially because of the Victorian view that "scholarship and ladylike behaviour were incompatible" and that education restricted a woman's chance for marriage.[34] An outstanding student, Bell soon became bored with lessons aimed at acquiring social rather than intellectual skills. Instead she developed a serious interest in history, reading many noncurricular books and writing special essays for her history teacher. In November 1885 she wrote to her father, "I have a burning ambition to go to Girton to read History . . . [and] I want to know one thing in the world at last. I'm tired of learning in this sort of dilettante way—it would be so nice to know something thoroughly."[35] Lonely and homesick, she disliked the all-female environment at school and missed her father, brother, and cousins as well as the luxuries she was accustomed to at home. Reading and visiting museums and exhibitions filled her spare time in London. According to her sister Elsa Richmond, Bell's interest in art and architecture dated to her school days in London.[36] Apparently at the age of seventeen (many of her letters are undated) she began discussing politics with her father, another of her lifelong interests.[37]

In March 1886 Bell wrote home that she would rather go to Lady Margaret Hall in Oxford than Girton to study history.[38] Her parents were hesitant about this extraordinary request, for young women, as a rule, were expected to be introduced to society at seventeen and married by twenty. But they ultimately consented, and in May 1886, after two years at Queen's College, Bell enrolled in Lady Margaret Hall, one of the two women's colleges in Oxford. She enjoyed her studies as well as the sports and social events.[39] Rules for women at Oxford were strict: they were not allowed to go out unchaperoned; and were segregated from men in classes, sitting on the podium either next to or with their backs turned to the teacher. Additionally, conduct for women included being forbidden to appear at meetings, write signed articles and letters to the press, speak in public, and act independently.[40] Women's education was trapped in what Sarah Delamont calls a "double conformity," requiring "ladylike" behavior as well as rigorous male academic standards.[41] But Bell successfully mastered the challenges and thrived at Oxford. According to her fellow student and close friend, Janet Hogarth (later Courtney), she was the youngest and also the most brilliant student.[42] In spring 1888 she took her orals a year ahead of time and graduated with "one of the most brilliant" first-class honors in modern history, the first woman at Oxford to do so.[43] David Hogarth remembered that, as a candidate at nineteen, she asked examiners more searching questions than they asked her.[44] She was not, however, awarded a degree, as women were ineligible to receive degrees until 1920.[45]

Conflicting Desires

Before she went to Oxford, Bell imagined that a university education would provide a career, and according to Janet Hogarth she studied with an "aim" and "concentration of purpose."[46] But, at age nineteen, she returned home with no prospect of a career, for in Victorian Britain even educated women were supposed to consider marriage as their sole vocation.[47] Whatever her career dreams may have been, it is difficult to believe Bell was satisfied with a life of social visits, dinners and dances, summers in the country, social work, and occasionally teaching history to her siblings. In her mother's absence she assumed responsibility for her younger siblings and the household. There are, however, no signs of despair or rebellion in her cheerful letters, suggesting that she tried to accept the gender script for young Victorian ladies.[48] But in some areas she continued her nonconformity—displaying her intelligence, utilizing her knowledge, voicing criticism, and being contentious when she thought she was right. In the words of her mother and Janet Hogarth Courtney, she was "entirely" or "disconcertingly honest" and had independent, although not always infallible, judgment.[49] Janet Wallach (her most recent biographer) believes that Bell gave the impression of "a snob, a bluestocking, a woman with an 'attitude,' haughty and self-important."[50] Her mother concedes that Bell was capable "on occasion of definite hardness, and a deliberate disregard of sentiment," but she also had the "capacity for deep emotion," wit, and play.[51] Her notably lively spirit, athletic figure, and rapid movements did not conform to Victorian gender stereotypes, and she apparently did not internalize the feminine gender script.[52] Extremely intelligent and aspiring to be a dutiful daughter, she was considered by Janet Hogarth Courtney "an odd mixture of maturity and childishness, grown-up in her judgements of men and affairs, child-like in her certainties, and most engaging in her entire belief in her father and the vivid intellectual world in which she had been brought up [and to which she had returned]."[53] Bell may have felt useless and insecure, torn between developing her talents and conforming to the feminine gender role of her time. Her frenetic activities, including serious reading and learning languages, demonstrate a search for a meaningful direction. Only once did she reveal the contradiction between her intellectual and her daily life:

> I discussed religious beliefs all the way there and very metaphysical conceptions of truth all the way back—that sounds rather steep doesn't it. I love talking to people when they really will talk sensibly and about things which one wants to discuss. I am rather inclined to think however that it is a dangerous amusement, for one's so ready to make oneself believe that the things one says and the theories one makes are really guiding principles of one's life where as a matter of fact they are not at all. One suddenly finds that one had formulated

> some view from which it is very difficult to back out not because of one's interlocutor but because the mere fact of fitting it with words engraves it upon one's mind. Then one is reduced to the disagreeable necessity of trying even involuntarily to make the facts of one's real life fit into it thereby involving oneself in a mist of half-truths and half-falsehoods which cling about one's mind do what one will to shake them off.[54]

Bell developed a sense of elegance, not exceptional for educated women who used dress to their advantage.[55] She certainly noticed that an elegant exterior enhanced people's perception of her, but she never ostentatiously displayed her wealth. She also learned to apply charm, be entertaining, converse amiably, and use her gifts to make friends easily.[56] Since she did not have to earn a living and had not yet a clear vision of how to use her intelligence and physical energy professionally, she experimented with a variety of activities. Her conviction that any activity diligently pursued would yield successful results (languages, riding, gardening, mountaineering, travel, writing, and archaeology) did not make her choice easier.

The Experience of Travel

A year before she went to Oxford, Bell had acquired her first taste of foreign travel when she visited Germany in 1887 to improve her German. It must have come as a revelation that knowledge could be acquired through travel. In her orals she corrected a professor on the precise location of a German city, remarking, "I know, I have been there."[57] After graduation she was invited to Bucharest by her aunt, Mary Lascelles, whose husband, Sir Frank Lascelles, had been appointed British ambassador to Romania.[58] During her visit there she befriended two men who would play a decisive role in her future, Charles Hardinge, future viceroy of India, and Valentine Chirol, eventually her most intimate friend, adviser, and supporter.[59] The Bell family was exceptionally well connected—either related to or friends with important and powerful people all over the world. Bell usually stayed at a British embassy or consulate and had friends in the highest political and social circles.[60]

On the journey home from Romania, Bell, accompanied by Billy Lascelles[61] and Valentine Chirol, visited Constantinople for the first time (April 1889); although she enjoyed the city, this initial visit to the Orient did not leave a lasting impression. Back in England she was introduced to society and for three years attended balls, dances, and tea parties seeking a suitable husband. She filled her free time by visiting museums and the British Library, reading, and learning Latin.[62] Wealthy, brilliant, university-trained, multilingual, and well traveled, Bell, as well as her parents, had certain expectations in a future husband, but no eligible young men compared favorably with her father. Although she feared remaining single and lonely, she would not compromise.

Given her large, close, and supportive family—and the example of her mother's rare combination of marriage and motherhood with a writing career—it is not surprising that Bell never found a man who satisfied her expectations. Of the three men she loved, her parents rejected one; one was married; and one rejected her proposal.[63] Perhaps she unconsciously fell in love with men who were not available. Although her celibacy was involuntary and she often admitted feeling lonely and missing family, she may have feared dependency on a man less intelligent, indulgent, liberal, and generous than her father. Moreover, her need for appreciation as a person in her own right, as well as her independent and adventurous way of life, were hardly congenial to Victorian marriage. She may have sensed this incompatibility and thus never fallen in love with a suitable man.

Travel was one possible means of locating an appropriate husband. In particular, travel to the "Orient" (that is, the non-European lands of the Ottoman Empire) had become fashionable in the nineteenth century. In the 1890s travel was no longer considered an educational task but a pleasure, a means to self-fulfillment and individualism that enriched the personality. Steamboats and trains facilitated transportation; bookshops and newspapers offered a wealth of information.[64] Europeans derived an unrealistic image of the Orient from such colorful romances as *The Arabian Nights* as well as from picturesque travel books. Fascination with everything "oriental" had begun with Napoleon's Egyptian campaign and continued into the 1930s.[65]

"Persia is the place I have always longed to see," wrote Bell, and the opportunity arose in 1892 with the appointment of her uncle, Sir Frank Lascelles, as ambassador to Persia.[66] Invited to accompany her aunt and Lascelles cousins to Teheran, Bell prepared for her journey, not only by reading books, but also by taking lessons in Persian. When it became known that she wished to learn Persian, Lord Henry Stanley, her aunt Maisie's brother-in-law, offered to teach her.[67] But it is unlikely that the deaf Lord Stanley taught Bell Persian.[68] More likely, it was the orientalist and art historian Arthur S. Strong (1863–1904), who wrote the introduction to her "Poems from the Divan of Hafiz," or possibly E. Dennison Ross (1871–1940), with whom she later studied Arabic and Persian.[69]

In Teheran, Bell met the German diplomat and oriental scholar Dr. Friedrich Rosen, whose wife, Nina, was an old friend of her mother's. The Rosens would become close friends and later offer her the chance to become intimately acquainted with the Orient.[70] Persia did not disappoint her romantic expectations. At the British embassy she befriended Henry Cadogan, a junior diplomat and grandson of the earl of Cadogan. They shared interests in poetry, Persian, riding, and tennis, and he accompanied her on tours, including her first journey into the desert. They fell in love and became engaged. But Henry had an income inadequate to support a family, no professional future, a problematic character, and gambling debts. Bell's father thus forbade the match, and she returned to England. Her hope of eventual parental consent was dashed by Cadogan's sudden death nine months later.[71]

To overcome her grief, Bell engaged in a life of study and travel. In addition to Persian and Latin, she began studying Arabic. While in Persia she had written down some of her impressions, and after her return, urged by a publisher, she added six more chapters to an emerging book. She considered her work, written for "her amusement," "extraordinarily feeble."[72] Was it insecurity, modesty, or fear that compelled her to distrust the judgment of both her author-mother and her publisher? Eventually, in 1894, she agreed to have *Safar Nameh. Persian Pictures. A Book of Travel* published anonymously for fear of disappointing her parents.[73] It was so well received that it was reprinted in 1928 with a preface by Sir E. Dennison Ross, and in 1937 with an introduction by Vita Sackville-West.

Drawing on her advanced fluency in Farsi, Bell published her first scholarly book in 1897—this time under her name. Her translation and analysis of fourteenth-century Persian poems by Hafiz, together with an historical introduction, was praised by reviewers for its poetic quality and description, and is still considered one of the best English translations.[74] In 1929 A. J. Arberry, professor at Cambridge University, wrote that "although about twenty people have translated Hafiz into English, her adaptations are still the best."[75] Despite praise for her "rare poetic gift," Bell never returned to poetry, and ten years would elapse before she published another book (in 1907).[76] The pattern of devoting all her energy to an activity until achieving near mastery, only suddenly to abandon it for something new, remained one of Bell's primary characteristics. Early on she condemned this proclivity as dilettantish, and hoped university education would lend permanency to her academic efforts.[77] Yet, as her sister observed, she was a restless person (playing with her hair as a youth and smoking as an adult).[78] Achieving mastery apparently bored her.

In her midtwenties Bell embarked on a series of journeys, accompanied either by her father or, occasionally, by one of her brothers or other relatives. She traveled through Europe, to North Africa and Constantinople, and twice around the world, arranging for language lessons whenever possible or teaching herself.[79] In constant search of a challenge, she became an accomplished mountaineer, climbing the highest Alpine peaks (one in the Bernese Alps is named after her).[80]

Invited by the Rosens to visit them in Jerusalem, where Friedrich Rosen was now German consul-general, Bell left England in November 1899 for her first prolonged visit to the Near East.[81] She transformed a room of her hotel suite (close to the Rosen's house) into a study, hired a teacher for Arabic, and bought a horse. Six hours a day she studied Arabic, which she admitted was more difficult than she had anticipated. She took hundreds of photographs, explored Jerusalem and its environments, and practiced Arabic.[82] The profound impact of her first encounter with the Orient is evident in a letter written to her sister Elsa from Jerusalem:

> The more you see, the more everything falls into a kind of rough and ready perspective, and when you come to a new thing, you haven't so much difficulty in placing it and fitting it into the rest. I'm awfully glad you love the beginning of things—so do I, most thoroughly, and unless one does, I don't believe one can get much pleasure out of ends. (April 9, 1900)[83]

When the Rosens could not accompany her on an excursion to Petra, she proceeded alone with a guide, a cook, and two muleteers. Previously, she had always traveled accompanied and in luxury, the path smoothed by good connections. But, in the hills and deserts of Palestine and Jordan, there were no hotels and little respect for law or life. There were no British officials in high positions to proffer assistance for those venturing beyond the cities and territories under Ottoman control. Yet, on her own, she handled tricky, dangerous, sometimes life-threatening situations, outwitted Turkish officials, made friends with Druze and Bedouins, Muslims and Christians, and endured extreme weather conditions.

British citizens were forbidden to travel to Petra because Turkish authorities thought they were all spies trying to instigate an Arab uprising against the Ottomans. But Bell found a way:

> I am going on to Petra! What with giving out that I'm German (for they are desperately afraid of the English), I have got permission and

a soldier from the Governor and this is always difficult and often impossible . . .

One of the great difficulties of this journey is that no one knows the distances even approximately and there is no map worth a farthing. Another is that the population is so scant we can't get food! This is starvation camp to-night, we have nothing but rice and bread, a little potted meat. No charcoal and no barley for our horses . . .

In all this country there is practically no water, there are a few cisterns scattered over the hills and, I should think, emptied before the middle of summer, and where we are camping a couple of wells, and that's absolutely all! I nearly went to sleep on my horse this morning, but was wakened up by hearing Ayoub relating to me tales of Ibn Rashid. One gets so accustomed to it all that one ceases to be bored. Medeba, in proportion to its size, must have the largest number of mosquitoes and fleas of any inhabited spot on the globe. Chiefly owing to the mosquitoes, my night was rather a restless one, it also rained a great deal and rain makes an unconscionable noise on the tent, besides the fact is I was troubled to think of my poor people outside . . . I broke up my camp here, and rode myself into Jericho . . . In one little fortnight the sun had eaten up everything but the tall dry daisy stalks. It was almost impossible to believe that it had been so lovely so short a time ago.[84]

At the end of April 1900 Bell left for the Druze mountains:

I wear a big white keffieh bound over my hat and wound round me so that only my eyes show, and they are partly hidden by a blue veil; but the chief comfort of this journey is my masculine saddle, both to me and my horse. Never, never again will I travel on anything else; I haven't known real ease in riding till now. Till I speak the people always think I'm a man and address me as Effendim . . . I am deep in intrigues!

Bell informed the Mudir, the governor of Basrah, that she intended to follow the eastern route via Salkhad in the Druze country to Damascus, which he forbade. But she "slipped through their fingers."

I dined early and as I was sitting reading in my tent I heard the voice of the Mudir. I blew out my light and when Hanna came to tell me of his coming, I sent him a message that I was very tired and had gone to bed. I heard this conversation: Hanna. "The lady has been awake since the rising of the sun; all day she has walked and ridden, now she sleeps," Mudir. "Does she march to-morrow?" Hanna. "I couldn't possibly say, Effendim." Mudir. "Tell her she must let me know before she goes anywhere." Hanna. "At your Pleasure, Effendim." And he left, but not without having assured me that he meant to stop me. I hastily re-arranged my plans. He knew I was going to Salkhad and when he found that I had flown, he would send after me along that road as far as he dared; I decided, therefore, to strike for a place further north. [When Bell rose at 2:00 she] prayed Heaven that no soldier would look over the castle wall, see our lantern. At 4 we were off. It was a ticklish business finding our way in the dark round the walls to the east . . . suddenly we would find ourselves heading inwards and were obliged to retrace our steps. It took us near an hour, but at last we were past the N.E. corner and hit on the Jemurrin road.

By sunrise they had reached the ruins of Jemurrin, whence they followed the ancient Roman road:

It seemed long to the first Druze village, Muhammed was trembling lest he should see either a Druze or a soldier. I feared the latter only, but much . . . The road rose gradually; we could see nothing ahead but the top of the west slope of corn, and a black village where I hoped we should find Druze, but which turned out to be only a ruin—Deir Zubeir was its disappointing name. There was a man among the corn, however, with the white turban and black keffieh of the Druze and I greeted him thus (it is the right form) "Peace be upon you! oh, son of my uncle!" He put us into the path, which we had missed. At length we came to the top of the last slope and saw in front of us the rolling fertile, watered country, scattered over with little volcanic hills, and behind it, higher hills and the pointed peak of the Kulieb rising over all—the Little Heart, the highest of the Jebel Druze.[85]

On her travels in the Orient, and apart from polite visits to the harems of her hosts, she spent her time with men—eating, drinking coffee, smoking, discussing politics. She was treated as a man, a role that suited her because it granted freedoms far beyond those considered acceptable in

Britain.[86] She did not, however, reflect upon her experiences in a broader social context. Her letters convey the impression that she relished being considered as exceptional, as an honorary man—for her synonymous with being a person and not in the same gender group as the local women. Her hatred of Islam had its roots in the status of women in Arabic societies.[87]

Bell's journeys would have been daring and trying for any man. Aside from determination and physical strength, she possessed cunning, excellent intuition, and a particular cleverness—eventually an expertise—in dealing with people and circumstances. "Obstacles had a trick of melting away when she encountered them," wrote Janet Hogarth Courtney.[88]

Travel and the Orient were associated with Bell's first great love, with tragedy, and with accomplishment. After she lost the man she loved, her attachment to her father became even stronger, reinforced by frequent joint travel without her mother or siblings. Aside from Constantinople and Egypt, the Near East was the only region where Bell traveled alone, perhaps needing the distance from her father to find something of her own to master—the more so because she was not financially independent. Requesting her father's permission for expeditions while already on the road was not just a formality—he financed them. Bell was not independently wealthy like other women travelers, although her father was unusually generous. Money is rarely mentioned in her letters home but appears in her description of travel costs. This dependence meant that Bell did not feel entirely free to do what she wanted (when at home she always assumed family duties, substituting as hostess or presiding over the household during her mother's absences). One result was that she accompanied her half-brother Hugo on a (her second) world tour.[89] They departed in December 1903, journeying eastward to India, Burma, Java, and Japan and returning via Canada and the United States. During this trip she made important contacts with British imperial officials that would change her life during World War I, in particular with the British consul in Muscat, Sir Percy Cox, who would become her superior and mentor in 1916.[90] Endowed with an amazing talent for languages—she spoke German, French, Italian, Persian, Arabic, and Turkish—she learned sufficient Hindustani and Japanese during the voyage to make herself understood.[91]

Exploration and Archaeology

Gertrude Bell's interest in archaeology increased after her first visit to the Near East, and in 1902 she visited, alone, all the ancient sites in Western

Anatolia. From Izmir (Smyrna) she took a boat to Haifa, where she studied Arabic and Persian for several months with two sheikhs as teachers. She visited Jerusalem by way of Syria, taking more Arab lessons there.

Finally she had exhausted traveling for travel's sake, and mountain climbing or studying languages could no longer satisfy her needs. Archaeology offered a new challenge. It was a field in which she could combine intelligence, talent, and skills with a love for adventure; and she possessed all the prerequisites to excel at it: training in history, excellent language skills, broad knowledge, an eye for detail, interest in art and architecture, physical endurance, and determination. Archaeology not only fascinated her but also gave her explorations a meaningful purpose. Her knowledge of and love for Arabic made Near Eastern archaeology the logical choice. Thus, in 1904 she began a systematic study of archaeology, art, architecture, and Greek manuscripts. She embarked, well prepared, in January 1905 on her first archaeological expedition to Syria and Asia Minor. Her reports home make it clear how much at ease she already felt:

> I'm deep in the gossip of the East! It's so enjoyable. I thought to-day when I was strolling through the bazaar . . . what a pleasure it was to be in the East almost as part of it, to know it all as I know Syria now, to be able to tell from the accent and the dress of the people where they come from and exchange the proper greetings as one passes.[92]

In the nineteenth century a new approach to the Near East had evolved, as scholars and archaeologists published detailed descriptions of their explorations and the Orient became a literary theme.[93] A. W. Kinglake's "Eothen" (1844) introduced a new form of travel narrative based on informal personal impressions and anecdotes but did not include descriptions of ancient ruins and sites.[94] As "a born archaeologist and historian," Bell combined both, describing informal personal experiences as well as geography and archaeology.[95] She kept enough detailed diaries and notes for several archaeological articles and the book that made her famous, *The Desert and the Sown* (1907). The book, which took two years to write, describes her journey, the landscape, people, and customs. A great success, it was translated into German and established Bell as a traveler and writer; it is still reprinted today.[96] According to David Hogarth, "it takes the rank among the dozen best books of Eastern travel," and, in 1995, Robert D. Kaplan praised it as "unsurpassed to this day as a traveller's account of the towns and people of Syria."[97]

Between 1907 and 1914 Bell conducted four expeditions to the Near East, crossing mountain ranges and deserts to regions no other European woman had ever visited. She mapped and recorded archaeological sites, geography, customs, culture, and personal conversations, including politics.[98] In 1911 she published another travel book, *Amurath to Amurath,* which did not achieve the popular success of *The Desert and the Sown* but exhibits "maturer science."[99] Gertrude Bell's travels and expeditions in the Near East became well known through her books as well as her studies on Arabists, orientalism, and Victorian women travelers.

By 1913 Bell was an experienced desert traveler and recognized archaeologist. But she had another ambition, a journey into the center of the Arabian desert, where few male explorers and only one European woman, Lady Anne Blunt accompanying her husband, had penetrated.[100] Although warned by British and Ottoman officials of the turmoil and dangers in the Arabian desert, Bell and her caravan of twenty camels, camel drivers, cook, guide, and escort left Damascus in January 1914.[101] In Ziza (Jiza south of Amman) Fatuh, a companion on all her expeditions, joined them. The journey was more difficult and hazardous than she had anticipated. Afterwards, she wondered if it had been worth it.[102] When she arrived at the end of February at Ha'il, the desert city ruled by the Rashid family, she was immediately imprisoned. In her diary she wrote:

> I feel as if I had lived through a chapter of the Arabian Nights during this last week. The Circassian women and slaves, the doubt and anxiety, Fatima[103] weaving her plots behind the qasr walls, Ibrahim[104] with his smiling lips and restless shifting eyes—and the whole town waiting to hear the fate of the army which has gone up with the Amir[105] against Jof. And to the spiritual sense the place smells of blood. The tales round my camp fire are all of murder. It gets on your nerves when you sit day after day between high mud walls.[106]

After ten days, she finally lost her patience and stormed out of a meeting with the powerful chief eunuch Sa'id. That tactic proved effective, and within a few hours she was granted permission to go wherever she wanted. Before her departure she spent a day photographing the medieval monuments. After eleven days, her caravan left Ha'il, and she proceeded north through the desert, reaching Baghdad by the end of March 1914.

In the published accounts of her journey, Bell rarely mentioned the dangers she encountered.[107] The entire story of her expedition to the Ha'il in the Arabian desert was not known until her correspondence with Charles Doughty-Wylie and the diary she kept for him became available in 1961.[108] To him she revealed her fears, depression, and dissatisfaction with the results. In a letter to Valentine Chirol, written before Bell left for Ha'il, she had been rather optimistic: "it is quite reasonable for an adventure, and yet exciting enough to divert me."[109] But after her return she admitted to Doughty-Wylie:

> The adventure always leaves one with a feeling of disillusion . . . Dust and ashes in one's hand, dead bones that look as if they would never rise and dance—it's all nothing, and one turns away from it with a sigh, and tries to fix one's eyes on the new thing before one. This adventure hasn't been successful either, [I] haven't done what I meant to do.[110]

How much this journey had changed her is revealed in a letter to Valentine Chirol:

> You will find me a savage, for I have seen and heard strange things, and they colour the mind . . . But whether I can bear with England—come back to the same things and do them all over again—that is what I sometimes wonder. But they will not be quite the same, since I come to them with a mind permanently altered. I have gained much, and I will not forget it.[111]

Although endowed with an "iron constitution" that could outlast any man, Bell appeared mentally weary and discouraged, her Ha'il experience having "dimmed her bright vitality."[112]

Two months after she returned to London, World War I broke out. During the summer and autumn she worked on her maps, photographs, and the report of her Ha'il journey for the Royal Geographic Society. In November 1914 she began working for the Red Cross office, tracing the missing and wounded, first in Boulogne (France) and then in London. But she really hoped for some occupation in the Middle East.

Opposition to Women's Emancipation

"She had no use for women in general, and was both unjust and unkind to many of them who crossed her path—a fact which I deeply deplored," wrote Dorothy Van Ess, one of Bell's few women friends.[113] And, to her father, Bell wrote from Baghdad: "Upon my soul I almost wish there weren't a desert route—it brings silly females, all with introductions to me."[114] Bell's attitude toward women in general and her rejection of equal rights have perplexed some biographers.[115] Many scarcely mention this aspect of her character in order to avoid discrediting her as a pioneering woman.[116] Winstone calls her antisuffrage activities "a brief diversion," although, between 1908 and 1912, Bell dedicated substantial time to them. To Max van Berchem she wrote, "anti-suffrage . . . is nearly as important as archaeology."[117] Her friend, Janet Hogarth Courtney, later admitted that they had been "on the wrong track" with their support of the Anti-Suffrage League.[118] Susan Goodman, like Bell a member of Lady Magaret Hall at Oxford, was the first biographer who tried to explain the disparity between Bell's unconventional pursuits and her conventional views about women. According to Goodman, most women and men of her social class were antisuffrage, including her mentors David Hogarth, Lord Cromer, and Lord Curzon; but, above all, her father. Educated, intelligent women who had already gained civil rights and could exercise political influence feared the effect of uneducated women on policymaking.[119]

Dea Birkett proposes a relation between the more adventurous travelers and their opposition to women's emancipation. The more daring explorers like Bell fought their public image "of a challenging New Woman."[120] Birkett goes on to write:

> Rather than opting for portraits as strong and ground-breaking women, they reinforced . . . their feminine attributes and the unthreatening nature of their claims. While they had imitated the male explorer and acted as white men, . . . in Britain the women travellers felt they had to be 100 per cent feminine. With the acute consciousness of this dilemma in mind they set out to defend and bolster their feminine reputations against all those who dared to question them.[121]

These women perceived their accomplishments as individual achievements, fearing the suffragists would usurp their reputation and professional recognition. According to Birkett, the motives for their explorations were highly personal and private, thus preventing them from ascribing their experiences to a broader sense of gender. (These fears were not spurious considering that Mark Sykes wrote in a letter about Bell: "What damned fool, silly chatting windbag of conceited, gushing, flat-chested man-woman, globe-trotting, rump-wagging, blethering ass, bitch, terror of the desert.")[122]

Birkett's analysis probably describes Bell, who, after the publication of *The Desert and the Sown,* had been portrayed as a role model even for men—a status she did not welcome, preferring the status of an extraordinary woman. Her own role models were all male, and in her publications she often used the pronoun "he" to refer to herself. There were no role models for female explorers and archaeologists; the few women archaeologists prior to World War I worked in "virtual isolation."[123]

On the Political Arena

"For, after all, to the best of our ability, we were making history," Bell wrote home in July 1921.[124] With the war, Bell's expertise in Arabian matters became valuable to military intelligence, and her wish to be "more usefully employed" was finally fulfilled.[125] In November 1915 she was assigned to Cairo as the first female political officer, working at the newly formed Intelligence Bureau for Arab Affairs. The Arab Bureau, as it became known, had been established to harmonize political activities in Arabia: to provide information to the military and the governments in London and India; to bring Arabs onto the British side of the war; as well as to collect and distribute intelligence information on Turkish and German activities.[126]

Arriving in Cairo, Bell met not only old friends, but also several archaeologists: the chief of the bureau, David G. Hogarth, T. E. Lawrence, and Leonard Woolley.[127] At first, she primarily compiled intelligence files about Arab tribes but soon became involved in policy issues. Relations between the Indian government—which had opposed the formation of the Arab Bureau—and the Cairo office were tense.[128] Intending to improve the situation, Hogarth sent Bell on a semiofficial mission to Delhi in February 1916 to confer with her old friends Viceroy Lord Hardinge and Valentine Chirol. On her return she was appointed Cairo's representative to Mesopotamia, which fell under India's authority. This appointment was considered inspired, as "Bell was unassailable in her credentials and suitably Cairene in her sympathies."[129] After being transferred to Basra, the main British navy base in the gulf and the seat of the general headquarters of the Mesopotamian forces, she encountered another archaeologist, R. Campbell Thomson. After a few weeks she was transferred to the personal staff of Sir Percy Cox, chief political officer in the gulf. According to Westrate's study of the Arab Bureau, her "contribution to the Arab Bureau's Mesopotamian branch was no mean one; . . . Bell provided a touch of éclat to the Mesopotamian intelligence scene—she was a font of energy and scholarship."[130] Eventually her commitment to the Cairo Arab Bureau loosened under the influence of Cox, who regarded her an "enormous asset."[131] When, in March 1917, the British defeated the Ottoman army in Mesopotamia, the political officers moved to Baghdad, where Bell bought her first house and lived for the rest of her life.[132]

British involvement in the Middle East and Gertrude Bell's influence in Middle Eastern politics are well documented.[133] As Percy Cox's right hand and his Oriental Secretary, Bell became a (some claim "the") major force in the creation of the new state of Iraq and the installation of the Hashemite prince Faisal as king of Iraq. Harry St. J. Philby, who was also stationed in Basra (and later became adviser to King Ibn Saud) noted:

> Officially, Miss Bell was a political officer for the British Arab Bureau in Mesopotamia. In truth, she was emerging as the dominant force behind a new state being assembled from a rump of Kurdistan and the Sunni and Shiite areas of Mesopotamia.[134]

Having reported the awakening of Arab nationalism long before the war, Bell now changed her views concerning Arab independence, supporting British guidance of the Arab government on the premise that the Arabs sought and needed British help.[135] Always agreeing with Cox on important issues, she clashed with his deputy, Sir A. T. Wilson when Cox was absent between 1918 and 1920. Wilson favored British rule and eventually asked Cox, in vain, for her dismissal.[136] Bell had on occasion given secret information to her father and unhesitatingly bypassed Wilson by sending reports directly to London.[137] The issue finally resolved itself with Cox's nomination as High Commissioner in Iraq in 1920.

Although some resented a woman meddling in political affairs, Bell encountered relatively little gender bias.[138] When she received an invitation to an all-male official dinner given in honor of King Faisal, she asked the host, Sir Percy Cox, "as man to man, whether he wanted me to come. He said, 'Yes of course if you won't feel smothered.' I said, 'I thought, as a high official in this office, I was sexless and that I ought to come and would.' Sir Percy, on these occasions (levees and so on) always treated me simply as an official and I don't think there's any other way. So I'm going."[139]

In working for the British High Commissioner and advising the Iraqi king, Bell occupied a unique and sometimes ambiguous position. Some questioned her political judgment.[140] Lord Cromer, a personal friend to whom she had dedicated *Amurath to Amurath*, noted this weakness in his recommendation letter to Balfour in 1915:

> She is a clever woman and undoubted authority on everything connected with the Arabs of Arabia and Mesopotamia. I do not on this account mean to say that her political judgement on the broader issues of Near Eastern politics is altogether to be trusted.[141]

But Sir Ronald Storrs, who worked with Bell, noted in his diary: "her first class brain, universal knowledge, her level judgement, outstanding."[142]

When Cox retired in May 1923, Bell's political power and influence began to decline. To King Faisal she once remarked, "I was a servant of Sir Percy and could hold no opinion apart from his."[143] Cox's successor, Sir Henry Dobbs, brought a new administration and atmosphere to the office. Bell no longer had access to secret information, and her expertise and connections were less sought after. Following the transition from British rule to an Iraqi government in 1923, the British were more involved in local administration, with the political issues decided in London. Further, the anomaly of a woman in a high position, unhesitatingly accepted during war, became much more obvious in "normal" times. After being instrumental in the establishment of the Iraqi state, the British mandate by the League of Nations in 1920, the coronation of King Faisal in 1921, and the Treaty of Lausanne in 1923, Bell became more and more an administrator. She felt she "was not necessary in the office," and "as far as my annals, they are now becoming very tame."[144] Lacking the temperament for routine work, she returned to archaeology and writing but kept her position as Oriental Secretary to the High Commissioner until her death.[145]

Bell's health deteriorated during her last years, and her psychological condition seems to have become volatile. She felt increasingly lonely, often depressed, unsure about her future, and reluctant to return to England.[146] Neither England nor Iraq offered a future as brilliant and exciting as the past. To her father she confided: "It will be dreadfully flat when I return to London, not to be consulted about all Cabinet appointments!"[147] Two days before her fifty-eighth birthday, on the night of July 11, 1926, Bell took a fatal overdose of barbiturates.[148]

A year after her death, the Royal Geographic Society held a memorial meeting at which David Hogarth remembered Bell as a woman who combined charm with qualities associated with men. Several men speaking at this memorial admired the "masculine" side of her personality.[149] Her androgynous nature, emphasized by a boyish figure and already evident in her tomboyish behavior as a child, perhaps facilitated acceptance in the "masculine" arena. With the financial, educational, and psychological support of her parents, particularly her father, she had developed enormous self-confidence, which, combined with intelligence, strength, talent, and individualism, led her to extraordinary accomplishments.

On her chosen stage of the Orient, she was the only female star. But a star in such diverse roles—explorer, archaeologist, political officer, royal adviser, law enforcer, museum founder and director—can suffer from isolation, loneliness, and depression. Despite awe-inspiring brilliance and achievements, she also felt an urgent need for compassion, love, and friendship.[150] What motivated her to end her life (as an avowed atheist, Bell would have had no religious scruples) remains an enigma—no hints in letters and no farewell note. But deteriorating health, vanishing political power, increasingly routine life, a sense of isolation, fear of the future, and lack of emotional support seem to explain her suicide.

Archaeology, an Absorbing Occupation

Gertrude Bell believed that "an absorbing occupation is the best resource,"[151] and archaeology provided it for her. In 1907, while digging with William Ramsay, she wrote home, "it is very nice to be completely absorbed in the thing one is doing." And when she returned to archaeology in the 1920s, she remarked, "I always feel well when I am back to archaeology." No other occupation provided this satisfaction.[152] Her contribution to Near Eastern archaeology falls into two phases, first as a field archaeologist (1905–14) and second as director of the Department of Antiquities in Iraq and founder and director of the Iraq Museum (1922–26).

Bell's first encounter with archaeology dated back to her student days in Oxford (1886–88), where she attended meetings of the Oxford Archaeological Society and was introduced to David G. Hogarth by his sister Janet.[153] Hogarth, who would become her friend and mentor, excavated in Egypt, Cyprus, Crete, Ephesos, and Carchemish; was director of the British School in Athens from 1897 to 1900; and succeeded Sir Arthur Evans as keeper of the Ashmolean Museum in Oxford (1908–27). His diverse publications included excavation reports and archaeological studies, as well as writings on the history of Arabia and geography.[154] While at Oxford, Bell probably heard of the British excavations in the Nile delta and the new discoveries in Palestine—in particular, Lachish—as well as the numerous sites excavated in Greece and Asia Minor.

Although she pursued many interests after graduation, Bell jumped at every opportunity to visit ancient sites, museums, and even private collections. Her father shared this interest.[155] While in Greece in November and December 1899, she observed the excavation of the German archaeologist

Wilhelm Dörpfeld, and, on visits to the Athens museum, Hogarth and Dörpfeld explained recent finds.[156] Fascinated by some ancient pottery, Bell wrote her mother, "Doesn't that make one's brain reel?" And about her tour of the Acropolis, accompanied by her father and uncle, Thomas Marshall, she marveled: "[Dörpfeld] took us from stone to stone and built up a wonderful chain of evidence with extraordinary ingenuity until we saw the Athens of 600 B.C. I never saw anything better done."[157]

By the time Bell was coming into closer contact with field archaeology in 1899, the era of treasure hunting and antiquarianism had practically ended. Archaeologists were becoming more interested in a cultural-historical approach, which led to the development of more refined methods and excavation techniques.[158] In Dörpfeld, Bell encountered one of the pioneers of these modern techniques. Studying his excavations in Greece and those of his colleagues in Asia Minor, she learned about the new emphasis on stratigraphy, chronology, and typology, as well as cultural and historical changes and variations. This must have been an exciting approach for an historian interested in antiquity.

During her visit to Greece, Bell also met Oskar van Lennep, the Dutch collector of antiquities, and he invited her to visit him on her way to Jerusalem. Lennep, who lived on an estate near Smyrna, showed Bell his collection of coins, gems, Greek terra-cottas, original and fake vases. She also learned that he conducted private digs on his property, which included parts of the ancient site of Colophon.[159] When she arrived in Jerusalem in the middle of December 1899, she was so fascinated by ancient sites that she took some six hundred photographs of the city and on her tours into the country. Mschatta, Petra, and Palmyra impressed her most of all the sites she visited.[160]

Two years later, in 1902, again invited to stay with the van Lenneps, she noticed that they "had opened a Byzantine tumulus . . . Professor Ramsay had also assisted."[161] In her diary she noted:

> We [Bell and friends of van Lennep] walked up to the tumulus. They were still clearing away the sides, so we determined to fetch our lunch and watch proceedings. Very merry picnic, after which we watched the men at work. At about five metres we came to a layer of very big stones; below (we dug down to five and a half metres), was earth, with small stones. We dug along the trench, but found nothing; but the site is extremely interesting . . . I should like to do an article about it for Newbolt when I get home. It's an enormous mound.

> They have got below the earth, and through a belt of stones which are calcinated by sacrificial fires. But as yet we have not seen the king of Colophon, or whoever it was that they buried so deep. Mr. Van Lennep is undismayed; the work is to be continued while I am away, in the hope that we may meet with a treasure in the end.[162]

References to the excavation in Colophon in 1902 are misleading because, according to this passage, she did not "participate in an excavation" but rather observed a private dig.[163] While staying with the van Lenneps, Bell went alone on a six-day tour to study the ruins of Pergamon, Magnesia, Sardis, and the Byzantine site, Philadelphia (Alaşehir), and Phrygian tombs. She also visited Ephesos twice and watched German archaeologists excavating in Menemen.[164]

In preparation for travels and expeditions, Bell perused all the archaeological, art historical, geographical, and travel literature available, and always traveled with a trunk full of books. Her published references range from classical authors to the latest in archaeology, art history, and geography.[165] By 1902, her knowledge of art must have already been considerable, as she reported home: "I lunched yesterday with the Strongs. He wants me to write a book for him in a series on art he is bringing out for Gerald Dunckworth. He gave me my choice of subject."[166]

At age thirty-six, Bell decided to study archaeology with Salomon Reinach (1859–1932) in Paris. Like Hogarth, Reinach was a scholar of broad scope who had excavated in Myrina near Smyrna and in Tunisia; as well as publishing on ancient Greek philology, archaeology, art history, myths, religion (even on Schopenhauer), not to mention travel guides for archaeologists and the *Chronique d'Orient.*[167] For some years he was Bell's teacher and mentor, placing his private library at her disposal and lecturing to her in museums. After a visit to the Louvre she wrote, "I think there is nothing more wonderful than to go to a museum with my dear Salomon."[168] But she also noticed that Reinach's impressive knowledge had its price: "He does nothing but work—never goes out, never takes a holiday except to go and see a far away museum."[169] Reinach's first scholarly assignment for Bell was a review for the *Revue Archéologique* on a "Syrian subject."[170] The subject was J. Strzygowski's *Mschatta* and not *Kleinasien,* as some biographers claim.[171] On her way to Petra in 1900, Bell had visited Mschatta, a palatial Ummayed country house on the western fringe of the Syrian desert.[172] Later, in 1905, she detoured around Mschatta because the decorated facades had been dismantled and shipped to Berlin, a gift from the Ottoman Sultan Abdulhamid to Emperor William II. In her review she does not mention the dismantling, but she describes her feelings in *The Desert and the Sown:*

> No one who knew it in its loveliness could have borne to revisit those ravished walls, it must be not forgotten that there is something to be said for the act of vandalism that stripped them. If there has been good prospect that the ruin should stand as it had stood for over a thousand years, uninjured save by the winter rains, it ought to have been allowed to remain intact in the rolling country to which it gave so strange an impress of delicate and fantastic beauty.[173]

Bell's review of Strzygowski's *Mschatta* testifies to her great appreciation for Strzygowski. She had read his *Kleinasien, ein Neuland der Kunstgeschichte* (1903), which influenced her archaeological work. Like Hogarth and Reinach, Strzygowski (1862–1941), professor of art history in Vienna, was a scholar of broad scope. His method, however, was criticized by Alois Riegl and Franz Wickhoff, the leading exponents of the art historical "Vienna school," prompting him to concentrate on Near Eastern ancient art. Strzygowski's approach was unconventional, especially his advocacy of interdisciplinary research.[174] Bell was probably attracted to his reevaluation of Near Eastern cultures, which most classical archaeologists still considered "primitive" or provincial.

Inspired by *Kleinasien* and encouraged by Reinach, Bell undertook her first archaeological expedition to Asia Minor and northeastern Syria in 1905 to examine Roman, Byzantine, and medieval ruins. She also discovered Hittite remains on the peak of Mehaletch and copied a number of inscriptions.[175] This work pleased her, and she reported home, "I had the most delightful day playing at being an archaeologist," and "it's the most fascinating study."[176] But she also experienced the unpleasant side of fieldwork:

> I shall not forget the misery of copying a Syrian inscription in the drenching rain, holding my cloak round my book to keep the paper dry. The devil take all Syrian inscriptions, they are so horribly difficult to copy. Fortunately they are rare, but I have had two today.[177]

When an expert told her that her copy was faultless, she exclaimed, "That was rather a triumph . . . for I remember as I did it all the Druzes and my Bedouin guide on his camel were standing round impatiently and crying 'Yallah, yallah! Oh, lady!'"[178]

One of her main tasks was a preliminary survey of the late Roman and Byzantine architecture of Binbirkilise (Turkish for "one-thousand and one churches") on the foot of the Kara Dagi mountain in the plain north of the Taurus, the ancient Lykaonia.[179] In a letter to her father she expressed her excitement: "If you had read the very latest German archaeological books you would be wild with excitement at seeing where I am."[180] On her return to Konya she met the British classicist William Ramsay, whose work she knew and admired; he agreed to collaborate on an excavation at Binbirkilise.[181] Contemplating her first serious involvement in archaeology, Bell experienced the contrast between what was perceived to have been the glorious past and the contemporary situation in the Ottoman provinces.

> What a country this is! . . . Race after race, one on top of the other, the whole land strewn with mighty relics of them. We in Europe are accustomed to think that civilisation is an advancing flood that has gone steadily forward since the beginning of time. I believe we are wrong. It is a tide that ebbs and flows, reaches a high water mark and turns back again. Do you think that from age to age it rises higher than before? I wonder—and I doubt.[182]

As a result of the 1905 expedition Bell published six richly illustrated articles, including plans for each building and copies of inscriptions, in the *Revue Archéologique* for 1906–7. Strzygowski reviewed them in the *Byzantinische Zeitschrift*.[183] In spite of Strzygowski's criticism of the badly reproduced photographs and sketchy descriptions (he understood it as preliminary work to be followed up by more thorough excavations), his final sentence is remarkable:

> I do not know Gertrude L. B. personally, I do not know if she is young or old, therefore my judgement is totally impartial: what she accomplished should set an example for men . . . she has presented the Christian art of Asia Minor in a way that hopefully the whole world will soon go there to see with their own eyes that Asia Minor is a very fruitful "Neuland" for art history.[184]

Certainly, Bell's research suited Strzygowski's efforts to promote the study of Near Eastern architecture and art. But this is still a highly unusual review of the first work of a woman archaeologist. Strzygowski was soon to become acquainted with Bell. To Max van Berchem she wrote, "I generally go and see Strzygowski on my way back [from the East] to tell him what I have done and found and I think I ought to come and talk over these things with you too."[185]

Before returning to the Near East, Bell worked for two years on her archaeological publications and her book, *The Desert and the Sown.* In April 1907 she left for Konya to prepare the excavation with Ramsay. By the time Ramsay arrived in Binbirkilise, the excavation was in full operation.[186] Bell's 1905 expedition and the Bell-Ramsay excavation represent the first and only systematic surveys of the Kara Dagi, and her photographs demonstrate how much has been destroyed since 1907.[187] Although their joint publication, *The Thousand and One Churches* (1909), is generally listed under Ramsay's name, Bell contributed 460 and Ramsay 80 pages.[188] The book is dedicated to Strzygowski, perhaps as a gesture of gratitude not only for providing a "constant companion" in his *Kleinasien,* but also for his encouraging review. Many churches, chapels, monasteries, mausoleums, and fortresses that had never been previously described or mapped were included; published but inaccurate plans were corrected; and a new chronology presented, based on an inscription Bell had discovered in 1905.[189] Bell's work contributed substantially to the recording of Byzantine monuments in Asia Minor, and the book became a standard reference for early Christian architecture.

By the time Bell came to the eastern Mediterranean and the Near East, archaeologists were digging in Greece, Crete, along the Turkish coast, in the Levant and Mesopotamia. She was interested in every site and period, even visiting Dalmatia in 1910. But she concentrated her own work on Roman, Byzantine, and early Islamic architecture, combining her exploration of relatively unknown regions with her archaeological work. By 1909 she felt confident enough to undertake her own research, cataloging monuments in the remote and dangerous Tur 'Abdin plateau, southwest of the Tigris between Diyarbakir (ancient Amida) and Nusaybin (ancient Nisibis).[190] *Tur 'Abdin* is Syriac for "mount of the servants of god," which Bell used as the title for a popular article.[191] The Tur 'Abdin is known for its numerous churches and monasteries dating from A.D. 300 to circa 1500.[192] Many buildings have been lost through destruction or rebuilding, so that Bell's publications, notes, and photographs are often the only remaining record.

Bell's publications attracted the attention of not only Strzygowski, but also Max van Berchem (1863–1921), the Geneva scholar and traveler to the Near East who was considered the founder of Islamic archaeology.[193]

According to Oleg Grabar, "van Berchem's intellectual rigour, scientific precision, breadth of information and range of deductions remain unsurpassed."[194] Bell's letters to van Berchem convey the circumstances under which she worked in England.[195] In September 1911 she wrote from Rounton Grange, "You must not think me very lazy; at this time of year work is not cozy (?) for we have a constant succession of guests."[196] She asked him to send her offprints that she "might possibly miss, . . . for though I diligently read a great number of periodical publications, I cannot, living in the country, keep pace with them all, and in London when I might see them, I cannot work."[197]

After studying the Tur ʻAbdin architecture, Bell traveled through the Syrian desert to southern Mesopotamia. Her destination was the Ukhaidir, west of Babylon. She had been told of this "unknown" ruin and had hoped to be its first discoverer. But, to her great disappointment, Ukhaidir had been visited by travelers since the seventeenth century, although it was barely known until 1908–9, when, a few months before Bell, M. Massignon surveyed and photographed the ruins, publishing a preliminary report in 1909.[198] After her first visit in March 1909, and the publication of an article "The Vaulting System of Ukhaidir" in 1910,[199] Bell returned in March 1911 for further studies. In the meantime, the German excavation team at Babylon had examined Ukhaydir and was preparing a book to be published in 1912.[200]

After Ukhaydir Bell went on to Karbalā:

> We left Kheidir on Tuesday and rode seven hours across awful desert. It was a horrible day—wind and dust haze everywhere, so that the desert loomed all the more terrible through the hot mist. I have told you of the drought this year. There is no grass, and the sheep and goats are all dying, and the people with them.[201]

From there she proceeded to the German expeditions at Babylon and Assur, where Robert Koldewey and Walter Andrae, both trained architects, had developed new excavation methods. Bell had long conversations especially with Andrae, who remembered her expressing "flaming interest" and extreme curiosity, wanting to know everything.[202] In the Assur guestbook, she signed in Arabic: "In those days even Miss Lowthian Bell was in Assur," the text being modeled after ancient cuneiform inscriptions.[203] She recounts her visit to Babylon and Assur in *Amurath to Amurath,* which also includes descriptions and photographs of many other sites she explored.[204]

In addition to Andrae and Koldewey, Bell met several other archaeologists on her travels: the Princeton team in 1905 (to whom she gave copies of inscriptions she had copied on the peak of Mehaletch), members of the Palestine Exploration Fund teams, Ernst Herzfeld, and Max von Oppenheim.[205] She was extremely generous with her material. Her correspondence with Max van Berchem demonstrates that she gave numerous photographs and plans to many scholars, once writing, "of course you must keep the photographs and I must, moreover, send you those which give the architectural details . . . But you must please clearly understand that it is a pleasure and an honor to send you photographs and you must always ask me for any that you want. Everyone asks me for photographs."[206]

An excellent observer, Bell studied the German excavations thoroughly, and when she later visited Carchemish, she noticed the difference[207] between British and German excavation techniques. Two young assistants, R. Campbell Thompson and T. E. Lawrence, were conducting the excavation in the absence of David Hogarth. While examining the site, she mentioned to them that their technique was "prehistoric" compared to that of the Germans, but Lawrence claims that they convinced her otherwise.[208]

Back home, Bell concentrated on her publications:

> I've finished the chapter for Strzygowski—only blocked out of course, there is a lot more work to be done on it, but the worst part is over and what is more I think it's rather neat. I have been so absorbed in it that I haven't had a moment to think of anything else.[209]

With the publication of the book, *The Thousand and One Churches* (1909); the chapter in van Berchem and Strzygowski's book, *Amida* (1910); and an article in the prestigious *Journal of Hellenic Studies* (1910), Bell gained considerable recognition as an archaeologist. No other women worked in field archaeology before World War I in such remote areas and under such hazardous conditions as Gertrude Bell. Working alone, with only locals for support, demanded courage, determination, stamina, and linguistic skills few possessed.[210] Yet, never satisfied with what she knew, she went to Rome in 1910 to study ancient architecture with Thomas Ashby, director of the British School; Richard Dehlbrück from the German Archaeological Institute; Eugénie Strong, assistant director of the British School (and widow of Arthur Strong with whom Bell had studied Persian and Arabic); as well as the American scholar Esther B. Van Deman.[211] She also gave a lecture in Rome.[212]

Bell's last archaeological books confirmed her professional status in the field: *Churches and Monasteries of the Tur 'Abdin and Neighbouring Dis-*

trict (1913) and *Palace and Mosque at Ukhaidir* (1914).[213] About her Tur 'Abdin monograph she wrote to van Berchem, "I hope it may be useful as I bring a lot of new material to it. In the light of the other churches which I saw this year I have modified my first opinion about the Tur 'Abdin buildings."[214] Her surveys and fieldwork from 1905 to 1914 focused on Byzantine and early Islamic architecture, although her interests ranged from ancient Mesopotamian to the Islamic periods. As a good draftswoman and photographer, she recorded many monuments, including Hittite reliefs, as well as various inscriptions, many now lost.[215] Her work is distinguished by thoroughness and precision. When in doubt, she returned to the site for verification (e.g., Tur 'Abdin and Ukhaidir), often discovering mistakes in others' publications.[216]

Except for her collaboration with Ramsay, Bell conducted all archaeological expeditions alone, accompanied only by her long-time servant Fatuh, a cook, muleteers or camel drivers, several other servants, and occasionally a guide, whereas most male archaeologists worked in teams that usually included philologists. Sometimes she would hire locals to help her dig. In spite of her experience, Bell was never invited to participate in an excavation. Excavation teams in the Near East were all male and not prepared to accept women colleagues. But they were not averse to collaborating with her, as is evident in the van Berchem correspondence. Bell enjoyed her independence and freedom of movement. As a team member she would have been subordinate to a director and been forced to remain stationary for a prolonged period.

Moreover, Bell apparently found her one experience of collaboration somewhat less than ideal. She was not enthusiastic about Ramsay's method: "It makes me laugh to think I could ever have had the idea of leaving things to the Ramsays," she wrote.[217] Her letters reveal that excavating in Anatolia, and with Ramsay, was not easy. He had been reluctant to work with her and only consented because she financed the excavation.[218] Bell's respect for scholars blunted her criticism, and she only hints about her experience with Ramsay. To van Berchem she wrote: "I'm so glad you are not a Professor! I feel now that I need not stand in such fear of you though my respect is not diminished."[219] By going her own way, she avoided the abuse and rejection that would otherwise have been caused by her wealth, gender, and lack of formal archaeological training. She is referred to repeatedly as an "amateur" archaeologist, a term rarely applied to Woolley, Campbell Thompson, or even T. E. Lawrence, who all lacked archaeological training prior to their first excavation. That her work is still consulted and reprinted is a tribute to her methodological thoroughness.[220]

Archaeology was only one of Bell's many interests, and while working with Ramsay in the Kara Dagi, she doubted her archaeological future:

> I have not the training for it; it demands the devotion of a life time, and that I cannot give—or I will not. Anyway circumstances are against it and I shall not struggle with them. No, I shall go back to Arabia, to the desert where I can do things and see things that Ramsay and his learned like could scarcely do and see because they have not time enough or money enough for such enterprises.[221]

This passage, written in 1907, has led some biographers to suggest that Bell lacked the temperament and patience of a scholar and archaeologist.[222] But her archaeological work after 1907—long intervals in England researching and writing scholarly books and articles, studies in the British Library and Museum, or with Reinach in Paris and in Rome—prove the contrary. On expeditions in 1909, 1911, and 1913, she recorded more ancient monuments than any other archaeologist and visited many excavations to garner information from experienced field archaeologists. She communicated with such eminent scholars as Max van Berchem, Marcel Dieulafoy, René Dussaud, Ernst Herzfeld, W. M. Flinders Petrie, Friedrich Sarre, and William Hayes Ward.[223] Although archaeology was her primary concern until the war, she believed that because she would not commit herself wholly to it, she could not become a true scholar like Ramsay, Reinach, or van Berchem. The war prevented her from publishing more archaeological work, and she was not convinced of the value of what she had done, writing to van Berchem that his flattering words "fill me with shame." She continued:

> I feel them to be so very much undeserved. No one knows one's own faults as well as oneself, but you will find them out some day and when you do, don't forget that I warned you of them from the first! I feel most acutely the truth of your saying that only the manner of work matters not the work accomplished and every year I make myself promises of reform. And then come the hard labour of travel and the temptation of laziness and the promises sail down the wind.[224]

Despite these self-doubts, Bell made the finding and recording of unknown archaeological monuments one of the purposes of her last expedition—the journey to Ha'il.[225] She recorded and photographed ancient monuments on the way to and from Ha'il on the Syrian desert frontiers, in Eastern Jordan, and in the Mesopotamian desert. It is regrettable that these were never published, for her descriptions, plans, and photographs are the only documents that survive today.[226]

During World War I, all archaeological activities stopped. In January 1918 Sir Percy Cox asked Bell to advise on the preservation of antiquities.[227] The same year, R. Campbell Thompson, still in uniform, undertook trial excavations in Ur and Eridu.[228] The following year H. R. Hall was sent by the British Museum to survey and excavate in Ur.[229] He also met Bell:

> At the Political Offices I found . . . Miss Gertrude Bell, directing the Arab Bureau, and every day deep in negotiations with the Chiefs with whose mind she sympathized so deeply. Her interest in possible archaeological work in Iraq was intensely keen, . . . and many were the discussions I had with her on the prospects of archaeology under the new régime.[230]

But until 1922 no further excavations were conducted in Iraq. By the time Woolley started to dig at Ur, Bell had returned to archaeology in an official position as honorary director of the Department of Antiquities in Iraq.[231] For the last three years of her life she devoted most of her time to Iraqi archaeology.[232]

The Law of Antiquities enacted in 1924, progressive for its times, was her idea. Until then excavators had kept most of their finds, especially the most important ones, for their universities and museums. The Ottoman government had demanded a very minor portion for the museum in Constantinople, and nothing had been left in the provinces. Bell wanted to avoid the kind of stripping and dismantling of monuments she had observed in 1905 at Mschatta and to ensure that the new Iraq Museum, of which she was the director, had first choice.[233] So she made regular visits to Ur and Kish, selecting objects to take back to Baghdad—a practice that sometimes aroused excavators' resentment, especially when they had found unique objects, such as the milking scene from the Temple of Ninhursag at Ubaid.[234] She described the experience:

> Before 9 we [Bell and Woolley] started the division (it began by my winning the gold scarab on the toss of a rupee) and we carried on until 12:30, when I struck. It's a difficult and rather agonizing job, you know. We sat with our catalogues and ticked the things off. But the really agonizing part was after lunch when I had to tell them that

> I must take the milking scene. I can't do otherwise. It's unique and it depicts the life of the country at an immensely early date. In my capacity as Director of Antiquities I'm an Iraqi official and bound by the terms on which we gave the permit for excavation. J. M. [Wilson] backed me but it broke Mr. Woolley's heart, though he expected the decision . . . I took very little of the bronze; we can't preserve it properly, and I gave them the choice with the door post stones.[235]

Bell felt compelled to write a letter of explanation to Sir F. Kenyon. She then received a letter from him and proudly reported home that "he holds up the Iraq Department of Antiquities as the model for the manner in which the division of finds is made between excavators and local government and that as long as things remain in my hands he will be perfectly satisfied."[236]

The antiquities law also detailed the requirements for excavation permits, such as staff, equipment, and time allocated for publication.[237] One major clause forbade excavating without a permit even on privately owned land. It was hoped this clause would stop illicit digging, but when Bell visited Warka, the ancient Uruk, she encountered a group of illicit diggers.

> When we reached the mound [Warka] we found quantities of people digging and rounded them up. They all screamed and cried when they saw me, but I gave them the salute and they were comforted. I said, "Have you any anticas?" "No," they answered, "by God no." I observed, "What are those spades and picks for? I'll give you backsheesh for anything you have." At that a change came over the scene and one after another fumbled in his breast and produced a cylinder or a seal which I bought for the museum at a few annas. The people came from a little village, Hasyah, about a mile away and I sent them off to bring all that was there while I examined the mounds. They returned while I was lunching on the zigurrat and I bought a quantity of terra cottas.[238]

Once she was looking for a house with an Assyrian statue on its roof that Herzfeld had described to her:

> I found the house, standing outside the town, but nothing on the roof. But as I rode around it I espied half an elephant planted on top of the courtyard wall over the door. It's unusual to see half an ele-

> phant standing on a wall, . . . this one was only three feet high—so I rode into the courtyard and asked who lived there. It was a very tumbledown place and the proprietor, or rather caretaker, was to match; but when he appeared he greeted me with joy . . . I asked if there were an idol in the house. "Oh, yes," he said, and taking me into the inner court, lifted up a mat, and there was the Assyrian statue. It's very roughly blocked out but so like a statue of Semiramis that was found at Assur that Herzfeld thinks it may be no other than she. It is said to have been brought from Babylon. Only the upper part remains, down to about the waist . . . But I must have it for the museum. This may be easy for the house belonged to the late Sir Iqbal al Daulah, a British subject, and I understand that we administer his property. (I shall have the elephant; it was brought from India 60 years ago by Sir Iqbal).[239]

During Bell's tenure as director of antiquities and the Iraq Museum, British and American archaeologists returned to Iraq.[240] Two major excavations were started: the joint excavation of the British Museum and the University Museum in Philadelphia at Ur in 1922; as well as the joint excavation of Oxford University and the Chicago Field Museum at Kish under Stephen Langdon and Ernest Mackay in 1923.[241] Bell, who persuaded the American professor Edward Chiera to survey the area around Kirkuk, where Mitanni tablets had been sold on the local market, initiated a third one.[242] In 1925 Chiera began the first excavation at Yorgan Tepe— the ancient Mitanni city, Nuzi—where, over the next few years, a large archive of tablets was found.[243] There were also plans for excavations involving Walter Andrae and Yale University.[244]

Bell worked relentlessly for the museum, with only one assistant, J. M. Wilson, an architect, who often accompanied her on visits to excavations.[245] She organized an exhibition of the finds from Ur for July 1924, and invited Woolley to give a lecture to a select audience, hoping to gain more support for a building to house the museum.[246] Her efforts paid off two years later when one of the most beautiful buildings in Baghdad was given to the museum.[247] She organized and supervised substantial renovation and installations for the exhibition of objects; she also cataloged, classified, and numbered most of the objects herself; and she wrote the first museum's catalog.[248] Mallowan remembered that "in 1926 she was hard at work classifying seals," and that "at one time she even thought of enlisting Walter Andrae in arranging the Iraq museum."[249]

In June 1926 King Faisal opened the first room of the museum. Since its modest beginnings Bell had referred to the Iraq Museum as "my" museum, and she took enormous pride in showing people around the "wonderful place" where "such wonderful things are to be seen." Until the end of her life the museum represented a "very grave responsibility" for her.[250] On her future as director she wrote to her father:

> I don't feel justified in asking the Iraq Government to give me anything like a permanent post. The Director here should know cuneiform and be a trained museum official . . . What I vaguely think of doing . . . is to . . . ask the Iraq Government to take me on as Director of Antiquities for six months or so. (I'm only Hon. Director now, as you know.) . . . the Department of Antiquities is now a full time job . . . [she describes plans with Andrae and Deutsche Orient-gesellschaft] far too much work to be treated as a secondary employment.[251]

As the museum's founder, antiquities administrator, director, and chief curator, Gertrude Bell became a legend in Iraq and among archaeologists. But, as time passed, her work was viewed more critically. Iraqi archaeologists claimed she gave away too many objects, although many of her decisions were guided by her concern for saving objects from decay, as the museum lacked the specialists and equipment needed for restoration or preservation.[252] That is why she offered the German excavators the confiscated finds from Babylon, which would have disintegrated had they not been treated in Berlin.[253] Because there were no Iraqi cuneiform philologists, nearly all tablets were allocated to the excavators' institutions so that they could be published and made available to students.[254] All things considered, she admirably balanced the divergent interests of nascent Iraqi archaeology and the museum; foreign excavators accustomed to keeping most finds; and the advancement of historical and archaeological knowledge.[255] To her father she wrote that she felt not "merely a responsibility to Iraq but to archaeology in general."[256]

For Gertrude Bell the past was part of the present. History was always on her mind, although sometimes she felt "that I am nothing better than an antiquarian."[257] When she saw the milking scene from Ubaid, she immediately associated it with contemporary life in Mesopotamia. When she traveled, she imagined Alexander the Great, the Parthians, or the Romans marching along the routes she was following or passing the Cilician Gates, or she envisioned the Babylonians and Assyrian armies crossing the Syrian desert. Because antiquity was part of her worldview, every visitor—interested or not—was taken to Babylon, Ctesiphon, or Ur, where she lectured about the glorious past and about the future revival and prosperity of Iraq. For archaeologists such as Bell, ancient history had a different significance than it has for contemporary archaeologists: the past was romanticized, ever present, a point of departure for a vision of the future. Gertrude Bell cannot be understood without considering her fascination with and enthusiasm for archaeology, and her training in modern history. In her last years she wrote to her friend, Janet Courtney, "my natural desire is to slip back into the comfortable arena of archaeology and history."[258] Thus, in spite of all her other activities, archaeology gave her a unique satisfaction.

In her will Bell bequeathed fifty thousand pounds ($220,000)—a fortune in 1926—to the Iraq Museum and six thousand pounds to the British Museum for the foundation of a British School of Archaeology in Iraq, which was established in 1932 as the "Gertrude Bell Memorial." In 1930 the team for the Diyala excavations arrived in Baghdad, just in time for the unveiling of the Gertrude Bell memorial plaque. Seton Lloyd, one of the members, reported the event:

> You wouldn't believe it how real her "Letters" suddenly became. Many of her best friends were there . . . The High Commissioner made a speech, which was replied to by the King . . . He spoke quietly and very sincerely, with an English interpreter: "The founding of this museum was not Miss Bell's only great work. She was, I consider, mainly—I will even say entirely responsible for establishing the Iraq Nation." Then the tablet was unveiled, surmounted by a bronze bust of G. B.[259]

Fifty-five years later, in 1985, the British archaeologist Michael Roaf visited Bell's grave:

> The grave lies in a small cemetery where Christians are buried . . . There are (or were in 1985 when I last visited the grave) a number of trees including date palms in the cemetery and the sandy earth was partly covered with grass, which makes it a pleasant place in the excessively sunny and dusty Baghdad summer.
>
> The grave itself is a rectangle made out of sandstone with a gabled top with an inscription in English along the long side and one in Arabic on the short side. Part of the Arabic inscription had eroded

and I remember there was some discussion when it was to be restored as to what the text might have been.

I find the grave rather sad: the setting is pleasant with trees and shade but her grave seems to be surrounded by strangers and in some way Gertrude Bell in death is as alone as she was much of her life.[260]

WORKS BY GERTRUDE L. BELL
A SELECTED BIBLIOGRAPHY

Books, Monographs, and Articles

"An Eastern Kingdom." *Daisy* 8 (1890).

Persian Pictures. 2d ed, London: E. Benn, 1928. Reprint, New York: Boni and Liveright, 1928. Reprint, London: Jonathan Cape, 1937. 3d ed., London: E. Benn, 1947. Originally published anonymously as *Safar Nameh. Persian Pictures. A Book of Travel* (London, 1894).

Translation of *Poems from the Divan of Hafiz,* by Hafiz. London: Heinemann, 1897. Reprint, London: Heinemann, 1928.

"In the Alps of the Dauphine." *Nineteenth Century and After* 47 (1900): 330–38. Also in *Living Age* (New York) 224 (January–March 1900): 780ff.

"Turkish Rule East of the Jordan." *Nineteenth Century and After* 52 (1902): 226–38.

"Islam in India—a Study at Aligarh." *Nineteenth Century and After* 60 (1906): 900–908.

"Notes on a Journey through Cilicia and Lycaonia." *Revue Archéologique,* 4th ser., 7 (1906): 1–29, 385–414; 8 (1906) 7–36, 225–52, 390–401; 9 (1907): 18–30.

The Desert and the Sown. London: Heinemann, 1907. Reprint, London, 1919; Salem, N.H., 1973; London, 1985; Boston, 1987.

William Ramsay, coauthor. *The Thousand and One Churches.* London: Hodder and Stoughton, 1909.

"The Churches and Monasteries of the Tur Abdin." In *Amida,* by Max van Berchem and Josef Strzygowski, 224–62. Heidelberg and Paris: 1910. Reprint with additional photographs by Bell, London: Pindar Press, 1982.

"The East Bank of the Euphrates from Tel Ahmar to Hit." *Geographical Journal* 36 (1910): 513–37, map, 636.

"The Vaulting System of Ukheidir." *Journal of Hellenic Studies* 30 (1910): 69–81.

"Palace in the Syrian Desert." *Quarterly Review* 212 (April 1910): 339–68.

"The Mount of the Servants of God." *Blackwood Magazine* 189 (September 1910): 354–65.

D. G. Hogarth, coauthor. "Druses." *The Encyclopaedia Britannica.* 11th ed. (1910–11), 7:603–6.

Amurath to Amurath. London: Heinemann, 1911.

"Damascus." *Blackwood Magazine* 189 (April 1911): 539–49. Also in *Living Age* (New York) 269 (May 1911).

"Asiatic Turkey under the Constitution." *Blackwood Magazine* 190 (October 1911): 425–40. Also in *Living Age* 271 (November 1911).

"Responsibility of the Committee: The Danger in Asia." *Times* (London), January 27, 1913, 5.

Churches and Monasteries of the Tûr 'Abdîn and Neighbouring Districts. Heiderberg, 1913. Reprint, with additional photographs by Bell, London: Pindar Press, 1982.

Palace and Mosque at Ukhaidir: A Study in Early Mohammadan Architecture. Oxford: Clarendon Press, 1914.

"A Journey in Northern Arabia." *Geographical Journal* 44 (1914): 76–77.

"Post-Road through the Syrian Desert." *Living Age* 280 (February 7 and 21, 1914): 329–42, 458–69.

———. "An Englishwoman's Desert Journey: Arab Intrigues." *Times* (London), June 13, 1914, 7.

The Arabs of Mesopotamia. Basra: Government Press, 1918. Published anonymously.

Review of the Civil Administration of Mesopotamia. Cmd. 1061. Series of Great Britain, Parliament. London: HMSO, 1920.

"Great Britain and Iraq: An Experiment in Anglo-Asiatic Relations." *Round Table* 53 (1923): 64–83. Published anonymously.

"Iraq." *The Encyclopædia Britannica.* 13th ed., suppl. vol. (1926), 2:510–14.

P. Z. Cox, coauthor. "Iraq." *The Encyclopaedia Britannica.* 14th ed. (1929–36), 12:587–90.

D. G. Hogarth, coauthor. "Druses." *The Encyclopaedia Britannica.* 14th ed. (1929–36), 7:681–82.

The Arab War: Confidential Information for General Headquarters Cairo from Gertrude Bell. Dispatches for the Arab Bulletin. London: Golden Cockerel Press, 1940.

Ich war eine Tochter Arabiens: Das abenteuerliche Leben einer Frau zwischen Orient und Okzident. Bern: Scherz, 1993.

"From *The Desert and the Sown.*" In *Maiden Voyages: Writings of Women Travellers,* edited by Mary Morris. New York, 1993.

Reviews

Mschatta, by J. Strzygowski. *Revue Archéologique,* 5th ser., 4 (1905): 431–32.

Binbirklisse: Archäologische Skizzen aus Anatolien, by Karl Holzmann. *Revue Archéologique,* 5th ser., 7 (1906): 219–20.

Suggested Readings about Gertrude L. Bell

Bell, Lady [Florence], ed. *The Letters of Gertrude Bell.* 2 vols. London, 1927.

Burgoyne, Elizabeth. *Gertrude Bell: From Her Personal Papers, 1889–1914.* London, 1958.

———. *Gertrude Bell: From Her Personal Papers, 1914–1926.* London, 1961.

Richmond, Elsa, ed., *The Earlier Letters of Gertrude Bell.* London, 1937.
Selected Letters of Gertrude Bell. Selected by Lady Richmond from Lady Bell's standard edition. Harmondsworth: Penguin, 1953, 1987.
The University of Newcastle upon Tyne Library, http://www.gerty.ncl.ac.uk.

NOTES

For advice, help, and information, I wish to thank Lesley Gordon (Robinson Library, University of Newcastle), Antoinette Harri (Fondation Max van Berchem, Geneva), Normann Yoffee (University of Michigan, Ann Arbor), Albert de Pury (University of Geneva), Michael Roaf (Munich University), and Claudia E. Suter (Oriental Institute, University of Chicago). I am particularly indebted to Jenai Wu (clinical psychologist at Massachusetts General Hospital), who discussed the problems of psychological interpretations with me. I also wish to express my gratitude to A. Lawrence Asher for aid and encouragement.—J. M. A.-G.

1. Written in 1934 by her close friend Janet Hogarth Courtney, this tribute to Gertrude Bell turned out to be prescient. No other woman archaeologist has received as much attention in print as Bell. Publications include eleven full biographies; three dissertations; scores of biographical articles; numerous entries in collective biographies, dictionaries, and encyclopedias; countless listings in the indices of autobiographies, biographies, and in editions of letters from Bertrand Russell, Virginia Woolf, Harold Nicolson, Mark Sykes, Vita Sackville-West, T. E. Lawrence, Walter Andrae, and Max Mallowan, to name a few. See, especially, Janet H. Courtney, *The Women of My Time* (London, 1934), 77; *The University of Newcastle upon Tyne Library,* http://www.gerty.ncl.ac.uk. The Gertrude Bell web site was initiated after the completion of this manuscript. The site contains all Bell's unpublished material as well as all of her letters and diaries.

2. See H. V. F. Winstone, *Gertrude Bell* (London, 1978), 93–312; Janet Wallach, *Desert Queen: The Extraordinary Life of Gertrude Bell: Adventurer, Advisor to Kings, Ally of Lawrence of Arabia* (London, 1996), 393–401; Billie Melman, *Women's Orients: English Women and the Middle East, 1718–1918. Sexuality, Religion, and Work* (London, 1992), 376–97. Melman, however, did not incorporate Bell into her analysis of Victorian women abroad because "she received so much scholarly and popular attention" (21).

3. *Orient* was the common term used for what is now called "Near" or "Middle East." It refers to the territories under Ottoman rule, including modern Turkey, Syria, Lebanon, Israel, the West Bank, Gaza, Jordan, the Arabian Peninsula, and Egypt. See Roger Adelson, *London and the Invention of the Middle East* (New Haven, 1995), 17–26, for the origin of the term *Middle East,* which was first used by the U.S. naval officer Alfred T. Mahan in 1902.

4. One of the nastiest descriptions is that of Mark Sykes, who had been outwitted by Bell in Aleppo. See Roger Adelson, *Mark Sykes: Portrait of an Amateur* (London, 1975), 108–9; cf. Susan Goodman, *Gertrude Bell* (London, 1985), 34–35; Winstone, *Gertrude Bell,* 96–97; Sarah Graham-Brown, introduction to G. Bell, *The*

Desert and the Sown (Boston, 1985), viii; excerpts from unpublished letters are quoted in most biographies on Bell.

5. E.g., Edward W. Said, *Orientalism: Western Conceptions of the Orient* (London, 1978), 224, 229, 231, 237–38, 245–55; for a critique of Said's method and interpretations, see James Clifford, "Review of *Orientalism* by Edward W. Said. New York: Pantheon Books, 1978," *History and Theory* 19 (1980): 204–23, and Robert Heussler, "Imperial Lady: Gertrude Bell and the Middle East, 1889–1926," *British Studies Monitor* 9, no. 2 (1979): 18 n. 1; Robert D. Kaplan, *The Arabists: The Romance of an American Elite* (New York, 1992), 59–62, 281; Melman, *Women's Orients,* 5. Many authors take Bell's vivid descriptions too literally, without taking into account the style of the time or addressee (mostly parents, siblings, intimate friends, and her lover Doughty-Wylie). That Bell was too passionate, emotional, and romantic is a recurrent topic; but, e.g., Lawrence and Philby were no less emotional and romantic. None of the biographies is scholarly.

6. Cf. J. E. Courtney, *An Oxford Portrait Gallery* (London, 1931), 51–52; Courtney, *Women of My Time,* 80.

7. Max Mallowan, "Gertrude Bell—the Last Years in Iraq: Archaeological Activities," *Iraq* 38 (1976): 81–84.

8. E. Walter Andrae and Rainer M. Boehmer, *Bilder eines Ausgräbers: Die Orientbilder von Walter Andrae 1898–1919* (Berlin, 1992), 34–36, 139–40 (English translation of German text); Walter Andrae, *Lebenserinnerungen eines Ausgräbers* (Berlin, 1961), 174. According to Andrae, Bell insisted on seeing everything during her visits to Assur. He claims he already then suspected that the reason for her visit was political rather than archaeological. Andrae's memoirs were written in the late 1950s, when Bell's work for British intelligence was well known. Andrae himself worked for the German intelligence, as did many other archaeologists (cf. Andrae and Boehmer, *Bilder eines Ausgräbers,* 32 with n. 50). Bell was not working for intelligence when she met Andrae in 1909 and 1911. But she was interested in Arab politics; she talked with and wrote to friends and people in high positions about the political situation in the countries where she traveled; cf. Goodman, *Gertrude Bell,* 72–75; G. Bell, *Amurath to Amurath* (London, 1911), 221–26.

9. L. Woolley, "Review of *The Letters of Gertrude Bell* (1927)," *Antiquity* 2 (1928): 496–98; cf. H. V. F. Winstone, *Woolley of Ur: The Life of Sir Leonard Woolley* (London, 1990), 125, 129, 144, about Woolley's discontent with Bell.

10. *A Change of Perspective: The Letters of Virginia Woolf,* ed. Nigel Nicholson, vol. 3, *1923–1928* (London, 1977), 235.

11. Quoted from V. Sackville-West, *Passenger to Teheran* (London, 1927), 57–62. Doubled question marks have been converted to single question marks for the sake of readability.

12. David G. Hogarth, "Gertrude Lowthian Bell," *Geographical Journal* 68 (1926): 363–68; Hogarth, "Miss Gertrude Bell: An Appreciation," *The Times* (London), July 14, 1926; Hogarth, "Bell, Gertrude Margaret Lowthian," *Dictionary of National Biography, 1922–1930* (London, 1937), 74–76; Salomon Reinach, "Gertrude Bell," *Revue Archéologique,* 5th ser., 24 (1926): 265–67.

13. Hogarth, "Gertrude Lowthian Bell."

14. For a list of institutions and archives holding unpublished material, see Winstone, *Gertrude Bell,* 265–66; Wallach, *Desert Queen,* 394–95. See also the

archive of Max van Berchem, containing thirty-two letters from Gertrude Bell, in the Bibliothèque Publique et Universitaire de l'Université de Genève (boîte no. 3, feuillets 89–166) and 177 photographs by Bell in the Fondation Max van Berchem in Geneva. The majority of Bell's diaries, letters to her family, notes, and photographs are in the Robinson Library at the University of Newcastle. The first biographer who made full use of the unpublished material (with the exception of the material in Geneva) was Winstone, *Gertrude Bell* (1978), ix–x.

15. Florence Bell, ed., *The Letters of Gertrude Bell,* 2. vols. (London, 1927) (hereafter cited as *Letters*); E. Richmond, ed., *The Earlier Letters of Gertrude Bell* (London, 1937) (hereafter cited as *Earlier Letters*); E. Burgoyne, *Gertrude Bell: From Her Personal Papers,* 2 vols. (London, 1958, 1961) (hereafter cited as *Personal Papers*); Courtney, *An Oxford Portrait Gallery,* 51–88; Courtney, *Women of My Time,* 77–89, 116, 119, 164, 173; Vita Sackville-West, introduction to G. Bell, *Persian Pictures* (London, 1928), 9–22; T. E. Lawrence, *The Selected Letters,* ed. M. Brown (New York, 1989), 36–37, 350, 351, 352–53; Valentine Chirol, *Fifty Years in a Changing World* (London, 1927), 332; Nigel Nicolson, ed., *Vita and Harold: The Letters of Vita Sackville-West and Harold Nicholson* (New York, 1992), 131; Ronald W. Clark, *The Life of Bertrand Russell* (London, 1975), 78; recollections of Percy Cox, Gilbert Clayton, William Goodenough, and David. G. Hogarth, *Geographical Journal* 70 (1927): 17–21.

16. A psychological study of Bell poses some problems because, as Julia Keay, *With Passport and Parasol: The Adventures of Seven Victorian Ladies* (London, 1990), 100, notes, "even Vita Sackville-West could not penetrate her emotional camouflage"; cf. also Graham-Brown, introduction to *Desert and the Sown,* xi; Nicola Walker, "A Woman of the Anglez," in *Times Literary Supplement,* no. 4889, January 31, 1997. Of the three newer biographies, Winstone, *Gertrude Bell* (1978), Goodman, *Gertrude Bell* (1985), and Wallach, *Desert Queen* (1996), none includes psychological speculation or analysis; cf. Walker, "Woman of the Anglez," 28; Julie Wheelwright, "Writer, Explorer, Spinster, Spy," *Middle East,* February 1996, 35–37.

17. A plaque on the house commemorates Gertrude Bell's birthplace; cf. Winstone, *Gertrude Bell,* 1.

18. "Bell, Sir Isaac Lowthian," in *Dictionary of National Biography,* 2d suppl., vol. 1 (London, 1912), 132–35.

19. Among her grandfather's regular guests were Charles Darwin, Thomas Huxley, John Ruskin, William Morris, and Edward Burne-Jones.

20. "Bell, Sir Hugh (1844–1931)," in *Who Was Who, 1929–1940,* ed. Adam Black and Charles Black (London, 1941), 90.

21. On her family, see Courtney, *An Oxford Portrait Gallery,* 53–54; Winstone, *Gertrude Bell,* 1–5, 90–95.

22. *Earlier Letters,* 4. Photographs of Red Barns, Rounton Grange, and its rock garden are reproduced in *Letters.* Bell was a passionate gardener and even in Baghdad tried to simulate an English garden; cf. *Letters,* 429, 442, 467, 486; *Earlier Letters,* 7, 13, 16; Sackville-West, *Passenger to Teheran,* 57.

23. Janet E. Courtney, "Gertrude Bell," *North American Review* 223 (1926). Melman, *Women's Orients,* 36, 347 with n. 28; cf. Goodman, *Gertrude Bell,* 1. Caroline T. Marshall, "Gertrude Bell: Her Work and Influence in the Near East

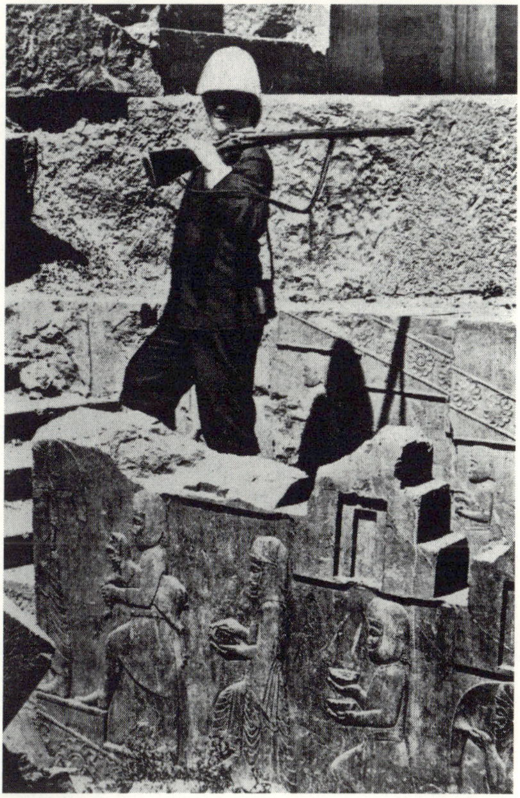

1.1. Jane Dieulafoy at Persepolis. (Courtesy of l'Association Dieulafoy, Paris.)

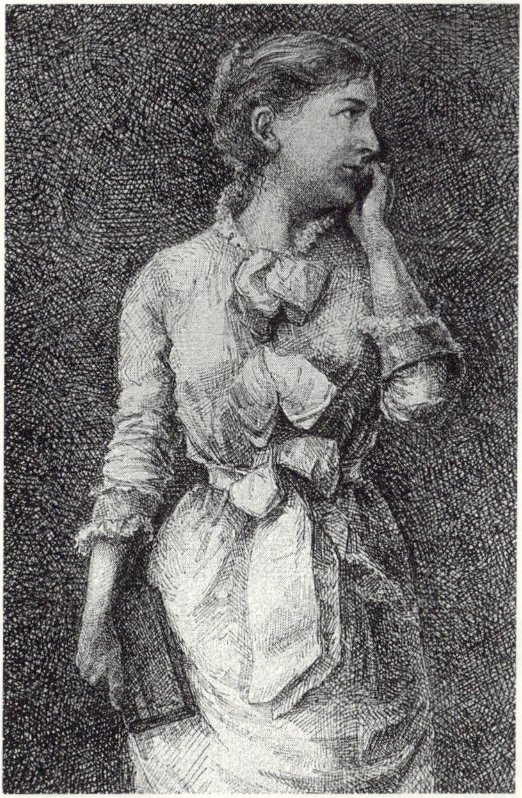

1.2. Portrait of Jane Dieulafoy. (Courtesy of l'Association Dieulafoy, Paris.)

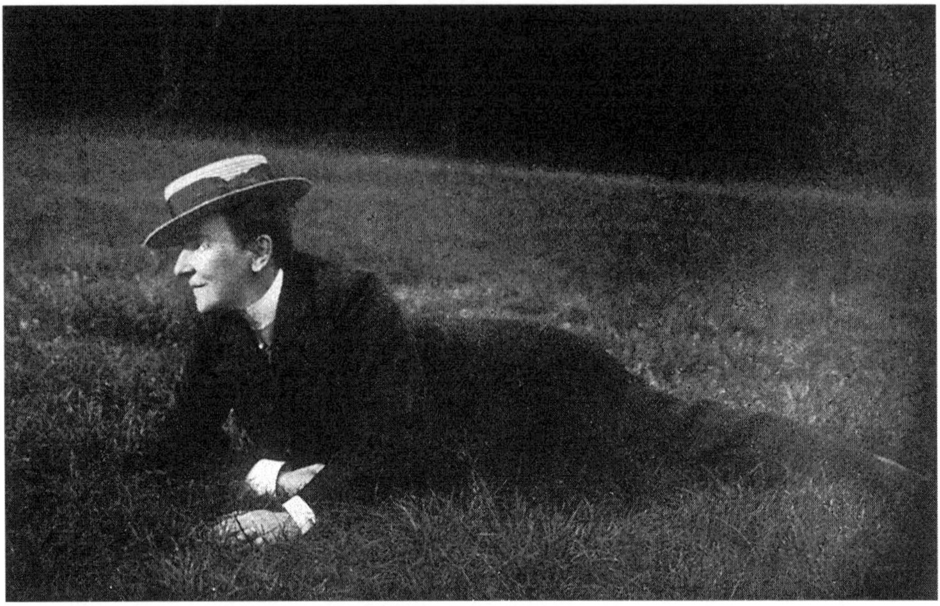

1.3. Jane Dieulafoy at leisure in masculine clothing. (Courtesy of l'Association Dieulafoy, Paris.)

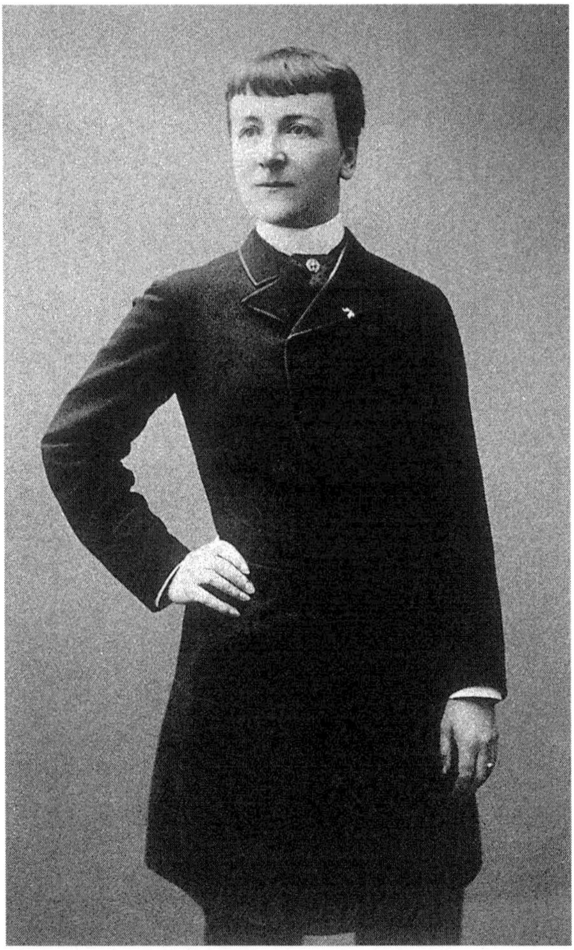

1.4. Jane Dieulafoy. (Courtesy of l'Association Dieulafoy, Paris.)

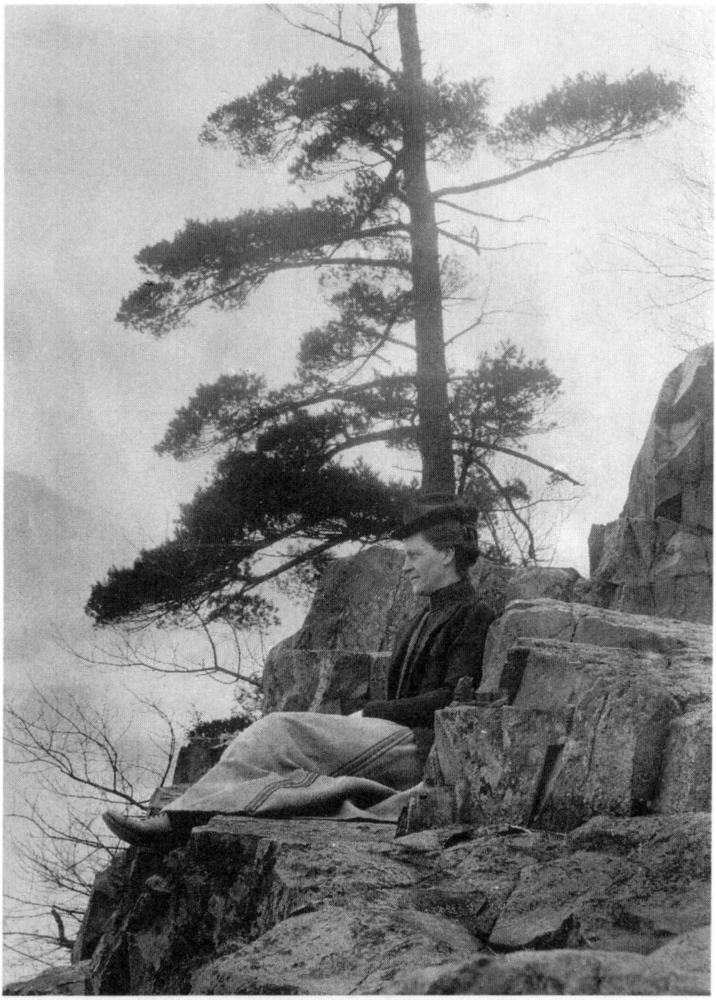

2.1. Self-portrait of Esther Van Deman in the Alps. (Courtesy of the American Academy in Rome, AAR, VD 2709.)

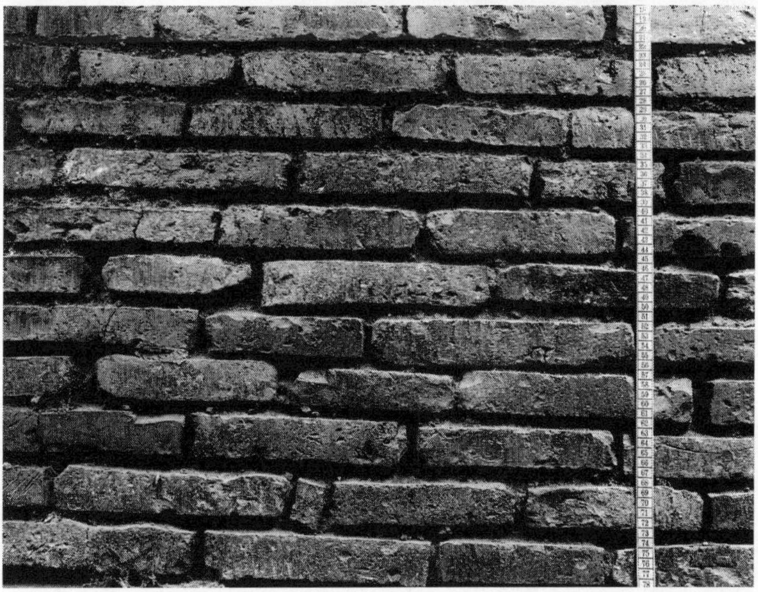

2.2. Brickwork of the Domus Aurea, 1911. (Courtesy of the American Academy in Rome, AAR, VD 29.)

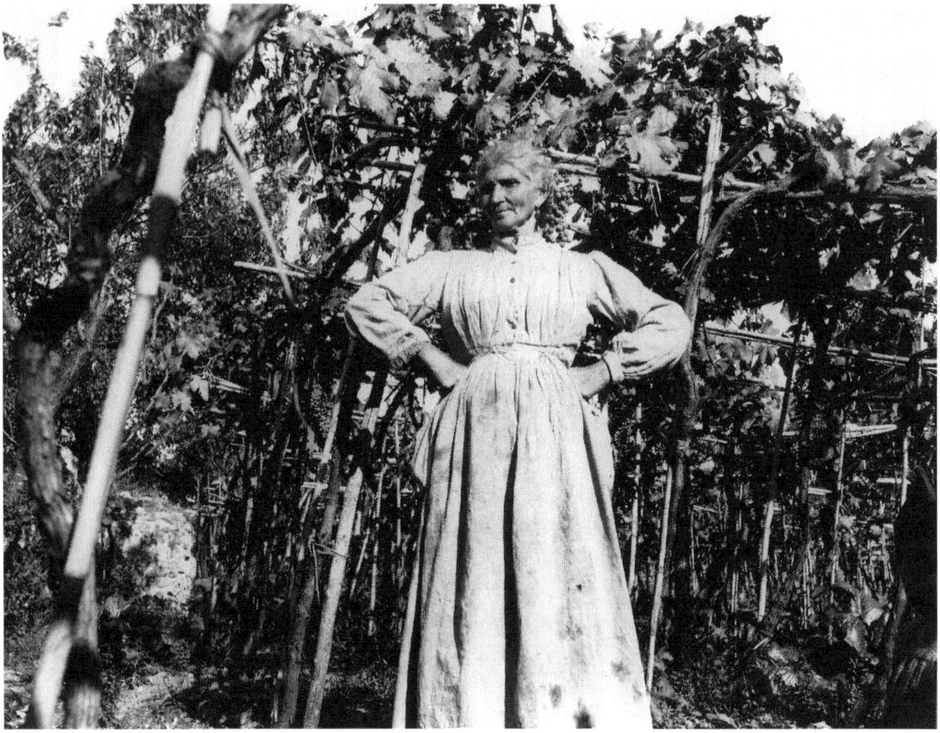

2.3. Anna Salviati in her vineyard, photograph by Esther Van Deman. (Courtesy of the American Academy in Rome, AAR, VD 1259.)

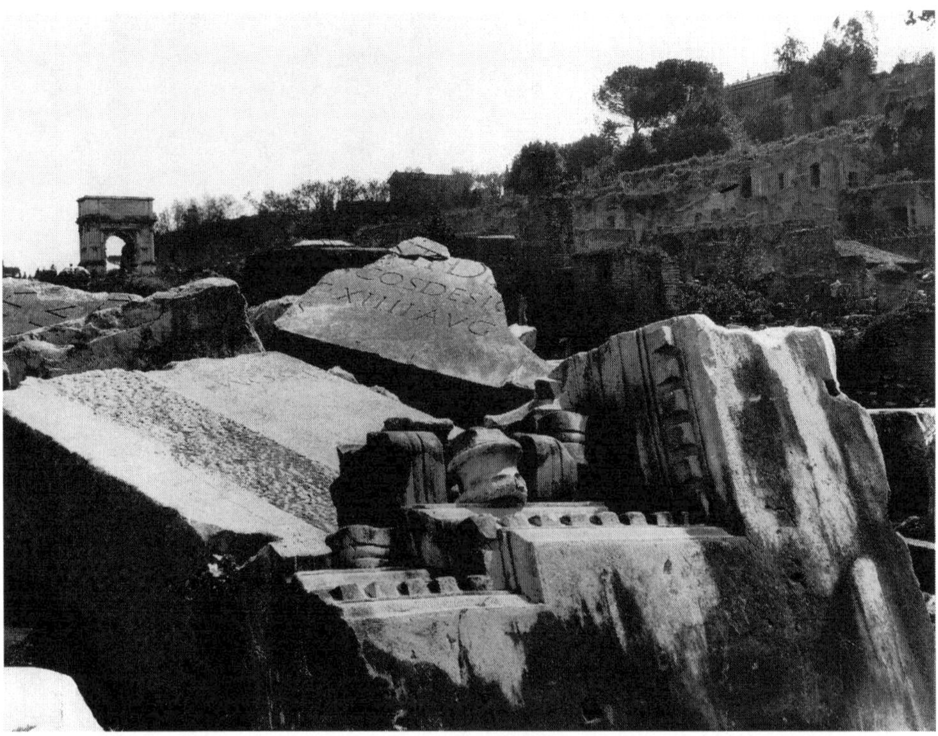

2.4. Forum Romanum, Portico of Gaius and Lucius, photograph by Esther Van Deman. (Courtesy of the American Academy in Rome, AAR, VD 526.)

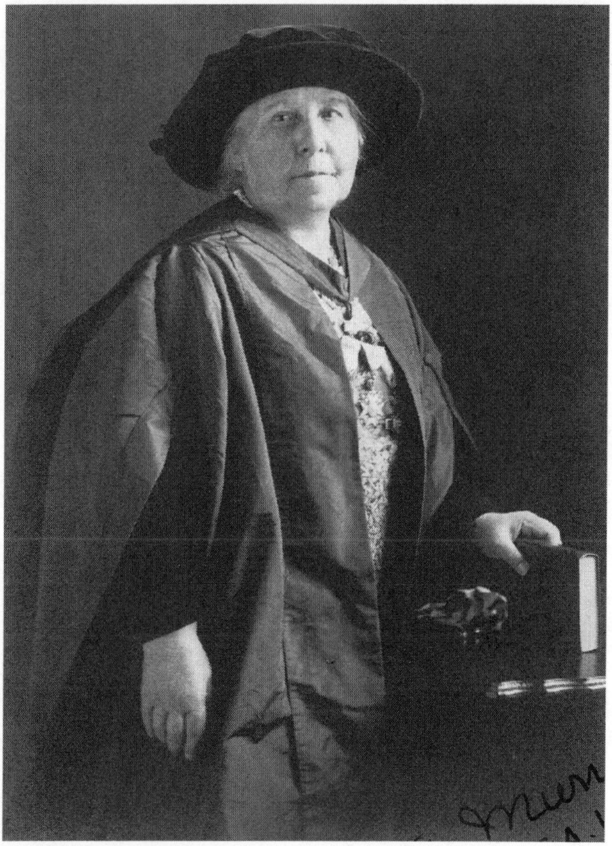

3.1. Margaret Murray in her Doctorate Robes, 1933. In 1931 Murray was awarded an honorary doctorate by the University College London. Because she was financially strapped, her students bought her robes. (Courtesy of M. S. Drower.)

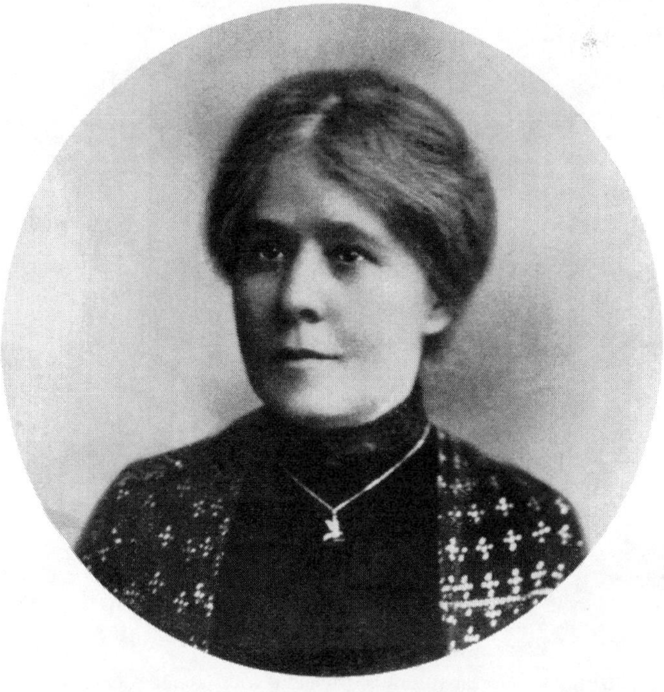

3.2. Margaret Murray in 1913, at age fifty. (Courtesy of M. S. Drower.)

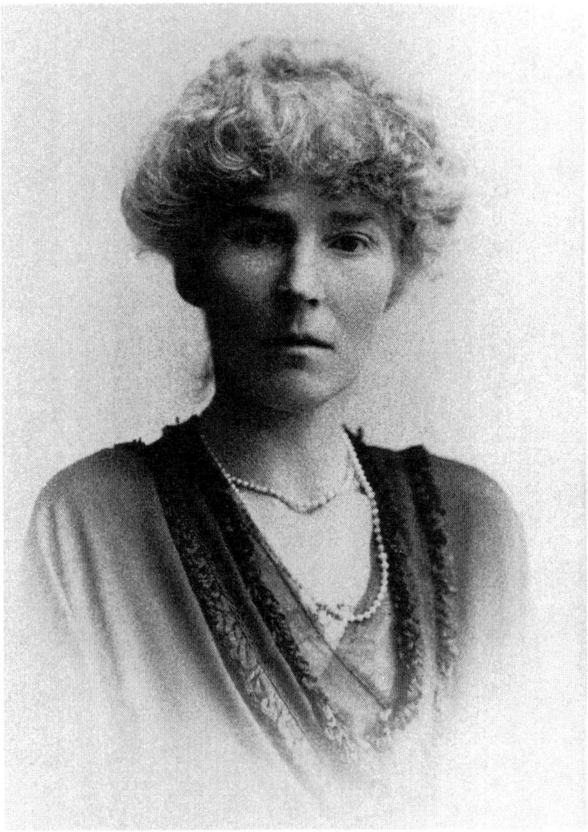

4.1. Gertrude Bell, 1921. (Courtesy of the University of Newcastle upon Tyne.)

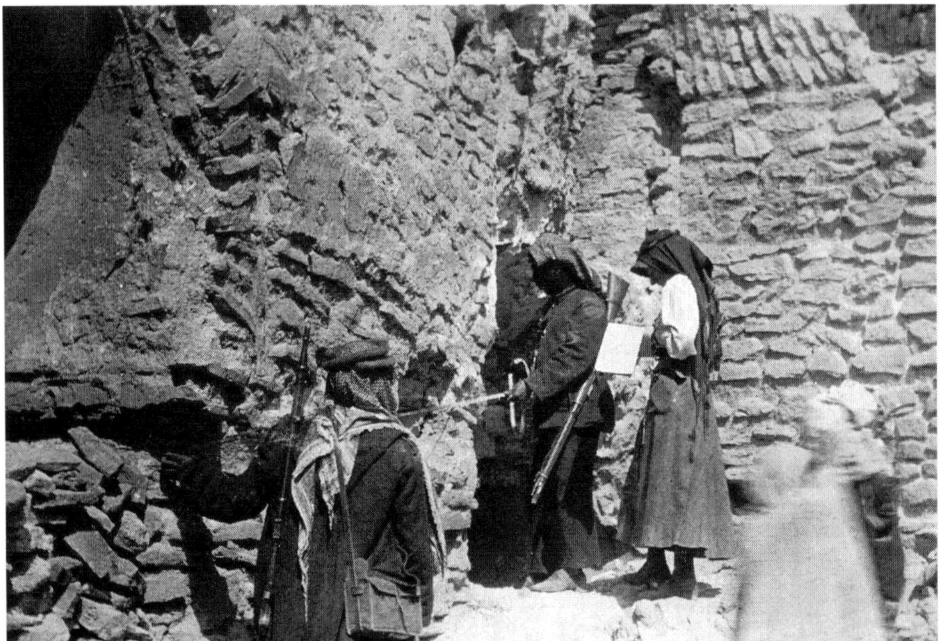

4.2. Gertrude Bell taking measurements at Ukhaidir, Iraq, 1909. (Courtesy of University of Newcastle upon Tyne.)

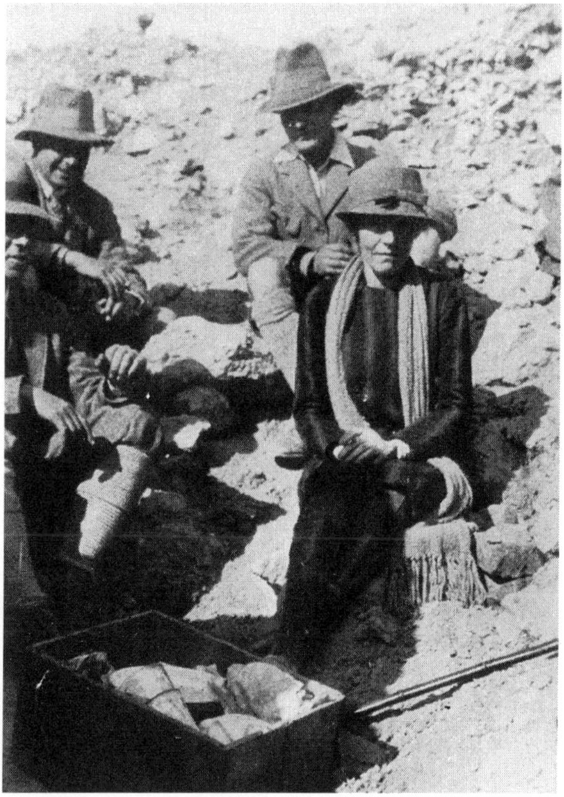

4.3. Gertrude Bell at Ur. Seated, *left to right,* are Sir Leonard Woolley and J. M. Wilson with Gertrude Bell. (Courtesy of the University of Newcastle upon Tyne.)

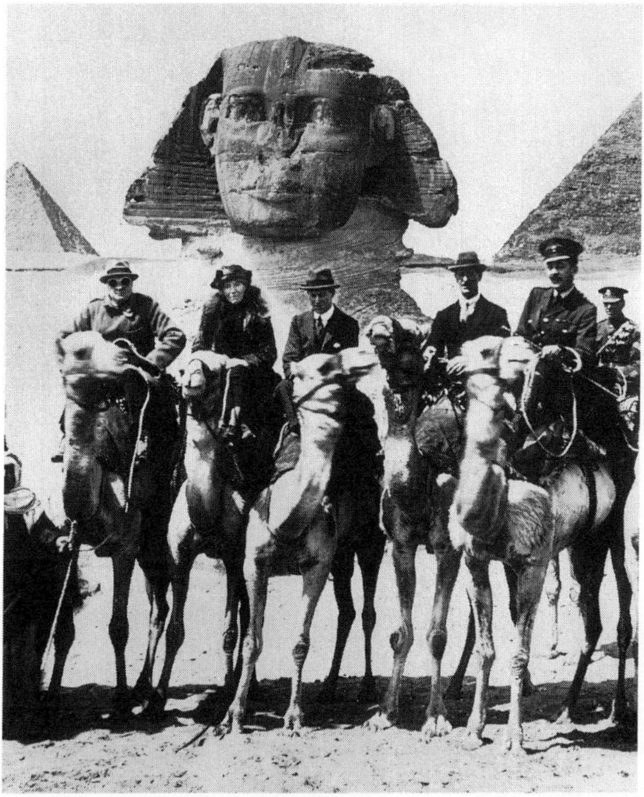

4.4. Gertrude Bell with, *left,* Winston Churchill and, *right,* T. E. Lawrence at the Pyramids during the Cairo Conference. (Courtesy of the University of Newcastle upon Tyne.)

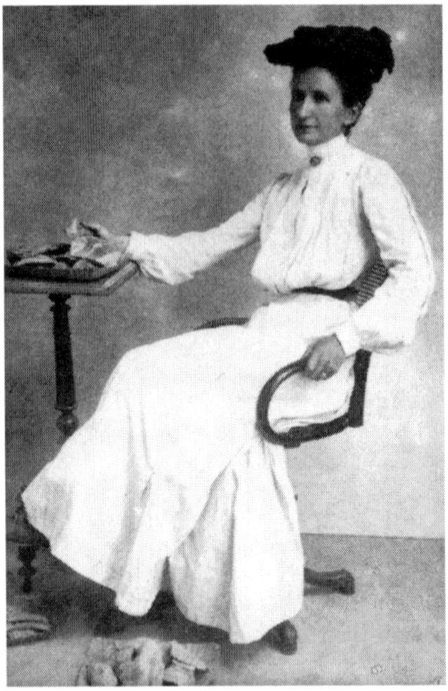

5.1. Harriet Boyd Hawes studying sherds at Herakleion, probably 1904. (Smith College Archives, Smith College.)

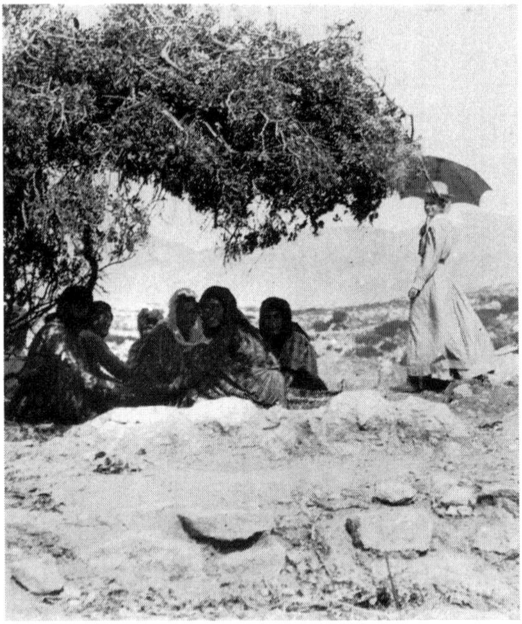

5.2. Girls washing sherds at Gournia and Harriet Boyd Hawes on the right under a parasol. (Archive of The Duckworth Collection, Department of Biological Anthropology, Cambridge University.)

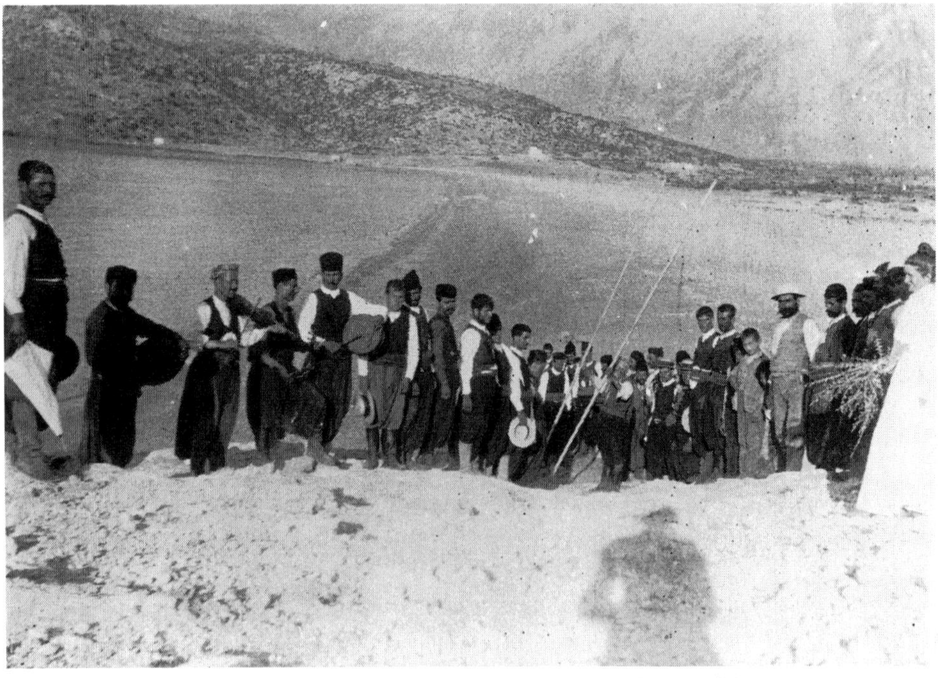

5.3. Harriet Boyd Hawes holding an olive branch during games at the end of the 1901 campaign. (Archive of The Duckworth Collection, Department of Biological Anthropology, Cambridge University.)

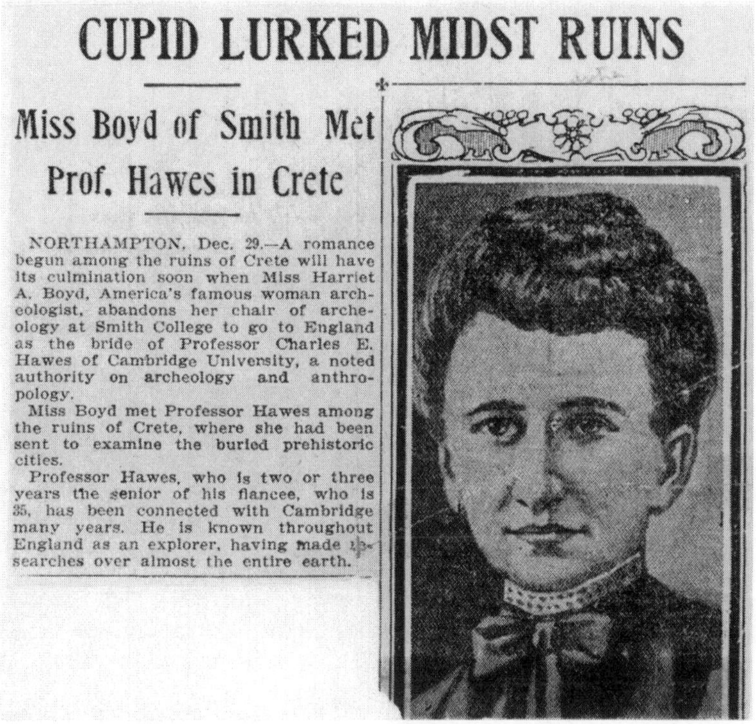

CUPID LURKED MIDST RUINS

Miss Boyd of Smith Met Prof. Hawes in Crete

NORTHAMPTON, Dec. 29.—A romance begun among the ruins of Crete will have its culmination soon when Miss Harriet A. Boyd, America's famous woman archeologist, abandons her chair of archeology at Smith College to go to England as the bride of Professor Charles E. Hawes of Cambridge University, a noted authority on archeology and anthropology.

Miss Boyd met Professor Hawes among the ruins of Crete, where she had been sent to examine the buried prehistoric cities.

Professor Hawes, who is two or three years the senior of his fiancee, who is 35, has been connected with Cambridge many years. He is known throughout England as an explorer, having made re-searches over almost the entire earth.

5.4. Marriage announcement of Harriet Boyd to Charles Henry Hawes, December 29, 1905.

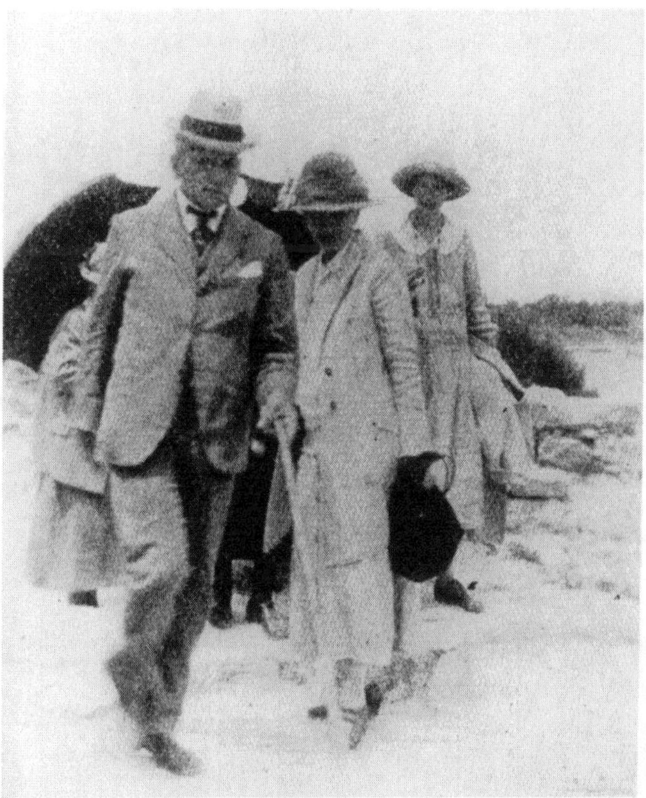

5.5. Harriet Boyd Hawes being shown around Knossos by Sir Arthur Evans, followed by her daughter Mary, 1926. (R. V. D. Magoffin, E. C. Davis, *The Romance of Archaeology* [London, 1930], fig. p. 31.)

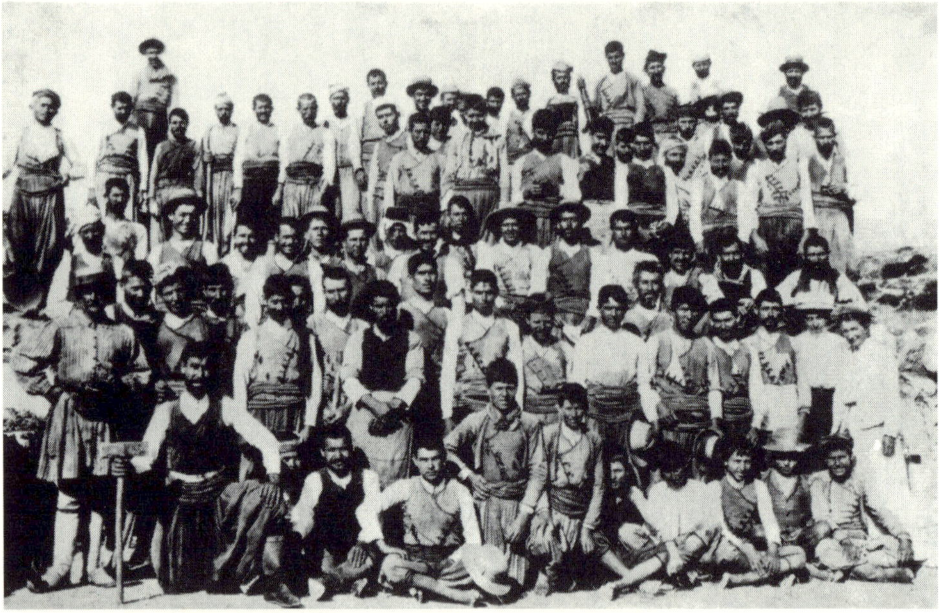

5.6. *Right,* Harriet Boyd Hawes with Edith Hall next to her and eighty workmen including, *left, front row,* Aristides Pappadhias during the 1904 campaign. (University of Pennsylvania Museum Archives.)

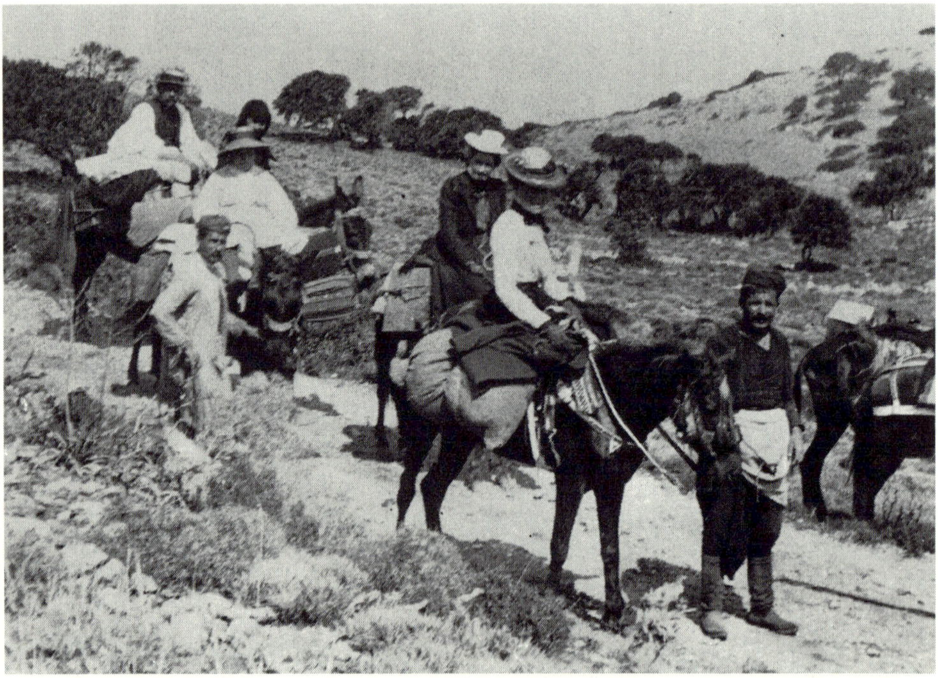

5.7. Harriet Boyd Hawes in dark dress riding behind Blanche Wheeler, with Aristides Pappadhias and Manna at rear, 1901. (Archive of the Duckworth Collection, Department of Biological Anthropology, Cambridge University.)

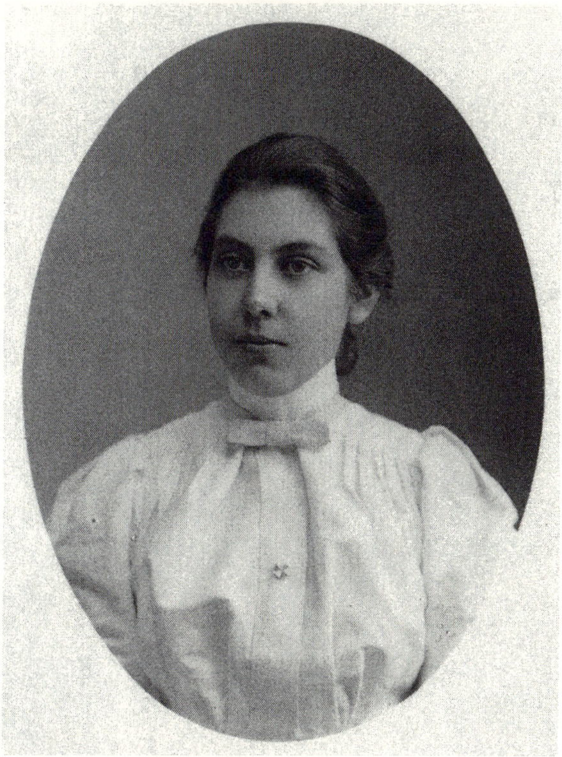

6.1. Edith Hall Dohan, as a graduate of Smith College, 1899. (Courtesy of Katherine D. Morrow, author's family photograph personal collection.)

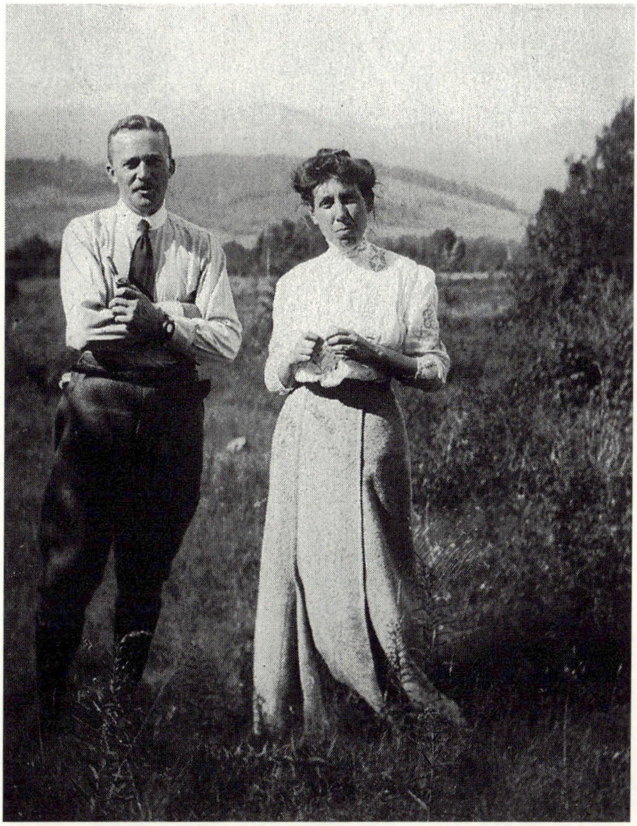

6.2. Edith Hall Dohan with Richard Seager, 1910. (Courtesy of Katherine D. Morrow, author's family photograph personal collection.)

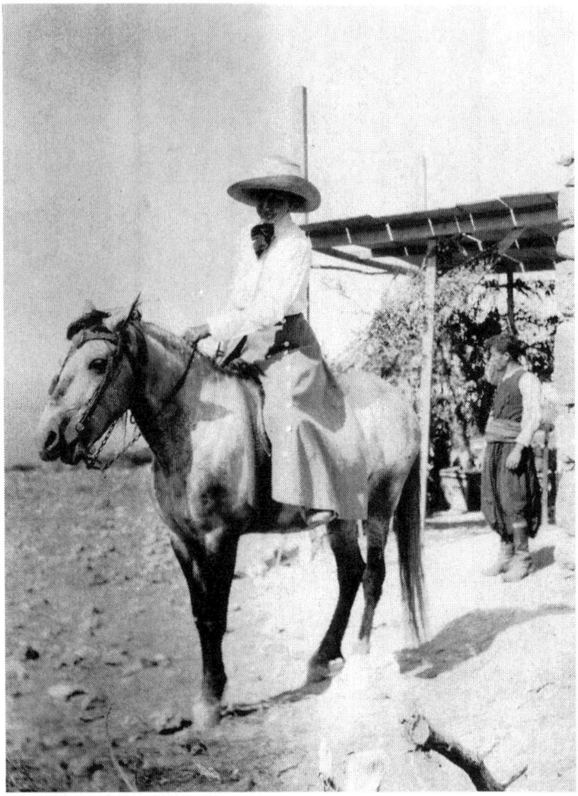

6.3. Edith Hall Dohan on horseback in Vrokastro, 1912. (Courtesy of Katherine D. Morrow, author's family photograph personal collection.)

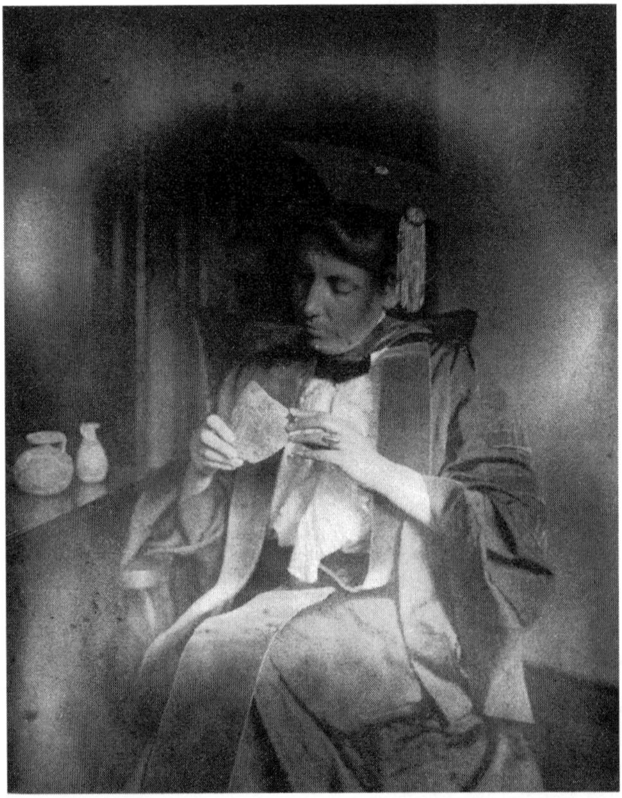

6.4. Edith Hall Dohan in academic regalia, 1922. (Courtesy of Katherine D. Morrow author's family photograph personal collection.)

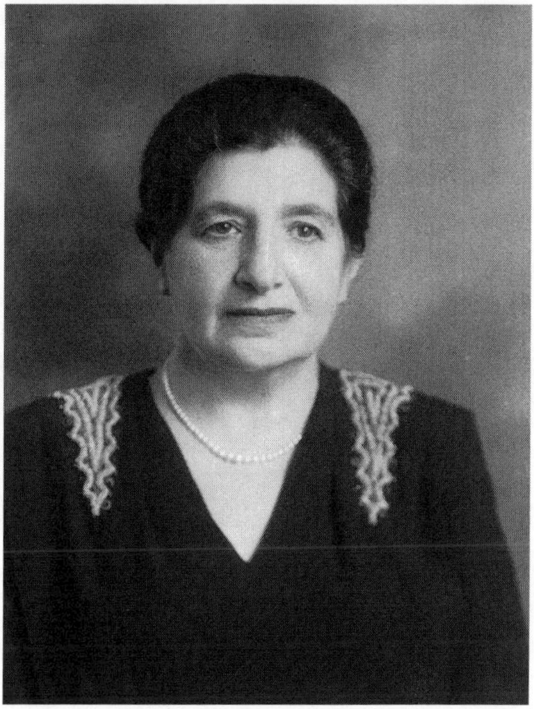

7.1. Hetty Goldman. (Clearose Studio, Princeton, N.J., Courtesy of Bryn Mawr College Archives.)

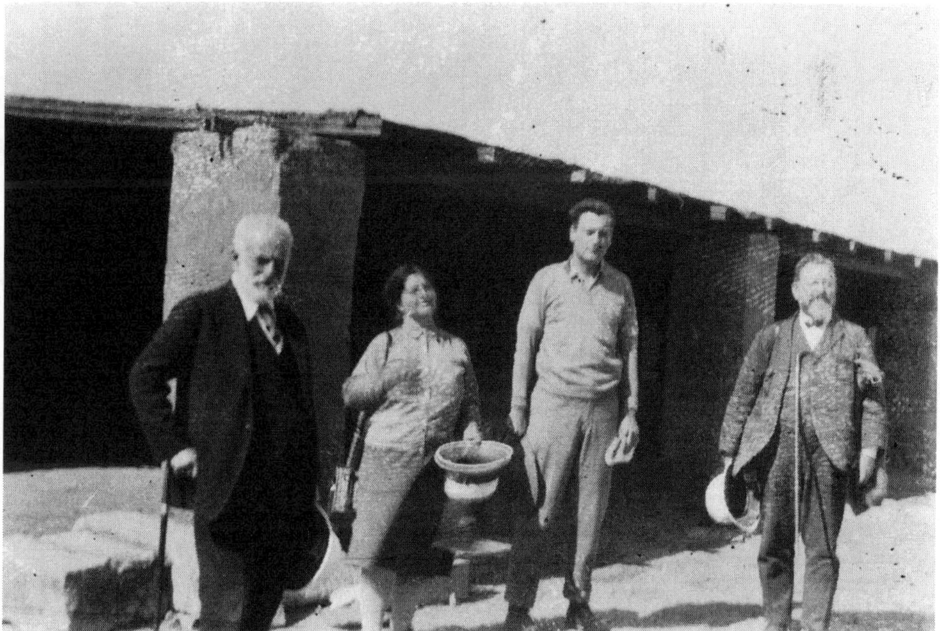

7.2. Senna East, Sudan, February 1930; *left to right,* Julius Goldman (Hetty's father), Hetty Goldman, Phelps Clawson, and Jean Capart. (Courtesy of Sarah Sanborn Moench.)

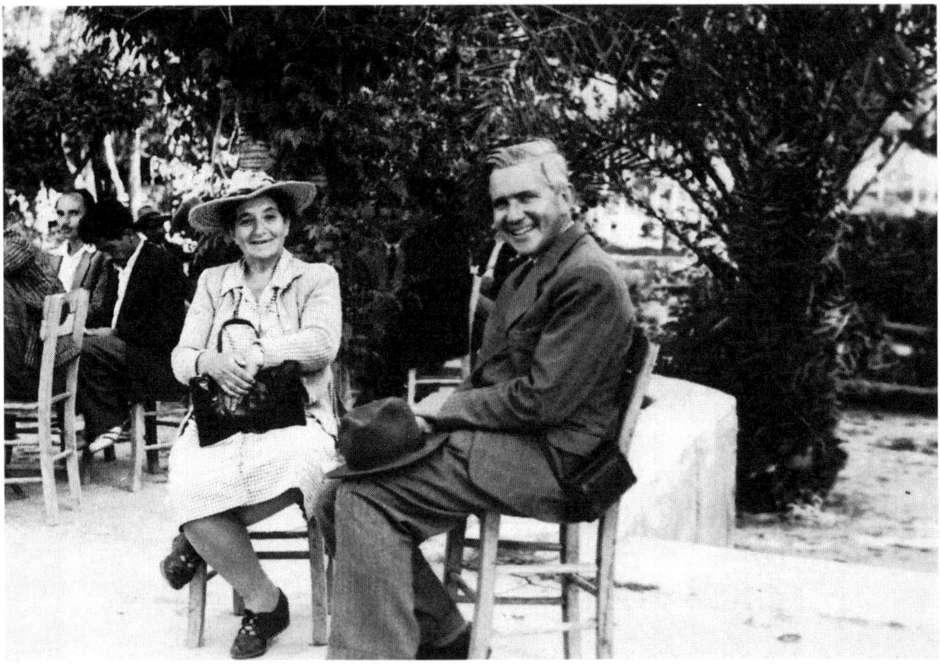

7.3. Professor Hetty Goldman and Professor Hans Güterbock in the Public Gardens at Tarsus. (Photograph by Theresa Goell, courtesy of Bryn Mawr College Archives.)

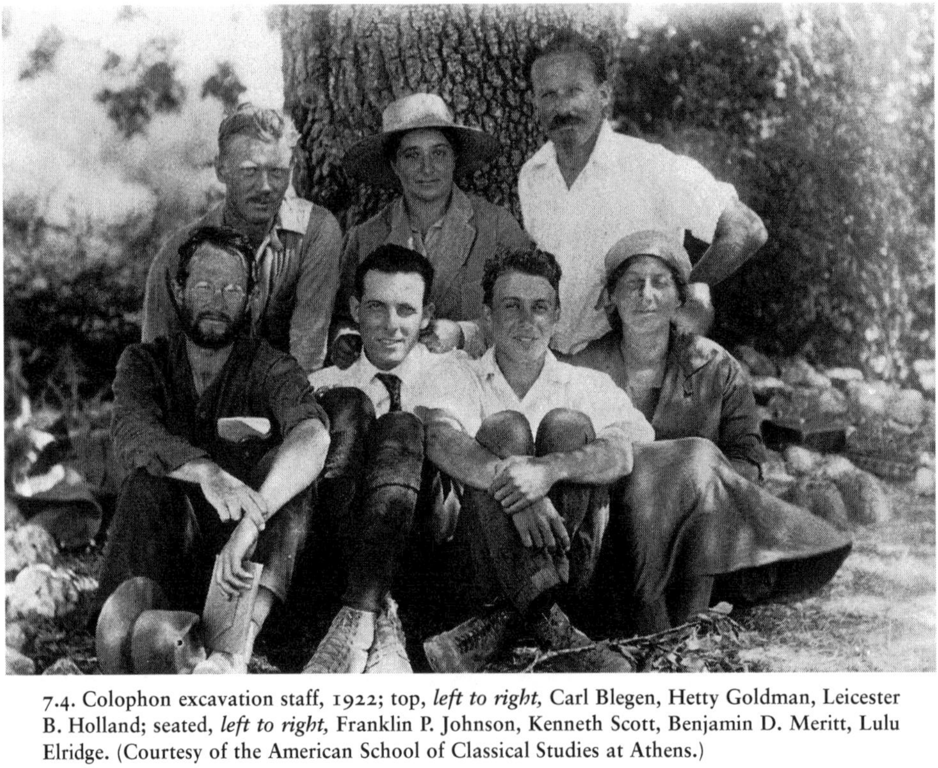

7.4. Colophon excavation staff, 1922; top, *left to right,* Carl Blegen, Hetty Goldman, Leicester B. Holland; seated, *left to right,* Franklin P. Johnson, Kenneth Scott, Benjamin D. Meritt, Lulu Elridge. (Courtesy of the American School of Classical Studies at Athens.)

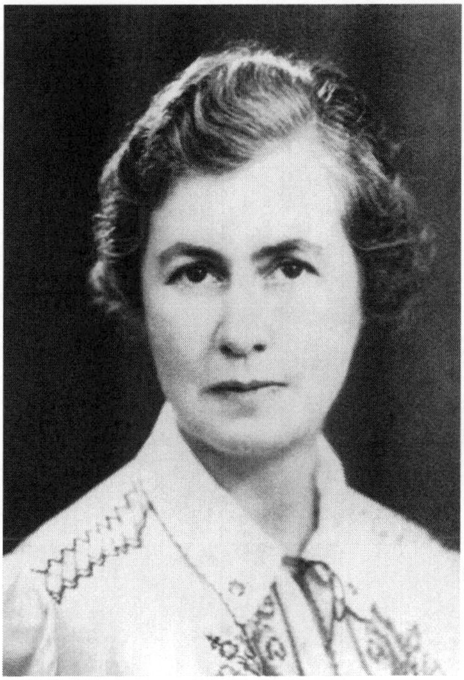

8.1. Gertrude Caton-Thompson, Fellow of Newnham College. (Courtesy of Newnham College, Cambridge.)

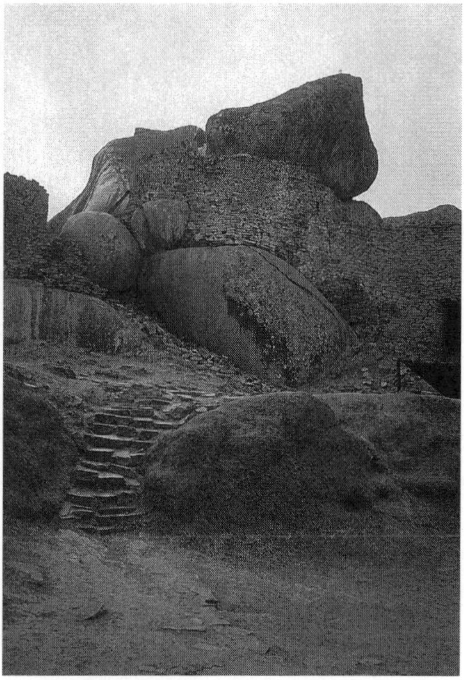

8.3. The western enclosure of the Hill Complex, Zimbabwe. (Courtesy of M. S. Drower.)

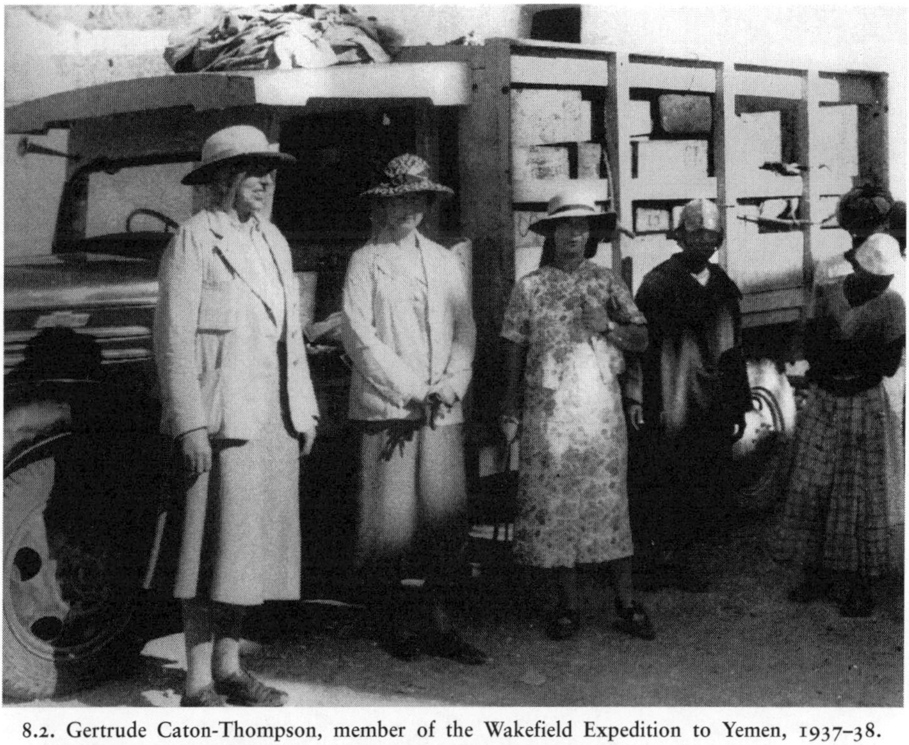

8.2. Gertrude Caton-Thompson, member of the Wakefield Expedition to Yemen, 1937–38. Caton-Thompson is shown in the middle with Elinor Gardner and Freya Stark as they set off for the Hadhramaut. (Courtesy of the Royal Society for Asian Affairs.)

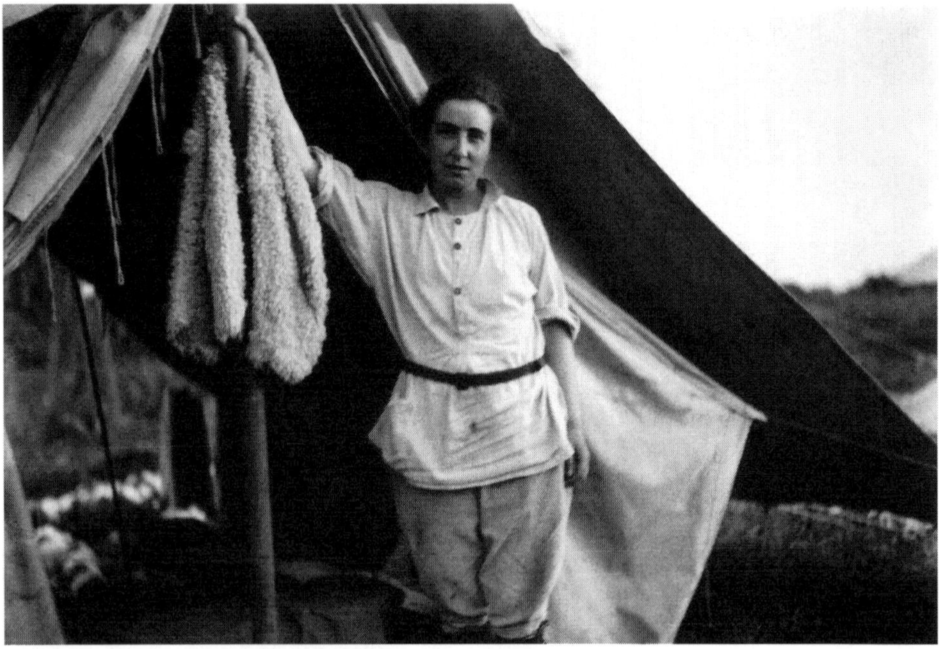

9.1. Dorothy Garrod in camp at Wadi Mughara during her first season, 1929. (Courtesy of Fonds Suzanne Cassou de Saint-Mathurin, Bibliothèque du Musée des Antiquités Nationales de Saint-Germaine-en-Laye, France. © Photo MAN. L. Hamon.)

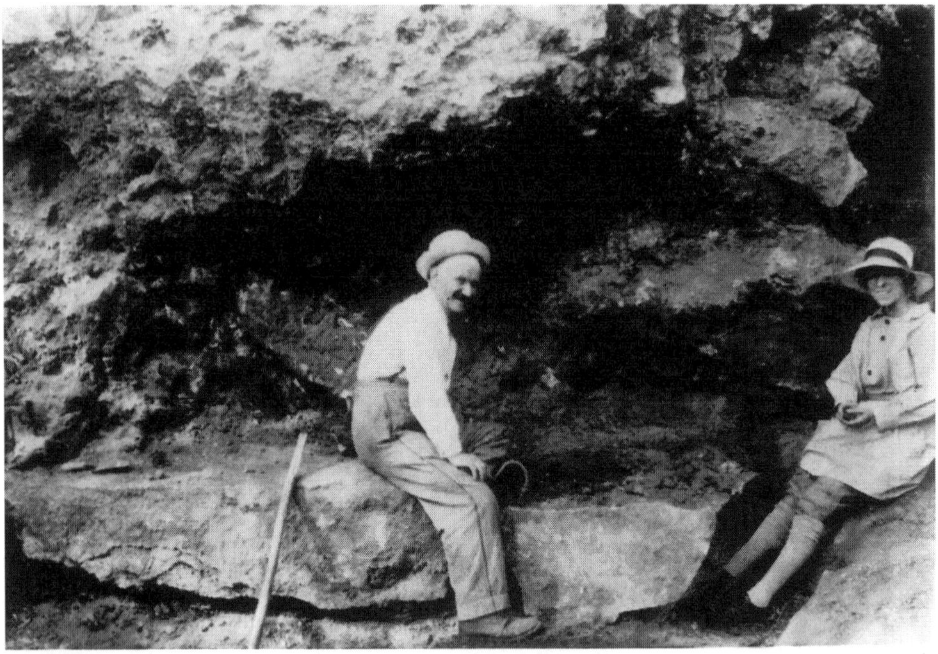

9.2. Dorothy Garrod learning fieldwork at LaBattu rockshelter, Sergeac, in 1921. (Courtesy of Fonds Suzanne Cassou de Saint-Mathurin, Bibliothèque du Musée des Antiquités Nationales de Saint-Germaine-en-Laye, France. © Photo MAN. L. Hamon.)

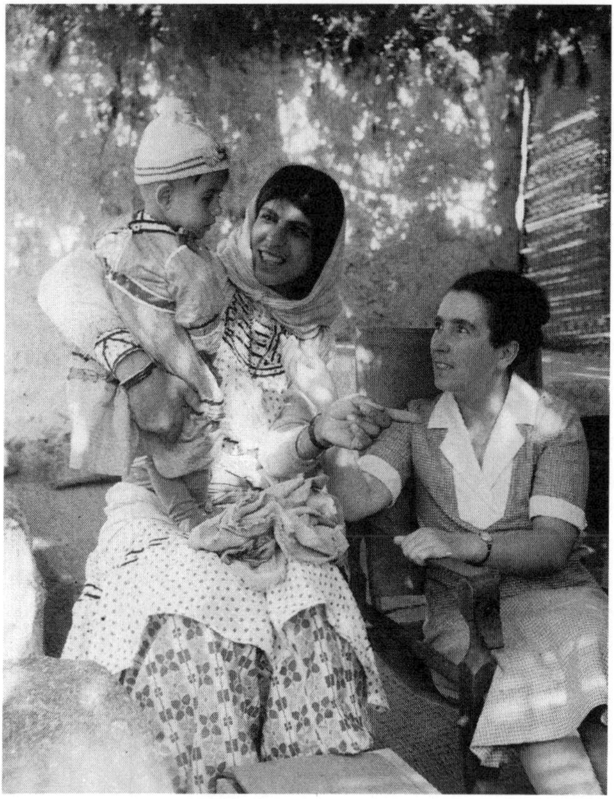

9.3. Dorothy Garrod with Yusrah, discoverer of Tabun I Neanderthal cave burial, 1934. (Courtesy of the Pitt Rivers Museum, University of Oxford.)

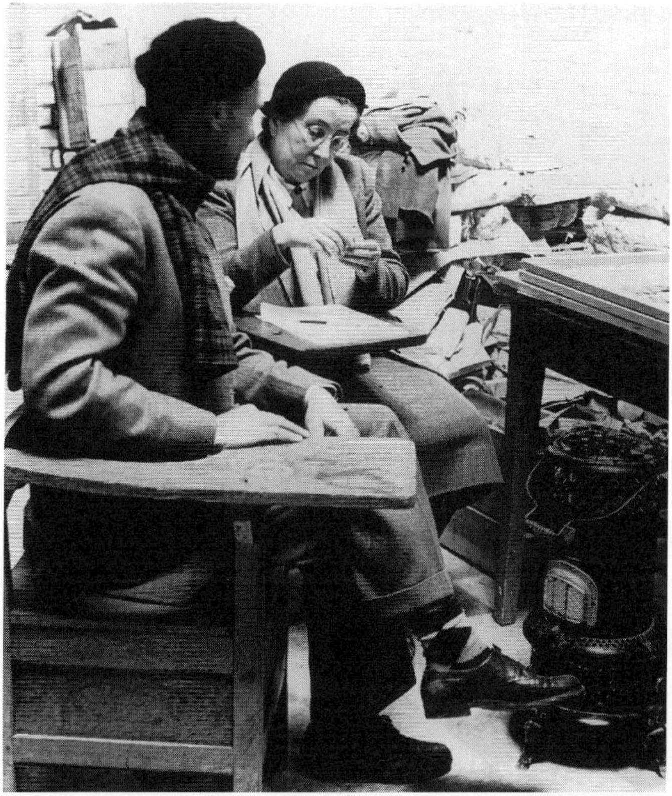

9.4. Dorothy Garrod in Baghdad, 1952 with Paleolithic archaeologist Ralph S. Solecki, looking at the Shanidar Cemetery Collection. (Courtesy of Dr. Ralph Solecki and Dr. Rose Solecki.)

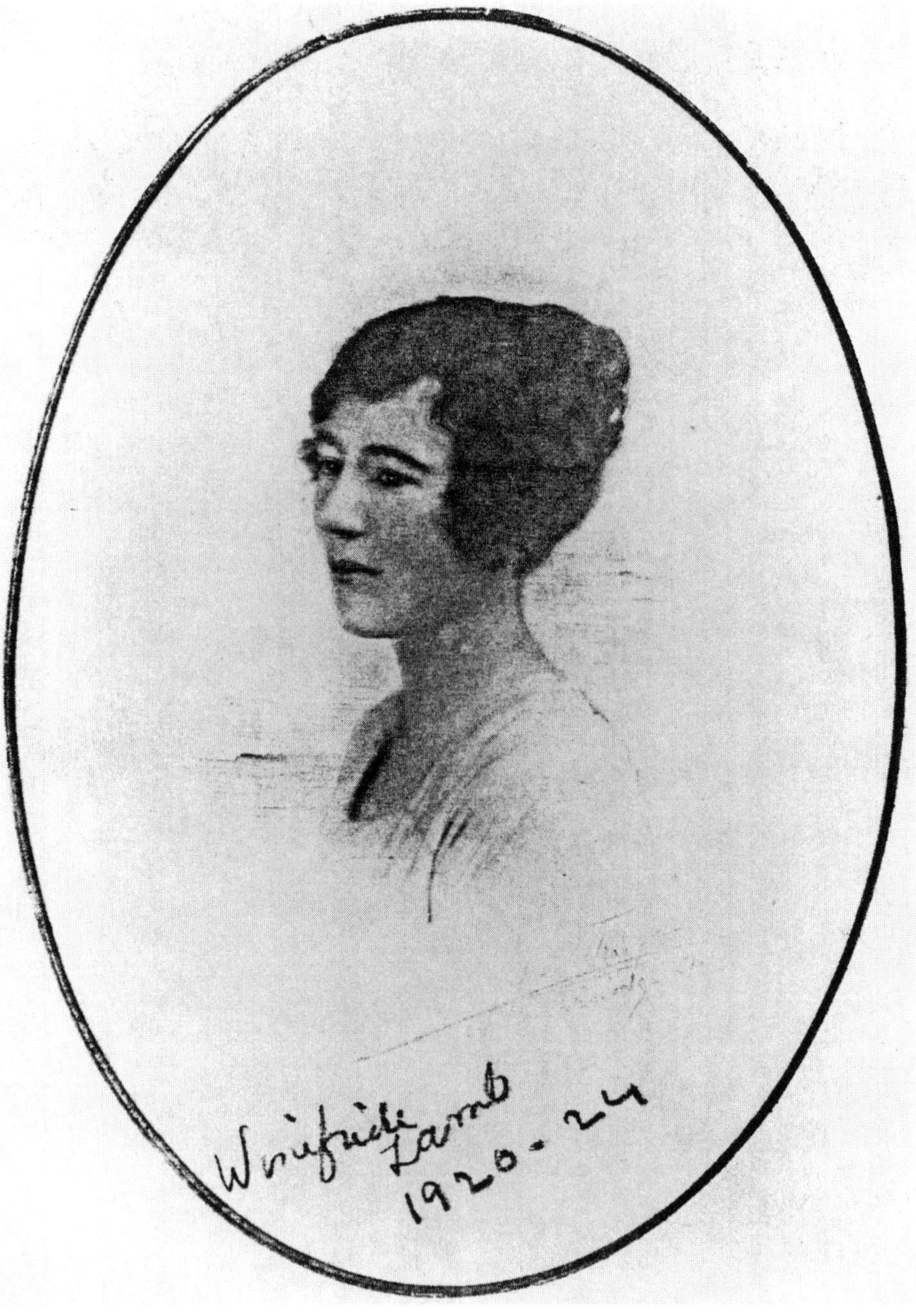

10.1. Winifred Lamb, Honorary Keeper of Antiquities. Photograph ca. 1920. (Courtesy of the British School at Athens.)

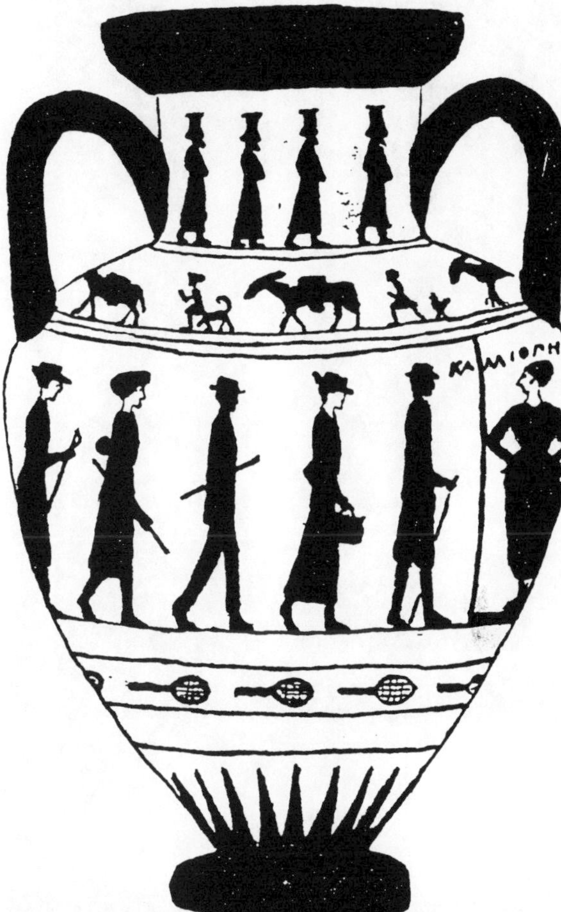

10.2. Drawing by Winifred Lamb, 1920, showing Kalliope, the housekeeper of the British School at Athens confronting, *right to left,* F. B. Welch, Mrs. Ashmole, Bernard Ashmole, Mary Herford, and Lilian Chandler. (Courtesy of the British School of Athens.)

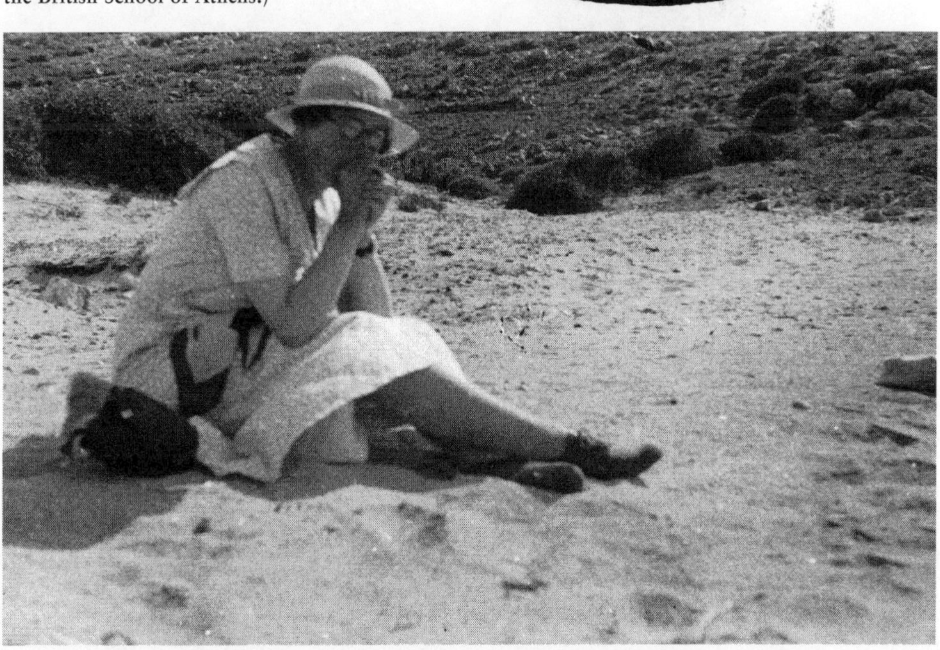

10.3. Winifred Lamb on Chios. (Photograph James Brock.)

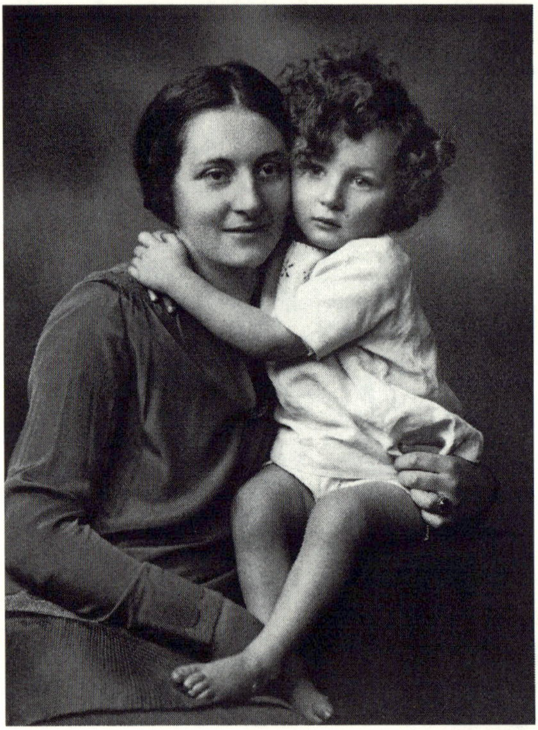

11.1. Theresa Goell with her son Jay Levinthal ca. 1927. (Theresa Goell Archives, Semitic Museum, Harvard University.)

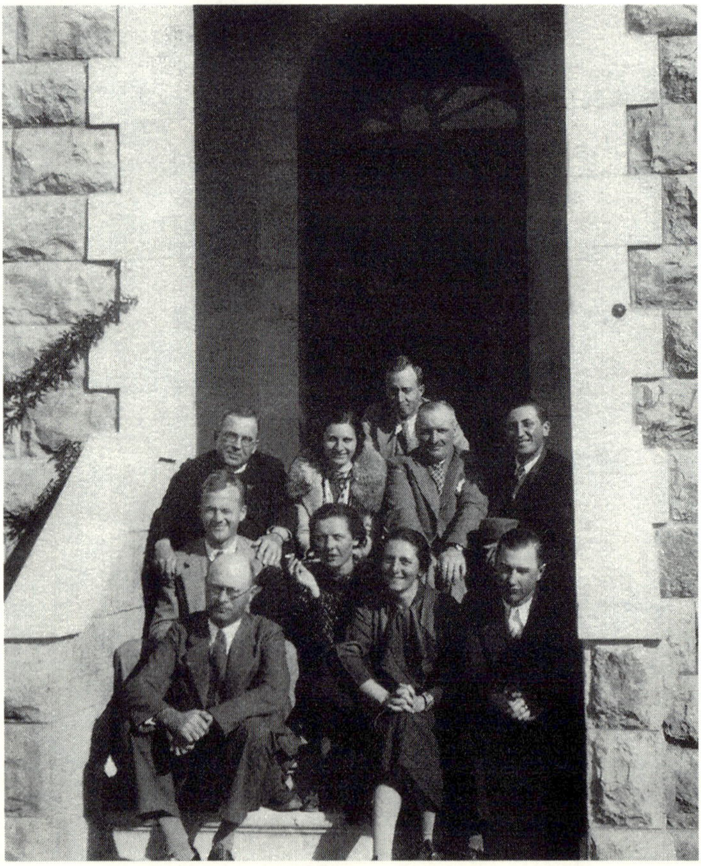

11.2. Theresa Goell, second from right in front row, with William Foxwell Albright, seated far left front row, and colleagues at the American School of Oriental Research in Jerusalem in the early 1930s. (Theresa Goell Archives, Semitic Museum, Harvard University.)

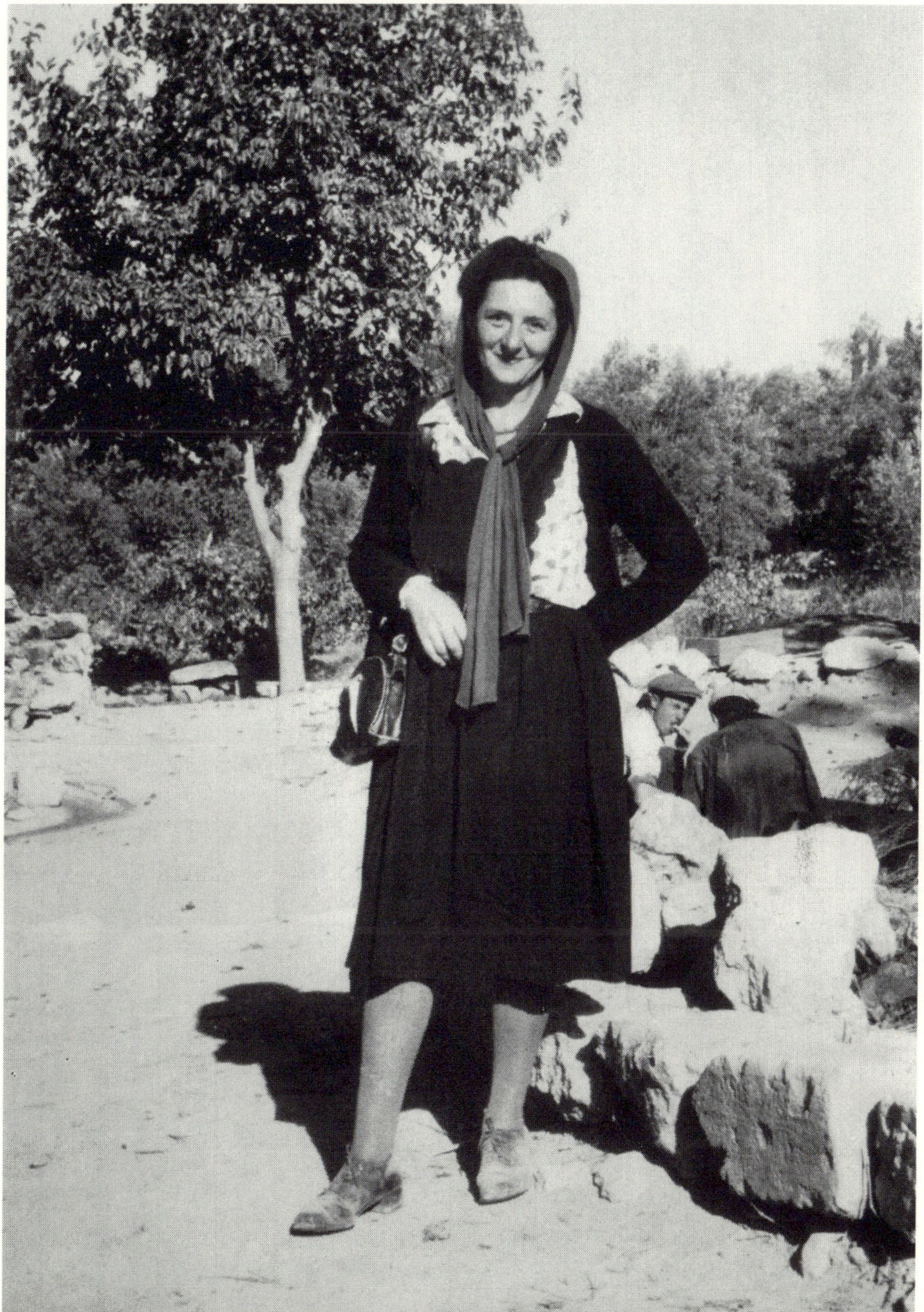

11.3. Theresa Goell at the Tarsus excavations directed by Hetty Goldman in 1947. (Theresa Goell Archives, The Semitic Museum, Harvard University.)

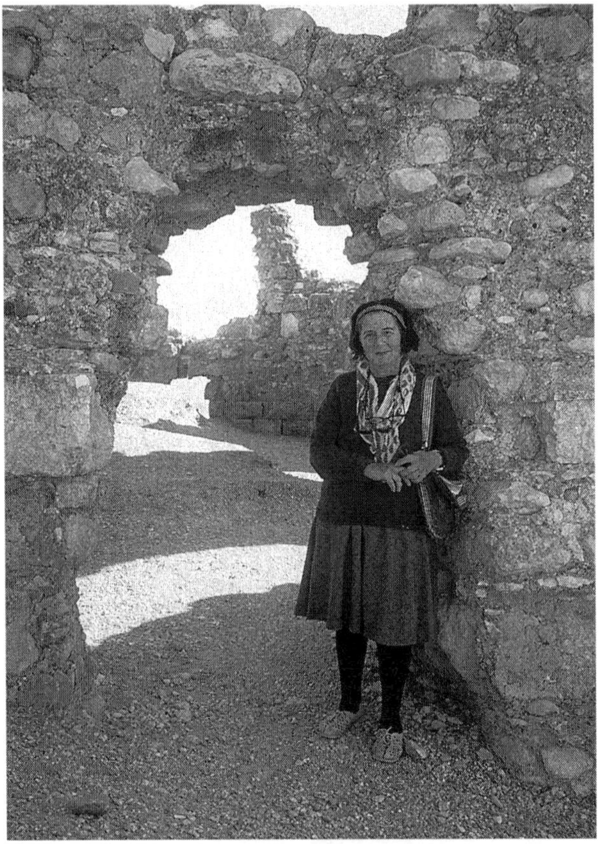

11.4. Theresa Goell at her excavations in Samosata, Turkey, 1970. (Courtesy of Jon Goell, Theresa Goell Archives, Semitic Museum, Harvard University.)

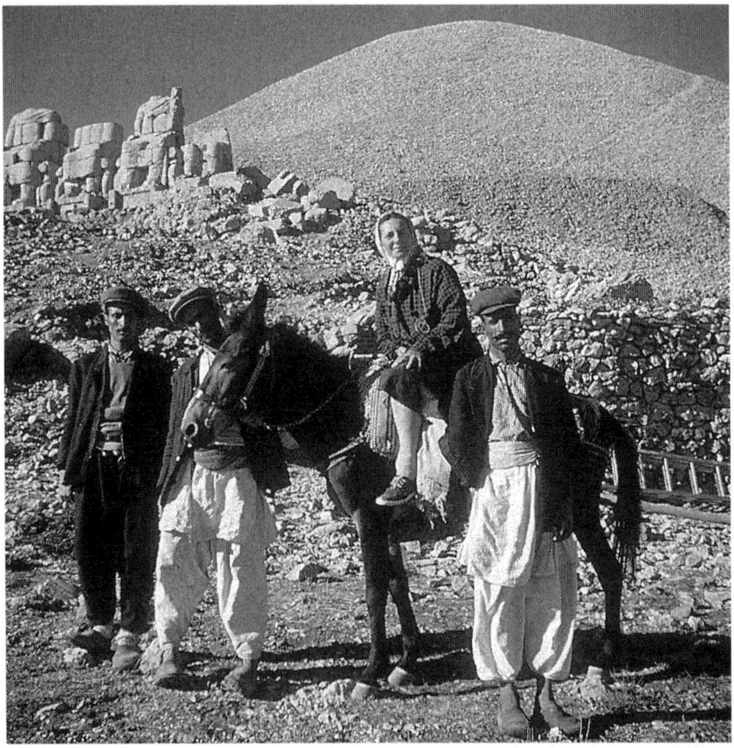

11.5. Theresa Goell with workers at the excavations of Nemrud Dagi, southeast Turkey, 1953. (Courtesy of Jon Goell, photograph by Kermit Goell, Theresa Goell Archives, Semitic Museum, Harvard University.)

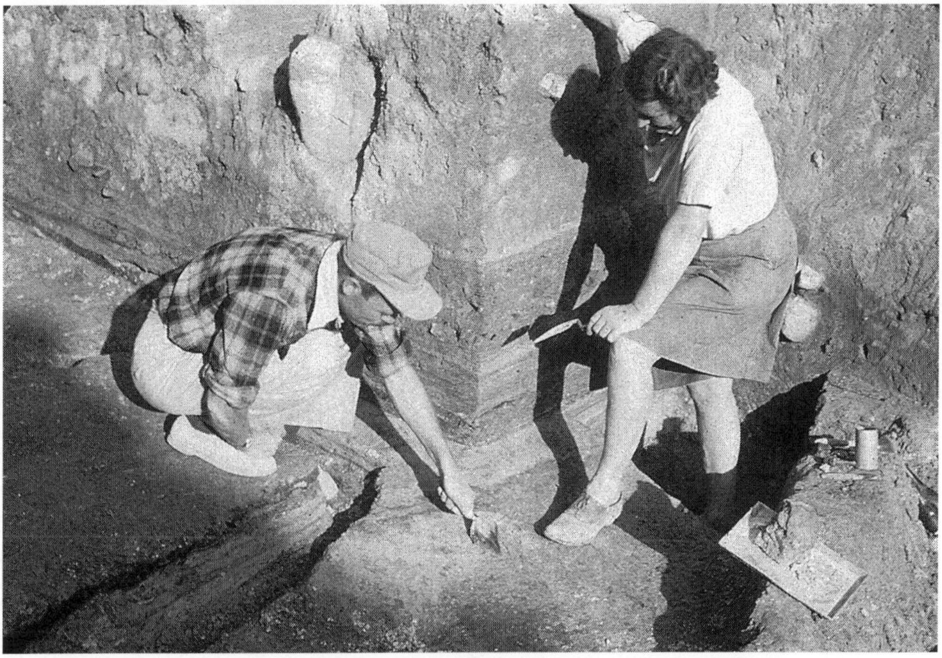

12.1. Kathleen M. Kenyon in the 1950s at Jericho. (Courtesy of the Kathleen M. Kenyon, Jericho-Jerusalem Archives, Institute of Archaeology, University College London.)

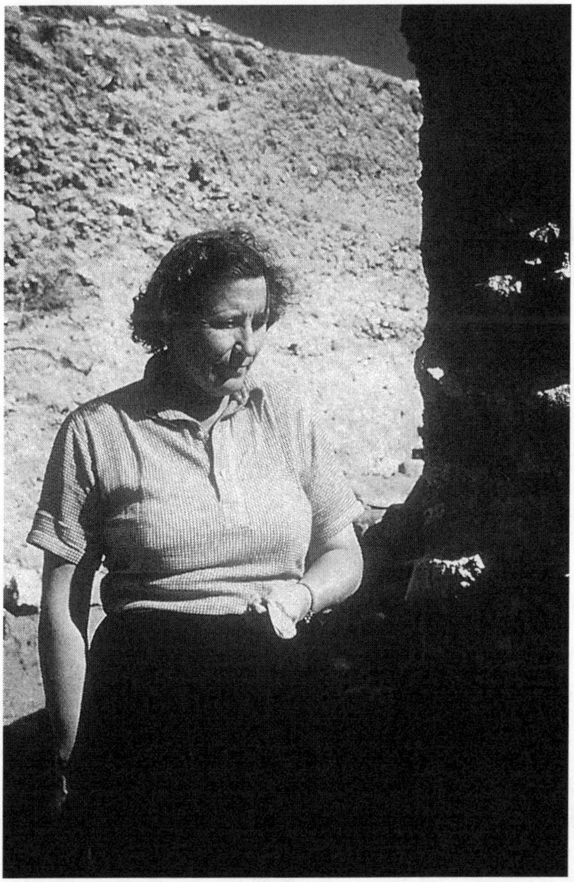

12.2. Kathleen M. Kenyon in the 1950s working at Jericho. (Courtesy of the Kathleen M. Kenyon, Jericho-Jerusalem Archives, Institute of Archaeology, University College London.)

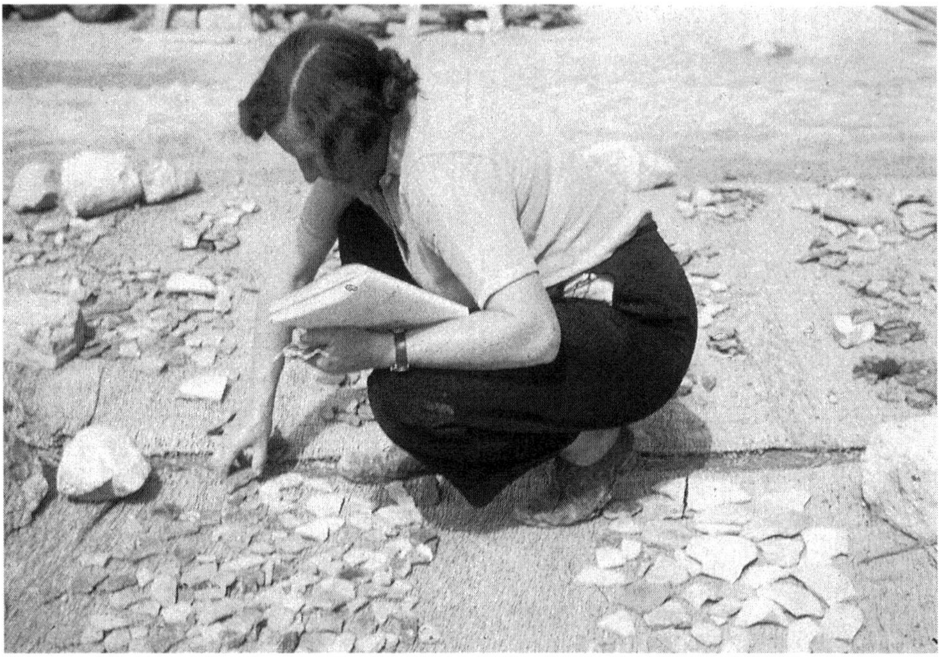

12.3. Kathleen M. Kenyon in the 1950s examining pottery at Jericho. (Courtesy of the Kathleen M. Kenyon, Jericho-Jerusalem Archives, Institute of Archaeology, University College London.)

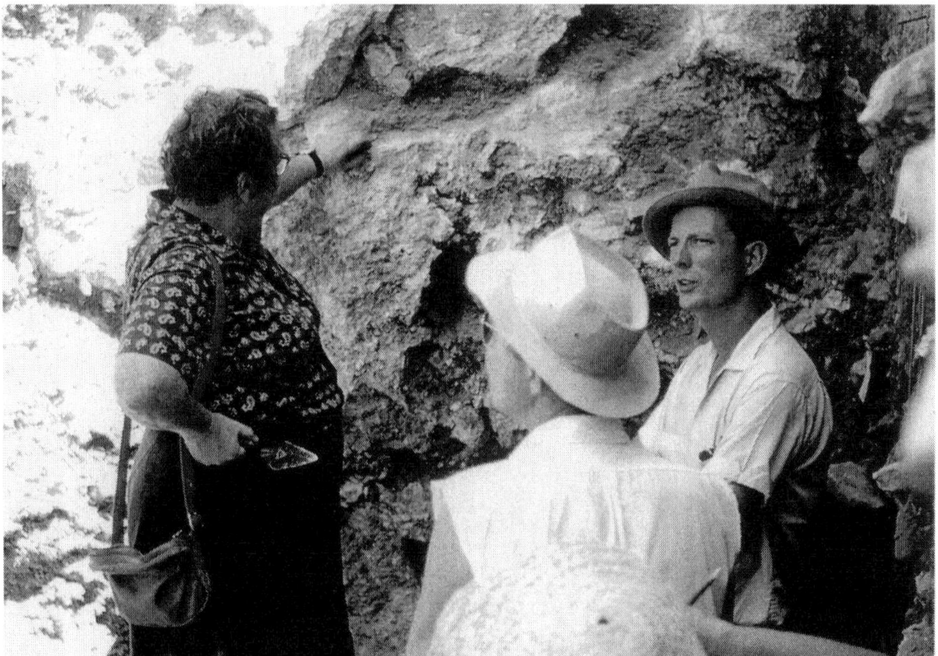

12.4. Kathleen M. Kenyon at Gezer, 1967, with William Dever. (Photograph by Robert B. Wright, courtesy of William Dever.)

1914–1926," Ph.D. diss., University of Virginia, 1968, 45, states: "The Bell family was of a Liberal turn of mind with Radical overtones . . . Lowthian Bell was a member of the Reform Club . . . Her [Gertrude's] family was wealthy, respected and unusually well educated."

24. *Letters,* 5, 428, 639, 664, 702.

25. Hugh Bell in *Geographical Journal* 70 (1927): 20; and see the memorial lecture given by David Hogarth, an account of Bell's "Journey to Hayil," published in *Geographical Journal* 70 (1927): 1–21.

26. Goodman, *Gertrude Bell,* 6–7.

27. On Florence Bell, see Courtney, *An Oxford Portrait Gallery,* 91–104; Linda Fitzsimmons and Viv Gardner, *New Woman's Plays: "Alan's Wife" (by) Florence Bell and Elizabeth Robins, "Diana of Dobson's" (by) Cicely Hamilton, "Chains" (by) Elizabeth Baker, "Rutherford and Son" (by) Githa Sowerby* (London, 1991), 3–5; Angela V. John, preface to Florence Bell, *At the Works: A Study of a Manufacturing Town* (London, 1985), ix–xxiii.

28. Because Bell always addressed her stepmother, half sisters, and half brother as "mother," "sister," and "brother" (in her letters usually prefaced with "dearest"), they will be referred to as such here.

29. *Earlier Letters,* 20, 30, 39–40, 69–71, 80–81, 85; cf. Dea Birkett, *Spinsters Abroad: Victorian Lady Explorers* (Oxford, 1989), 27–31.

30. *Letters,* 9; cf. Woolley, review of *Letters.*

31. *Earlier Letters,* 5.

32. *Letters,* 8, 10.

33. *Earlier Letters,* 44. For a list of books she read in one week, see *Earlier Letters,* 14–16; Goodman, *Gertrude Bell,* 7; Winstone, *Gertrude Bell,* 11–12.

34. *Earlier Letters,* 17; Goodman, *Gertrude Bell,* 8 (on Queen's College). See Sara Delamont, "The Contradiction in Ladies' Education," and "The Domestic Ideology and Women's Education," in *The Nineteenth-Century Woman: Her Cultural and Physical World,* ed. S. Delamont and L. Duffin (London, 1978), 134–74. On education, see Jane Mackay and Pat Thane, "The Englishwoman," in *Englishness: Politics and Culture, 1880–1920,* ed. R. C. Colls and P. Dodd (London, 1986), 191–229; Delamont, "Contradiction in Ladies' Education," 152–53, 174, 180–81. According to Delamont, the majority of female students came from the professional class. Even good schools strictly adhered to standards of ladylike comportment, and schools were often stricter than parents because attending school was still exceptional. It is not surprising, therefore, that Bell's letters to her stepmother quite often hint at quarrels concerning appropriate behavior and etiquette; cf. Joanna Trollope, *Britannia's Daughters: Women of the British Empire* (London, 1983), 24–29, on Bell's parents progressiveness; see also Sackville-West, introduction to *Persian Pictures,* 10–11.

35. *Earlier Letters,* 73; cf. Birkett, *Spinsters Abroad,* 9. Girton at Cambridge University, founded in 1869, was the first women's college in Britain. Bell felt a little guilty not having chosen Girton because Lady Stanley, mother of her uncle Lyulph, was one of its founders; cf. *Earlier Letters,* 2, 99–100; *The Autobiography of Bertrand Russell, 1872–1914* (London, 1967), 34.

36. *Earlier Letters,* 35, 38, 41–42, 54, 84.

37. *Letters,* 13; *Earlier Letters,* 54, 75–76.

38. *Earlier Letters,* 75–77, 89–89; cf. Goodman, *Gertrude Bell,* 10–12.

39. Courtney, *An Oxford Portrait Gallery,* 51–57. For her letters from Oxford, see *Earlier Letters,* 75–175.

40. *Earlier Letters,* 96–97 Delamont, "Contradiction in Ladies' Education," 145; cf. also *Earlier Letters,* 96–97, 112–13; Mackay and Thane, "The Englishwoman."

41. Delamont, "Contradiction in Ladies' Education," 159–60; cf. Goodman, *Gertrude Bell,* 10–12. The principal of Lady Margaret Hall, Elizabeth Wordsworth, was an extraordinary woman who was later knighted; cf. Courtney, *An Oxford Portrait Gallery,* 225–40; Courtney, *Women of My Time,* 25–30. Practically all of Bell's teachers from her history teacher at Queen's College in London to the archaeologist had been people of broad interests.

42. Courtney, *An Oxford Portrait Gallery,* 51–57.

43. F. Bell, in *Letters,* 4.

44. Hogarth, "Gertrude Lowthian Bell," 364.

45. Delamont, "Contradiction in Ladies' Education," 158; Goodman, *Gertrude Bell,* 12.

46. Courtney, *An Oxford Portrait Gallery,* 77; and see *Earlier Letters,* 88–89.

47. Trollope, *Britannia's Daughters,* 25–29.

48. For her activities from 1888 to 1889, see *Letters,* 4, 13–24; *Earlier Letters,* 11, 176–82. Because her mother was an authority on "manners," it is claimed that she was very strict with her daughters; cf. Lady Bell, "A Plea for the Better Teaching of Manners," *Nineteenth Century and After* 44 (1898): 281–95. But Bell was brought up in a relatively liberal environment given Victorian standards; she was allowed many exceptions to the rules, such as strolling alone with her cousin Horace, who also studied at Oxford. Nor was she punished when she went out unchaperoned with a man. Cf. also *Letters,* 15; *Earlier Letters,* 96–97, 217–18; Sackville-West, introduction to *Persian Pictures,* 4; Goodman, *Gertrude Bell,* 6. She was never pressured into marriage. The content of her letters from 1888 to 1892 is rather superficial, but her sister Elsa thinks that this period was "the last chapter of absolute happiness in Gertrude's life" (E. Richmond, in *Earlier Letters,* 215).

49. F. Bell, in *Letters,* 13, 29; Courtney, *An Oxford Portrait Gallery,* 57.

50. Wallach, *Desert Queen,* 25, with no corroborating references. Sources for this period (1886 to 1892) are primarily Bell's mother and Janet Courtney, who mentions Bell's "over-sureness" and that she was "conspicuous and animated, intensely vital, perfectly dressed and entirely self-possessed" (*An Oxford Portrait Gallery,* 55, 57).

51. F. Bell, in *Letters,* 31–32; Courtney, *An Oxford Portrait Gallery,* 51, 55, 84.

52. For new theories of formation of gender identity and its influence on personal development, see Sandra Lipsitz Bem, *The Lenses of Gender: Transforming the Debate on Sexual Inequality* (New Haven, 1993), 133–75.

53. *Letters,* 11; Courtney, *An Oxford Portrait Gallery,* 51; cf. Birkett, *Spinsters Abroad,* 27–28.

54. *Letters,* 15–16, dated July 5, 1889.

55. Delamont, "Contradictions in Ladies' Education," 146. Janet Courtney reports that the classical archaeologist Jane Harrison "took great pains about

clothes and in later life at Cambridge used 'to dress the part' when she lectured on Greek art" (*Women of My Time,* 72).

56. Courtney, *An Oxford Portrait Gallery,* 54, 77, 84.

57. Courtney, "Gertrude Bell," 657; Courtney, *An Oxford Portrait Gallery,* 57.

58. Frank Lascelles was the husband of Florence Bell's sister Mary; see "Lascelles, Frank (1841–1920)," in *Dictionary of National Biography, 1912–1921* (London, 1927), 323–24.

59. *Earlier Letters,* 181. Valentine Chirol, referred to by his nickname "Domnul," became Bell's most trusted friend; he had studied at the Sorbonne, traveled widely, became foreign editor at *The Times,* and wrote several books on political issues; see *Dictionary of National Biography, 1922–1930,* 182–83. For Bell's letters from Bucharest, see *Earlier Letters,* 176–215.

60. See the indices in *Letters, Earlier Letters,* Winstone, *Bell;* Wallach, *Desert Queen;* Courtney, *An Oxford Portrait Gallery,* 53–54.

61. Billy courted Gertrude Bell for some time, but she lost interest in him (*Earlier Letters,* 182, 215).

62. Ibid., 217–51.

63. Bell's love affair with Charles Doughty-Wylie was kept secret by her family and Doughty-Wylie's wife, who died in 1960. See Winstone, *Gertrude Bell,* ix–x, 118–25; Goodman, *Gertrude Bell,* 54–60, 65–68; Wallach, *Desert Queen,* 80, 96–98, 138–42. For Bell's relationship with Sir Kinahan Cornwallis, the British adviser to King Faisal, see Wallach, *Desert Queen,* 340, 351–56, 366–67; on Cornwallis, see *Dictionary of National Biography, 1951–1960* (Oxford, 1971), 257–58; Bruce Westrate, *The Arab Bureau: British Policy in the Middle East, 1916–1920* (University Park, Pa., 1992).

64. R. Bevis, *Bibliotheca Cisorientalia: An Annotated Checklist of Early English Travel Books on the Near and Middle East* (Boston, 1973); P. G. Adams, ed., *Travel Literature through the Ages: An Anthology* (New York, 1988); J. Shattock, "Travel Writing Victorian and Modern," in *The Art of Travel: Essays on Travel Writing,* ed. P. Dodd (London, 1982), 151–64; Anonymous, "From Kinglake to Lawrence," in *Times Literary Supplement,* no. 2691, August 28, 1953, xxxviii–xl.

65. Robin Fedden, *English Travellers in the Near East* (London, 1958); Rana Kabbani, *Europe's Myths of the Orient: Devise and Rule* (Basingstoke, 1986); Kathryn Tidrick, *Heart-Beguiling Araby: The English Romance with Arabia* (London, 1981, 1989). For overviews and analysis of women's travels, see Melman, *Women's Orient;* L. Hamalian, ed., *Ladies on the Loose: Women Travellers of the Eighteenth and Nineteenth Centuries* (New York, 1981); Dorothy Middleton, *Victorian Lady Travellers* (London, 1965); Annette Deeken and Monika Bösel, "An den süssen Wassern Asiens," in *Frauenreisen im Orient* (Frankfurt am Main, 1996), 14–16.

66. *Letters,* 24.

67. Ibid., 21; *Earlier Letters,* 244–45; Goodman, *Gertrude Bell,* 15.

68. Lyulph Stanley (later Lord Stanley of Alderley, Lord Sheffield) was married to Hugh Bell's sister Maisie; Lyulph's brother Henry had converted to Islam. Lyulph and Henry Stanley were uncles of Bertrand Russell, who remarks in his autobiography that his uncle Henry was "almost stone deaf" (34).

69. "Strong, Sanford Arthur (1863–1904)," in *Dictionary of National Biography,* 2d suppl., vol. 3 (London, 1912), 442–44. For E. Dennison Ross see *Letters,* 21, 39–40, 47. There is no evidence in *Letters* that Bell worked with Ross before 1898 (p. 47). Ross became professor of Persian at London University in 1896 and in 1916 was appointed director of the School of Oriental Studies; see "Ross, Sir (Edward) Dennison (1871–1940)," in *Dictionary of National Biography, 1931–1940* (London, 1949), 750–51.

70. Friedrich Rosen, *Oriental Memories of a German Diplomatist* (New York, 1930), 156–58, 273–77, 279–81.

71. Courtney, *An Oxford Portrait Gallery,* 60. Cadogan died of pneumonia after falling into a river; it remains unclear whether this was accidental or intentional. For Bell's letters from Persia, see *Letters,* 25–32; *Earlier Letters,* 252–342; cf. also Rosen, *Oriental Memories,* 156–61.

72. *Letters,* 24; E. Dennison Ross, preface to G. Bell, *Persian Pictures* (1928), 5; Sackville-West, introduction to *Persian Pictures,* 20–22; cf. review by D. W. F. in *Geographical Journal* 72 (1928): 283–84.

73. Ross, preface to *Persian Pictures;* Sackville-West, introduction to *Persian Pictures.* Throughout her life Bell shunned publicity; in addition to *Persian Pictures, The Arabs of Mesopotamia* (1918) and her article "Great Britain and Iraq" (1923) were published anonymously. To her mother she wrote, "I always throw all letters asking for an interview or a photograph straight into the waste paper basket and I beg you to do the same on my behalf" (*Letters,* 424); in another letter she describes a meeting with a distinguished Italian journalist, Mr. Cipola, who asked her "if he might photograph me for his paper. I said the best way in which he could express thanks was not to photograph or mention me and he dropped the idea" (quoted from Burgoyne, *Personal Papers,* 2:378).

74. Burgoyne, *Personal Papers,* 1:24–26; Winstone, *Gertrude Bell,* 37–38; Goodman, *Gertrude Bell,* 15–16, 21.

75. A. J. Arberry, afterword to G. Bell, *Persische Reisebilder* (Hamburg, 1949), 179.

76. On her literary talent and writing style, see Ross, preface to *Persian Pictures,* 7; Courtney, *An Oxford Portrait Gallery,* 61, 70–71, 73, 77; Graham-Brown, introduction to *Desert and the Sown,* viii; Hogarth, "Gertrude Lowthian Bell," 365; *Letters,* 31.

77. *Earlier Letters,* 73.

78. Ibid., 50, 217.

79. *Letters,* 32, 33.

80. She took up mountain climbing on a family holiday in the Dauphiné in April 1897. *Letters,* 46; *Earlier Letters,* 2–3; Winstone, *Gertrude Bell,* 66–73, 78–80; E. L. S[trutt], "In Memoriam," *Alpine Journal* 38, nos. 232, 233 (1926): 298–99; Hogarth, "Gertrude Lowthian Bell," 364.

81. Rosen, *Oriental Memories,* 273–77, 281. Rosen's recollections of Bell end with the following remarks: "I cannot repress the melancholy reflection that all the knowledge and experience of the East which she owed to a great extent to the aid of the Germans was afterwards employed against my country. I do not blame her for this, for her motive was love of her country, and she has tried, whenever she has been able, to help those of my countrymen, mostly orientalists and archaeologists,

at a time when the hatred of everything German was, so to speak, an article of the political creed of the great majority of the English." Actually, Bell acquired nearly all her knowledge of the Middle East after 1900 and, apart from a few archaeologists, Germans played a negligible role in her education, if we exclude books. Indeed, her feelings toward her former colleagues were more benign: she regretted that the war had broken friendships; see, e.g., *Letters,* 441.

82. *Letters,* 55–120; Burgoyne, *Personal Papers,* 1:82–94; Goodman, *Gertrude Bell,* 24–29; Winstone, *Gertrude Bell,* 53–65; Birkett, *Spinsters Abroad,* 52–54, 68, 117–18.

83. *Letters,* 30–31.

84. Ibid., 73–80.

85. For these excerpts from her travels to Petra, see ibid., 84–90.

86. Birkett (*Spinsters Abroad,* esp. 80, 11, 114–21, 137) demonstrates that this kind of travel allowed women unknown freedoms; see also Melman, *Women's Orients,* 7–8.

87. Cf. Dorothy F. Van Ess, "Pioneers in the Arab World (Gertrude Bell)," in *The Historical Series of Reformed Church in America,* no. 3 (Grand Rapids, Mich., 1974), 98; Heussler, "Imperial Lady," 15.

88. Courtney, "Gertrude Bell," 661; Courtney, *An Oxford Portrait Gallery,* 52, 85.

89. Burgoyne, *Personal Papers,* 1:112–32; Winstone, *Gertrude Bell,* 75–78.

90. *Letters,* 151–66; Burgoyne, *Personal Papers,* 1:137–83. According to Wallach, *Desert Queen,* 67, Bell met Cox on this trip; Cox himself gives a different story in *The Geographical Journal* 70 (1927): 17–18; cf. "Cox, Sir Percy Zachariah (1864–1937)," in *Dictionary of National Biography 1931–1940,* 196–99.

91. *Letters,* 155, 163.

92. Ibid., 174 (dated January 18, 1905).

93. See nn. 64 and 65; cf. Karl U. Syndram, "Der erfundene Orient in der europäischen Literatur vom 18. bis zum Beginn des 20. Jahrhunderts," in *Europa und der Orient 800–1900,* ed. G. Sievernich and H. Budde (Gütersloh, 1989), 324–41.

94. Fedden, *English Travellers,* 15–22.

95. Courtney, *An Oxford Portrait Gallery,* 82.

96. See bibliography in this article; for Bell's style, see n. 76.

97. Hogarth, "Gertrude Lowthian Bell," 365; Kaplan, *The Arabists,* 59–60.

98. *Letters,* 227–306; Burgoyne, *Personal Papers,* 1:239–78; Winstone, *Gertrude Bell,* 94–116;

99. Hogarth, "Gertrude Lowthian Bell," 366; cf. also Hogarth's "G. L. Bell, Amurath to Amurath (1911)," *Geographical Journal* 37 (1911): 435.

100. Melman, *Women's Orients,* 276–305, 321. By 1906 Blunt was divorced from her husband and lived in Cairo, where Bell visited her several times; cf. Burgoyne, *Personal Papers,* 1:235, 237, 2:30.

101. The Ottomans, who governed the Arabian peninsula from Baghdad, kept garrisons in the larger towns but could never control central Arabia. At the end of the nineteenth century the most powerful family were the al-Rashid of Ha'il, whose emir ruled as governor under Turkish authority. In 1902 Abdul Aziz Ibn Saud captured Riyad from the Rashids and expanded his control from Kuwait to Qatar. Wars among the various tribes lasted until 1915, when three leaders controlled most

of Arabia: Sharif Hussain in the Hajez (he controlled Mecca and Medina), Ibn Saud in Nejd with the capital Riyad, and Ibn Rashid in the Jebel Shamar, with the capital Ha'il, a caravan city at the crossing of the north to south and east to west routes. See Westrate, *The Arab Bureau,* 113–14.

102. Cf. Wallach, *Desert Queen,* 119. Her letters to Valentine Chirol and Charles Doughty-Wylie written during and after this journey contain signs of severe depression, partly triggered by her experiences during the journey.

103. Sa'ud, the ruling emir, was away fighting in the desert. His grandmother Fatima, who held the power, was rumored to have been involved in many of the recent murders.

104. Ibrahim, uncle of the emir, was officially in charge during his absence and feared Fatima.

105. The sixteen-year-old emir was the oldest male of his family after all his older brothers and paternal uncles had been murdered. Bell had intended to proceed from Ha'il further south to meet Ibn Saud but had to abandon her plan.

106. Quoted from Goodman, *Gertrude Bell,* 61.

107. Especially in her report of her most dangerous expedition, "A Journey in Northern Arabia," *Geographical Journal* 44 (1914): 76–77; cf. also Hogarth's "Journey to Hayil." Her "Hayil Diary, 1913–1914," in the University of Newcastle-upon-Tyne, was never published.

108. Excerpts of this diary were used and published in the biographies and studies written after 1961.

109. Quoted in Goodman, *Gertrude Bell,* 58.

110. Quoted in ibid., 62.

111. Cited by Winstone, *Gertrude Bell,* 144; Goodman, *Gertrude Bell,* 62–63; Wallach, *Desert Queen,* 128.

112. Courtney, *An Oxford Portrait Gallery,* 65–66, 82.

113. Van Ess, "Pioneers," 118.

114. *Letters,* 725; cf. also Burgoyne, *Personal Papers,* 2:368; Mallowan, "Last Years."

115. Goodman, *Gertrude Bell,* 44–53; Graham-Brown, introduction to *Desert and the Sown,* xiv; Mallowan, "Last Years"; Wallach, *Desert Queen,* 81–83.

116. E.g., Hogarth, "Gertrude Lowthian Bell," 363; Burgoyne, *Personal Papers,* 1:274, dedicates two sentences to the issue, claiming that Janet Courtney told her that Bell "much later was amused by her attitude"; cf. Courtney's brief mention in *An Oxford Portrait Gallery,* 86–87, and *Women of My Time,* 164. For accounts of Bell's life that omit her antisuffragist stand, see, e.g., Courtney, "Gertrude Bell"; Keay, *With Passport and Parasol;* Margaret E. Tabor, *Pioneer Women* (London, 1930); Marion Tinling, *Women into the Unknown: A Sourcebook on Women Explorers and Travellers* (New York, 1989), 39–46.

117. Winstone, *Gertrude Bell,* 110; unpublished letter to Max van Berchem, feuillets 89–90 in Max van Berchem Archive.

118. Courtney, *Women of My Time,* 173–74.

119. Goodman, *Gertrude Bell,* 44–53. In addition to Goodman, see two recent studies on the importance of Queen Victoria's different roles for the ideology of women: Alison Booth, "Illustrious Company: Victoria among Other Women in

Anglo-American Role Model Anthologies," and Sharon A. Weltman, "'Be No More Housewives, But Queens': Queen Victoria and Ruskin's Domestic Mythology," in *Remaking Queen Victoria,* ed. M. Homans and A. Munich (Cambridge, 1997), 59–78 and 105–22.

120. On "The New Women," see E. J. Hobsbawm, *The Age of Empire 1875–1914* (London, 1987), 192–218.

121. Birkett, *Spinsters Abroad,* 197–202.

122. Adelson, *Mark Sykes,* 108–9.

123. Cf. Cheryl Claassen, ed., *Women in Archaeology* (Philadelphia, 1994), 4–5, 41–43.

124. *Letters,* 609.

125. In a letter to Doughty-Wylie; cf. Wallach, *Desert Queen,* 119. The best analysis of Bell's work from 1915 to 1926 is still R. Heussler's "Imperial Lady"; cf. also Van Ess, "Pioneers."

126. For a recent analytical study of the Arab Bureau, see Westrate, *The Arab Bureau;* cf. also Winstone, *Gertrude Bell,* 162–64; Goodman, *Gertrude Bell,* 69–75; Tidrick, *Heart-Beguiling Araby,* 163–92.

127. For the people assigned to the Arab Bureau, see Westrate, *The Arab Bureau,* 39–53. The involvement of many archaeologists (including French and Germans) in intelligence work still haunts archaeologists today because in certain countries they are still looked upon with suspicion. T. E. Lawrence destroyed most of the letters he received; see Lawrence, *Selected Letters,* ed. Brown, xix; David Garnett, ed., *Selected Letters of T. E. Lawrence* (London, 1941); Thomas E. Lawrence, William G. Lawrence, and Frank H. Lawrence, *The Home Letters of T. E. Lawrence and His Brothers* (Oxford, 1954). He was with Hogarth and Bell at the Paris Peace Conference in 1919 and served as Winston Churchill's advisor at the Colonial Office from 1921 to 1923.

128. Westrate, *The Arab Bureau,* 11–38, 57–100.

129. Ibid., 84–85.

130. Ibid., 85.

131. Cox, in *The Geographical Journal* 70 (1927): 18; Cox, in *Letters,* 504–41. Cf. Westrate, *The Arab Bureau,* 86. Bell loved working for Cox and wrote home, "Sir Percy gives me a lot of thrilling things to do and is the kindest of chiefs" (*Letters,* 406); cf. also Philip Graves, *The Life of Sir Percy Cox* (London, 1941).

132. *Letters,* 406.

133. For the many books and articles on this theme, see the bibliographies of Wallach, *Desert Queen;* Tidrick, *Heart-Beguiling Araby;* Kaplan, *The Arabists;* Sarah Searight, *The British and the Middle East* (London, 1969); C. J. Edmonds, "Gertrude Bell in the Near and Middle East," *Journal of the Royal Central Asian Society* 56, no. 3 (1969): 229–44. See esp. Heussler, "Imperial Lady," and Van Ess, "Pioneers." For recent studies on Iraq, see Liora Lukitz, *Iraq: The Search for National Identity* (London, 1995), and on the Arab Bureau, Westrate, *The Arab Bureau* (1992). For a general history, see Bernard Lewis, *The Middle East: 2000 Years of History from the Rise of Christianity to the Present Day* (London, 1995), 338–48, and for an introduction to Iraq with many illustrations and quotations from Gertrude Bell, see Gavin Young, *Iraq: Land of Two Rivers* (London, 1980).

134. Quoted from Kaplan, *The Arabists,* 59.

135. See, e.g., Winstone, *Gertrude Bell,* 169ff.; Goodman, *Gertrude Bell,* 93–111; Graham-Brown, introduction to *Desert and the Sown;* cf. also Heussler, "Imperial Lady."

136. Winstone, *Gertrude Bell,* 191–92, 206–27, 262; Goodman, *Gertrude Bell,* 93–103; cf. John Marlowe, *Late Victorian: The Life of Sir Arnold Talbot Wilson* (London, 1967).

137. Goodman, *Gertrude Bell,* 98; Heussler, "Imperial Lady"; Marlowe, *Late Victorian.*

138. In Britain gender bias was more overt; when her white paper, "Review of the Civil Administration of Mesopotamia" (1920), was presented to Parliament, there was "a fandango about my report," and Bell remarks sarcastically that "the general line taken by the press seems to be that it's most remarkable that a dog should be able to stand on its hind legs—i.e., a female write a white paper. I hope they'll drop that source of wonder and pay attention to the report itself, it will help them understand what Mesopotamia is like" (*Letters,* 583–84; cf. also 461; Burgoyne, *Personal Papers,* 2:189–99).

139. *Letters,* 678. In nearly all official photographs she is the only woman participant.

140. This criticism is unfair because it concerns several military matters and weighs her opinion against that of men with military experience; cf. Heussler, "Imperial Lady."

141. Quoted from Graham-Brown, introduction to *Desert and the Sown,* xiii.

142. Quoted from Wallach, *Desert Queen,* 199. Storrs was Oriental Secretary to General (then Colonel) Clayton in Cairo when Bell worked there; see Westrate, *The Arab Bureau.*

143. Burgoyne, *Personal Papers,* 2:242.

144. *Letters,* 701.

145. She also worked on guides for Iraq and Baghdad; *Letters,* 682, 685, 687, 710, 718; Burgoyne, *Personal Papers,* 2:356.

146. In her letters from September 1923 onward she repeatedly mentions feeling depressed and lonely (*Letters,* 669–774, especially 735, 743–44, 747). Although it is well documented that Bell had depressions, she still appeared enthusiastic and vital; Mallowan, "Last Years"; Sackville-West, *Passenger to Teheran,* 57–62. Bell's tendency to severe mood swings may have been aggravated by symptoms of menopause. Also see Courtney, "Gertrude Bell," 662; Courtney, *An Oxford Portrait Gallery,* 86, Burgoyne, *Personal Papers,* 2:391–92.

147. *Letters,* 663; cf. also Courtney, "Gertrude Bell," 662.

148. Victoria Glendinning, *Vita: The Life of V. Sackville-West* (New York, 1983), 174.

149. The following men spoke at the memorial: Sir Percy Cox, Brigadier-General Sir Gilbert Clayton, Admiral Sir William Goodenough, and David G. Hogarth (*Geographical Journal* 70 [1927]: 17–21).

150. Nearly all her friends had left Baghdad. And she particularly missed a woman friend; cf. Wallach, *Desert Queen,* 369–71.

151. Burgoyne, *Personal Papers,* 1:84.

152. *Letters,* 245, 750. To Janet Courtney she said: "my natural desire is to slip

back into the comfortable arena of archaeology and history" (*An Oxford Portrait Gallery,* 86).

153. *Earlier Letters,* 159; Courtney, *An Oxford Portrait Gallery,* 3–16 (David Hogarth), 51–88 (Gertrude Bell).

154. F. G. Kenyon, "Hogarth, David George (1862–1927)," in *Dictionary of National Biography, 1922–1930,* 421–23; A. H. Sayce, "David George Hogarth," in *Proceedings of the British Academy* (1927), 379–83; C. R. L. Fletcher, "David George Hogarth," in *Geographical Journal* 71 (1928): 321–44; Richard D. Barnett, "Hogarth," *Reallexikon der Assyriologie* 4 (1972–75): 452–53.

155. *Letters,* 259.

156. Wilhelm Dörpfeld (1853–1940) was trained as an architect and sent to Olympia in 1877 to help develop better methods. Many German archaeologists emerged from the school he started, including Koldewey and Andrae. Dörpfeld became one of the most important excavators of his time; he excavated in Olympia, Athens, Tiryns, and together with Schliemann in Troy; cf. *Neue Deutsche Biographie* (Berlin, 1969), 35–36; Lothar Wickert, *Beiträge zur Geschichte des deutschen Archäologischen Instituts 1879–1929* (Mainz, 1979).

157. *Letters,* 49.

158. Bruce G. Trigger, *A History of Archaeological Thought* (Cambridge, 1989), 196–206.

159. Burgoyne, *Personal Papers,* 1:78–79, 109ff., 239; cf. Winstone, *Gertrude Bell,* 75–76.

160. *Letters,* 31, 57, 75–76, 108–9; Burgoyne, *Personal Papers,* 1:92.

161. Burgoyne, *Personal Papers,* 1:110 (March 1, 1902); cf. Winstone, *Gertrude Bell,* 75–76.

162. Burgoyne, *Personal Papers,* 1:110.

163. Winstone, *Gertrude Bell,* 75–76: "She spent several weeks with them (the Van Lenneps), . . . joining archaeological digs at a Byzantine tumulus and at the ancient Ionian city of Colophon where the shrine of Claros Apollos was unearthed." Stephen Hill, "Gertrude Bell," *Antiquity* 50 (1976): 190: "worked on excavations at the site of Colophon. Unfortunately, her notes and photographs for this expedition cannot be found." According to Wallach, *Desert Queen,* 61, "she joined an archaeological dig in Malta." But Bell only stayed a week in Malta, and Wallach (not an archaeologist) may have mistaken taking photographs, drawing plans, and making detailed descriptions of ruins for being engaged in a dig; cf. diary entries in Burgoyne, *Personal Papers,* 1:103.

164. Burgoyne, *Personal Papers,* 1:112–21.

165. For the 1902 tour in western Turkey see Burgoyne, *Personal Papers,* 1:104. Bell's library was given to the University of Newcastle; see Winifred C. Donkin, *Catalogue of the Gertrude Bell Collection in the Library of King's College Newcastle upon Tyne* (Newcastle upon Tyne, 1960). A partial impression of her reading material can be obtained from the bibliography in Winstone, *Gertrude Bell,* 293–312, where books from Bell's library are marked by an asterisk. There are, however, many books missing that are mentioned in her letters.

166. *Letters,* 150, August 13, 1902.

167. Wickert, *Beiträge,* 192; *Index Bibliographique Français* (London, 1993), fiche 881:337–42.

168. *Letters,* 172.

169. Ibid.

170. Ibid., 171–73; Burgoyne, *Personal Papers,* 1:234; Reinach, "Gertrude Bell," 265–67; Keay, *With Passport and Parasol,* 106–7; reviews of G. Bell in *Revue Archéologique,* 5th ser., 4 (1905): 431–32; 7 (1906): 219–20.

171. G. L. Bell, "Review of J. Strzygowski, *Mschatta.* Festschrift zur Eröffnung des Kaiser Friedrich-Museums. *Jahrbuch der königlich-preussichen Kunstsammlungen* (Berlin 1904)," *Revue Archéologique,* 4th ser., 5 (1905): 431–32.

172. *Letters,* 71.

173. G. L. Bell, *The Desert and the Sown* (London, 1907), 43–48.

174. Edwin Lachnit, "Strzygowski, Josef," in *The Dictionary of Art,* ed. J. Turner (London, 1996), 29:795–96. The Max van Berchem Archive contains several unpublished letters from Strzygowski, Herzfeld, and Bell that hint at the controversial and problematic nature of Strzygowski.

175. Hogarth, "Gertrude Lowthian Bell," 365; and *Letters,* 175–223.

176. *Letters,* 173, 208.

177. Ibid., 208.

178. Ibid., 197–99.

179. In the modern Turkish province of Karaman in south central Turkey (*Letters,* 220–22; Mark Whittow, "Binbirkilisse," in Turner, *The Dictionary of Art,* 4:66–67).

180. *Letters,* 220, dated May 13, 1905.

181. *Letters,* 223–24. For Sir William Ramsay (1851–1939), see *Dictionary of National Biography, 1931–1940,* 727–28.

182. *Letters,* 209–10.

183. In *Byzantinische Zeitschrift* 16 (1907): 378–81. Reviews of articles are rather exceptional.

184. Ibid., 381.

185. Unpublished letter to Max van Berchem dated November 20, probably 1910, feuillet 111 in Max van Berchem Archive.

186. *Letters,* 223–24, 239.

187. Cf. Whittow, "Binbirkilisse."

188. See review by Salomon Reinach, "W. Ramsay et G. L. Bell, *The Thousand and One Churches* (1909)," *Revue Archéologique,* 4th ser., 15 (1910): 200–201.

189. *Letters,* 232–51; Burgoyne, *Personal Papers,* 1:221–23, 243–45; Winstone, *Gertrude Bell,* 98–105; W. M. Ramsay and G. L. Bell, *The Thousand and One Churches* (London, 1909). The chronology and development of Byzantine architecture is still not very well known; see Hans Buchwald, "Early Christian and Byzantine Art: II. Architecture," in Turner, *The Dictionary of Art,* 9:527–28; Whittow, "Binbirkilisse," 4:67.

190. Bell, *Amurath to Amurath,* 300–317; Burgoyne, *Personal Papers,* 1:252–73; Winstone, *Gertrude Bell,* 106–16.

191. "The Mount of the Servants of God," *Blackwood Magazine* 189 (September 1910): 354–55.

192. M. Mundell Mango, "Tur 'Abdin," in Turner, *The Dictionary of Art,* 31:433–36. Called the Mount Athos of the Orient, Tûr 'Abdin has been the center of

Syrian Christians since the fourth century; its main city is Midyat in the border region of Iraq, Syria, and Turkey.

193. Oleg Grabar, "Berchem, Max van," in Turner, *The Dictionary of Art,* 3:757.

194. Ibid. According to Jonathan M. Bloom, van Berchem, who studied Islamic architecture and art in its historical context, initiated the idea of understanding Islamic art as a product of its culture ("Islamic Art and Architecture: Historiography," in Turner, *The Dictionary of Art,* 16:548).

195. The van Berchem–Bell correspondence covers approximately ten years from ca. 1908–9 to 1919 (Bell's letters usually give only the day and month, not the year); the last letter was written from Baghdad on November 21, 1919 (feuillets 163–64 in Max van Berchem Archive); on many letters Max van Berchem noted when he answered it or what he received or sent as publications, photographs, inscriptions, etc. The letters from Bell in the Max van Berchem Archive also contain references to her correspondence and meetings with other scholars. Her unpublished correspondence in Geneva and Newcastle-upon-Tyne includes letters to and from Ernst Herzfeld, Reinach, and Strzygowski and mentions meetings with Viollet, Millet, and Dieulafoy in Paris, as well as with Herzfeld and Sarre. She probably met van Berchem at the great Islamic art exhibition in Munich (May–October 1910), which was organized by Herzfeld and Sarre; cf. unpublished letter, feuillets 129–30 in Max van Berchem Archive; van Berchem visited her in London, probably in June 1912 (letters feuillets 151–54, 157–58 in Max van Berchem Archive).

196. Unpublished letter, feuillets 159–62 in Max van Berchem Archive.

197. Unpublished letter, feuillets 145–48 in Max van Berchem Archive.

198. *Amurath to Amurath,* 86, 88, 100, 131, 140–58; G. Bell, *Palace and Mosque at Ukhaidir* (Oxford, 1914), xi. Ukhaydir is the earliest known Abbasid palace (ca. A.D. 775), located in the desert ca. fifty kilometers west of Karbalā. L. Massignon had spent about an hour at Ukhaydir on March 31 and a day on April 3, 1908; see L. Massignon, "Notes sur le château d'al Okhaider," in *Comptes Rendus de l'Académie des Inscriptions et Belles-Lettres* (1909), 202–12; cf. K. A. C. Creswell, *Early Muslim Architecture: Umayyads, Early 'Abbasids, and Tulunids,* 2 vols. (Oxford, 1932–40), 2:50–100; Creswell considered Bell's plans "excellent" (2:52) but also remarks that the state of conservation had deteriorated between Bell's last visit in 1911 and his own in the 1930s (2:57 with n. 1).

199. *Journal of Hellenic Studies* 30 (1910): 339–68.

200. The German team researched Ukhaydir in October and December 1910; cf. Oskar Reuther, *Ocheïdir: Nach Aufnahmen von Mitgliedern der Babylon-Expedition der Deutschen Orientgesellschaft* (Leipzig, 1912); Reuther used information received by Bell (cf. p. 42 n. 2, p. 48 n. 1) but does not acknowledge this. Bell was the first to identify the mosque, which Reuther also does not acknowledge (cf. Reuther, 22–23). Compared with Reuther's study, Bell's *Palace and Mosque at Ukhaidir* (1914) is more comprehensive, with more than three times the text and many more illustrations.

201. Burgoyne, *Personal Papers,* 1:262–63.

202. Andrae, *Lebenserinnerungen eines Ausgräbers,* 174–75; Andrae and Boehmer, *Bilder eines Ausgräbers,* 34–37, 138–42.

203. In *Mitteilungen der Deutschen Orientgesellschaft* 42 (1909): 34; cf. Bell, *Amurath to Amurath,* 221ff.

204. Bell, *Amurath to Amurath,* 221ff.

205. Cf. Winstone, *Gertrude Bell,* 101–2.

206. Unpublished letter, feuillets 145–48 in Max van Berchem Archive. The Fondation Max van Berchem (Geneva) holds 177 of Bell's photographs; cf. Solange Ory, *Catalogue de la photothèque,* Archives Max van Berchem (Geneva, 1975); cf. M. van Berchem, "Note sur l'avancement du recueil des inscriptions Arabes en 1910–1911," in *Opera Minora,* vol. 1 (Geneva, 1978), 53ff., 57 (reference to Bell).

207. Cf. Winstone, *Gertrude Bell,* 101–2.

208. Winstone, *Woolley of Ur,* 33–34; W. D. Hogarth, "T. E. Lawrence and Gertrude Bell," in *Times Literary Supplement* no. 3153, August 3, 1962, 557; Lawrence, *Selected Letters,* ed. Garnett, 104, 106–7, 543, 556; Lawrence, *Selected Letters,* ed. Brown, 36–37; Lawrence, Lawrence, and Lawrence, *Home Letters,* 161–62.

209. *Letters,* 256 (dated September 13, 1909).

210. Claassen, *Women in Archaeology,* 5, remarks that "women . . . appear to have worked in virtual isolation from other women and even from more than one or two other professional archaeologists." Most women who dug in the Near East or the Mediterranean accompanied their husbands. To my knowledge there were just two women who directed excavations, both in Crete: Harriet Boyd Hawes in 1900 and Edith Hall in 1910. Both were Americans, younger than Gertrude Bell, and had Ph.D.'s, whereas Bell was denied a degree in 1888. Cf. also Diane. L. Bolger, "Ladies of the Expedition: Harriet Boyd Hawes and Edith Hall in Mediterranean Archaeology," in Claassen, *Women in Archaeology,* 44; Louise E. Lord, *A History of the American School of Classical Studies at Athens, 1882–1942* (Cambridge, Mass., 1947), 84, 94–95, 111; and biographies in this volume.

211. *Letters,* 259–61. Strong had died in 1904; cf. "Strong, Eugénie (1860–1943)," in *Dictionary of National Biography, 1941–1950* (Oxford, 1959), 848–49; Katherine A. Geffcken, "Esther van Deman and Gertrude Bell (1910)," in *Esther B. Van Deman: Images from the Archive of an American Archaeologist in Italy at the Turn of the Century,* ed. K. Einaudi (Rome, 1991), 24–27.

212. Geffcken, "Esther van Deman and Gertrude Bell." See also the biography of van Deman in this volume.

213. According to Creswell, Bell's work on Ukhaydir is "dispassionate," and her "only argument is the logic of facts, conveyed by means of beautiful literary expression" (*Early Muslim Architecture,* 1:2, 145–60).

214. Unpublished letter; probably written in 1911 or 1912, feuillets 145–48 in Max van Berchem Archive.

215. Cf. *Letters,* 222, 237, 239.

216. For example, her 1909 expedition along the ancient road from Aleppo to Urfa and across the middle Euphrates; she discovered Latin and Hittite inscriptions, tombs, sarcophagi, and reliefs, as well as a lion's head near Tell Ahmer, which prompted her to dig into the mound and uncover a large block with a relief depicting legs; cf. Bell, "The East Bank of the Euphrates from Tel Ahmar to Hit," *Geographical Journal* 36 (1910): 514–18; Bell's Hittite material is still used in scholarly

publications, e.g., J. D. Hawkins, *The Hieroglyphic Inscription of the Sacred Pool Complex at Hattusa,* Studien zu den Bogazköy-Texten, vol. 3 (Wiesbaden 1995); K. Kohlmeyer, "Felsbilder der hethitischen Grossreichszeit," in *Acta Praehistorica et Archaeologica* 15 (1983 Washington, D.C.); M. Wäfler, *Bibliographie der hieroglyphenluwischen Inschriften,* vol. 1, unpublished Habitilationschrift, Berlin.

217. Quoted from Burgoyne, *Personal Papers,* 1:246; cf. Winstone, *Gertrude Bell,* 103–4.

218. *Letters,* 232–51; Burgoyne, *Personal Papers,* 1:244–50.

219. Unpublished letter, feuillets 89–90 in Max van Berchem Archive; Bell admired van Berchem's work and wrote to him: "I have read Amida with care & I must write to congratulate you about it. It is the most remarkable book & adds greatly to our knowledge" (unpublished letter, feuillets 143–44).

220. G. Bell, *The Churches and Monasteries of the Tur 'Abdin,* with an introduction and notes by M. M. Mungo (London, 1982); cf. also Jean-Pascal Fourdrin, "Les églises à nef transversale d'Apamène et du Tûr 'Abdin," *Syria* 62 (1985): 319–35. Bell's work on Ukhaidir has been analyzed by Creswell, *Early Muslim Architecture.*

221. "It" apparently refers to the survey work she did for Ramsay. Burgoyne, *Personal Papers,* 1:245.

222. E.g., Goodman, *Gertrude Bell,* 43; Graham-Brown, introduction to *Desert and the Sown,* x.

223. Unpublished letters in the Robinson Library of the University of Newcastle.

224. Unpublished letter, June 9, possibly 1912, feuillets 120–21 in Max van Berchem Archive.

225. Bell, "Journey in Northern Arabia," 76.

226. Hill, "Gertrude Bell," 190–93; Mungo in Bell, *Tur 'Abdin.*

227. *Letters,* 440–41 (dated January 1, 1918).

228. R. Campbell Thompson, "The British Museum Excavations at Abu Shahrain in Mesopotamia in 1918," in *Archaeologia or Miscellaneous Tracts Relating to Antiquity,* Society of Antiquaries of London, vol. 70 (Oxford, 1918–20), 101–41; H. R. Hall, *A Season's Work at Ur. Al-'Ubaid, Abu Shahrain (Eridu), and Elsewhere. Being an Unofficial Account of the British Museum Archaeological Mission to Babylonia, 1919* (London 1930), vii–viii; Seton Lloyd, *Foundations in the Dust: The Story of Mesopotamian Exploration,* rev. ed. (London, 1980), 180.

229. H. R. Hall, "The British Museum Archaeological Mission in Mesopotamia, 1919," *Journal of the Central Asian Society* 9–10 (1922–23): 119–26; Hall, *Season's Work at Ur,* vii–x, 9, 19, 49–51, 54, 59.

230. Hall, *Season's Work at Ur,* 19.

231. Cf. *Letters,* 645, 652–55. At King Faisal's request the cabinet appointed Bell director of antiquities on October 24, 1922; as her first duty on November 1, 1922, she had to defend the Law of Antiquities to the cabinet.

232. *Letters,* 664–67, 673–75, 679–81, 683, 686, 687, 690–92, 694, 697, 707–8, 711, 724–27, 742, 747, 748, 754–55, 759–65, 767–69, 771, 772; Burgoyne, *Personal Papers,* 2:290, 302, 311–12, 316, 325–26, 333, 335–37; Brian M. Fagan, *Return to Babylon: Travellers, Archaeologists, and Monuments in Mesopotamia* (Boston, 1979),

241–53; Fagan, "Bell of Baghdad," *Archaeology* 44, no. 4 (1991): 12–15; Lloyd, *Foundations in the Dust,* 177–81; Nicholas Postgate, *The First Empires* (Oxford, 1977), 55; Winstone, *Woolley of Ur,* 119–20, 122, 124–25, 128–29, 135; Mallowan, "Last Years"; Hill, "Gertrude Bell."

233. Cf. *Desert and the Sown,* 24, 55.

234. From March 1924 her letters home contain many references to her visiting excavation sites and dividing the finds: *Letters,* 686ff., esp. 690–91 (Kish), 730 (Nuzi), 754–55 (statue of the goddess Bau [Baba] from Ur); cf. Lloyd, *Foundations in the Dust,* 181–82. Also see *Letters,* 679–81, 708 (Ubaid); Winstone, *Woolley of Ur,* 125; Postgate, *The First Empires,* 48.

235. *Letters,* 686–87.

236. Ibid., 687, 707–8.

237. Ibid., 645, 654–55; Svend Aage Pallis, *The Antiquity of Iraq: A Handbook of Assyriology* (Copenhagen, 1956), 278–81.

238. *Letters,* 681.

239. Ibid., 683.

240. Pallis, *Antiquity of Iraq,* 368–71; cf. also her report on the inauguration of the American School of Archaeology in Baghdad in 1923 (*Letters,* 674).

241. Cf. *Letters,* 645, 664, 681, 787, 790; Winstone, *Woolley of Ur,* 115–16; P. R. S. Moorey, *Kish Excavations, 1923–1933* (Oxford, 1978), 13–16; McGuire Gibson, *The City and Area of Kish: Field Research Projects* (Miami, Fla., 1972), vii–viii.

242. *Letters,* 730. Edward Chiera, "Report of the Professor in Charge of the School in Baghdad," *Bulletin of the American School of Oriental Research* 20 (1915): 21–25.

243. Martha A. Morrison, "Nuzi," in *The Anchor Bible Dictionary,* ed. David N. Freedman, vol. 4 (New York, 1992), 1156–62.

244. *Letters,* 765.

245. J. M. Wilson also supervised the preservation work at Babylon and Ctesiphon and did work for King Faisal; he left in autumn 1925; cf. *Letters,* 773; Hall, *Season's Work at Ur,* x, 52, 57.

246. Winstone, *Woolley of Ur,* 128.

247. *Letters,* 749.

248. *Letters,* 750, 755–56, 761–62, 766–68, 721–34; Mallowan, "Last Years."

249. Mallowan, "Last Years," 83; cf. also *Letters,* 766, 768–69, 771–72. Walter Andrae was the principal force behind the Vorderasiatische Museum in Berlin, which at that time was regarded as a model for displaying Near Eastern antiquities.

250. *Letters,* 694, 696, 697, 772; cf. Mallowan, "Last Years."

251. *Letters,* 764–65; cf. Burgoyne, *Personal Papers,* 2:389.

252. *Letters,* 687, 691, 725.

253. Andrae and Boehmer, *Bilder eines Ausgräbers,* 33–34.

254. *Letters,* 269–70, 690, 725.

255. Cf. Mallowan, "Last Years"; Fagan, *Return to Babylon,* 241–53; Hill, "Gertrude Bell."

256. *Letters,* 773.

257. *Letters,* 750; cf. also 455.

258. Courtney, *An Oxford Portrait Gallery,* 86; Graham-Brown, introduction to *Desert and the Sown,* xv.

259. Seton Lloyd, "Excavating the Land between the Two Rivers," in *Civilizations of the Ancient Near East,* ed. J. M. Sasson, vol. 4 (New York, 1995), 2732. For a photograph, see Burgoyne, *Personal Papers,* facing 2:337.

260. Michael Roaf, personal communication. According to Prof. Roaf the British ambassador to Iraq, Terence Clarke, and the archaeologist John Curtis were organizing the restoration of Bell's grave just before Saddam Hussein invaded Kuwait; the restoration had not yet begun.

Harriet Boyd Hawes

(1871–1945)

Vasso Fotou and Ann Brown

HARRIET BOYD HAWES'S DUAL ROLE as a scholar and humanitarian sets her apart from many of her peers. Her activities were not confined to archaeology. Her strong character, selfless courage, and natural compassion, reinforced by her commitment to Christian beliefs, found expression and fulfilment in humanitarian work. She nursed the wounded in three wars. She championed social causes raising funds for refugees and lobbying for justice for the downtrodden. Further, her generous spirit extended to political action and social reform.

Boyd's scholarly work embraced two fields at different times in her life. Her early years in archaeology were devoted to active excavation. At a time when opposition to women's participation in fieldwork was the prevailing attitude in archaeological institutions, she proved that a woman could lead an excavation successfully, make important discoveries, and maintain a good record of publication. She was to turn to theoretical archaeology after retiring from fieldwork and raising a family. Little is known of this later work since almost all is unpublished. Her fame and contribution to archaeology have always been measured by her Cretan discoveries.

The First Years (1871–96)

Harriet Ann Boyd was born in Boston on October 11, 1871, the fifth and last child of Alexander Boyd, a businessman of Scottish-Irish descent, and Harriet Wheeler Boyd (née Harriet Fay Wheeler) of English Colonial stock. Her mother died when Boyd was ten months old, and her father raised her, along with her four brothers, James, Alexander, Harry, and Allen. Her father never remarried and, as Boyd later wrote, although "The loss [of our mother] clouded our lives . . . his constancy gave a touch of splendor to our home."[1] Living in an all-male environment reinforced Boyd's natural independence and determination. It is little wonder that in later life she did not conform to convention. In the absence of their mother a strong bond grew up among the children. With her youngest brother, Allen, four years her senior, she played "soldiers" and "politics."[2] These games kindled Boyd's interest and prepared her for nursing two generations of soldiers in three wars. Her second brother, Alex, "the leader, disciplined and inspired," was her idol, dearly loved.[3] Although only eleven years older, he seems to have replaced her mother.[4] He graduated with honors in history from Harvard (1882), admired classical art, and was a devout Christian whose beliefs and interests became her own. Nine months after Alex's premature death she changed from the Unitarian to the Episcopal Church and found "great happiness" in being confirmed by Bishop Brooks, her brother's ideal of a Christian preacher, whose teachings came to have a profound influence on her.[5] It was Alex who planted the first seeds of her love for the Hellenic world and introduced her to the classics.[6]

Harriet Boyd spent the first year of her secondary education at a boarding school in Morristown, New Jersey, then attended Prospect Hill School (Stoneleigh-Burnham), in Greenfield, Massachusetts.[7] To her delight she was able to study classics. One of her classmates, Jean Patten, became a lifelong friend and accompanied her to Crete in 1900.[8] After receiving her diploma from Prospect Hill in June 1888, Boyd entered Smith College, in Northampton, Massachusetts.[9] She followed classics, concentrating in particular on Greek. Archaeology was not an option, but a lecture by the British Egyptologist Amelia B. Edwards gave Boyd her first glimpse into this discipline.[10] During her college years she made two particular friends: an artist and social worker, Adelene Moffat, eleven years her senior, who later drew pottery from Boyd's excavations, and a fellow student, Blanche E. Wheeler, who joined her in Crete in 1901 and shared in the discovery of Gournia. Saddened by the death of her brother Alex on August 26, 1891, Boyd nevertheless graduated in June 1892.[11]

Although she inherited her brother's estate, Boyd was determined to use her degree to support herself. For the next four academic years she taught ancient and modern languages, first in Henderson, North Carolina (1892–93), and then in Wilmington, Delaware (1893–96).[12] In Wilmington she enjoyed the school, but started thinking of further study to go on to college teaching. Upon enquiring, she learned of the American School of Classical Studies at Athens. In her third year in Wilmington the illness of her father and his death on April 4, 1896, proved a turning point. She soon resolved that now was the time to pursue her plans for further studies.[13]

In June 1896, still undecided between history and classics, England or Greece, she set off to tour Europe.[14] On the steamer her chance acquaintance with the brother of the archaeologist Louis Dyer ultimately determined her future. He argued, "Why go to England and study Homer and Plato under dull, grey skies, when Greece is there to teach you more than you can ever learn in books?" Boyd recalled Amelia Edwards' lecture—the fascination and reassurance she felt from her experience working in the field. By the end of her travels she had decided to study classics at the American School of Classical Studies at Athens.[15]

The First Year in Greece (1896–97)

On October 8, 1896, Boyd had her "first sight [of] Greece, sailing betw. Laconia & Cythera. Land Piraeus."[16] The next day she called at the American School and eagerly started exploring Athens and its monuments on her bicycle. This immediately won her the title of "Famous Bicyclist," under which a national newspaper reported: "From Europe arrived yesterday the famous American bicyclist Miss Boyd, and she stayed at the hotel 'Grande Bretagne.'" Her stylish life at this prestigious hotel only lasted a few days.[17] She soon accepted the invitation of Aikaterini McCraith, a chance acquaintance from her trip to Greece, and moved into her home, a large mansion close to the palace in the center of Athens. There she stayed as a paying guest for the rest of the year.[18] Aikaterini, who was married to James McCraith, an Irish doctor, came from the prominent Greek family of Damala, which had built up a fortune from commerce and shipping. Her mother had been maid of honor to Queen Amalia, and she herself entertained politicians, diplomats, journalists, officers, and wealthy businessmen. At her home Boyd was introduced to the Athenian upper class and heard firsthand accounts of the important political events of 1897. This was a great chance for Boyd and she was the first to acknowledge the influence her acquaintance to Mrs. McCraith had on her life.[19]

At the school that year the two women among nine students, Boyd and Anna L. Perry of Cornell University,[20] were barely tolerated—occasionally excluded from field trips and always from excavations. The school's program combined lectures with field trips, usually led by the director, Rufus B. Richardson, but, exceptionally, for this year by the visiting professor, J. R. Sitlington Sterrett of Amherst College.[21] Boyd joined the two long field trips led by Professor Sterrett, who considered such trips an important part of the course (specifically in relation to the topography and remains of sites), in contrast to Richardson, who seemed to take a more touristic than scholarly interest in them.[22] These trips were the best introduction Boyd could have to Greece and to prehistoric sites, suiting her preference for field rather than library research.

The first trip, beginning October 13, was a five-day tour of Argolid during which two major prehistoric sites, Tiryns and Mycenae, were closely investigated.[23] A second trip, at the end of October, took Boyd to Delphi and to Boeotia. She visited sites already excavated, such as Plataea and the shattered remains of the colossal stone lion at Chaeronea, as well as towns and sites known from ancient Greek texts but still unexcavated. On November 1 the party climbed Mt. Helicon. Professor Sterrett, knowing that this was the first time non-Greek women had climbed the mountain, wrote, "The women members of the School took part in all these tours and ascended Helicon with the rest of us; their pluck and courage deserve high praise." From Boeotia they crossed to Euboea to see the American School's excavation at Eretria before sailing to Piraeus.[24] By February 1897, long field trips of all the schools had been suspended because of the impending political crisis created by the situation in Crete and on the northern frontier.[25] To make up for the cancellation of trips in the rest of Greece, the school organized tours by bicycle in Attica. One such tour ended with a visit to Marathon, its past glory having been revived with the inauguration of the modern Olympic Games a year earlier. The students retraced the great battle—a favorite exercise of Boyd, reminiscent of her childhood games with her brother Allen.[26]

Boyd attended Richardson's classes at the museum and at the archaeological sites in Athens and Wilhelm Dörpfeld's Saturday lectures on the

Acropolis Museum and Athens topography. She also went to Professor Sterrett's lectures on epigraphy.[27] But her interest was not confined to her work at the American School. Anxious to be involved in Greek life, she started lessons in modern Greek, at first with a tutor at home and later at the all-girls school, Arsakeion, where the students translated ancient Greek texts into modern Greek.[28]

By 1897, the political situation in Greece had started to escalate, gradually distracting Boyd from academic work. Macedonia and Epirus on the mainland, and Crete, where the population was predominantly Greek, deeply resented Turkish rule, and the desire for union with Greece was strong. In February the Greek army landed near Hania to support the uprising of the Christian Cretans and claim the island in the name of King George of the Hellenes. The impact on Athens of events in Crete was dramatic, and Boyd listened to passionate debates in Parliament.[29] In March she started first-aid classes, run daily by Dr. Maria Kalopothakis on behalf of the Union of Greek Women. Her aim was to volunteer as a nurse in case of war, but her hope of becoming a Red Cross nurse evaporated after a poor performance at the final test. Disappointed, she tried to catch up with exam work for the 1897–98 American School fellowships. However, in April, the outbreak of the Greco-Turkish War on the northern frontier put an end to her studies. After an appeal to the queen, she was allowed to join the first group of Red Cross nurses chosen to leave for the front.[30] This was the first of the humanitarian activities that went hand in hand with her archaeological work for the rest of her life.

Boyd's first task was to organize a new hospital in a schoolhouse at Volos, where she served until forced by the Turkish invasion to flee with the wounded troops on a ship converted to hospital, bound for Piraeus. During these difficult times Boyd made an influential friend, Sophie A. Baltazzi, a Greek from Constantinople, who managed to reach the Greek side and join the Red Cross nurses. In 1901 Baltazzi became private secretary and maid of honor to Queen Olga; her friendship with Boyd never faded.[31] Soon the two women returned to the front at Domokos where, on May 5/17, they witnessed the greatest battle of the war and joined in the subsequent retreat of the Greek army to Lamia, and thence to Athens.[32] According to her memoirs of the war:

> Doubtless there were people in Athens in that later part of May when truce had been declared, resumed at once the interests and occupations that had been interrupted by the war. The fellowship examinations of the American Archaeological School were held at

> the appointed time; the students continued to ponder over vases and inscriptions. The past was not less rich because the present was poorer, and the crop of college degrees that grows on the stony soil of Greek ruins would flourish even if the grapes and olives failed. The Acropolis rising above the city against the perfect blue of the Attic sky seemed nobler and grander to me than ever before, a glory that the Turks could not take away from this poor land but my feet led me as if bewitched not to libraries and museums but still to hospitals.[33]

Boyd spent only three days nursing in Athens before leaving with Miss Baltazzi for Vonitsa on the western front, where help was greatly needed after the Turks blockaded the entrance to the Ambracian Gulf. When the blockade was lifted, the two friends went back to Lamia, where they nursed victims of the typhoid epidemic that had broken out in the Greek army. Boyd's nursing ended with a pilgrimage to the ancient battlefield of Thermopylae. After a few days in Athens she left for America on September 3.[34]

In the report of the director of the American School for 1896–97, Boyd is mentioned in relation not to her studies or to specific research but only to her war work.[35] She had embraced selflessly the Greek cause, driven by both a "natural desire to relieve . . . suffering"[36] and a romantic view of the Greeks fostered by her brother Alex and her study of classics. As a fellow archaeologist put it, "Miss Boyd . . . [is] an idealist who thinks all Greeks Pericles!!!"[37] This love and devotion endeared her greatly to the Greek people. She was to receive a letter of commendation from the Greek Society of the Red Cross and the Red Cross medal from Queen Olga.[38] Her classes in nursing and her work at the front brought her into contact with Athenian women of high society: Mme. Schliemann and Miss Sophie Baltazzi; Mrs. Rallys, Mrs. Cassavetti and Dr. Kalopothakis, who were in charge of the hospitals at the front; and, above all, the queen. Both her exceptional devotion to the Greek cause and her newfound friends were the best credentials Boyd could have when, three years later, she applied for a permit to pursue archaeological research in Crete.

The Fellowship Years (1897–1900)

Boyd spent the academic year 1897–98 in America mainly studying for a fellowship examination which, the previous year, she had dropped in favor of nursing with the Red Cross.[39] Two fellowships, each carrying a stipend of six hundred dollars, were available for study at the American School in

Athens. The Archaeological Institute of America offered one, and the American School offered the other. Successful candidates were chosen according to the results of the written examination (which covered subjects on Mycenaean art, Greek art, archaeology, and epigraphy) and to "other evidence of ability and attainments."[40] In Boyd's case, the chairman of the Managing Committee of the school, T. D. Seymour, spelled out such evidence, when he praised her war efforts in his annual report.[41] Early in July she heard that she had been awarded the fellowship of the Archaeological Institute, but at the same time the outbreak of the Spanish-American War over Cuba called for action. Again she gave precedence to the Red Cross and left for Florida. But the war was short-lived, and so she was able to take up her fellowship.[42]

On September 10 Boyd sailed from New York with two friends, Blanche E. Wheeler, her contemporary from Smith who was to be a student at the American School in Rome during 1898–99, and Mary K. Waring, known to her friends as Mame. On September 30, they reached Athens.[43] Boyd found the political climate much changed. Peace and calm had returned, and there was confidence in the future. The peaceful atmosphere meant that all Boyd's energy could be channeled into her studies. Her appointment as a fellow of the Archaeological Institute of America began a promising new period for her at the school. The chairman and the director of the school acknowledged the "unsought distinction" she had won by her service in the war.[44] Although it did not win her any direct concessions from the director, who was prejudiced against women members,[45] it did improve her status.

In the year 1898–99 the number of women (four out of fifteen), as well as the total number of students enrolled, was the largest so far. More importantly, women held two of the school's three fellowships—Boyd and May Louise Nichols, also from Smith.[46] Also for the first time one of the three faculty members, the annual professor, was a woman, Angie C. Chapin, professor of Greek at Wellesley College.[47] The course as usual combined lectures and field trips. Richardson's lectures in the museums started with the Mycenaean collection.[48] His main topic was sculpture, supplemented by Chapin's lectures on the grave reliefs. Chapin also lectured on epitaphs in addition to the main lectures on epigraphy given by Alfred Emerson of Cornell University and the subsequent ones by Wilhelm of the Austrian Archaeological Institute. The monuments of Athens and Eleusis were mainly examined during the "peripatetic lectures" given on Saturdays by Dörpfeld but also by Richardson. Boyd took meticulous notes and examined these monuments in great detail—for the Parthenon she had even obtained permission to climb up the scaffolding.[49] She probably went with Miss Chapin to Salamis, where they retraced the topography of the battle—a favorite exercise for Boyd.[50]

Generally, Boyd seems to have organized her own trips, as was apparently typical.[51] Blanche Wheeler and Mame Waring, who stayed in Greece until the middle of November, provided the necessary companionship for a two-day trip to Aegina and an eight-day tour of Phocis and Phthiotis.[52] A year and a half later the comments of the guide she had hired illustrated the lasting impression Boyd made on people.[53] In spring Boyd had her first trip around central and southern Peloponnese with Wheeler and a party of friends.[54] She joined Dörpfeld's party in a visit to Eleusis; she revisited Delphi and went to see the American School's excavations at Corinth. In June she made a last trip to Eleusis, the site relevant to her research.[55] Her subject, "Inscriptions from Eleusis Relating to Building," demanded long hours of work in the library, which made Boyd realize that she was not "cut out for a Library student."[56] Outings and other activities were kept to a minimum and, by staying at the Grand Hotel and the American School, she was barely distracted by domestic worries.[57] Thus Boyd passed the year 1898–99 in total dedication to her studies, trying to find her own way in archaeology.

After a summer holiday in Germany, Boyd returned to Greece in October 1899 bringing with her an old highschool friend, Jean Patten, to stay with her in Athens.[58] At Volos they were met by a Greek from Epirus, Aristides Pappadhias, hired by Miss Baltazzi as their servant. Pappadhias, outlawed by the Turks for his activities in the 1897 war, served Boyd during the year in Athens as housekeeper and cook and later, during all the years that she excavated in Crete, as her right-hand man, foreman, and pot-mender. An imposing figure who dressed in the traditional Greek kilted skirt, the foustanella, he made a great impression on the villagers in Crete and on the Athenians alike, boosting Boyd's status.[59]

For her third year at the American School Boyd was appointed Agnes Hoppin Memorial Fellow, with a stipend of one thousand dollars.[60] In the year 1899–1900 the school had fifteen students, with the women (eight of them) for the first time outnumbering the men.[61] The program was similar to that of the previous year, combining lectures by Richardson, H. W. Smyth Professor of Greek at Bryn Mawr College, and Wilhelm, with field trips.[62] A novelty in Smyth's lectures in epigraphy was to explore the history of primitive writing in Greece in connection with Cretan linear writing,[63] thus introducing Boyd to a subject of great importance for her subsequent work in Crete. In addition, she went to lectures outside the school and took private lessons daily, perfecting her Greek and expanding her knowledge of Greek civilization and modern Greek life.[64]

In the months preceding her Cretan expedition, Boyd should have completed her paper on the inscriptions from Eleusis, begun the previous year, but she "never found Mr. Richardson stimulating or helpful."[65] The completed part of the work was in her judgment "far from satisfactory," but in April she decided to send it to Seymour, admitting, "it will be an immense load off my mind."[66] Her new study, "The Coinage of Eleusis," had a better outcome, resulting in "an excellent paper."[67] This study was responsible for her renewed interest in the small coin collection she had begun in 1897. She resumed making purchases in the years 1898 through 1900. The collection amounted to eighty-one coins, but only one, given to her daughter, can be found today.[68] This was the only collection Boyd is known to have made. She was one of the few archaeologists of her time whose interest was to discover and to study antiquities, not to acquire them: "I never was a *collector* but a detective & cared for what *fed* my mind & heart."[69] During the years she excavated in Crete she did look for antiquities to purchase, but always for museums or other institutions. In any event these purchases were limited—as the law-abiding Boyd was quick to point out in one of her first letters from Crete:

> The Cretan law is very strict about purchasing antiquities but the Ephors are lenient toward purchases that are made for the express purpose of learning what a site yields.[70]

Boyd left for Crete in the spring of 1900. This trip was the beginning of the most brilliant chapter in Boyd's professional life, full of great discoveries that placed her among the greatest figures of Aegean archaeology.

The Background of the Cretan Expedition (1899–1900)

In the last decades of the nineteenth century Crete had been in the forefront not only of Greek politics but also of archaeological circles in Athens, particularly of the foreign schools. But plans for systematic excavations never materialized, blocked either by the Cretan Christians, who feared that any treasures discovered would be taken to Constantinople, or by the Turks, who did not wish to bring to light the Greek past of the island.[71] In December 1898 the autonomy of Crete removed the reasons for obstructing excavations. With the finalization of the Antiquities Law of the Cretan State six months later,[72] petitions from the British and French schools and the Italian Archaeological Mission to Crete poured in.[73] The American School, despite the previous ties of the Archaeological Institute of America with Crete,[74] did not show any interest, but the British School, which had decided to concentrate all its resources on excavating in Crete,[75] certainly stirred the students' interest. Boyd was reminded of a conversation with a guardian of antiquities and Cretan refugee who, pointing to the Acropolis, claimed that "Crete is full of ruins much finer than those, to be had for the digging,"[76] but any thoughts about the prospects of her excavating in Crete were still far off.

Boyd had first thought of excavating at Corinth—the only site in Greece where the school was then digging. But her proposition, in the spring of 1899, to use some of her fellowship money to "try to find tombs in the neighbourhood of Corinth" was not approved by Richardson.[77] Corinth was "his" excavation,[78] and he was unlikely to allow Boyd to excavate on "his" site. There was also of course his "dictum that a woman could not endure the hardship of active excavation"[79]—a dictum he consistently put into practice, as Ida Thallon's testimony suggests,

> Tonight, we are to dine with Mrs. Richardson, we think it is a joke. Whenever Mr. R. rather slights the girls, Mrs. R. asks us up there to dinner or something. This time he has gone off to Corinth to excavate without taking us along. Not that we care much . . . but it is funny, as the girls belong to the School as much as the men.[80]

Richardson's attitude may not have reflected the school's policy, but as director he was invested with the power to impose his beliefs, which were shared by most of his peers.[81]

Richardson's objections did not deter Boyd. By 1900 she was convinced of her "failure in 'research' work," for which she came to believe she was not fitted.[82] Certain that her studies of neither the coinage nor the inscriptions of Eleusis could reach the high standard required by the fellowships,[83] she reported to Seymour that only excavation would give "some return for the honor and opportunity as well as the money which the Fellowship bring."[84] She repeatedly expressed the same feelings and hopes in her private correspondence. Characteristically she wrote to Wheeler, "You know that the Fellowships have been often a real burden to me . . . The commandment 'Thou shalt not steal' came to have an awful meaning for me, for I did not like to take money without giving any return."[85]

Boyd was fully conscious that she had only theoretical training in the "art of excavating,"[86] and she was the first to admit that the knowledge of topography of known sites could not solve the problems of identifying a site to excavate.[87] However, she had faith in her ability to carry out an excavation successfully. Eventually, her meticulous records and the prompt and (for their time) fully published results of all her excavations proved that active fieldwork was her vocation.

It was a fortunate coincidence that the door to archaeological excavation in Crete opened at the very time Boyd was seeking an opportunity to excavate. With the arrival in Athens of Hogarth and Evans on their way to Crete to begin excavations, Boyd saw the possibility of realizing her plans and overcoming Richardson's objections. In a letter to Blanche Wheeler, she recorded:

> One Sunday morning last February I lay in bed in one of those delicious dreamy moods when everything seems possible. Mr. Hogarth was in town on his way to Crete to dig. The plan took shape. That afternoon I went up to see him alone and told him I wanted to dig in Crete. To my great surprise he did not hoot at the idea but advised me "to come over and see." A week later, by great luck Mr. Arthur Evans passed through town. I met him at the British School and he too was encouraging.[88]

The support of the two leading foreign figures in Cretan archaeology was crucial in obtaining the consent of Richardson. He could no longer oppose her argument that "Americans ought, if possible, to have a share in the exploration of Crete," particularly since Boyd was herself funding any excavation with half her Agnes Hoppin Memorial Fellowship.[89] (Although the fellowship money came earlier than usual and in time to take care of the expenses, it was thanks to a satisfactory return from a private investment that Boyd could press on with her plans at the right time.)[90] The backing of the Archaeological Institute of America came from Seymour, the acting president, who approved the project while also acknowledging that it was a contribution to the school,[91]—boosting Boyd's morale and, in her own words, removing "any last misgivings as to the wisdom of coming to Crete."[92]

Early in April, headlines in Boyd's favorite newspaper, *To Asty,* read "Spring has come officially." For Boyd this was "a call to action." She immediately wrote to Hogarth her intention to sail for Crete in the next week, and began preparing for her expedition.[93] The contribution of her friend Sophie Baltazzi was vital. She provided Boyd with letters of introduction addressed to 'key' people: one was the bishop of Rethymno; another, the wife of the influential Andreas D. Pappadiamantopoulos, a distinguished member of the legal profession and a diplomat, now serving as private secretary of Prince George; and, most importantly, Nikolaos Stavrakis, general director of customs in Crete and a scholar in his own right, well respected by the Cretan archaeological community.[94] In the field, three trusted friends helped make the expedition a success. The first was Jean Patten, a botanist by training. She was to study the plant life of the Kavousi region and aid the expedition by "her tact and good judgement and her keen powers of observation."[95] The Epirot, Aristides Pappadhias, joined them as foreman and his mother Angeliki (whom they too called "Manna" [mother]) as cook and "chaperon."[96] The rumor of the impending all-women expedition spread in Athens, and farewell parties were given to wish Boyd "God-speed" and success for the expedition—one by Mrs. Richardson and another by Mme. Schliemann, at which, to Boyd's delight, Dörpfeld was also present.[97] These celebrations were a happy note in the midst of the last days' preparations, helping Boyd to counter her doubts about the daring, nonconformist task that lay ahead.

The 1900 Campaign in Crete

On April 10 Boyd and her team embarked on a "dingy little Greek boat" bound for Herakleion, via Hania. The stop at Hania was lucky. Boyd could send her letter of introduction to Stavrakis; in return he wrote her a letter of introduction to Iosif Hazzidakis, the ephor of antiquities of central and eastern Crete, whose support was fundamental in obtaining an excavation permit.[98] Arriving at Herakleion on the evening of April 12, Boyd was handed a note from Hogarth. Although he had encouraged her to come to Crete, he now suggested there were great difficulties in obtaining an excavation permit, concluding:

> Dr. Hazzidaki in whose hands is the fate of your projects, is, I believe, leaving for Canea tonight. If you come over to us [i.e., to Knossos] we can talk the matter over. But I am inclined to think you will find a journey of exploration more practicable than a dig at present.

Boyd may have been surprised by this change of attitude, but not deterred. Without losing a moment, she sent Stavrakis's letter to Hazzidakis. He came immediately to see her, and the meeting was a complete success. She wrote, "He was most cordial . . . puts me in high spirits by promising help in excavations. . . . Nothing could have been more opportune than my seeing him that first night."[99] Undoubtedly Hazzidakis's attitude was influenced by Stavrakis's letter, which, as Boyd readily acknowledged, was an immense help. This and the other letters of introduction gave concrete evidence of Boyd's connections.[100] It was clear that the fervent philhellenism she demonstrated on many occasions, and above all through her service in the 1897 war, had won her the sympathy, respect, and support of many influential Greeks; such credentials weighed heavily with the Cretans, especially Hazzidakis. Of course, her academic background would have commended her to Hazzidakis, and he may have been favorably predisposed to an American request for excavation, as he had recently (1893) served as American consul. Hazzidakis's immediate and positive response to Boyd's project came as a surprise to all, not least to Hogarth. He had clearly misjudged Boyd's case and abilities, as his reaction to the news of her meeting with Hazzidakis suggests: "Miss B. has evidently got round H. [Hazzidakis] and will get her dig."[101]

The next day Boyd and Patten had their first sight of Cretan antiquities in the Museum of the Syllogos and of the extraordinary discoveries at Knossos. Their arrival on the site at Knossos could not have been timed better, for the excavators were finishing clearing the Throne Room and uncovering the throne itself, which Evans "immediately named in sport 'the throne of Ariadne.'" Spirits were running high and with them the prospects of Boyd's "little project."[102] Hogarth and Evans gave Boyd much practical advice and confirmed the suggestion first made in Athens about the Kavousi area being the best for sites. Boyd acknowledged Evans's help: "Mr. Evans . . . in the moment of his great success at Knossos yet found time to read me his notes on the Kavousi region."[103]

Thus on Tuesday, April 17, Boyd, accompanied by Patten, Pappadhias, and a Cretan guide set off on mules for their first destination, Gortyna, where the longtime explorer of Crete, F. Halbherr, was conducting excavations. Two days later, with further advice from Halbherr, Boyd began her quest for a site along the route crossing the Messara plain toward Viannos, thence along the south slopes of Dicte to Ierapetra and from there across the isthmus to Kavousi. This route "was planned by way of sites" suggested by Hogarth, Evans, and Halbherr; they had also urged Boyd "to learn as much as possible from the peasants," and although in practice peasants' tales often proved to be worthless gossip, she persistently followed every clue she was given.[104] In each village they entered, villagers brought her varied objects and showed her many sites, not only because they hoped that an excavation would bring work and "untold wealth to the community," but also because Boyd's party made a great impression upon them. Pappadhias's contribution was vital in orchestrating their arrival at each village.

> On nearing a village, he would ride ahead, go to the inn, and order coffee for himself and any peasants who received him kindly. He would then question them about antiquities in the neighbourhood. By the time we arrived, an altogether exaggerated opinion of our importance had spread throughout the village, helped largely by the national Greek costume worn by Aristides [Pappadhias], which Cretans had seen, if at all, only in patriotic plays representing heroes of the Revolution of '21. Ladies attended by a man in this garb must be great indeed! Soon sealstones, fragments of pottery and bronze would be brought to us quietly, and men would offer to show the fields where these had been unearthed.[105]

Pappadhias's foustanella never lost its effect, becoming the hallmark of Boyd's expeditions. Although in Athens he dressed in a suit, during the campaigns in Crete Pappadhias always wore a foustanella, made specifically for this purpose and included in the excavation's expenses.[106]

Boyd had been "tempted to put in the spade at more than one of the sites" they visited "had it not been for the salutary laws which forbid unauthorized digging" and her wish "to defer judgment until . . . Kavousi, which had been specially recommended by Dr. Evans."[107] In fact Kavousi was not the only site recommended by Evans. Boyd was also anxious to visit Arvi, a site on the southern coast, west of Ierapetra, because of the "quantity of good material cited by Evans in his 'Cretan Pictographs' as well as his spoken praise of the site." She bought two Hellenic vases and one bronze found there and saw architectural remains that made her "believe that Arvi would make an excellent site—The first finds would be Roman but there is good reason to believe that under the Roman, one might find Greek remains."[108] Two other sites, one near the village of Ligortino, already investigated by Evans, the other near the village of Viannos, already described by L. Mariani and from where Boyd obtained two lentoid carnelian sealstones, also seemed promising and favorable for an excavation.[109]

At Ierapetra the party was hospitably received by the eparch (county governor), Emmanuel Aggelakis, who was to be assigned to supervise the dig at Kavousi on behalf of the government.[110] He wrote a letter of introduction to the authorities at Kavousi so that, when the party reached

Kavousi on April 24, the vice-demarch welcomed them "in pompous speech," procured lodgings for them at a cobbler's shop, and gave them every other help.[111] Soon the necessary preparations were made for visiting the sites on the neighboring heights mentioned by Evans, and the mule train, guided by peasants who knew the sites, began the hour-long ascent to the Kastro (citadel) some seven hundred meters above the sea. They followed a "fearful path" and just before the top had to abandon the mules, so that the summit "was reached by a hand and foot scramble."[112] There they saw "early polygonal walls," and on the adjacent slope, Plaï tou Kastrou, the peasants showed them the tholos tomb investigated a year earlier, as well as other places where Boyd believed similar tombs would be found.[113]

Early the next morning, April 25, "an old *old* man" brought Boyd three small bronze objects and showed her where they had been found: Mouri t'Azorià, a rocky hill commanding the direct route between central and eastern Crete, and Aghios Antonios, a hillside near the sea, west of Kavousi plain. Mouri t'Azorià, where a bronze stag was found, "had especially pleased" Boyd "for the slope is covered with ancient walls some of which deserve to be called 'Cyclopean,'" and she "noticed a 'very promising earth platform on top, which ought to be dug.'" At Aghios Antonios, where "the forepart of a small bronze lion of excellent workmanship and the upper half of a small bronze figure" were found, Boyd noticed "Megalithic walls." She thought they "must yield something beside the little idol and the lion's head," which she was convinced "could not occur alone."[114]

Boyd finally made up her mind to excavate at Kavousi. She had considered all the evidence from the four sites and concluded that this "seemed to preclude the possibility of failure."[115] Apart from strong evidence from these specific sites and Evans's recommendation, Kavousi also presented, like no other area she had seen during her trip, a good prospect for finding new sites. Since excavation permits were granted not for one particular site but for an area,[116] in petitioning to excavate at Kavousi she was reserving the right to excavate in the whole isthmus, the diachronic importance of which and its prospects for archaeological research became immediately clear to her. As the letters she wrote soon after her trip suggest, she hoped "to find evidence of regular traffic across the isthmus to the South coast and thence to Egypt etc. in early days."[117] Thus, compared to the other sites she saw, particularly to Arvi, which only gave "later things," the Kavousi area "proved particularly rich in good παραδείγματα [antiquities]" and offered sites covering a larger chronological span.[118] The clues from Aghios Antonios pointed to the Bronze Age, the "Golden Age of Crete," and tipped the balance in favor of Kavousi. Although the trial subsequently carried out there "was to all appearances a complete failure,"[119] Boyd continued to believe that there must be a Bronze Age settlement, and this belief brought her back to the isthmus in 1901. Kavousi offered another important advantage. "The sites are almost entirely waste land so there will be no crop complications. The land slopes so that a dump will be easy."[120] Moreover, she felt that Geometric sites like those at Kavousi suited her limited experience.[121]

Boyd did not, however, begin with these mountain sites but with Aghios Antonios. The attraction of an apparently Bronze Age site was great, and she had a genuine fear of heights, which she acknowledged on many occasions.[122] This fear also deterred her from even considering excavating on Mt. Keraton ("not for all the King's treasures would I excavate on that Mt. top—I should permanently lose my breath in getting there!");[123] and from inspecting what appeared through the spyglass to be characteristic Iron Age walls at a site in the gorge of Ha.[124] It is therefore surprising that she ever decided to go up this "fearful path" and undertake excavations on the heights of Kavousi, but such must have been her determination to make a success of her expedition and thus to have a chance to return for further excavations.[125]

With no doubt remaining in her mind about her choice of Kavousi, Boyd returned "as quickly as possible to Herakleio" to put in her petition.[126] She was further encouraged by Hogarth's comments on the finds from Kavousi: "Mr. Hogarth thought the bronzes good indications."[127] On April 29, she sent her petition (drawn up with Hazzidakis's help) to the Ministry of Education at Hania, requesting permission to conduct trial excavations in the district of the villages of Kavousi and Episkopi, as representative of the American School at Athens. Earlier on the same day she went to the museum to be introduced by Hazzidakis to Ioannis Perdekaris, secretary general of the Ministry of Education. Wearing white to show up her little Red Cross pinned on, she explained that she was known to the queen and once to Prince George. The meeting gave Boyd enough assurance that the permit would be granted, to begin immediately organizing the expedition.[128] She was "full of her undertaking" and "full of ideas and enthusiasm."[129] Hogarth helped her to hire an overseer, and again on his advice and on the basis of an estimated workforce of thirty men, Boyd bought her excavation equipment, "20 pick-axes, 20 spades, 50 baskets, 10 large knives, plenty of rope." She replenished the supplies of food, "canned things, jams, meat, biscuit, etc.," since only the fresh food could be obtained at Kavousi. By May 10, when the permit arrived, everything was ready.[130]

Boyd and Patten, with Pappadhias, "Manna," and the overseer, arrived at Kavousi May 12.[131] The excavation's headquarters were immediately established in a small house rented from "the chief capitalist and shopkeeper of Kavousi": three or four small stone sheds built around a narrow courtyard and an upper room with a wooden floor, "one of the two in the village." Its simplicity was compensated for by the "never to be forgotten" view from the terrace roof, where the women had their breakfast and evening meal: "a magnificent outlook over the plain to the sea."[132] The next day, Boyd went to inspect four sites (Aghios Antonios, Khordakia, Kastro, and Avgos),[133] having instructed Pappadhias to ask villagers "who cared to dig" to come later to the excavation house. Boyd chose ten of the thirty who came, "selecting them for vigor of body and for good qualities revealed in the face." With one exception, these men, known as Firsts, formed the basis of Boyd's workforce throughout all her campaigns.[134]

The excavations started May 14 and ended June 6.[135] During this time Boyd, assisted by Patten and the workforce of men, explored ten sites from the Late Bronze Age to the Roman period.[136] The first site was Aghios Antonios. Two days' work and twelve trial pits yielded only potsherds belonging to the end of the Middle and beginning of the Late Bronze Age and used by later occupants to build up terraces. These potsherds indicated the existence of a Bronze Age settlement in the vicinity, but realizing the risk of searching for this settlement, especially since "the indications above ground were very slight," she turned her attention to the heights. There, an excavation was certain to find better-preserved remains even if these were of the Geometric period.[137]

The next week was spent excavating at Mouri t'Azorià, the site she thought very promising on her first visit. Work revealed structures of three different periods, the oldest dating to the Geometric period, yet Boyd described this excavation as "dull, perplexing and comparatively fruitless."[138] The complex stratigraphy, the intricacy of the architectural remains and puzzling existence of round structures were too much for a novice, and Boyd was relieved when workmen "sent to reconnoiter the Kastro . . . returned with several extraordinary and ludicrous figures representing animals."[139] She immediately moved camp to Kastro. The "ludicrous figures" of animals proved to be the contents of a shrine at Plaï tou Kastrou, found while the workmen were looking for tholos tombs like the one shown to Evans.[140] At Kastro, Boyd uncovered thirteen rooms belonging to various buildings of a small settlement of the Geometric period—today still one of the best examples of a settlement from this period yet excavated in Crete.

But the sites that yielded "the best returns" to the expedition were Skouriasmenos ("Rusty Ridge") southeast of Kastro and Vronda ("Thunder Hill") south-southwest of Kavousi. At Skouriasmenos, Boyd reinvestigated a Geometric tholos tomb illegally excavated forty years before. The looters had left many objects—vases, iron swords, spearheads and belt attachments, bronze arrowheads, a gold button, pieces of gold leaf and glass, glass beads, and above all fragments of a thin bronze plate engraved with sphinxes, griffins, lions, and human figures.[141] At Vronda the excavation began with the discovery of a badly preserved building and five tholos tombs largely or entirely plundered. One day before the campaign was to close, two boys, who thought they were clearing stones blocking a trench, were, in fact, removing masonry from the side of a tholos tomb. The tomb proved to be intact: forty vases, a large pithos, a clay and a steatite spindle whorl, parts of iron swords and spearheads, a bronze bracelet, five bronze fibulae, and a bronze ring were found.[142]

Just before the excavation closed Boyd sent a letter to Hogarth "asking for [Theodore] Fyfe," the architect working at Evans's excavations at Knossos. Fyfe could not be spared, and R. C. Bosanquet, then assistant director of the British School, went instead to help her with planning the remains.[143] The published plans, although not made by an architect, and at least the one of Mouri t'Azorià traced by Wheeler, show accuracy and a careful record of details unusual at that time, especially for what were considered poor remains.[144] However, the discoveries made at Kavousi were enough to satisfy Boyd:

> Not only were we pleased, but what was more important, . . . the villagers were now satisfied. They would have much to discuss through the winter, . . . and could claim for Kavousi an importance it had never before enjoyed among the villages of Eastern Crete.[145]

The archaeological community, to judge by Hogarth's note, did not apparently share her feelings: "Miss B's stuff evidently poor but she is quite content."[146] As for the villagers, a letter dated May 31 (June 13) written by the demarch of Kavousi stated:

> We certify that Mrs. [*sic*] Harriet Boyd, member of the American School at Athens, who arrived here a month ago and carried out

excavations at various places in our district, worked with the required impartiality, with which the people were pleased. She also paid 60 francs for the damage to the crops, trees and terrace walls made for the excavation of the antiquities.

Having packed the finds, to be sent to Herakleion by boat from Pachyammos, Boyd and her team left for Herakleion via Lasithi to visit Hogarth's excavation of the sacred cave on the side of Mt. Dicte above Psychro, and take part of the material with her to the Museum of the Syllogos.[147] At Herakleion, after a few days of anxious waiting, the boat with her own finds arrived, and Boyd spent a few weeks writing an excavation report for the Managing Committee of the American School and sorting out her material. She was anxious to present a full study of her excavations with drawings and photographs of her material, but she had not made provision for an artist. Again Hogarth "arranged with Gilliéron about copying the vases" and, apparently, the engraved bronze plate from Skouriasmenos.[148] On July 9 Boyd was back in Athens.[149]

During these few weeks at Herakleion, Boyd reflected on her experiences as a woman in the field. Her genuine modesty could hardly disguise the fact that, in financing and successfully conducting these excavations, she had disproved Richardson's belief that women were incapable of carrying out fieldwork. Aware of how widespread this belief was, she wrote that her work in Crete would probably never have been undertaken had it not been for her experience in the Greco-Turkish War, which resulted "in an intimate acquaintance with Greek peasant character & a warm liking for the people." She further makes the point that having learned to control hospital wards in dire circumstances, she had no difficulty in directing excavations.[150]

Difficulties due to the specific time and place of her excavations, also a widespread concern, were unfounded. She wrote:

> It might be supposed that such an enterprise, conducted by women, would be fraught with serious difficulties in a land which had just issued from Turkish bondage, and which for centuries has been noted for the turbulent character of its people.[151]

But traveling round Crete searching for sites or excavating did not seem to have presented any more difficulties for Boyd as a woman than for any of her male colleagues.[152] There was, in her words, "a remarkable security of person and property . . . throughout the island." Difficulties were practical, such as "those one expects to meet in a country of limited resources and no comforts," which many men would have thought unfit for a woman but which never worried Boyd.[153] As for the Cretan villagers, not only did they not discriminate against a woman prospecting for a site or directing an excavation, but they were pleased and genuinely respectful. The presence of foreign women was "the proof . . . that Crete . . . was a safe, orderly land in which even ladies might travel without fear of molestation."[154] Moreover, being a foreigner, particularly from a powerful country, as well as disposing of wealth, outweighed any disadvantages the villagers associated with female gender. In their minds and those of the authorities Boyd was not comparable to a Cretan woman. It is telling that in church Boyd and her female companions were offered places in front, although the custom for women was to take places at the back.[155] On the other hand, Richardson completely ignored Boyd's excavations in his report, although this was the only other excavation of the school apart from Corinth in the year 1899–1900.[156] The only official recognition of Boyd's expedition came from Seymour in his annual report as chairman of the Managing Committee of the American School and two years later in his history of the school.[157]

The Discovery of Gournia (1901)

By September 1900 Boyd was back in America, appointed to the post of instructor at Smith College,[158] a position she was to hold, with appropriate leaves of absence for excavations and research, until her resignation at the end of 1905. She taught Greek archaeology, modern Greek, and epigraphy.[159] Boyd was determined to resume her work in Crete, but she needed institutional backing and sponsorship. It was clear to her that she could not expect support from the American School. As she had confessed to Ida Thallon, there was "no chance for a woman to excavate with the Amer.[ican] School & she must do it for herself."[160]

In December, at the Archaeological Institute of America general meeting held in Philadelphia, Boyd read a paper on the results of her excavations at Kavousi.[161] It was a decisive moment for the future of her work in Crete. *The Philadelphia Press* praised her "scientific presentation," noting that it "attracted the attention of one of those in charge of the scientific interest of the American Exploration Society."[162] This was its secretary, Sara Yorke Stevenson (Mrs. Cornelius Stevenson), who was also a member of the council of the Archaeological Institute and president of the Pennsylvania Branch.[163] Mrs. Stevenson, convinced of the importance of Crete through her own studies, immediately saw in Boyd's Cretan project the opportunity to promote the interest of the society in this particular corner of the Mediterranean.[164] This was the turning point, not only for Boyd's work but also for American research in Crete, which now secured a firm base. Stevenson forwarded Boyd's project to the society. Within a month the society confirmed its support, but reconciling its interests with those of the Archaeological Institute and its school at Athens proved impossible (despite the exchange of several letters between Stevenson, Boyd, Seymour, representing the school at Athens, and J. W. White, president of the institute).

In February Boyd decided to "cut the Gordian knot" and leave for Crete on March 16, at her own expense and in the hope that the authorities would not insist on an affiliation with a national body such as the Archaeological Institute and the school at Athens. She further hoped they would agree to an excavation under the auspices of the American Exploration Society. The society cautiously retained the funds (one thousand dollars provided by two of its members) until a permit to excavate under its auspices was obtained.[165] Meanwhile Boyd made arrangements for a leave of absence from Smith College and for Blanche Wheeler to join the expedition. She was also hard at work on the results of her 1900 campaign, preparing a report for the journal of the institute and a thesis on the basis of which Smith College awarded her an M.A. in June 1901.[166]

On April 7 Boyd and Wheeler, along with Pappadhias and "Manna," arrived at Herakleion. Boyd saw Hazzidakis, who urged her to find a large undertaking, otherwise "Americans would be permanently discouraged from digging in Crete." He had already written to her suggesting important sites in west Crete, but these did not appeal to Stevenson nor to Boyd, who preferred east Crete.[167] At their meeting Hazzidakis suggested four new sites including two in east Crete, Dreros and Palaikastro, the latter, however, being immediately taken by Hogarth.[168] Boyd thought it safer to petition for renewal of her permit to excavate at Kavousi while looking for a new site.

Armed with information from Hazzidakis and Evans, she set off with Wheeler, Pappadhias, and a muleteer on an eight-day round trip through Hersonissos, Malia, Neapolis, Lato, Elounda, Kavousi, Episkopi, Mesoleri, Kalamavka, Mallais, Psychro, and back to Herakleion. They particularly investigated a site thought to be Homeric, near the village of Malia, mainly prompted by Hazzidakis's opinion that Malia is "the greatest centre in Crete for seal-stones." The site, "a rocky rise of ground not far from the sea," was the very site of the palace Hazzidakis was to discover in 1915—subsequently excavated by the French School. Boyd noted that it was covered with sherds but she could not find good examples, and there were no walls visible on the surface. They carried on to investigate the known ancient sites in the area of Neapolis—Anavlochos (particularly recommended by Evans), Dreros and Milatos, and further on, ancient Olounda. Finally, at Kavousi, Boyd showed Wheeler Aghios Antonios and Avgos, which she considered most promising.[169] Of the new sites, Boyd chose Dreros, on the hill of Aghios Antonios, apparently hoping to extend her rights to the neighboring Anavlochos and Milatos, thus securing a large area for Americans if "a second year's luck at Kavousi" did not bear fruit. As it happened, the Dreros permit was granted on May 21, the day after she discovered Gournia.[170] A few years later she was asked by the French School for her rights on Dreros, and probably gave them.[171]

On April 26 Hazzidakis handed Boyd the permit to continue work at Kavousi, advising her to "let it be known among archaeologists that Americans take Isthmus & Mirabello."[172] This must have sounded ironic to Boyd, who wrote that when the party set off for Kavousi to excavate Geometric or at best sub-Mycenaean sites, their quest "excited pity rather than envy among the archaeologists at Herakleion."[173] Boyd's spirits were kept up by the hope of locating the Bronze Age settlement at Aghios Antonios on the evidence of the previous year's excavations. But she kept her hope secret, knowing that the chances of being proved right were small.

The party established themselves in small stone huts in the upland valley of Avgos, and on May 7 the excavations began with twenty-five men and two new overseers. They revealed a "megalithic homestead" of the end of the Bronze Age, but Boyd's search for tombs at Avgos, based on ornaments, sealstones, and fragments of a larnax found by the peasants, was unsuccessful.[174] New evidence for the existence of tombs in this area came two years later with a chance discovery by one of her workmen of an assemblage of objects, but by then Boyd was too busy at Gournia to follow it up.

As the second week at Avgos was drawing to a close, the outlook was bleak. Living conditions were hard to bear, especially with the atrocious weather; the excavations were proving disappointing; and the search "up and down Kavousi plain and the neighboring coast hills" for the Bronze Age settlement, which she was convinced existed in the lowlands, had been unsuccessful.[175] A small excavation at Aloni near Kastro, which revealed two tombs, could hardly compensate for their efforts. Boyd was heartbroken, and the prospect of Dreros seemed the only hope.[176] Then a hopeful message reached her. George Perakis, "peasant antiquarian of the neighbouring village of Vasiliki," claimed that at a place called Gournia, four miles west of Kavousi, he could show Boyd "a hill close to the sea, where there were broken bits of pottery and odd walls." To substantiate his claim he sent Boyd an excellent sealstone found near the hill.[177]

On May 19 Boyd and Wheeler, guided by George Perakis and his brother Nicholas, visited Gournia. They were first shown massive walls of a building near the sea. Then four hundred meters south of the sea, on a hill "commanding a magnificent view between rocky headlands over the Gulf to the peninsula [of] Spinalonga," they noted, well disguised beneath dense undergrowth, "Ancient walls, some massive slabs [of] smooth stone w.[ith] holes cut in them, mounds that look like tombs, fields strewn w.[ith] sherds." Some of the potsherds had patterns similar to those from Aghios Antonios, which indicated a Bronze Age settlement. This was enough to raise Boyd's hopes. As Gournia fell within the limits of the area allowed by her permit, she decided to begin immediately "a thorough exploration of the new site."[178]

The next morning one of the overseers took all their workmen to Gournia, while Boyd and Wheeler returned to the previous year's house at Kavousi, "for it was mail-day and important letters had to be written." When they rode out to the site in the afternoon, their "astonishment . . . was indeed great," for the workmen had already found "fine fragments of pottery . . . traces of many houses, a paved road w.[ith] clay gutter, a bronze spear, bronze sickle, broken stone vases & a small clay jug." Fifteen additional men were engaged, making a force of fifty-one, including the two overseers. By May 22, nineteen trial pits had exposed houses and paved roads and "enough vases and sherds bearing octopus, ivy-leaf, double-axe and other unmistakably Minoan designs as well as bronze tools, seal impressions, stone vases, etc. to make it certain that we had found what we were seeking, a Bronze Age settlement of the best period of Cretan civilization."[179] A jubilant telegraph was sent to Stevenson.[180]

The preparations for extensive systematic excavations began in earnest. Barrows, baskets, fine wire for sieves, aqua fortis, and other needed items were brought from Ierapetra and Herakleion. The first task was to dig "trial trenches etc. in order [to] find places for dump." The tests were "in general unsuccessful—walls everywhere." On May 25 one of these tests revealed an ashlar wall and fallen ashlar blocks—the first remains of what proved to be a small palace occupying the summit of the hill.[181] The next day the expedition's headquarters moved from Kavousi to Pachyammos to be nearer Gournia. Two rooms over a storehouse at the coast-guard station rented for "thirty cents a day, an exorbitant rate" (undoubtedly the best available accommodation at Pachyammos, then a small hamlet), became the main residence. In addition "two adjacent storehouses were hired, one for the antiquities, the other for those workmen who did not wish to trudge home to Kavousi every night."[182]

Large-scale excavations on a particular site required a special permit, as the general permit covered only trial or small-scale excavations on sites within a defined area. On May 15 (May 28) Boyd petitioned for such a permit for Gournia. Hazzidakis, who had arrived the previous day and was pleased with the excavations, promptly supported Boyd's petition. The permit, under the auspices of the American Exploration Society, was granted with the least possible delay on May 21 (June 3).[183] The number of workmen soared to 96 (100 to 110 was the average number for the rest of the season and for the 1903 and 1904 campaigns), the usual workforce for large-scale excavations at that time. Many trenches were dug simultaneously with only intermittent supervision by an archaeologist—so much of the work depended on the judgment of the workmen. According to their specific task the workmen at Gournia were divided into four classes.[184] The Firsts, on average fifteen workmen, carried out the digging and included the first men from the 1900 campaign. They were assisted by a slightly larger number who shoveled, and were supervised by Boyd and one assistant (two in 1904). Apart from a small number of men knowledgeable in carpentry or wall building, the rest, representing half the workforce, were unskilled laborers. In addition, eleven girls washed the finds.[185]

Keeping the accounts and preparing the payroll became a major task, particularly in 1901 when the wages were paid in a variety of currencies—Turkish, French, Italian, and British. But Boyd persisted with her policy of dealing directly with all matters concerning the workmen and kept full charge of their pay.[186] This direct dealing helped to establish a cordial relationship between Boyd and the workmen. Four weeks after the beginning of the excavations N. B. Pantoulas, teacher at the Ierapetra elementary school and acting supervisor of the excavations on behalf of the state, reported:

> The workmen, over 120, are entirely content both with the kind behaviour of the Misses and with the recompense of their labour in these scheming penniless days, and the Misses are completely thrilled with their luck.[187]

Just as the site of Gournia surpassed everyone's hopes, so the expenses of the excavation exceeded the original fund of $1,000. By June the expenses amounted to $250 a week. Boyd wrote to Stevenson explaining that she "could not have foreseen such good fortune" when she estimated the budget, and additional funding was necessary if the campaign was not to be cut short. She stressed that "the opportunity is too good a one to lose."[188] Meanwhile, she continued excavating using her own and Wheeler's money, but the American Exploration Society proved willing to contribute additional funds.[189]

One building after another came to light. By the end of the campaign an almost complete picture of the north part of the town had emerged, consisting of small, "humble" houses, which Boyd recorded carefully, considering them a prime source of information on how the Bronze Age people lived and worked. To the discovery of the palace was added, on June 6, the discovery of a shrine—a simple rectangular room standing in the middle of the town. In this room, enmeshed within the roots of a carob tree, was found "a set of objects more curious than beautiful": a low three-legged offering table, five "snake tubes," a female idol, and various parts of others in coarse clay.[190] Sacred to the earth goddess, this shrine was the first, and still is the best, example of a Minoan town shrine yet discovered.

Trenches were also opened in the area surrounding the acropolis. A large building was excavated across the small valley on the opposite hill east of the acropolis, and an investigation of the walls visible on the surface near the sea revealed another building.[191] The settlement was therefore not confined to the acropolis but extended to the surrounding area. The imposing construction of these peripheral buildings and the ambitious plan on which they were built emphasized the importance of the town.

As the palace had been thoroughly plundered, its excavation did not produce the rich finds one might have expected. In fact, "in proportion to its size it yielded much less than some of the poorer houses."[192] But the finds, mainly of stone, clay, and bronze, "unusually good and complete,"[193] and in great numbers, were more than satisfactory. The tools, in particular, appeared in such numbers and variety that the workmen readily adopted the name *viomichaniki polis* (industrial town), which Pappadhias wrote on an ashlar block with wood charcoal from the destruction of the palace.[194] Boyd immediately attached much importance to these tools, as they testified to the daily activities of the inhabitants of Gournia—farming, pasturing, fishing, building, weaving, shoe making, bronze casting, stone carving, and potting. The bronzesmiths, stone carvers, and potters possessed high technical and artistic skills, to judge from the objects found, especially the bronze weapons, stone, and ceramic vases.[195]

Hogarth was one of the first archaeologists to visit Gournia. During Boyd's 1900 campaign he had kept "a paternal eye" on her,[196] and it was doubtless with genuine pleasure that, after seeing Gournia, he reported in *The Times:*

> [Gournia] is the most perfect example yet discovered of a small "Mycenaean" town, uncontaminated with later remains, and at this moment after the two great palaces, it is the "sight" best worth visiting in Crete.[197]

But had really the existence of a "Buried City"[198] on this hill close to the main road from Herakleion to Siteia, so often taken by so many archaeologists and explorers, passed by "unobserved," as Hogarth noted in the same article, and Boyd confirmed repeatedly in her notes? Hogarth had passed along this road with Bosanquet only three weeks before the discovery of the site, and Boyd also recalled that in 1900 she had even stopped for lunch within two minutes' walk from the site, all unaware.[199] However, Arthur Evans, who had visited the area of Gournia in 1896, wrote that he had observed a "prehistoric polichna at a spot called Gurnia."[200] Boyd was aware of his article, but what Evans described there does not fit the site Boyd was to excavate.[201] Consequently, this information did not help her to locate the site. Evans's original notes (now untraced) appear to have presented a more explicit version of the evidence he saw, which could have given Boyd a clue both to the existence of significant remains and to their location, but she was not aware of these notes.[202] The discovery of Gournia was truly her achievement or, as Hogarth rightly put it in *The Times,* the result of her perseverance.

On July 3, after six weeks' work, the excavations came to a close, and to mark the event a fête with games and a dinner was held the next day to coincide with Independence Day.[203] Boyd and Wheeler remained at Pachyammos for another week, settling the accounts and paying compensation while continuing to study the material and the remains.[204] Boyd had arranged for the photographer, G. Maraghiannis, to come and take pictures of the site and finds, for the museum's artist to make casts of the most important finds, and for Theodore Fyfe, the architect of the excavations at Knossos, to help with planning the architectural remains. During the excavations she had sketched and measured every building and noted many details (paving, built-in furnishing, etc.), thus supplementing the architect's basic outlines.[205] On July 11 Boyd left Gournia in the care of Anagnostis Koïnas, an old peasant from Vasiliki, whom she employed as a guard during the excavations. From July 18 (July 31) he was officially appointed by the government and remained guard until after the 1903 campaign, when

Markos Perakis replaced him. Thus Boyd established a tradition that made Gournia the only guarded site other than the great palaces.[206]

Resumption of Excavations after a Year Away (1902–3)

In September 1901 Boyd returned to Smith College and spent the next months teaching, writing excavation reports, and preparing a paper entitled "Mycenaean Discoveries at Gournia, in the Neighborhood of Kavousi, Crete" for the Archaeological Institute of America general meeting in December. Her paper "showed and explained a series of views" illustrating the excavations at Gournia and was followed by Wheeler's paper on the pottery. With her discoveries already publicized by the press, Boyd enthralled her audience.[207] For the first time in its history the executive council of the AIA recognized the work of a woman by inviting her to lecture in January before ten of its regional societies.[208] Thus, aged only thirty, Boyd found herself in the public eye, praised by both journalists and colleagues. Stevenson wrote in her report:

> So few women have achieved distinction as field archaeologists that Miss Boyd's success must be greeted with peculiar pride by Americans. Several women have done important original work in archaeology, others have distinguished themselves in Museum work, others again as Mme Schliemann, Mme Dieulafoy and Mrs Flinders Petrie have accompanied their distinguished husbands and shared their labours in the field—but it was reserved to an American woman to undertake singly the business responsibility and scientific conduct of an expedition.[209]

Yet the title of Boyd's lecture to the societies—"American Excavations in Crete, 1901: The Discovery of a Mycenaean Provincial Town"—reflects her modesty and level-headedness. Having spent scarcely any time after the excavation campaign studying the material, she was too much aware of the gaps in her understanding to attempt anything more than general public lectures. In a letter to Hazzidakis dated March 9, 1902, she wrote, "There is no official report as yet, and I shall not try to make more than a brief preliminary report before examining our finds more carefully."[210] But soon she abandoned even the idea of a brief report.

As she lectured and taught, Boyd started preparing for her next campaign. Hazzidakis had advised her to postpone her excavation until autumn. Boyd agreed, hoping to have one campaign in autumn 1902 and another in spring 1903, but she was still concerned that this postponement might jeopardize the continuation of the excavations. Seeking reassurance, she wrote to Hazzidakis,

> I should be most unhappy if there were no prospect of a return to Crete . . . I hope that in view of my intention to resume work at Gournia next autumn, the Cretan government will protect our rights to the site and that no one will seek to excavate on the Isthmus of Hierapetra. I understood from you that the isthmus would be reserved for Americans for a reasonable length of time. I have every reason to believe we shall have funds adequate for the work.[211]

But securing excavation funds was not easy. Negotiations with the American Exploration Society went on throughout the spring and summer of 1902. Boyd believed that large-scale excavations required a scientific team of at least two archaeologists, an artist, and an architect who should be paid accordingly. As part of the team, she had already chosen Miss L. Maverick, a colleague from Smith, to replace Wheeler, who could not go, and Adelene Moffat, an artist friend from her undergraduate years in Northampton. In a note to Sara Stevenson accompanying her budget, she wrote:

> I feel very strongly about this whole matter, Mrs. Stevenson. If our services for 3 months . . . are not worth $300 to science, we must all try something else, for really it touches one's dignity. Scientific expeditions are not charitable affairs . . . we are working women . . . Our education has cost us much . . . No, Mrs. Stevenson, if such expenditure seems to the Society unjustifiable, we must give up the work.[212]

Boyd's negotiations with the society ended successfully. But in July her health started deteriorating in a way that she labeled "break-down."[213] Soon thereafter Miss Maverick got engaged and, when her fiancé declared that "she would go to Greece over his dead body," withdrew from the expedition.[214] It was clear that the autumn campaign had to be postponed. On September 26, Boyd wrote to Hazzidakis, "We have funds in hand . . . for continuing the excavations at Gournia and I hope that nothing will prevent our renewing work early in the spring."[215] By the time she wrote this letter, Boyd had begun a year's leave from Smith and moved to Washington, to stay with her brother Allen. She was still convalescing, the condition of her eyes forbidding much reading, writing, or any other work.

Departing on January 3, 1903, Boyd, fully recovered, first visited Egypt for three and a half weeks to study its antiquities. She relished the opportunity of spending an entire evening with Flinders Petrie at Abydos learning firsthand of his methods of excavation and publication, and discussing Gournia with him. She then spent four weeks in Athens.[216] Richardson, who was in his last year as director of the American School, no longer ignored Boyd's work and invited her to speak on her excavations at Gournia on March 6. Her talk, "Excavations at Gournià in Crete, 1901," particularly impressed Mr. and Mrs. Houston, an affluent Philadelphia couple who were wintering in the Mediterranean on their yacht. A few weeks later they visited Boyd at the site. Mrs. Houston must have been greatly impressed, for she provided funds for the next season and later for the publication.[217]

While in Athens, Boyd was met by her teammate, Adelene Moffat, and her new assistant, Richard Berry Seager, a friend of one of her cousins. Seager had no academic qualifications but was interested in Mexican archaeology. When Boyd suggested that he join her in Crete, he readily agreed. Although he was only twenty years old, he had a large personal fortune and contributed funds to the excavation. Under Boyd's tutelage he was also to assist in the field, but this first year his main work was the pottery.[218] Later, a second artist, a Dane, Halvor Bagge, joined the team. The following year he was to take complete charge of the drawings. Harold R. Hastings helped with architectural drawings, as this time Fyfe could not be spared from Knossos.[219]

On March 15 Boyd and her party left for Crete. At Pachyammos they were welcomed to a new house built for them by the locals and boasting the luxury of a few chairs, tables, shelves, plates, forks and spoons.[220] The excavation lasted from March 30 until June 6, and the organization of the work followed the same pattern as in 1901, with two new overseers and a similar workforce.[221] The excavation was concentrated mainly on the palace and the east slope, but some further work was also done on the north part of the west slope. The palace and the adjacent area to the south (including three buildings and a large public open space) were completely cleared. Excavation on the east slope of the acropolis uncovered enough to give a clear picture of the town's layout.[222] The houses were laid out in as many as three levels, following the slope of the land. Owing to the accumulation of the fill, largely caused by the same drop, the lowest and often the middle level of the houses were preserved in such good condition that Gournia immediately earned the name "Mycenaean Pompeii"—or, in the terminology established a year later, "Minoan Pompeii."[223] The general view of the remains was impressive, attracting travelers and fellow archaeologists. Gournia was definitely put on the map.

The excavation of this part of the town yielded some of the best finds of all the campaigns. A clay roundel with Linear A signs, the only document with writing from the site, was found in House Cf. What Boyd described as "our most remarkable piece of pottery" was found in House Cc. This three-handled stirrup jar, decorated with sea creatures, remains one of the most characteristic examples of Marine Style pottery. Also, a cellar in House Cm (Cm 58) yielded the astonishing number of eighteen vases, most finely decorated.[224] The collection of tools and other objects from the 1901 campaign was considerably enlarged. Among those found was a cracked stone mold for casting chisels, nails, bars, or awls. This object, Boyd wrote, "more than any other made the distant past live in our imaginations . . . the owner used the utmost care in mending it. First he drew a narrow strip of bronze twice around the block binding this fast with turns of the strip, and then he drove in flat stones as wedges between the strip of metal and the block . . . a neat piece of work, that brings us in very close touch with the everyday life of the burghers."[225]

Almost immediately after the beginning of the excavations at Gournia, Boyd started promoting new plans for other excavations on the isthmus. She specifically targeted Bronze Age sites that could provide evidence for understanding the chronological sequence leading to the period represented by Gournia.[226] In the spring, she was granted a permit to excavate on the hill of Kefali near the village of Vasiliki, a site she had eyed since 1901.[227] She was granted another permit to excavate in the entire district of the Isthmus of Ierapetra.[228] But the excavations at Gournia left little time for other ventures. Boyd conducted one day's work in a cave west of Gournia that uncovered a Late Mycenaean burial and a four-day trial dig at Pachyammos, which revealed a large Graeco-Roman building.[229] Vasiliki was left to Seager. In a three-day trial excavation, he uncovered part of a building of the Gournia period and poor Roman tombs, but no indication of the site's earlier occupation whose brilliant remains would be unearthed the next year.[230] Her second petition mainly targeted the caves of Aghia Photia and Aghios Ioannis, following a clue given by peasants who had found there samples of Early Bronze Age pottery.[231] Seager visited the caves, and they were excavated the next year.[232]

After the close of the excavations on June 6, Boyd stayed for two weeks to study, pay compensation, and dispatch household goods and finds to Herakleion.[233] The 1903 campaign had cost 12,736.80 francs (about $2,550), of which the American Exploration Society contributed 10,190 francs, Seager 2,200, with Boyd assuming the balance of 346.80 francs—a quarter of what she had asked for her salary.[234] In July, Boyd left Greece, but she did not arrive in America until late September. She first visited Constantinople and spent a month and a half in England. There she attended the annual meeting of the British Association for the Advancement of Science. She followed the sessions of the Anthropology Section, where the British archaeologists working in Crete—Evans, Bosanquet, and Myres—presented their work and participated in the Sectional Committee meetings. She must have felt that this was a forum par excellence to debate new ideas on Cretan archaeology and planned to return next year to present her conclusions on the classification of the Cretan Bronze Age pottery.[235] Back in America, with a further leave of absence from Smith, Boyd gave her time to causes close to her heart. From November until mid-February she worked at Hull House, helping with the integration of Greek immigrants, while she wrote up the financial and archaeological reports of her 1903 excavations and prepared for her spring season.[236]

Last Excavation Season (1904)

Mrs. S. F. Houston and the Hon. Calvin Wells funded a third campaign at Gournia for twenty-five hundred dollars.[237] Boyd arrived in Athens in March 1904, where she met Richard Seager and the assistant he had recruited, Edith Hayward Hall, a Smith graduate.[238] On March 25 Boyd, Hall, Seager, and Pappadhias left for Herakleion, whence they set off on a two-week trip around western Crete. After returning to Herakleion for a few days, the party, joined by Manna and the new overseer, finally reached Pachyammos on April 16.[239] The excavations lasted from April 18 until June 24 and intermittently for another month with only Boyd, who had remained at Pachyammos, camping out with Manna. At Gournia regular work went on until June 4, then intermittently until June 21.[240]

The work at Gournia was organized on the same pattern as in previous years with a new overseer and a similar workforce.[241] The first task was to gain a complete picture of the town. Until mid-May almost all effort was concentrated on the eastern slope, particularly on exposing a new quarter (D) adjacent to the south of quarter C.[242] The addition of quarter D to the already exposed part of the remains gave the town a striking appearance, which still impresses the visitor today. After mid-May the excavation expanded on the southern slope, and the southern part of the western slope, exposing more buildings of quarters H and E.[243] The excavation in quarters H and E, and subsequently A, unearthed remains of two settlements. One was of the period preceding and the other following the main Gournia period, thus fulfilling another of this season's aims: to establish the history of the site's occupation and consequently a classification of pottery in chronological sequence from the third millennium B.C. to the full Iron Age.[244] Further exploration of one of the very first trenches on the acropolis (North Trench) linked the pottery series of the successive Gournia settlements to those of earlier periods found in tombs at Gournia, as well as at other sites excavated this season. Gournia had fulfilled both Boyd's wishes: it gave evidence of stratification of various stages of Minoan civilization and extended the remains of a wonderfully preserved town of the golden age of this civilization.

Boyd must have taken great pride in showing visitors around. One of these was Charles Henry Hawes, her future husband. Henry, as she was to call him, was a widower who, at the age of thirty, went up to Trinity College, Cambridge University, and became an anthropologist.[245] This was his first trip to Greece and Crete. Of his May 10 visit to Gournia, Boyd wrote:

> At about 11 a.m. Mr. Hawes appears. Mr. H. is an Englishman who has traveled extensively thr.[ough] Asia & has written a book [*In the Uttermost East* (1903)] wh.[ich] is much read to-day in Eng.[land]—about a Russian penal colony—We show him the site—after lunch he has a sea bath & I arrange shelves for to-morrow—Then we have tea together & he tells me about British India, the native Congress, etc.[246]

The next day they had their only other meeting of 1904, at Palaikastro.[247]

As the excavations at Gournia were ending, Boyd could turn her attention to other sites on the isthmus.[248] Time was too short for her to carry out systematic excavations, but by trial digs she aimed first to complete the picture of the occupation of the isthmus she had drawn up in her 1903 report[249] and second to supplement the evidence afforded by Gournia on the classification of pottery. Permits for excavation at Vasiliki and other sites along the isthmus had already been secured in 1903. On May 24 (June 6) Boyd was granted a permit to excavate at Aghios Ioannis, on the island of Pseira, and in the district of Kalo Khorio (presumably at Vrokastro).[250] Time, and perhaps funds, allowed work on only some of these sites; no exploration was conducted on Pseira and at Vrokastro, later excavated by

Seager and Edith Hall respectively.[251] Nevertheless the sites finally explored afforded enough evidence for Boyd to achieve both her goals.

At Vasiliki, trials resumed on May 7 with a few workmen under Seager's supervision, and by May 10 the first evidence for the existence of important remains of an early occupation was noted.[252] On visiting the site early that day Boyd decided to stop the excavations at Gournia for three days to allow Seager to carry out extensive trials with the full workforce.[253] The results of the Vasiliki excavation surpassed all expectations. Well-preserved remains of a settlement preceding the earliest settlement at Gournia were found together with "about one hundred whole specimens of a very early style of pottery hitherto unknown in the Aegean except by one or two isolated pieces never published."[254] Evidence of the period preceding Vasiliki was obtained from the discovery in July of tombs at Gournia, on the acropolis and the promontory to the northeast (Pera Alazzomouri), as well as from the excavations at Aghios Ioannis and Aghia Photia in June.[255] In July, the excavation of tombs at two locations near Pachyammos (Pothe Alazzomouri and Aïsa Langadha) enriched the pottery series represented by the reoccupation of Gournia.[256]

By July 25 excavation of the various sites on the isthmus came to an end. Having paid compensation and packed the finds from the last excavations, Boyd, accompanied by Manna, left for Herakleion.[257] There she petitioned the minister of education with a list of objects from her excavations that she wished to export. These, she thought, "might fall under the wording of the new Cretan law that grants to excavators such material as is 'without any scientific value or interest whatever for Cretan Museums.'"[258] While awaiting a decision, she continued to study the finds at the museum. Halvor Bagge assisted her with the drawings.[259] Eventually, part of Boyd's petition was granted, and she felt that "the net result was gratifying."[260] More objects were allowed for export in 1905, although Boyd did not excavate during that season.[261]

On August 19 Boyd left Crete with nine cases and one gunny sack of finds from Gournia and Vasiliki—the very first antiquities to leave Crete with the permission of the government.[262] A month later, she arrived in New York and went straight to Philadelphia to "present her curios to the Museum [the Free Museum of Science and Art of the University of Pennsylvania]."[263] "Her curios" were the only Minoan collection in America at that time.[264] There were "several thousand fragments and several hundred unbroken objects [the numbers inflated by an overenthusiastic journalist]" among which were many whole pieces of Vasiliki pottery, of which "there isn't a sample . . . in the whole wide world outside Crete."[265]

Boyd had hoped to present a scheme of classification of the pottery she had excavated from the beginning of the Bronze Age to the full Iron Age at the annual meeting of the British Association for the Advancement of Science.[266] But arranging for the export of her "curios" kept Boyd in Crete past the time of the meeting. This question of classification had totally absorbed Boyd during the 1904 campaign. She had excavated a great number of sites, and the creation of such a general chronological framework was the result, and, at the same time, was made imperative by, the distribution of her finds over both space and time.[267] She had prepared a paper and sent a précis to J. L. Myres, recorder of the Anthropology Section, from which he "invented" an abstract printed by the association.[268] This paper would have been the first public presentation of a classification of the Cretan Bronze Age pottery series. It was, therefore, unfortunate that she did not present it, but her intention to do so seems to have prompted Evans's presentation on the same subject.[269]

Evans arrived at the meeting the day he was due to speak, and it was only then that he announced his intention to give, instead of his excavation report scheduled for that day, a paper on the classification of pottery.[270] There is no question as to the wider character of Evans's scheme, with the reintroduction of the term *Minoan* to designate the Bronze Age civilization in Crete and the threefold division of this period into Early, Middle, and Late.[271] But his eagerness to present his scheme at this meeting was clearly prompted by Boyd's work. Furthermore, Evans did not have any stratified Early Minoan material, and he would not have been able to define the Early Minoan series without having been aware of Boyd's work.[272] Since Boyd's paper was not actually presented, the abstract could not be published in the "Proceedings," leaving Evans's "first" on the matter unchallenged, and her role emerges only now through the study of Evans's and her own personal archives.

Study Season (1905)

Boyd returned to her post at Smith College, where she was to teach for one semester before returning to Crete. At the AIA general meeting in December, she again hoped to present her paper on the classification of pottery from Gournia and the other sites on the isthmus, but Wheeler had to give the paper on her behalf.[273] She did further work on the subject during winter 1905 as part of her report on the 1904 campaign and for a paper for the International Congress of Archaeology to be held in Athens in the spring.[274] Meanwhile she was making arrangements for the final publication. She was also concerned with the publication of Hall's and Seager's articles on the pottery from the North Trench at Gournia and on the excavations at Vasiliki respectively.[275] A letter from Sara Stevenson dated January 13 reveals the responsibility Boyd felt toward the American Exploration Society and toward her assistants:

> I am sorry that you should have been so overworked . . . With your work represented in the next "Transactions" by Mr. Seager's and probably Miss Hall's papers, there is no reason why you should kill yourself. Just take your time and let this winter go before you undertake any report. All we want is a brief introduction from you, as head of the expedition, to your assistants' papers.[276]

True to character, Boyd wrote a complete report.[277]

By January Boyd's plans to return to Crete to study for the final publication began to take shape. To Sara Stevenson she wrote:

> As to the large publication . . . I have not wanted to get full estimates . . . until I know the opinion of the Society but I have made enquiries & will pledge myself not to go beyond the $6000 limit of expense to the Society . . . President Seelye has granted me leave of absence for the second semester & has said that he will this week recommend the Finances Committee to continue my salary for the express purpose . . . to work on our excavation material. What he recommends usually goes—This . . . means that I will not have to teach after next week and can give all my time to the publication if the Society agrees to issue it. It will be an immense relief to my mind.[278]

With Stevenson's help the American Exploration Society agreed to the publication, with the excavation's patrons, Mrs. S. Houston and the Hon. Calvin Wells, sharing the costs.[279]

Boyd left America in March. In Naples, "cheated & perhaps robbed!" when she lost "a letter of credit . . . 100 £," she missed her boat. This turned out to be a piece of "Boyd luck." By catching a later boat she was to renew her acquaintance with Henry Hawes, who was on his way "to Crete 'head-hunting' for the British Association for the Advancement of Science, to make measurements and thus to try to trace racial origins."[280] He noted laconically, "Met Miss Boyd on board." During the three-day trip the two evidently spent considerable time together, and their conversations, Henry noted, ranged from Cretan politics to marriage customs on the island and to Boyd's site at Gournia.[281] Boyd, writing to her friend Blanche Wheeler, described the voyage and the "unique!" company on the steamer, adding "Great friendliness & a noticeable degree of intelligence marked the atmosphere"—but no mention of Henry's name.[282]

After landing at Piraeus on April 3, Henry sailed to Crete while Boyd remained in Athens to attend the International Congress of Archaeology. Almost all the scholars who had been or were working in Crete were present. Boyd was one of the two women speakers in the whole conference and the only woman speaker in the section on Prehistoric and Oriental Archaeology.[283] Here she was finally able to deliver a revised version of the paper on the classification of the pottery from Gournia and the other sites she had explored in the isthmus that she had been unable to present publicly in 1904.[284] Two days earlier Evans had presented his revised version of the paper he gave at the British Association meeting.[285]

Characteristically, Boyd acknowledged Evans's contribution in her talk and promptly adopted his period divisions in her classification.[286] Following her talk Evans made some observations on the classification of vases and their dating, also admitting that he had himself been helped by Boyd's discoveries.[287] Relieved and satisfied with her presentation, she wrote to Wheeler, "My awful forebodings were all groundless; as far as people and all the essentials have gone, I have had a happy time . . . I gave a paper myself & don't regret it yet!"[288] News of her reappointment at Smith College for the following academic year came as a further boost to her morale.[289]

Shortly thereafter, Boyd returned to Crete for three and a half months to study the finds in the Museum at Herakleion and the building remains at Gournia.[290] She started with the site, and soon after, on April 20, Henry arrived from Palaikastro, where he had been working since they parted company. His long twelve-hour ride was rewarded when, as he wrote, "half way from Kavousi [to Pachyammos] . . . I see and hear a pony galloping and have my suspicions but on looking a second and third time I think I see a Turk with [a] red fez or rather turban, when suddenly my man sees 'Kuria' and I am met by Miss Boyd who was riding out to Kavousi for a constitutional." He noted proudly, "I am known to many to be a friend of Miss Boyd who is almost as the lady of the manor here or Lady Bountiful."[291] Henry set to work measuring, and Boyd noted, "I have had great fun furnishing the material, mostly our workmen & acting as a clerk."[292] They decided to go to the island of Spinalonga, but found this once-Turkish outpost "not possible. Lepers already put there and Moslems gone." They returned to the mainland, where measuring went on apace, and

Henry noted with admiration that Boyd "did wonders for me in helping me through, without her it would have been impossible and she made all sorts of suggestions and worked hard at taking down." Measuring continued the next day at Vasiliki and Kavousi, and they "rode home [to Pachyammos] by starlight" escorted by a local man.[293]

On April 26 Boyd received a party of 110 participants from the International Congress of Archaeology on the official trip led by Dörpfeld. Gournia had become one of the main sites to be included in this program or indeed in any tour of Crete, together with Knossos, Palaikastro, Phaistos, and Agia Triada.[294] Henry sailed with Dörpfeld's party to Palaikastro, and after six days of work there he returned to Pachyammos to help Boyd with planning the remains at Gournia.[295] On May 7 he accompanied Boyd and Daphne Kalopothakis, sister of Dr. Kalopothakis, to Aghios Nikolaos. The next day the ladies sailed for Herakleion, where Boyd resumed work in the museum on the material from the excavations. Kalopothakis helped with the drawings for a few days, but it was a professional draftsman, Halvor Bagge, who worked intermittently throughout the summer to produce the enormous amount of drawings and additional color plates Boyd wanted for the publication.[296] Henry arrived at Herakleion on May 11, and they saw more of each other, particularly since he was also working at the museum on the skulls from various excavations including Boyd's.[297] On May 23 he "went to dine with Miss Boyd and sat on terrace." They talked politics; Boyd was "very strong on the union. Wanted genuinely she says by the peasants and wanted because must belong to a greater Power, cannot stand by itself," while Henry favored autonomy.[298] On May 29 Henry left for a month in western Crete.

While Henry was away, Boyd returned to Pachyammos. She had been offered $150 by the Museum of Fine Arts in Boston for a short dig, and although she had unused permits to excavate at a number of sites (e.g., Pseira, Vrokastro), she preferred to concentrate on publishing Gournia.[299] Thus she resumed work on the site with the German architect W. Sejk, who completed a full plan of the remains.[300] With the site plans and a detailed description of the remains completed, Boyd's work at Gournia was finished, and she left at the end of June. Her concluding words in an article published posthumously sound a farewell to the forgotten prehistoric city she brought back to light:

> Almost one seems to have known the gentle folk, whose household gods and household goods have puzzled us, and the thought comes whether they have not pitied our restlessness and striving and will

> not be glad when again trees and wild flowers cover their habitations.[301]

Back in Herakleion to work for a further month, Boyd again met Henry, who noted with some surprise, "She seems almost to have changed places with me in her views of Cretans and their political aims. She is probably a bit tired . . . She tells how they did not wait for (her) to get away from Pachyamos [*sic*] but they rushed in and stripped the house of everything available." Moreover, her departure had been dogged by difficulties. Laden with luggage and material from the excavation, her caique had to turn back because of rough weather. Traveling overland, the baggage mules were slow and the captain of the boat she hoped to catch from Agios Nikolaos refused to wait. Then a French gunboat gave her a passage to Souda, where it arrived "just a ¼ hour too late to catch the Austrian boat [for Herakleion]."[302] It is little wonder that she was tired upon her return. Anxious to complete the study of her material and feeling that she might be leaving Crete, perhaps forever, she spent a stressful last month at Herakleion. The arrival of a young archaeologist and student at the British School at Athens, Gisela Richter, seems to have given her some pleasure. They became lifelong friends. In August, accompanied by Richter, she left for a holiday in Brittany, during which time she received a letter from Henry proposing marriage. Boyd did not make up her mind to accept immediately, for she would have to choose marriage over career and would probably have to live in England. In 1925 she was to write:

> A woman should expect her intellectual life to be interrupted, i.e. she should be prepared to give the first 10 years after marriage . . . to her family interests . . . Perhaps she can keep alive her intellectual interests and return to them with new zest and judgement after the ten years. Throughout life a woman's work should be more or less interruptible or family and society will suffer. Her happiness in accepting this interruption will depend largely on her having anticipated it as part of the Good Life.[303]

Boyd spent September and October in England with Richter and met Henry frequently. Of one of these meetings she noted, "Henry entertains me at Cambridge in his charming rooms . . . In walk nr. river learn of Henry's marriage at 21 to Carrie Heath & her death 5 yrs later . . . Memorable bus ride: Henry conscientiously recites his financial assets. English!"[304] Without a permanent position Henry's finances were precarious, and for four years after their marriage Boyd was to worry about money. On November 7 Boyd sailed to America with Richter.[305] Soon after landing at Boston, she made up her mind to marry Henry, abandoning her planned "2nd semester return" to Smith College.[306] At the end of December the couple formally announced their engagement. Headlines in one newspaper read, "Cupid lurked midst ruins," and Boyd was described as "America's famous woman archaeologist."

At the time Boyd was about to announce her engagement to Henry, she felt it her duty to make clear her plans concerning the work in Crete. She had decided not to return to the island, but she was eager to see American work continued in order to establish an American tradition of research in Crete. With this aim in view, she transferred to Seager the permit that gave her the right to excavate, in the name of the American Exploration Society, on the Isthmus of Ierapetra.[307] His premature death in 1925 ended American excavations in Crete, and, apart from a short dig in 1959 by Gladys Weinberg in western Crete, they were not resumed until 1976. Since then, there is an ever increasing number of projects all over Crete, and particularly in the isthmus. The continuing interest in the area remains a tribute to Boyd's perceptive choice and extraordinary efforts.[308]

Publishing, Family, and Wars (1906–19)

Time and chance, faith and perseverance were key elements in the success of Boyd's pioneering excavations in Crete. Perseverance was needed even more in the following years as she tried to reconcile three different goals: publishing her excavations, raising a family, and war work. On March 3, 1906, Henry Hawes and Harriet Boyd were married at St. John's Church, Washington, D.C., settling in New York in time for the birth of their first baby. Boyd anticipated the arrival of her baby with great excitement, and some trepidation. Although she no longer held an academic position, she kept herself busy with work.[309] She had begun preparing the prospectus for her book on Gournia, Vasiliki, and the other sites she had explored on the isthmus. She was also writing a paper on Minoans and Mycenaeans for the Archaeological Institute of America general meeting. The birth on December 3, 1906, of Alexander Boyd, named after Harriet Boyd Hawes's favorite brother, seems to have barely interrupted her work.[310] But as she had to miss the institute meeting in January, Gisela Richter read her paper on her behalf.[311] Less than four months after Alex's birth the prospectus for the publication of her excavations was published.[312]

From the following September until spring 1909 the Haweses lived in

Madison, where Henry taught at the University of Wisconsin. Throughout 1907 and 1908 Boyd continued to work, as she wrote, "under the necessity of publishing excavation results and having the days filled with care of my son."[313] Her book came out in November 1908.[314] This monumental volume is a testament not only to Boyd's scholarship but also to her character. She always presented the excavations as teamwork, and the long list of authors bears witness to her generosity toward all who assisted with her excavations—particularly so since she provided background information and the illustrations for their studies. Crediting the contributions of assistants was not common practice and did not pass unnoticed by reviewers. The *New York Nation* called the volume "a monument of self-denying."[315]

The scholarly contribution of the volume is twofold. In the three introductory chapters Boyd went beyond the scope of a publication of excavations to give a comprehensive account of Minoan civilization and to review Homer in light of the Cretan discoveries. These chapters attracted the favorable attention of contemporary scholars.[316] More importantly, however, Boyd's well-documented publication put "ordinary sites" on the archaeological map, balancing the picture provided by the palace sites.[317] The attention she paid to the remains of humble houses, providing a site plan full of information and details on the layout of the settlement as well as on the architecture of individual houses, was, and long remained, unparalleled.[318] Gournia also became the site where everyday objects of the Minoans could best be studied, not only because they were found in great numbers but also because the publication, unlike other publications, drew particular attention to them through descriptions, drawings, and numerous color plates of the highest quality.[319] Boyd's ambition "was to produce artistic plates which should take the place in museums of objects which cannot be seen outside of Crete"—an ambition she had to pay for by going to great lengths to secure the necessary funds.[320] This latter task was not her only contribution to the business side of this publication. She also put considerable efforts in organizing the sales of the book, keeping track of the payments from subscribers and repaying the sponsors.[321]

While Boyd spent the spring and summer of 1909 in Cornwall with little Alex, Henry Hawes took a last trip to Crete alone.[322] On his return to England, with the family settled near Oxford, he was able to incorporate up-to-date information in the book that he was writing with his wife. *Crete the Forerunner of Greece,* aimed at a general readership, was published in December 1909, and has long held its own as the best, most compact and most readable survey of the subject.[323]

Their stay in England was cut short in February 1910 when Henry

Hawes was appointed assistant professor of anthropology at Dartmouth College, New Hampshire, and the family moved to Hanover. On October 5, Harriet Boyd Hawes was awarded the degree of doctor of humanities (L.H.D.) from her alma mater. The ceremony had to be fitted around the needs of her six-week-old daughter, named Mary Nesbit after Henry Hawes's mother.[324] For the following two years Boyd's life revolved around her children.

The outbreak of the Balkan War in 1912 motivated Boyd to change her priorities. She raised funds to send to Greece for the care of the wounded and relief of the refugees. Her friend Sophie Baltazzi wrote to thank her. Her long letter is a testimony to a strong and true friendship rooted in love for Greece and the cause for independence, best illustrated in the last lines, "Do come over to us some day. Now Crete is free. You can go to Gournia again or begin excavations at Samothraki, or Pella, or Argyrokastro, or Nikopolis. All that is Greece now."[325]

Boyd's dream to resume archaeological work in Greece revived, and momentarily, in December 1914, when the post of the director at the American School became vacant, she thought her dream would materialize. In her diary she noted, "Henry & I decided pretty well to try for [the] post at Athens," and she drew up a list of new ideas for a joint candidacy.[326] But with the escalation of the hostilities in Europe, events took another turn. A year later, Boyd was on her way to Greece, not to Athens and the school, but to the little island of Vidos, off Corfu. It had been transformed into a vast transit camp for the Serbian soldiers who, defeated and driven away by the German army, were arriving there by the thousands, ill, starved, and exhausted from their long journey. From February to April 1916 Boyd organized the feeding of the camp and care for those who were ill. By April the situation had improved, and Boyd returned home.[327] A year later she wrote:

> Comparing my war memories of many years ago as a young woman without home ties with my experiences of last year, I realise how much easier it is for a woman who has not children to be fearless and persistent in an enterprise of this sort.[328]

Yet her personal life never prevented her from acting on her compassion for human suffering.

On April 6, 1917, the United States declared war. Boyd immediately set up a relief unit for the devastated districts of France. In August, Boyd became director of the Smith College Relief Unit and for the second time in less than two years she left for the war zone with seventeen volunteers, trucks, portable houses, food, and clothes, leaving the children with their "nanny" Marie. Her husband had obtained sabbatical leave from Dartmouth College, where he had been appointed full professor only a few months before, and had already left for England to serve in an administrative capacity during the war.[329]

The relief unit was established at Grécourt and began to help the surrounding villages. There were inevitable delays in getting aid, the unit's supplies were held up, and Boyd was under a great deal of pressure. She had had what she described as a short attack of indigestion. The doctor, who was also deputy director, advised her to stay in Paris and had written behind her back to Henry that she was on the verge of a breakdown. Although she denied this, Boyd found that her position as director had been undermined and she therefore resigned. By the time of her resignation the relief unit was fully operational and continued its work for three more years with almost fifty volunteers and nearly two hundred thousand dollars in funds.[330] In September Boyd left Grécourt for Paris, where she ran a canteen for the YMCA and later at the American Red Cross Military Hospital. Among the wounded soldiers was a Greek whose father had died from wounds at Domokos: "He thought she had nursed his father. Three wars and two generations of wounded. 'This,' she felt, 'is my swan song in war nursing!'" The war was drawing to a close and, in June 1918, Boyd left for America.[331]

In July 1919 Henry Hawes was appointed assistant director-bursar at the Museum of Fine Arts in Boston, and the family moved to Boston. The return to Boyd's hometown was the start of a new era that lasted the rest of the Hawes's professional life. Henry Hawes became associate director of the museum in 1924 and held this position until his retirement in 1934. Boyd returned to teaching, taking up a lectureship at Wellesley College.

Teaching, Theorizing, and Social Reforms (1920–36)

Boyd's return to teaching also meant a return to archaeological research. With no prospect for field archaeology, she turned to theoretical archaeology, which could be studied in a library. In September 1920 Boyd joined the art faculty of Wellesley College as lecturer in pre-Christian art. For the next sixteen years, until her retirement in June 1936, she taught the artistic achievements of successive civilizations from the Paleolithic to early Christian times.[332] In addition, she gave many lectures pertaining to classical archaeology and occasionally to Minoan archaeology at the Museum of Fine Arts.[333] Classical archaeology was hardly new ground for her. During her three years at the American School at Athens she had studied many aspects of this field.[334] It now became the focus of her research through the study of five subjects. However, her approach to these subjects extended, where possible, to their prehellenic background. It was the idea of cultural continuity from Bronze Age to Classical Greece and from there to Christianity, that attracted her more in her new research. She called her five subjects *riddles.* A paper on the "Ludovisi throne" and the "Boston Relief" marked her return to the Archaeological Institute of America general meeting in 1921. This was the only one of her "riddles" to be published in full. Two more, the Parthenon pediments and the Erechtheum, were presented at the AIA general meeting in 1923.[335]

In 1926, almost twenty-one years after Boyd had last left Greece, an opportunity arose for a return trip. She was invited to represent Wellesley College at the April 23–24 inaugural ceremonies of the new Gennadeion Library of the American School of Classical Studies at Athens, along with sixty-four other delegates from American colleges and universities.[336] Boyd arrived in Athens well before the ceremonies hoping to conduct a trial excavation under the auspices of the Museum of Fine Arts. She obtained a permit and excavated for four days at Stavros, in the area of ancient Phyla, seat of the ancient mysteries of the Great Goddess—a tradition with Cretan connections. She hoped to find there proof that the marble of the Boston Relief was a local variant of Pentelic marble. This she did, but otherwise the excavation proved fruitless.[337] After the ceremonies, she left Athens with her two children and a party of friends for a cruise of the islands and the long-awaited return to Crete. Of her landing at Herakleion on April 30 she wrote to her husband, Henry:

> I was alone on deck watching sun-rise light the coast towards Mirabello Bay. You know how Crete looked, the beauty of Mt Ida. Mary Waring [Mame] joined me as we entered the harbor. Iron cranes & railways encumber the Venetian fort & sea wall. We steamed in close to the quay. Some new buildings are good, but oh Henry I'm glad we antedate modernity in Crete! I'll not lament on paper but that morning when we came ashore & found only a few sections of the great wall, *no* gates, no mosque on the bastion, my heart ached for the beauty gone![338]

Over the next few days Boyd alone or with her children and the rest of the party made several visits to Knossos and the museum at Herakleion. She found Knossos "much *improved* by the reconstructions" and saw

Evans and his assistant Duncan Mackenzie, who "aged & softened came over for a pleasant chat."[339] On May 7 she and her children set off on horses for the isthmus, stopping at various new sites along the way.[340] They then sailed from Agios Nikolaos to Pachyammos, where they spent the night at Seager's house, empty since his death the year before. The next morning, May 9, they rode out to Gournia, twenty-one years after she had last left it.

> First view a surprise! Never looked better! Even the calm Alex's face glowed—Thoroughly satisfactory return. We talk over roads, houses, shrine, ways of reconstructing palace. Rest in a well-shaded ancient house—then walk back in a blazing sun.

In Kavousi, Boyd was received by the "aged demarch of 1900" and invited for coffee and sweetmeats into so many houses that her daughter exclaimed, "Never had I been kissed and hugged so many times, nor felt such a warm welcome." Their trip to the isthmus ended with a visit to Vasiliki.[341] Back at Herakleion Boyd went to the museum to "select sherds" (probably for the Museum of Fine Arts) and spent a day with Evans at Knossos debating his new ideas.[342] The visit to her old Cretan haunts was complete. Back in Athens she returned to her riddles, studying and checking in situ her ideas on the Erechtheum and the Parthenon. Yet the trip would not have been complete without showing her children the other parts of Greece she so loved, the Peloponnese, Eleusis, Delphi and many other sites.[343]

This was to be Boyd's last trip to Greece, but her love for the past and present of the country where, in her daughter's words, "she seemed to feel, and was made to feel, at home," never faded.[344] She would support Greek causes right up until the time of her death in 1945. For few others would the inscription on top of the Gennadeion Library be more fitting:

> ΕΛΛΗΝΕΣ ΚΑΛΟΥΝΤΑΙ ΟΙ ΤΗΣ ΠΑΙΔΕΥΣΕΩΣ ΤΗΣ ΗΜΕΤΕΡΑΣ ΜΕΤΕΧΟΝΤΕΣ
> ELLINES KALOUNTE OI TIS PAIDEFSEOS TIS IMETERAS METEHONTES
> [Greeks are all those who take part in Greek culture.]

Now that the children were grown, Boyd's scholarly work intensified. She completed the study of the four remaining riddles (the so-called Theseum; the Erechtheum; the Parthenon pediments; the Poros sculptures of the Acropolis), and presented her conclusions on the first two at the Archaeological Institute of America general meetings in 1929 and 1935 respectively.[345] But her hope to publish the complete study of the Erechtheum and her two books (*Five Riddles of Greek Art,* and *The Hellenic World and Christianity: An Historical Study*) based on the studies of the five riddles, never materialized.[346]

During all the Wellesley years, but especially after 1926, archaeology was intermittently overshadowed by Boyd's activities in social justice and politics, and the serious scholarly research was intermingled with lighthearted writing. Always attracted by theater, opera, and concerts, Boyd became enamored of the new medium of film, and it was not long before she tried her pen at scenarios: *Ivanhoe,* as well as more than one version of a tale set in prehistoric Athens and Crete (*The Minotaur and the Maiden; Theseus, Prince of Athens;* and *Theseus and Ariadne*). In the late 1930s came the mystery story *When the Mummy Moves,* the subject of a newspaper competition some twenty-eight years before in which she had won first prize for finding the solution, and *Amalasuntha, Daughter of Theodoric King of the Goths.*[347] All remained unscreened. A less glamorous enterprise but one that reached the bookstores was a guidebook of the Boston area, published in 1936.[348]

In the period 1920–36, and particularly after 1926, the burning issues of the present were to consume much of Boyd's energy. She supported the socialist Norman Thomas for president in 1932 and she wrote countless letters to people in positions of power on a range of domestic and foreign issues.[349] All this activity culminated in her support of a strike in an East Cambridge shoe factory in spring 1933. The help and advice she gave the strikers was so efficient that the company turned against her. At first they tried to scare her off by sending gunmen to trail her; later they filed a one-hundred-thousand-dollar lawsuit against her, which was eventually withdrawn.[350] Meanwhile two happy events occurred in Boyd's family life: the marriage of her son Alex in June 1934 and the birth, in July 1935, of her first grandchild, named Harriet Boyd, after her.[351]

The Last Years (1936–45)

Boyd retired from Wellesley College in June 1936, the year in which she would turn sixty-four. As her husband had already retired, Boyd decided that they should move to Washington, not only to be nearer their children but also to enable her to attend "the most interesting and curious university" she had "ever known—the sessions of Congress."[352] She spoke before the House Committee on Banking and Currency and bombarded congressmen with her ideas. In autumn 1937 she and Henry moved to Belle Haven, near Alexandria, Virginia, where they acquired property.

It was not long before local issues were overshadowed by the threat of war in Europe. As protest against events in Germany, she resigned from membership in the German Archaeological Institute in February 1938. In her letter of resignation she wrote, "The ascendancy of Nazi-Fascism over the mind of Germany and Italy, permitting it to threaten violence to its neighbours . . . is so repugnant to me that I have wished for some time to dissociate myself entirely from it." Although no friend of Communism, she attended House Un-American Activities Committee meetings and wrote to Representative Martin Dies on August 23, 1938:

> It is a fact of present day history that Hitler, Mussolini, Franco and the Japanese high command justify their evil deeds on the ground that they are saving the world against Communism. Are we to see a similar drama enacted in the U.S.?[353]

Following international events from afar and issuing written protests did not suit Boyd, who always longed to be an eyewitness. In August 1938, when Hitler was turning his attention to Czechoslovakia, her daughter Mary went to Prague to report for *The Washington Post,* and Boyd, becoming increasingly concerned for her daughter's safety, determined to act with the courage she had shown all her life. Sweeping aside all difficulties, she telegraphed Mary, "I have passport ready, God bless you, Mother" and set sail on September 22.[354] On October 1, attempting to buy a ticket for Prague after arriving in Paris, she was told, "We have instructions not to sell tickets to Czechoslovakia."[355] She obtained a ticket for Eger but was forced to break her journey at Schorning, "the last station that day in legal possession of the Third Reich." She managed to get to Eger late in the evening of the next day. In the morning she found "every man, woman and child" busy decorating the town for Hitler's arrival in the afternoon. At last she had a view of Hitler himself "moving quickly forward from the army side [on the platform]—alone, strikingly simple. Great emotion! Some women, many small boys wept." To her surprise Boyd, usually affected by such devotion, "remained absolutely cold, unillusioned." She attempted to withdraw from the crowd saluting Hitler, but "withdrawal was not permitted"; she "heard it all and witnessed the oath of the people, in the awkward position of a non-participant in a religious rite."[356]

Boyd left Eger and hired a car at Karlsberg to take her to the border.

Stopping at Buchov for the night, she awoke the next morning to find that the Czechs had left. She decided to walk the next leg of her journey and finally arrived in Prague on October 8. A journey that should have taken twenty-two hours "had taken a week, but a week of adventure passing from a democracy through Hitler's Germany into a no man's tract, and at last reaching a beleaguered but dauntless land of freedom."[357] Seven weeks later Boyd and Mary left via Vienna, where they witnessed the terrible effects of the hatred stirred up against the Jews.

Boyd felt that "in no other three months of a long life" had she learned "so much live history." Upon her return to America, she put this knowledge to practical use by seeing Mrs. Roosevelt, hoping she would pass on her views to the president. She had concluded that the only path to lasting peace was for Europe to form federations that would eventually lead to a World Federation—far-sighted ideas. Intensely embarrassed by the aim of the isolationists, she wrote to the Keep America Out of War Committee: "The idea of the U.S. surviving in lonely moral grandeur strikes me as silly and Pharisaical. Every Christian is per se a citizen of the world and rises or falls with the world community."[358]

In September 1939 the invasion of Poland signaled the beginning of World War II. When Italy invaded Greece in autumn 1940, Boyd wrote, "Greece takes the place of Britain as the first line of defense for democracy and that is tragically fitting, since Greeks invented democracy . . . I phoned my concern and admiration to the Greek Embassy." When six months later the Greeks and fifty-three thousand British troops sent to their aid from Libya were overwhelmed by German panzer divisions and the Luftwaffe, she wrote in spring 1941 that she was "as proud of the Greeks in defeat (by overpowering odds) as in victory."[359]

Boyd's energies were funneled into writing to opinion-forming broadcasters about the current crisis and into learning Russian. In a practical way she kept goats, chickens, and pigs and discovered that "for exercise, nothing excels pig-chasing."[360] But more and more of her time was spent looking after her husband Henry, whose failing health led to his death on December 13, 1943. Boyd later regretted "immensely every unkind, impatient word and act . . . he did help himself all he could." She continued, "I knew him better and loved him more those last six months than ever before. He had a glimpse of it—I wish he had had far more."[361]

Her own health deteriorating, Boyd nevertheless wrote to the British ambassador in January 1945 asking for permission to visit Greece. As Europe struggled to emerge from the ruins, her thoughts turned to her "adopted" country. In a letter dated February 18, 1945, she praised Greece as the country with "a cleaner record before and during this war than any other country in the world." She added, "I believe I couldn't do better with the rest of my life short or long than to help Greece all I can."[362] She had recently written an eloquent plea for the return of the Dodecanese to Greece, which was published by the American Friends of Greece.[363] She also wrote to Alex, who was working for the United Nations Relief and Rehabilitation Administration in Italy, urging him to go to Greece for the same work.[364] She was undeterred by the Greek Civil War and hoped to make a "future expedition to Crete, carrying fine stock, chickens etc."[365] Two months after she had planned to visit Greece, Boyd was in the hospital and after an operation died on Easter eve, March 31, 1945, her two children at her bedside. She was buried in the family plot at Forest Hills, Boston.[366]

Epilogue

Harriet Boyd Hawes's professional achievements reveal a person of great intelligence and stamina. She was, in the words of Edmond Pottier a "bel exemple de féminisme intelligent."[367] Due to her devotion, perseverance and single-mindedness she was able to overcome the barriers of the profession and enter the realm of field archaeology. However, her strive to lead her own excavation would have been jeopardized had she no access to private funds. The fact that in 1900 Boyd was paying for her own excavation was a crucial factor in overcoming the objections of Rufus Richardson, the director of the American School of Classical Studies at Athens. Equally, in 1901, it was the fact that she and Blanche Wheeler were able to advance a considerable sum of money, which made the expedition, and ultimately the discovery of Gournia, possible. Of course, time and chance were also on her side from the moment she chose to come to Greece.

Many scholars, of both genders, shared the attributes that bring success but Boyd stands out from her peers because of three further traits: modesty in her achievements, honesty in the way she credited those who advised and helped her, and finally loyalty to institutions and to those who worked with her. Boyd's qualities may have marginalized her, for she never "blew her own trumpet." The fact that two major publications—the *Encyclopaedia Britannica* and Arthur Evans's *The Palace of Minos*—claimed that Richard Seager discovered Gournia is instructive.[368] The error in the entry in *Encyclopaedia Britannica* was corrected after Boyd's daughter Mary pointed it out in a letter to the editor. The case of *The Palace of Minos,* must have saddened Boyd, as she felt she herself ought to set the record straight.[369] In a letter to Evans she pointed out:

> The item [in the index] under Seager "discoveries at Gournia" is misleading (see *Gournia,* Preface). I wonder if you realize that when Richard came to Gournia the town, palace and shrine had been discovered 2 years earlier, that the first burials at Gournia and Pachyammos were found by me, that I took him to Vasiliki and Pseira and Edith Hall to Vrokastro, that in fact the only site discovered independently by R. B. S. was Mochlos; we were returning from a visit to Palaikastro and he halted on the way to follow a clue given him personally by a peasant, which led to his great success at Mochlos. I hope this doesn't seem petty—it is just meant to keep the record clear—a record which Mr. Wace obscured when he came to Boston.[370]

It must be said that Seager would not have made such a claim. However, he never acknowledged, in print, Boyd's part in his later work or gave her credit as the founder of American research in Crete. But in a letter to Boyd, although understated, he admitted that "it is all due to you really and your giving me a chance to get started."[371]

Boyd's traits of modesty, honesty, and loyalty also shone through her war nursing and humanitarian work. They gained her the love, respect, and admiration of the many people she encountered, from ordinary soldiers and villagers to high officials, politicians, and even the queen of Greece. In her personal life they won her firm friends. Boyd's human aspect was best epitomized by one of these friends, Gisela Richter:

> Her loyalty to her friends and students, her keen sympathy for those whose cause she espoused, and her imaginative approach to problems made her an inspiring and dynamic personality.[372]

WORKS BY HARRIET BOYD HAWES
A SELECTED BIBLIOGRAPHY

Books, Reports, and Articles

Articles on the 1897 Greco-Turkish War. *Philadelphia Public Ledger.* Spring 1897.

Articles on the 1897 Greco-Turkish War. *New York Journal.* April and May 1897.

"Excavations at Kavousi, Crete, in 1900." *American Journal of Archaeology* 5 (1901): 125–57.

"Houses and Tombs of the Geometric Period at Kavusi, Crete." *American Journal of Archaeology* 5 (1901): 14–15.

Letter reporting on the 1903 campaign. *Records of the Past* 3 (1904): 92–94.

"Gournia. Report of the American Exploration Society's Excavations at Gournia, Crete, 1901–1903." *Transactions of the Department of Archaeology, Free Museum of Science and Art, University of Pennsylvania* 1, no. 1 (1904): 7–44.

"Gournia. Report of the American Exploration Society's Excavations at Gournia, Crete, 1904." *Transactions of the Department of Archaeology, Free Museum of Science and Art, University of Pennsylvania* 1, no. 3 (1905): 177–90.

Article on the Archaeological Congress 1905. Παρθενών, Boston, June 3, 1905.

"The Pottery of Gournià Vasiliki, and other prehistoric sites on the isthmus of Hierapetra (Crete)." In *Comptes Rendus du Congrès International d'Archéologie. Ire Session, Athènes 1905*, 226. Athens, 1905.

"Minoans and Mycenaeans: A Working Hypothesis for the Solution of Certain Problems of Early Mediterranean Race and Culture." *American Journal of Archaeology* 11 (1907): 57–58.

B. E. Williams, R. B. Seager, and E. H. Hall, coauthors. *Gournia, Vasiliki and Other Prehistoric Sites on the Isthmus of Hierapetra, Crete.* The American Exploration Society, Free Museum of Science and Art. Philadelphia, 1908.

C. H. Hawes, coauthor. *Crete the Forerunner of Greece.* London, 1909. 2d ed., 1911. 3d ed., 1916.

"A Gift of Themistocles: Two Famous Reliefs in Rome and Boston." *American Journal of Archaeology* 26 (1922): 81–82.

"A Gift of Themistocles: The 'Ludovisi Throne' and the Boston Relief." *American Journal of Archaeology* 26 (1922): 278–306.

"The Parthenon Pediments and the Original Plan of the Erechtheum." *American Journal of Archaeology* 28 (1924): 74–75.

"The Ancient Temple of the Goddess on the Acropolis." *American Journal of Archaeology* 40 (1936): 120–21.

Ready-Guide: Boston, Cambridge, Brookline. Boston: Marshall Jones Company, 1936.

"Memoirs of a Pioneer Excavator in Crete." *Archaeology* 18, no. 2 (1965): 94–101.

"Memoirs of a Pioneer Excavator in Crete." *Archaeology* 18, no. 4 (1965): 268–76.

Reviews

Excavations in the Island of Mochlos, by R. B. Seager. *Classical Philology* 3 (1912): 366–69.

Fouilles exécutées à Mallia. Premier Rapport: Exploration du Palais (1922–1924), by F. Chapouthier and J. Charbonneaux. *American Journal of Archaeology* 34 (1930): 107–9.

Suggested Reading about Harriet Boyd Hawes

Allsebrook, Mary. *Born to Rebel: The Life of Harriet Boyd Hawes.* Oxford: Oxbow Books, 1992. Paperback ed. 2002.

Archival Material: Notes

Two articles published posthumously in 1965 in *Archaeology* (see bibliography above) were extracted from two holograph documents titled "Second article = Crete: Exploring Trip: Trial Excavations," and "Third article = Excavations at Gournia," respectively, which form part of a lengthy unpublished work by Boyd, titled "The Quest of a Buried City." A general outline of the work with lists of photographs and a fragment of the first part, dated 1906, and typescript or manuscript versions of the three articles are in the Smith College Archives, kept separately in folders 58, 63, 108, 109, 112, 115. Also available in the Smith College Archives are a number of articles on wars or social issues, and on archaeological matters, that have been published in various newspapers and in Smith College magazines. See especially "The School of Excavations," *Smith College Monthly,* April 1901, 430; "An Account of the Excavations at Gournia, Crete," *Smith College Monthly,* January 1904, 262; "A Trip through Western Crete, 1904," *Smith College Monthly,* November 1904, 119; and "Archaeology and Literature," *The Nation,* April 18, 1907. A manuscript version—titled "A Cretan Pompeii,"—of an article about the 1901 campaign that appeared in *The Nation,* November 7, 1901, p. 356, and in the *American Journal of Archaeology* 6 (1902): 71–72, is also housed in the Smith College Archives. The archives also include a number of finished or nearly finished manuscripts on a diverse range of subjects—e.g., classical archaeology, war memoirs, scenarios for films, etc. as well as correspondence.

The Ashmolean Library, Oxford, has a proof of the unpublished abstract "The Pottery of the Prehistoric Settlement at Gournià and Its Neighbourhood in Crete," *British Association for the Advancement of Science, Cambridge Meeting, 17th–24th August, 1904.*

NOTES

The writing of Harriet Boyd Hawes's biography would not have been possible without the constant help and generosity of her daughter Mary Allsebrook. She not only read the manuscript and gave us much advice but also supplied us with photographs and other material. We are very grateful to Mary and her husband Colin. We are also grateful to Boyd's grandchildren, Hat Hawes B. Savage and Alexander B. Hawes Jr., for searching for and making available new archival material. We are also indebted to Helen Hughes-Brock for reading the final draft and making many useful comments and suggestions.

In addition to Harriet Boyd Hawes's family members, we would like to thank the following individuals and institutions who made archival material accessible to us. In England: Caroline Barron, for allowing Ann Brown to consult D. G. Hogarth's diaries; Maggie Bellatti, in charge of the C. H. Hawes Archive, Department of Biological Anthropology, University of Cambridge, for the reproduction of photographs kept in that archive; Roger Moorey, Keeper of the Department of Antiquities, Ashmolean Museum, for giving us access to the A. Evans Archive. In Greece: Alexandra Karetsou, director of Herakleion Archaeological Museum, for giving

Vasso Fotou access to the museum's archives and for much practical help during her study; Marina Panagiotaki for alerting us to the existence of documents in the Herakleion Archaeological Museum Archives; James D. Muhly, Director of the American School at Athens, for allowing Vasso Fotou to study the school archives and the archivist Natalia Vogeikoff for helping her with this study. In the United States: Alessandro Pezzati, Acting Senior Archivist of the University of Pennsylvania Museum Archives, for helping Vasso Fotou during her study there; Nanci A. Young, Archivist of Smith College Archives, and Kathleen B. Nutter and Karen Eberhart, Archives Specialists, for supplying us with photocopies of relevant material and for helping Vasso Fotou during her study there. Vasso Fotou's study of Harriet Boyd Hawes's archives at Smith College Archives and the University of Pennsylvania Museum Archives in January 2001 was made possible thanks to a grant from the Institute for Aegean Prehistory, and she is grateful to Philip Betancourt and the INSTAP Review Committee. Permission to publish archival material has been obtained from the above individuals and institutions wherever possible. Unfortunately the number of illustrations had to be drastically reduced.

Not least we are extremely grateful to our families for their invaluable support, most particularly David and John.

Reference note: For the documents from Harriet Boyd Hawes's archive published in V. Fotou, *New Light on Gournia: Unknown Documents of the Excavation at Gournia and Other Sites on the Isthmus of Ierapetra by Harriet Ann Boyd, Aegaeum* 9 (Liège, 1993) (hereafter cited as Fotou, *New Light*), a reference to this publication is given where the reader can find all the necessary details. All these documents are now in the University of Pennsylvania Museum Archives (hereafter cited as Penn).

1. Autobiographical notes titled "Memoranda" (hereafter cited as *HB/Memoranda*), Smith College Archives (hereafter cited as Smith). A letter from Alex Boyd to his sister-in-law Ellen Slade, November 18, 1872 (possession [2001] of Hat H. Savage), is particularly touching, revealing his feelings.

2. Autobiographical notes titled "Memories & Opinions," covering the years 1871–84, 1892–96, dated December 31, 1944–January 1945 (typescript copy by and in possession [1998] of Mary Allsebrook; original at Smith), 2 (hereafter cited as *HB/Autobio*); M. Allsebrook, *Born to Rebel: The Life of Harriet Boyd Hawes* (Oxford: Oxbow Books, 1992), 4–5.

3. Holograph notebook by M. Allsebrook, with occasional notes by Boyd, presented as a calendar for the years 1871–1945, indicating events of Boyd's life with corresponding dates in margin (possession [1997] of M. Allsebrook) (hereafter cited as *MA/Calendar*), s.v. 1871–72. Also *HB/Autobio*, 1.

4. Allsebrook, *Born to Rebel*, 7, and *HB/Memoranda*, 5; see also five letters from Alex to Harriet Boyd, dated from 1890 to 1891, Smith.

5. Allsebrook, *Born to Rebel*, 8, 14–15, 232–35; *HB/Autobio*, 11. For her religious beliefs at that time see Diary for 1892, Smith.

6. *HB/Autobio*, 11; Allsebrook, *Born to Rebel*, 7–8.

7. Allsebrook, *Born to Rebel*, 9; *Stoneleigh-Burnham Alumnae Bulletin* 1, no. 3 (1968): 1.

8. Holograph notebook by Boyd presented as a calendar for the years 1871–1937, indicating events of her life (possession [1997] of M. Allsebrook) (here-

after cited as *HB/Calendar*), s.v. Oct. 1 [1885]. See also letter from Boyd to Jean Patten, July 13, 1886, Smith.

9. *Stoneleigh-Burnham Alumnae Bulletin* 1, no. 3 (1968): 1; P. W. Lehmann, "Harriet Boyd Hawes: Introductory Remarks," in *A Land Called Crete: A Symposium in Memory of Harriet Boyd Hawes, 1871–1945, Smith College Studies in History* 45 (Northampton, Mass., 1968) (first published under the title "Indomitable Scholar and Humanitarian," *Smith Alumnae Quarterly* 59, no. 1 [1967]: 11).

10. Twelve years later she dedicated her first lecture at Smith on Gournia to Amelia Edwards. Document titled "Lecture on 'Gournia' Smith College. Nov. 1902," by Boyd, Smith, 1–2 (hereafter cited as *HB/Smith Lecture* 1902). Edwards visited America in 1889–90, giving lectures on Egypt (published in 1891 with the title *Pharaohs, Fellahs and Explorers*); she must have left a strong impression at Smith College, which honored her with a L.H.D.

11. *MA/Calendar,* s.v. Aug. [1891], June [1892].

12. Allsebrook, *Born to Rebel,* 15–16; *HB/Calendar,* s.v. Aug., Sept. [1892], Jan. [1893 to 1896]; *HB/Autobio,* iii.2.

13. *HB/Autobio,* iii.3–5.

14. *HB/Calendar,* s.v. June, July, Aug., Sept., Oct. [1896] and *HB/Autobio,* iii.5–9; Allsebrook, *Born to Rebel,* 16–18.

15. *HB/Autobio,* iii.5, 8. On her early thoughts on archaeology see *HB/Smith Lecture* 1902, 1–2. On the American School see L. E. Lord, *A History of the American School of Classical Studies at Athens, 1882–1942* (Cambridge: Harvard University Press, 1947), esp. 4–6, 10. For a description of the school at that time, see M. C. McClellan, *Three Americans in Greece: The Early Years of the American School* (Athens: ASCS, 1981), 5–6; T. D. Seymour, *The First Twenty Years of the American School of Classical Studies at Athens. Bulletin of the School of Classical Studies at Athens* 5 (1902), 45.

16. *HB/Calendar,* s.v. Oct. [1896].

17. *HB/Calendar,* s.v. Oct. [1896]; cf. R. B. Richardson, "Report of the Director 1896–97," *American Journal of Archaeology* (hereafter *AJA*) 1 (1897): 107. For her first days in Greece see her letter to her family, October 18, 1896, Smith. The "announcement" appeared in *To Asty* (daily illustrated newspaper, Athens), Sunday Sept. 29 (Oct. 11), 1896, no. 2105, p. 2. The dates correspond to Julian and Gregorian calendars respectively, which differ by thirteen days for dates in the nineteenth century, and by fourteen days in the twentieth century. Wherever the Gregorian dates are not given, we have added them in parentheses.

18. *HB/Calendar,* s.v. Oct. [1896], Jan. [1897].

19. Allsebrook, *Born to Rebel,* 19, 21, 24, 36–37; A. Gold, R. Fizdale, *The Divine Sarah: A Life of Sarah Bernhardt* (London, 1992), 195–240 passim. For further glimpses of her life at Mrs. McCraith's home see her letters to her family, October 27, December 6, 21–29, 1896; to her aunt Ellen (Slade), December 10, 1896; to J. M. R. B., December 14, 1896; holograph document, "Experiences in Greek Lands," by Boyd, probably dated 1924, all at Smith. Additional information was given by Nanos Valaoritis, great-grandson of Mrs. McCraith, whom we thank.

20. *AJA* 1 (1897): appendix, 62; Richardson, "1896–97," 107; Lord, *American School,* 90.

21. Richardson, "1896–97," 108. Richardson used to exclude women from

some trips , or parts of trips (Richardson, "1896–97," 108), but this was not uncommon. Dörpfeld would admit women only for part of his excursion in the Peloponnese (R. B. Richardson, "Report of the Director 1898–99," *AJA* 3 [1899]: 679 and cf. Lord, *American School,* 94; T. Peck, "Report of the Director 1898–99," *AJA* 3 [1899]: 707–8; R. B. Richardson, "Report of the Director 1899–1900," *AJA* 4 [1900]: supplement, 20–21). Women's inability to travel in Greece was a widespread belief among male archaeologists; see e.g., Emerson's report in T. D. Seymour, "Seventeenth Annual Report of the Managing Committee of the American School of Classical Studies at Athens," *AJA* 2 (1898): 488, cited below.

22. Lord, *American School,* 93. Richardson later published a popular account of these tours: R. B. Richardson, *Greece through the Stereoscope: A Tour Conducted by Rufus B. Richardson, Ph.D.* (New York: Underwood, 1907). See also R. B. Richardson, *Vacation Days in Greece* (London, 1903).

23. J. R. S. Sterrett, "Report of the Professor of the Greek Language and Literature, 1896–97," *AJA* 1 (1897): 120. For Boyd's description of the trip see letter to her family, October 18, 1896, Smith (extracts in Allsebrook, *Born to Rebel,* 22–23).

24. Sterrett, "1896–97," 120–21; letters from Boyd to her family, December 6 and 14, 1896, Smith (extracts in Allsebrook, *Born to Rebel,* 26–28).

25. Richardson, "1896–97," 110, 112–13; T. D. Seymour, "Sixteenth Annual Report of the Managing Committee of the American School of Classical Studies at Athens," *AJA* 1 (1897): 91.

26. Richardson, "1896–97," 109, and Allsebrook, *Born to Rebel,* 34–35; also Lord, *American School,* 70–71.

27. Richardson, "1896–97," 108; Sterrett, "1896–97," 121; Lord, *American School,* 90–91; *HB/Calendar,* s.v. Dec. [1896], and letters from Boyd to her family, December 21–29, 1896, and to J. Boyd, January 10, 1897, Smith. Dr. Wilhelm Dörpfeld was the director ("first secretary") of the German Archaeological Institute in Athens from 1887 to 1912.

28. Letter from Boyd to her family, October 27, 1896, Smith; Allsebrook, *Born to Rebel,* 24, 30.

29. Allsebrook, *Born to Rebel,* 30.

30. *HB/Calendar,* s.v. Mar. [1897], and letter from Boyd to her family, March 8, 1897, Smith; Allsebrook, *Born to Rebel,* 34, 39–43. A small notebook with notes taken during these classes and starting March 9, 1897, exists at Smith.

31. Allsebrook, *Born to Rebel,* 44–55; I. N. Καρόλου, *Ὄλγα, ἡ Βασίλισσα τῶν Ἑλλήνων. 22 Αὐγούστου 1851–19 Ἰουνίου 1926,* (Athens, 1936), esp. 238, 260, 308, 335, 354. Also, letter from Blanche to Mame (Mary K. Waring), April 9, 1901, and letters from S. Baltazzi to Boyd, various dates, Smith.

32. Allsebrook, *Born to Rebel,* 56–63.

33. Holograph draft for a book by Boyd on her experiences of the Greco-Turkish War, from the preliminary activities before March 1897 to end of August 1897. Probably written in 1898 (typescript copy by and in possession [1998] of M. Allsebrook; original at Smith) ch. 6, p. 1. Original material on Boyd's activities in 1897 includes entries in her Diary for 1896–1900, and a great number of letters to her family and friends written during the period she served in the Greek army, all at Smith.

34. Allsebrook, *Born to Rebel,* 64–75.

35. Richardson, "1896–97," 109, 113.

36. Allsebrook, *Born to Rebel,* 47.

37. Comment by F. Halbherr to her future husband; see Diaries of Charles Henry Hawes describing his trips to Crete, Greece and elsewhere (1904 [2 vols.], 1905 [6 vols.], 1909 [2 vols.], typescripts by M. Allsebrook and originals in Bodleian Library, Oxford) (hereafter cited as *CH/Diary*), 1905, 5:458.

38. Allsebrook, *Born to Rebel,* 76–79, and entries for January 1, 2, 1899, in Diary for 1896–1900, Smith.

39. Seymour, "Seventeenth Report," 484.

40. Seymour, "Sixteenth Report," 99–101; Lord, *American School,* 81, 82.

41. Seymour, "Sixteenth Report," 92.

42. Fragment of a document attached to an outline of her work "The Quest of a Buried City," and forming part of the same work (see Archival Material: Notes); Lord, *American School,* 94, 363.

43. *HB/Calendar,* s.v. Sept. [1898]; *AJA* 3 (1899): appendix, 53.

44. T. D. Seymour, "Eighteenth Annual Report of the Managing Committee of the American School of Classical Studies at Athens," *AJA* 3 (1899): 669. Also, "Sixteenth Report," 92; "Seventeenth Report," 484; Richardson, "1896–97," 113.

45. Lord, *American School,* 94.

46. Nichols held the first Agnes Hoppin Memorial Fellowship established by Joseph C. Hoppin with the aim of increasing the activity of the school for women students. It was awarded on the basis of merit, without examination.

47. *AJA* 3 (1899): appendix, 43; Seymour, "Seventeenth Report," 480. Cf. Lord, *American School,* 94–95.

48. The Mycenaean civilization was becoming a regular subject in teaching and examinations; see Seymour, "Seventeenth Report," 482; *AJA* 2 (1898): appendix, 101; cf. 3 (1899): appendix, 101, 104.

49. Richardson, "1898–99," 680–81; *HB/Calendar,* s.v. Nov. [1898], and further on her notes see infra; letter granting permission to Boyd to climb up the scaffolding of the Parthenon, dated April 9 (April 21), 1899, issued by the Department of Antiquities, possession (2001) of A. B. Hawes Jr.

50. Richardson, "1898–99," 680; cf. *HB/Calendar,* s.v. Oct. [1898].

51. According to Emerson's report, "The travelling work of our own membership has been too scattered and individual to make it the subject of systematic report" (Seymour, "Eighteenth Report," 672).

52. *HB/Calendar,* s.v. Oct., Nov. [1898]. This tour included Delphi as well as Thermopylae and Lamia—Boyd's wartime haunts. A few snapshots from this trip and probably also from the trip to Peloponnese (see below) exist at Smith.

53. On a trip from Delphi to Volos, Ida Thallon, a fellow student, recalled that it was "great fun" to hear the same guide "talk about the Kuria Boyd" and how "everything she ever said or did was perfect" (letter from Ida Thallon to her mother, April 13, 1900, typescript in American School of Classical Studies [ASCS] Archives); see also Boyd's complimentary comments on him, e.g., in her letter to her family, December 6, 1896, Smith.

54. Entries for March 30 to April 9, 1899, in Diary for 1896–1900, Smith; it is not clear if this was Professor R. Norton's trip of the American School in Rome, in which Blanche Wheeler was a student, the first official tour women could follow throughout (Peck, "1898–99," 707–8, and above, n. 21).

55. *HB/Calendar,* s.v. Feb., Mar., May, June [1899].

56. Letter from Boyd to her family, April 28, 1900, Smith; Richardson, "1898–99," 681.

57. *HB/Calendar,* s.v. Oct. [1898], May [1899]. According to a circular on the 1898–99 fellowships of the school the men fellows were allowed to occupy furnished rooms in the school on payment each of twenty dollars per annum (Seymour, "Seventeenth Report," 482); Boyd was probably a paying guest of Mrs. Richardson, as her note suggests: "Board Mrs. Richardson 290 dr." (*HB/Calendar,* s.v. March [1899]; see also letter from Boyd to her friends, December 16, 1898, Smith).

58. Letters from Boyd to Blanche, July 11, December 3, 1899, Smith; on her route see entries July to October 1899, in her Diary for 1896–1900, Smith.

59. A fellow student remarked: "The only other fustanella servants in town belong to the Queen and the Schliemanns, but Miss Boyd looks far too grand when she has him on the box" (letter from Ida Thallon to her mother, Feb. 19, 1900, typescript in ASCS Archives). See Boyd's introduction of Aristides Pappadhias in her letter to Blanche (December 3, 1899, Smith). A few letters from Aristides to Boyd, spanning from 1905 to 1927, are in possession (2001) of Hat H. Savage.

60. J. R. Wheeler, "Twenty-Second Annual Report of the Managing Committee of the American School of Classical Studies at Athens," *AJA* 7 (1903): supplement, 13; Seymour, "Seventeenth Report," 481.

61. *AJA* 4 (1900): supplement, 84; Lord, *American School,* 95.

62. Richardson, "1899–1900," 20–21; T. D. Seymour, "Nineteenth Annual Report of the Managing Committee of the American School of Classical Studies at Athens," *AJA* 4 (1900): supplement, 10–11.

63. Seymour, "Nineteenth Report," 10.

64. Her studies included Byzantine history, Orthodox religion, folklore, modern literature, and politics (letter from Boyd to Blanche, Dec. 3, 1899, Smith; letter from I. Thallon to her mother, Feb. 19, 1900, typescript in ASCS Archives).

65. Letter from Boyd to Blanche, April 28, 1900, Smith.

66. Letters from Boyd to Blanche, April 28, 1900, and to Seymour, May 1–10, 1900, and draft of a letter from Boyd to Seymour, May 1, 1900, Smith.

67. Richardson, "1899–1900," 20; Lord, *American School,* 7, 95; cf. Seymour, "Nineteenth Report," 11. Lord's comment suggests that he had seen the paper, but we were not able to trace it in the ASCS Archives.

68. All the coins are listed in a small notebook titled "Greek Coins of HBH listed" (in papers containing writings by Boyd, both unpublished and published, relating to her scholarly work [nine files, classified by V. Fotou in 1994], file III, Smith; hereafter cited as *HB/Papers* 1994). According to comments by I. N. Svoronos, director of the Numismatic Museum Athens, to whom she showed her collection, some of the coins were rare or good specimens. Boyd rechecked the collection in 1902 and noted a couple of coins missing and one given to Blanche. To judge from the title of the notebook, she still had the collection after her marriage. The notebook also lists two vases probably bought in Athens in March 1900. Ida Thallon, describing Boyd's and Jean's rooms, noted "a good many interesting things they have picked up" (letter to her mother, February 23, 1900, typescript in ASCS Archives).

69. Notes written on verso of a draft of a letter to M. S. Grierson, February 27, 1943, Smith.

70. Draft of a letter from Boyd to Seymour, May 1, 1900, Smith. In this same letter and in her letters to her family and to Blanche (both April 28, 1900, Smith) she refers to objects bought during her first exploration trip in central and eastern Crete: two ceramic and one stone vase, four (?) bronzes, four (?) sealstones, and a few coins. In her financial accounts for 1904 (see *HB/FinRec* B, doc. 2: Fotou, *New Light,* 52–53), Boyd lists a number of Minoan, Greek, and Roman objects bought at Axos, Kalyviani, Palaiokastro (Polyrrinia), and Eleutherna during her journey across western Crete before her campaign. E. Hall, who also joined this trip, mentions in her letters home the purchase of coins and "Mycenaean gems" (K. Page, "Memoirs of an Archaeologist in Crete," *Archaeology* 31, no. 2 [1978]: 8, 10) and Boyd's attempt (?) to buy illuminated books: "we have been looking over the old books of the monastery [at Gonia]; some are illuminated and go back to 1613. Miss Boyd wants to buy some for the Library of Congress" ("Memoirs," 8). In the same year she also bought chance finds from Avgos, which she donated to the museum at Herakleion.

71. Federico Halbherr and Arthur Evans, who among modern scholars worked most continuously on the island, mainly limited themselves to extensive surveys and the reconnaissance of sites. Limited excavations were carried out at such sites as Idean Cave, Gortyna, even Knossos; see De Luca, ed., *Creta antica: Cento anni di archeologia italiana (1884–1984)* (Rome: Italian Archaeological School at Athens, 1984), 52–68, 73, 84, 101. On the conditions regulating archaeological research in Crete before 1898, see A. Brown, "'I Propose to Begin at Gnossos': John Myres's Visit to Crete in 1893," *Annual of the British School at Athens* (hereafter cited as *BSA*) 81 (1986): esp. 37–38, 42–44. On the position of Cretan Christians see I. Hazzidakis's comments on his 1881 travels in Crete, quoted in S. Hood, "An Early British Interest in Knossos," *BSA* 82 (1987): 88. On the conditions of travel in pursuit of antiquities in Crete during the last decade of the last century see Brown, "Begin at Gnossos," and A. Brown, *Before Knossos . . . Arthur Evans's Travels in the Balkans and Crete* (Oxford, 1993), 35–84; also De Luca, *Creta antica,* 27–28, 52–68.

72. The law was finalized on June 18 (June 30) and promulgated on June 21 (July 3), 1899.

73. By the beginning of 1900, eighteen sites were allocated to these institutions, half of them (including Knossos) to the British School—an achievement brought about by the persistent efforts of its director D. G. Hogarth and A. Evans, along with Prince George's support. Cf. H. B. Hawes, "Memoirs of a Pioneer Excavator in Crete," *Archaeology* 18, no. 2 (1965): 95, 97 (hereafter cited as *Memoirs I*), and J. Evans, *Time and Chance, the Story of Arthur Evans and His Forebears* (London, 1943), 326–27.

74. J. W. Shaw, "North American Archaeological Work in Crete, 1880 to 1990," *Expedition* 32, no. 3 (1990): 6–8; H. A. Boyd, "Excavations at Kavousi, Crete, in 1900," *AJA* 5 (1901): 125.

75. *BSA* 5 (1898–99): 1, 102, 104; a further step was the establishment of the Cretan Exploration Fund under the management of Hogarth and Evans and the patronage of Prince George.

76. Fragment of a document attached to an outline of her work "The Quest of

a Buried City," and forming part of the same work (see Archival Material: Notes).

77. Fragment of a document attached to an outline of her work "The Quest of a Buried City," and forming part of the same work (see Archival Material: Notes), and letters from Boyd to Blanche and to her family, both April 28, 1900, Smith. It is not known whether Boyd submitted a formal petition; no such document could be found in the ASCS Archives.

78. Cf. Lord, *American School,* 84, 298–99.

79. Ibid., 95.

80. Letter to her mother, April 5, 1900, typescript in ASCS Archives.

81. *AJA* 3 (1899): appendix, 72 (esp. Regulation XV); cf. comments *re* Agnes Hoppin Memorial Fellowship in Wheeler, "Twenty-Second Report," 13.

82. Letter from Boyd to her family, April 28, 1900, and draft of a letter to Seymour, May 1, 1900, both at Smith.

83. Cf. *AJA* 3 (1899): appendix, 73 (esp. Regulation XX), and Seymour, "Eighteenth Report," 670.

84. Draft of a letter, May 1, 1900, Smith.

85. Letter dated April 28, 1900, Smith.

86. Cf. H. B. Hawes, B. E. Williams, R. B. Seager, and E. H. Hall, *Gournia, Vasiliki, and Other Prehistoric Sites on the Isthmus of Hierapetra, Crete* (Philadelphia: American Exploration Society, Free Museum of Science and Art, 1908), v (hereafter cited as *Gournia*). There is no record of any comments on her lack of experience, but, a few years earlier, excavations conducted by inexperienced students had been the subject of serious concern resulting in a drastic reduction of the school's fieldwork (Lord, *American School,* 81, 84–85).

87. Cf. *Memoirs I,* 98.

88. Letter of April 28, 1900, Smith (passage published in *Memoirs I,* 97); the same but more concise version of events is given in a letter from Boyd to her family, April 28, 1900, Smith. Hogarth's meeting with Boyd, in Athens, followed his lecture on his latest excavations at Naukratis (Egypt), at the British School open meeting on Friday 16. Evans was in Athens between February 20 and 27; see holograph diaries by D. G. Hogarth containing various notes and describing his travels and excavations, 3 vols., 1898–1901 (in possession of his granddaughter Caroline Barron) (hereafter cited as *DGH/Diary*), entries for February 1900. Also Boyd's entry for February 16, 1900, in Diary for 1896–1900, Smith; the invitation to the British School open meeting exists at Smith.

89. *Memoirs I,* 97. H. A. Boyd, "Gournia. Report of the American Exploration Society's Excavations at Gournia, Crete, 1901–1903," *Transactions of the Department of Archaeology, Free Museum of Science and Art, University of Pennsylvania* (hereafter cited as *Trans*) 1, no. 1 (1904): 26.

90. Cf. letter from Boyd to her family, April 28, 1900, Smith.

91. See Seymour's comments quoted in a letter from Boyd to her family, April 28, 1900, Smith.

92. Draft of a letter to Seymour, May 1, 1900, Smith.

93. Draft of a letter from Boyd to Hogarth, 1900, Smith, and cf. fragment of a document attached to an outline of her work "The Quest of a Buried City," and

forming part of the same work (see Archival Material: Notes). *To Asty* was the newspaper that had announced her arrival in Athens, back in 1896 (see n. 17). Luckily this letter did not reach Hogarth, who, by that time, had become less optimistic for the success of Boyd's plans (see infra).

94. Letter from Boyd to her family, April 28, 1900, and draft of a letter from Boyd to Seymour, May 1, 1900, Smith; also holograph document by Boyd describing her first weeks in Crete in 1900 (see Archival Material: Notes).

95. Boyd, "Crete, in 1900," 126; letters from Boyd to her family, and to Blanche, both April 28, 1900, Smith. Jean's report was published in *Gournia,* 58.

96. Seymour, "Nineteenth Report," 15; cf. Lord, *American School,* 95.

97. Letter from Boyd to her family, April 28, 1900, Smith, and *Gournia,* v. Dörpfeld was involved in Schliemann's attempt to excavate at Knossos in 1886 (Hood, "British Interest," 92–93, and cf. report by A. S. Koumanoudis to the Archaeologiki Etaireia at Athens, dated July 15, 1886, published in *Γ. Σακελλαράκης, 'Αρχαιολογικές ἀγωνίες στὴν Κρήτη τοῦ 19ου αἰώνα 51 ἔγγραφα γιὰ τὶς κρητικὲς 'αρχαιότητες (1883–1898)* [Herakleion, 1998], 50); he retained a keen interest in the island, and from 1900 he paid, as part of his Inselreise, yearly visits to the new excavations, including Gournia.

98. *Memoirs I,* 97. For original sources on this trip see: leaves dated April 10, 11, 12, cut from Diary for 1900 and inserted in Diary for 1896–1900, and letter from Boyd to her family, April 28, 1900, Smith.

99. *DGH/Diary* 1900, Thursday April 12; letter from Hogarth to Boyd, April 12, 1900, possession (2001) of Hat H. Savage. The entry in Hogarth's diary responding to the news that she was actually coming to Crete is similar: "Wire from Miss Boyd, saying 'delayed' but referring to what letter? Must leave her to Hazzidaki. I'm sure he will not be able to sanction another dig" (Wednesday April 4, 1900). For the arrival at Herakleion and the meeting with Hazzidakis see letter from Boyd to her family, April 28, 1900 (extracts in Allsebrook, *Born to Rebel,* 86–87, and *Memoirs I,* 97), and leaf dated April 12, cut from Diary for 1900 and inserted in Diary for 1896–1900, both at Smith.

100. See draft of a letter to Seymour, May 1, 1900 and letter to the Boyd family, April 28, 1900, both in Smith. The contributions of these connections to Boyd's success first in obtaining the permit and then in carrying out the excavations were acknowledged in her reports. See Boyd, "Report of 1901–1903," 26; *Gournia,* v; see also Seymour, "Nineteenth Report," 15.

101. *DGH/Diary* 1900, Friday April 13.

102. Letter from Boyd to her family, April 28, 1900 (extracts in *Memoirs I,* 97), and leaf dated April 13 cut from her Diary for 1900 and inserted in Diary for 1896–1900, both at Smith. Evans, in his reports, reconsidered his earlier opinion on the throne and suggested that it was "better adapted for a man" (*BSA* 6 [1899–1900]: 38), and that on this throne "Minos may have declared the law" (*Cretan Exploration Fund. Report to the Subscribers,* November 1900, 2).

103. Evans had repeatedly explored this area during his trips in 1894, 1896, and in particular 1899. During the last visit he was shown Plaï tou Kastrou, where a tomb had been discovered accidentally by a peasant in 1895; subsequent investigation resulted in the discovery of vases and bronze objects that Evans obtained and presented to the Museum of the Syllogos. *HB/Notes* 2, 5–6: Fotou, *New Light,* 47;

holograph document by Boyd describing her first weeks in Crete in 1900 (see Archival Material: Notes); Boyd, "Crete, in 1900," 127; leaf dated April 13, cut from Diary for 1900 and inserted in Diary for 1896–1900, Smith; also *DGH/Diary* 1900, Sunday April 15.

104. For this trip see accounts by Boyd in *Memoirs I,* 97–99; Boyd, "Crete, in 1900," 127, and "Report of 1901–1903," 26–28; also Allsebrook, *Born to Rebel,* 88–93. These published accounts are largely based on the letters from Boyd to her family, April 28, 1900, and to Seymour, May 1, 1900, Smith.

105. Boyd, "Report 1901–1903," 27, 28.

106. Fotou, *New Light,* 21–22; also cf. supra, p. 205.

107. *Memoirs I,* 98.

108. Draft of a letter from Boyd to Seymour, May 1, 1900, Smith. According to this draft letter, at the nearby village of Aghios Vasilios she bought a three-sided steatite sealstone "with excellent pictographs," which she used to stamp the envelope with the letter to Blanche (April 28, 1900, Smith); the envelope is lost and there is no indication as to the provenance of this seal, but it is clear she did not connect it with Arvi.

109. Holograph document by Boyd describing her first weeks in Crete in 1900 (see Archival Material: Notes); also letters cited in previous footnote.

110. Boyd, "Report of 1901–1903," 28, and *HB/Corresp.* B, doc. 1: Fotou, *New Light,* 54. Also Aggelakis's letter to Boyd (April 30 [May 13], 1900, possession [2001] of Hat H. Savage) acknowledging with obvious delight his appointment. The appointment of a supervisor of the excavations on behalf of the Cretan state was a condition in all the permits, and the task was usually entrusted to one of the ephors (Hazzidakis or Xanthoudidis), but often it was carried out by an administrative officer or a teacher (Fotou, *New Light,* 22). The supervisor was paid by the government and had to report on the progress of the excavations (some of these reports can be found in Herakleion Archaeological Museum Archives [hereafter cited as HM Archives]; one, by N. Pantoulas, supervisor of the excavations in 1901, is given below).

111. *Memoirs I,* 98, 99, from a letter from Boyd to her family, April 28, 1900, Smith. Letters of introduction were common practice, a kind of "passport" that would secure hospitality and help for the bearer during his journey. Aggelakis's letter must have been very similar to the one that still exists in Boyd's archives; see *HB/Corresp.* B, doc. 2: Fotou, *New Light,* 54.

112. Boyd, "Crete, in 1900," 137; Allsebrook, *Born to Rebel,* 93.

113. *Memoirs I,* 99.

114. *HB/Notes* 2, 20: Fotou, *New Light,* 47; Boyd, "Report of 1901–1903," 21; *Memoirs I,* 99, after a letter from Boyd to her family, April 28, 1900, Smith.

115. Boyd, "Crete, in 1900," 127.

116. Fotou, *New Light,* 22.

117. Draft of a letter from Boyd to Seymour, May 1, 1900, and letter from Boyd to her family, April 28, 1900 (extracts in *Memoirs I,* 99), both at Smith; also cf. *HB/Notes* 2, p. 6: Fotou, *New Light,* 47. For a short account on early antiquities she noted at Episkopi, in the isthmus, see holograph document by Boyd describing her first weeks in Crete in 1900 (see Archival Material: Notes).

118. *DGH/Diary* 1900, Friday April 27, and draft of a letter from Boyd to Seymour, May 1, 1900, Smith. In her plans for the 1901 campaign Boyd was still con-

sidering Arvi (her letter to Stevenson, Feb. 2, 1901, Penn), but again when she came to put in an alternative petition she chose Dreros.

119. Boyd, "Report of 1901–1903," 21.

120. Letter from Boyd to her family, April 28, 1900 and draft of a letter from Boyd to Seymour, May 1, 1900, both at Smith.

121. Boyd, "Crete, in 1900," 126, and holograph document by Boyd describing her first weeks in Crete in 1900 (see Archival Material: Notes).

122. E.g., when she climbed Mt. Helicon in 1897 (Allsebrook, *Born to Rebel,* 28, and supra) or when she visited the monasteries at Meteora in 1899 (letter from Boyd to Blanche, December 3, 1899, Smith [extracts in Allsebrook, *Born to Rebel,* 82]).

123. Letter from Boyd to her family, April 28, 1900, Smith; similar statement in draft of a letter to Seymour, May 1, 1900, Smith.

124. Boyd, "Report of 1901–1903," 18. The site was located on the eastern side of the isthmus.

125. Cf. Ida Thallon, Diary 1900–1901, May 8, 1900, p. 8 (ASCS Archives) *re* Boyd's plans for carrying on her work next year "if it is a success."

126. Draft of a letter from Boyd to Seymour, May 1, 1900, Smith; see also Boyd, "Report of 1901–1903," 28, and *Memoirs I,* 99.

127. Letter from Boyd to her family, April 28, 1900, Smith. Cf. Hogarth's comments: "Saw Miss Boyd anxious to dig Kavousi and had some nice little bronzes & γαλόπετρες ["milkstones," a nickname for sealstones]" (*DGH/Diary* 1900, Friday April 27). Boyd had bought the bronzes from Kavousi as well as a few other objects from other sites she visited; see especially draft of a letter from Boyd to Seymour, May 1, 1900, Smith.

128. On the petition see draft of a letter from Boyd to Seymour, May 1, 1900, Smith; in this letter she makes two interesting comments on the permit's terms: (1) Her capacity to act under the auspices of the American School required written confirmation from Richardson; (2) The excavations "are called δοκιμαατικαί [trial] but may be made όριστικαί [permanent] any time by my buying the land if it seems best to keep them open." Further on the petition and her morning meeting, see entry dated April 29, 1900, under same date and under April 28, in Diary for 1896–1900, Smith; *Memoirs I,* 99, after a letter from Boyd to her family, April 28, 1900, Smith. The covering letter accompanying the petition, addressed to Hazzidakis and dated April 16 (April 29), 1900, exists in HM Archives.

129. Letter from Ida Thallon to her mother, May 11, 1900, typescript, and Ida Thallon, Diary 1900–1901, May 7, 1900, p. 4, ASCS Archives. Ida Thallon, who was visiting Crete with Dörpfeld's tour on May 7, witnessed the preparations, and her comments in the same documents are a testimony to Boyd's competence: "If anyone ought to succeed, she should, for she has great ability," "and ought to find something good for she is not going at it in the dark. Good luck to her."

130. *DGH/Diary* 1900, Friday April 27 and Wednesday May 9. On her preparations see her letter to her family, April 28, 1900, and draft of a letter to Seymour, May 1, 1900, both in Smith, and letter from Ida Thallon to her mother, May 11, 1900, typescript in ASCS Archives. Further on the permit see n. 128; note that the date on the permit, April 25, is of the Greek calendar (May 7 of the Western calendar).

131. On their trip see entries in Boyd's Diary for 1900 on leaves dated May 10, 11, 12, cut from this diary and inserted in Diary for 1896–1900, Smith.

132. *Memoirs I,* 99.

133. Leaf dated May 13, cut from Boyd's Diary for 1900 and inserted in Diary for 1896–1900, Smith. Khordakia and Avgos were two further sites mentioned to her by Evans (Boyd, "Report of 1901–1903," 28).

134. *Memoirs I,* 100.

135. *Gournia,* 19.

136. Boyd, "Crete, in 1900," 128 and passim.

137. Entries dated May 14, 15, 1900, in Boyd's Diary for 1896–1900, Smith; Boyd, "Crete, in 1900," 130–31.

138. *Memoirs I,* 101.

139. *Memoirs I,* 101, and see Boyd, "Crete, in 1900," 150–54.

140. Boyd, "Crete, in 1900," 149–50.

141. Ibid., 143–48.

142. *HB/Notes* 2, p. 26–28: Fotou, *New Light,* 47; Boyd, "Crete, in 1900," 131–36. Along with or between the investigation of these six sites Boyd made smaller trials at four other sites (Khondrovolakes, Cape Tholos, Khordakia, and Kefalolimnos) with, however, poor results.

143. *DGH/Diary* 1900, Wednesday June 6, and letter from Hogarth to Boyd, June 6, 1900, possession (2001) of Hat H. Savage.

144. Entry for March 26, 1901, in Boyd's Diary for 1901–5, Smith.

145. *Memoirs I,* 101.

146. *DGH/Diary* 1900, Thursday June 14.

147. *Memoirs I,* 101, and cf. *DGH/Diary* 1900, Thursday June 14; also letter from Hogarth to Boyd, June 6, 1900, possession (2001) of Hat H. Savage.

148. Gilliéron's drawing of the plate appeared in the publication (Boyd, "Crete, in 1900," fig. 11, p. 148). *DGH/Diary* 1900, June 21, July 1.

149. *HB/Calendar,* s.v. July (1900).

150. Fragment of a document attached to an outline of her work "The Quest of a Buried City," and forming part of the same work (see Archival Material: Notes). Her letters written during her first months in Greece in 1896 and later, e.g., letter to Blanche, December 3, 1899 (all at Smith), testify her feelings for Greece, how deeply enchanted she immediately became with the land, the light, the people, the food, the way of life—and of course the antiquities.

151. *Gournia,* 19.

152. Cf. Boyd, "Report of 1901–1903," 26.

153. *HB/Notes* 4, p. 1: Fotou, *New Light,* 47, and *Gournia,* 19; Boyd refers specifically to the period between the expulsion of the Turkish troops, May 1898, and the uprising of 1905. On the "discomforts" of travel in Crete at that time see M. J. Becker and P. P. Betancourt, *Richard Berry Seager: Pioneer Archaeologist and Proper Gentleman* (Philadelphia: University of Pennsylvania Museum of Archaeology and Anthropology, 1997), 17–18, 36, and cf. Emerson's statement on traveling in Greece in his report as professor of archaeology at the school in 1898: "Greece is still a wild country . . . Women and delicately nurtured men may well recoil from the annoyances and hardships incident to travelling much in the interior [of

Greece], and indeed by the coastwise steamboats" (in Seymour, "Seventeenth Report," 488).

154. *Memoires I,* 98.

155. E.g. letter from Boyd to her family, April 28, 1900, Smith; holograph document by Boyd describing her first weeks in Crete in 1900 (see Archival Material: Notes); Page, "Memoirs," 10.

156. Cf. Lord, *American School,* 298. Richardson's report of the following year does include summary accounts of the excavations, other than Corinth, which were conducted by members of the school. R. B. Richardson, "Report of the Director, 1900–1901," *AJA* 5 (1901): supplement, 26–27.

157. Seymour, "Nineteenth Report," 15–17; Seymour, *First Twenty Years,* 2, 42.

158. *HB/Calendar,* s.v. Sept. [1900].

159. A. Murray, "Harriet Boyd Hawes. Boston 1871–Washington 1945," in *A Land Called Crete: Minoan and Mycenaean Art from American and European Public and Private Collections,* exhibition organized by the Smith College Museum of Art, Northampton, Massachusetts, 1967.

160. Ida Thallon, Diary 1900–1901, May 8, 1900, p. 8, ASCS Archives.

161. See abstract in *AJA* 5 (1901): 14–15.

162. Allsebrook, *Born to Rebel,* 99.

163. The American Exploration Society was an organization founded in 1897 to act as a feeder and adjunct to the Egyptian and Mediterranean Section of the Free Museum of Science and Art of the University of Pennsylvania. As cofounder of the Mediterranean Section of the AES, Stevenson had a special interest in Mediterranean archaeology. Further on Stevenson (1847–1921) and her work at the University Museum, see D. P. Winegrad, *Through Time, across Continents: A Hundred Years of Archaeology and Anthropology at the University Museum* (Philadelphia: University Museum, University of Pennsylvania, 1993), 20–21, 37.

164. Report by Stevenson titled "Philadelphia's Archaeological Expedition to Crete" (1901), Penn, 1–2, and *Gournia,* v. The society was dissolved by 1910; see holograph diary notes by Boyd for December 11 to 23, 1909, January 1, 31 and February 1, 1910, Smith, entry for December 12 (hereafter cited as *HB/Diary* 1909–10). Apart from Stevenson, Edward Robinson of the Museum of Fine Arts in Boston also offered to support her future plans for work in Crete, but withdrew in the belief that Stevenson had the first right (letters from Boyd to Stevenson, January 6, 20, 21, 1901, Penn, and letter from Robinson to Boyd, January 9, 1901, possession [2001] of Hat H. Savage).

165. See correspondence from January 6 to March 15, 1901 (total thirty-four items including a draft of a memorandum, and a typewritten memorandum with covering letter, March 13), Penn, and entries for February 14, 15, March 15, 1901, in Boyd's Diary for 1901–5, Smith. Also Boyd, "Report of 1901–1903," 29; J. S. Silverman, "Excavating Gournia," in *Gournia, Crete: The Seventy-fifth Anniversary of the Excavations,* ed. P. Betancourt (*Temple University Aegean Symposium* 4 [1979]), 3.

166. Diary entries for January 26–29, 1901, on loose leaves, and entries for January 26–29, February 6, 14, 16, March 7, 9, 10, 26, 1901, in Diary for 1901–5, Smith; letters from Boyd to Stevenson, January 6, 20 and February 2, 1901, Penn. From

these entries it is clear that work on her report went on well after March 6, 1901 (noted in Boyd, "Crete, in 1900," 157). On her M.A. see Lehmann, "Introductory Remarks," 12, and short c.v. in Boyd's hand, Smith; also *MA/Calendar,* s.v. June 1901, and cf. entry for June 17, 1901, in Boyd's Diary for 1901–5.

167. Letters from Boyd to Stevenson, January 20, February 2, April 5, 1901, and letter from Stevenson to Boyd, January 27, 1901, Penn.

168. Holograph notes by Boyd, on six leaves torn from a notebook, describing her daily experiences starting with her trip from America to Crete and stopping short on the second day of her prospecting trip in Crete, in 1901, Smith (hereafter cited as *HB/Notes* 1901); letters from Boyd to Stevenson, April 9, 13, 1901, Penn.

169. *HB/Notes* 1901, and entries for April 17–24, May 4, 1901, in Boyd's Diary for 1901–5, Smith; also Boyd, "Report of 1901–1903," 29. The letter of introduction in *HB/Corresp.* B, doc. 2: Fotou, *New Light,* 54, was written during their stay at Neapolis. For a history of research at Malia, see H. Van Effenterre, *Le Palais de Mallia et la cité minoenne,* vol. 1 (Rome, 1980), 5–9.

170. *HB/Corresp.* B, doc. 4: Fotou, *New Light,* 55. According to the permit her petition was dated April 11 (April 24), but it was not submitted until April 20 (May 3) (date on a cover letter from Boyd to Hazzidakis accompanying most certainly the petition for Dreros, HM Archives), and forwarded to the ministry by Hazzidakis soon after (see date on his letter of support April 21 [May 4]). Lengthy negotiations took place before this petition could be submitted, which explains Boyd's belated departure for Kavousi. There were practical difficulties from Hazzidakis's side and uncertainty about Evans's plans for Milatos (entries for April 25, 26, 30, May 1, 2, 1901, in Boyd's Diary for 1901–5, Smith). The permit would have been issued earlier, before the discovery of Gournia, had it not been for delay in the ministry receiving the credentials from the American Exploration Society (letter from Boyd to Stevenson, May 13, 1901, Penn). On Boyd's plans concerning the area of Neapolis, see also letter with photograph of Anavlochos from Wheeler to Stevenson, May 7, 1901, Penn.

171. Letter from A. Reinach to Boyd, June 25, 1910, possession (2001) of Hat H. Savage.

172. Entry for April 26, 1901, in Boyd's Diary for 1901–5, Smith. The permit, dated April 11 (April 24), and a letter from the director of education to Hazzidakis appointing supervisors for the excavations, exist in HM Archives; for a similar letter to Boyd see *HB/Corresp.* B, doc. 3: Fotou, *New Light,* 54–55. In connection to the wording of this permit referring to Boyd as "representative of the American School at Athens" and not of the American Exploration Society, see letter from Boyd to Hazzidakis asking to have this amended (letter in Greek, dated May 8 [May 21], HM Archives), and letter from Boyd to Stevenson (May 13, 1901, Penn) assuming the responsibility and expense of the excavation at Avgos. Both new permits (for Dreros and Gournia) and all subsequent permits referred to Boyd as "representative of the American Exploration Society."

173. Boyd, "Report of 1901–1903," 29.

174. The excavations at Avgos were never fully published. In early July 1902 she apparently was working on Avgos (entry for July 5, 1902, in Diary for 1901–5, Smith), but only a short account is included in her published report (Boyd, "Report of 1901–1903," 18–20). Part of the original records of the excavations at Avgos has

survived; see holograph loose leaves by Boyd with extracts from Wheeler's and her own daybooks of the excavation at Avgos, the investigation of the Kavousi area, and the discovery of and the first days of excavations at Gournia, May 7–22, 28, 1901, Smith (hereafter cited as *HB/DBextracts* 1901).

175. H. B. Hawes, "Memoirs of a Pioneer Excavator in Crete," *Archaeology* 18, no. 4 (1965): 269 (hereafter cited as *Memoirs II*), and Allsebrook, *Born to Rebel,* 101. On her investigation of the Kavousi area and the sites she discovered, see *HB/DBextracts* 1901, and entries for May 5–18 in her Diary for 1901–5, Smith. Among these sites are Alykomouri and Chrysokamino, recently explored by D. C. Haggis and P. P. Betancourt respectively; see J. D. Muhly and E. Sikla, eds., *One Hundred Years of American Archaeological Work on Crete* (Athens, 2000), 59–74.

176. *HB/DBextracts* 1901, 7–8; letters from Blanche to Mame, May 15, 1901, and to Alan, May 20, 1901, Smith.

177. Boyd, "Report of 1901–1903," 30.

178. *HB/NB* I, 40: Fotou, *New Light,* plates 18–19, and *HB/DBextracts* 1901, 9; *Memoirs II,* 269.

179. *HB/DBextracts* 1901, 10 (partly reproduced in *Memoirs II,* 269); *HB/NB* I, 40: Fotou, *New Light,* plates 18–19; *HB/Notes* 3, passim: Fotou, *New Light,* 47.

180. *HB/NB* I, 38: Fotou, *New Light,* 43, 44. The original telegraph (May 23, 1901) is at Penn.

181. *HB/NB* I, 38, 38 verso: Fotou, *New Light,* 43, 44, plates 6–7.

182. Becker and Betancourt, *Richard Berry Seager,* 22; Allsebrook, *Born to Rebel,* 103.

183. On the permit see *HB/NB* I, 38 verso and *HB/Corresp.* B, doc. 5: Fotou, *New Light,* plates 5–7; postal from Boyd to Stevenson, June 10, 1901, Penn. On Hazzidakis's visit see entry for May 28, 1901, in Boyd's Diary for 1901–5, Smith, and letter from Wheeler to Stevenson, May 28, 1901, Penn.

184. Fotou, *New Light,* 21, plate 1a.

185. Letter from Boyd to Stevenson, June 6, 1901, Penn; *Memoirs II,* 271; Boyd, "Report of 1901–1903," 33; H. A. Boyd, "Gournia. Report of the American Exploration Society's Excavations at Gournia, Crete, 1904," *Trans* 1, no. 3 (1905): 177; Fotou, *New Light,* plate 1b.

186. The wages remained the same throughout the excavations, but varied according to class. The Firsts were paid two francs per day (about forty cents), reduced to 1.25 francs for the men of the fourth class and to less than one franc for the girls who washed the finds. Finding sealstones and other special objects earned a separate reward. On the different currencies see in particular Allsebrook, *Born to Rebel,* 103–4. Boyd kept meticulous accounts, as a number of documents testify; e.g., for 1901 see *HB/DBextracts* 1901, 2, 11–13, and holograph notebook titled "American Exploration Society. Crete. 1901," by Boyd, Penn; for 1903 and 1904: *HB/FinRec* A, docs. 1–4 and B, doc. 1: Fotou, *New Light,* 52, plates 1b, 2.

187. Report dated June 4 (June 17) 1901, HM Archives.

188. Letter from Boyd to Stevenson, June 6, 1901, Penn.

189. Letters from Boyd to Stevenson, June 12, August 7, 25, 1901; six telegraphs from Wells to Stevenson and from Boyd to Stevenson, July–August 1901, and letter from Cramp to Stevenson, August 6, 1901; letter from Boyd to Wells, October 11, 1901; all at Penn.

190. *HB/Notes* 3, p. 6: Fotou, *New Light,* 47, and *Gournia,* 47. "Snake tubes" are cylindrical objects with two opposing rows of vertical serpentine loop handles, and represent a distinctive type of Postpalatial cult objects.

191. Fotou, *New Light,* 28–30, 97–98.

192. *HB/Notes* 3, p. 7: Fotou, *New Light,* 47.

193. *DGH/Diary* 1901, Wednesday June 19.

194. *HB/Smith Lecture* 1902, 13; *Gournia,* pp. 31–32 and plate 3, pp. 33–34 and plate 4.

195. Letter from Boyd to Stevenson, June 6, 1901, Penn.

196. P. Lock, "D. G. Hogarth (1862–1927): '. . . A Specialist in the Science of Archaeology,'" *BSA* 85 (1990): 194.

197. *The Times,* Saturday, August 10, 1901, 12; similar comment in *DGH/Diary* 1901, Wednesday June 19. For Boyd's own newspaper report on the discovery of Gournia, see *The Nation,* November 7, 1901.

198. From the title, "The Quest of a Buried City," of a work by Boyd (see Archival Material: Notes).

199. Document titled "Some Experiences and a Moral," by Boyd, 1924 (supplemented 1943), Smith, 19; *HB/Smith Lecture* 1902, 10.

200. *The Academy,* July 4, 1896, no. 1261; also *AJA* 11 (1896): 459.

201. Boyd, "Crete, in 1900," 127 n. 1.

202. Boyd, "Report of 1901–1903," 28. Boyd would have never failed to acknowledge Evans's help in the discovery of Gournia if he had indeed helped; on the contrary she repeatedly pointed out both in private letters (letter to Stevenson, June 6, 1901, Penn) and in her reports (Boyd, "Report of 1901–1903," 30, 31; *Gournia,* 19) that she was the first to locate the site.

203. Letter from Boyd to Wells, October 11, 1901, Penn; *Memoirs II,* 271.

204. *HB/FinRec* C, docs. 2–3: Fotou, *New Light,* 53.

205. Letters from Boyd to Stevenson, June 12, August 7, 25, 1901, May 19, 1902, and from Boyd to Wells, October 11, 1901, Penn; letter from Blanche to Mame, August 2, 1901, Smith; Boyd, "Report of 1901–1903," 33. A scaled plan in pencil of Gournia in 1901 by Fyfe, probably a first draft, exists in the Evans Archive, Ashmolean Museum. For Boyd's sketches see holograph draft daybook titled "Gournia Notes" with sketches and plans, describing the excavations at Gournia in Crete, 1901, 1903, possession of M. Allsebrook (hereafter cited as *HB/draftDB* 1901, 1903); also *HB/NB* II, passim: Fotou, *New Light,* 44–45.

206. Cf. letter from Boyd to Wells, October 11, 1901, Penn, where she expressed her concern on this matter, and letter from Boyd to Hazzidakis, March 9, 1902, HM Archives, where she stressed the need to keep a guard at Gournia. The contracts of employment of Anagnostis and Markos exist in HM Archives (copy of contract, dated Oct. 29 [Nov. 11], 1901; contract dated June 3 [June 16] 1903). Boyd reemployed Anagnostis during the 1904 excavations (*HB/FinRec* B, doc. 2, pp. 5, 7: Fotou, *New Light,* 52–53).

207. *AJA* 6 (1902): 48–49. For references to newspaper and magazine articles see *AJA* 6 (1902): 71, 72. For Boyd's opinion on the meeting and her contribution see her letter to Stevenson, January 9, 1902, Penn.

208. For the invitation see letter from Boyd to Stevenson, December 5, 1901, Penn; for the schedule of the tour see loose leaf titled "Arch. Inst. Lecture Tour [of]

1902," Smith. Also P. S. Sheftel, "The Archaeological Institute of America, 1879–1979: A Centennial Review," *AJA* 83 (1979): 14, and *MA/Calendar,* s.v. Jan.–Mar. 1902. The Pennsylvania society was the only one not to ask for the lecture, an incident that caused some turbulence in Boyd's relations with the institute; see her letter to Stevenson, January 9, 1902, and letter from White to Stevenson, January 28, 1902, Penn. A further invitation came in April from the newly formed Washington society; see prospectus issued by the society announcing the lecture, Smith, and letter from Boyd to Stevenson, May 4, 1902, Penn. The content of the lecture must have been similar to *HB/Smith Lecture* 1902.

209. Manuscript version of the report on Cretan Expedition, 1901, Penn; also Allsebrook, *Born to Rebel,* 110–11.

210. Letter in HM Archives.

211. Letter dated March 9, 1902, HM Archives; cf. letter from Boyd to Stevenson, May 4, 1902, Penn.

212. Memorandum of agreement between Boyd and the American Exploration Society, drawn up by Boyd, July 8, 1902; see also letters from Boyd to Stevenson, May 4, 19, 30, July 18, 19, 25, 1902, and from Stevenson to Boyd, July 19, 1902, Penn; *HB/Calendar,* s.v. Sept. [1901].

213. *HB/Calendar,* s.v. July [1902]; cf. letter from Boyd to Stevenson, August 29, 1902, Penn.

214. Letter from Boyd to Stevenson, September 18, 1902, Penn.

215. Letter to Hazzidakis, September 26, 1902, HM Archives; *HB/Calendar,* s.v. Sept. [1902].

216. Entries for January 19–March 14, 1903, in Boyd's Diary for 1901–5, Smith; Allsebrook, *Born to Rebel,* 112. Further on her meeting with Petrie, see letter from Boyd to Stevenson, February 14, 1903, Penn, and short c.v. written in Boyd's hand, Smith.

217. R. B. Richardson, "Report of the Director, 1902–1903," *AJA* 7 (1903): supplement, 18; Allsebrook, *Born to Rebel,* 112, 113.

218. For a biography of Seager see Becker and Betancourt, *Richard Berry Seager.* On his joining Boyd's expedition see Allsebrook, *Born to Rebel,* 112; Becker and Betancourt, *Richard Berry Seager,* xi, 7–8. On his work in 1903 see Boyd, "Report of 1901–1903," 33; also Becker and Betancourt, *Richard Berry Seager,* 11, where the authors point out that he was considered by Boyd as a student.

219. Boyd, "Report of 1901–1903," 33, fig. 5, p. 14, and letter from Evans to Boyd, April 15, 1903, possession (2001) of Hat H. Savage. For line plans by Moffat and Hastings see *HB/NB* II, passim: Fotou, *New Light,* 44. Further on Hastings (holder of the Charles Eliot Norton Fellowship at the American School) see T. W. Heermance, "Twenty-third Annual Report of the Managing Committee of the American School of Classical Studies at Athens," *AJA* 8 (1904): supplement, 20; Lord, *American School,* 379.

220. Letter from Boyd to Blanche, May 6, 1903, Smith.

221. *HB/FinRec* B, doc. 1, p. 2: Fotou, *New Light,* plate 1b, and entry dated March 30, 1903, on a loose leaf, Smith.

222. Cf. Boyd, "Report of 1901–1903," fig. 23, and for an early tracing see line plans accompanying letter from Boyd to Stevenson, September 4, 1903, Penn.

223. Boyd, "Report of 1901–1903," 22.

224. On the roundel: *HB/NB* III, 35: Fotou, *New Light,* 45–46, 68. On the stirrup jar: *Gournia,* 24; Allsebrook, *Born to Rebel,* 107. On the vases from Cm: *Gournia,* 39.

225. *Gournia,* 32.

226. This could also explain her decision not to investigate further the chance discovery of an assemblage of bronze tools, knife blades, rings, sealstones, and beads, made at Avgos at that time. She did, however, inspect the spot, acquired the objects for Herakleion Museum and entrusted their study and publication to H. R. Hastings ("A Bronze-Age 'Pocket' from Avgo (Crete)," *AJA* 9 [1905]: 277–87). See also letter from Boyd to Blanche, May 6, 1903, Smith; and Boyd, "Report of 1901–1903," 20.

227. *HB/Corresp.* B, doc. 6: Fotou, *New Light,* 22, 55; Boyd, "Crete, 1904," 178.

228. *HB/Corresp.* B, doc. 7: Fotou, *New Light,* 55.

229. Boyd, "Report of 1901–1903," 13, 20, fig. 5, p. 14.

230. *Gournia,* 49. The excavation of the building of the Gournia period was completed in 1904 (Fotou, *New Light,* 104).

231. *HB/Corresp.* B, doc. 8: Fotou, *New Light,* 55; cf. Boyd, "Crete, 1904," 183.

232. Boyd, "Report of 1901–1903," 21.

233. See *HB/draftDB* 1901, 1903, 141–44, notes on a number of buildings including the palace dated June 11. For the dispatch of the finds see telegraph by Boyd to the Eforia Archeotiton, Herakleion, dated June 9, 1903 (May 27 of the Greek calendar) and another by an official (?) of the Eforia to S. Xanthoudidis, also dated May 27 (June 9), 1903, both in HM Archives; cf. entry for June 8, 1903, in Boyd's Diary for 1901–5, Smith.

234. *HB/FinRec* B, doc. 1, p. 3: Fotou, *New Light,* 52.

235. Entries for July 8–28, August 13, 1903, in Boyd's Diary for 1901–5, Smith. For her participation in the meetings of the Anthropology Section Committee, see *Southport 1903. British Association for the Advancement of Science. Seventy-Third Annual Meeting. Journal of Sectional Proceedings,* no. 3 (issued Friday, September 11, 1903, at 8 A.M.), 13; no. 4 (Monday, September 14, 1903, 8 A.M.), 13; no. 5 (Tuesday, September 15, 1903, 8 A.M.), 12; no. 6 (Wednesday, September 16, 1903, 8 A.M.), 10; for summaries of the papers see *Report of the Seventy-Third Meeting of the British Association for the Advancement of Science Held at Southport in September 1903* (London, 1904).

236. Allsebrook, *Born to Rebel,* 114; *HB/FinRec* B, doc. 1: Fotou, *New Light,* 52.

237. Boyd, "Crete, 1904," 177; Page, "Memoirs," 10. Boyd tried, but failed, to obtain a research grant from the Carnegie Institution.

238. Becker and Betancourt, *Richard Berry Seager,* 32–33, 34, 35.

239. Holograph cards of a diary by Boyd describing her trip from Naples to Herakleion, her journey to western Crete, and her excavations at Gournia and other sites, March 19–June 1, Smith (hereafter cited as *HB/CardDiary* 1904); for shorter accounts of the trip see *Memoirs II,* 272; Allsebrook, *Born to Rebel,* 116–17; also Page, "Memoirs."

240. Boyd, "Crete, 1904," 177; *HB/FinRec* A, doc. 3: Fotou, New Light, 52. Pappadhias left first on May 22 (*HB/CardDiary* 1904, May 22, and letter from Boyd to Blanche, July 10, 1904, Smith), but probably came back on July 12 for a few days

(*HB/FinRec* B, doc. 3: Fotou, *New Light,* 53). Seager, having fallen ill, left on June 6 (Becker and Betancourt, *Richard Berry Seager,* 48–49); Hall followed after the closure of the main campaign when also all the finds and household goods were sent off to Herakleion. On the dispatch of the finds see letter from Xanthoudidis to Hazzidakis, June 14 [June 27], 1904, HM Archives; also holograph loose leaves by Boyd, probably part of or copied from a daybook, describing the excavations at Gournia, April 18, 19, May 23, June 5, 16, 20, 21, July 8, 1904, Smith, entries for June 16, 20 (hereafter cited as *HB/DBextracts* 1904).

241. *HB/DBextracts* 1904, April 18; also letters from Hall and Boyd to Stevenson, March 28 and April 21, 1904, respectively, Penn; letter from Boyd to Mame, August 27, 1903, Smith. The payroll lists 110 workmen, not all working at the same time (*HB/FinRec* A, doc. 3: Fotou, *New Light,* 52).

242. See dates of discovery of finds listed in *HB/NB* III, 56–58: Fotou, *New Light,* 45.

243. *HB/NB* III, 58, 59, 60–70: Fotou, *New Light,* 45, 46.

244. Boyd, "Crete, 1904," 178.

245. Charles Henry Hawes (1867–1943) was awarded a B.A. degree in 1899 and M.A. in 1902. An expedition in 1900–1901 through Asia provided material for his first book, *In the Uttermost East* (1903). In 1904 he began anthropological research in Crete, where he met Boyd. See also Allsebrook, *Born to Rebel,* 126–27.

246. *HB/CardDiary* 1904, May 10. Henry's account in his diary is very similar (*CH/Diary* 1904, 2:153–55).

247. *CH/Diary* 1904, Wednesday May 11, 2:159–60.

248. Cf. letter from Boyd to Stevenson, April 21, 1904, Penn.

249. Boyd, "Report of 1901–1903," 8–22 and esp. 12.

250. *HB/Corresp.* B, doc. 10: Fotou, *New Light,* 55; cf. *HB/CardDiary* 1904, May 22.

251. Shaw, "Crete, 1880 to 1990," 11; and cf. B. J. Hayden and J. A. Moody, "The Vrokastro Survey Project," *Expedition* 32, no. 3 (1990): 45; also Fotou, *New Light,* 22.

252. *HB/CardDiary* 1904, May 5, 7, 10; *Gournia,* 49.

253. *HB/CardDiary* 1904, May 10 (for the sketch of the building of the Gournia period at Vasiliki made by Boyd on this day and noted in her diary see Fotou, *New Light,* 104, plate 44). The trials were carried out by Seager alone, Boyd and Hall being on a visit to Palaikastro.

254. Boyd, "Crete, 1904," 178.

255. Boyd, "Crete, 1904," 179–85, and Fotou, *New Light,* 99–101, 104. An intermittent journal of these excavations can be found in *HB/NB* V (Fotou, *New Light,* 42, 46); cf. J. Silverman, "A Lost Notebook from the Excavations at Gournia, Crete," *Expedition* 17, no. 1 (1974): 12, 14.

256. *Gournia,* 46; Silverman, "Lost Notebook," 17–20, and Fotou, *New Light,* 101–2.

257. Certificates for these payments exist in Boyd's archive: *HB/FinRec* C, docs. 4–14: Fotou, *New Light,* 53 (Greek calendar dates); see also receipt from Xanthoudidis confirming deposit of five hundred francs for payment of compensation, dated July 30 (August 12), 1904, *HB/FinRec* E, doc. 4: Fotou, *New Light,* 54. The finds of

the excavations up to June 24 had been already sent from Pachyammos to the Herakleion Museum.

258. Boyd, "Crete, 1904," 177; on the amendment of the Cretan law of antiquities see also Becker and Betancourt, *Richard Berry Seager,* 33–34. A letter acknowledging Boyd's petition, dated July 16 (July 29) and appointing a four-member committee (including Hazzidakis and Xanthoudidis) that would decide on the objects for export exists in HM Archives, but the list of objects she chose for export could not be found. For a partial list of the objects she was allowed to export see her letter to Stevenson, August 29, 1904, Penn.

Unlike Evans, who was pressing for "original" pieces to enhance his museum's collections, Boyd was happy to have only "duplicates." See letter from Boyd to Stevenson, April 21, 1904, Penn, and cf. letter from Evans to Boyd, January 11, 1905, possession (2001) of Hat H. Savage.

259. *HB/FinRec* E, doc. 3: Fotou, *New Light,* 53; the receipt concerns work done in 1903 and August 1904.

260. Boyd, "Crete, 1904," 177.

261. Letter acknowledging petition by Boyd for the export of antiquities, dated 1905, in HM Archives. There is much correspondence to and from Boyd in respect of these antiquities, which arrived in America with much delay and were shared between museums.

262. Letter from Boyd to Stevenson, August 29, 1904, Penn. Also Boyd, "Crete, 1904," 177, and journal for August 19, 20, 21, 1904, included in *HB/NB* V: Fotou, *New Light,* 42, 46.

263. Article dated September 19, 1904, *The New York Times.*

264. Boyd, "Crete, 1904," 177. On the University Museum collection and its importance see P. P. Betancourt and J. S. Silverman, *The Cretan Collection in the University Museum, University of Pennsylvania,* vol. 2, *Pottery from Gournia, University Museum Monograph* 72 (Philadelphia: University Museum, 1991), 1. Among the other Minoan collections in America, the Metropolitan collection includes material from Gournia granted to Boyd in 1905 and obtained through exchange with the University Museum thanks to her efforts (Becker and Betancourt, *Richard Berry Seager,* 66, 71–72, 75). She also presented a potter's wheel from Gournia to the British Museum; see letter from C. Smith to Boyd, June 6, 1905, Smith.

265. *The New York Times,* September 25, 1904, quoted in Allsebrook, *Born to Rebel,* 123.

266. The meeting took place in Cambridge, August 17–24, and already by May 15 Boyd had been invited to give a paper on the pottery; see her letter to Stevenson, August 29, 1904, Penn, and cf. her letters to Mame, May 15, 1904, and to Blanche, July 10, 1904, both in Smith.

267. An extensive summary of her classification of pottery is included in a letter Boyd wrote to Blanche, dated July 10, 1904, Smith. From a letter Boyd wrote to Stevenson, May 9, 1904 (Penn), it is clear that she was already fully preoccupied by this question. Also from a letter by Hall to her parents we learn that by May 22 she and Seager were already writing up their reports on the early pottery series from the North Trench at Gournia and from Vasiliki respectively (Becker and Betancourt, *Richard Berry Seager,* 46). This was undertaken at Boyd's suggestion and with her

encouragement, and undoubtedly under her supervision; given her assistants' inexperience, one may assume that many of her ideas were reflected. Indeed her role in the creation of, for example, Seager's report was critical, if only for his use of the evidence gained from the excavations at Gournia, Aghios Ioannis, and Aghia Photia, in order to establish a framework for the Vasiliki material. It is interesting to note that when Seager finalized his paper, late in 1904 (*HB/Corresp.* A, doc. 1: Fotou, *New Light,* 54), Boyd had already established the full classification of pottery. Cf. Becker and Betancourt, *Richard Berry Seager,* 50–51, where the authors entirely pass over Boyd's role and give Seager the full credit. The same could be said for Hall's paper; see letter from Boyd to Stevenson, August 29, 1904, Penn.

268. Part of the paper has survived; see *HB+BW/Notes* 5, doc. 1: Fotou, *New Light,* 48. The précis could not be found, but it is acknowledged in a letter from Myres to Boyd, August 27, 1904, Smith; it was probably similar to that included in Boyd's letter to Blanche (July 10, 1904, Smith). The printed abstracts were forwarded by Myres to Boyd; one copy exists in Smith and another in the Ashmolean Library—the latter coming from Evans's bequest: H. A. Boyd, "The Pottery of the Prehistoric Settlement at Gournià and Its Neighbourhood in Crete," *British Association for the Advancement of Science, Cambridge Meeting, 17th–24th August, 1904.*

269. Fotou, *New Light,* 24–26.

270. The title for the paper was "Preliminary Scheme for the Classification and Approximate Chronology of the Periods of Minoan Culture in Crete, from the Close of the Neolithic to the Early Iron Age." However, according to the program, which was updated daily and the new issues published every morning, the paper scheduled for Tuesday 23 was "Knossos 1904" (*Cambridge 1904. British Association for the Advancement of Science. Seventy-Fourth Annual Meeting. Journal of Sectional Proceedings,* no. 5, issued Tuesday, August 23, 1904, at 8 A.M., p. 16; cf. programs issued the previous days [nos. 1–4]). Evidently Evans replaced this paper with the one on the classification of pottery at the last moment. According to the meeting's report the paper read by Evans as scheduled was on the classification of pottery. It is not clear whether he also read his 1904 report, a summary of which was published elsewhere in the volume (*Report of the Seventy-fourth Meeting of the British Association for the Advancement of Science Held at Cambridge in August 1904* [London, 1905], 321–24, 719–21).

271. The term was introduced as early as 1823 by Karl Hoeck in a three-volume history of Crete based on philological evidence; see A. A. Ζώης, *Κνωσός. Το εκστατικό όραμα. Σημειωτική και ψυχολογία μιάς αρχαιολογικής περιπέτειας* (Herakleion, 1996), 38–39, 257–80, 413–86.

272. In his 1904 report Evans establishes three Early Minoan strata/floor-levels (*BSA* 10 [1903–4]: 2, 18–26, esp. fig. 7, p. 19). Mackenzie who was not consulted on this issue (see letter from Hogarth to Boyd, January 17, 1905, possession [2001] of Hat H. Savage), thought that the material from Knossos was far too scanty to support such conclusion (see letter from Mackenzie to Evans published in L. Palmer, *The Penultimate Palace of Knossos, Incunabula Graeca* 33 [Rome: ed. dell'Ateneo, 1969], 149–51). Clearly Evans's interpretation of this material as representing three floor levels was not coincidental and could only be based on evidence on three Early Minoan phases gained from elsewhere. A comparison of the final version of his scheme presented at the Athens Congress in spring 1905 (see below) and that pre-

sented in the 1904 meeting is enlightening: the former is understandably more elaborate, but for the early pottery series the representative material comes mainly from Boyd's sites—and yet in a letter to Boyd he affirmed "At Gournia I know little beyond 'Late Minoan I'" (Jan. 11, 1905, possession [2001] of Hat H. Savage; also cf. Becker and Betancourt, *Richard Barry Seager,* 58).

273. For a summary of the paper see *AJA* 9 (1905): 77. For the manuscript of the paper see *HB+BW/Notes* 5, doc. 2: Fotou, *New Light,* 48; a note on the last page of Wheeler's manuscript reads: "I would like to preface my talk by saying that this paper is compiled . . . from notes furnished me by Miss H.A.B. & that I have undertaken to present it at her request." The meeting held sessions in both Boston and Cambridge, Mass.; Boyd may have attended the Boston sessions while her paper was scheduled for the Cambridge sessions (letter from Boyd to Stevenson, December 27, 1904, Penn; *AJA* 9 [1905]: 65).

274. Boyd, "Crete, 1904," 178–79.

275. Letter from Boyd to J. McHugh, October 16, 1904, Penn; *Trans* 1, no. 3 (1905): 191–205, 207–21.

276. *HB/Corresp.* A, doc. 1: Fotou, *New Light,* 54.

277. Boyd, "Crete, 1904."

278. *HB/Corresp.* A, doc. 2: Fotou, *New Light,* 54. Also *HB/Calendar,* s.v. Jan. [1905]. Laurenus Clark Seelye, first president of Smith College, held that office from 1873 to 1910.

279. Cf. *HB/Corresp.* A, doc. 3: Fotou, *New Light,* 54; *HB/Notes* 6, doc. 2, p. 3: Fotou, *New Light,* 49.

280. Letter from Boyd to Blanche, April 24, 1905, Smith; *HB/Calendar,* s.v. Mar. [1905]; Allsebrook, *Born to Rebel,* 124, 127.

281. *CH/Diary* 1905, 1:6–10.

282. Letter dated April 24, 1905, Smith.

283. The other woman was Miss J. E. Harrison, a scholar with a well-established reputation and already the author of five books. *Comptes Rendus du Congrès International d'Archéologie. Ire session, Athènes 1905* (Athens, 1905).

284. Her paper was not announced in the program (letter from Boyd to Stevenson, April 27, 1905, Penn), but a summary was published in the proceedings of the Congress. See H. A. Boyd, "The Pottery of Gournià, Vasiliki and other prehistoric sites on the isthmus of Hierapetra (Crete)," in *Comptes Rendus,* 226; the manuscript of the paper and the summary exist in Boyd's archive: *HB+BW/Notes* 5, docs. 3 and 4: Fotou, *New Light,* 48.

285. Fotou, *New Light,* 25–26 and n. 39 with references.

286. See Boyd, "Pottery of Gournià," and *HB+BW/Notes* 5, doc. 4: Fotou, *New Light,* 48; cf. Allsebrook, *Born to Rebel,* 125, and holograph report by Boyd on the congress, Smith.

287. Letter from Boyd to Stevenson, April 27, 1905, Penn; see also editorial comment following Boyd, "Pottery of Gournià."

288. Letter dated April 24, 1905, Smith.

289. *MA/Calendar,* s.v. Apr.–June 1905.

290. Letter from Boyd to J. McHugh, December 17, 1905, Penn.

291. See *CH/Diary* 1905, 1:93–94, 2:90–91.

292. Letter from Boyd to Blanche, April 24, 1905, Smith.

293. *CH/Diary* 1905, 1:99, 100, 102, 2:103–7.

294. *Comptes Rendus,* 69–74, 83.

295. *CH/Diary* 1905, 2:169–70; for the plans see Fotou, *New Light,* plates 20, 42.

296. *HB/Calendar,* s.v. May [1905]; letter from Boyd to J. McHugh, December 17, 1905, Penn.

297. *CH/Diary* 1905, 2:200; 3:204, 205, 210, 211, 228, 250–51, 254.

298. *CH/Diary* 1905, 3:254–55.

299. Letter from Boyd to Stevenson, April 27, 1905, Penn; letters from E. Robinson and E. Forbes to Boyd, May 5 and 21, 1905, Smith.

300. Following on the lines already set out by Boyd on a preliminary version of the plan traced during the winter by the architect of the British School, Heaton Comyn, Sejk incorporated in the final plan a wealth of architectural details and made chronological distinctions not usual for what were then considered humble houses. Letter from Boyd to H. Comyn, not dated (1904–5?), Smith; *Gournia,* v; letter from Boyd to J. McHugh, December 17, 1905, Penn. Sejk's receipt for his plans of Gournia exists in Smith.

301. *Memoirs II,* 276. Boyd's 1904 campaign saw the last excavations at Gournia. Seager's plans to resume the excavations in 1921 (*Bulletin de Correspondance Hellénique* 44 [1920]: Chronique, 401) never materialized. Limited investigations in the area of the tombs on the north extremity of the acropolis summit were undertaken in 1971–72 by C. Davaras and J. S. Soles (C. Davaras, *Αρχαιολογικόν Δελτίον* 28 [1973], Chron. B2, 588–89; J. S. Soles, "The Gournia House Tombs: A Study of the Architecture, Chronology, and Use of the Built Rectangular Tombs of Crete," Ph.D. diss., University of Pennsylvania, 1973). In the town the Archaeological Service carries out regular cleaning, consolidation, and restoration of the remains.

302. *CH/Diary* 1905, 5:436–39.

303. Original letter untraced; typescript copy of part of the letter by and in possession (1998) of M. Allsebrook.

304. *HB/Calendar,* s.v. Sept. [1905].

305. Letter from Boyd to A. Evans, October 7, 1905, Evans's Archives, Ashmolean Museum.

306. *HB/Calendar,* s.v. Nov.–Dec. [1905]. On her reaching this decision see her letter to her cousins, December 20, 1905, Smith.

307. R. B. Seager, "Report of Excavations at Vasiliki, Crete, in 1906," *Trans* 2, no. 2 (1907): 111. For the next twenty years, Seager, alone or with Edith Hall, continued the archaeological research on the isthmus, mainly on sites already excavated or identified by Boyd: Vasiliki, the promontory northeast of Gournia, Pachyammos, Pseira, and Vrokastro—Mochlos being the only major new site to be discovered and excavated by Seager.

308. Further on the history of recent American research in Crete see Shaw, "Crete, 1880 to 1990," 11–14. See also H. A. Thompson, "In Pursuit of the Past: The American Role, 1879–1979," *AJA* 84 (1980): 263–70, esp. 267.

309. *HB/Calendar,* s.v. Mar., Sept. [1906], and letter from Boyd to her cousins, November 19, 1906, Smith.

310. Allsebrook, *Born to Rebel,* 133; postal from Henry to J. McHugh, December 6, 1906, Penn.

311. *AJA* 11 (1907): 57–58; cf. *Gournia*, 7–13.

312. *MA/Calendar*, s.v. March 25, 1907; letter from Boyd to Stevenson, March 21, 1907, Penn.

313. Letter from Harriet to Stevenson March 14, 1907, Penn.

314. *Gournia*. 300 copies were printed.

315. Quoted in a leaflet published by the University Museum for the promotion of the book. See also opening remark in E. Pottier's review, *Journal des Savants*, n.s. 8 (April 1910): 145.

316. See, for example, the eloquent review of Edmond Pottier in the *Journal des Savants*, n.s. 8 (April 1910): 147, 154–55.

317. Cf. J. L. Fitton, *The Discovery of the Greek Bronze Age* (London, 1995), 196.

318. Cf. Fotou, *New Light*, 23–24. A comparison with Seager's publications, in particular of Pseira, is instructive; see Becker and Betancourt, *Richard Berry Seager*, 91–92.

319. Some of the original color drawings and their reproductions were exhibited in Dresden in 1909 by the printing company as examples of the high quality of their photogravure process (correspondence *re* loan of originals at Penn). However, these illustrations meant large format and high price for the book, two facts deplored in the reviews (e.g., S. Reinach in *Révue Archéologique* 2 (1909): 163; A. J. Reinach in *L'Anthropologie* 21 (1910): 671 n. 1, 679; E. Pottier in *Journal des Savants*, n.s. 8 (April 1910): 146.

320. Many letters mainly to or from Boyd, spanning the period 1904 to 1908 (Penn), bear witness to her efforts to secure the highest quality for the publication, particularly the plates, and to raise the necessary funds; see esp. the first and one of the latest of these letters, both from Boyd to McHugh, July 7, 1904, and February 20, 1908; also Allsebrook, *Born to Rebel*, 133–34.

321. A great amount of correspondence, receipts, etc., exists at Penn.

322. See *CH/Diary* 1909; also C. H. Hawes, "My Wanderings in Crete," *The Wide World Magazine* 26 (1910): 509–15 (part 1), 595–600 (part 2); C. H. Hawes, "Cretan Anthropometry," *AJA* 15 (1911): 65–67.

323. See *HB/Diary* 1909–10. See Arthur Evans's laudatory preface to the volume. Also G. M. A. Richter, "Necrology: H. B. Hawes," *AJA* 49 (1945): 359. The book was re-edited twice (1911, 1916).

324. Letters from Boyd to J. McHugh, February 8, July 22, 1910, Penn. On the L.H.D. see correspondence at Smith.

325. Letter dated April 12/25, 1913, Smith (also quoted in Allsebrook, *Born to Rebel*, 138); see also telegraph from Queen Olga to Boyd, December 19, 1912, Smith, and letter from Daphne Kalopothakis to Boyd, December 4, 1912, possession (2001) of Hat H. Savage.

326. Diary notes covering a few days of years 1908 to 1945, entries for December 15 and 19, 1914, and notes on three loose leaves titled "Ideas for School," Smith.

327. Allsebrook, *Born to Rebel*, 141–51; a number of documents including photographs, some very disturbing, are kept at Smith.

328. Allsebrook, *Born to Rebel*, 158. In the year following her return from Vidos Boyd had received many invitations to speak about her experiences—one,

from the Dartmouth Commons, was particularly significant. Her speech, on March 18, 1917, entitled "My Work with the Serbian Army" was the first speech in Commons by a woman. Allsebrook, *Born to Rebel,* 155–56; *MA/Calendar,* s.v. Jan.–Mar. 1917.

329. Allsebrook, *Born to Rebel,* 156–58.

330. Allsebrook, *Born to Rebel,* 161–69; E. L. Kohler and P. S. Boyer, "Hawes, Harriet Ann Boyd," in *Notable American Women, 1607–1950: A Biographical Dictionary,* ed. E. T. James (Cambridge: Harvard University Press, 1971), 2:161. A great number of documents related to this unit exist at Smith.

331. Allsebrook, *Born to Rebel,* 167, 169–75.

332. Richter, "Necrology," 359; Allsebrook, *Born to Rebel,* 178–79.

333. See *Forty-fourth Annual Report of the Museum of Fine Arts, Boston* (1919) and subsequent issues; Minoan subjects included "The Genius of Minoan Art" (1919) and "The Minotaur" (1920). Her lectures culminated in a course of ten lectures, "Greek Art and Culture of the Fifth Century and Its Origins in the Prehistoric Past," given in 1931; see *Fifty-sixth Annual Report of the Museum of Fine Arts, Boston* (1931), 96–97.

334. Her studies included classical monuments (from the lectures of Dörpfeld and Richardson as well as visits to all major classical sites); sculpture (from Richardson's lectures in the museum); grave reliefs (from Chapin's lectures); and epigraphy (from Sterrett's, Emerson's, Chapin's, Smyth's, and above all Wilhelm's lectures).

335. *AJA* 26 (1922): 81–82, and H. B. Hawes, "A Gift of Themistocles: The 'Ludovisi Throne' and the Boston Relief," *AJA* 26 (1922): 278–306; *AJA* 28 (1924): 74–75.

336. In the program of the festivities Boyd, referred to as "A.M., L.H.D., Lecturer in Wellesley College," appears as one of the two representatives of Wellesley College, but at the dedication she found herself representing also the Museum of Fine Arts (see *The Opening Exercises of the Gennadius Library of the ASCS at Athens. April the 23rd and 24th 1926;* letter from Boyd to Henry, April 13, 1926, Smith). On the festivities see *AJA* 30 (1926): 203; letter from Boyd to her husband, April 25, 1926, Smith.

337. At Stavros Boyd found "a local variety of Pentelic, less compact, more crystalline than usual Pentelic . . . exactly matching" the chip from the Boston Relief given to her for this purpose by the museum. However, she did not publish this finding and recent research did not examine this possibility. See letters from Boyd to Henry, April 13 and 19, 1926, both at Smith; Allsebrook, *Born to Rebel,* 180–81, 185; The Museum of Fine Arts authorization is at Smith. For recent research on the marble's origin see W. J. Young and B. Ashmole, "The Boston Relief and the Ludovisi Throne," *Boston Museum Bulletin* 66, 346 (1968): 124–66.

338. Letter from Boyd to Henry, May 2, 1926, Smith; see also *MA/Calendar,* s.v. Apr.–June 1926.

339. Letters from Boyd to Henry, May 2 and 13, 1926, Smith.

340. Eight pages of notes by Boyd on these sites, including Nirou Hani, Pyrgos Cave, and Malia, exist at Smith.

341. Letter from Boyd to Henry, May 13, 1926, Smith, and Allsebrook, *Born to Rebel,* 188.

342. Letters from Boyd to Henry, May 13 and 25, 1926, both at Smith.

343. Letter from Boyd to Henry, June 3, 1926, Smith; *MA/Calendar,* s.v. Apr.–June [1926]; Allsebrook, *Born to Rebel,* 189.

344. Allsebrook, *Born to Rebel,* 189.

345. "The Route of Pausanias in Athens and the East Frieze of the 'Theseum,'" *AJA* 34 (1930): 51; unfortunately no abstract was published. "The Ancient Temple of the Goddess on the Acropolis," *AJA* 40 (1936): 120–21.

346. The manuscripts of both books and the final draft of her study of the Erechtheum complete with drawings, exist at Smith.

347. Allsebrook, *Born to Rebel,* 134–35, 201; the manuscripts of all these scenarios are at Smith.

348. H. B. Hawes, *Ready-Guide: Boston, Cambridge, Brookline* (Boston: Marshall Jones Company, 1936).

349. Allsebrook, *Born to Rebel,* 194; the correspondence is at Smith.

350. Allsebrook, *Born to Rebel,* 194–98.

351. Ibid., 198; *HB/Calendar,* s.v. July 24 [1935].

352. Allsebrook, *Born to Rebel,* 199.

353. Ibid., 204, 205.

354. Ibid., 206.

355. Typescript copy by and in possession (1998) of M. Allsebrook of Boyd's manuscript "A Trip to Prague at the Time of Munich," nine pages, followed by a further account of the same trip, unpaginated; original version, typed with annotations and corrections in Boyd's hand, at Smith.

356. Ibid.

357. Ibid.

358. Allsebrook, *Born to Rebel,* 215, 217.

359. Ibid., 218.

360. In times of crisis Boyd's reaction was to raise livestock (ibid., 222).

361. Ibid., 225.

362. Typescript copy by and in possession (1998) of M. Allsebrook; original probably at Smith.

363. Richter, "Necrology," 359; unfortunately we have not been able to trace this publication.

364. *MA/Calendar,* s.v. Jan.–Mar. 1945.

365. Allsebrook, *Born to Rebel,* 226.

366. Mary Allsebrook, personal communication.

367. *Journal des Savants,* n.s. 8 (April 1910): 146.

368. Allsebrook, *Born to Rebel,* 230; Mary Allsebrook, personal communication.

369. The problem becomes more obvious in the index compiled by Joan Evans than in the text.

370. Typescript copy (date unknown) by and in possession (1998) of M. Allsebrook.

371. Letter dated October 12, 1906, possession (2001) of Hat H. Savage.

372. Richter, "Necrology," 359.

Edith Hayward Hall Dohan

(1879–1943)

Katherine Dohan Morrow

AS ONE OF THE FIRST AMERICAN women to become a field archaeologist, Edith Hall Dohan excavated in Crete, on behalf of the University of Pennsylvania Museum, at Gournia (1904), Sphoungaras (1910), and Vrokastro (1912). She was instrumental in collecting and cataloging materials for the Mediterranean Section at the University Museum established a short time before, under the direction of Sarah Yorke Stevenson. In her lifetime, Hall published more than fifty articles and four books. Her repertoire of knowledge ranged from Minoan and Mycenaean decoration to classical Greek sculpture and vase painting to Etruscan tombs and later Roman statues.

Edith Hall's "love of all things Greek" infused every aspect of her life. Her abundant letters to her parents and to her beloved older sister, Anne, convey this philhellenic philosophy. She was a superior correspondent, writing letters in the form of week-long diaries. These letters offer a glimpse of life, in Athens and at the excavation site, for a woman archaeologist in the early 1900s. Her poetic descriptions and honest evaluations paint a vivid picture of her undertakings in Greece and on Crete.

The Early Years, 1877–1903

Edith Hall Dohan was born on New Year's Eve 1877 in New Haven, Connecticut, the second of three children and the youngest daughter. She was very close to her older sister, Anne, who, to judge by her letters, served as confidante and friend in a family in which emotions were kept to oneself. Edith Hall grew up in a household strictly administered by a tyrannical yet loving father, Ely Ransom Hall, a Yale graduate and mathematics teacher who bestowed upon his children an unwavering belief in the importance of a fine education and a well-founded Christian ethic. He instilled the "Emersonian ideal of plain living and high thinking" in all his children.[1]

In 1888, Ely Hall became principal of the then financially strapped Woodstock Academy in Woodstock, Connecticut. During his twenty-six years in that position he pulled the school out of an economic and academic slump, turning it into one of the finest secondary schools in New England. Along with her brother and sister, Hall attended Woodstock Academy, where she excelled academically. She also exhibited a tomboyish nature and an unquenchable zest for sports that would later prove their worth in Greece and Crete. She loved horseback riding and also rode her bicycle whenever possible. In addition, she enjoyed tennis, but golf was an obsession. Her niece, many years later, recalled stories of Hall pedaling furiously down the Woodstock sidewalks with her golf clubs strapped across the handlebars of her bike. Pedestrians had to jump out of the way of her wide load as she breathlessly fought to arrive in time to tee off. Such physical exertion certainly helped prepare her for the rigors of life at an excavation.

Hall's love of the Greek language and culture first became apparent at the Woodstock Academy under the tutelage of her father. She graduated with a "love of classic literature" and a "moral accountability of herself."[2] Although many of the graduating girls married local farmers and businessmen rather than attending college, Hall chose to follow an independent route and entered Smith College in Northampton, Massachusetts. Out of three majors offered at that time at Smith, Hall selected the "Classical

Course" as her major. Her classes included Greek, Latin, Mathematics, Biblical Literature, English, Physiology, and Elocution. Along with her academic pursuits, Hall found time to appear in a number of dramatic productions as well. She graduated with honors in 1899.[3]

Study and Travel 1903 and 1904

After graduation, Hall returned to Woodstock to teach alongside her father. But it did not take long for her to realize that she needed to expand her horizons. Teaching on a secondary level left her unfulfilled. Graduate studies brought her to Bryn Mawr College in Bryn Mawr, Pennsylvania. There, in the Department of Classical Archaeology, she began intense studies of Greek, Latin, and Greek archaeology. The college has no record of her professors' names, but, as she wrote to her sister, Anne, "Miss Jordan is democratic and interested in every individual girl. Miss Thomas is aristocratic and critical."[4] Hall thrived at Bryn Mawr and grew to "love Greek more everyday."[5] She was among young women who had also decided to devote themselves to higher learning, and she consequently developed many close friendships.

Because the Hall family could spare no resources to send a daughter to graduate school, Hall supported herself by taking jobs as a tutor at the neighboring Shipley School and as a chaperone to Miss Baldwin's girls at the Baldwin School. She often wrote about her poverty and the poor state of her clothing, although material possessions on the whole meant little to her. When, for example, she lost everything in a dormitory fire, she had risked her life to save what she deemed more important—another student's thesis. She herself had sounded the alarm, helped clear out the building, and then, realizing the magnitude of her friend's potential loss, coolly wrapped herself in wet towels, reentered the building, and made her way through smoke-filled rooms to retrieve her friend's thesis. Her own possessions were replaceable, but she would not let three years of work be lost. Her friends at the school rallied around her and started a collection. The thirty dollars raised would carry her through the rest of the semester, and the much-needed used clothing was gratefully received.[6]

In the spring of 1903, Hall was granted the Mary E. Garrett Fellowship, a five-hundred-dollar stipend "intended to defray the expenses of one year's study and residence at some foreign university."[7] In May, she was granted another one thousand dollars to become the Agnes Hoppin Memorial Fellow at the American School of Classical Studies in Athens. The fellowship, intended to allow women to study abroad, had been established "to help remove the limitations of women students."[8] Hall was the only woman to apply. Consequently, she felt she could "take no satisfaction in it as a great honor."[9] Choosing a difficult life course for a turn-of-the-century woman, Hall had already refused two marriage proposals because she had decided to pursue scholarship. And she did so despite pressure by her parents and friends. As she admitted to her sister, it was an "awfully hard course to steer if [a woman] keeps herself scholarly for a teaching career or womanly against the chance she may marry."[10]

The fall session of the American School officially opened on October 1, 1903. Hall arrived a week early after a journey of more than two weeks by boat. Her trunk and bicycle would arrive a few days later. She used these free days to explore the Greek capital and visit the sites she had studied for so many years. Hall was the only female student at the school. The only other women present were the wives of her professors, and, as she was to discover, they were not always up to the arduous excursions that were part of the school's program. Throughout all her work and travels, Hall had to maintain propriety, especially since she was the only woman participating in the program with six young men. Whenever possible, Hall liked to bicycle to the sites around Athens and so save carriage fare, but she could not decorously pedal with only one man. To solve this problem, groups were organized on her behalf. For instance, when Lacey Caskey invited her to bike with him to Eleusis, Professor Fowler proposed that the whole group go.

Hall's rooms were located a short walk away from the school in Merlin House, a privately owned boarding house where the daily routine was quite different from that at Hall's home in Connecticut. In a letter written shortly after she arrived in Athens, she described the start of her day:

> And since last Friday, when I came, my days have been all the same . . . The maid calls me at seven, and brings a pitcher of hot-water. By half past seven when my breakfast comes, I have my bath taken, my physical culture exercises done, and . . . go on to the balcony for breakfast. I sit in my big comfortable rocker, and put the tray in a straight chair in front of me, and very happily eat my roll and honey, and drink my two cups of chocolate. Between bites I can look at the Acropolis . . . By half past eight I . . . am on my way to the school . . . The way leads through crooked and very dusty streets, in which little donkeys, laden on each side with great baskets of grapes may be seen, or carts filled with skins of wine.[11]

At noon she headed back to Merlin House for lunch and then again in the late afternoon for a lonely dinner at 6:00 P.M. She yearned to participate in the dinner conversations of her fellow male students at the school's dining facility, but for that she would have to wait for a private invitation.

In those early days, life in Athens was fairly solitary for Hall. However, her sense of purpose kept her optimistic:

> My trunk is not here yet, so I can not make calls, and there is no one here at the house or at the school to "play with." So I think I am doing pretty well when I say that I have not been lonely since I came. Work begins at the school tomorrow, and we take our first excursion next week, so things will soon be changed. I think I shall be the only serious woman student at the school.[12]

At the American School, Hall attended lectures given by Dr. Theodore Woolsey Heermance, the director, and Harold North Fowler, professor of Greek language and literature. Hall's fellow full-time students were William Battle, Lacey D. Caskey, Fritz S. Darrow, Harold Hastings, Robert C. McMahon, and Gorham Phillip Stevens. Another man, an associate member who would have the most influence on her archaeological career, arrived a few months later. His name was Richard B. Seager.[13] Hall mentioned his arrival in a letter home, explaining that "a Mr. Segur [*sic*] . . . is going to help Miss Boyd in Crete for a second season. He is good-looking and carefully dressed, but may be nice."[14]

Within the first week, Dr. Heermance and Hall had discussed a topic for her doctoral thesis. He advised her to take the year to write a thesis and perhaps a few months of the following year as well.[15] It would be a tight schedule; Hall's money would not last much longer. Indeed, her time exploring and studying seemed to fly by.

The first school-sponsored trip, in early October, was a three-day journey to Delphi. Not only students and professors but also the professors' wives usually participated in the school outings. The group went first by boat to Corinth to pass through the canal, disembarking at Itea, then by horseback to Delphi. Scorching heat and bug-ridden hotel rooms were only two of the discomforts they endured. Hall learned especially to beware of insects—"to look before you sleep."[16] At Delphi, Heermance and Fowler lectured at the newly excavated site. The group returned to Athens via Thermopylae—on horseback as far as Lamia and then to Athens by boat. Such trips were always an adventure, and Hall learned quickly to deal with the poverty and squalor she faced each day. In her letters home she wrote of infestations of bedbugs so awful that she would often find the insects crawling on her gown at dinner. She also described "a rabbit . . . hopping about last evening on the dining table not far from where our party sat," and it was a common occurrence to find mangy dogs and other animals underfoot.[17]

Interspersed with traveling and studying at the school and local museums, protocol demanded that Hall establish a somewhat time-consuming social schedule. As the only woman at the American School, she was expected to call upon and make friends with other foreign women in the city. When foreigners living in the city heard that an American girl was at the school, they would often come for tea and leave their calling cards. This ritual enabled her to befriend Mrs. Bosanquet, wife of the director of the British School. In addition, she received visitors such as Madam Sophia Schliemann and the governess to the royal children of Prince George, future king of Greece. By January, with social credentials in place, Hall was presented to the queen of Greece:

> Well, I've been to the court ball and made my curtsey to the Queen of Greece . . . Mr. and Mrs. Fowler and Dr. Heermance took me in their carriage with them. We left the Merlin at a little after nine, I clad in my green . . . low neck gown. Mrs. Lotjohann lent me a long fur-lined cape for the occasion. Arrived at the palace, we were relieved of our wraps by footmen in gold-braided knicker-bockers and white stockings, and were ushered into the ball room itself, where a large number of people was assembled waiting for royalty. The ladies were on one side and the gentlemen were on the other, while up and down the space between them pranced the master of ceremonies, trying to keep a good generous path clear for their majesties. At last they came, to the strains of the Greek National Hymn; first the king and queen, then a long line of princes and princesses and archduchesses, and then the diplomats led by our minister, Mr. Jackson . . . Twice the presentations stopped for royal quadrilles, which we had great fun watching . . . At last our turn came, and we made our low bows as well as the rest of them. I doubt if I made any great impression on her majesty, enough to secure an intimate friendship in the future, but she at least chatted graciously to us for the few minutes we talked to her.[18]

In addition to the social interchanges, there seems to have been a steady intellectual interchange among the students and faculty of the various archaeology schools in Athens. The students had the privilege of joining one another's groups. Hall often heard Dr. Wilhelm Dörpfeld, of the German Archaeological Institute, speak on the Acropolis and Dr. Bosanquet lecture at the National Museum. Hall found it "difficult launching out on a thesis topic. [There were] so many lectures to hear and things to do."[19] After all she was "having the chance of a lifetime."[20] Nevertheless, Dr. Heermance proposed a dozen subjects, and by early November she had settled on one. She wrote to her sister:

> When I am not hearing lectures at the museum, I am in the Mycenean room, leaning on the cases, and drawing patterns from the gold and ivory ornaments. I like my work much better now, and am beginning to see a bit what I am to try to do. Some of the patterns are drawn free hand from nature; others are entirely conventional.[21]

The main question she hoped to illuminate was: "Are they conventionalized natural patterns or are they developed from linear motives?"[22]

At first, work was slow and time in which to do it was rare, but by the beginning of 1904 research for her thesis became all-consuming. In the moments between lectures, classes, and excursions out of the city, Hall found time to accumulate more than two hundred designs for her thesis. She drew, cataloged, and studied the various naturalistic motives on "Mycenaean" vases.[23] Soon it became clear that the amount of material from both the mainland and Cretan sites would be too much to manage, and she was forced to limit her scope to Cretan designs. The work was fascinating and timely since, until then, only generalizations had been made about the motives. But the exciting new discoveries at Knossos, Phaistos, and Agia Triada warranted intensive study. The fresh material that abounded in 1904 was badly in need of organization and analysis. Soon Hall was ready to travel to Crete for firsthand study of the pieces in the museum at Candia (modern Herakleion). For this first trip to Crete, she traveled unaccompanied—her mother would have been aghast.

Nearly thirty years earlier, in 1878, Furtwängler and Löschcke had published *Mykenische Vasen.* At the time, it was the definitive study on pottery in Athens from the various "Mycenaean" sites in Greece.[24] The two Germans had concluded that, with a few exceptions, "all the patterns of vase with lustrous paint were representations of natural objects."[25] With all the new material coming to light, Hall set out to improve on or disprove Furtwängler's statement, especially in relation to Cretan pottery designs. Her conclusions were significant. In relation to lustrous painted vases, she felt the Germans were correct. Lustrous paints, however, had a limited time frame, correlating mainly with the Late Minoan periods, "when naturalistic designs prevailed."[26] Simple curvilinear motives on wares from the Early Minoan period developed into conventionalized naturalistic and nonimitative designs of the Middle Minoan period. Finally, Late Minoan pottery displayed the naturalistic depiction observed by Furtwängler. Thus Hall showed unqualifiedly that Furtwängler's "statement . . . needs modification."[27] More importantly for future archaeology, in the process of drawing this conclusion, Hall had outlined a chronology of Minoan pottery based on design. This chronology would later prove to be an important tool for the excavation of Knossos and other Cretan sites.

Gournia, 1904

By the time Edith Hall traveled to Crete to study the vases in the museum, she was anticipating joining Harriet Boyd's excavation at Gournia. Richard Seager had worked at the Gournia excavation and knew Boyd well. It was he who acted as liaison for his friend and set up Hall's appointment. Her experience researching Minoan pottery enhanced her qualifications for the job.

> Further, and best of all, I think there is little doubt now but what Miss Boyd will take me to excavate in Crete with her for the whole campaign from March till June. I shall have no board to pay for all that time, and . . . I shall have a squad of men to watch and shall keep an eye on every clod upturned so as to watch for the vases that may appear. Who knows but that I may help Miss Boyd in the publication of her finds? . . . All I'm sure of now is that she is coming, that she wants a woman for a companion, and one trained in archaeology, and that Athens possesses no one else besides myself in these lines.
>
> Mr. Seager will make the other member of the party. We will have a nice comfortable house built by Miss Boyd near the excavations, where we will live with three servants, and entertain the scholars who come to pay visits to the excavations.[28]

Hall joined the Gournia expedition for its third season of excavation in the spring of 1904.[29] Richard Seager telegraphed her with the news at the end of February, "Miss Boyd authorizes invite you Gournia, "and followed that message with a letter in which he wrote "enthusiastically of the season before us."[30] Hall felt very fortunate to have this opportunity "to get familiar with the 'art of digging.' "[31] Hall's primary role was to serve as an assistant to Harriet Boyd. Since propriety frowned on a lone single woman among so many workmen, especially in the back area of impoverished Crete, having a second female at the excavation was reassuring.

Although Hall had not met Harriet Boyd prior to landing in Crete, she knew the appointment would prove extremely beneficial, not only on an intellectual level but also on a practical level as well. Richard Seager had warned Hall that Miss Boyd was a "hard person to get in [*sic*] with . . . She is absent-minded and says one thing one day, and another, the next. She is, evidently, sharp-tongued too."[32] Hall was willing to take the risk. Part of the excavation grant from the American Exploration Society was specified for the room and board for Boyd's aide.[33] With her living expenses covered, Hall could, thus, not only gain invaluable experience in the field; she would also save enough money from her fellowships to allow her to stay in Greece for another year to finish her thesis. At least for now her financial worries had eased.[34]

In Edith Hall, Harriet Boyd had found a person she would later come to consider an ideal companion. Known for her short-fused temper, Boyd had unknowingly hired her foil. Hall's calm, patient, and quiet nature uniquely counterbalanced Boyd's lively personality. In addition, no time was needed to train her new aide, for Hall was an able horsewoman, could speak reasonable Greek, and had studied Minoan and Mycenaean pottery designs in preparation for her thesis. Boyd was prepared to let Hall undertake those tasks that she did not have time for and that Hall wanted to do. In fact, Harriet Boyd admitted to being bored with "the museum work of piecing endless pots together."[35] It was an ideal arrangement.

Gournia is located on the eastern end of Crete on the Isthmus of Ierapetra on the Gulf of Mirabella. While the Italians were at Phaistos, the English at Knossos, and the Germans at Agia Triada, Gournia was the American site.[36] The town was not a royal seat, and, unlike Knossos or Phaistos, it had no palace. "Gournia was a settlement of the common people."[37] Its importance lay in "the light it throws on the history of labor and the common life of the Mycenaeans."[38]

At first, Boyd's agenda would take them not to Gournia but rather westward. They were to travel for two weeks on horseback exploring parts of western Crete "for the purpose of finding a site for next year's digging."[39] It was a small party that set out for the northwest corner of the island: Harriet Boyd, Richard Seager, Edith Hall, a guide and Aristides Pappadhias, Boyd's foreman. ("While Miss Boyd was studying at the American School, he [Pappadhias] was her servant, cooking her meals, and eating his own at a little side table.")[40]

Their guide led them to the end of the island. Hall and Boyd traveled on horseback, Seager by carriage. Aristides Pappadhias and the guide went on foot, leading the pack mules.

> Miss Boyd learned to ride horseback on a wooden pack saddle, so she helps the two men in carrying some of the luggage on her saddle. We have four beds with us, the same ones we shall use later at Gournia. They consist of narrow strips of canvas stretched across supports. Sheets, pillows, blankets, a marvellous tea-basket, individual sets of knife, fork and spoon in leather cases, canned goods etc etc, (all of these are tied on in a circle to the three pack saddles, while Miss Boyd . . . sits triumphant in the middle. I am very thankful I learned how to ride last year. Mr. Seager and Miss Boyd are old hands at it, and I should be very sorry to keep them behind. I have a good comfortable man's saddle.[41]

Provisions were loaded on the mules—tea and food baskets and a rubber bathtub for the women.[42] The party was headed for Dictyna and the western end of Crete, chasing rumors of unexcavated sites. It was said that in the western part of the island there were graves and caves with good Mycenaean sherds.[43] The trip took at least ten days and was complicated by unpredictable living conditions. At Palaikastro, they could get only one room. A sheet was hung to divide the space in two and the men from the women.[44] On other nights, the weary archaeologists slept at local monasteries. Boyd's reputation as an excavator preceded them (perhaps the appearance of Pappadhias, a local hero, as well), and they were welcomed by the locals. In the villages, Boyd and Hall bought ancient coins and gems from the needy townsfolk, who had found them in the fields they tilled.[45] In the end, it was felt that the trip had been in vain, despite the visible ruins they had found at Phalarsena.

> The ancient harbor is now land, and we longed for spades to try our luck. The site is not yet excavated. I was never more excited in my life than when after climbing a neighboring mountain to see the ruins of an old temple, we found the old dump heap where terra cottas and vases were thrown, and picked up several fragments of very decent terra cottas and vases.[46]

The site proved to be Roman, too late in date for Boyd's purposes. She then decided to turn back to Candia and prepare for Gournia.

> It seemed quite like getting home again when yesterday Miss Boyd and I finally . . . reached the mountain top west of Candia, and could look down on the plains and the sea, with the town in between. We had a splendid wild gallop along the good road across the lowlands; then we tidied up, sat sidesaddle and approached the town as demure as you please. We had decided that Mr. Seager and Aristides should go to Candia by boat while Miss Boyd and I should stick to the horses. I was a little doubtful of the success of the trip . . . yet on the whole we got along splendidly. I could be of more use on the trip, for I understood better the packing and unpacking of baggage and could do a good deal toward planning the route . . .
>
> The next day was a troubled one, because of difficulties in finding the road. Miss Boyd got angry with the guide, and she can get angrier than any woman I ever saw . . .
>
> [In Candia] Miss Boyd and I are rooming together, and the room is disorderly with muleteers and servants and what not coming in every few minutes for instructions.[47]

At Candia, the team restocked and prepared to go east. The mules were reloaded and a guide hired to oversee them on the road. Boyd's and Hall's belongings were also loaded, but the two women traveled by sea along with Aristides Pappadhias and his mother, who served as cook and housekeeper for the excavators. The sailboat arrived at Aghios Nickolaos in the early morning, having sailed all night. The women had passed the time "looking up at the stars, singing, and reciting Greek poetry."[48] From the port they would ride over to Richard Seager's house at Pacchyammos. Seager himself would meet them there. The house at Pacchyammos was a new, well-built seven-room house looking out over the sea. There, only a short ride by horseback to the site, they set up the excavation headquarters.

> Miss Boyd breakfasted at 5:30 this morning, and was ready at six to interview the hundred or so men who had come for work. She had already posted the names of those she wished to employ, so she merely called a roll-call for the first fifty and sent them flying over the hill with wheel-barrows, baskets, picks, and shovels. I saw their tail feathers as I was dressing. Mr. Seager and I breakfasted at seven and went over to the field of action immediately. My day's work was to

> measure and locate every large terra-cotta jar and stone basin. Many of the latter are just inside the front door of the houses. We (!) find many stone grinders, and pestles, and even some wash-boards, and many clay lamps, and perforated weights for looms. Just before noon I . . . went down to the place where the men were digging, just in time to see them taking out a very nice standard to a stone vase.[49]

Boyd asked Hall to write up the stone vases and tables, admitting that she did not enjoy the publishing part of excavation reports.[50]

Seager and the women took a few days to decipher the mechanics of a photographic developing machine, then a new invention, which had been granted to the 1904 campaign. After several attempts, the three were able to use it very effectively, thus saving much time and money. They had, in effect, a "dark room" at Pacchyammos where "every available space is filled with beakers of water or developing fluids or other apparatus."[51]

At times the tedium of the task at hand and the "burden of dealing with Boyd's temper" proved almost too much.[52] Seager, well aware of Boyd's short-fused temper and "peppery tongue," had forewarned Hall on several occasions.[53] He admitted, however, that she got along with Miss Boyd "better than anyone he had ever seen." Hall, herself, felt "quite triumphant" that she and Harriet Boyd had never had a real quarrel.[54]

The grant from the American Exploration Society allowed the team to hire about one hundred local men. The workers either stayed in tents at the site or went home into the village each evening. All the overseers, including Hall, were to be in the field by 7:30 A.M. They would watch and direct the men until they broke at around 11:00, the hottest time of day, for lunch and siesta. Hall would return at 3:00 and stay until sunset.[55] A quick gallop back to the house, followed by a swim in the sea before dinner, would conclude her day.

Hall dutifully fulfilled her daily tasks at the excavation—meticulously locating and measuring jars and basins throughout the site. In addition, she cleaned and recorded pottery sherds that came her way. "Things have to be cleaned, measured and labeled according to the exact spot and depth at which they were found."[56] She found much of the work purely mechanical. At times, Boyd would ask for help pasting photographs of the finds into her excavation scrapbooks—usually photos of vases, bronzes, fishhooks, fibulae, knives, and daggers. Each artifact had first to be cleaned with hydrochloric acid before it was photographed. At day's end, Hall's hands were often sore and raw from the chemicals.

Obligations for the women at the dig were more than merely archaeological. On some days they did not get to the excavation at all but instead had to go into town to call on the local dignitaries, or participate in village life, such as attending village weddings. The importance of keeping up good relations with the local villagers should not be underestimated. The success of future excavations might depend heavily on the contentment and well-being of the locals. It was they who worked the site and also reported pottery finds or, better yet, gravesites they spotted while tilling their fields or digging their wells. That goodwill manifested itself in many ways. For example, Hall served as bridesmaid at the wedding of one of her workers. She was also a favorite among the village children. One such child, four years old at the time, remembered her eighty years later when Hall's granddaughter visited the site and the boy, now the entrance guard, reminisced about "his lady." He still had her photograph pasted to the guardhouse wall. Such affection served the excavation well. The villagers were more than willing to lead the archaeologists to more finds. Another obligation, which took the women away from their archaeological tasks, was showing the work in progress to visitors at the site. On several occasions, Dr. Wilhelm Dörpfeld brought his "Inselreise" tour to the Gournia excavations and lectured there as well. The women also visited neighboring sites where friends and colleagues were excavating: Dr. Bosanquet at Palaikastro and Sir Arthur Evans at Knossos. They caught a glimpse of the steatite "Harvester's vase" at Agia Triada shortly after the Italians had unearthed it.[57]

The job of measuring the large Gournia jars was soon completed. Uncharacteristically, Hall grew impatient. She wanted a dig of her own. After much persuasion, Boyd assigned her to oversee a pile of pottery sherds in the northwest end of the ancient town. This "waste heap," uncovered in 1901 "when one of the first trial trenches was sunk," was packed with thousands of bits of broken pottery. It had previously been passed over as not worth any effort, and Boyd had considered it not a main focus of the excavation.[58] Hall was given a "little job" to dig it out. It was "thick with sherds down to the native rock." The site, although somewhat disappointing, was of some interest to Hall:

> At first we thought that if a record were kept according to the depth at which the sherds were found, that we might get different kinds of pottery at different depths, and so get evidence as to the successive settlements of the town; but as it appeared, when all the sherds were washed, there was no difference at all in the successive layers. However, the sherds were unusually good ones, and some of them remarkable both for their color and patterns.[59]

A few weeks later, she was even more enthusiastic about her finds:

> The sherds I have been digging have proved as important as anything else we have dug. I have spent some time this week in drawing off the patterns from the best of them. They are the very earliest painted pottery that is known in either Greece or Crete, dating from about 2000 B.C.[60]

Hall was to dig out and record the entire waste heap. The shoveling alone took more than a week to complete. She had three men, one wheelbarrow, and four village girls to get the job done. The findspot of each piece of pottery was recorded, and then it was washed. Not one intact vase was recovered; and, out of twenty thousand fragments, only five joins were made.[61] It became clear after the first sherds had been cleaned and studied that the pottery would prove to be of major importance for the excavation. The decoration of the simple, curvilinear geometric designs pointed to an early "pre-Mycenaean" period. Some of the fragments appeared to predate the main occupation of the town. Indeed, stratification indicated that the place had been a popular dump site for many years before Gournia had been built.[62]

In the town itself a few similarly decorated pottery sherds had been found along with Kamares ware in several Mycenaean foundations, thus providing a *terminus ante quem* for Hall's "dump ware."[63] In the end, this dump site provided the main evidence for the chronology of the once-thriving coastal town. Hall concluded that the Gournia fragments belong "midway between the Early Geometric ware from Knossos and the later Kamares pottery."[64] Boyd later wrote that the finds from "Gournia and Vasiliki and other neighboring sites [reveal] a new pottery series which included eight distinct styles from the Third Millennium B.C. down to the full Iron Age."[65] Hall's publication was a "pioneering work which seemed to have preceded and triggered Evans' classification" of the Knossos wares.[66] The significance of her findings earned Hall an invitation to present her results at the International Archaeological Congress in Athens in early 1905. The honor of such an invitation should not be understated. Very few women archaeologists were asked to present, let alone one in the dawn of her career.

The excavation came to a halt at the end of May. Boyd and Hall had managed to ship to the United States artifacts that eventually formed the first Mycenaean and pre-Mycenaean collection ever seen in America. At this time, it was permissible to take artifacts out of the country of origin.

Cretan law required that petitions be submitted to the government listing all the objects to be shipped.[67] The Cretan authorities held Boyd in high esteem and granted her requests "with as much magnanimity toward a foreigner as conscience would permit."[68] These women had sought out evidence of the common life in ancient Crete and had recognized the need to document daily life in ancient times. In doing so, the two had left an indelible mark on the history of archaeology.

Teaching, Sphoungaras, and Vrokastro, 1905–12

Edith Hall left the American School in Athens in the early spring of 1905. During the following years she taught at the Shipley School outside Philadelphia. Then from 1908 to 1912 she held the position of professor in Classical archaeology and Greek at Mount Holyoke College in South Hadley, Massachusetts.[69] Course catalogs for those years indicate she taught Greek Archaeology, Greek Sculpture, and Roman Archaeology. This position required her to teach during the fall semester but allowed her to continue digging in Crete in the spring. She would return to Crete in the spring of 1910, when, under the directorship of her friend Richard Seager, she excavated at Sphoungaras. In 1913 she returned to Mount Holyoke as a guest lecturer to discuss her recent excavations in Crete.

During her 1910 campaign at Sphoungaras, Hall was to excavate several gravesites found in 1904 during one of Harriet Boyd's hunts for burials. Boyd had married in 1906 and stopped doing field archaeology the following year. The excavation permits for the site, already granted to the American Exploration Society and to Harriet Boyd, were transferred to Richard Seager. He, in turn, requested Edith Hall to excavate. The campaign lasted only three weeks. Seager, in increasingly poor health, directed the dig from his house at Pacchyammos while Hall took charge at the site.

Located not far from Gournia, Sphoungaras revealed an extensive cemetery dating from the Early Minoan period down to the Bronze Age. Hall and her crew uncovered more than 150 burial jars and many simple interments. The two types of burials were dated differently according to the grave contents. The interments without pithoi spanned the Early Minoan periods II–III. The burials in pithoi ranged from Middle Minoan III to Late Minoan I. This was the first time Late Minoan graves had been found, and the site was undeniably important in revealing the use of pithoi as a burial method of the Late Minoan period. "Sphoungaras shows that the highly developed Minoan civilization as well as the older more primitive societies of the mainland sometimes buried their dead in jars."[70]

Toward the end of this campaign, Hall moved her men to the cliffs at Vrokastro. As at Sphoungaras, Boyd and Seager had previously designated this site as potentially significant because they had seen evidence of numerous walls and readily picked up potsherds from the ground surface. It was a promising place for Geometric remains.[71] Hall's indebtedness to Seager continued. He supplied not only his expertise at Vrokastro, but also tents and supplies for the workmen. Hall also continued to use his house as headquarters.[72] The last three weeks in the 1910 campaign were devoted to excavating the loftier parts of the area. Hall had "hoped to excavate the summit and to find a shrine perhaps. Nothing save the tangle of house-walls appeared."[73]

Edith Hall and Richard Seager returned to Vrokastro in 1912 with a threefold goal. Hall planned to clear more houses on the mountainside in order to ascertain the date of the walls as well as to find any tombs associated with the lower ancient town. The very first day a chamber tomb was discovered. Hall expected it to indicate the ancient cemetery, but only house walls surrounded its location. She and her men located several other tombs during the campaign, all in among the house walls. Tombs of several types were found scattered throughout the site: chamber tombs, cave burials, and pithoi interments. Burial remains and potsherds indicated an Iron Age site; that is, that the "main settlement lasted from the end of the Bronze Age to the dawn of Classical Greece."[74] The majority of the tombs dated "slightly earlier than the Seventh Century."[75] Hall went on to propose three different influences, based on the variety of styles of pottery, fibulae, and tripods found in the graves. As she explained the phenomenon: "The remains at Vrokastro record three great invasions of Crete from the North, those of the Mycenaeans, the Achaeans and the Dorians."[76]

Hall sailed back to the United States on August 20, 1912, on a small merchant ship. A letter written in May 1912 explained her travel arrangements. "Since the fearful news of the Titanic, I have concluded that the smaller the ocean steamer the safer." She would not return to Greece again until 1936 when she took a pleasure cruise with her children. This was to be her last trip to Greece.[77]

Family Life and Museum Work, 1912–43

Hall returned to America as a staff member at the University of Pennsylvania Museum. She wrote the director that she felt she could "convey her enthusiasm about Greece in a museum just as much, if not more, than in a college."[78] She had already imagined plans for the Cretan room. As assistant curator, she supervised the cataloging and arranging of the classical collections. As curator, she would see her ideas come to fruition over the next thirty years.

On May 12, 1915, at the age of thirty-six, Edith Hall married Joseph M. Dohan, a Philadelphia attorney. A year later, she gave birth to a son, David, and shortly after that to a daughter, Katharine.[79] While her children were small, Hall temporarily retired. Then, in 1921, she joined the teaching staff at Bryn Mawr College as a part-time instructor in Greek and Roman art.[80]

Several of her students at Bryn Mawr went on to have careers in archaeology. One of them, Lucy T. Shoe (later Lucy Shoe Meritt), was a student in 1926. In a letter written in 1995, she recalled Hall's "great humanity" and "the warm, caring, generous, loyal friend she was as well as the excellent effective teacher."[81] Another archaeologist, Dorothy Burr Thompson, who was also a former student, remembered Hall "with admiration and affection . . . she was a wonderful woman."[82]

Hall also continued lecturing at the University of Pennsylvania and later, in 1931, returned to the museum as associate curator. She was promoted to curator in 1942. At the same time she became review editor for the *American Journal of Archaeology.* She held both positions until her death in 1943.

Hall's last work encompassed both curating a show and publishing its catalog. The exhibition and the catalog, both entitled *Italic Tomb Groups,* extensively explained the contents of several Etruscan tombs that had been stored haphazardly at the museum since 1897. The nineteenth-century excavation of twenty-seven tombs near Narce, Pitigliano, and Vulci had been poorly recorded, and it was unclear whether the integrity of the tomb groups could be relied upon. Hall organized the catalog *Italic Tomb Groups* as if it were an excavation report, and "the scheme of the book could hardly be improved . . . The high scholarly character of the work makes the book one of the highest importance for the period of the tombs."[83] In the exhibition, Hall had "succeeded in reconstructing the contents of the tombs" and had "bestowed exemplary care upon the scrutiny of every object found in the tombs. Her exemplary detective skills and scholarly ways contributed toward a better understanding of Italian regionalism."[84]

Unfortunately, Edith Hall Dohan did not live to read the many glowing reviews of her magnum opus. Collapsing at her desk in the museum during the brutal heat wave of the summer of 1943, she died surrounded by the artifacts she had spent her life excavating and researching.

Conclusion

Edith Hall Dohan had devoted her life to her "love of all things Greek." As an independent woman, she defied the protocol of her era and traveled afar. Her work in remote areas of Crete, where few foreigners had ventured before, earned her the title "explorer."[85] She willingly started at the bottom of her profession performing the most menial of tasks (from washing sherds in acid to making photographic records of every artifact discovered) so that she could learn more about excavating and ancient Greek life. From the beginning, as an assistant to Harriet Boyd, to the time when she excavated her own sites, and through the years as writer, teacher, and curator, Edith Hall never wavered in her devotion to archaeology. At the culmination of her career, first as assistant designer of the Cretan Room and later as the curator of the Classical Collections at the University of Pennsylvania Museum, she helped build the collections that today are known throughout the world. Her knowledge burst the boundaries of Greece and Crete to include Roman and Etruscan art. She was a woman admired and respected by her colleagues and loved by her friends and family. As George Hanfmann eulogized:

> Of the fullness of her life she gave unstintingly: one could not meet her as a scholar without becoming a devoted friend.[86]

WORKS BY EDITH HAYWARD HALL DOHAN
A SELECTED BIBLIOGRAPHY

Books, Monographs, and Articles

"Archaeology in Crete." *The Independent,* June 23, 1904, 1438–40.

"Early Painted Pottery from Gournia, Crete." *Transactions of the Dept. of Archaeology, Free Museum of Science and Art* 1, no. 3 (1905): 191–203.

"The Decorative Art of Crete in the Bronze Age." *Transactions of the Dept. of Archaeology, Free Museum of Science and Art* 2, no. 1 (1906): 5–49.

The Decorative Art of Crete in the Bronze Age. Philadelphia, 1907.

"Recent Excavations in Crete." *The Independent,* January 21, 1909, 138–44.

"Archaeological Research in Greece." *The Independent,* November 24, 1910, 1143–48.

"Excavations in Eastern Crete, Sphoungaras." *Anthropological Publications of the University Museum* 3, no. 2 (Philadelphia, 1912).

"Two Black-Figured Amphorae with Scenes Portraying the Birth of Athena." *Museum Journal* 3, no. 4 (1912): 68–75.

"The Graeco-Roman Section." *Museum Journal* 4, no. 4 (1913): 117–41.
"A Roman Relief from Pozzuoli." *Museum Journal* 4, no. 4 (1913): 142–46.
"Attic Vases from Orvieto." *Museum Journal* 4, (1913): 147–61.
"A Red-Figured Kylix." *Museum Journal* 4, no. 4 (1913): 162.
"A Seated Dionysos." *Museum Journal* 4, no. 4 (1913): 164–67.
"Excavations in Eastern Crete, Vrokastro." *Anthropological Publications of the University Museum* 3, no. 3 (Philadelphia, 1914).
"A Neo-Attic Relief and a Roman Portrait Head." *Museum Journal* 5, no. 1 (1914): 26–30.
"A Red-Figured Amphora Signed by the Potter Meno." *Museum Journal* 5, no. 1 (1914): 31–37.
"A Granite Sphinx from Memphis." *Museum Journal* 5, no. 2 (1914): 49–54.
"A Colored Marble Statuette." *Museum Journal* 5, no. 2 (1914): 116–21.
"A Roman Portrait Head." *Museum Journal* 5, no. 2 (1914): 122–24.
"Examples of Mycenaean and Minoan Art." *Museum Journal* 5, no. 3 (1914): 145–68.
"A Bronze Blade from the Dictaean Cave, Crete." *Museum Journal* 5, no. 3 (1914): 169–72.
"A Pair of Bits from Corneto." *Museum Journal* 5, no. 4 (1914): 213–17.
"Some Greek and Italian Vases in the Museum." *Museum Journal* 5, no. 4 (1914): 218–30.
"Fresco Representing a Hunt from the Later Palace at Tiryns." *Museum Journal* 5, no. 4 (1914): 231–35.
"Two Black-figured Amphorae from Orvieto." *Museum Journal* 6, no. 2 (1915): 85–93.
"Four Covered Bowls from Orvieto." *Museum Journal* 6, no. 4 (1915): 173–79.
"An Archaic Head from Cyprus." *Museum Journal* 12, no. 3 (1921): 200–203.
"An Amphora by the Berlin Painter." *University Bulletin* 3, no. 2 (1921): 53–54.
"Coins from Magna Graecia and Sicily." *Museum Journal* 14, no. 2 (1923): 162–69.
"Recent Additions to the Collections of Greek Vases." *Museum Journal* 19, no. 1 (1928): 72–84.
"Three Greek Grave Monuments." *Museum Journal* 19, no. 3 (1928): 249–60.
"Four New Geometric Vases." *University Bulletin* 2, no. 1 (1930): 11–14.
"An Amphora from the Hope Collection." *University Bulletin* 2, no. 3 (1931): 90–94.
"Two Plastic Vases." *University Bulletin* 2, no. 4 (1931): 123–27.
"Two Greek Sculptures." *University Bulletin* 2, no. 5 (1931): 150–53.
"A Greek Cup by the Foundry Painter." *University Bulletin* 3, no. 1 (1931): 23–26.
"A Head of a Youthful Herakles." *University Bulletin* 3, no. 2 (1931): 55–56.
"Four Vases from the Henry C. Lea Collection." *Museum Journal* 23, no. 1 (1932): 23–24.
"A Late Minoan Pyxis." *Museum Journal* 23, no. 1 (1932): 55–59.
"A Lydian Imitation of a Laconian Vase." *Museum Journal* 23, no. 1 (1932): 62–63.
"Two Vases from the Hegeman Collection." *Museum Journal* 23, no. 1 (1932): 64–74.
"The Cyprus Expedition." *University Bulletin* 4, no. 1 (1932): 12–17.
"A Corinthian Amphora." *University Bulletin* 4, no. 2 (1933): 48–49.

"Exekias." *University Bulletin* 4, no. 3 (1933): 66–67.
"The Gallery of Italic and Etruscan Art." *University Bulletin* 4, no. 6 (1933): 149–75.
"A Pair of Earrings from Cyprus." *University Bulletin* 5, no. 2 (1934): 41–44.
"An Italic Head." *University Bulletin* 5, no. 3 (1934): 90.
"Some Unpublished Vases in the University Museum, Philadelphia." *American Journal of Archaeology* 38 (1934): 523–32.
"Attic Vases from Memorial Hall." *University Bulletin* (1935): 70–76.
"A Statue of Athena." *University Bulletin* 5, no. 6 (1935): 75–78.
"A Daphnae Situla from Memphis." *University Bulletin* 6, no. 1 (1935): 15–17.
"A Ziro Burial from Chiusi." *American Journal of Archaeology* 39 (1935): 198–209.
"A Recent Acquisition of the University Museum, Philadelphia." *American Journal of Archaeology* 39 (1935): 451.
"Two Syrian Sculptural Portraits." *University Bulletin* 6, no. 5 (1936): 20–22.
"A Bell Krater by the Christie Painter." *University Bulletin* 6, no. 4 (1936): 126–28.
"A Bronze Statuette from Delphi." *American Journal of Archaeology* 40 (1936): 520–21.
"A Mosaic from Cento Celli." *University Bulletin* 7, no. 4 (1939): 18–20.
"Locrian Terracotta Plaques." *University Bulletin* 8, nos. 2–3 (1940): 12–17.
"Three Inscriptions in the University Museum, Philadelphia." *American Journal of Archaeology* 46 (1942): 532–34.
"An Italiote Krater in the University Museum, Philadelphia." *American Journal of Archaeology* 47 (1943): 171–73.
Italic Tomb Groups in the University Museum. Philadelphia, 1942.

Suggested Readings about Edith Hayward Hall Dohan

Allsebrook, Mary. *Born to Rebel: The Life of Harriet Boyd Hawes.* Bloomington, Ind., 1992.
Fotou, Vasso. *New Light on Gournia—Unknown Documents of the Expedition at Gournia and Other Sites of the Isthmus of Ierapetra by Harriet Ann Boyd.* Austin, Tex., 1993.
Thompson, Dorothy Burr. "Dohan, Edith Hayward Hall." *Notable American Women, 1607–1950: A Biographical Dictionary,* ed. E. T. James, J. W. James, and P. S. Boyer, 496–97. Cambridge: Harvard University Press, 1971.
Winegrad, D. P., *Through Time, Across Continents—A Hundred Years of Archaeology and Anthropology at the University Museum.* Philadelphia 1993.

NOTES

This biography is based mainly on the letters written by Edith Hall Dohan over the years 1903–12 and now on file in the archives of the University of Pennsylvania Museum. Deep thanks to Alessandro Pezzati, archivist at the University Museum in Philadelphia, for providing copies of letters and manuscripts. Except where otherwise stated, letters written by Edith Hall Dohan between 1903 and 1912 are referred to by their date only. Secondary sources not cited in the notes include Gisela Richter and Mary Swindler, "Necrology—Edith Hall Dohan," *American Journal of Archaeology* 47 (1943): 466; Joseph W. Shaw, "North American Archaeological Work in Crete, 1880–1990," *Expedition* 32, no. 3 (1990): 8–11; Jean Silverman, "A Lost Notebook from the Excavations at Gournia, Crete," *Expedition* 17, no. 1 (1974): 11–20; Jean Silverman, "In The Footsteps of Harriet Boyd Hawes," *Ms.*, January 1980, 13–20; and D. P. Winegrad, *Through Time, across Continents: A Hundred Years of Archaeology and Anthropology at the University Museum* (Philadelphia, 1993), 37–42.

1. Robert J. Smith, *A History of Woodstock Academy* (Woodstock, 1986), 57–81, esp. 58.

2. Smith, *History of Woodstock Academy,* 81.

3. Smith College curriculum (1895–99), Smith College Archives. (The Reverend Henry M. Tyler was professor of Greek.) Thanks to Joanne C. Dougherty, archives specialist at Smith College.

4. My thanks to Lorett Treese, Bryn Mawr College archivist, for searching the files for me. Professors' names are mentioned in Edith Hall's letter of December 15, 1902.

5. Letter of November 11, 1901.

6. A letter of March 2, 1902, relates the entire ordeal.

7. Bryn Mawr College Course Catalogue (1903), 33.

8. Louis E. Lord, *A History of the American School of Classical Studies in Athens, 1882–1942* (Cambridge, Mass., 1947), 111. Edith was the last recipient since the donors felt the purpose of the prize had been met (111).

9. Letter of May 7, 1903.

10. Letter of December 29, 1903.

11. Letter of September 30, 1903.

12. Ibid.

13. *American Journal of Archaeology Annual Reports* (1903–4), 108–9. Richard Seager later introduced Edith to Harriet Boyd. My thanks to Natalia Vogeokoff, archivist to the American School of Classical Studies in Athens, who sent me this information and copies of several letters heretofore unknown.

14. Letter of January 18, 1904.

15. Letter of October 2, 1903.

16. Letter of November 15, 1903.

17. Letters of November 1, 6, and 13, 1903.

18. Letter of January 18, 1904.

19. Letter of November 1, 1903.

20. Letter of November 13, 1903.

21. Letter of December 20, 1903.

22. Ibid.

23. Edith's trip to work at Gournia was to interrupt her progress, and it would not be until she returned to the American School in the fall of 1904 that she would be able to continue her writing.

24. See E. Hall, *The Decorative Art of Crete in the Bronze Age* (Philadelphia, 1907), 3.

25. Ibid.

26. Ibid., 47.

27. Ibid.

28. Letter of February 15, 1904.

29. Harriet Boyd had started the dig in 1901 and had continued in 1903. Under the auspices of the American Exploration Society and with a grant of twenty-five hundred dollars, the dig was allowed to continue into 1904, its last season. H. Boyd, "Gournia. Report of the American Exploration Society's Excavations at Gournia, Crete 1904," *Transactions of the Department of Archaeology, Free Museum of Science and Art, University of Pennsylvania* 1, no. 3 (1905): 177 and 191 (hereafter cited as *Transactions* 1905).

30. Letter of March 6, 1904.

31. Ibid.

32. Ibid.

33. Interestingly, one of the major supporters of the excavation and the American Exploration Society was Mr. Sam Houston, then a Philadelphia resident (*Transactions* 1905, 177).

34. Letters of February 15, 1904; April 10, 1904.

35. Mary Nesbit Allsebrook, *Born to Rebel: The Life of Harriet Boyd Hawes* (Bloomington, Ind., 1992), 115.

36. Crete at the time was governed by "the Powers." Each city or town on the island was occupied by one of four nations; see Allsebrook, *Born to Rebel,* 116. The island was not yet annexed to Greece and had just won its independence from Turkey.

37. Letter of April 18, 1904.

38. Ibid.

39. Letter of March 20, 1904.

40. Letter of March 28, 1904.

41. Ibid.

42. Letters of March 28 and April 18, 1904.

43. Letter of March 28, 1904.

44. Edith hinted to her sister how difficult it was to sleep so near to Richard Seager. All her writings suggest she was a little in love with him. He, in turn, was a sickly man, having a congestive heart disorder and possibly malaria. He lived in Greece for his health, finding the climate easier on his lungs and heart.

45. Letter of April 10, 1904.

46. Letter of March 28, 1904.

47. Letter of April 10, 1904.

48. Letter of April 18, 1904.

49. Ibid.

50. Ibid.

51. Letter of April 24, 1904.

52. Letter of April 13, 1904.

53. Letter of April 24, 1904.

54. Letter of May 1, 1904.

55. Letter of April 13, 1904.

56. Ibid.

57. E. Hall, "Archeology in Crete," *The Independent,* June 23, 1904, 1438–39.

58. E Hall, "Early Painted Pottery from Gournia, Crete," *Transactions* 1905, 191.

59. Ibid.

60. Letter of May 1, 1904.

61. Hall, "Painted Pottery," 194.

62. Ibid.

63. Allsebrook, *Born to Rebel,* 119. At Vasiliki, Seager uncovered more evidence. His preliminary excavations brought up sherds with similar decorative motives. Several graves found at the end of the season substantiate Edith's observations; see "Painted Pottery," 193.

64. Hall, "Painted Pottery," 204, 205. At the time, pottery from Knossos had not been fully published, thereby limiting Hall's conclusions.

65. Boyd, *Transactions* 1905, 178.

66. Vasso Fotou, *New Light on Gournia: Unknown Documents of the Excavation at Gournia and Other Sites on the Isthmus of Ierapetra by Harriet Ann Boyd* (Austin, Tex., 1993), 25.

67. *New York Times,* September 25, 1904, as quoted in Allsebrook, *Born to Rebel,* 123. For government regulations, see Boyd, *Transactions* (1905), 177. See also *Women in Archaeology/Anthropology in the University Museum,* an undated exhibition brochure.

68. Fotou, *New Light,* 22.

69. For this information, I am indebted to Patricia J. Albright, archives librarian at Mount Holyoke College.

70. E. Hall, "Excavations in Eastern Crete, Sphoungaras," *Anthropological Publications of the University Museum* 3, no. 2 (1912): 72.

71. E. Hall, "Excavations in Eastern Crete, Vrokastro," *Anthropological Publications of the University Museum* 3, no. 3 (1914): 80–81.

72. Ibid., 80.

73. Ibid., 83.

74. Ibid., 179.

75. Ibid., 180.

76. Ibid., 182.

77. Personal communication and notes from Edith's niece, Marjorie Gaylord Brink.

78. Letter of October 27, 1911.

79. David Hayward Warrington Dohan was born August 31, 1916, and Katharine Elizabeth Dohan was born March 5, 1918.

80. Bryn Mawr College course catalogs 1922–24, 1926–27, 1929–30. Course titles over the years included Greek Sculpture, Hellenistic Towns, Ancient Architecture, Minor Arts, and Aegean Archaeology.

81. Letter to the author dated July 14, 1995. Lucy Shoe Meritt is known for her comprehensive study of architectural profiles of Greek buildings.

82. A personal note to Edith's niece, Margorie Brink. Unfortunately neither Meritt nor Thompson give any detail about teaching style.

83. F. P. Johnson, review of Edith Hall Dohan, *Italic Tomb Groups in the University Museum* (Philadelphia, 1942), *Classical Philology* 38 (October 1943). Other

reviews include those by Paul Jacobstahl in *Journal of Roman Studies* 32–33 (1942–43): 97–100 and by Raymond T. Ohl in *Classical Weekly* 36, no. 1 (1942): 7–8.

84. George M. A. Hanfmann, review of E. H. Dohan, *Italic Tomb Groups in the University Museum* (Philadelphia, 1942), *American Journal of Archaeology* 48 (1944): 114–16. See also Dorothy Burr Thompson, "Dohan, Edith Hayward Hall," *Notable American Women,* ed. E. T. James (Cambridge, Mass., 1971), 497, where she recalls that the "set up [of the] exhibition was "acclaimed by experts."

85. *Philadelphia Press,* May 13, 1915.

86. Hanfmann, review, 116.

Hetty Goldman

(1881–1972)

Machteld J. Mellink
and Kathleen M. Quinn

HETTY GOLDMAN'S CAREER in archaeology was conducted against the backdrop of a series of world upheavals, yet throughout, she persevered not only in her desire to engage in field archaeology, but also in her philanthropic devotion to those people in the Mediterranean touched by turbulent times. Goldman was part of the first generation of American archaeologists to work in the Mediterranean, and she became the first American woman to direct an archaeological excavation on mainland Greece. Remembered as a woman of exceptional wit and humor and a scholar of unshakable principles and determination, Goldman left behind a legacy worthy of her pioneering spirit.

Throughout her long career, Goldman made significant contributions to the development of archaeology as a scholarly discipline in terms of techniques employed and questions asked. She supported regional archaeological surveys, discouraged looters from pillaging artifacts from sites, and penned comprehensive final publications that served as models for other scholars in the field. Although she played many roles during her career—

relief worker, archaeologist, and mentor—Goldman is best remembered for her contributions to the study of trade contacts between Greece and the Near East during the prehistoric period.

> Let me make the humiliating confession at once. I have never raised a pick-axe, I have never wielded a shovel. Cherish no fond regard for the female excavator as a subtle compound of brain and brawn, who at will can raise a boulder or decipher the inscription upon its face. Here you shall have her true portrait and the chronicle of her days, and if they are poor in deeds of prowess, you still may find them full of varied experiences, half poetic, half practical, and of precious human contacts.
>
> —Hetty Goldman, "With the Spade in Greece," 1918

Family Background and Education

Hetty Goldman was born on December 19, 1881, in New York City.[1] She was the daughter of Sarah Adler and Julius Goldman, both of whose families were actively involved in the social and intellectual movements of the late nineteenth and early twentieth centuries. Her maternal grandfather, Samuel Adler, was a university-educated man who, in 1856, had been called as a Reform rabbi from Germany to Temple Emanu-El in New York City. Isaac Adler, Samuel Adler's son and one of Goldman's maternal uncles, became a doctor, while Felix Adler, another of Goldman's uncles, founded the New York Society for Ethical Culture, out of which sprang the New York Ethical Culture schools and the national and international Ethical Culture movements.[2] He later served as professor of social and political ethics at Columbia University from 1902 until 1933.

Goldman's paternal grandparents, Bertha and Marcus Goldman, had emigrated from Germany to Baltimore, Maryland, during the 1850s. After living briefly in Baltimore, they moved to New York City, where Marcus Goldman founded the investment banking house of Goldman, Sachs, and Company with two brothers, Julius and Samuel Sachs. Bertha and Marcus Goldman had four children: Julius, Rebecca, Rosa, and Louisa. They eventually found themselves linked to the Sachs family through both business and personal ties. Rosa Goldman married Julius Sachs, and Louisa married Samuel Sachs.

Julius Sachs, like Felix Adler, was committed to improving secondary and university education in New York City. He founded the Sachs School for Boys in 1871 and the companion Sachs School for Girls in 1891. Julius Sachs's academic interests were in classics and archaeology. He had studied classics in Germany with Hermann Sauppe at the University of Göttingen and had assembled an extensive library of books on these subjects, which his niece, Hetty Goldman, eventually inherited. Julius delivered a lecture entitled "Echoes of Greek Epic Poetry in Vase Painting" to the newly formed Archaeological Institute of America (AIA) in May 1893 and served as president of the AIA's New York Society from 1900 to 1903. Julius Sachs was also a member of the Auxiliary Fund board of directors for the American School of Classical Studies in Athens from 1912 to 1922, during the early years of Goldman's archaeological career.[3]

Julius Goldman married Sarah Adler in 1878. He worked as a lawyer, and Sarah devoted her time to her friends and family. The Goldmans had four children: Bertha, Marcus, Hetty, and Agnes. All four attended the Sachs School for Boys and Girls, where they learned, among other subjects, Greek and Latin. It was this training in ancient languages at the secondary level, coupled with her uncle Julius Sachs's own personal interests in classics and archaeology, that may have prompted Hetty to pursue classics in college.[4]

Hetty Goldman entered Bryn Mawr College in 1899 as the recipient of the Second Scholarship for the State of New York. While at Bryn Mawr, she double majored in English and Greek. After graduating in 1903, she embarked on a year of graduate study (1903–4) at Columbia University, where she continued to improve her ancient Greek. At the same time, she worked as a manuscript reader with the Macmillan Company, a job that complemented her interest in writing and her major in English. For a short time she considered a career in writing, later lamenting to friends that "though she enjoyed writing she had as yet nothing to say."[5] Goldman's interest in classical studies was further inflamed in the spring of 1906 when she made a three-month tour of the archaeological sites of Italy. She followed this excursion with a second year of graduate study in classics at Columbia University from 1906 to 1907.

In addition to her interests in writing and the classics, Goldman enjoyed music. She played both the piano and violin. Frances Jones, a longtime friend and colleague, recalled that Goldman often performed for others, especially on her violin. Goldman realized, however, that her diminutive hands made her unsuited to play either instrument professionally, something that Frances Jones reported "was a real disappointment to her."[6]

In 1909 Goldman enrolled at Radcliffe College as a graduate student in classical languages and archaeology. While at Radcliffe, she lived in a dormitory with other women graduate students, all supervised by a housemother. Goldman worked for one year on her master's thesis, "The *Oresteia* of Aeschylus as Illustrated by Greek Vase-Painting." In this paper Goldman demonstrated her understanding of Aeschylus's poetry and sentiments and presented a courageous analysis of the iconographic inspiration and elaboration of the Oresteia in Attic vase-painting and other artistic comparanda.[7] This thesis, published in *Harvard Studies in Classical Philology,* showcased Goldman's talents as a writer, a student of literary expression, and an archaeologist familiar with the iconographic repertoire of vases in collections from Boston to St. Petersburg. It demonstrated that she was a student worthy of her uncle Julius Sachs's archaeological pioneering.

Halae

Goldman submitted her Radcliffe thesis on the *Oresteia* as part of her application for Harvard University's Charles Eliot Norton Fellowship in Greek Studies at the American School of Classical Studies in Athens for the 1910–11 academic year. Her application was successful, and she became the first woman to hold this prestigious Harvard fellowship, an honor that was eventually extended for a second year (1911–12). There were eleven students at the school during the first year of Goldman's fellowship, among them five women. Goldman's fellow students included, among others, Carl W. Blegen, William Bell Dinsmoor, Cyrus Ashton Rollins Sanborn, and Alice Leslie Walker.[8] The students attended lectures by Professor Dörpfeld on Athenian topography and by Professor Karo on the Neolithic and Archaic objects in the National Museum.[9] During her first year at the American School, Goldman's special project focused on the votive reliefs in the Athenian museums.[10]

Goldman later recalled that there was, upon her first arrival in Greece, "in my heart a great desire for that experience which up till then had been denied women: some share in the field work of the School."[11] This interest in archaeological excavation was at odds with the beliefs of some of the early directors of the American School, who suggested that "women [could not] travel well in the interior of Greece, nor share in the active work of excavation."[12] This attitude seemed to prevail at the school despite the fact that Harriet Boyd (later Hawes) and Edith Hall (later Dohan) had already directed excavations on Crete for the American Exploration Society and the University of Pennsylvania Museum of Archaeology and Anthropology, respectively. The novelty of women being interested in archaeology even prompted some teasing from Goldman's male colleagues at the school, including her future brother-in-law, Ashton Sanborn. After all, they would tease, what did women know about archaeology?[13] Yet such teasing only made Goldman more determined in her efforts to excavate. Goldman, although a diminutive five feet, two inches, is remembered as being both feisty and stubborn by family and colleagues alike.[14]

So despite discouraging encounters with colleagues at the school, Goldman's enthusiasm for excavation never wavered; in fact, it was further inflamed by the extensive and sometimes arduous explorations of archaeological sites by students and faculty during the various field trips of the American School. Goldman wrote: "I cannot remember the exact process by which . . . I was transformed into a passionate excavator who was either turning up the soil of Greece, or planning to return to it; but complete conversion took place on top of a hill in Boeotia."[15] Here, on one of the school trips, Goldman spied "an eminence in the field, which suggested, not a natural hillock, but the kind of mound formed by the debris of an ancient town."[16]

The mound that had so delighted Goldman turned out to be the ancient city of Eutresis, a site with which she was later to become intimately familiar. During the fall of 1910 she eagerly sought permission to excavate the mound, but she was eventually denied. Writing in 1923, Goldman lamented,

> The ruins of Eutresis still sleep beneath the soil, for although the director of the School was open-minded enough to meet our desire to excavate half way—I worked with another woman student—it was deemed advisable to choose a site nearer to where the men of the School were working that year, so that we should not be left to meet unaided the many difficulties, both practical and archaeological, which our inexperience was certain to encounter.[17]

Yet Goldman's determination paid off, so that in May 1911 she and Alice Leslie Walker came to the site of Halae-by-the-Sea, more commonly referred to simply as Halae. The gentlemen of the school on whom Goldman was to call in case of emergency were, under the direction of Professor Carl D. Buck, excavating in East Locris at both Kyparissi and Atalante "with a mind towards identifying ancient Opus."[18] In her later years, Goldman acknowledged the hesitancy of the American School to assign her a site for excavation by joking to friends that she and Walker were permitted to excavate at Halae only because the director of the American School wished to locate them as far from Athens as possible.[19]

The excavation at Halae was the first for the thirty-year-old Goldman, although Alice Walker, a graduate of Vassar College, had worked on the American School excavations at Corinth as a pottery analyst. The excavations at Halae were conducted under the auspices of the American School of Classical Studies. The school provided Goldman and Walker with some resources (books, large excavation equipment, and professional personnel like architects), but for the most part, Bert Hodge Hill, director of the American School, reported that the women "worked at their own expense."[20] Thus, the directors were responsible for the payment of workers, their lodging for the season, miscellaneous excavation equipment, notebooks, and the like. Goldman was well aware that her archaeological work would require private funding. Many years later she wrote to her niece, Elizabeth Gutmann, the daughter of her sister Bertha Goldman Gutmann, about becoming an archaeologist:

> First of all be sure that they do not get the impression in Athens that you are in the same position as myself and can work without pay. When I took up the special kind of archaeology I pursue—that is field work—your Grandad and I clearly understood that to mean that I would not be earning my living thereby, and I asked him whether he was sufficiently interested in the results of such a career to finance me. It was only with his consent that I embarked upon it, for otherwise I should have turned to teaching or museum work.[21]

By assuming the directorship of the excavations at Halae, Goldman and Walker became the third and fourth women ever to direct an excavation in Greece—Harriet Boyd having been the first (at Gournia, 1901) and Edith Hall the second (at Vrokastro, 1910).[22] And should anyone at the American School have doubted that women could travel well in Greece, Harriet Boyd had "scaled a mountain and scrambled up a forked tree into a cave" in her pursuit of archaeological sites.[23] During the numerous seasons of excavation at Halae, both Goldman and Walker lived in tents close to the Bay of Atalante. There they had to deal with "the case of the delinquent postman . . . a trying day of high winds, blowing dust into one's eyes and cold into one's limbs . . . [a] dilapidated alidade . . . [and] a dynamite explosion in the sea, [which] disturbs the dawn."[24] According to Frances Jones, Goldman eagerly accepted all the difficulties of an excavation, and she "made no great matter of what might be considered unusual circumstances for a woman."[25] She tackled fieldwork much as she did everything else—with intelligence and a sense of humor.

Today the acropolis of ancient Halae hugs the northern shoreline of the Bay of Atalante in the province of Locris in north central Greece. The site is located within the modern town of Theologos, a resort for Greeks on vacation. Yet in the early part of the century, when Goldman first put spade to soil, Theologos was a sleepy fishing village in the middle of nowhere with few amenities. Goldman and Walker traveled to the site by steamboat up the Euripus Straits. Goldman later described the journey as one filled "with shepherds, peasants, and goats, in superb but ill-smelling democracy, [filling] whatever space on the first class deck [was] not encumbered by our fifty-odd pieces of hand-baggage."[26] And just as the Roman general Sulla had stopped at Aidepsos centuries before to rest from travel, so, too, did Goldman and Walker stop to change boats before finally reaching the Bay of Atalante and the site of Halae.

Upon arriving at Halae in the spring of 1911, Goldman and Walker encountered a certain Demetrios, owner of the only available house in Theologos. After extended negotiations, the women finally agreed to pay his exorbitant price for shelter, happy "with visions of the Abercrombie and Fitch tents with which we mean to defy the Haliotes when next we return to their shores."[27] Next, the two women began the process of acquiring the rights to excavate on the parcel of land where the presence of walls had been noticed. These dealings were necessary even though the American School had already obtained a government permit for excavation. With not a little irony Goldman once wrote, "the government permit does no more than permit us to try and get the permission to dig from the actual owner of the soil."[28] So after more negotiations, conducted with much the same success and loss of funds that the encounter with Demetrios had produced, Goldman and Walker finally began their excavations.

In an article written for the *Bryn Mawr Alumnae Bulletin* in 1955, Goldman recalled Halae as "one of the loveliest sites that could be found."[29] She described the bucolic peace of life and work at the site, remembering that the bay was both "good for swimming" and for the local fishing industry. Yet despite the beauty of the surroundings, for Goldman the "fascination of this site from the archaeological point of view was that it gave so good a picture of the ancient Greek Polis in miniature form."[30]

Excavations in 1911 focused on parts of the acropolis wall that were already exposed. Goldman and Walker traced the so-called sea wall (the southern fortification wall that bordered the bay) from a tower discovered on the east end toward the west. Work was also conducted at the summit of the acropolis inside a ruined Late Roman church. In the area west of the church, the women found a large well filled with Archaic terra-cotta figurines and building fragments associated with a small sanctuary to Athena, identified by a charming third-century B.C. inscription, which spoke of hangings made for the cult statue.

In addition to the acropolis trenches, Goldman and Walker excavated on a hill northeast of the acropolis proper to look for graves in hopes of establishing "a more exact chronology for some of the vases and terra-cottas of the sixth and later centuries before Christ."[31] To aid them in locating the graves, they employed some of the local peasants, who were "known to have dealt lucratively, if illicitly, in antiquities filched by night from the old cemetery of Halae."[32] Once she hired these men, Goldman tolerated none of their illegal activities. She wrote,

> These too canny employees for the most part conveniently provided for their own dismissal, by concealing some precious bit in the ample folds of their shirts, and then naïvely offering it, still damp with fresh soil, to [us] on the following day, as a treasure long in the possession of their family, with which they would be willing to part—for a consideration—to such zealous and persevering investigators.[33]

Despite the frustrations caused by these local "archaeologists," Goldman and Walker excavated a number of unrobbed tombs, finding inside terracotta masks, lamps, and other small personal items. Most of the movable artifacts were transported to the Archaeological Museum at Thebes for storage; jewelry was taken to the National Museum in Athens.

Goldman later spoke of archaeology as an "adventure," and indeed her descriptions of life at Halae suggest a challenge that she eagerly embraced:

> It was a simple life we led at "Theologou." Labor laws being unknown—they have since been enacted—work started at sunrise and ended at sunset, with a short pause for breakfast and a long noonday rest. For us the day began with a swim in the bay and often ended at night with another swim in the path of the moon or the golden trail of the planet Jupiter. We were in the field as long as the men worked, guiding their digging, recording exact positions of finds, stratifications of soil which might help in determining relative dates, measuring and photographing. Evenings were for cataloguing and writing, or if an inscription had been found, it was hardly possi-

> ble to go to bed, no matter how tired, until one had some clue to its meaning. Our neighbors were kindly folk, helpful, and even generous when it was not a matter of business. As women engaged in the strange pursuit of excavating, we were hardly of our sex. Great was the speculation as to the actual object of our work, the most favored hypothesis being that somewhere on the acropolis was an ancient treasure of gold guarded by serpents of which our "map" told us. Archaeologists are supposed to carry always with them a map—the result of our devotion to Pausanias, I doubt not—which tells them the precise location of antiquities. I have often had a workman raise himself from a trench to enquire, "And what does your map say we shall find at this spot?"[34]

Goldman's fellowship to the American School was renewed for the academic year 1911–12. During this academic year, plans were being formulated to enlarge the American School's facilities in Athens to include a "women's room" since "women were beginning to play a larger role in the activities of the school."[35] During her second year in residence at the school, Goldman worked in the National Museum with the objects she and Alice Walker had excavated the preceding spring.[36] Her newfound excavation experience also resulted in invitations to participate in a few days of digging at Delphi and on the Acropolis. Goldman and Walker returned to Halae in the spring of 1912, this time focusing most of their energy on the graves north and northeast of the acropolis.

The annual report of the American School for 1912–13 indicated that the first of the two Balkan Wars "had made all excavations impossible, but Miss Walker and Miss Goldman have spent much time in work upon their finds of previous years at Halae."[37] After a short trip home to the United States, where she presented the preliminary results of her work at Halae at the Archaeological Institute of America's annual meeting, Goldman returned to Athens. She continued to be in residence at the school during the year, although her fellowship had ended. Goldman and Walker were the only women present at the school during the Balkan Wars (1912–13). When not studying the Halae material, Goldman was involved in social concerns during the war. As a member of the American Red Cross Commission to Greece, she served as a nurse. As her sister, Agnes Goldman Sanborn, wrote later in a report to Bryn Mawr College:

> In 1913, during her summer vacation in Switzerland, while the second Balkan War was on, Hetty Goldman felt called upon to volun-

> teer as a nurse with the totally inadequate Greek medical service. They accepted her eagerly and sent her back to Salonika, the only woman on a troop ship. She stepped into her duties and into almost the first hospital ward she had ever seen, over the prostrate figure of a dying officer. For six weeks she worked at tending the wounded, and in doing anything that was possible for a totally untrained person. Her experience with the peasant soldiers, who scarcely knew why they were fighting, left an indelible impression, and rendered her for all time peculiarly responsive to the appeal of suffering.[38]

After the cessation of hostilities, Goldman and Walker returned to Halae during the fall of 1913 and again in the spring of 1914. These two seasons of work focused on the acropolis, particularly the western end. Goldman and Walker excavated the north gate of the fortification wall and its associated shops, dug several trenches inside the Late Roman church and Byzantine chapel, and identified the western fortification wall and tower.

During 1915 Goldman published the first of several articles on her work at Halae. One was a brief description of the excavations at the site prior to the outbreak of the Balkan Wars, and the second presented the epigraphic material so far found at the site.[39] After the outbreak of World War I, Goldman returned to America, having studied further in Greece and for some months in Munich. More work at Radcliffe College led to her Ph.D. in 1916. Her dissertation, entitled "The Terracottas from the Necropolis of Halae," included an exhaustive catalog of the hundreds of figurines excavated during her first two campaigns, which had focused on the cemeteries outside the small, seaside acropolis. In all, Goldman and Walker unearthed more than 280 graves, most dating from the late sixth century to the third century B.C., although a few graves of Roman date also were found. The graves were easily dated by the well-documented pottery that emerged from them, and this allowed Goldman to establish a fairly reliable chronology for the terra-cottas she found. This chronology was especially important, as Frances Jones has noted, since "certain types had been associated for decades with Boeotia," but because they had been looted, their contexts were unknown. "Here at last," Jones wrote, "in the stone graves of Halae, were the means to follow the evolution of the youth with cock, the draped female figure, and the other regional favorites."[40]

During the forced hiatus from digging at Halae, Goldman and President Thomas of Bryn Mawr College became involved with the Women's Building Fund at the American School of Classical Studies in Athens. The purpose of the fund was to raise money for the purchase of some land opposite the American School grounds upon which to construct a residence hall for the female students at the school. As in most of her endeavors, her father (Julius Goldman), her uncle (Samuel Sachs), and her cousin (Paul Sachs), supported Hetty Goldman in her efforts. By the end of the academic year 1915–16, the Women's Building Fund had grown to fifty-seven hundred dollars.[41]

Although she remained enmeshed in the study of antiquity and causes archaeological, Goldman's concern with the miseries of the contemporary world led her into further public service. Shortly after America entered World War I in April 1917, she joined the newly organized Red Cross Home Service Department. As part of her Red Cross work, she visited the families of soldiers from New York City during the summer months. The following winter she worked in Washington, D.C., for the Department of Public Information, and she returned to New York in the summer to work with the Colonel House Commission.[42]

In the autumn of 1918 Goldman joined a Red Cross unit headed for Greece under the direction of Professor Capps of Princeton University. She joined as a representative of the Joint Distribution Committee for the Relief of Jewish War Sufferers, and her sister Agnes Goldman Sanborn noted:

> Her duties included recommendations for the distribution of funds, the formation of non-partisan distributing committees among Jewish communities and the negotiations with the government when, as in Salonika after the fire, the Jews, still living in half-destroyed hovels, were to be supplied with temporary living quarters. Of all the work she had done, none was more exacting, or involved greater responsibility. It demanded tact, sound judgment, and ready perception.[43]

Goldman's work with the Red Cross unit and the Relief of Jewish War Sufferers took her to Jewish communities in Greece, Serbia, Bulgaria, and Romania. She made a final report on her observations in Paris before returning to America in July of 1919, where she continued to devote considerable attention to the problems of the Near Eastern Jews.

Although the war ended in November 1918, further fieldwork at Halae was delayed. Alice Walker married the foreman of the excavation team, George Kosmopoulos, and remained permanently in Greece. Goldman undertook supplementary work at the site in 1921 with the assistance of Piet de Jong, artist and architect associated with the American School. She returned to Halae again in 1923, focusing her work on the northeast part of the site. Here Goldman found several wells, houses or shops, and a possible Roman bathing establishment. Excavations on the east side of the acropolis revealed a row of Early Roman shops. From materials inside, she tentatively identified the shops of a metalworker, a grocer, and a statue seller, in whose establishment she found a miniature marble copy of the Aphrodite of Knidos. Goldman returned for one final season of work in 1931 with Virginia Grace. While Goldman examined the streets of the town, Grace worked in a trench focused on the Neolithic levels. Alice Walker Kosmopoulos returned to examine the prehistoric materials in 1935, although she never completed her final publication of the Neolithic period at Halae. Goldman published a final site report in 1940 and revised her Ph.D. dissertation with the assistance of Frances F. Jones for publication two years later.[44]

The preliminary results of the Halae excavations and the importance of the site as a Locrian coastal station both in prehistoric and classical times attracted a team of archaeologists from Cornell University to make a new survey of the region. The Cornell Halai and East Locris Project, under the direction of John E. Coleman of Cornell, conducted two seasons of survey in 1988 and 1989. Excavations began in 1990. Work at the site continues, both in study seasons and in excavation.[45]

Colophon

In 1920 the American School of Classical Studies at Athens declared a moratorium on all excavations in Greece until "the School should have had time to catch up with arrears in the matter of publication" of various sites previously excavated.[46] An exception to the new policy was reached with the Fogg Museum of Harvard University. Under an agreement with the American School, the Fogg would supply no less than ten thousand dollars per year, for no fewer than five years of excavation. In return, the school would be responsible for making arrangements with the Greek government, including obtaining deeds to the site. Both the Fogg Museum and the school agreed to provide a representative for the excavation; Hetty Goldman was named Fellow of the Museum and chosen as the representative for the Fogg. During her fellowship, Goldman reported to the museum and to her cousin, Paul Sachs, director of the Fogg Museum, who received many letters about her travels and excavations. Paul Sachs had preferred the study of prints to banking and made his distinguished academic and museum career at Harvard from 1917 to 1948.

The school welcomed Goldman's choice as representative, citing her tenure as a student at the school, her excavations at Halae, her fluency in modern Greek and familiarity with the country, and her dedication to community service during the wars.[47] During the summer of 1921 Goldman traveled with Bert Hodge Hill, director of the school, to scout out a suitable site for excavation.[48]

They first traveled to Asia Minor where they began their journey at Smyrna (modern Izmir) on June 14, 1921, accompanied by Konstantinos Kourouniotes, who was the Greek superintendent of antiquities for the Greek-organized archaeological service. They arrived in the area of Colophon and Notium two weeks later after visiting several other sites, including Sardis, Clazomenae-Urla, Erythrae, and Ephesus. Goldman and Hill also visited the site of Colophon, which had been identified by Carl Schuchhardt in 1885 but had not been studied in detail. After their trip to Asia Minor, Goldman and Hill remained undecided on a new site. They set off again, this time in Greece. Goldman described their journey with humor:

> We made a preliminary trip which covered almost all of northern mainland Greece, a large part of Macedonia, the eastern end of Thrace with an excursion into Albania. Never did rickety Ford start out more gaily on perilous adventure. On the lonely plains of Thessaly it carried us away from under the noses of three brigands, and devotedly waited for its semi-breakdown until we were well out of their reach. I have much humiliation to record at the hands of brigands. Twice have I been at their mercy and rejected as unworthy of capture. Evidently there is nothing about me to suggest the possibility of fabulous ransoms.[49]

A decision was ultimately made to excavate at the site of Colophon in Ionia (a name long-associated with the west coast of modern Turkey) "after it was found that the British Museum, which had a clear claim to this site from Turkish times, would be glad to waive its rights to dig there, and that the French, who intended to dig at Notium, would welcome an American undertaking at the nearby site of Colophon." Formal application was made to the Greek government in Smyrna in February 1922, and a permit was issued to dig there "under the laws of Greece."[50] Greece had, since 1919, occupied much of western Asia Minor, an area previously held by the Ottoman Empire, and lost following their defeat in World War 1.

At Colophon, Goldman recorded her impressions of the walls, inscriptions, and topography. Here, too, she must have first met members of the

Van Lennep family, the Swedish consul's family whose farm was at Malkaçik, north of Colophon. One of the Van Lenneps later gave her information on the robbery of the tholos tomb that she dug later in 1922; an ancestor of the same clan had given topographical advice to Carl Schuchhardt in 1885.[51]

Goldman returned to Greece in November 1921 to finalize arrangements with the American School. Both the Fogg Museum and the American School of Classical Studies at Athens made preparations for the excavation. Goldman and Lulu Eldridge represented the Fogg, while Carl W. Blegen, who was at the beginning of his distinguished career, having recently published the results of his first excavation at Korakou in 1921, represented the school in the field. Blegen was assisted by Leicester B. Holland, architect and surveyor, who was appreciated for his specialty and his active participation in the excavation as well as the publication of Colophon's ruins. American School students Benjamin D. Meritt, Franklin P. Johnson, and Kenneth Scott also assisted in the excavation. The Greek army lent the excavation "all the suitable light railway material it had in its stores" for use at Colophon and agreed also to send a cartographer to help create a good map of the site. "Decauville cars and section of track and track equipment" were shipped to Colophon from the Corinth excavations.[52]

Excavations began at Colophon on April 20, 1922. In a letter written more than forty years later, Carl Blegen described the natural beauty of the site:

> We lived in a little village called Değirmendere, a pleasant spot where a copious spring emerged from an almost vertical cliff, supplying water for a small river that flowed through a great grove of poplar trees. In the topmost branches were hundreds, or thousands, of nightingales who sang with enthusiasm all night long and made so much noise—like a waterfall—that our architect was unable to sleep.[53]

The site consisted of the Hellenistic acropolis and the outlying Geometric-period cemeteries. Both were explored during the ten-week season of 1922.

Goldman and Blegen uncovered numerous houses and buildings of the Classical period constructed on terraces along the slope of the mound. Dated to the fourth century B.C., many of the houses yielded complete plans; some were the earliest Greek houses known from excavation, the only earlier examples having been found at Priene. Colophon appeared to have been a well-planned city, much as Halae had been. The streets between the organized city blocks were paved with cobbles or dressed and fitted with stone. The excavators also explored the city's drainage system. Terra-cotta pipes were found below the level of the street, presumably to drain water and waste. In addition, the excavators discovered the remains of a stoa, a bathing establishment with at least fourteen bathtubs, and a sanctuary to Cybele. Coins found at the site proved the identification of the acropolis as that of Colophon.

George Hanfmann has noted that the "urbanistic fame of Colophon has been immensely heightened by an inscription found in the Metroon in 1922, which is one of the most revealing documents of classical Greek city planning."[54] The inscription records how the residents of Colophon began to rebuild following the liberation of the city by Alexander the Great and his general Antigonus. The decree provided for the construction of a common city wall and for the election of a committee of ten members whose role was to oversee urban planning and all construction jobs. These jobs included the appointment of an architect "to study the layout and leasing of streets and lots, to reserve land for sacred and public complexes, and to raise funds by subscription in order to build the city walls."[55]

The tombs excavated during 1922 were found beyond the city walls in three different locations. Many had already been looted. Those that had not been disturbed dated, for the most part, to the fourth century B.C. Others contained Geometric-style pottery of previously unknown types; these were tentatively dated to the ninth century. The most promising discovery was that of a small, built tholos of the Mycenaean period, which had received recent damage from tomb robbing, although fragments of pottery remained in the debris. This tomb, called Tomb 9, was dug by Goldman herself and drawn by Leicester Holland; the drawings were published by Robert A. Bridges Jr., in 1974.[56] According to Goldman, this "well-built beehive tomb . . . yielded pottery of a design strikingly like the late Minoan wares."[57]

In June 1922 excavations at Colophon were cut short by tensions leading to the outbreak of the Greco-Turkish war. The Turks, under the leadership of Mustafa Kemal (Atatürk), drove the Greeks out of Asia Minor. On September 11, 1922, Smyrna was destroyed by fire, and Goldman's hopes for the excavations at Colophon came to an abrupt end. Goldman recalled:

> We had closed down the excavation before [the fire], thinking to continue after a short interval, but when we returned all the antiqui-

> ties we had garnered by careful work, both in a part of the town site of post-Alexander times and in an important geometric cemetery of the ninth or eighth century B.C., had disappeared. All that remained was a single iron bedstead on which a local policeman was found taking his noon day siesta.[58]

Fortunately for the excavators, "the coins which had proved the identity of the town reached asylum in Istanbul."[59]

Supported by the Fogg Museum, Goldman returned for a short second campaign in the late summer and fall of 1925. Edward Capps Jr. and Dorothy H. Cox, who served as architect for the excavations, accompanied her.[60] Goldman and Cox recorded the plan of the impressive Metroon, published in a general study of architectural results by Leicester B. Holland.[61] The rich epigraphic harvest, with its ample confirmation of the identity of the site as Colophon and which Goldman recalled "we had the foresight to re-bury,"[62] prior to the war was published by Benjamin Meritt in 1935. Included among the epigraphic material was the important fourth-century inscription about the rebuilding of Colophon.[63]

The Mycenaean phase of activities at Colophon came as quite a surprise to the excavators in 1922, but a Mycenaean presence in the area was recently confirmed by the discovery of another Mycenaean built chamber tomb. The tomb was found on Baklatepe near Bulgurca in 1997 by Hayat Erkanal, also excavator of Limantepe-Clazomenae with its third and second millennium B.C. strata and Mycenaean ceramic evidence. Erkanal believes that the Baklatepe discovery may lead to further study of the topography of Colophon in the Mycenaean period, since the newly discovered chamber tomb may be another "elite" burial belonging to Late Bronze Age Colophon. Erkanal suggests that the Bronze Age citadel at Colophon may have been located on a nearby hill not identical with the acropolis investigated by Goldman in 1922. Other tholoi of a format resembling that of Colophon Tomb 9 have come to light at Panaztepe near Menemen north of Izmir.[64]

Although no excavations were carried out in Colophon in 1923, Goldman remained in Greece. She arrived in August 1923 and conducted supplementary excavations at Halae, continued to study the previously excavated Halae material, and prepared materials for publication. In June 1924 she assisted with the excavations of the American School at Phlius and began to make plans to excavate at the site of Eutresis in Boeotia for the fall campaign of 1924.[65]

Eutresis

After the upheavals in Ionia forced Goldman to move her activities back to mainland Greece, she began a new excavation in the fall of 1924. The joint funding from the Fogg Museum and the American School that she had procured for Colophon was transferred to the new site. The site selected was Eutresis in Boeotia, the mound some seven miles southwest of Thebes that had first caught her interest in 1911 during a trip with the American School. In 1911 the school would not allow her to excavate at the site. Yet just over ten years later her position in the archaeological world had changed, and she was granted sole leadership of the project. The excavation at Eutresis was to usher in a new phase of Goldman's archaeological career: her interest in prehistory and trade connections in the prehistoric Aegean.

Goldman chose Eutresis because the mound "seemed . . . an excellent site to examine with a view of determining the cultural relations of a small Boeotian town in prehistoric times."[66] At the symposium held after Goldman's death, John L. Caskey recalled that the field of Aegean prehistory had, in 1924, been little studied outside of the Argolid in the Peloponnese. "The picture in Central Greece," he wrote, "was still very dim. Miss Goldman, with her flair for seeing the right thing at the right time, chose well" in her selection of Eutresis.[67]

The excavation team for the five-week fall campaign of 1924 consisted of Goldman, Dorothy Burr (later Thompson) of Bryn Mawr College, and Hazel D. Hansen, Fellow of the Archaeological Institute of America and student at the American School.[68] Both women assisted Goldman with excavation and pottery analysis. Piet de Jong served as architect for the project. Goldman and Burr spent the winter months in Thebes working on the finds from the fall work. A longer, three-month campaign was held from the end of April until July 1925. Burr accompanied Goldman during this season, and Dorothy H. Cox, an associate member of the school, assisted during the latter part of the spring excavation. "Dorothy [Burr] found Goldman a strict disciplinarian and a most exacting and careful director. This archaeological experience was, she recognized, excellent training, and she deeply respected her teacher."[69] Yet Goldman's businesslike approach to archaeology never prevented the team from enjoying the pleasures of the Greek countryside, including the weddings and dances held in the village of Parapoungia where they lived among Albanian peasants.[70]

The main site was a mound located directly above and east of the spring of Arkopodi. The work of the first two seasons concentrated on the prehistoric levels that were readily accessible near the surface below limited strata of the historic period. Byzantine settlement at the site had greatly disturbed the underlying Late Archaic, Classical, and Early Hellenistic remains of fifth- and fourth-century B.C. date. Nevertheless, the excavation team unearthed the remains of a small shrine to a goddess and an inscription that confirmed the name of the site as Eutresis. A historic-period cemetery was found on a hill northwest of Eutresis on the road to Thespiae closer to the main historic town that lay to the north of the prehistoric mound. Near this cemetery, "which, for lack of promise, was not pursued," Goldman found the remains of a Roman villa.[71] Built into the walls of the villa were five inscriptions, one of the early fifth century and the others of the fourth century B.C. All had originally been used as gravestones and no doubt were mined from the nearby cemetery. Among the excavated material from the villa's courtyard Goldman found "the torso of an excellent marble statue of a youth and the lower part of a seated female figure, both of late Archaic style."[72] Both must have been "antiques appreciated by the owners" of the villa.[73]

The remains of a Mycenaean settlement of the Late Bronze Age lay directly under the shallow and badly disturbed deposits of the historic period, but they had suffered severe destruction from later building activity at the site. The first undisturbed layers at the site revealed Middle Helladic (MH) material. Most important of the early work in these levels at Eutresis was "the discovery, usually at a depth of slightly over two meters, of an excellent series of Middle Helladic houses, which establish the rectangular house with small antechamber and long main room and hearth sometimes central, but more often in or near a corner, as the prevailing type."[74]

At least seven of the excavated houses had plans that could be reconstructed; one had an apsidal end that was modified in a later stage to be straight. Some of the houses had forecourts of either paved or beaten earth construction, and most contained large pithoi, presumably for the storage of water. The excavations also revealed evidence for the wooden roof supports of the houses as well as storerooms or shops that contained bins and jars filled with the remains of charred wheat.[75] A series of MH flexed burials located within the settlement was also excavated.

The Early Helladic (EH) settlement at Eutresis appeared to be larger than that of the Middle Helladic. Goldman noticed that the walls of the EH settlement were thicker and more carefully constructed and that the houses were bigger. In addition, bronze and marble objects, which had been noticeably absent from the MH levels, appeared more frequently in the EH settlement. Goldman believed these factors pointed to "greater prosperity and contacts with the outside world" during this earlier phase of habitation at the site. Two of the houses from the EH settlement at Eutresis were similar to those found by Carl Blegen at Zygouries. Several test pits were dug to sterile soil levels, and the lowest EH strata revealed pottery showing affinities to Late Neolithic wares.

Based on the successful results of the first two seasons of work, Goldman hoped to dedicate another campaign solely to the remains of the EH period at Eutresis. She had been unable to excavate as deeply into the EH levels as she wanted because the EH strata were buried beneath up to six layers of MH occupation. Yet despite the difficulties of digging through the MH levels, Goldman was convinced that "the stratification [of the EH period] is undisturbed and ought to yield important results."[76]

Goldman returned to Eutresis from mid-May to mid-July 1926 and again in April, May, and June 1927. Dorothy Burr, Dorothy Cox, and Barbara P. McCarthy of Brown University assisted her in the excavation and ceramic study of 1926. Miss Lacey von Wagenen joined the team as photographer. Working alone with Goldman in 1927, Cox served both as architect and as a trench supervisor. As she had planned, Goldman focused the excavation on the EH strata, although some attention was paid to the northern slope of the mound, where the Classical period shrine was located. Digging in the fill for a terrace wall yielded pottery and numerous terra-cottas, particularly figurines of women with pigs and various hydrophoroi often associated with Demeter sanctuaries. Other areas revealed Boeotian figurines of types similar to those found at Halae. Excavations in the EH levels yielded houses of three successive periods as well as pottery that contributed further to the chronology of the site.[77]

Eutresis contributed solid stratified data for the study of domestic architecture, pottery, and trade of the Early and Middle Helladic periods in Boeotia. Goldman and her staff members carefully studied the material in the context of what had been excavated and published in the late 1920s for Thessaly, Korakou, Zygouries, and the Cyclades. Goldman's volume *Excavations at Eutresis in Boeotia* was a well-organized account of the result of the four seasons of excavation in clear, comfortable prose. Published by Harvard University Press, the volume was fully illustrated with photographs, drawings, and plans, as well as color plates by Piet de Jong and Dorothy H. Cox. The introductory statement by George H. Chase, then curator of Classical Antiquities at the Fogg Museum, mentioned both the anonymous gift to the museum for research in Greece and Goldman's appointment in 1920 as Fellow of the Fogg Museum for research in Greek lands. "All the essential information was thus made available quickly, and [the excavation report] has formed a basic building block in all subsequent studies of the Bronze Age in Greece."[78]

Yet Goldman regretted her inability to investigate the mound more fully, especially its earliest deposits. "We were wrong," she once told John Caskey, "too timid about destroying anything."[79] In 1958 John L. Caskey and Elizabeth Caskey, the successful excavators of Lerna from 1952 to 1958, persuaded Goldman to revisit Eutresis for a day and to explain what she considered inadequate information about the earlier levels at the site.

> It was agreed that a further test of the most ancient strata was worth undertaking, and a suitable region was noted for another deep sounding, considerably larger than any of the pits that had been excavated in 1927. Miss Goldman asked us to make this supplementary excavation, a proposal which we eagerly accepted. She generously provided the necessary funds.[80]

A brief campaign followed in September 1958. Some of the workmen employed by the Caskeys were the sons of Goldman's original Eutresis workmen. The Caskeys reached Neolithic levels, and the succession of architectural as well as ceramic features of the following Early Helladic I and II levels was clearly reanalyzed, as was the uneventful beginning of Early Helladic III. The 1958 postscript to the Eutresis excavations was fully published as an addendum at Goldman's request.[81]

Yugoslavia

Following the excavation at Eutresis, Hetty Goldman did not settle into a regular academic teaching appointment. In 1928, while she was involved with the study and publication of the Eutresis material, she was a visiting lecturer in archaeology at the Johns Hopkins University. She also continued to be involved with the Women's Building Fund at the American School of Classical Studies.

The land for the women's dormitory had been purchased jointly with the British School, and eight women's colleges had made contributions for the erection of the facility. From 1916 to 1926, however, plans had been produced and rejected. The original plan called only for rooms for eight female students, a number that "was thought . . . would take care of all the women students who were likely to present themselves for a good many years to come."[82] Yet the addition of the Gennadius Library and increased enrollment in the American School's programs "and especially the increase in the proportion of women students" led to the creation of a committee of women organized by President Thomas of Bryn Mawr. This committee "had a larger conception of the opportunity which the School offers to women" and wanted the dormitory to be able to house up to twenty female students.[83] A larger structure would not fit on the land available, and so the American School acquired the British School's half of the property in order to move forward with building plans. The final arrangement for the Women's Building Fund was that a larger facility would be constructed for use by all students.[84]

In the meantime, Goldman's interest in prehistory and trade took her to Yugoslavia in 1932.[85] Vladimir Fewkes and Robert W. Ehrich, both interested in the prehistory of Europe, had conducted soundings in Czechoslovakia (1929–31) and Yugoslavia (1931). Their work was sponsored by the Peabody Museum, at Harvard University, the American School of Prehistoric Research and the University Museum in Philadelphia. When the latter institution pulled out in 1932 because of financial strains brought about by the Depression, the Fogg Museum of Harvard University accepted part of the burden for excavation. Paul Sachs, Goldman's cousin and director of the museum, alerted her to the possibility of prehistoric research comparable to her work at Eutresis.

Goldman became involved in this project after archaeological testing at Starčevo by Vladimir Fewkes and Miodrag Grbić, official liasion to the National Museum in Belgrade, revealed Neolithic painted pottery "not only analogous to that purportedly found in the deepest levels of Vinca [one of the few well-stratified sites in this area], but also showing some striking similarities to the Dhimini wares of Thessaly."[86] She joined Fewkes, director of the project, Grbić, Robert W. Ehrich, and Branimir Bugarčić on a survey through Yugoslavia. The survey season began on May 6, 1932, and lasted until June 19. The group of five traveled via Model A Ford, recording evidence of cultural remains as well as geographic, topographic, economic, and other information about 144 sites ranging in date from Neolithic to modern times.[87] Ehrich recalled,

> It was a rough trip, but Miss Goldman took it in good part and was a valued, respected, functioning member of the party, particularly after an early down-to-earth session in which she strongly objected to being inadequately consulted and generally not given sufficient consideration. She rapidly and affectionately became "Aunt Hetty" and remained so to us for the rest of her life.[88]

Goldman and the other team members traveled nearly 4000 miles by car during their reconnaissance of the Yugoslavian countryside.[89] The trip was temporarily suspended while Vladimir Fewkes led a tour for the American School of Prehistoric Research. During the four-week hiatus from the survey, Goldman visited Paris. When she returned to Yugoslavia, full-scale excavation began at Starčevo, a site on the northern side of the Danube not far from Belgrade where the group believed there were prehistoric fortifications. The excavation season ran from July 15 to September 20.[90] Goldman supervised the excavation of one of the areas under investigation, helping the students in the trench to understand and map the stratigraphic sequences. Robert Ehrich recalled that when the students reached the bottom of the trench, they found "bars of decomposing wood which overlay a fairly recent cow bell. In the history of the site this became known as 'the Goldman trench.' "[91]

Goldman stayed on at Starčevo, assisting with the excavation, answering questions where possible, and traveling to various museums in Yugoslavia, Romania, and Bulgaria to look at comparative prehistoric material. The site proved to be of Neolithic date and may have been founded as early as the first half of the third millennium B.C. Its rich ceramic deposits helped the excavators establish ties with neighboring sites and suggest possible trade patterns.[92] Goldman continued to work at Starčevo until called home by news that her mother was ill, and she did not return for the 1933 season. She published two articles on the work in Yugoslavia in conjunction with Fewkes and Ehrich, who remembered,

> Although she always said that her signature on our two reports was only window dressing, this is considerably less than the truth. She did participate in the basic work, she did read the drafts of the articles, and she did make very valuable comments, most specifically with regard to the sites with classical materials and with regard to routes of cultural contact and transmission.[93]

Goldman was so impressed with the work she observed at Stobi, one of the many sites the survey team visited while in Yugoslavia, that she volunteered to publish an article reviewing the excavations. The article's subject matter took Goldman far afield from her new interest in prehistoric archaeology. "It is my enthusiasm rather than my competence," she wrote, "which has lead [sic] me to write about a site whose chief glory is its Byzantine architecture and the light it throws upon the period of transition from Roman to Byzantine."[94] The article, although brief, presented the information on Stobi's finds to an English-speaking audience. She described the bishop's church at Stobi and its elaborate decoration, but she reserved much of her enthusiasm for the secular architecture from the site. The decorative schemes of the palatial residences uncovered by the excavators rivaled that of the church and revealed, on the part of their ancient owners, a fondness for earlier Macedonian and Roman sculpture.

It was also after the completion of the excavations at Eutresis that Goldman became involved with the excavations of the Athenian Agora. She spent three seasons from 1932 to 1934 as a member of the Agora staff. Returning to her classical roots, she oversaw the analysis of the Greek and Roman pottery.

Tarsus

The next excavation project would take Goldman to Cilicia on the southeast coast of Anatolia, close to Cyprus and northern Syria. The impetus to return to Turkey was the new discovery of Mycenaean pottery in Cilician coastal sites and renewed historical discussions of Hittite references to Mycenaean Greeks (Achaeans) as Ahhiyawa. This identification was first advocated by Emil Forrer in his 1924 article and debated as the "Ahhiyawa question" by Aegean and Hittite scholars alike.[95]

Goldman and Mary Hamilton Swindler of Bryn Mawr's Department of Archaeology discussed these new scholarly questions in the context of Bryn Mawr's plan to give its archaeology students experience in excavation. Funds were raised in 1933, and a survey expedition to Cilicia was organized jointly with the Fogg Museum of Harvard and the Archaeological Institute of America. Early in April 1934 the group gathered in Istanbul. The team consisted of Goldman as field director; Ann Hoskin, who had recently been in Athens working on the techniques of Greek sculpture as the Workman Fellow of Bryn Mawr College; and Robert Ehrich, Goldman's colleague from the Yugoslavian expedition. Emil Forrer, who was surveying archaeological sites along the coast of Syria, joined the group later at the site.

Goldman recalled how the group departed Istanbul, full of questions about what they would find in Cilicia:

> Our objective was Adana, the somewhat shabby queen of the Cilician plain, lying in the angle formed by Syria and the southeast corner of Asia Minor . . . There is Cilicia as a possible starting point for the culture which spread westward over the Aegean and more immediately to Cyprus; Cilicia as one of the roads by which the Hittites of

> the Asia Minor high plateau passed over into Syria. How far in conquering Cilicia had the Hittites left the imprint of their own civilization upon the land? Would it prove in its essential features to be a part of Cappadocia or was it more nearly allied to northern Syria? Would there be connections with the Troad? How much of Mycenaean civilization had taken root in a land linked to the Achaeans by Hittite texts, whose inhabitants Herodotus tells us were known, long before his day, as Hypachaeans?
>
> It is easy to pose questions. It takes many years of patient investigation to answer them even partially. No one understands this better than Hâmit Zübeyr Koşay [the director-general of antiquities of Turkey]. Together we worked out a program for this, our preliminary visit to Cilicia, which was to include reconnoitering the sites which stand up conspicuously as hillocks in the otherwise flat Cilician plain, test digs or soundings at promising mounds, and finally on the basis of these soundings the selection of a site or sites as the field of our future operations.[96]

The group spent the first adventurous weeks of the survey in an automobile with Halil Kamil Bey, director of the Adana Museum. Goldman described their journey:

> At every promising site we stopped our car, climbed the mound and like gleaners in a field gathered up the sherds which lay about on the surface. These with observation in height, preservation and other superficial evidence helped us to estimate the importance of the site. When we had to cross rivers it was usually by the most primitive type of ferry, little more than a raft, which we shared with the water buffaloes and flocks of sheep. Once on a rainy day the swift current of the Pyramus (Ceyhan) started the ferry on its way while the hind wheels of the car were still firmly embedded in the mud of the embankment and amid the alarmed shrieks of our fellow passengers we leaped to safety on the shore.[97]

The first site the surveyors visited was Zeytin, but although they found the mound to be rich with painted pottery from the Bronze Age, the site had been extensively disturbed by ancient storage pits and modern war trenches. By May, the group had moved on to Kabarsa, a site nine kilometers from Tarsus. At Kabarsa, testing revealed an archaic cylinder seal, engraved bone, bronze and stone artifacts, pottery, and foundation walls for houses. Goldman led her group on to Domuztepe on the eastern bank of the Pyramus River, where "no village offered attractive lodging so we camped out in tents and did nightly battle with scorpions and giant spiders. Here we came for the first time upon pottery which could unmistakably be identified as Hittite."[98]

The Greek-Hittite connection having been the goal of the survey, Goldman found it tempting to stop the group before the full summer heat began. Nevertheless, the group pressed on to Tarsus (Gözlü Kule), where the ancient capital of Cilicia had been located. In Tarsus, the survey team found lodging in an old Franciscan monastery.

> Our host [was] the sole remaining monk with the auspicious name of Paul[;] we spent three weeks of July in driving a deep pit into the summit of the mound and a mighty gash into its side. Again we found traces of the Hittites, some pieces of Mycenaean pottery, and at a depth of some fourteen meters pottery which recalls that of Cyprus in the Early Bronze Age. Heavy walls had appeared in one trench and pithoi numerous and large enough to belong to some palace-storehouse.[99]

The success of the trial trenches left the survey team eager to return to Tarsus the following year for full excavation.

Goldman was named director of excavations at Tarsus on behalf of a joint venture among several institutions. Bryn Mawr College pledged a three-year annual contribution of twenty-five hundred dollars toward the project, while the Archaeological Institute of America and Harvard's Fogg Museum each contributed five thousand dollars annually for three years.[100] According to this agreement, "Dr. Goldman is not to be paid any salary, but her expenses to and from America and for the duration of the excavation season shall be paid out of the funds contributed toward the joint enterprise." In return, Goldman agreed "to give preferential consideration to Bryn Mawr Students recommended by the Bryn Mawr Faculty of Archaeology," with the understanding that the final choice would reside with the director.

Goldman departed for Turkey at the beginning of February 1935. Her excavation team consisted of Dorothy H. Cox (who continued as architect as at Eutresis), Virginia Grace, Ann Hoskin, and Robert Ehrich. Ann Hoskin (later Ehrich) complemented her work of excavation and recording with photography; Robert Ehrich combined fieldwork with the duties of anthropologist and foreman as well as accountant and assistant field director. The two were to marry in 1937 and, with Goldman, formed the core staff of the Tarsus team.[101]

The work at the mound of Tarsus developed into the kind of project Goldman foresaw in the preliminary statement. She had not planned initially to make a sounding at Tarsus since the mound had been developed as a public park and planted with trees. Nevertheless, the sensible invitation from the citizens of Tarsus to dig there anyway was accepted and the site's historical perspective confirmed by the 1935 campaign. The excavations exposed sections of a Hittite building on the highest part of the mound, a sample of Hittite Empire pottery, and bullae with impressions of Hittite hieroglyphic stamp seals. The principal bulla was marked with the seal of Išputaḫšu, previously known from the Boğazköy archives as king of Kizzuwatna. The discovery of the bulla with seal promptly linked Tarsus with the archives of the Hittite capital.[102] This bulla is bilingual, with the name of Išputaḫšu on the outer rim in Akkadian cuneiform. Hittitologists began to comment on Tarsus-Tarša and Adana-Adaniya in Cilician and Kizzuwatnan contexts.[103] I. J. Gelb and A. Goetze accompanied Goldman's annual reports with articles on the emerging cuneiform and hieroglyphic inscriptions from Tarsus; in Ankara, H. G. Güterbock and B. Landsberger provided advice after examination of further originals that emerged in 1936.

Other Hittite material from the first campaign included a miniature statuette of rock crystal labeled by Goldman "certainly from the point of view of art our most important find."[104] This is indeed a fine piece of Hittite art, originally provided with a precious metal crown. It is comparable in style to rare instances of Hittite sculpture in the round such as a statue found in Alaca Höyük in 1964.

For the 1936 campaign at Tarsus, Dorothy H. Cox continued as architect. New staff members were Margaret S. Woods (later Keith), Sara Anderson (later Immerwahr), and Maynard Riggs from Bryn Mawr; J. Franklin Daniel from Cyprus; and Florence Day from Beyrouth. The Hittite potential of the site became even clearer through the discovery of a Hittite land deed and additional finds of Hittite hieroglyphic bullae, most notably that of Queen Puduhepa, the wife of Hattusili III.[105] Hittite pottery began to clarify itself in stratigraphic order. Mycenaean sherds of Late Helladic IIIC1 type were amply represented in the area of Section B and were analyzed by J. F. Daniel and Goldman in historical context.[106]

Goldman returned from the excavations of 1936 at the beginning of August and then planned a holiday in California with her father. She reported that the campaign "was most satisfactory, yielding an immense amount of material in the way of pottery, bronzes, seals, terracottas and other small objects, as well as buildings, one of which was preserved to a height of more than thirteen feet."[107] As to the significance of the excavation, Goldman recalled a meeting with the late Professor Breasted:

> Our meeting took place on the platform of a train in the Grand Central Station and although it was very brief, it was long enough for an interesting exchange of ideas. He told me then that he hoped sometime to excavate a site at which the Hittite civilization met the Greek and that if he did so, he would like to call upon me to head the undertaking. His intention, which remained unfulfilled, has now actually been fulfilled by our work at Tarsus. For we found this year a sealed deposit in which there were both Hittite royal seals, a Hittite royal deed and Mycenaean pottery, much of which was imported from the Greek mainland. This is what archaeologists have been eagerly expecting of Tarsus and I think on the whole that it represents the most significant contribution of the 1936 campaign.[108]

In 1936, shortly after her brief report to Abraham Flexner at the Institute for Advanced Study (IAS) in Princeton, New Jersey, Goldman was offered a position as the institute's first woman professor. In accepting the position, she wrote:

> I am sure you realized that your offer of a position at the Institute came to me as such a complete surprise that I felt literally "stricken" and was incapable of any reaction at the moment. Such hesitation as I felt was due solely to doubts of my own capacity, but I have decided to put the most flattering interpretation upon it and to believe that no person of integrity and imagination faces a great opportunity without self-questioning.[109]

In making her final decision, Goldman spoke with former colleague Benjamin Meritt, who was instrumental in persuading her that there was "before [her] the possibility of undisturbed work under conditions which certainly could not be equalled anywhere in America."[110] Goldman graciously accepted the position at the institute and suggested that she could teach a course in Mediterranean and Near Eastern prehistory as her workload permitted.[111] For her appointment as professor in the School of Humanistic Studies of the Institute for Advanced Study, Goldman received an honorarium of two hundred dollars per month,[112] with the understanding that she was to spend half of her time at the institute and half in the field.[113]

During this period of great changes in her career, Goldman had given some thought to resigning her directorship of the Tarsus excavation but in November 1936 wrote to her cousin Paul Sachs of the Fogg Museum that she was withdrawing her tender of resignation from the project. She had become dissatisfied with the lack of interest in the project on the part of its sponsors and complaints about a proposed increase in the budget, which she felt was necessary. As justification for the increase in the budget, Goldman cited the results of the Tarsus project. These included the stratigraphic level with both Late Helladic pottery and Hittite royal seals and land deed, and she noted that only two other land deeds were known from archaeological work at the time and that both were from the Hittite capital of Boğazköy. She also called attention to the other finds, including "a rich deposit of bronze daggers and utensils of about 1400 B.C.," a first millennium B.C. house with walls preserved to a record height, pottery, and fine terra-cottas from the Early Roman period. She was also frustrated by the devaluation of the dollar between the time when the original funding agreement was made and the beginning of the fieldwork. In addition, she noted that, as director, she "not only served without salary, but paid [her] own travelling expenses and met for two years a not inconsiderable annual deficit." Goldman also argued that the original agreement made no provisions for the payment of a professional photographer, draftsperson, colorist, or clerical help for the excavation. She pointed to the timely manner in which the material was being prepared for publication despite all the drawbacks she faced. The conclusion of her discussion cited the opinions of several learned archaeologists, including Claude Schaeffer, the director of Ras Shamra excavations in Syria, who felt the Tarsus excavations were much needed and should be continued.[114]

In early May 1937 Goldman wrote a preliminary report of the 1937 campaign at Tarsus for Abraham Flexner of the IAS. Her spirits appeared to have lifted, and she wrote to Flexner that she had "just the kind of staff I like, small but experienced and the site itself still full of surprises."[115] The excavation season had begun on March 23 and was to run until July 8. The staff of 1937 included Dorothy Cox, who served as a trench supervisor and draftsperson; Ann Hoskin Ehrich, who worked in the field and served as photographer; Robert Ehrich, assistant field director, who had taken over the accounts and labor management; Maynard Riggs, secretary of the dig, who also helped with developing film, conservation, and inventory; and Edgar Lindstrom, formerly of the Peabody Museum of Harvard, as conservator.[116]

Excavations resumed, and almost immediately more Hittite bullae began to appear. A particularly noteworthy example, large in size and decorated with cylinder seal impressions, remains unparalleled in quality and iconography.[117] Middle Bronze Age levels began to emerge, and soundings along the south edge of the mound revealed several Late Chalcolithic jar burials. Pottery ovens along the southern slope of Section A had been used in the Iron Age. Roman and Islamic levels were also dug and analyzed. At the end of the 1937 report, Goldman explained the series of events and contacts exposed archaeologically at Tarsus as "years of prosperity attributed to the first extension of Hittite power over Cilicia." She also commented: "I think it probable that, in the heyday of their power, it was the strong arm of the Hittites which kept both Mycenaeans and Cypriote merchants from settling in the Cilician plain."[118] This conclusion remained valid. The "Ahhiyawa question" took a different direction after the discovery that Mycenaean pottery at Tarsus was largely of the Late Helladic IIIC1 period.

Yet despite the archaeological importance of the site, funding difficulties continued to plague Goldman and the Tarsus team. The original budgeted amount of $12,500 fell short of the $16,000 actually spent on the 1937 excavations. In a letter from Abraham Flexner to Paul Sachs in April 1937, the Institute for Advanced Study agreed to contribute $20,000 to the project over a period of four years, with Bryn Mawr to contribute $7,500 over the same period. Flexner inquired of Sachs whether the Fogg "will commit itself now to supplying this fund over a four-year period or will, as the Institute proposes to do, make its contribution in full now. We will thus have in hand the money which will see [Goldman's] task through and permanently remove from her mind all uncertainty and anxiety such as have hitherto increased the burden she has borne."[119] Unfortunately, the Fogg was unable to continue its support of the Tarsus project.

The excavations of 1938 were conducted around the emerging conflict in Europe. The season began on March 9 and ran through July 4. The original plan had been to return home following the end of the campaign to avoid what Goldman described as "the next universal explosion."[120] She changed her mind, however, writing that "we were naturally somewhat anxious after the seizure of Austria by Germany, but the world having apparently taken that act calmly we have decided to follow a good example and do likewise."[121] The decision was made to extend the excavations at Tarsus into the fall and winter seasons. Goldman wrote,

> In many ways I regret the long absence, primarily on account of my Father, but also because I was beginning to enjoy the feeling of belonging to the Institute community. However, the excavation is my first love and fundamentally I fear I am a wandering spirit.[122]

With the threat of war again looming, as during excavations at Halae and Colophon, a second campaign was conducted from September 15, 1938, to the beginning of January 1939. In November, Goldman had to return to the United States because of her father's terminal illness, but the excavation ran smoothly under the direction of the Ehrichs. They conducted major excavations in both Sections A and B of the mound. Maynard Riggs continued to act as secretary for the project. Frances F. Jones, a 1934 graduate of Bryn Mawr, had been hired as Goldman's assistant in August and remained in Tarsus to assist with the pottery analysis. Piet de Jong, a colleague of Goldman's from Halae and Eutresis, arrived in the fall and "performed the arduous task of drawing trenches, profiles, all of the seals and bullae and making watercolors of selected pieces of pottery." Effie (Mrs. Piet) de Jong was in charge of the bronze cleaning.

Despite the tensions caused by the outbreak of war, Frances Jones recalled that life in the Tarsus excavation house ran smoothly and efficiently. Goldman rented the two-story house that served as the headquarters for the dig. The work areas were located on the ground floor. The pottery room was filled with pottery laid out chronologically "for the benefit of interested visitors," including the Turkish officials from the Department of Antiquities. There were separate areas for pottery mending, cooking, and laundry. Members of the team slept in the upper story. Frances Jones recalled that the Ehrichs had a room on one end of the building, while Frances and her roommate slept on the opposite end. Goldman's room occupied the middle of the house, and there were spare rooms for visiting scholars as well.[123]

While Goldman was at Tarsus in 1938, Frances Jones remembered that she would supervise both students and scholars in the field, watching their work, offering suggestions on excavation, and asking questions about objects that had been unearthed. Ann and Robert Ehrich served primarily as the field directors, and Goldman would lay out the plan for the day with them each morning. The team rose early to avoid working in the afternoon heat, and once a week the group would travel to the local Turkish baths for a real scrubdown. In addition to excursions to the baths, Goldman would allow the students and scholars time off from excavation and study, something that Frances Jones termed "pleasant interruptions which kept things from getting too organized." Often Goldman would appoint one of the Turkish potmenders to chaperone the young women who worked at the excavation as they walked around the modern city of Tarsus.[124]

During the spring campaign, much progress was made with the stratigraphic analysis of the Middle and Early Bronze Age levels of the mound in Section A. Architecturally, the Early Bronze Age (EBA) levels revealed a regularly laid-out street with well-appointed houses on either side and repeated attempts at fortification in EBA II. After a destructive conflagration at the end of the EBA II, ceramic innovations showed affinities to the Troy II period: with Tarsus originality in two-handled goblet shapes of the early stage; later adoption of the West Anatolian depas; and interaction with the North Syrian and Amuq goblet tradition continuing beyond the Troy II period. This ceramic evidence opened the way for chronological linkage from Tarsus to the northwest corner of Anatolia, while in the deeper EBA levels was evidence of contacts with Cyprus and central Anatolia. Additional exploration of the large building (temple?) in Section A, with its additional harvest of bullae and seals, further confirmed the Hittite aspect of Tarsus. One of the bullae found in this area was impressed by a seal ring carrying a name written in both hieroglyphic and cuneiform.[125] The results of the excavation impressed Goldman and excited the local media. While excavating in strata dated to the third millennium B.C., the team discovered "some gold earrings [that] were turned into four large gold cups by the local press and have caused consequently great excitement and almost continuous knocking at our front door to view the treasure!!!"[126]

Yet despite the promising results in the field and her enthusiasm on site, Goldman continued to be frustrated by the funding of the Tarsus project. In a letter to Flexner in early May 1938, she was upset by the recent release of the *Bulletin of the Institute* (no. 7) with no mention of the institute's association (via an anonymous donor, her father, Julius Goldman) with the Tarsus excavations. She wrote,

> When my Father decided no longer to make his gift through Harvard University, I urged him to come forward and make it personally. As all such enterprises must be supported by individuals of means, I saw no reason why he should not be known as part-supporter of my work. He has, however, always shunned publicity and so, without in any way consulting me first, he made his offer to the Institute which you accepted. This satisfied and pleased me; as it seemed appropriate

> that the Institute at which I am professor should be connected with what is and will remain for a number of years my chief interest and occupation. It is true that my father stipulated that his name should not be mentioned, but I feel quite sure that he made no stipulation that the connection of the Institute with Tarsus should remain equally anonymous. Indeed, the announcement of such a connection is the only satisfaction he could have had and it should not have been withheld in fairness both to him and to myself. I had thought that I was done with answering the oft-repeated and tiresome question, "Why is the Institute connected with Antioch and not with Tarsus?"[127]

Further difficulties arose in November 1938 when President Park of Bryn Mawr College wrote to Goldman that the college would no longer be able to support the excavation despite its 1937 promise.[128] Goldman's disappointment was clear in a letter to Flexner in early December 1938 in which she describes herself as "almost shock-proof in these [financial] matters."[129] The disintegrating political situation cut short the double season of digging before the entire mass of EBA ceramic evidence could be studied. As at Colophon, the artifacts were placed in a storehouse, the excavators unsure of the objects' fate. Frances Jones remembered that she had to carry all of the Tarsus data back to the United States since Goldman had already gone to be with her dying father.[130]

After her father died at the end of 1938, Goldman settled into her life at Princeton at the Institute for Advanced Study. She became a friend of Albert Einstein's daughter Margo, and she helped to bring other archaeologists to the institute.[131] In its early days the institute had no buildings and thus rented various houses and other buildings scattered around Princeton. Goldman, Frances Jones, and the Tarsus materials were housed in one such accommodation. The two worked on the publication of the Hellenistic and Roman materials from the earlier seasons of digging at Tarsus; this was to form the core of the first volume of *Excavations at Gözlü Kule, Tarsus.* Both Dorothy Cox and Virginia Grace, long-time colleagues of Goldman's from previous excavations, contributed to this volume.

The prolonged nature of World War II drastically changed the routine at the institute. Frances Jones continued to assist Goldman as she was able but was appointed to the art museum at Princeton University. Goldman continued to work on the Tarsus material as well as preparing her final publication of the excavations at Halae. Much of her time, however, was spent working on war relief issues.[132] Although she was no longer able to serve as a traveling nurse as she had in earlier crises, Goldman continued to offer support generously and without ostentation.

Early on during the war, Goldman and other American School alumni (like T. Leslie Shear, Oscar Broneer, Louis E. Lord, and Benjamin D. Meritt) living in and around Princeton formed the American School Committee for Aid to Greece to assist with war relief. The group guaranteed funds for the purchase of an ambulance for the Greek Red Cross and raised approximately $3,000 for efforts along the Albanian front. The committee continued to raise funds through written appeals to private individuals as well as to the American School of Classical Studies at Athens, the Archaeological Institute of America, the American Philological Association, and the American Philosophical Society. Additional moneys were raised through benefit concerts and royalties from the photographic essay "This is Greece" by Lucy Talcott, Alison Frantz, and the staff of the Athenian Agora. By the end of January 1942, the group had raised over $21,500 for hospital and medical supplies, woolen clothes, and food for four canteens that had been established on the front by the Princeton-based committee and the American School. The group disbanded shortly after the war's end, and the balance of the funds raised was transferred to the treasurer of the American School to use for relief purposes as needed.[133]

In 1943 Goldman became a member of the Committee on Education for the Community War Services Committee of Princeton.[134] Before and during World War II, she generously supported and sponsored academic refugees from the Nazi regime who continued their archaeological careers in the United States. One such friend and colleague was Margarete Bieber, a classical archaeologist whose appointment to Barnard College Goldman ardently supported.[135] Goldman's outreach to war-torn peoples greatly influenced her colleagues. Many of her junior colleagues offered work to the Red Cross or strategic services, as many archaeologists did to help Greece and the Allies.

The war had also given Goldman a chance to catch up on the paperwork that assails an active field archaeologist.[136] She completed the first volume of the Tarsus material and the final report on Halae. She also published several articles on Tarsus, including one on some painted ceramics for the *Bulletin of the American Schools of Oriental Research;* two on the Sandon Monument for the *Journal of the American Oriental Society;* and one on two terra-cotta figurines for the *American Journal of Archaeology.* George Hanfmann called particular attention to her two papers about the "Cilician god, Sandon, based on a close and careful interpretation of Hellenistic terracotta plaques and coins of Tarsus of the mid-second century B.C. which, as Goldman rightly argued, perpetuated an Anatolian, indeed, a Hittite art type."[137] The study of the Sandon monument gave Goldman the opportunity to explore the "persistence of religious traditions" at the site of Tarsus.[138] During the war years, she also reworked her Ph.D. dissertation on the terra-cottas from the cemeteries at Halae with Frances Jones. And she published an article on the origin of the Greek herm, which enabled her to return to her classical archaeology roots, using both ancient literary texts and archaeological evidence to explore the "underlying attitude" of ancient religion.[139]

In October 1945 Goldman wrote to Dr. Aydelotte of the School of Humanistic Studies at the institute to request a leave of absence during the academic year 1946–47. This would allow her to return to Tarsus to complete the study of the excavated material that had been interrupted by the outbreak of World War II. Although she and Frances Jones had brought many notes, architectural plans, and photographs with them to Princeton, the prehistoric materials desperately needed to be examined to facilitate writing the final report for the second volume of the Tarsus series. In particular, very little of the EBA pottery had been studied or analyzed. Goldman also hoped that a "limited amount of supplementary excavation aimed at completing such data as study has shown to be inadequate" would also be possible. She stated in her appeal:

> This will not be the fulfillment of the original program which envisaged excavation on a larger scale than has been possible of the earliest levels, but it will give us sufficient data to write an authoritative report on the early archaeological history of Tarsus and, in view of the many years lost through the war, that seems all that I can undertake.
>
> The excavations at Tarsus represent a pioneer study of this region of Anatolia and I feel that it is my professional duty to complete it before I undertake any other work.[140]

The institute granted Goldman's request for leave, and in February 1947 she found herself in Alexandria, Egypt, awaiting the Turkish boat that would take her to Mersin, a port within a half hour of Tarsus.

Goldman had arranged for a new team to meet her at the site for the spring season. In particular, she had organized a group to complete the study of the pottery stored at the end of the 1938 seasons and to continue exploring the early third millennium B.C. fortification walls and houses. In

Ankara, Hâmit Zübeyr Koşay still held the position of director-general of antiquities and happily welcomed Goldman back to Tarsus. New staff for the dig included architect Theresa Goell, who devoted herself to the assignment and Tarsus with energy and enthusiasm; and Aşkidil Akarca, a student of classical archaeology at Istanbul University, who worked as a digging assistant. The official representative for the 1947 season was classical archaeologist Necati Dolunay, who would later become director of the Ankara and Istanbul museums.

At Tarsus, the group investigated the sequence of Early Bronze Age houses with their hearths, benches, and cupboards. They also dug around the fortifications, which appeared to have been erected in some haste in order to protect the core of the settlement as a citadel.[141] Interruptions in the course of the EBA II phase continued to be evident in two conflagrations. The excavation revealed even more aspects of the protohistory of the Cilician region in contact with other Anatolian regions, and there was also evidence of a local tradition in spite of some evidence of hostile assaults.

The 1947 season was Goldman's last at Tarsus. She wrote to Frank Aydelotte at the conclusion of the excavation that, although there were still areas where sterile soil had not been reached, she had decided to stop excavating. "I can still get away with it but I no longer have that margin of energy and enthusiasm which I think should go into this type of work. I am ready for the more contemplative life."[142] Shortly thereafter Goldman was diagnosed with a nonmalignant brain tumor and underwent surgery that prevented her from returning to Tarsus in the fall of 1947. She downplayed the nature of her illness for friends at the institute but admitted that she had also been deceived in the seriousness of the illness by her own "invincible optimism."[143] It was at this time that she resigned from her professorship at the institute and became a professor emerita for the remainder of her life. During her recovery, Goldman occupied herself with the proofs of the Tarsus volume and "the ever increasing literature of my profession."[144]

The final Tarsus campaign was held from May 4 to July 3, 1948. The team, led by Theresa Goell, included: Ahmet Dönmez, representative of the Department of Antiquities; Machteld J. Mellink, recruited at Bryn Mawr; and Arlette Cenani, a student from Istanbul. Goldman returned to Tarsus in September 1948 to study the results of the final digging campaign, which had included probes of the EBA I, Chalcolithic, and Neolithic levels. The study of the pottery, newly excavated as well as resurrected from storage units left in 1938, was completed as basic evidence for the final publication of volume 2 of *Excavations at Gözlü Kule, Tarsus* (or *Tarsus II*). George and Ilse Hanfmann had studied the Iron Age materials intensively at Tarsus during winter and spring 1948.

While in Turkey, Goldman made several trips to study comparative material at sites like Kusura, dug by Winifred Lamb in 1935–36, as well as pottery and other artifacts on display in the Afyon Museum. Other important comparanda from several mounds in the Amuq region, dug by teams from the Oriental Institute at the University of Chicago and published by Robert and Linda Braidwood, were available in the galleries and study rooms of the Antalya Museum. Sir Leonard Woolley welcomed Goldman to the excavations in progress at Alalakh (Tell Atchana) and discussed questions of chronology with her.

After the close of the excavations at the end of the 1948 season, the mound at Tarsus continued its role as a public park. It was planted with a limited selection of trees and offered an open-air café for visitors. The trenches in Sections A and B had been partially filled in for protection before the war; in order to prevent collapse and other damage, the local authorities filled them even more.

The nearby site of Mersin-Yumuktepe, under excavation from 1937 by the British Neilson Expedition under John Garstang, presented the closest comparanda for architecture, ceramics, small artifacts, and general cultural-economic development. Goldman was familiar with the material from Mersin-Yumuktepe because she had collaborated with Garstang on an article about Cilician pottery that appeared in the *American Journal of Archaeology* in 1947. She and Garstang had begun their article with an explanation of how they came to work together:

> One of those happier circumstances which sometimes lighten the gloom of dark events brought the excavators of Tarsus and Mersin together at Princeton during the years of World War II, and so gave opportunity for a fruitful exchange of ideas on the problems of ceramic history and development in Cilicia from the earliest prehistoric times to approximately 1100 B.C.[145]

The contacts made in Turkey continued throughout Goldman's later life. Her junior colleagues at Tarsus had all risen within the archaeological community. By 1947 John F. Daniel had succeeded Mary H. Swindler as editor-in-chief of the *American Journal of Archaeology*. Daniel had supervised a trench and studied Mycenaean and Iron Age Cypriote pottery at Tarsus during the 1936 campaign. Another Tarsian, Dorothy H. Cox, was book review editor for the *American Journal of Archaeology* at this time.

The excavations at Mersin were closed in 1946, and a concise final volume on *Prehistoric Mersin* by John Garstang appeared in 1953, while the final publication of *Tarsus II* was progressing at Princeton. The first volume, covering the Greek and Roman occupation of the site, had appeared in 1950 after the World War II study sessions, with separate volumes for text and plates. *Tarsus II* was to cover the prehistoric and Bronze Age phases of the site. After the last study and digging season, the center of effort was relocated to the Institute for Advanced Study, where the Tarsus records were assembled in a large study room and in Goldman's office. In addition to the drawings, plans, photographs, catalogs, and excavation notebooks, a ceramic collection was available for study. The ceramic samples, donated by the director of antiquities in Turkey, had been selected from the large study collection housed in an annex of the original museum at Adana. They were set up in labeled trays and repeatedly consulted by traveling archaeologists. The restored pottery and the small artifacts of clay, bone, stone, and metal, as well as the by-now famous seals and bullae, were displayed in glass cases of the museum's exhibition halls next to the Mersin material, which was especially strong in Neolithic and Chalcolithic pottery. The museum curator had created stepped platforms to show their correct stratification.

The preparation of *Tarsus II* required a wide range of special studies spanning the Neolithic to the end of the Late Bronze Age. I. J. Gelb wrote the chapter on Hittite (Luwian) hieroglyphic seals and seal impressions, clearly the most important historical evidence of the Hittite period at Tarsus; this material is still being analyzed and interpreted in further detail. Goldman dealt with the non-hieroglyphic seals and seal impressions, pointing out the early use of stamps on clay plugs, weights, and pottery in the EBA II and III periods. For pottery study, Frederick R. Matson provided an appendix on techniques of the potters at Tarsus. Machteld J. Mellink, who had participated in the final pottery study of the pre–World War II stored pottery lots, wrote about the Neolithic and Chalcolithic pottery.[146]

All of these collaborative efforts benefited greatly from Goldman's questions and suggestions. Her assistants and associates have invariably praised her as a generous, precise, and sensible adviser. Frances F. Jones has commented on her joint work with Goldman:

> I do wish to mention what a pleasure and privilege it was to work with Miss Goldman and how much I enjoyed the years of friendship that continued after our Tarsian project. If asked the journalistic

> question of the particular qualities which made her a special person, I would choose her generosity, her integrity, and her resilience, all of them spiced with wit and wisdom. The extent of her material generosity I doubt that anyone, even the family to which she was devoted, really knows. She was generous in her hospitality, in her time, and in her interest in other people. Her insistence that my name be added to hers in the revision of her thesis on the terracotta figurines from Halae and on the chapter on the Greek and Roman lamps from the excavation at Tarsus, although I was doing the work in my capacity as her assistant, was a facet of this quality. She was forthright, but considerate, in dealing with people and meticulous in her scholarship.[147]

The publication of *Tarsus II* in 1956 presented a rich assemblage of new archaeological data in Anatolian and foreign context, with material for further analysis of historical-cultural interrelations and chronological guidelines. In the preface, Goldman explained the nature of the enterprise and thanked the many team members who aided her in bringing the data to light and presenting them in words, drawings, photographs, and plans. At a 1952 symposium on relative chronologies in Old World archaeology, organized by Robert Ehrich in Philadelphia and published in 1954, Goldman discussed the relative chronology of southeastern Anatolia on the basis of the new evidence from Tarsus and Mersin, much of it carefully excavated by Ehrich.[148]

The third and final volume of the Tarsus publication was prepared with the substantial collaboration of George Hanfmann, who had spent the winter and early spring of 1947–48 at Tarsus studying the Iron Age pottery lots from the pre–World War II excavations. The third Tarsus volume became a precious resource to many Iron Age archaeologists, with the architecture, terra-cotta figurines, metals, bone, and stone dealt with by Goldman and the important collection of seals by Edith Porada. The discussions of the pottery culminate in a solid essay on historical development and a summary conclusion. The role of Tarsus in international contact, especially with Cyprus, the Levant, and Assyria, is evident in Hanfmann's study and remains a subject of discussion in all Iron Age studies of the coastal Levant and Cyprus, as well as early trade with the Aegean. Goldman was praised for her contributions later in her career when the Archaeological Institute of America remarked that she "brought archaeological method to the Cilician coast and laid the foundations for South Anatolian archaeology of the

Classical and Preclassical periods with the monumental publication of her excavations at Tarsus-Gözlü Kule."[149]

Legacy

The Tarsus excavations had thus been fully published by 1963, in a format created by Goldman in cooperation with the Princeton University Press. The Institute for Advanced Study had become a lively center of publication and discussion, starting with two archaeologists working in the Near East, Goldman and Ernst Herzfeld, whose work in Iran formed another courageous aspect of pioneering research at the Institute. Over the years many assistants—in both the field and the laboratory—had worked to complete the Tarsus volumes, and Goldman had a respectable number of alumnae in her Anatolian research school. Ann Hoskin Ehrich, one of Goldman's colleagues from Tarsus, recalled:

> I met Hetty Goldman through her niece, and from the very beginning she was to me "Aunt Hetty." . . . Aunt Hetty was a very warm and caring person. She quickly made a loyal and cohesive "family" out of any working group of which I was a part, and I have learned that this was also true in her early days in Greece and later in Yugoslavia. It included the humblest workmen and their families as well as testy government inspectors and everyone in between. If they needed help she did not send it—she delivered it herself—and in return she got response.
>
> Every man knew his job and how she wanted it done and he did it to the best of his ability. She did not coax or bribe, and her word was good wherever given. She related to all she accepted.
>
> In the same way she personalized her relationships to her site. When she walked down the street we excavated in Tarsus, she lived there. She saw the fire on the hearth, the women squatting at the quern. One could almost expect her to nod a greeting to the neighbors![150]

Goldman is remembered as a firm and forthright person but one with a great sense of humor. Frances Jones recalled a dinner at Tarsus when the cook brought out a large bowl of stew with a nice crust on top. "As first lady of the room, [Goldman] picked up the spoon and fork and dove right into the middle; but she immediately met up with resistance. She then turned to the cook with a critical eye and began to prod around, only to discover that the cook, in attempting to make a nice presentation, had inserted an inverted cup in the center of the stew to keep the crust from collapsing. At that, everyone laughed and the dinner was a great success."[151]

While excavating at Tarsus in 1935, Goldman had obtained a collection of 815 coins from a local collector who had acquired them from various dealers in Mersin and Tarsus. By purchasing the collection, she prevented the coins from being further divided up and removed from Turkey. She donated them to the local Adana Museum, setting an example of archaeological responsibility in the recovery of stolen or looted objects. Dorothy H. Cox later published the most important coins from the collection in a monograph of the American Numismatic Society entitled *A Tarsus Coin Collection in the Adana Museum.*[152]

Apart from the personal affection and admiration of the family of scholars who worked with her, Goldman received many honors in the wider world of scholarship. Her professorship at the Institute for Advanced Study from 1936 on was a signal honor for the first woman so appointed. In May 1950, Goldman was elected a fellow of the American Academy of Arts and Sciences. Citations followed at her graduate alma mater Radcliffe, with a medal for distinguished achievement in June 1953, and at her undergraduate alma mater Bryn Mawr College in June 1960. Goldman also served as a trustee for the Archaeological Institute of America and was a member of the Archaeological Society of America, the American Numismatic Society, and the American Association of University Women.

In 1956 Goldman's colleagues presented her with a festschrift, *The Aegean and the Near East,* on the occasion of her seventy-fifth birthday.[153] Many of her fellow excavators and coauthors from Colophon to Tarsus contributed to this volume, as did the Turkish director-general of excavations and antiquities, Dr. Hâmit Zübeyr Koşay. It was also in 1956 that Goldman became chair of the Auxiliary Fund Association of the American School of Classical Studies at Athens, serving in this capacity until 1962. Started in 1917, this fund had raised an average of one thousand to two thousand dollars in donations annually. Under Goldman's leadership, it began to collect donations of up to sixty-three hundred dollars annually.[154]

In December 1966, at the Archaeological Institute of America meeting in Toledo, Ohio, Goldman received the Gold Medal for Distinguished Archaeological Achievement. She was only the second recipient of the institute's highest award, her colleague from the American School, Carl W. Blegen, having been the first. She was lauded at the ceremony as an "excavator, author, mentor of archaeologists . . . [and] a pioneer in many fields and in many lands." She was praised for her contributions to the study of contacts between the Aegean and the eastern Mediterranean and for her "unbiased scholarly curiosity."[155] Although unable to attend the meeting, Goldman sent a written response, read by a fellow scholar:

> I really cannot imagine why I should be rewarded for the pursuit of a profession which has given me so much happiness over so many years. I can honestly say that I have enjoyed not only the field work which brought with it the companionship of younger people whose enthusiasm, devotion and fresh point of view so largely contributed to the success of our work, but also the long hours of study of excavated material. This is often referred to as inevitable drudgery, but to me it was like working my way through a dark tunnel with a light glimmering at the end, and gradually finding my way, by organization and comparative study, into the full light of a final arrangement that seemed to me valid. Was I assailed by doubts? Of course, at times; but today I lay aside all thoughts of self-criticism and accept with gladness and I hope some humility this great gift of your medal. I take it joyfully as a symbol of your affection and esteem which I heartily reciprocate, and I shall place it among my treasures.[156]

Goldman continued to participate in discussions and meetings at the Institute for Advanced Study and nearby archaeological centers and she was an active member of the small Archaeology Club, a group of professionals from the East Coast, that met on Sundays once a month to discuss work in progress. The club included many of Goldman's friends and colleagues from a lifetime of archaeological work, including Margarete Bieber, Edith Hall Dohan, William Dinsmoor, Benjamin Meritt, Gisela Richter, and Leslie and Josephine Shear.[157] She still had her piano and enjoyed concerts as well as theater performances—serious and frivolous—and was much amused by the musical *La Plume de ma Tante* in New York in 1960. She kept in touch with her former colleagues from excavations and was a gracious hostess in Princeton.

Goldman often gave lectures on her archaeological work, but Frances Jones recalled that popularizing archaeology for the general public was not her forte. "Hetty really felt that archaeology was a business."[158] She was an engaging lecturer with a good sense of humor, and although she wrote primarily about her own excavations, she occasionally took up other topics "which would catch her eye."[159] Goldman was adept at incorporating philology, art history, numismatics, epigraphy, and archaeology into her work, a practice that had begun as early as her master's thesis for Radcliffe and that continued into her work on the Sandon Monument at Tarsus. She was well versed in the cultures of the ancient Mediterranean and was easily able to find comparative material from Phoenician, Hittite, Egyptian, Greek, or Roman sources, among others.

Hetty Goldman's dedication to "discrimination and attention to detail" was another hallmark of her archaeological scholarship. She expected careful organization and planning not only from herself but also from her colleagues and students. Describing a particularly frustrating experience at the 1922 annual meeting of the Archaeological Institute of America in New Haven, Goldman wrote:

> While I enjoyed foregathering with so many old archaeological and classical friends, the sessions for reading papers were rather unsatisfactory. Too many papers, too hasty reading, absolutely no discussion . . . I made an absurd attempt to tell all about Colophon, or more correctly all that I knew about Colophon, in twenty minutes; fairly gabbled towards the end, and showed slides so fast that it looked like an unsuccessful attempt at motion pictures.[160]

Goldman was a self-described "wandering spirit" who loved to travel.[161] Even after she had given up active excavation, she still enjoyed visits to the Mediterranean. In 1958 she traveled with Effie (Mrs. Piet) de Jong to visit the Gordion excavations in Turkey. Rodney Young met the women at the train station in Beylikköprü and took them to the excavations in the battered old excavation Jeep. Since this conveyance was without roof or doors, Young had improvised some safety ropes to reassure his passengers that they could safely ride to the citadel mound and the Midas tumulus. This was sheer delight to Goldman, always the intrepid traveler.

Yet Goldman was immensely loyal to her family and spent many of her later years in residence at a home built by her grandfather, Marcus Goldman, in 1889, only eight years after she was born. She had inherited the house, a Swiss chalet located in Keene Valley, New York, after her father's death. Finding the chalet too big and too much trouble, Goldman had a smaller house built on the property in 1941. Rationing during World War II forced a hiatus in building her new house, but it was finally completed in 1946. Her niece, Sarah Sanborn Moench, recalls that Goldman spent many relaxing hours in the solitude and peace of her "little house" while the nieces and nephews had the run of the chalet nearby.[162]

Goldman's declining strength and a brief illness led to her death in Princeton on May 4, 1972. The following memorial resolution was read at the June 17 meeting of the Executive Committee of the Archaeological Institute of America:

> Hetty Goldman . . . was one of the great archaeologists of the first half of the twentieth century. She was also, by determination, one of the pioneers among women in field archaeology. A student of literature . . . a classicist and archaeologist . . . she approached antiquity with the interest of an historian, prehistorian, and art historian, with a sense of the relative importance and unimportance of human achievements, with an appreciation of beauty in literature, the visual arts, and the Mediterranean setting, with a sense of humor to temper romantic inclinations, and with a felicitous command of language spoken and written. She combined her scholarly and artistic gifts with human courage in all circumstances, whether in peace, war, or politics.[163]

Goldman's obituary, prepared by Mrs. Paul Bortell Jr. of the Institute for Advanced Study in Princeton, recalled her accomplishments in archaeology:

> Dr. Goldman's conscientious and penetrating mind made itself felt on every facet of her life. Her excavations were meticulous, but imaginative in approach; her publications thoughtful. She always maintained a sense of balance between the precision of her observations and the brilliance of her hypotheses. Her books are concise and unassuming, but they are incredibly useful and effective and serve as models for archaeological publications. Perhaps she gave even more as a teacher to the many students and colleagues who never failed to see more clearly and to dig more deeply under her keen eye . . . She liked to think of herself as a catalyst, helping to draw out or create ideas in others, a role in which she was paramount.[164]

A year after her death, her former colleagues held a memorial symposium in her honor at the Institute for Advanced Study in Princeton.[165] In her will, Goldman left generous bequests to the Archaeological Institute of America and Bryn Mawr College to further the study of classical and prehistoric archaeology in the United States. Both of these institutions had received gifts from her in previous years, for the *American Journal of Archaeology* and the archaeology program of Bryn Mawr College, respectively.

Hetty Goldman was a woman of uncompromising strength of mind and spirit. Her pioneering spirit opened the doors for many women who came after her at the American School in Athens. Her anthropological interests in the prehistoric Aegean helped to pave the way for today's prehistorians. She once thought that, as a writer, she had little to say. Yet her articles are full of life and reveal much about her character. In a speech she gave to Bryn Mawr students in 1955, she said about her career:

> I am, as perhaps you know, not only an archaeologist but one of that happy band of excavators whose work takes them to many different lands, usually very different in background and cultural pattern from our own. It has been this interplay of contrasting patterns, this attempt on the part of the excavator and stranger to learn and understand what others live by and what to them is basically important and morally significant which constitutes the intensely fascinating by-product of archaeological excavation.[166]

Hetty Goldman's archaeological career spanned more than sixty years. In the beginning she was young, inexperienced at fieldwork, yet unwilling to accept that she was not just as capable of participating in archaeological excavation as her male colleagues. By the end of her career, she had traveled to many lands, spoken several different languages, and discovered the joys and challenges of archaeological excavation. It is not really remarkable that she was a woman and accomplished these things; what is remarkable is that she had the patience, the wit, and the tenacity to do what she set out to do. Hetty Goldman's achievements and her contributions to the field of classical and prehistoric archaeology continue to live on over thirty years after her death.

WORKS BY HETTY GOLDMAN
A SELECTED BIBLIOGRAPHY

Books, Monographs, and Articles

Many of the items dated 1910–56 in the bibliography appear in *The Aegean and the Near East: Studies Presented to Hetty Goldman on the Occasion of Her Seventy-Fifth Birthday,* ed. Saul Weinberg, (Locust Valley, NY: J. J. Augustin, 1956) xiii–xvi. This served as the foundation for the present list to which has been added the items from the alumnae magazines and papers delivered at conferences.

"The *Oresteia* of Aeschylus as Illustrated by Greek Vase-Painting." *Harvard Studies in Classical Philology* 21 (1910): 111–59.

"Two Unpublished Oedipus Vases in the Boston Museum of Fine Arts." *American Journal of Archaeology* 15 (1911): 378–85.

"Excavations at Halae." Paper presented at the 14th annual meeting of the Archaeological Institute of America, Washington, D.C., Dec. 30, 1912. *American Journal of Archaeology* 17 (1913): 92.

Alice L. Walker, coauthor. "Report on Excavations at Halae of Locris." *American Journal of Archaeology* 19 (1915): 418–37.

"Inscriptions from the Acropolis of Halae." *American Journal of Archaeology* 19 (1915): 438–53.

"The Terracottas from the Necropolis of Halae." Ph.D. diss., Radcliffe College, 1916.

"With the Spade in Greece." *Radcliffe Quarterly* 2, no. 2 (1918): 34–36.

"Archaeological Excavation—a Profession and an Adventure." *Bryn Mawr Alumnae Bulletin,* June 1923, 6–11.

"Excavations of the Fogg Museum at Colophon." Paper presented at the 24th annual meeting of the Archaeological Institute of America, Washington, D.C., Dec. 29, 1922. *American Journal of Archaeology* 27 (1923): 67–68.

"The 'Ludovisi Throne' and Boston Relief Once More." *American Journal of Archaeology* 30 (1926): 464–68.

"Aspects of the Early Helladic Settlement at Eutresis." Paper presented at the 28th annual meeting of the Archaeological Institute of America, Cambridge, MA, Dec. 29, 1926. *American Journal of Archaeology* 31 (1927): 94.

"Excavations at Eutresis: Preliminary Report on the Excavations at Eutresis in Boeotia." *Fogg Art Museum. Notes.* Special number. Cambridge: Harvard University, Sept. 1927.

"A Metrical Inscription from the Necropolis of Eutresis." *American Journal of Archaeology* 32 (1928): 179–81.

"Votive Offerings from the Acropolis of Halae." Paper presented at the 29th annual meeting of the Archaeological Institute of America, Cincinnati, OH, Dec. 28, 1927. *American Journal of Archaeology* 32 (1928): 56.

"Some Votive Offerings from the Acropolis of Halae." In *Festschrift für James Loeb,* 67–72. Munich: F. Bruckmann AG, 1930.

Excavations at Eutresis in Boeotia. Cambridge, Mass., 1931.

V. J. Fewkes and R. W. Ehrich, coauthors. "Excavations at Starčevo, Yugoslavia, Seasons 1931 and 1932." *Bulletin of the American School of Prehistoric Research* 9 (1933): 33–54.

"Excavations at Stobi in Yugoslavia." *American Journal of Archaeology* 37 (1933): 297–301.

V. J. Fewkes and R. W. Ehrich, coauthors. "Preliminary Report on an Archaeological Reconnaissance in Yugoslavia, American Expedition, Season 1932." *Bulletin of the American School of Prehistoric Research* 9 (May 1933): 16–32.

"The Activities of the Expedition Sent by Bryn Mawr College and the Archaeological Institute of America to Cilicia in Asia Minor." *Bryn Mawr Alumnae Bulletin,* November 1934, 4–8.

"The Bronze Age Pottery of Greece." *Bulletin of the American Ceramic Society* 13 (1934): 301–8.

"Bryn Mawr in Asia Minor: Excavations at Tarsus in Cilicia, 1935." *Bryn Mawr Alumnae Bulletin,* November 1935, 5–7.

"Preliminary Expedition to Cilicia, 1934, and Excavations at Gözlü Kule, Tarsus, 1935." *American Journal of Archaeology* 39 (1935): 526–49.
"Preliminary Investigations in Cilicia by the Expedition Sent Out under the Joint Auspices of Bryn Mawr College and the Archaeological Institute of America, 1934." Paper presented at the 36th annual meeting of the Archaeological Institute of America, Toronto, ON, Dec. 27–29, 1934. *American Journal of Archaeology* 39 (1935): 115.
"Excavations at Tarsus, 1935." Paper presented at the 37th annual meeting of the Archaeological Institute of America, New York, NY, Dec. 26–28, 1935. *American Journal of Archaeology* 40 (1936): 123.
"Preliminary Expedition to Cilicia, 1934, and Excavations at Gözlü Kule, Tarsus, 1935." *Bryn Mawr Alumnae Bulletin,* April 1936, 7–19.
"Excavations at Gözlü Kule, Tarsus, 1936." *American Journal of Archaeology* 41 (1937): 262–86.
"Excavations at Gözlü Kule, Tarsus, 1936." Paper presented at the 38th annual meeting of the Archaeological Institute of America, Chicago, IL, Dec. 28–30, 1936. *American Journal of Archaeology* 41 (1937): 111.
"Excavations at Gözlü Kule, Tarsus, 1937." *American Journal of Archaeology* 42 (1938): 30–54.
"Excavations at Gözlü Kule, Tarsus, 1937." Paper presented at the 39th annual meeting of the Archaeological Institute of America, Philadelphia, PA, Dec. 28–30, 1937. *American Journal of Archaeology* 42 (1938): 127.
"The Mound of Tarsus." *Asia* 39 (1939): 413–18.
"A Note on Two Painted Sherds from Tarsus with Representations of Birds." *Bulletin of the American Schools of Oriental Research* 76 (1939): 2–5.
"The Acropolis of Halae." *Hesperia* 9 (1940): 381–514.
"Excavations at Gözlü Kule, Tarsus, 1938." *American Journal of Archaeology* 45 (1940): 60–86.
"The Sandon Monument of Tarsus." *Journal of the American Oriental Society* 60 (1940): 544–53.
"The Origin of the Greek Herm." Paper presented at the 42nd annual meeting of the Archaeological Institute of America, Baltimore, MD, Dec. 26–28, 1940. *American Journal of Archaeology* 45 (1941): 89.
"The Origin of the Greek Herm." *American Journal of Archaeology* 46 (1942): 58–68.
Frances F. Jones, coauthor. "Terracottas from the Necropolis of Halae." *Hesperia* 11 (1942): 365–422.
"Two Terracotta Figurines from Tarsus." *American Journal of Archaeology* 47 (1943): 22–34.
John Garstang, coauthor. "A Conspectus of Early Cilician Pottery." *American Journal of Archaeology* 51 (1947): 370–88.
"Sandon and Herakles." Commemorative Studies in Honor of Theodore Leslie Shear. *Hesperia Supplement* 8 (1949): 164–74.
"Tarsus, First Report of the 1947 and 1948 Excavations at the Site of Gözlü Kule." *American Journal of Archaeology* 53 (1949): 46–49.
Editor, *Excavations at Gözlü Kule, Tarsus.* Vol. 1, *The Hellenistic and Roman Period.* 2 pts. Vol. 2, *From the Neolithic through the Bronze Age.* Vol. 3, *The Iron Age.* 2 pts. Princeton: Princeton University Press, 1950–63.

"Buildings and Habitation Levels." In *Excavations at Gözlü Kule, Tarsus,* 1: 5–28. Princeton, 1950.
Frances F. Jones, coauthor. "The Lamps." In *Excavations at Gözlü Kule, Tarsus,* 1: 84–134. Princeton, 1950.
"The Terracotta Figurines." In *Excavations at Gözlü Kule, Tarsus,* 1: 297–383. Princeton, 1950.
"A Crystal Statuette from Tarsus." In *Archaeologica Orientalia in Memoriam Ernst Herzfeld,* 129–33. Locust Valley, N.Y.: J. J. Augustin, 1952.
"The Relative Chronology of Southeastern Anatolia." In *Relative Chronologies in Old World Archaeology,* ed. by R. W. Ehrich, 69–84. Chicago: University of Chicago Press, 1954.
"Golden Moments in Greece." *Bryn Mawr Alumnae Bulletin,* summer 1955, 4.
"So You Want to Become an Archaeologist?!" *Newsletter of the American School of Classical Studies,* fall 1987.

NOTES

The authors gratefully acknowledge the following individuals who provided access to and gave permission for the use of archived materials in the present work: Lorett Treese, Archivist, Bryn Mawr College; Natalia Vogeikoff-Brogan, Archivist, American School of Classical Studies at Athens; and James R. Fein, Archivist for Historical Studies and Social Sciences at the Institute for Advanced Study in Princeton. We also thank Jan Trembley, editor of the *Bryn Mawr Alumnae Bulletin,* and Doreen Spitzer who alerted us to published articles written by Goldman appearing in the *Bryn Mawr Alumnae Bulletin* and the *Newsletter of the American School,* respectively. We acknowledge Jeanny Vorys Canby, who interviewed (on our behalf) Frances F. Jones, a longtime friend and colleague of Goldman's. Jones provided valuable information on Goldman's personality and on the excavations at Tarsus. Frances F. Jones died (less than a year after that interview) on February 14, 1999.

We also extend our gratitude to John E. Coleman of Cornell University for allowing Kathleen M. Quinn access to the records of the Cornell Halai and East Lokris Project. The field diaries of Hetty Goldman and Alice L. Walker were invaluable tools in the research for Quinn's M.A. thesis ("Late Roman and Byzantine Halai," Cornell University, 1996) which served as a springboard for the historical background of the present work and for the section on Halae. Thanks also to Jack L. Davis of the University of Cincinnati for his advice and for sharing with us a forthcoming article on American archaeology in Greek-occupied Asia Minor.

We would especially like to thank Sarah Sanborn Moench, daughter of Ashton and Agnes Goldman Sanborn and niece of Hetty Goldman. Mrs. Moench generously provided genealogical information about the Adler and Goldman families as well as personal anecdotes and favorite memories about Goldman, including several photographs of her aunt.

1. Sarah Sanborn Moench, personal communication with Kathleen M. Quinn, May 5, 1998.

2. Ethical Culture Society, "Who Was Felix Adler?" http://www.ethicalsociety.org/FAQs/answer10.htm, accessed June 18, 2003.

3. *Thirty-Ninth Annual Report of the Managing Committee of the American School of Classical Studies at Athens, 1919–1920,* extract from the *Bulletin of the Archaeological Institute of America,* 1919, 17.

4. Hetty Goldman, Bryn Mawr Alumnae Survey, 1961. Archives of Bryn Mawr College, Bryn Mawr, PA.

5. Homer A. Thompson, "Introductory Remarks," *A Symposium in Memory of Hetty Goldman, 1881–1972, Held at the Institute for Advanced Study, Princeton, New Jersey, May 4th, 1973* (Princeton: Princeton University Press, 1974), viii.

6. Interview with Frances F. Jones, conducted by Jeanny Vorys Canby, May 1, 1998.

7. Hetty Goldman, "The *Oresteia* of Aeschylus as Illustrated by Greek Vase-Painting," *Harvard Studies in Classical Philology* 21 (1910): 112.

8. *Thirtieth Annual Report of the Managing Committee of the American School of Classical Studies at Athens, 1910–1911,* extract from the *Bulletin of the Archaeological Institute of America,* 1912, 137. Ashton Sanborn was eventually to marry Hetty Goldman's younger sister, Agnes.

9. Ibid., 131.

10. Ibid., 133.

11. Hetty Goldman, "Archaeological Excavation: A Profession and an Adventure," *Bryn Mawr Alumnae Bulletin* (June 1923), 7.

12. Louis E. Lord, *A History of the American School of Classical Studies at Athens, 1882–1942* (Cambridge: Harvard University Press, 1947), 94, 362.

13. Sarah Sanborn Moench, personal communication.

14. Ibid.

15. Hetty Goldman, "With the Spade in Greece," *Radcliffe Quarterly* 2, no. 2 (1918): 34.

16. Goldman, "Archaeological Excavation," 7.

17. Ibid., 7–8.

18. *Thirtieth Annual Report,* 134.

19. Thompson, "Introductory Remarks," viii.

20. *Thirtieth Annual Report,* 135.

21. Hetty Goldman, "So You Want to Become an Archaeologist?!" *Newsletter of the American School of Classical Studies,* fall 1987, 12.

22. Lord, *American School,* 298, 300.

23. Mary Allsebrook, *Born to Rebel: The Life of Harriet Boyd Hawes* (Oxford: Oxbow Books, 1992), 91.

24. Alice L. Walker, Halae Field Journals, 1911 and 1913, Archives of the Cornell Halai and East Lokris Project, Cornell University, Ithaca, NY.

25. Jones, interview.

26. Goldman, "With the Spade," 35.

27. Ibid.

28. Ibid.

29. Hetty Goldman, "Golden Moments in Greece," *Bryn Mawr Alumnae Bulletin,* summer 1955, 4.

30. Ibid.

31. Goldman, "With the Spade," 35.

32. Ibid.

33. Ibid., 35–36.

34. Goldman, "Archaeological Excavation," 9–10.

35. *Thirty-First Annual Report of the Managing Committee of the American School of Classical Studies at Athens, 1911–1912,* extract from the *Bulletin of the Archaeological Institute of America,* 1912, 217.

36. Ibid., 218.

37. *Thirty-Second Annual Report of the Managing Committee of the American School of Classical Studies at Athens, 1912–1913,* extract from the *Bulletin of the Archaeological Institute of America,* 1913, 8.

38. Agnes Goldman Sanborn, personal communication with Machteld J. Mellink.

39. Hetty Goldman and Alice L. Walker, "Report on Excavations at Halae of Locris," *American Journal of Archaeology (AJA)* 19 (1915): 418–37; and Hetty Goldman, "Inscriptions from the Acropolis of Halae," *AJA* 19 (1915): 438–53.

40. Frances F. Jones, "A Quartette of Excavations," in *Symposium in Memory of Hetty Goldman,* 3.

41. *Thirty-Fifth Annual Report of the Managing Committee of the American School of Classical Studies at Athens, 1915–1916,* extract from the *Bulletin of the Archaeological Institute of America,* 1916, 7, 22–23.

42. Sanborn, personal communication.

43. Ibid.

44. Hetty Goldman, "The Acropolis of Halae," *Hesperia* 9 (1940): 381–514; also Hetty Goldman and Frances F. Jones, "Terracottas from the Necropolis of Halae," *Hesperia* 11 (1942): 365–422.

45. John E. Coleman, "Excavations at Halai, 1990–1991," *Hesperia* 61 (1992): 265–89; John E. Coleman, Patricia S. Wren, and Kathleen M. Quinn, "Halai: The 1992–1994 Field Seasons," *Hesperia* 68 (1999): 285–342.

46. *Fortieth Annual Report of the Managing Committee of the American School of Classical Studies at Athens, 1920–1921,* extract from the *Bulletin of the Archaeological Institute of America,* 1921, 19.

47. Ibid., 19–20.

48. Ibid., 20.

49. Goldman, "Archaeological Excavation," 10.

50. *Forty-First Annual Report of the Managing Committee of the American School of Classical Studies at Athens, 1921–1922,* extract from the *Bulletin of the Archaeological Institute of America,* 1922, 17.

51. Hetty Goldman, Colophon Notebook, June 22, 1922, Archives of the Department of Classical and Near Eastern Archaeology, Bryn Mawr College, Bryn Mawr, PA.

52. *Forty-First Annual Report,* 17.

53. Carl W. Blegen, letter, February 14, 1965, *His Letters Home,* ed. Robert D. Blegen, 1995, 2: 208–9.

54. George M. A. Hanfmann, "Hetty Goldman and the Iron Age," in *Symposium in Memory of Hetty Goldman,* 16.

55. Ibid., 17.

56. Robert A. Bridges, Jr., "The Mycenaean Tholos Tomb at Kolophon," *Hesperia* 43 (1974): 264–66.

57. *Forty-First Annual Report,* 18.

58. Goldman, "Golden Moments in Greece," 4.

59. Jones, "A Quartette of Excavations," 4.

60. *Forty-Fifth Annual Report of the Managing Committee of the American School of Classical Studies at Athens, 1925–1926,* extract from the *Bulletin of the Archaeological Institute of America,* 1926, 27.

61. Leicester B. Holland, "Colophon," *Hesperia* 13 (1944): 91–171.

62. Hetty Goldman, "By-Products of Scholarship: An Address Given at Bryn Mawr College on 5 April 1955," in *Symposium in Memory of Hetty Goldman,* 51.

63. Benjamin D. Meritt, "Inscriptions of Colophon," *American Journal of Philology* 56 (1935): 358–97.

64. Y. E. Ersoy, "Finds from Menemen/Panaztepe in the Manisa Museum," *Annual of the British School at Athens* 83 (1988): 55–82; Hayat Erkanal, "1994 Panaztepe Kazilari Sonuçlari," *Kazi Sonuçlari Toplantisi* 17 (1995): 329–35.

65. *Forty-Third Annual Report of the Managing Committee of the American School of Classical Studies at Athens, 1923–1924,* extract from the *Bulletin of the Archaeological Institute of America,* 1924, 23.

66. Hetty Goldman, *Excavations at Eutresis, September 1927,* pamphlet published by the Fogg Museum of Art, 3–4.

67. John L. Caskey, "Hetty Goldman: Excavations of Preclassical Sites in Greece," in *Symposium in Memory of Hetty Goldman,* 26–27.

68. *Forty-Third Annual Report,* 23.

69. Claire Richter Sherman, *Women as Interpreters of the Visual Arts, 1820–1979,* with Adele M. Holcomb, Contributions in Women's Studies no. 18, (Westport, CT: Greenwood Press, 1981) 360–61.

70. Ibid.

71. Jones, "A Quartette of Excavations," 5.

72. Caskey, "Hetty Goldman," 27.

73. Jones, "A Quartette of Excavations," 6.

74. Hetty Goldman, "Excavations at Eutresis in Boeotia, 1924–1925," in *Forty-Fourth Annual Report of the Managing Committee of the American School of Classical Studies at Athens, 1924–1925,* extract from the *Bulletin of the Archaeological Institute of America,* 1925, 32.

75. Ibid.

76. Ibid., 33.

77. *Forty-Fifth Annual Report,* 34.

78. Caskey, "Hetty Goldman," 26.

79. Ibid., 27.

80. John L. Caskey and Elizabeth Caskey, "The Earliest Settlements at Eutresis: Supplementary Excavations, 1958," *Hesperia* 29 (1960): 126.

81. Ibid., 126–27.

82. *Forty-Seventh Annual Report of the Managing Committee of the American School of Classical Studies at Athens, 1927–1928,* extract from the *Bulletin of the Archaeological Institute of America,* 1928, 15.

83. Ibid.

84. Ibid, 15–20.

85. Much of the information on Yugoslavia is presented in Robert W. Ehrich, "The Yugoslavian Interlude," *Symposium in Memory of Hetty Goldman,* 38–42. This is the only source that discusses Goldman's personal experiences outside of Greece and Turkey.

86. Ibid, 39.

87. V. J. Fewkes, Hetty Goldman, and R. W. Ehrich, "Preliminary Report on an Archaeological Reconnaissance in Yugoslavia, American Expedition, Season 1932," *Bulletin of the American School of Prehistoric Research* 9 (1933): 26.

88. Ehrich, "The Yugoslavian Interlude," 40.

89. Fewkes et al., "Preliminary Report," 25.

90. V. J. Fewkes, Hetty Goldman, and R. W. Ehrich, "Excavations at Starćevo, Yugoslavia, Seasons 1931 and 1932," *Bulletin of the American School of Prehistoric Research* 9 (1933): 36.

91. Ehrich, "The Yugoslavian Interlude," 40.

92. Fewkes et al., "Excavations at Starćevo," 48.

93. Ehrich, "The Yugoslavian Interlude," 40.

94. Hetty Goldman, "Excavations at Stobi in Yugoslavia," *American Journal of Archaelogy* 37 (1993): 297.

95. Emil Forrer, "Vorhomerische Griechen in den Keilschrifttexten von Boghazköi," *Mitteilungen der deutschen Orient-Gesellschaft* 63 (1924): 1–22.

96. Hetty Goldman, "Bryn Mawr in Cilicia," informal report to Bryn Mawr College, late summer 1934. Archives of Bryn Mawr College, Bryn Mawr, PA.

97. Ibid.

98. Ibid.

99. Ibid.

100. "Agreement for Tarsus Excavations," Hetty Goldman Papers, Archives for Historical Studies and Social Sciences, Institute for Advanced Study, Princeton, New Jersey.

101. Jones, "A Quartette of Excavations," 7; Hetty Goldman, "Preliminary Expedition to Cilicia, 1934, and Excavations at Gözlü Kule, Tarsus, 1935," *AJA* 39 (1935): 526–27, nn. 2 and 4.

102. Goldman, "Preliminary Expedition," 535–36, fig. 18; I. J. Gelb, "Hittite Hieroglyphic Seals and Seal Impressions," in *Excavations at Gözlü Kule, Tarsus,* vol. 2, *From the Neolithic through the Bronze Age,* ed. Hetty Goldman (Princeton: Princeton University Press, 1956), 246–47, no. 1.

103. A. Goetze, *Kizzuwatna and the Problem of Hittite Geography* (New Haven: Yale University Press, 1940), 49–56, 73–74.

104. Goldman, "Preliminary Expedition," 542–43, figs. 33–34; Hetty Goldman, "A Crystal Statuette from Tarsus," in *Archaeologica Orientalia in Memoriam Ernst Herzfeld* (Locust Valley: J. J. Augustin, 1952), 129–33; *Tarsus II,* figs. 456a–d.

105. Hetty Goldman, "Excavations at Gözlü Kule, Tarsus, 1936," *AJA* 41 (1937): 271, 280; I. J. Gelb in *Tarsus II,* 289–91; H. G. Güterbock, "Observations on the Tarsus Seal of Puduhepa, Queen of Hatti," *Journal of the American Oriental Society* 117 (1997): 143–44; A. Goetze, "Cuneiform Inscriptions from Tarsus," *Journal of the American Oriental Society* 59 (1939): 1–5.

106. Goldman, "Excavations, 1936," 281–83.

107. Letter to Abraham Flexner, Institute for Advanced Study, Princeton, New Jersey, August 10, 1936, Goldman Papers.

108. Ibid.

109. Letter to Abraham Flexner, Institute for Advanced Study, October 8, 1936, Goldman Papers.

110. Ibid.

111. Ibid.

112. Abraham Flexner, letter to Hetty Goldman, October 15, 1936, Goldman Papers.

113. Letter to Frank Aydelotte, Institute for Advanced Study, October 16, 1945, Goldman Papers.

114. Letter to Paul Sachs, November 5, 1936, Goldman Papers.

115. Letter to Abraham Flexner, Institute for Advanced Study, May 5, 1937, Goldman Papers.

116. Hetty Goldman, "Report on the Excavations at Gözlü Kule, Tarsus, March 23–May 1," 1937, Goldman Papers.

117. *Tarsus II,* 243–44, fig. 403, no. 44.

118. Hetty Goldman, "Excavations at Gözlü Kule, Tarsus, 1937," *AJA* 42 (1938): 54.

119. Abraham Flexner, letter to Paul Sachs, April 20, 1937, Goldman Papers.

120. Letter to Mrs. Bailey, April 9, 1938, Goldman Papers.

121. Letter to Abraham Flexner, Institute for Advanced Study, April 12, 1938, Goldman Papers.

122. Ibid.

123. Jones, interview.

124. Ibid.

125. Hetty Goldman, "Excavations at Gözlü Kule, Tarsus, 1938," *AJA* 44 (1940): 76, fig. 33; I. J. Gelb in *Tarsus II,* 253, no. 58.

126. Letter to Mrs. Bailey, May 26, 1938, Goldman Papers.

127. Letter to Abraham Flexner, Institute for Advanced Study, May 3, 1938, Goldman Papers.

128. President Park, letter to Hetty Goldman, November 29, 1938, Goldman Papers.

129. Letter to Abraham Flexner, Institute for Advanced Study, December 6, 1938, Goldman Papers.

130. Jones, interview.

131. Moench, personal communication.

132. Jones, interview.

133. Meritt, "Inscriptions of Colophon," 7.

134. Frank Aydelotte, letter to Mr. Stoll, March 11, 1943, Goldman Papers.

135. Sherman, *Women as Interpreters,* 87.

136. Full references to the articles mentioned here can be found at the end of the article in the bibliography of Goldman's published works.

137. Hanfmann, "Hetty Goldman," 20.

138. Ibid., 21.

139. Ibid.

140. Letter to Frank Aydelotte, October 16, 1945, Goldman Papers.

141. Hetty Goldman, "Tarsus, First Report of the 1947 and 1948 Excavations at the Site of Gözlü Kule," *AJA* 53 (1949): 46–48.

142. Letter to Frank Aydelotte, June 6, 1947, Goldman Papers.

143. Letter to Frank Aydelotte, October 4, 1947, Goldman Papers.

144. Ibid.

145. Hetty Goldman and John Garstang, "A Conspectus of Early Cilician Pottery," *AJA* 51 (1947): 370.

146. *Tarsus II,* 65–91, 230–41, 352–61.

147. Jones, "A Quartette of Excavations," 10.

148. "The Relative Chronology of Southeastern Anatolia," in *Relative Chronologies in Old World Archaeology,* ed. R. W. Ehrich (Chicago: University of Chicago Press, 1954), 69–85.

149. "Notes from the Sixty-eighth General Meeting of the Archaeological Institute of America," *AJA* 71 (1967): 182.

150. Ann Hoskin Ehrich, letter to Machteld J. Mellink, 1997.

151. Jones, interview.

152. Dorothy H. Cox, *A Tarsus Coin Collection in the Adana Museum* (New York: American Numismatic Society, 1941).

153. Saul Weinberg, ed., *The Aegean and the Near East: Studies Presented to Hetty Goldman on the Occasion of Her Seventy-Fifth Birthday* (Locust Valley, NY: J. J. Augustin, 1956).

154. Lucy Shoe Meritt, *History of the American School of Classical Studies at Athens, 1939–1980* (Princeton: American School of Classical Studies at Athens, 1984), 80–81, 385.

155. *AJA* 71 (1967): 182.

156. Archives of the Archaeological Institute of America, Boston University, Boston, MA.

157. Sherman, *Women as Interpreters,* 252.

158. Jones, interview.

159. Ibid.

160. Letter to Carl W. Blegen, January 9, 1923, Carl W. Blegen Papers, American School of Classical Studies at Athens, Athens, Greece.

161. Letter to Flexner, April 12, 1938, Goldman Papers.

162. Moench, personal communication.

163. Archives of Bryn Mawr College, Bryn Mawr, PA.

164. Mrs. Paul Bortell Jr., obituary for Hetty Goldman, May 5, 1972, Goldman Papers.

165. *Symposium in Memory of Hetty Goldman.*

166. Goldman, "By-Products of Scholarship," 43–44.

Gertrude Caton-Thompson

(1888–1985)

Margaret S. Drower

GERTRUDE CATON-THOMPSON MUST BE considered one of the most outstanding archaeologists of her generation, all the more remarkable because she was born into a well-to-do family, privately educated, and had sufficient means to lead a comfortable life of leisure. Not until she was in her midthirties did she begin seriously to study archaeology, first distinguishing herself as a prehistorian in the Nile valley, the Fayum, and the Kharga Oasis in Egypt; next in Central Africa, in what was then called Rhodesia (now Zimbabwe); and, finally, as the first archaeologist to conduct a scientific excavation in Arabia. She never held a professional or academic post but was honored by several universities and a number of learned societies. In her role as a generous patron, she was the benefactor of several academic foundations devoted to the prehistory of Africa. Always a very private and retiring person, she kept a diary throughout her life and in her nineties was prevailed upon by friends to write the memoirs of her remarkable life.[1] Careless of discomfort and danger, she pursued her fieldwork with a meticulous regard for accuracy and an acute perception of the problems involved.

Early Years

Born in February 1888, Gertrude Caton-Thompson was only five when her father, William Caton-Thompson, head of the legal department of the London and North-Western Railway, died at the age of fifty-seven. The youngest of her mother's four brothers, a lawyer, became the family's guardian and adviser. William's will divided his estate into three, one part for the widow and one each for young Gertrude and her brother Arthur. Shrewd investment ensured that the family would continue to live comfortably in their house at Camberley in Surrey, then at Maidenhead on the Thames, not far from London. Arthur was sent to Eton to be educated, while Gertrude had a series of governesses, learned to play the violin, and was taught to ride and groom a horse. Holidays abroad in France, Malta, Sicily, and Italy broadened the children's horizon. In Rome, in particular, Caton-Thompson remembered feeling "the first stirrings of interest in past civilizations."[2]

At the age of thirteen, Caton-Thompson was sent to a small boarding school on the south coast. Looking back on her school years, she later concluded that the standard of teaching had been poor, lacking in the "precision subjects"—science in any form, mathematics, Latin, and Greek. Nevertheless, during the prolonged and frequent school visits to cities like Dresden and Florence, she was encouraged to keep neat and careful notebooks in museums and art galleries, fostering an orderliness to which she later attributed her methodical recording of archaeological field notes. She continued to study the violin and for a time played in a small orchestra near her home. She never lost her love of music and in later life counted several eminent musicians among her friends. Her education culminated with a finishing school in Paris, where she visited art galleries and museums and went riding with her companions in the Bois de Boulogne.

Her education completed, Caton-Thompson embarked on a life of carefree enjoyment—rowing on the Thames; riding and hunting; playing tennis; visiting relatives and friends; attending parties and dances; going to London for the occasional play or concert; and, from time to time, traveling abroad with her mother. In 1910, after her mother had divorced her second husband, the two of them bought an apartment in central London at Kensington Gardens near Hyde Park. This was to be Caton-Thompson's base for much of her future life. Now for the first time she became involved with the movement for women's suffrage, becoming a joint secretary of the London branch of the association. In 1911, she helped organize a meeting at the Albert Hall that raised four thousand pounds.

War Work

During the early months of World War I, when she was already twenty-six, Caton-Thompson, for the first time, found herself employed, in a voluntary capacity, with the Soldiers and Sailors' Families Association. Then, returning to London in the Women's Emergency Corps, she helped raise money for refugee organizations, which she regarded as a futile task. It was not until 1916 that she found war work that fully occupied her energies and talents: while stationed at Woolwich arsenal, she worked hard organizing canteens for munitions workers. One evening at a dinner party in London, Caton-Thompson chanced to meet a civil servant named Arthur Salter, who invited her to join his staff in the newly formed Ministry of Shipping and Supply. This was a turning point in her life.[3]

Early in 1917 she found herself working in a government office as "a very lowly cog" in the wheels of a body without which England would have been starved out of the war by enemy action at sea. Before the end of 1917 she was promoted to be Salter's private secretary in a wider organization, the Allied Maritime Transport Council and Executive, with a common shipping pool and an agreed allocation of all raw materials. Salter himself acted as executive chairman as well as secretary of the council. He worked his staff hard: "a less dynamic personality could not have succeeded . . . I was proud to serve such a man."[4] She had neither typing nor shorthand; others, he said, could provide these services. When the war ended, she took a much-needed holiday, but then Salter asked her to accompany him to the Peace Conference in Paris in March 1919 as his personal assistant. He was to be secretary of the Supreme Economic Council. Caton-Thompson records buying a "ravishing evening dress" for this trip.[5] The negotiations took some months, during which time she met a number of important people, including Gertrude Bell, T. E. Lawrence, and Maynard Keynes. In the intervals between meetings, she and her new friends visited the local battlefields (which filled her with horror), frequented such museums and galleries as were open, and enjoyed a frivolous day or two at the Longchamp races. The Treaty of Versailles was finally signed on June 23, 1919, and Caton-Thompson returned to London.

Visits to friends in Ireland that autumn and to France in the spring of 1920 filled the time pleasantly. Salter pressed her to stay on in the civil service, but she had other ideas and another career in mind: archaeology, in particular paleontology, and the world of the ancient Near East.

Beginnings of a Career in Archaeology

The Near East was not unfamiliar to Caton-Thompson. An early susceptibility to bronchial infections, coupled with her mother's love of foreign travel, had led the two of them more than once to the Mediterranean sunshine. In 1906, when Caton-Thompson was only fourteen, they had taken a Cook's tour to Athens, to Jaffa (for Jerusalem and Jericho), and to Alexandria, where their boat had docked for several days, enabling them to visit Cairo and the usual sights. The tour concluded with stops at Naples and Pompeii on the way home (although she later confessed to having been more interested in the local aquarium than in the museum).[6]

Caton-Thompson and her mother made a much longer second visit to Egypt in 1911. They stayed in Luxor for a time and then in Aswan, where Caton-Thompson had made the acquaintance of a Mrs. Ella Stephens, who was to prove a lifelong friend. These early encounters with antiquity may have kindled her interest in archaeology. About a year afterward she had attended a course of lectures at the British Museum on Mycenae and early Greece, which she later said "enthralled her."[7] But it was prehistory that finally captured her enthusiasm. In 1915, taking a short holiday from war work at Menton in the south of France, where Mrs. Stephens had a villa, she had discovered an excavation going on nearby at the Rochers Rouges, where the Chanoine de Villeneuve was excavating a Paleolithic site. Caton-Thompson volunteered her services as a "bottle-washer" in the early mornings before breakfast.

In April 1921 she went back to Menton and again helped on the excavation. She had now determined to train for a career in archaeology, and in the summer of 1921 enrolled in Egyptology classes at University College London with Flinders Petrie and Margaret Murray. She also studied paleontology with Dorothea Bate at the Natural History Museum in Kensington; took Arabic lessons at the School of Oriental Studies; and arranged for lessons in surveying from a young man at the School of Mines. Thus equipped, she applied in October to join Petrie's excavations for the British School of Archaeology in Egypt. She had found her career.

The Nile Valley

In 1921 the Petries were back in Abydos, where they had excavated the royal cemetery of the First Dynasty in 1901–3. Now Flinders Petrie had his eye on another area that promised early finds.[8] Several other helpers were coming, including two young men and two women. Caton-Thompson traveled out with the Petries and had her first experience of Petrie economy: "second class on trains, boats and hotels." Petrie was very amiable, taking her and another student to Luxor for "an educational three days." He was a wonderful guide. At Abydos they settled into tents, and most of the party started excavating a cemetery that appeared to contain some hundreds of archaic tombs. Caton-Thompson was left to roam the high desert all day, accompanied by one of Petrie's trained native assistants, a Qufti (Quftis were originally from Quft in Upper Egypt and became professional excavators, trustworthy and efficient) whose name was Mahmud. Together they searched the desert for flint artifacts.

Previously, on their way through Cairo, Caton-Thompson had met Dr. Hume, director of the Geological Survey of Egypt, who had assured her that the Paleolithic did not exist in Egypt. But she soon found quantities of flint implements of Mousterian date. On one of these excursions into the numerous cavelike apertures high up in the cliffs, she discovered a Christian hermit's cell. Hilda Petrie took charge of the recording, excavation, and publication of this hideaway; the party thereafter used it as a convenient place to store water and food in case of an insurrection, for there was political unrest in Egypt at this time, and the sound of shooting could be heard occasionally in the distance. Nothing untoward happened, however, and the dig moved, for the last part of the season, further north to Behnesa, the site of the city of Oxyrhynchus. Here the remains were Graeco-Roman, and the desert was too far away to visit.

After about a week Caton-Thompson left the Petries and returned to England. On the way she stopped in Helwan to collect microliths and stayed in Cairo for a few days to study the Old Kingdom exhibits in the museum. On the journey home she stopped for an exciting few days at Les Eyzies in the Dordogne to see the cave paintings and the museum. During the summer she helped the Petries at University College with their exhibition of the recent season's finds, among which were the best of her two thousand paleoliths.

Malta

In August, Margaret Murray, her former teacher, invited Caton-Thompson to join a small excavation in Malta, where, with the help of Murray's friend, Dr. Edith Guest, she planned to investigate the megalithic temple of Borg en Nadur, in the Marsaxlokk near St. George's Bay. Caton-Thompson's inclusion in the expedition had been the idea of Dr. Themistocles Zammit, director of Maltese antiquities. In the deep stalactitic cave of Ghar Dhalam nearby, sporadic excavation in the 1890s and later had revealed pottery of the Neolithic period, but underneath was a great mass of animal bones, including red deer, pigmy elephant, and hippopotamus. Several human teeth had also been found: all molars with a rare feature known as taurodontism, in which the roots are fused together—a characteristic found in Neanderthal skulls. This evidence suggested that at some time there must have been a land bridge between Malta and the African continent.[9]

In the late summer, the three women stayed for two months in a rented house in Birzebugga village, where they were visited from time to time by Dr. Zammit. While the temple party toiled in the heat, Caton-Thompson, with two men and four basket boys, worked in the shade and comparative coolness of the cave. She excavated with care, level by level, and found hippopotamus bones but not a single paleolith. Her conclusions were guarded, but she found no evidence to support the Neanderthal theory. (Subsequent digging elsewhere in the island has revealed that taurodontism was a feature of normal *Homo sapiens* Maltese skulls: the Ghar Dhalam teeth may well have belonged to a later level than the animal bones and have worked their way down.) As for the animals, the smallest were apparently later than those lying below, implying that they had become separated from the African continent during some remote geological age and that their descendants had grown smaller and smaller owing to worsening climatic conditions.[10]

The geological questions raised by this investigation convinced Caton-Thompson that if she wanted to become an expert in the prehistory of a region, she must seek training in order to understand questions of geology and physiography. She had already had this in mind, for before going to Egypt she had discussed the possibility with the principal of Newnham College, Cambridge. Now, in January 1933, she became a research fellow at Newnham, studying geology, zoology, paleontology, and anthropology with A. C. Haddon; prehistory with Miles Burkitt; and surveying with the polar explorer Frank Debenham. Privileged to live as a guest of Lady Darwin in Newnham Grange, she enjoyed to the full the social and intellectual life of Cambridge.

Egypt Again

At the end of her three-term fellowship, Caton-Thompson left Cambridge to return to Petrie's camp in Egypt. He was now excavating at Qau in Middle Egypt, the site of ancient Antaeopolis, some ten miles north of Asyut, where he was clearing Middle Kingdom tombs. Caton-Thompson was allotted sleeping quarters in an empty rock tomb, which she shared with three cobras whom she refused to disturb. As in Abydos, she slept with a revolver under her pillow in case of an unwelcome visit from a hyena. Her first assignment was to investigate the source of a find that had puzzled Petrie: a large collection of bones, both human and animal, which he assumed must have been washed down from the high desert in prehistoric times. Caton-Thompson went off into the eastern desert with camels and a Bedouin guide but returned two days later having found no evidence of a bone deposit. The collected bones, she suggested, represented the stock-in-trade of some early bone carver. Petrie, unconvinced, arranged for a geologist to come and see the bones the next winter, but this expert came to the same conclusion.[11]

Caton-Thompson next joined the camp of Petrie's assistants, Guy and Winifred Brunton, who were excavating at Badari, a few miles north of Qau. There they were finding tombs containing a handsome black-topped pottery different from the early prehistoric ware Petrie had called First Prehistoric. They named it Badarian. Caton-Thompson was convinced that more could be learned from an occupied village settlement than from a cemetery. She wrote:

> Whenever an early settlement is found, the habitation area furnishing that cemetery should be sought as well . . . Graves give us their special, quite invaluable contribution: the physical aspect of a people, the spiritual aspect, as seen both in burial habits and in artistic achievements, and lastly, a wealth of cultural information concerning them; a settlement, on the other hand, gives us of this last in an amplified form, contributing details of a people's everyday avocations and cultural status; and further it may, if reasonably undisturbed and continuously occupied, give us with a certainty to be achieved by no other method whatsoever the typological and chronological relation of one succeeding civilization to another.[12]

So she set out to find a village. Fortune favored her: along the base of the cliffs above the cemetery, spurs of limestone scree projected from the talus slopes into the cultivated plain. The sharp eyes of Ali Suefi, Petrie's most trusted and experienced digger, spotted Badarian sherds on one of these spurs at a place called Hammamiya. Caton-Thompson set her six men to work, each with his basket boys. She leveled and contoured the site, then subdivided it into strips ten feet wide and thirty-five feet long, pegged at five-foot intervals, within which the exact position and depth of every find was recorded. She sieved the soil from hearths and floors, searching for seeds and tiny artifacts. Then the strips were cleared, six inches at a time, by a gentle combing motion of the hoe. She never left the site while work was in progress and could safely say: "In no single instant was the position of an object taken on trust."[13] Six small circular huts built of mud and rubble were found, some containing a hearth, others possibly pens for sheep or goats. They had probably had domes or conical roofs of reeds or straw.

Caton-Thompson's methods were revolutionary. No prehistoric settlement site had ever before been scientifically excavated in Egypt. The care that Petrie and his followers took in recording the contents of a tomb was being, for the first time, applied to the houses of the living. It produced clear stratigraphic proof that his "sequence dating" for the remains of the prehistoric period had not been mistaken.[14] Her meticulous attention to detail, endless patience, and imaginative insight mark Caton-Thompson out as one of the pioneers of archaeological method more than sixty years ago. The excavation delighted Petrie and also Egyptologist Gerald Wainwright, who came to look at the site and declared the work "to rival in importance Carter's discovery of the tomb of Tutankhamen." It was to be many years before Caton-Thompson's methods would again be followed on a prehistoric site in Egypt.[15]

She was now anxious to establish whether the finely worked flints found in the Fayum, and often to be seen in dealers' shops in Cairo, could be related to those found in a Badarian context at Hammamiya. Petrie promised that his organization, the British School of Archaeology in Egypt, would underwrite the expense of an expedition and offered her five of his best Qufti workmen from Upper Egypt. For reasons of propriety she needed a female companion to keep her company in her camp. Miss Hughes, the sister of an old friend, volunteered to come; she had a little Arabic and would cook and occupy herself with sketching.

When the two arrived in Egypt in November 1924, they were warned that the political situation was tense: the British governor of the Sudan had been murdered in the streets of Cairo, and British troops patrolled them now. Undeterred, they bought a secondhand car and set off. For two months they explored an area of the Fayum, discovered a Neolithic occupation site, identified the shore level associated with the flints, and excavated a Middle Kingdom cemetery. Later Caton-Thompson looked back on these months as "utter bliss."[16] In February she went back to the Bruntons in Hammamiya for a few weeks, then traveled home by way of Crete and Greece, seeing for the first time the civilizations of the Minoans and Mycenaeans.

The Fayum

Caton-Thompson now decided that the Fayum needed further investigation. There were questions still to be answered by a trained geologist; someone better qualified than Caton-Thompson herself. Again, because she was working in a Muslim country, it would have to be a woman. Finding such a person was not easy, but at length Caton-Thompson was fortunate. Elinor Gardner, a Cambridge graduate who was teaching at a girls' school, was so eager to come that she relinquished her job; she had excellent credentials and some fieldwork experience in Africa. "From my first encounter," Caton-Thompson wrote later, "I was satisfied she would make a thorough job of the Pleistocene geology of the Fayum, and thus began a working alliance of thirteen nearly consecutive years and a friendship of over fifty."[17]

Petrie had disagreed with Caton-Thompson about her findings of the previous year. He had worked in the Fayum himself in the 1880s and had firmly adhered to the opinion of Herodotus that the depression had in his own time been filled with a great lake, which had been there since the Nile had broken into it in prehistoric times. Caton-Thompson believed that the evidence supported several different lake levels, of which the second, that of Herodotus's time, "showed a history of recession from an already low level."[18]

Her concession for 1925–26, as in the previous year, was a strip of desert north of the Birket Karun (Lake Moeris). While Gardner made a contoured map of the whole area, Caton-Thompson, with twenty-five basket boys, finished clearing the site, Kom W., of the Neolithic village. Sixty-five complete pots were found there, and on a ridge some miles away were found fifty-six basket-work granaries containing cereal grains, fine wicker baskets, and remains of linen textiles. As for the lake levels, their report identified two: a Paleolithic one and a lower Neolithic one, on both geological and archaeological grounds.[19]

Although Petrie still disagreed, he withdrew Caton-Thompson's financial support less because of his disapproval than because he had now, in

1926, removed his work altogether from Egypt on account of difficulties with the authorities of the Antiquities Department. He had, in fact, transferred his team and his funds to Palestine.[20] With sponsoring by the Royal Anthropological Institute, Caton-Thompson spent the next year (1927–28) writing her report. Elinor Gardner obtained a post as lecturer in geology at Bedford College for Women in London, where Caton-Thompson also had been given a room in which to work.

In October 1928 Caton-Thompson and Gardner were ready to set out again under the sponsorship of the Royal Anthropological Institute and several other learned bodies. They were to be joined by Elinor's brother, Captain Guy Gardner, whose experience in practical matters such as the running of a car was to be of great use to them. All was not to be clear sailing, however. Earlier that year they had learned that, after reported discoveries by an unauthorized research party (including one Count Byron de Prorok, who claimed to have found a cave, lake dwellings, and even dolmens), the concession Caton-Thompson applied for had already been given to the Oriental Institute of the University of Chicago. After some difficulties, she applied for two different concessions: one at the extreme west and one to the north of the lake. In Cairo she picked up eleven Quftis, an Arab cook, and Captain Gardner.

While excavating an Old Kingdom village after a heavy rain, Caton-Thompson noticed a line of green in the sand that proved to betray the presence of an irrigation channel leading to the houses of a Graeco-Roman settlement. She tried to enlist the help of the Royal Air Force in Cairo: aerial photography under these conditions should reveal the whole Ptolemaic irrigation system. But no help was forthcoming—a great opportunity, she felt, had been lost. While the two Gardners marked in this settlement area, Caton-Thompson reconnoitered a quarry of pure gypsum, in which earthenware jars, as well as thousands of flint picks and drill-cores, testified to a dynastic use from the Old Kingdom onward. The director of irrigation for the Fayum, Ahmed Ragheb Bey, was so impressed that he ordered the party to ignore the limits of their concession and gave them the services of ten more workmen. They were thus able to excavate 109 more Neolithic silos. Due to Elinor Gardner's astute observation of a "single grain of wheat on the desert surface," they were able to prove Prorok's discoveries nonsense.

The two Fayum expeditions had added a new chapter to the history of agriculture. Later, in 1951, the newly discovered method of dating by carbon 14 placed the wheat and barley from the silos at approximately 4000 B.C.[21] Assuming the contents of each granary to be the property of one family, Guinness's grain expert calculated that these Neolithic people were not essentially an agricultural folk but must have subsisted largely on fowling and fishing.

One incident during the season, which Caton-Thompson records in her memoirs, illustrates both her toughness and the hazards of camp life in the wilderness. Gardner, excavating with a few workmen some twenty miles away, sent a messenger to the camp with the news that her Ford truck had broken down. That same day the other vehicle in the camp, a six-wheeled Morris, also broke down, leaving the party without transport and creating the possibility that Gardner's party might run out of water. The nearest telephone was eighteen miles away. Caton-Thompson, who had had a difficult day, decided to walk there. She set off by fitful moonlight, accompanied by a trusty Qufti, and they reached Karanis at 5:30 the next morning. After a short rest she was able to contact Ragheb Bey at Medinet el-Fayum, and he immediately sent lorries to the aid of the stranded party.[22]

An extract from Caton-Thompson's report serves to illustrate the care with which she conducted her excavation of Kom W.:

> The mound was first planned to a one foot V.I. [vertical interval] and fixed bases were established. On this framework excavation proceeded on a latitude and longitude system; my ten men clearing shoulder to shoulder methodically across the mound, in measured strips 160 ft. long and 20 ft. wide, pegged out at 5-ft. intervals, with checks on the general contours by dumpy level readings on the pegs. Each strip was worked in layers until true bottom was reached. Each object was given a section letter, latitude and longitude figure and vertical depth, and its position recorded on squared paper and in field book. When each section was stripped, the bottom was levelled and a north to south section across the mound was made for every 20 ft. of longitude. Objects may thus be considered in their relative position *above the bottom,* which, rather than relative *depth from the top,* has always seemed to me the desideratum in stratigraphical work.[23]

Zimbabwe

Caton-Thompson's career now took an unexpected turn. The British Association for the Advancement of Science was due to meet in South Africa in the following year, 1929. One of the most pressing problems on their agenda was that of the remarkable field of stone-built ruins at Zimbabwe near Masvingo, some 150 miles south of Salisbury (now Harare) in what was then called Rhodesia. Much controversy surrounded this site and a number of smaller groups elsewhere.[24] No Bantu people, it was believed, could have been responsible for such an elaborate and sophisticated complex of buildings. The theory that Zimbabwe was the ancient Ophir, the source of King Solomon's gold, according to the Book of Kings, went back to the Portuguese missionaries of the sixteenth century. It was particularly popular with the devout Boer settlers and enthusiastically embraced by a young German geologist, Karl Mauch, who in 1871 made several investigations of the site and left plans of some of the buildings. The few artifacts he found convinced him that Zimbabwe had been the home of a "civilized nation"; and a piece of wood that he believed to be cedar confirmed his belief in the link with Solomon and the Queen of Sheba (in fact, it proved later to be a local African hardwood). In 1890, Cecil Rhodes had occupied Mashonaland for the British/South African Company, and many white settlers had come to live there. The idea of Zimbabwe as Ophir had been compared with the Sabaean temple of Marib in Yemen.

Several very inexpert excavations had been carried out with little regard for stratigraphy, and a number of objects had been found. These included some remarkable bird forms in soapstone, quite unlike anything known from the ancient Near East; gold beads and pottery akin to those still made in the area; as well as a number of foreign imports: fragments of oriental porcelain and Indian beads. One of the excavators was R. N. Hall, whose book, *The Ancient Ruins of Rhodesia,* had earned him the post of curator of the ruins in Zimbabwe.[25] His investigations, which eventually extended over most of the area, were carried out with an almost total disregard for stratigraphy, and the conclusions he drew from them confirmed the generally held opinion that the best workmanship was the earliest and that it derived directly from the ancient Orient.

It was clear that more scientific excavation was necessary. In 1904, the British Association had invited an old student of Flinders Petrie, David Randall MacIver, who had a record of careful excavation in Egypt, Nubia, and northern Italy, to carry out the first scientific excavation of Zimbabwe. He concluded that the ruins were medieval in date and entirely native Bantu in origin.[26] His verdict had evoked a storm of protest, especially among South Africans, who had difficulty in accepting such impressive monuments as the work of a people whom it was their custom (and in their interest) to regard as inferior.

As "a trained and experienced excavator," Caton-Thompson was now invited to undertake fresh investigations in an endeavor to establish, once and for all, the true identity of the builders. It was a formidable challenge, and she met it with characteristic determination. The journey to Zimbabwe was itself horrendous: from Suez by boat to Beira; a long train journey delayed by hurricane-force winds, then by a railway strike; roads made impassable by torrential rains; and flooded rivers to cross. It took her "a month's continuous endeavour" to reach her destination.[27] In Zimbabwe at last, she was joined by her two chosen helpers, both young women, who had come by sea via the Cape of Good Hope. Kathleen Kenyon, daughter of the director of the British Museum, Sir Frederick Kenyon, had recently graduated from Oxford and had a little excavating experience in England. She was to be responsible for photography and for maintaining the car, an old Dodge lorry obtained locally. D. Norie (Caton-Thompson always referred to them by their surnames), an architectural student, drew the plans and sections and did the pen and ink drawings for the final publication, many of them illustrating details of masonry more clearly than photographs. The curator of Zimbabwe, a Mr. Wallace, was helpful in recruiting local labor for the dig (Caton-Thompson's Arabic being useless here), and the three women stayed in a small tourist hotel not far from the site.

Apart from Zimbabwe they visited, planned, and photographed five other sites, and, in each, exploratory trenches were excavated for dating material. Most of these hilltop sites—Matendere, Chiwona, Mshosho, Hubvuni, and Dhlodhlo—presented difficulties in surveying, since they were perched on precipitous crags and built between huge boulders. One day, in Hubvuni, Caton-Thompson disturbed a leopard as she set up her plane table on the edge of a sheer drop. His growl and roar so startled her that she knocked the plane table over the edge and had to make a long detour down the steep hillside to recover it. The leopard fortunately went back to sleep.

Zimbabwe itself, by far the most complex and extensive site, is where most of her energies were spent. Here three groups of ruins are spread over a large area: the "Elliptical Building," otherwise called the Great Enclosure, whose high walls enclose several buildings and a high conical tower; the Acropolis or Hill Complex, a walled enclosure on the summit of a steep hill crowned with massive granite boulders that determined its contours; and a series of enclosure walls known as the Valley Ruins, which appear to be enclaves of hut dwellings and are named after various past investigators of the site. Studying their reports, she concluded that, with the exception of MacIver, former excavators had been "scandalously indifferent to stratigraphical record."[28]

A complete clearance to bedrock, she decided, was the only way to solve the problems raised by the excavations of earlier explorers. So she dug through the cementlike floors of huts and, for the first time, reached bedrock. On and even below the floors, she found fragments of glass beads and china dated by experts at the British Museum to the thirteenth or fourteenth century and traced to China, Persia, and India. Many fragments of pottery showed remarkable similarity with the wares of the modern villagers of the neighborhood, both in their simple bowl shapes and in the application of a graphite wash that gives a metallic shine to the surface of the vessel. On the summit of the acropolis she decided not to reexcavate in the main occupation area, which had been "ravaged" by the ill-advised excavations of previous investigators. Instead she cut trenches into the middens on the western side to a depth of twenty-four feet. All produced pottery, iron implements, and animal bones, and, again, a number of small glass beads, some of which the British bead expert Horace Beck pronounced to be early and probably Indian.[29]

Dating the Elliptical Building, where Hall and others had dug extensively, was more difficult. To date the huge Conical Tower, which proved to be solid, she tunneled underneath it with the assistance of a mining engineer. Here again, there was "still not one single item that is not in accordance with the claim of Bantu origin and medieval date."[30] Former investigators had been bewildered by the apparent sophistication of the stonework in the walls, which had been thought to indicate an origin in brickmaking. But the rectangular stone blocks, laid in courses, showed no attempt at bonding—mortar was never used, and the general design seemed to be based on sweeping curves, not, as in brick buildings, on rectangular shapes. She observed, moreover, that the granite boulders of the neighborhood, from which the stone must have been cut, tended when shattered to flake into slabs, which easily cracked into oblong shapes of the required size. The extensive use of daga (red clay mixed with granite particles) was, she pointed out, a feature unknown in any building in the Mediterranean world or anywhere in the ancient Near East, as was the incorporation of large boulders in the structures. Her report, published in 1931, concluded:

> Examination of all the existing evidence, gathered from every quarter, still cannot produce one single item that is not in accordance with the claim of Bantu origin and mediaeval date. The interest in Zimbabwe and the allied ruins should, on this account, to all educated people be enhanced a hundred fold; it enriches, not impoverishes, our wonderment at their remarkable achievement; it cannot

> detract from their inherent majesty; for the mystery of Zimbabwe is the mystery which lies in the still pulsating heart of native Africa.[31]

In April 1930, a loan exhibition of the finds from "Zimbabwe and Other Ancient Sites in Southern Rhodesia" was held in the Assyrian basement of the British Museum. Caton-Thompson's dating was not universally accepted, and there were lively exchanges in the press.[32] The introduction of the new method of dating by radiocarbon isotopes in the early 1960s, and the subsequent excavations by a number of archaeologists working for the National Museum and Historical Monuments of Southern Rhodesia, have to some extent modified Caton-Thompson's dates for the earliest occupation of the site. The deposits under the hut floors, which she recognized as predating any building, are now dated as early as the fourth or fifth century A.D., somewhat earlier than she had thought, but the earliest buildings have been dated, by the same method, to 1075–1440 (plus or minus 150 years). The "best period" of building, to which the Elliptical Building or Great Enclosure must be assigned, yielded glass beads carbon dated to the fifteenth to seventeenth centuries, more or less confirming Caton-Thompson's dating of the structures. In the preface to the second edition of her book *The Zimbabwe Culture,* she concluded:

> I am as confident as ever that the great buildings, as well as the lesser ones, are African in conception and execution, remembering that their builders even at their eventual best, though excellent dry stone masons were never architects. Their craft, I believe, developed at Zimbabwe from very small fragmented beginnings in the Early Iron Age of Period II (or possibly I) and grew gradually in building skill and size, in Periods II and IV under the stimulus of expanding ivory and gold exports and the import of desirable articles of which glass beads and ceramic fragments also survive. This expansion would be the expression of a stable, centralized, administrative system which reached its zenith in the 16th and 17th centuries under the energy and power of an autocratic and paramount dynasty centered at Zimbabwe, but controlling through semi-independent provincial chieftains, such as those at Ingombe and Mapungubwe, the extensive area of the "Golden Triangle" and perhaps beyond.[33]

The Kharga Oasis

The next area to demand Caton-Thompson's attention was the oasis of Kharga in the Libyan desert west of Egypt. Something was known of the area's history in the Dynastic period but nothing of its archaeological records in prehistoric ages. In historic times the inhabitants of the oasis had subsisted on water obtained from deep artesian wells. But she wanted to know whether human life existed here before that technique had been developed.

Kharga lies in a depression eighty miles long and twenty miles wide, about one hundred miles west of the Nile Valley. It could be reached only by camel or by one narrow-gauge truck railway built by the army during World War I. On her way south to Zimbabwe in 1928, and with an American friend, Mrs. Stout, for company, she collected her camping gear from Karanis in the Fayum and started by train southward, arranging to be dropped off at the place where the Kharga line branched off. It was Christmas morning; and before starting out they had enjoyed on the train the contents of a dinner basket containing cold turkey, plum pudding, and champagne. Caton-Thompson's best Qufti, Nasr el-Din, met them at the rendezvous and, when they reached Kharga, they spent many hours every day for a week prospecting for likely sites. Caton-Thompson obtained the promise of camels and found a place to store her gear until she should return.

Encouraged by what she saw, she wrote to Elinor Gardner that it was "full of Palaeolithic and Neolithic interest."[34] On her return to England from Africa, she reported finding quantities of flint implements. She argued that there must have been a camping ground where a group of numerous flaked tools were found together. She had persuaded the Royal Anthropological Institute of London (to whose council she had recently been elected) to support her expedition financially, and Gardner took a leave of absence from Bedford College, London. This time they started from Abydos; camels were not to be found in Kharga owing to an outbreak of illness. Accordingly, on December 9, 1930, they set off from Baliana with eight camels, tanks of water, three Quftis, and a cook. The 170-kilometer crossing of the desert took five and a half days. Reaching the scarp, they found paleoliths abundant in the cliffs. When their water ran out, they went down to the oasis to find a well and fodder for the camels.

Almost on the first day they discovered a fact of great importance: curious rounded mounds of hardened sand-rock tended to cap ridges. On some of these there were flint implements in profusion:

> Cores and flakes of china-white patination unlike anything I had seen in Egypt except "in situ" were concentrated round the base of a "crater." A trench across it disclosed a "floor" of Palaeoliths deeply

> buried, and further sections showed the "crater" to be spring deposits of Pleistocene age nine metres in depth of alternating clays, loams and pure white sands. The character of deposition suggests successive phases of quiescence and discharge under terrific pressure, the loam beds indicating a placid pool fringed by reeds and vegetation, the comminuted and distorted clays periods of violent activity. The water, almost without doubt, was sealed in the surface-water sandstone, and we have thus gained an insight into the capacity of this stratum to discharge under pressure in Pleistocene times.[35]

The excavation of some of these springs produced a fine collection of hand axes and also flakes, which she assumed to be arrowheads (though some later prehistorians disagreed on the grounds that they were too big—it may have been too early for the invention of the bow and arrow). Caton-Thompson and Gardner were also able to fly over the oasis a number of times, a piece of good fortune that they had scarcely dared to hope for. The enterprising wife of a wealthy South African, Sir Abe Bailey, whom Caton-Thompson had met in London, telegraphed them that she was coming out to join them. She flew solo from England to Tunis and thence along the North African coast in her De Havilland Moth aircraft. Hearing that she was coming, they made a landing strip for her with water on the sand, keeping six camels going to and fro from a well for six days, But this was not a great success, and the governor of the oasis helped them to find a better spot. Lady Bailey, who stayed for two weeks, was very welcome, for her airplane made it possible to take many aerial photographs and thereby obtain what Caton-Thompson called a "physiographic comprehension" of the area. This was the first time an airplane had ever collaborated in an archaeological expedition in Egypt.

The following winter (1932–33), Caton-Thompson had intended to return to Kharga, but her mother's serious illness kept her at home. Instead Gardner went with two assistants. They found several new mound-springs and a new pass into the oasis. At an International Congress of Anthropological and Ethnological Studies in University College London, attended by delegates from thirty-four countries, Caton-Thompson was able to mount an exhibit for Kharga Oasis, with a model fossil spring. The publication of all the results, the monumental *Kharga Oasis in Prehistory,* had to wait until after World War II, when, thanks to the sponsorship of Professor Gordon Childe, it was accepted as the first publication of the new Athlone Press of the University of London. Childe stipulated that the flints Caton-Thompson was allowed by the Egyptian government to bring home should be permanently housed in the Institute of Archaeology in London. To this she gladly agreed. A young student, Mary Nichol (who would marry Louis Leakey in 1936 and, with him, make the important discoveries of the Olduvai Gorge in Africa), skillfully drew the flints in the publication.

After her mother's death in 1934, Caton-Thompson moved back to Cambridge, deciding to live not with Lady Darwin but in the college itself, where there were fewer social interruptions. She was asked by the Royal Anthropological Institute to present the Rivers Lecture on her recent work. In view of her proposed title, "A Revision of Recent Research upon Stone Age Problems in Northern Africa," she realized she must broaden her knowledge. So she traveled to Oran to look at what was in the museum there, then to Algiers and Constantine by train, and finally to Tunis, where she spent two happy days in the Musée Alaoui examining its excellent collections of Aterian and Capsien Typique. Unfortunately, snow prevented any visit to a prehistoric site. After delivering the Rivers Lecture in April 1935, Caton-Thompson was presented with the Rivers Medal—the first time it had been granted to a woman.[36]

In January 1937, Caton-Thompson and Elinor Gardiner reluctantly decided that they must return to the Fayum in order to review the conclusions reached by the Geological Survey of Egypt, which in 1934 had again explored the Fayum depression. The survey team had excavated a number of sections and, while accepting the two women's interpretation of the successive levels of the Paleolithic lake, had concluded that the twenty-four-meter level, instead of being Neolithic, was that of the historical Lake Moeris, attributed by Herodotus to the Twelfth Dynasty pharaohs. They had sunk bore holes in the Hawara channel linking the Nile with the Fayum depression and found bedrock silt at seventeen meters below sea level.[37] The two women decided to reopen the investigation with the cooperation of an Egyptian geologist, Dr. Sulaiman Huzzayin, working for five weeks in February and March. Their good friend Ragheb Bey put the Irrigation Rest House at their disposal. In their report, assembled in April in a hotel in Jerusalem, Caton-Thompson set out, under the headings "Physiographical," "Structural," and "Archaeological," the difficulties they had encountered in accepting the survey's conclusions and ended with the words:

> We are aware of many obscure points and uncertainties in our interpretation of events. Indisputable proofs for the existence of a high-level historic Lake Moeris may yet be found, but we do not think, for the reasons stated in this paper, that they have yet been offered.[38]

Arabia

Gertrude Caton-Thompson now turned her mind to a project that she had long been contemplating: the Arabian peninsula had been little explored, and nobody had yet excavated an ancient site. For her publication of the Zimbabwe ruins she had asked Kathleen Kenyon to write a short survey of Arabian sea trade. It might, Caton-Thompson hoped, be possible to establish the existence of early trade contacts between Africa and southern Arabia. It was to be her last field expedition.

In London in 1934, she had first met Freya Stark, a writer of travel books, whose reputation rested not only on her very readable account of her explorations in Iran (*The Valley of the Assassins,* 1934), but also of her solo journey in search of the remote city of Shabwa.[39] Stark had not reached Shabwa, having contracted measles en route, but on the way she had passed through Hureidha, where, before again falling ill, she had noted monumental ruins with an appearance of considerable antiquity. In the end, Stark had to be evacuated by air by an RAF bomber squadron, which returned her to Aden on a stretcher. Stark's description of the trip, *The Southern Gates of Arabia,* was warmly received and awarded a medal by the Royal Scottish Geographical Society.[40]

A mutual friend, the orientalist Rhuvon Guest, introduced the two women. At that meeting Stark told Caton-Thompson that she intended to return to Arabia in the winter of 1937–38. Thenceforward they met fairly frequently, although their acquaintance can hardly be said to have blossomed into friendship, for they were temperamentally far too dissimilar. Stark may have thought that an expedition in the company of a distinguished archaeologist would enhance her own reputation as a scientific explorer. Caton-Thompson, for her part, would have relied on Stark's previous experience in a hitherto unfrequented country and her reputation as an Arabist to smooth the path of the scientists in this alien region so unaccustomed to Europeans. On the practical side, Stark's acquaintance with the influential Besse family in Aden could give the travelers a useful start. They both discussed the project with their mutual friend, Sydney Cockerell, curator of the Fitzwilliam Museum in Cambridge. He used his influence to procure substantial financial backing from Lord Wakefield (fifteen hundred pounds), while the Royal Geographical Society agreed to sponsor the expedition.

In 1936 Stark stayed with Caton-Thompson in her London flat while they planned the trip. Elinor Gardner was to accompany them as geologist, and Stark would act as liaison with the local people, from whom she had already enjoyed much hospitality. They would start from Makalla, where

Harold Ingrams was the British resident adviser to the sultan of Makalla and Seyun; his wife Doreen was, in those days, the only European woman living in the Arabian peninsula outside Aden.

During the summer of 1937, Caton-Thompson worked hard to improve her Arabic. In Egypt and in the oases, Petrie's "kitchen Arabic" had been serviceable enough, but in Arabia a more classical tongue would be spoken. Not having a great facility for languages, she compared herself unfavorably with Gertrude Bell. From March to May of that year she was in Palestine. While Gardner was helping Dorothea G. Bate in the Bethlehem excavation, finding Pleistocene vertebrates, Caton-Thompson went sightseeing for a week in the company of archaeologist friends. At Petra they found Margaret Murray at work, and at Tell Duweir they visited J. L. Starkey, who, with Olga Tufnell as his assistant, was excavating the large mound claimed to be Lachish.

The expedition started from Port Said in October.[41] After an uncomfortable journey though the Red Sea, they landed in Aden, where they met Ingrams, who was in Aden on business. He was somewhat dubious at the prospect of having to be responsible for three Englishwomen in an area of Arabia much subject to tribal disturbance. Part of their luggage had been lost owing to the incompetence of the shipping company and had gone on to Singapore. The fast of Ramadan imposed further delays. Finally they reached the port of Makalla by air on November 7, and were hospitably received by the Ingrams. For a few days, while their onward transport was being organized, Caton-Thompson walked about the neighborhood collecting flints—the first paleoliths from southern Arabia and an assortment of microliths.

On November 13 they set off in a two-ton lorry over the Jol with a large collection of packages, a native servant, a driver, and several hitchhikers, all heading for their first stop at Terim. It took them three days to reach the Wady Hadhramaut, 130 miles from the coast. Negotiating the precipitous descent into the wady, they stopped at Seiyun, where Caton-Thompson and Gardner prospected for several days around the town. Thereafter they traveled to Shibam, the headquarters of the Qa'iti sultans and the commercial center of the Hadhramaut. Between the picturesque tall houses piles of rubbish and open sewage defeated their search for a salubrious lodging, and all three women developed sore throats. Stark had a high temperature and with Ingrams' help was flown by one of Besse's planes back to a hospital in Aden. She was to rejoin the others later at Hureidha, their final destination ninety-two kilometers from Shibam. There the Mansab, head of the local Sayyids and an educated and traveled man, welcomed them. He put lodgings at their disposal in the town. Fearing more throat infections, they asked for accommodation out of town and were given a small, clean house on a hillside. They were also presented with a huge African who proved to be a most efficient and pleasant servant; he often accompanied Gardner on her mapping expeditions in the Wady Amad. Freya Stark rejoined them after Christmas, but she still was not well. At the end of January, Ingrams came to see her and advised a return to Aden. A plane was sent, but to the pilot's disgust she refused to go.

Earlier, before Christmas, Gardner had set out to explore the whole area and decide where they were going to excavate. Of two possible mounds, she chose the more promising. Under a huge heap of sand, about ninety minutes' walk from the town, was a stone building that proved to be an oblong stone-paved platform covering a deep pile of boulders. It was confined by a wall of ashlar masonry and reached by two flights of stone steps. Little remained of the superstructure but the bases of five stone pillars. At the foot of one was a heavy libation table with archaic lettering. A number of inscribed stones lay about, and many earlier dedications had been incorporated into the superstructure. Fifty-eight monumental inscriptions in archaic Hadhramoutic script were found. These, when later translated by Professor Ryckmans of Louvain, gave the name of the temple as Madabum or Madhab; the god to whom the dedications were made was the Semitic moon-god, Sin. Rough limestone images, incense burners, and offering tables with votive inscriptions were found.[42] Extramural shrines outside the latest of the three facades contained offering slabs on which ritual meals had been eaten. About the crudity of early Arabian sculpture, Caton-Thompson added a wry footnote to her publication: "I like to delude myself with the idea that Muhamed's ban on the fashioning of images was due to aesthetic distress at the result."[43]

In mid-January Caton-Thompson switched her workmen to the scree slopes of the cliffs bordering the valley, where several artificial caves had been observed; these might provide a clue to the date of the temple. Some were still inhabited by families, and many had clearly been used as tombs. In some, she found burials; most had been disturbed, the bones "as intermingled as spillikins." Among the grave goods were scraps of faience and gold, obsidian and flint microliths, and nearly five hundred beads. These, examined in England by Horace Beck and other experts, were dated to between the seventh and fifth centuries B.C. by comparison with similar beads from Syria and Iraq. Other distinctive glass beads and two sealstones showed Achaemenid influence. Therefore the tombs, and presumably also the temple, were probably to be dated to between the seventh and fifth centuries B.C. Forty-two skulls, submitted to Dr. Morant, were small and of low cephalic index.

At the beginning of February, choked by dust and exhausted by the heat, Caton-Thompson succumbed to acute bronchitis, and, as she suspected, malaria. She was forced to stop working and retire to bed. Stark, also, was still in and out of bed. Only Gardner carried on with her work and completed her intensive survey of the ancient irrigation system and geology of the region. On March 3, Caton-Thompson decided to start packing up. Stark announced her intention of returning to the coast by camel and by a different route in order to trace another incense road from Shabwa to Cana—the ancient incense port on the Red Sea at Husn al Ghurab. She urged the others to come with her, but both refused; the undertaking seemed not only difficult but also dangerous in view of the unsettled state of the tribes. Moreover, they were anxious to get home to report their findings, and Caton-Thompson was unwilling to deviate from the route agreed upon with Harold Ingrams. Stark's journey took three weeks and was not without danger. Joining a caravan, she reached Husn al-Ghurab, which she identified as the Himyaritic incense port of Cana. Because of the hostility of the local people, she had to retreat, riding through the night to Balhaf, where she was rescued by sea to Aden.

Predictably, the collaboration had not been a success, as Caton-Thompson and Stark were not temperamentally compatible. Caton-Thompson had been irritated by Freya's lack of interest in the excavation, her constant fraternizing with the women of Hureidha, and her frequent demands for attention. Stark, perhaps defensive because she lacked academic status and training, professed to find the scientists' attitudes toward their workmen unfeeling. She also disapproved of women wearing trousers, as Caton-Thompson and Gardner did. In her account of the expedition, *A Winter in Arabia,* published the following year, she drew an unflattering portrait of her companions.[44] Both Cockerell and her publisher John Murray tried in vain to get her to tone down her portrayal of "the archaeologist" whom everyone recognized. The geologist, whom she calls "Alinur," got off rather more lightly but was included in her general charge of insensitivity and tactlessness toward their Arab hosts. Many years later, when Caton-Thompson published her autobiography, she was able to retaliate, depicting Stark as a hypochondriac whose contribution to the scientific results of the expedition had been negligible.

Later Years

With World War II intervening, Caton-Thompson was not able to publish her report on her last archaeological venture until 1944. Early in the war she returned to Newnham College, Cambridge, and worked on her various publications. Her afternoons were spent planting and growing vegetables, and keeping bees to supplement the meager rations of the college. For a time she was far from well and suffered spells of dizziness. Most of her possessions from the London flat, including the notes of her published excavations, were destroyed by enemy action when a furniture depository in London received a direct hit. The report on her latest results, a catalog of the first Paleolithic implements to be found in Arabia, was ultimately published by the Prehistoric Society.

In 1945, when the tenure of her Cambridge fellowship expired, she bought a house in Cambridge, which she shared with a friend and colleague, Dorothy Hoare, a university lecturer in Anglo-Saxon. Hoare eventually married an archaeologist, Toty de Navarro, also a Cambridge don, who was an authority on the European Iron Age, and he shared the house during term time. During the vacations, they invited Caton-Thompson to join them in their beautiful seventeenth-century manor house, Court Farm, in the town of Broadway in Worcestershire. In 1956 they all retired from Cambridge and went to live permanently at Court Farm. This was to be Caton-Thompson's home for the rest of her life. Here she could share her friends' enjoyment of gardening and love of music, but when she wished to be private, she could retire to her own comfortable sitting room. Court Farm had a large room that could serve as a concert hall, and many of their musical friends came to give recitals, including (later Dame) Myra Hess, the pianist, and the young cellist, Jacqueline du Pré. Here Caton-Thompson was supremely happy, sharing holidays in the countryside with her friends; sailing in Norfolk; fishing in Wales and Scotland; and watching the de Navarros' son, Michael, grow up. London was easily accessible, and she could attend the meetings of such learned societies as commanded her attention while continuing to enjoy concerts and theater.

Hureidha had been her last excavation, but in July 1955 Caton-Thompson returned to South Africa for the Third Pan-African Congress. This time she flew to Nairobi, with an overnight stop at Wady Halfa on the way, and thence traveled by car to Bulawayo. She toured the excavations at Khami, which had revealed the same architectural features as her site at Dhlo-Dhlo, and took a party of archaeologists to Zimbabwe. The conference itself opened on July 19 at Livingstone, Victoria Falls. Caton-Thompson was elected to the Committee for Cultural Terminology, charged with clarifying the nomenclature applied to Stone Age civilizations. There were many lectures and excursions to the falls, culminating in a banquet. For the second part of the Congress, in August and September, the delegates traveled to Lusaka in Northern Rhodesia (now Zambia) and to Broken Hill and other Paleolithic sites. In all, their journey took them about two thousand miles. Caton-Thompson, now sixty-seven years old, was suffering from an ear infection picked up on the journey, but was much admired for never flagging or giving up on the most exhausting of excursions.

Finally, when the Congress had dispersed, she flew to Nairobi, where she called on Louis Leakey, then curator of the museum, who had been a friend since early Cambridge days. He took her around his own creation, the Coryndon Museum, and showed her a number of paleontological sites in the vicinity. She was much impressed by his enthusiasm and determination, against all odds, to found a national park; and admired his championship of the Kikuyu people, in the troubled days leading up to Kenyan independence. When she returned to London, she was forcefully involved in the negotiations between Nairobi and London, which eventually led to the foundation of the British Institute of the History and Archaeology of East Africa, on the governing council of which she served until 1971.

Throughout her life Caton-Thompson kept a diary, and her autobiography records the friendships, occupations, and pleasures of her daily life as well as her archaeological preoccupations. Her family circumstances had not been altogether happy: her father's early death, the failure of her mother's second marriage, the mental decline of her only brother, who died in 1940 after an eleven-year stay in a nursing home, where he had been frequently visited by his sister. The one deep love of her life, a childhood friend who (unaware of her feelings for him) had been posted to Egypt at the start of World War I as an Intelligence officer in the British Army, was murdered by the Senussi in the Libyan desert in 1916 (could it have been this that drew her to Kharga?). She confessed to "feminist sympathies," which led her to prefer women doctors; and many of her close friends were women archaeologists: Dorothea Bate, the paleontologist and ornithologist, "a really intimate friend"; Mary Leakey, whose work in East Africa, with her husband Louis, Caton-Thompson deeply admired; Winifred Lamb, at whose house in Borden Wood with its beautiful grounds she was a frequent visitor; and Dorothy Garrod, in whose company she explored the Paleolithic sites in the Dordogne and whose cave excavations at l'Angle sur l'Anglin she visited in 1950. It was with Winifred Lamb that she had once embarked on a walking tour of the Peloponnese—an expedition that had been brought to an abrupt end when Lamb developed whooping cough.

Conclusion: Honors and Accolades

The intellectual community recognized Caton-Thompson's archaeological achievements, and she received many honors. In 1932 she was given the Peake Award of the Royal Geographic Society, and in 1934 and 1946 the Rivers and Huxley Medals of the Royal Anthropological Institute. In 1944, she was elected a member of the British Academy—the second woman to be accorded that honor (the first had been the economist Beatrice Webb, twenty years earlier). In that same year she was made an honorary doctor of literature (D.Litt.) by the University of Cambridge; she and one of the other recipients at the ceremony, the diseuse Ruth Draper, were the first women to be awarded honorary degrees by that university. She was elected a Fellow of University College London, and an honorary Fellow of Newnham College, Cambridge. In 1954 she received the Burton medal of the Royal Asiatic Society "for eminent services in oriental exploration and research." She was several times reappointed governor of Bedford College, University of London, and also of the School of Oriental Studies at the same university. Although she was never involved in formal academic teaching, she strongly influenced the Board of Studies in Archaeology of London University, owing to her admiration for Sir Mortimer Wheeler, who founded the Institute of Archaeology in the years before World War II.

The war had ended Caton-Thompson's active career as a field excavator, but she continued to travel widely and to attend scientific conferences all over Europe. To archaeology she was a generous benefactor. In 1968 she bought an annuity and with the surplus was able to donate twenty thousand pounds to the National Trust for the preservation of the English countryside and the same amount to the British Academy, with the proviso that it should be allocated, preferably to Fellows, for work in North Africa. The income from this gift, the Caton-Thompson Fund for Archaeological Research, was allotted to the Society for Libyan Studies for their excavations.

In spite of arthritis and an eventual double hip replacement, Caton-Thompson was able to continue traveling in the company of the de Navarros and other friends, visiting France and Switzerland, Corfu and Cyprus, Spain and Greece, as well as New York, Washington, and Boston on one trip to America. Once she went to Ceylon, on the lookout for glass beads such as those she had found in Zimbabwe; she spent an afternoon hunting for beads in a field that had been cleared by a bulldozer, but to no avail. For years she enjoyed annual visits to the Highlands of Scotland, where she was an enthusiastic fly-fisher. In 1968, the death of Dorothy Garrod ended, as Caton-Thompson said, "my last direct link with pioneer fieldwork in the Near East and a friendship of forty-six years."[45] In 1974 she had the satisfaction of knowing that the results of the new "thermoluminescence" dating for her sequence of three pre-dynastic industries at Hammamiya confirmed their stratigraphic order to have been correct.[46]

The last event recorded in Gertrude Caton-Thompson's memoirs is the death of Toty de Navarro in February 1979, but she lived on with Dorothy in their tranquil house in Broadway. Her autobiography, *Mixed Memoirs,* was privately printed in 1983, circulating only to a few of her friends and to libraries of one or two universities. She died at the age of ninety-seven at Court Farm on April 18, 1985. In her will she left a generous legacy to University College for the scientific work of her old department, Egyptology. It has enabled students and staff to pursue their research in Egypt and to undertake urgent restorations in the Petrie Museum.[47]

Professor Harry Smith, in a recent talk to the Friends of the Petrie Museum, remembered his last visit to Gertrude. "I had the privilege," he said, "of visiting her in the late 1970s in her beautiful home in the Wiltshire village of Broadway, on the occasion of her munificent bequest to the Egyptology Department as it then was; already in her late 80s, her pose was as upright and her mind as razor-sharp as ever, and she had that ethereal form of beauty, unrelated to good looks, sometimes manifested by very old people of exceptional character."

WORKS BY GERTRUDE CATON-THOMPSON
A SELECTED BIBLIOGRAPHY

Books, Monographs, and Articles

"The Recent Geology and Neolithic Industry of the Southern Fayum Desert." "The Neolithic Industry of the Northern Fayum Desert." *Journal of the Royal Anthropological Institute* 56 (1926): 301–23.

"Explorations in the Northern Fayum." *Antiquity* 1 (1927): 326–40.

G. Brunton, coauthor. *The Badarian Civilisation.* London: British School of Archaeology in Egypt, 1928.

E. W. Gardner, coauthor. "Recent work on the Problem of Lake Moeris." *Geographical Journal* 73 (1929): 20–58.

"Zimbabwe, Based on the British Association Report." *Antiquity* 3 (1929): 20–28, 424–33.

The Zimbabwe Culture: Ruins and Reactions. Oxford: Clarendon Press, 1931.
"The Prehistoric Geography of Kharga Oasis." *Antiquity* 5 (1931): 221–26.
"Zimbabwe Culture: Guesses and Facts." *Man* 31 (1931): 77–84.
"The Royal Anthropological Institute's Prehistoric Research Expedition to 'Kharga Oasis, Egypt,' Preliminary Outline of the Season's Work." *Man* 31 (1931): 91ff.
"The Prehistoric Geography of Kharga Oasis." *Geographical Journal* 80 (1932): 369–406.
"The Royal Anthropological Institute's Prehistoric Research Expedition to Kharga Oasis, Egypt: The Second Season's Discoveries." *Man* 32 (1932): 129–35.
"Some Palaeoliths from South Arabia." *Proceedings of the Prehistoric Society* 19 (1933): 189–218.
E. W. Gardner, coauthor. *The Desert Fayum.* 2 vols. London: Royal Anthropological Institute, 1934.
"A Commentary on Dr. Laidler's Article on Beads in Africa South of the Zambesi." *Proceedings and Transactions of the Rhodesia Scientific Association* (1936): 10–18.
E. W. Gardner and S. Huzzayin, coauthors. "Lake Moeris: Reinvestigations and Some Comments." *Bulletin de l'Institut d'Égypte* 19 (1937): 243–303.
"Geology and Archaeology of the Hadhramaut, South-west Arabia: Preliminary Notes on Lord Wakefield's Expedition." *Nature* 142 (1938): 139.
E. W. Gardner, coauthor. "Climate, Irrigation, and Early Man in the Hadhramaut." *Geographical Journal* 93 (1939): 18–38.
The Tombs and Moon Temple of Hureidha (Hadhramaut). Research Report no. 13. London: Society of Antiquaries, 1944.
"The Levalloisian Industries of Egypt." *Proceedings of the Prehistoric Society* 12 (1946): 56–120.
"The Aterian Industry: Its Place and Significance in the Palaeolithic World." *Royal Anthropological Institute of Great Britain and Ireland* (1947).
"Some Palaeoliths from South Arabia." *Proceedings of the Prehistoric Society* 19 (1953): 189–218.
"The Evidence of South Arabian Palaeoliths in the Question of Pleistocene Land Connections with Africa." *Proceedings of the Third Pan-Africa Congress on Prehistory* (1955): 380–84.
"Zimbabwe, All Things Considered." *Antiquity* 38 (1964): 99–102.
The Zimbabwe Culture: Ruins and Reactions. 2d ed., with a new introduction by the author. London: Cass Library of African Studies, 1971.
Elizabeth Whittle, coauthor. "Thermoluminescence of the Badarian." *Antiquity* 49 (1975): 89–97.
Mixed Memoirs. Gateshead: Paradigm Press, 1983.
(Obituary) Graham Clark *Gertrude Caton Thompson 1888–1985* in *Proceedings of the British Academy* 71 (1935) 523–31.
Garlake, P. S. *Great Zimbabwe* London, Thames and Hudson. 1973, 80–83.
See also G. Clark, *Prehistory at Cambridge and Beyond* (Cambridge, 1989) 10, 43, 104.
———. *Proceedings of the British Academy* 71 (1985): 523–31.
G. Daniel, *A Hundred and Fifty Years of Archaeology* (Cambridge, 1975) 197–98, 279, 285, 315.

NOTES

1. G. Caton-Thompson, *Mixed Memoirs* (Gateshead: Paradigm Press, 1983).
2. Ibid., 40.
3. See Arthur Salter, *Memoirs of a Public Servant* (London: Faber and Faber, 1961).
4. Caton-Thompson, *Mixed Memoirs,* 74.
5. Ibid., 66.
6. Ibid., 78.
7. Ibid., 45.
8. See M. S. Drower, *Flinders Petrie: A Life in Archaeology* (London: Gollancz, 1985), 352ff.
9. See J. D. Evans, *Malta* (London: Thames and Hudson, 1959), 35–36.
10. *The Times,* November 20, 1922.
11. Flinders Petrie, *Antaeopolis: The Tombs of Qau,* British School of Archaeology in Egypt 43 (London, 1928).
12. Caton-Thompson, *Mixed Memoirs,* 91.
13. G. Brunton and G. Caton-Thompson, *The Badarian Civilisation,* British School of Archaeology in Egypt 46 (London, 1928), pt. 11.
14. Ibid., 73ff.
15. Michael Hoffman, *Egypt before the Pharaohs* (London: Routledge and Kegan Paul, 1980), 137ff.
16. Caton-Thompson, *Mixed Memoirs,* 100.
17. "The Neolithic Industry of the Northern Fayum Desert," *Journal of the Royal Anthropological Institute* 56 (1926): 309–23.
18. Gertrude Caton-Thompson, "The Desert Fayum," *Journal of the Royal Anthropological Institute,* 1954, 84.
19. Ibid.
20. Drower, *Flinders Petrie,* 363ff.
21. Caton-Thompson, *Mixed Memoirs,* 107–8.
22. Ibid., 110.
23. *The Desert Fayum,* 24.
24. For a history of the Zimbabwe controversy see Peter Garlake, *Great Zimbabwe* (London: Thames and Hudson, 1973).
25. R. N. Hall and W. G. Neal, *The Ancient Ruins of Rhodesia* (London: Macmillan, 1906).
26. D. Randall MacIver, *Mediaeval Rhodesia* (London: Macmillan, 1906).
27. Caton-Thompson, *Mixed Memoirs,* 137–38.
28. G. Caton-Thompson, *The Zimbabwe Culture: Ruins and Reactions* (Oxford: Clarendon Press, 1931), 1st ed. 2.
29. G. Caton-Thompson. *The Zimbabwe Culture,* 1st ed. 187–88.
30. G. Caton-Thompson. *The Zimbabwe Culture,* 1st ed., 99.
31. Caton-Thompson, *The Zimbabwe Culture,* 1st ed., 199.
32. R. Summers, "The Dating of the Zimbabwe Ruins," *Antiquity* 29 (1955).
33. *The Zimbabwe Culture: Ruins and Reactions,* 2d ed. (London: Cass, 1971), 31.
34. Caton-Thompson, *Mixed Memoirs,* 165.

35. Caton-Thompson, "The Prehistoric Geography of Kharga Oasis," *Antiquity* 5 (1931): 226.

36. Caton-Thompson, *Mixed Memoirs,* 165.

37. H. O. Little, "Recent Geological Work in the Fayum," *Bulletin de l'Institute d'Égypte* 18 (1935–36): 201–40.

38. Gertrude Caton-Thompson, E. W. Gardner, and S. Huzzayin, "Lake Moeris: Reinvestigations and Some Comments," *Bulletin de l'Institut d'Égypte* 19 (1937), 243–303. See further Fred Wendorf and Romvald Schild, *The Prehistory of the Nile Valley* (New York: Academic Press, 1976), 151ff.

39. Shabwa was said to have been the Himyaritic capital and center of the incense route. Stark's solo journey in search of Shabwa, in the interior of the Hadhramaut, was undertaken in the winter previous to her meeting Caton-Thompson.

40. Freya Stark, *The Southern Gates of Arabia* (London: John Murray, 1936).

41. For accounts of what follows, see Molly Izzard, *Freya Stark: A Biography* (London and Sydney: Hodder and Stoughton, 1993), 111ff; and Jane Fletcher Geniesse, *Passionate Nomad: the Life of Freya Stark* (New York: Random House (1999), 201ff.

42. G. Caton-Thompson, *The Tombs and Moon Temple of Hureidha (Hadhramaut),* Research Report no. 13 (London: Society of Antiquaries, 1944), 157ff.

43. Ibid., 91 n. 2.

44. Freya Stark, *A Winter in Arabia* (London: John Murray, 1940).

45. Caton-Thompson, *Mixed Memoirs,* 332.

46. Ibid.

47. Rosalind M. Janssen, *The First Hundred Years: Egyptology at University College, London, 1892–1992* (London: University College London, 1992), 86.

Dorothy Annie Elizabeth Garrod

(1892–1968)

Ofer Bar-Yosef and Jane Callander

DOROTHY GARROD, DISNEY PROFESSOR of Archaeology at the University of Cambridge from 1939 to 1952, was the first woman to hold a chair in either of Britain's ancient universities. Her name is well known to any prehistorian who works in the Old World and, more specifically, in the Mediterranean basin. Her excavations on Mount Carmel, which led to the uncovering of human fossils in the caves there, identify this undertaking as one of the most decisive in interpreting the course of human evolution. The finds from her excavations in Tabun and Skhul caves were, and remain, central to any discussion on the origins of modern humans and the demise of the Neanderthals. One of her main discoveries was the Natufian culture, first encountered in Shukbah cave and later in El-Wad. This prehistoric culture is now known to stand, as her original interpretation almost predicted, on the threshold of the origins of agriculture in the Near East, particularly in the Levant.

As we tell the story of her life as one of the founding prehistorians of this region, we will set it, as much as possible, in the social-historical context within which her career took a stellar trajectory.

The Early Years

Dorothy Annie Elizabeth Garrod was born in 1892 into the secure and comfortable world of the late Victorian English upper middle class, the only daughter in a devoted family with a fine inheritance of achievement in science and medicine. Her grandfather (Sir Alfred Garrod, physician), her father (Sir Archibald Garrod, physician and biochemist), and uncle (also Alfred, physiologist and zoologist) were all Fellows of the Royal Society. On her mother's side, her grandfather, Sir Thomas Smith, was a distinguished surgeon, particularly noted for the dexterity of his hands.[1] Her three brothers were expected to carry on the family scientific tradition. However, expectations for Garrod were perhaps different, though in the year of her birth higher education for women was slowly gaining ground, with five women's colleges already in existence at Oxford and Cambridge. Nevertheless, even in the most enlightened families, education for daughters was viewed differently from that of sons. Thus, until she was nine years old, Garrod was taught at the family home at Merton in Suffolk by a series of governesses. One of these, Isobel Fry, gave her young pupil such a thorough grounding in Latin, arithmetic, and history that Garrod remembered it with appreciation all her life. She would later say—only half joking—that their visit to Roman Verulamium (now the town of St. Albans) was the inspiration for her future career.[2] For an East Anglian family, Cambridge was the natural choice for higher education. She took the entrance examination at a boarding school in Hertfordshire and, in 1913, entered Newnham College to read History and Classics, beginning an association that would last for the rest of her life. No degree course in archaeology yet existed at either Oxford or Cambridge.

When Dorothy Garrod arrived at Newnham, the female students there (and at Girton, Cambridge's other women's college) were still denied full membership in the university. Women had been admitted in 1881 and could take the honors examination for the Bachelor of Arts degree, called the tripos at Cambridge. But it would take some twenty years before they were included in the official lists of results and a further twenty before—in 1921—they were admitted to take degrees. Full admission only came in 1948. In this reactionary practice, Cambridge—and Oxford also—lagged behind London and some provincial universities where, since the late nineteenth century, women could be full university members. Nevertheless, the women students at Newnham enjoyed the highest quality tuition, often responding with great distinction, though when they left, those seeking a professional career found many openings barred to them and were often advised to learn shorthand and typing.[3]

In her first year, this might have been the prospect facing Dorothy Garrod. In 1914, her second year, war turned her secure future upside down, as it would for so many of her generation and class. In 1916 her brother Thomas died of wounds at the age of twenty-one while serving in France. The next year her eldest brother, Alfred Nöel—already a qualified doctor aged twenty-nine—was also killed in France while serving with the Royal Army Medical Corps. It seemed that the youngest, Basil, would survive; then he too died just before demobilization in 1919, in the influenza pandemic that caused more death than the guns of the entire war.

Garrod had left Newnham in 1916 with a second-class degree—perhaps inevitable in that traumatic year—determined also to play her part in the Great War. She served briefly in the Ministry of Munitions, then followed her brothers to France with the Catholic Women's League, converting to that faith in 1917. When she was demobilized in Germany in 1919, she was alone in her generation—her brothers dead and the man she might have married also swept away. In her grief, she pledged that for her bereaved parents' sake her life should compensate in achievement for her lost brothers.[4] As yet it was not clear which direction she should take.

Garrod joined her parents in Malta, where her father was now head of war hospitals. It was his inspired suggestion that she should occupy her time and her mind among the island's spectacular prehistoric antiquities. When Archibald Garrod returned to England in 1921 as Regius Professor of Medicine at Oxford, the family's move there set Garrod on her lifetime's course. She registered for the university diploma course in anthropology under the direction of its legendary founder and Reader in Social Anthropology, Robert Ranulph Marett. Inspired by him, she later told her student Mary Kitson Clark, the "determination to be a prehistorian, and particularly in the Old Stone Age, came over her in one second, like a conversion . . . She was, after the war, in great turmoil—what was she to do with her life? And it came over her in a flash, that was what she was to do."[5]

Formative Influences and Studies

R. R. Marett realized his dream of founding a school of anthropology at Oxford with the help of the archaeologist and historian John Linton Myres, secretary of the Oxford Committee for Anthropology, whose love of archaeology ensured its place in the school's syllabus. In 1910 Marett persuaded the university to invite Émile Cartailhac, the doyen of French prehistory, to Oxford to accept an honorary doctorate and to lecture on Quaternary art. His visit was a triumph and indirectly shaped Garrod's future as a prehistorian. Cartailhac returned the university's compliment by inviting Marett and W. J. Sollas, Oxford's Professor of Geology and a keen scholar of ancient man, to tour the French Paleolithic caves with him. Count Bégouën, Denis Peyrony (archaeologist of La Ferrassie), Victor Commont (the legendary exponent of the Somme gravels), and, above all, the Abbé Henri Breuil were also included. Watching Breuil instantly recognize typologically important implements in a pile of assorted flint tools or define the outline of an animal in a mass of scratched lines on a cave wall, Marett "came to recognise that prehistory was no mere pastime for the irresponsible amateur, but a genuine branch of science."[6]

Garrod gained her diploma with distinction in 1921. Her contemporaries at Oxford were a mixture of generations, survivors of the war and those too young to have served in it. Among the latter was a young man nine years her junior from a Catholic family deeply rooted in English history, an aesthete and homosexual, Francis Turville-Petre. On his sudden—and apparently scandalous—departure from Oxford he went, with Marett's encouragement and inspired with his enthusiasm for prehistory, to Palestine where he and Garrod would later meet again.[7] Meanwhile, Newnham College rewarded her success in the diploma with a Travelling Scholarship. She went to France with Marett's introductions to the French prehistorians who had so fired his imagination before the war, when she was still a schoolgirl. Now she too saw the wonders of the Paleolithic caves. At Count Bégouën's house she met the Abbé Breuil, who agreed to take her as his pupil for two years at the Institut de Paléontologie Humaine in Paris. Writing his obituary forty years later, she remembered the first task Breuil set her. She was to study Victor Commont's extensive work on the Somme gravels. There, in the mid–nineteenth century, the customs officer and amateur antiquarian Jacques Boucher de Perthes had first identified flint bifaces, later established—with British help—as genuine artifacts from the Lower Paleolithic, the period that now preoccupied the Abbé Breuil. "I learned later," wrote Garrod all those years later, "that this was a test, and that if I had come back to him saying that I had understood, and had no particular difficulties, he would have taken no further interest in me." Breuil's teaching continued to be unorthodox.

> Twice a week . . . he would be available—either in the Library or in his room or among the prehistoric collections. It would then be up to me to present my problems, which he would discuss in a masterly way opening up all the time fresh perspectives. On the other hand, if no questions or ideas had been forthcoming from me, I do not think he would have suggested any. It was the pupil who must take the initiative and think for himself.[8]

As she settled to work in the Institut basement, she discovered shared experiences with the paleontologist and Jesuit priest working at the next table. Pierre Teilhard de Chardin had served as a wartime stretcher-bearer. He also knew R. R. Marett, having visited the Jersey Paleolithic cave La Cotte de Saint-Brelade with him in 1919.[9] Garrod was now finding her Catholic faith hard to reconcile with her new knowledge of human prehistory. The intellectual honesty that had obliged her to admit to Breuil that the Somme gravels left her baffled caused her to withdraw from the church. The Abbé Breuil could not help her, or she did not ask him. Teilhard, twelve years her senior, had reasoned his way through the conundrum to his own satisfaction (though not always that of his Jesuit superiors), and his philosophy of evolution showed her a way back to her faith.

During her two years with the Abbé Breuil, Garrod showed herself capable of sustained, intensive work. In this formative age of French prehistory, no chance could be lost to work with the great men who inspired her as they had inspired her tutor Marett. The French prehistorians were a powerful network and Breuil's patronage inestimable. It is a testament to her abilities and the potential they observed in her that they welcomed this still comparatively young Englishwoman in the field. In the summer of 1921 she was taking her first lessons in excavation with Louis Didon at his rock shelter site Labattu, near Perigueux. One evening, the American anthropologist George Grant MacCurdy, from Yale University, arrived at their hotel with students of his newly established American School in France of Prehistoric Studies. They were making an excursion to Labattu from their work at Dr. Henri-Martin's legendary site of La Quina (Charente). The school was Henri-Martin's idea and for MacCurdy, then aged fifty-eight, it was the realization of a long-held dream: "a prehistoric link that would bind the Old World to the New World." Already his friends included the major scholars of both worlds. MacCurdy showed an immediate interest in Dorothy Garrod, and the friendship that began as MacCurdy and his students worked the following afternoon at Labattu would have profound consequences both for her future and for prehistoric studies. When they met again the next year as guests of the Cambridge prehistorian Miles Burkitt (also a former student of Breuil), MacCurdy noted her rapidly developing interest and experience.[10] She had by then worked at Les Eyzies with Denis Peyrony; in Isturitz with the Saint-Periers; with Jean Bouyssonie in Corrèze; and at La Quina with Henri-Martin. La Quina was to produce remains of twenty-seven Neanderthal individuals: particularly important for Garrod's future work were fragments of a juvenile cranium. She also found a lifelong friend in Henri-Martin's daughter Germaine.

The First Book

Despite her enduring love of France and French prehistory, Garrod had not ignored her own country. Her name first appears in the membership list of the Prehistoric Society of East Anglia in 1922,[11] and she made good use of her contact with fellow members in her research for her first book, *The Upper Palaeolithic Age in Britain.* The Upper Paleolithic in Britain was a neglected area. "The reason for this," she explained, "is to be found in the fact that the literature relating to [sites] is buried for the most part in ancient numbers of scientific journals, while the collections themselves are dispersed in museums all over the country." This was a situation not helped by the fact that most sites were excavated before the de Mortillet system of classification by type-names, associated with French sites, came into use in Britain.[12] An opportunity thus presented itself that Garrod was ideally situated to seize, and she did so. In Paris, Marcellin Boule and Abbé Breuil gave her full access to the Institut collections and library, help matched—to judge from the people and institutions she acknowledged—by the archaeological community in Britain.

As Garrod worked on the book at her parents' Suffolk home in the summer of 1924, George Grant MacCurdy brought students from his renamed American School of Prehistoric Research to the region for their annual study tour in Europe. He was now director of the school, widened in scope and occupying fully half his time. Between visits to East Anglian scholars and sites, they were given tea at the Garrod home. MacCurdy recorded how "Miss Dorothy" added to their enjoyment with a lecture based on her research.[13]

The Upper Palaeolithic Age in Britain, published by the Oxford University Press in 1926, gained Garrod a B.S. from the university. The book was meticulous and comprehensive. Cave and open-air sites are surveyed in detail, with their archaeological remains listed, described, and drawn. This work created, for the first time, a synthesis uniting the British Isles culturally with the continent of which they were physically a part during the Upper Paleolithic. Breuil contributed a preface praising Garrod's sustained and enthusiastic labors in filling a genuine lacuna in the scientific literature of her own country. This was all the more praiseworthy, he added—somewhat pityingly—since Britain was deprived by its harsh climate of participation in the flowering of cave art in France and Spain. Only many years later did John Campbell make another attempt to summarize the Upper Paleolithic of Britain, and his work clearly shows that Garrod's conclusions remain essentially valid.[14]

The Excavations at Devil's Tower

The publication of her book established Garrod as a significant figure in British prehistory, and she was ready to begin her own field project. Breuil gave her the opportunity that arose from his wartime attachment to the French embassy in Madrid. In Spain he had, inevitably, combined prehistoric exploration with diplomatic duties whenever the chance arose. During a mission to Gibraltar, delivering dispatches for his embassy, he had spent a spare hour exploring a Mousterian rock shelter he had found at the foot of the northern front of the Rock, the nearby ruined and picturesquely named "The Devil's Tower." The discovery gave Breuil the right to excavate, but his interests at this time lay more in northern France and England. He therefore suggested that Garrod should take his place.

Gibraltar was a British Crown Colony and garrison, and had been de facto a British possession for some two hundred years. Thus, for a single woman undertaking her first major excavation, it was important to be able to rely on the local infrastructure. The goodwill, interest, and practical help of the government and military authorities were available to her, as they would also be during her later work in the Near East. She began the first of three seasons in November 1925, well aware of the site's potential: Forbes Quarry, site of the first Neanderthal skull found in Europe in 1848 (though only recognized in 1907) was 350 meters from the Devil's Tower, a narrow fissure in the rockface. Four workmen were employed to clear the site, and in her first season she identified seven layers of archaeological material, all containing Mousterian artifacts resembling, apparently, those of the Upper

Mousterian she had seen at La Quina while working with Henri-Martin.[15]

While at home in Oxford in spring 1926, Garrod received an invitation from the Abbé Breuil, as did Henry Field, the young American student whom she had proposed as secretary of the University Anthropological Society. Field found the Abbé's handwriting totally illegible and bicycled over to the Garrod house at 85 Banbury Road to find that Dorothy had already deciphered her copy: the Abbé required them to go with him to the decorated caves and rock shelters of southern Spain. Sir Archibald and Lady Garrod urged their daughter to accept.

In his vividly entertaining memoirs, Henry Field's account of their expeditions from Gibraltar to the Paleolithic sites graphically portrays Breuil's indefatigable energy, impatience with any second of wasted time, and extraordinary "gift of seeing" the images of long-extinct animals. In his company Garrod was very quiet, apparently overshadowed by her teacher and mentor, until pushed to the limit of endurance at La Pileta cave. In Field's revealing account, Breuil risked their lives down an eighty-foot fissure to collect specimens for a friend. Field pulled Garrod out of the abyss by her arms, "whereupon Dorothy lay down where she stood and closed her eyes . . . [Breuil] made the whole climb in record time. I doubt if an Olympic champion could have done better . . . Panting only slightly from his exertions he remarked 'Venez vite, vite.' Dorothy opened one eye and said, 'Je ne bouge plus.' I think the Abbé was a little surprised, even shocked. This was probably the first time anyone had been so definite with him."[16]

She resumed digging at Devil's Tower in April 1926. On June 11, a controlled explosion to remove a large rock extending into Layer 4 revealed the frontal bone and left parietal of a human skull in the surrounding travertine. During the final season in October, Layer 4 yielded a mandible, right maxilla, and right temporal 5.50 meters from the site of the first fragments. Despite this separation, Garrod concluded that they all belonged to the same, very young individual, whose skull had been removed and preserved "either as a trophy or in fulfillment of a pious rite." Some features were identical to the juvenile from La Quina, and she concluded that these were the remains of a male Neanderthal child aged about five years. This discovery, on her first major excavation, at once established Garrod in her chosen field of Paleolithic study. It also touched her deeply. A photograph surrounded by red stars in her album for 1921–27 is entitled "Abel," the name that she had chosen for the child. Garrod sits smiling on a rock with the skull fragments in her hands. Beneath the photograph she has written: "b. B.C. 20,000. d. aet. 5. Disinterred June 11, 1926." The child is now thought to be three to four years of age, and current dating of the fragments may show her estimation to be unexpectedly close. The late Neanderthals of Gibraltar were part of the population of the Iberian Peninsula south of the Ebro valley, living on the western margin of their range, apparently their final refuge before extinction. Sites such as Zafarraya are currently dated to twenty-seven thousand to twenty-five thousand years ago.[17] At the time of Garrod's discoveries at Devil's Tower, it was thought that Neanderthal territory extended across Europe to the eastern Mediterranean and beyond. From the late nineteenth century until quite recently, archaeologists and bioanthropologists equated them with the geographic distribution of the Mousterian industries. Today we know that the Neanderthals' territory was limited to Europe and the parts of western Asia that they invaded when climatic conditions during Isotope Stage 4 (some seventy-five to sixty-five thousand years ago) caused the expansion of the glaciers.[18]

The Glozel Affair

During her first season in Gibraltar, Dorothy Garrod had time to explore the Spanish neighborhood to the north of the Rock, where she found two promising sites containing evidence for Mousterian occupations. She published them in the *Proceedings of the Prehistoric Society of East Anglia* in 1927, the year her growing reputation was recognized by her election as vice president of the society, at the time that R. R. Marett was president. The French conferred a more dubious honor the same year by appointing her to an international Commission of Inquiry into "The Glozel Affair." This *cause célèbre* stemmed from the discovery, by a farm boy named Émile Fradin, of debris from a medieval glass furnace and a Neolithic ax-head that he found while he was plowing a field at Glozel near Vichy. These finds were apparently genuine. Books were given to the boy to encourage his interest in archaeology, but these, Garrod remembered more than forty years later, "instead had the effect of launching him on a career of organized forgery." The site began to yield an "improbable collection of objects," which resembled pieces illustrated in the books—inscribed clay tablets, "Bronze Age" pottery, and "Palaeolithic" animal engravings and tools—claimed locally to be evidence of an ancient indigenous "Glozelian" civilization. A few eminent French scholars were convinced; others—including the Abbé Breuil—were not; Garrod tried to keep an open mind. She and her fellow commissioners (she was the youngest and the only woman) were invited to dig at the site for three days: "Glozelian" objects conveniently appeared on the second and third days. Garrod, while checking their trench for evidence of suspected interference, was even accused by a local "excitable and uncritical" amateur archaeologist of manufacturing evidence herself to discredit the site. Despite the commission's verdict of fraud and a police raid that found unfinished objects on the Fradin farm, the "Glozel affair" has proved curiously persistent. Dating by thermoluminescence (TL) in the 1970s produced confusing results and revived the controversy. Even after her death, the accusations against Garrod were repeated. She herself always considered the whole affair absurd. At the time, Glozel quickly faded from her mind as she prepared to leave for the Middle East.[19]

Early Days in Palestine

The next step in Garrod's career as an archaeologist determined her lasting reputation. Although she was trained as a western European prehistorian, a sequence of events now led ultimately to an invitation to work in Palestine, a country ruled under British mandate since the dismantling of the Ottoman empire in 1918. During her excavation in Gibraltar, John Garstang, the director of the British School of Archaeology in Jerusalem as well as Director of Antiquities for the government of Palestine, had announced an International Congress of Archaeology to be held in spring 1926 in Beirut and Jerusalem. The impetus for organizing such a meeting was a number of archaeological discoveries—not least the fragmentary human skull, supposedly Neanderthal, found in 1925 in Zuttiyeh cave, just north of the Sea of Galilee. The discoverer was Francis Turville-Petre, once Garrod's contemporary in Marett's Oxford diploma classes, now a student of the British School of Archaeology in Jerusalem.[20] George Grant MacCurdy, who represented Yale University at the congress, had traveled in advance to Palestine to visit Zuttiyeh and other sites in the area. He left with "a deep sense of [Palestine's] importance as a fertile field for prehistoric research" and a desire to involve the American School in exploring the extent of the Neanderthal presence in the Near East.[21]

In the following year, 1927, the threads of Dorothy Garrod's life as a prehistorian, especially those that had intertwined with MacCurdy's interests and their mutual friendships, came together. He was visiting Oxford for the American School's summer term studies: she, working there on the fragments of the Neanderthal child "Abel," found time to help him. MacCurdy's close friend in Oxford, Sir John Linton Myres, chairman of the Council of the British School of Archaeology in Jerusalem, was anxious that the opportunities and possibilities opened up by the "Galilee Skull" from Zuttiyeh should be followed up. Future cooperation was clearly in the interests of their respective schools. In the temporary absence of Turville-Petre for medical reasons,[22] Myres proposed that Garrod be admitted to the British School as a student to continue his work. MacCurdy had already asked her to lead an expedition to Mesopotamia in the following year for the American School. Thus she could combine this project with research in Palestine.[23]

The years between the two world wars in Palestine had been the formative period in archaeology. In many ways, there has been no similar momentum since. The foundation for all fields of archaeology, from the Stone Age to the Islamic, was laid in the years of the British mandate. The necessary academic atmosphere was created by the establishment of the Department of Antiquities, the British School of Archaeology, the American School of Prehistoric Research, the Hebrew University, and the presence in Jerusalem of the French École Biblique. René Neuville, Garrod's contemporary at the Institut de Paléontologie Humaine in Paris, arrived at this time to serve in the French consulate in Jerusalem, where he could combine his duties with his interest in prehistory. Moshe Stekelis came as a Zionist exile from Russia and in 1928 excavated cave sites with Neuville in the Judean desert.

Now thirty-six years old, Garrod arrived in Palestine in 1928. Her Gibraltar report had been published, establishing her as a significant contributor to the expanding discipline of prehistoric investigation. Her sex was apparently no disadvantage. Arguably, it was even a benefit. The Middle East had held a particular attraction for aristocratic and intellectual Englishwomen since the eighteenth century, and Dorothy Garrod was following such remarkable figures as Lady Mary Wortley Montagu, Lady Hester Stanhope, and Gertrude Bell.[24] She had the added advantage in Palestine—as in Gibraltar—of a British government and would move with equal confidence among both its highest officials and her local (usually Arab) employees.

Garrod found that once again, for her first excavation, she would be indebted to a French priest with a taste for prehistory. Four years previously, the Jesuit Père Alexis Mallon had noticed the cave of Shukbah in the Wadi-en-Natuf while on a journey through the Judean hills northwest of Jerusalem. He collected flint artifacts nearby and noticed more embedded with many bones in a mass of breccia inside the cave. Père Mallon waived his own right to excavation in favor of Garrod. Before she could begin work, however, a preliminary visit to Mesopotamia (now the new kingdom of Iraq but governed, like Palestine, under British mandate) was necessary.

The original invitation to lead a joint Anglo-American expedition to southern Kurdistan had come from the British Honorary Director of Antiquities in Iraq. In March, Garrod set off on a preliminary survey in the Kirkuk region, then—as now—an area of persistent strife and unrest. With the enthusiastic help—and automobile—of T. F. Williamson, the Turkish (later Iraq) Petroleum Company geologist, she explored the local gravel spreads for promising signs. Three of these produced the first Paleolithic artifacts to be reported from the area, encouraging "hope that we may find remains of Palaeolithic man": caves sixty miles to the east would be the focus of the planned expedition later that year.[25] Leaving her application for a permit to excavate with the Department of Antiquities, she returned to Palestine and Shukbah cave.

The Excavations at Shukbah Cave

Garrod led the excavation, from April to mid-June 1928, with the collaboration of George and Edna Woodbury from MacCurdy's American School of Prehistoric Research.[26] The team concentrated on the main chamber, largest of three chambers in the cave. The layers identified were D, in situ deposit that contained a Levalloiso-Mousterian industry with a few human fragments; C, redeposited sediment containing mainly reworked pieces from layer D; and B, "a layer of black hearths containing a very abundant microlithic industry and animal remains." Evidently a major time gap separated Layer C from Layer B, which contained the main discovery of the site. "Small crescentic knives" (a term she used prior to "lunates") characterized the industry in B. These were reminiscent of the Tardenoisian, a Mesolithic culture in western Europe. Bone tools were carefully fashioned into points, and one (defined as a needle) retained the eye at its point. Eleven human burials, badly preserved but fairly complete (both primary and secondary), were also uncovered. Garrod's preliminary observations were published almost immediately after closing the dig, and a fuller description of the burials is given in her later report.[27] Most intriguing had been those of H (Homo) 6, 7, and 8: an adult male who seemed to be "half lying, half sitting," associated with fragments of two children so as to suggest they had been placed on his knees, all facing southwest.

The microlithic industry of Layer B had been noticed already in Palestine surface deposits, but this was the first time it had been found in stratified deposits. At first Garrod classified it, cautiously, "as a Mesolithic industry of Capsian affinities,"[28] but she later recognized the originality of the composition of this industry, which included sickle blades, lunates, and perforators, always accompanied by a rich bone industry. She therefore named it Natufian after the wadi in which the cave was located.[29]

The lithic assemblages of Layers C and D were referred to as Upper Levalloiso-Mousterian.[30] During that time it was common in western Europe to differentiate between two Middle Paleolithic industries, namely, the Levalloisian (which was known from northern France) and the Mousterian (which was common in the south). The two industries differed, according to the local scholars, in the extensive use of the Levallois technique and relatively low frequencies of retouched pieces in the "Levalloisian" and the paucity or absence of this knapping method from the "Mousterian" assemblages, which were often rich in retouched items. Faced with the mixed features of the Middle Paleolithic industries in Palestine, Garrod labeled them "Levalloiso-Mousterian." When she showed the finds to Abbé Breuil, he thought that the assemblage from Shukbah could be defined as "Aurignacio-Mousterian." Regarding this aspect, which directly relates to the origins of the Upper Paleolithic cultures, Garrod concluded that there was

> an earlier and much more intimate contact between the two industries (than in western Europe) and the inference which I would draw is that in Palestine we are much nearer to the centre of dispersion of the Upper Palaeolithic . . . But whether that centre of dispersion will prove, ultimately, to be situated in North Africa or in Asia is a question which cannot yet be answered.[31]

Hence, on her first Paleolithic excavation in the Levant, she faced two of the major archaeological problems that continue to challenge current research: (1) the origins of modern humans and the fate of the Neanderthals, and (2) the cultural origins of the Upper Paleolithic.

Field Project in Kurdistan

The Prehistoric Society of East Anglia unanimously elected Garrod president for the year 1928. She returned to London to deliver her presidential address on September 28 in the elegant rooms of the Society of Antiquaries: her title, "Nova et Vetera," reflected the widening experience and vision that Gibraltar and Palestine had given her. With confidence and authority she pleaded for a new method in Paleolithic archaeology, now at a "critical stage in its growth." The "heroic age" of her French teachers and their great predecessors was over, and now new discoveries outside Europe were increasingly difficult to fit into the "classic sequence from Chellean to Magdalenian" of de Mortillet's framework. She proposed an alternative system that would be "sufficiently generalised and elastic to accommodate new evidence as it comes to light . . . something more closely resembling the phyla of the paleontologist, a kind of family tree showing the inter-relation of the various Palaeolithic cultures." This proposal echoed the ideas developed by her French masters Breuil and Peyrony. The new evidence should be sought outside Europe where prehistory was still little known, she concluded, unaware that in Palestine events were already under way that would very soon present her with evidence of unimaginable importance to Paleolithic studies.[32]

Garrod did not return immediately to Palestine. Within three weeks of her address in London she had taken up her permit to excavate in southern Kurdistan and was traveling north from Baghdad. She traveled with a small Anglo-American party: Mrs. Charlotte Baynes (Francis Turville-Petre's colleague at Zuttiyeh cave); Turville-Petre himself; and MacCurdy's student, Robert A. Franks Jr., representing the American School of Prehistoric Research. Garrod's full report is prefaced with a vivid description of their journey toward the Zagros arc, through desolate badlands into an area of mountainous ridges and flat valleys. Archaeologists had rarely visited here—the legendary nineteenth-century European explorers of ancient Mesopotamia were more preoccupied with the spectacular historic remains. As the landscape changed to oak-forested hills and they reached the Persian-style town of Sulaimaniya, Garrod knew she was in country "which from the point of view of prehistory was virgin soil." Her hopes for the area had been raised by her own surveying that spring and the discovery in 1926 by her Gibraltar colleagues Henry Field and L. H. D. Buxton of Paleolithic-type flints in the North Arabian Desert. She considered this evidence of prehistoric "migrations" between Syria and Upper Mesopotamia, a theory she now hoped to prove by excavation in the limestone caves of Sulaimani province.[33]

The party set up a base camp within the safety of the air force compound and, although the district was in a period of relative calm, they remained under armed police escort throughout the expedition. Eleven days were spent in reconnoitering promising sites. Trusting Turville-Petre's experienced eye, she sent him with Robert Franks twenty miles north to make soundings in caves and rock shelters in the Surdash area, while she and Mrs. Baynes explored a group of six caves eight kilometers to the southwest at the village of Hazar Merd. Turville-Petre and Franks returned, having found traces of Paleolithic occupation in one small cave only—near the village of Zarzi—which Garrod decided to excavate first.

She began on November 3, employing the local Kurdish villagers for the heavy work. The small south-facing cave—barely more than a rock shelter—contained three identifiable layers. Layer A inside the cave was a mixture of pottery fragments and flint implements similar to those of Layer B, which spread from the cave mouth out onto the terrace and down the talus. There it covered a completely sterile layer (C). The abundant implements of Layer B seemed to Garrod to belong "to an Upper Palaeolithic industry of Aurignacian type." It was microlithic—nothing exceeding ten centimeters—and contained a high proportion of notched blades and scrapers. In the upper part of Layer B she noted an apparent development of the microliths to a geometric form. Zarzi contained no human remains and only sparse and fragmented animal bones and shells. Though at the time she had no terms of reference in the Middle East other than Shukbah and was in the very predicament she had identified in her presidential address, she nevertheless firmly concluded that the industry was "a typical Upper Aurignacian ensemble." *Aurignacian* was a term then used to define all early Upper Paleolithic entities. Today the lithic assemblages of this site are incorporated in the Epipaleolithic.[34] It is worth noting that when Zarzi cave was excavated again by G. Wahida, he reaffirmed Garrod's original observation of the basic stratigraphy of the cave.[35]

Soundings in only two caves in the Hazar Merd group had produced evidence of Paleolithic occupation. Identical Zarzian implements appeared in Layer B of the "Dark Cave," which she selected for excavation in preference to the heavily brecciated "Water Cave." The Dark Cave's Layer C was three meters thick and contained hearths and Mousterian implements. Garrod noted the resemblance between this industry at Hazar Merd, the Mousterian at Zuttiyeh, and at Shukbah. There was no way of knowing the length of the Mousterian occupation, but she considered it must date "from very far back in this part of the world." Ralph Solecki's excavations in 1950–60 in the large Shanidar cave, some two hundred miles to the northwest, bore this out. He noted the similarity of the industry he found in Shanidar D, the level of the Neanderthal burials (now dated at ca. sixty thousand years), to that of Hazar Merd C.[36]

The Excavations in Wadi El-Mughara (Nahal Hamearot)

At her remote Kurdistan site Dorothy Garrod was totally cut off from events in Palestine. There, prehistoric research, though still in its infancy, suddenly became a matter of concern at the highest level of the British

Mandatory government. This arose from the decision in 1927 that Haifa should become the main port of Palestine. New breakwaters would require massive quantities of good quality stone. Extensive surveys and test borings had identified the valley of Wadi el Mughara, Mount Carmel, as the best quarry site, particularly a bluff at the western end, some 150 ft. high. Caves in the cliffs, though known as antiquity sites, were considered unimportant by the engineers. But Ernest Richmond, now Director of Antiquities for Palestine, insisted on "soundings with the object of discovering the nature and importance of the antiquities on the site."[37] El-Wad cave showed the most interesting signs. A Department of Antiquities assistant named Charles Lambert (who was a coin specialist, not a prehistorian) opened five trial trenches in the cave and on its terrace. Inside the cave he found "the carved bone head of a bovine animal . . . the carving is extremely fine." This small object (now thought to be the head of a Natufian bone sickle haft) caused a sensation. It could stand comparison with the portable art of western Europe and was the first prehistoric art object found in the Near East.

Fortunately a close and sympathetic relationship existed between government and archaeologists in the mandate years. Thus a telegram, dated December 2, 1928, from the High Commissioner to the Secretary of State for the Colonies in London ensured that the quarry site was moved to the coastal area and the caves were protected for complete and expert excavation.[38] Meanwhile at Hazar Merd in Kurdistan the winter rains had begun and Garrod's funds were running low. Four days later she had closed down the excavation and begun the long return journey to Palestine.

In her absence, George Grant MacCurdy had become increasingly convinced by her discoveries at Shukbah, and his own explorations, that Palestine as "the meeting place of three great land masses" would be a rich field for prehistoric research. In light of this, he had formalized an alliance between his American School of Prehistoric Research and the British School of Archaeology in Jerusalem.[39] Their first joint project was to be a second season at Shukbah, but the discoveries in the Wadi el Mughara and the successful campaign to move the quarry site away from the caves changed this plan. It was essential to maintain the momentum. E. T. Richmond therefore asked both schools to postpone Shukbah and instead begin excavation at Mount Carmel under Garrod's direction.

One witness to the surprisingly modest beginnings of this vast undertaking was Mary Kitson Clark, then a young graduate of Girton College, Cambridge. She still has vivid memories of her first meeting with her director at Jerusalem railway station in spring 1929. She remembers feeling embarrassed at immediately having to borrow money from Garrod, and

Garrod's untroubled response.[40] The small team for this first season were entirely women, though this was fortuitous and not a deliberate choice. Elinor Ewbank from Lady Margaret Hall, Oxford, and Mary Kitson Clark joined the British School. Dean Harriet M. Allyn from Mount Holyoke College represented the American School, accompanied by her friend Dr. Martha Hackett. The latter set up a small clinic for the local Arab villagers and gave them an inspired explanation for the excavation: the stones and bones from the caves would be ground up in England and made into medicines for distribution in the clinic. With her inexperienced team and untrained workforce, Garrod bore the entire burden of setting up routines of living and working that would last—though they could not know it then—for seven seasons. Her Arabic grew fluent as this deceptively quiet and contained Englishwoman negotiated and argued, often fiercely, over the inevitable attempts to cheat her. Respect for her grew among the villagers. They called her Sitt Miriam—"Lady Mary" (Mary Kitson Clark thought this an allusion to her Catholic faith)—and gradually included her and her party in the important occasions of village life.

Garrod had wanted to rent a village house so the team could all live together. This was not possible, so they camped at first in tents pitched in the wadi below the caves. Later they lived in a row of *tibn* (mudbrick) cabins, nicknamed "Tibn Towers." Each day the Arab workforce walked the two or three miles from their village to the site. A few men did the heavy work with picks, while a large party of girls hand-picked the lithics and bones from the spoil, then shoveled it into baskets for dumping. Garrod was always present as they worked. Kitson Clark remembered, "She knew when the girls were bringing the baskets to her, just by the look of the things she was handling, that the stratification had changed." Under her tuition the Arab girls' powers of observation grew expert and stories of ground-up bones were no longer necessary. In the leisure time with her students Garrod's innate shyness disappeared, and her strong sense of humor emerged. Kitson Clark sensed the releasing effect of the close camaraderie of their camp life as they happily discussed music, art, literature—"I remember her saying how she liked Proust"—and the deep sympathy the two women had shared, as Christians, during an off-duty visit to Galilee.

This first season at Mount Carmel in 1929 lasted from April to June. The starting point was obvious: El-Wad cave, where Charles Lambert had made the first soundings and discoveries. Garrod began digging in the outer chamber, where he had found the beautiful carved animal head. Below the first disturbed Layer A she too came to the microlithic industry, in situ, with the bone points and beads, but this time associated with a collective human burial of ten young individuals, four adolescents and six children. Beneath one skeleton was a small fragment of calcite incised to represent a human head. Too crude to be a portrait in any real sense, it was nevertheless the second discovery of an art object this culture had produced.[41] In the first of her annual reports for the Palestine Exploration Fund's quarterly statements she noted that the microlithic industry at El-Wad resembled that of Shukbah: the assemblage at El-Wad appeared to be typologically more developed and was therefore a later phase of the same industry. No pottery was associated with either; thus the Mesolithic date she had suspected seemed valid. She concluded that "as it will be convenient to have a name for this culture, I propose to call it Natufian, after the Wady en-Natuf at Shukbah, where we first found it in place."[42] Garrod's rough notebook for this season, and Mary Kitson Clark's, both use the term *Natufian* for the microlithic industry at El-Wad. She had clearly realized at Shukbah that she had a distinctive culture that deserved its own identity, choosing the name before beginning work at El-Wad, rather than after the first season, as her published report implies.[43]

The Natufian Layer B in El-Wad cave spread across half the outer chamber, but elsewhere, under the disturbed Layer A, was "a crumbly breccia containing a Mousterian industry." Suspecting the degree of disturbance would be misleading, she moved into the inner chamber and found an undisturbed sequence of seven prehistoric levels. This was a vital step in her aim to establish, through the excavation of stratified sites, a chrono-cultural framework for the Near East. The stratigraphy of El-Wad contained remains classified as (A) Bronze Age to recent, (B) Natufian (originally referred to as Mesolithic but known today as Epi-Paleolithic), (C) Atlitian (a late Upper Paleolithic assemblage), (D and E) two Levantine Aurignacian layers (later called, by Garrod, Lower and Upper Antelian but originally known in the 1930s as "Middle Aurignacian" following the 1912 scheme established by Abbé Breuil),[44] (F) a partially mixed layer that, due to erosion, contained both early Upper Paleolithic finds (which Garrod later labeled the Emiran culture but first referred to as "Lower Aurignacian"), and (G) a Mousterian industry. With satisfaction she reported, "This is by far the most complete prehistoric sequence so far found in the Near East, and lays the foundations of a Palaeolithic chronology for this region."[45]

El-Wad terrace produced Natufian remains resting undisturbed on the terrace bedrock. Here Garrod noted the lunates, sickle blades, bone implements, and burials (there would eventually be some sixty). Several skeletons were ornamented with elaborate dentalium shell decorations, apparently associated with an artificially paved and walled area and a series of rockcut basins. A possible explanation for these, she tentatively suggested, was a cult of the dead. In the upper portion of this thick deposit was a level that resembled Shukbah B more closely. During her third season it became clear that El-Wad B must be subdivided, reversing her previous assumption that the richer phase (now Layer B2) must be the later. B2 was now designated Lower Natufian. Above it the cultural assemblage of B1 (Upper Natufian) had, unaccountably, shown what she noted as a decline into the less careful and varied workmanship that she had found in Shukbah B. This situation was the more puzzling since the sickle blades and their bone hafts in B2 had already suggested to her that "a primitive form of agriculture had been practised" by the Natufians.[46]

During her journeys by train between Haifa and Jerusalem, Garrod had noticed another cave, the Mugharet el-Kebara, at the southern end of the Carmel range. Considering it worth investigating, she had gone there at the end of her 1930 season with her American colleague Theodore McCown to make, as they then thought, a first sounding. They did not know that Moshe Stekelis, a new immigrant from Russia with an M.A. degree in archaeology from Odessa University, had already done the same three years earlier. However, without an academic position at the Hebrew University at that time, he could not raise funds for further excavation. Interestingly, Stekelis also did his Ph.D. thesis with Abbé Breuil in the early 1930s and, given this common mentor, he kept in touch with Garrod and even cooperated when she wrote up the reports of Shukbah and Kebara.

Dorothy Garrod and McCown identified a Lower Natufian level below the later deposits and then "an underlying level containing an unfamiliar microlithic industry characterized by long triangles."[47] She recommended to the British and American schools that Kebara be excavated while work continued at El-Wad. The schools accordingly invited her companions in Kurdistan, Francis Turville-Petre and Mrs. Charlotte Baynes, to dig Kebara during her 1931 season at Wadi Mughara and to share the camp there. This arrangement was practical from an academic point of view, but Garrod's personal relationship with Turville-Petre was deteriorating, adding to the difficulties of a busy season with four sites under excavation simultaneously. To Kebara, El-Wad, and et-Tabun were added the small cave and terrace of es-Skhul, with McCown in charge. Skhul also produced a Mousterian industry, which at first seemed to Garrod to be identical to Tabun, and the almost complete skeleton of a child. She gave most of her attention to et-Tabun, which had seemed on first investigation to be another small cave but in fact was vast and complex and would be excavated until the close of the project in 1934. Garrod quickly found that from the very top of the first undisturbed level (B) in the inner chamber at Tabun she had a Mousterian industry that corresponded to the lowest Level G at El-Wad. Tabun B thus showed the Mount Carmel sequence could be extended "to great depth, with the possibility of obtaining a still older industry than that already found."[48] The cave has borne out this promise. It contains the longest stratigraphic record in the region, spanning perhaps six hundred thousand years or more of human activity, and remains the archaeological yardstick for the Levantine Paleolithic.[49]

At Kebara, Turville-Petre had found a rich Lower Natufian assemblage of numerous sickle blades and lunates and some of the finest bone implements known from this culture, particularly exquisitely carved sickle hafts. Below the Natufian layer, Kebara Layer C was dominated by the microlithic industry of the new culture, which Garrod later named Kebaran. Turville-Petre's brief report did not refer to his work in the lower levels that contained Levantine Aurignacian assemblages.[50] Garrod, following his untimely death in 1941, published these.[51]

In October 1931, in London, Garrod and Turville-Petre together exhibited and discussed their finds at a meeting of the Society of Antiquaries. A serious rift that existed between them was not then apparent, though his season at Kebara was to mark the end of Turville-Petre's once-promising career as an archaeologist.[52] Illness, perhaps caused by the stresses of the summer, prevented Garrod from returning to Palestine in spring 1932. Thus she missed the discovery by T. D. McCown (serving as acting director of the expedition in her absence) of the Mousterian cemetery at Skhul cave. In this site, where the original limestone ceiling had collapsed in antiquity, the remains of nine (it was initially thought) individuals were embedded in consolidated Mousterian deposits (breccia). It was necessary to remove them in blocks and ship them to London for excavation and study in Sir Arthur Keith's laboratory at the Royal College of Surgeons. McCown accompanied and remained with them, depriving Garrod of experienced support for her next three seasons at Tabun.

In summer 1932 the young Jacquetta Hopkins (later Hawkes) had finished her exams at Newnham College and—realizing that her director of studies, Dorothy Garrod, would welcome help at her Mount Carmel excavations—became a member of the small team for the autumn season. Again the team was almost entirely female and included Mary Kitson Clark's cousin Elizabeth. Almost sixty years later, Jacquetta Hawkes also remembered the happiness and excitement of this time: Garrod again relaxed in their company despite her daily responsibilities and the constant anxiety of securing funds to continue the work. The Arab girls were now highly expert, after four years' training by Garrod, and some even dreamed of studying at Cambridge.

One of the best, named Yusrah, working in Tabun with Jacquetta Hawkes, noticed a human tooth in Level C just outside the small cave opening on the west side of the talus. Together they searched the spoil put aside for dumping and found the skull fragments in a lump, then realized the rest of the skeleton was in situ.[53] Uncertainty concerning the stratigraphic position still surrounds this Neanderthal female, Tabun I, the only relatively complete burial found in the cave. Did the burial belong in Layer C, or—since it was near the top of the level—was the grave dug down from Layer B? Garrod's final opinion was that "this must remain an open question."[54] Earlier in the same layer she had discovered the Tabun C2 isolated jaw. Her realization that this jaw closely resembled the skeletal remains from the cave of Skhul may have raised doubts in Garrod's mind concerning the attribution of two different human types to the same layer. She was not alone in her impression that the two humans should be classified as members of different populations. Originally, T. D. McCown had had similar thoughts.[55] This was not the opinion, however, of the senior researcher at the time, Sir Arthur Keith, who finally persuaded McCown to retreat from his original view. What essentially bothered Garrod, and probably motivated her to add that by now famous caveat, was Dorothea Bate's paleo-climatic sequence. Based on the combined Tabun and El-Wad fauna, and expressed in the famous *Dama-Gazella* graph, this sequence indicated a major faunal change at the onset of Layer B. It seems that Bate's conclusions, and the more or less overall consensus during the 1930s that Neanderthals were of the Last Glacial period, led Garrod to suspect that the Neanderthal woman (Tabun I) should be assigned to Layer B, at the onset of the Last Glacial cycle, while the Tabun II mandible actually belonged to Layer C, assumed to be of Last Interglacial Age. Garrod explicitly viewed the "Lower Levalloiso-Mousterian" as of Last Interglacial Age and the "Upper Levalloiso-Mousterian" as of Early Würm; however, Vaufrey, working at the Institut de Paléontologie Humaine in Paris, strongly suggested that the age of the Near Eastern Middle Paleolithic was retarded in comparison with the European sequence. In particular, he could not accept the idea that the Mousterian of the Levantine caves could be older than the Mousterian of the European caves.[56]

As Garrod's team excavated in 1932 and 1933, the cave walls gradually widened out, and the magnitude of the site of Tabun became clear. Layer D still contained a Levalloiso-Mousterian industry, but Layer E was found to be immensely thick (some seven meters), and the depth of the excavation now obliged Garrod to limit its extent. She subdivided Layer E into four (Ea–Ed), on the basis of the tool typology and arbitrary levels, first classifying the entire sequence as "Acheulo-Mousterian" but changing this to Upper Acheulean (Micoquian) in her final site report.[57] Years later, following the excavations of Alfred Rust in Yabrud rock shelter I (Syria) prior to World War II, but published only afterwards, Garrod again revised her views and terminology.[58] The lowermost levels of Layer E sank downward into a swallow hole, into which Layer F (Upper Acheulean) and Layer G (which Garrod named Tayacian, following Breuil's term for a pre-handaxe industry) plunged even more steeply to an unknown depth.

In her final 1934 season Garrod enlarged the excavated area. Then, having established that no layers older than G could exist, she decided that it was time to close the excavation and begin the huge task of preparing her data for publication. In considering her work of the last seven years, Garrod was aware of the need to fit what was essentially a typological sequence into a broader framework of geochronology. Only evidence of changes in sea level could relate the pluvial periods in the Near East to the sequence of glaciations in Europe, and this evidence might exist on the coast.

In April 1935 she spent a few days with the Newnham geologist E. W. Gardner examining the sandstone (known locally as the *kurkar*) ridge that runs parallel with the shoreline, thought to be a Pleistocene formation. It was here that the contractors for the Haifa harbor project had transferred their quarrying operations, creating extensive deep sections that revealed a layer of red loam, known as *hamra,* sandwiched between layers of aeolianites, in which Levalloiso-Mousterian flint implements were found. These corresponded to Layer G of El-Wad cave and Layer B of Tabun and were thus of a late Pleistocene age. Garrod and Gardner planned to return the next year for a more detailed study,[59] but the commencement of what would become the violent conflict between the Jewish and Arab populations of Palestine in 1936 prevented them from continuing this research. Only in more recent years have a number of geologists studied the different *kurkar* ridges along the coastal plain of Israel.[60]

On April 8, 1935, Garrod and Gardner visited the Jisr Banat Yaqub bridge area in the northern Jordan valley.[61] The bridge lay on the border between Palestine and Syria, where heavy machinery was employed to enlarge the channel of the Jordan River. In the dumps Garrod and Gardner found Acheulean bifaces. The typology and associated fauna convinced Garrod that these "were older, probably much older, than anything found in the caves."[62] Stekelis was informed of their discovery and, with the geologist P. Solomonica, continued the fieldwork. He conducted an excavation in 1937 but was stopped by the outbreak of war.[63] The frontline situation of this important locality remained the same for many years: only after 1967 could the late D. Gilead dig a small trench north of the current bridge, and more recently N. Goren-Inbar conducted an important project at the site.[64]

Garrod returned to England to work on the Mount Carmel publication, breaking her established pattern of summer fieldwork abroad and winters in Cambridge, where she was still Director of Studies in Archaeology and Anthropology at Newnham College. Her parents had moved to Cambridge when her father retired: his death in 1936 was a particularly hard loss, depriving her of a much-loved teacher (her knowledge of anatomy was learned from him) and a constant support. The bereavement and consequent responsibility for her mother perhaps explains why she did not return as planned to her coastal investigations in the Near East. There the community of Jesuit prehistorians of the University of St. Joseph in Lebanon was finding raised beaches with Mousterian artifacts, which she realized were potentially a part of the general scheme and might be the evidence she sought to clarify the chronology of the Mount Carmel succession.[65]

The publication of *The Stone Age of Mount Carmel* (volume 1) in 1937 marked a formidable achievement in the prehistory of the Levant. Only three major publications had previously appeared: the monograph on Wadi Amud by her colleague Turville-Petre (1927) and, prior to him, studies by G. Zumoffen (1900) and P. Karge (1917), which were based mostly on survey work and accidental collections.[66] Hence Garrod's volume established a new standard for its time. Oxford University recognized this achievement by awarding her a B.S. degree. Even today, the volume is a useful source of information, though readers are primarily interested in her field observations. The quantitative information is biased as she, like others at that time, kept only a selection of the collected artifacts, retrieved without the systematic use of a sieve.

Anatolia and Bulgaria

Dorothy Garrod did not return to the Levant for almost twenty years, but in 1938 she felt able to leave her widowed mother and travel again. George Grant MacCurdy asked her, on behalf of the American School of Prehistoric Research, to lead a reconnaissance for Paleolithic sites in Anatolia, which might establish evidence of links between the Near East and Europe. She would have two young companions from Harvard University, Bruce Howe and James H. Gaul. They took the Orient Express from Paris on

April 21. For the first time in the field Garrod had no British backup, nor—given her achievements and now secure reputation—did she need it. The German and French Archaeological Institutes (she was fluent in both languages) advised her and, along with the local American diplomats, helped with Turkish bureaucracy and delay. She asked permission to explore a wide area of the central Anatolian plateau, but only the eastern half was allowed. On June 6 they set off in a hired Plymouth with an experienced driver and the obligatory Department of Antiquities representative. Garrod, typically, ensured that he quickly became a friend.

In three and a half weeks they drove in a rough circle south and west of Ankara and to the Black Sea coast, making surface surveys and small soundings. Only two limestone caves showed faint promise, though both were remote and hardly worth the expense of excavation. The north shore of the shallow salt lake Tuz Gölü yielded a few flint artifacts and seemed worth further investigation. But facing more administrative delay and the prospect of working in the baking heat of an arid lake basin in midsummer, Garrod decided to cut her losses and withdraw her application to excavate.[67] Some funds, however, remained. Discussing with her young colleagues how best to spend them, she realized it was possible to return home via Bulgaria, where O. G. S. Crawford (editor of the British journal *Antiquity*) had seen many promising sites, which he had urged her to explore. The disappointments in Anatolia now made this possible. The friendly and constructive welcome they received in Sofia immediately justified the decision. In the National Museum she examined flints recently found by an amateur in Bacho Kiro cave (near Drénovo in the Balkan Mountains), and her application to excavate was quickly granted. Among Garrod's papers are numerous photographs showing that the local officials and the monks of the Sveti Arkhangel monastery, in whose guesthouse they stayed, repeated their welcome at the site.

Fortunately for Garrod, since she could only afford to dig for two weeks, local enthusiasts had carefully mapped the labyrinthine cave behind its deceptively small entrance, saving her precious time. She chose four areas, two inside the cave entrance and two in the remote depths where the flint tools had been found. In her Locus I, working with great speed, they reached bedrock at a depth of 4.80 meters, identifying eleven layers by feeling the change of texture with their fingers and seeing the changes of color by the light of a petrol pressure lamp. In the third, Layer C, she found the first flint flakes of an indeterminate Upper Paleolithic industry. As they worked downward, identifiable Aurignacian flints appeared in Layer E and continued, with gaps, until Layer J. There was then a change. In the two deepest layers, K and L, she found a Mousterian industry, mostly roughly made from quartzite and other pebbles from the riverbed, though she noted the beauty of the few flint implements. Most of the layers contained bone fragments, many deliberately modified for use. Deep in the cave Bruce Howe was investigating Locus III (site of the original finds) and IV: here were implements of comparable quality. Garrod had first thought these too were Mousterian, but as she found this industry stratified in her Locus I, the obvious differences now caused her doubts, and she found them very difficult to classify. Once again she was breaking new ground in "establishing for the first time the outline of a Palaeolithic sequence for Bulgaria." Bulgaria (with Rumania) lay in the center of an area that would undoubtedly provide useful comparisons but at that time was—with these two exceptions—"a blank on the Palaeolithic map."[68] The early Upper Paleolithic industry in the cave, named Bachokirian, was later dated to more than 43,000 B.P. during the excavations conducted by J. Kozlowski in the 1970s. It was shown to be one of the earliest Upper Paleolithic industries in eastern Europe, which could mark the migration of Cro-Magnons from western Asia.[69]

Professor at Cambridge and the War Years

Back in Cambridge, writing her reports for the ASPR *Bulletin,* Garrod was helped in the transliteration of her Bulgarian references by the Slavonic scholar E. H. Minns, now approaching retirement as the Disney Professor of Archaeology in the university. The megalithic specialist Glyn Daniel remembered Garrod inviting him to take a glass of wine in the Blue Boar Hotel opposite St. John's College and telling him she had applied for the Disney chair. There was, paradoxically, no bar to a woman's tenure of a professorial chair in a university still denying full status to women. "I shan't get it," she told Daniel, "but I thought I'd give the Electors a run for their money." Formidable applicants included Miles Burkitt (teacher and lecturer in prehistoric archaeology at Cambridge for twenty-five years) and Christopher Hawkes (who became professor of European archaeology at Oxford in 1946). Yet in May 1939 Garrod's election was announced.[70] Her colleague at Newnham, the archaeologist Gertrude Caton-Thompson, met her immediately afterward: "I wish my father had been alive," Garrod told her, perhaps thinking of the pledge she had made after the loss of her brothers "and the others."[71]

For the first years, after the declaration of war in September 1939, there was little opportunity for Garrod to use her new powers as professor to reshape the course of archaeological study in Cambridge and to be an active administrator on the Faculty Board. At this time she decided to write the full report of her excavation at Shukbah cave: there would be no further work there for the foreseeable future, and Shukbah should now be correlated with the caves in the Wadi el-Mughara.[72]

Despite her appointment as professor, Garrod had applied for war work, although she was approaching her fiftieth year, when such work would no longer be obligatory. In 1941 she was offered a commission in the Royal Air Force and the next year followed many of her colleagues into the Photographic Interpretation Unit at Medmenham on the River Thames (near Henley). Because of her sex, this distinguished woman could only be given the rank of Section Officer. In a special section for photographic reconnaissance showing the effects of bombing on German industry, the expert contribution she could make in the company of her fellow archaeologists (who included two future Disney professors) more than compensated for the lower rank, which seems to have amused rather than troubled her. She greeted her superior officer, Wing Commander Glyn Daniel, one day with a smart salute and a gentle warning: "Remember, Glyn, very soon our roles will be reversed and Assistant Lecturer Daniel will be saluting Professor Garrod!"[73] She returned to Newnham periodically to recruit archaeology students for the unit. Gertrude Caton-Thompson vividly described her on one of these brief visits. Garrod was only five feet, two inches but in her uniform seemed taller, with short dark hair and dark eyes; quiet in her voice and movements, she nevertheless combined energy and repose in a way that immediately attracted attention.[74] She was released from war service at Easter 1945. While she was glad to get back to her own work, she wrote to Sir Arthur Keith, "I would not have missed the other experience for anything."[75]

Back in Cambridge, her priority was to reorganize teaching in her department and to ensure fuller recognition of prehistory. Her successor as Disney professor, J. G. D. Clark, considered that it was Garrod whose influence most advanced the subject. Within three years, thanks to her efforts, archaeology and anthropology could be taken as a full-degree course. At this time archaeology was a small enough discipline for its participants all to know each other. The sympathy of shared backgrounds transcended gender: "Your brain, not your sex, mattered," said her secretary Mary Thatcher (herself a graduate in archaeology and anthropology from Girton College), "and hers was first class."[76] The pleasure of teaching for Garrod always lay in working closely with her students. With her innate shyness, her quiet voice and personality, she never overcame the ordeal of public lecturing and could seem dull to her listeners. Thatcher remembers her 1962 Huxley Lecture, so readable, clear, and meticulous in its published version, as a painfully nervous occasion. University administration was also a perpetual anxiety in an overspent faculty, and though always conscientious in her duties, she was increasingly distracted from her own research work.[77] In 1952 she was sixty, an acceptable age to retire from a position undertaken in part from a sense of duty. Her remaining years would be largely spent abroad, though she never abandoned Cambridge: the university, and especially Newnham College, continued to serve as a physical and intellectual base in England, enjoyed all the more in her freedom from professorial responsibilities.

Les Trois Graces

During the years of her professorship Dorothy Garrod did not abandon the archaeological fieldwork she loved. From 1946 until her retirement she spent the long summer vacations in France, excavating at two major sites under the direction of her closest friends. At Fontechevade cave (in the Charente region) she worked with Germaine Henri-Martin, sharing with her the excitement of finding human skull fragments in the Lower Paleolithic levels. Then in 1948 she started to work regularly with Suzanne de St. Mathurin at the Magdalenian rock shelter at Angles-sur-l'Anglin. The promise shown by a preliminary visit was fulfilled by their gradual discovery of sculptured, engraved, and painted rock fragments, then a superb frieze of animal and human figures carved in relief on the back wall of this site. The French recognized the achievements of this trio of eminent prehistorians by naming them affectionately Les Trois Graces. The pleasure the three women derived from their work is apparent in the photographs each preserved. The conditions were modest compared with Garrod's great operation at Mount Carmel: here all three are seen digging, and the records are often kept in Garrod's clear, meticulous handwriting.

Dorothy Garrod spoke and wrote French fluently and was always more at ease and light-spirited in France among a people who valued intellectual women more highly than did the British. Joan Crowfoot-Payne, a lithic specialist at Mount Carmel in 1934, had noticed there how Garrod's shyness fell away when French visitors came.[78] Thus it was a natural step, upon retirement, for Garrod to make her home in France. She had a comfortable private income and, since her mother's death, no immediate family left in England. She had a small house built near the Henri-Martin family home in the Charente and could have continued in the pleasant environment for many years. But Garrod was not a woman who willingly turned away from uncompleted work. In 1953 she left her new house for a three-month journey to the Near East that would tie up the loose ends of her prewar work and lay the foundations there for the final phase of her life in prehistoric archaeology.

Return to the Levant

Back in Jerusalem for the first time since 1935, Garrod found the city divided and much changed, the sites of Mount Carmel and Galilee (now in Israel) inaccessible to her from the Jordanian side. Her priority was to study the Aurignacian material from Kebara cave left by her troubled colleague Francis Turville-Petre, now dead. The Aurignacian of Kebara D and E had been dispersed to several museum collections in the custom of the time, but a significant amount of material remained in East Jerusalem in the Rockefeller Museum. Her published paper summarizing the Turville-Petre excavations and comparing the Levantine Aurignacian (as it is called today) from Kebara with similar assemblages in El-Wad added information to her basic scheme of the Upper Paleolithic sequence.[79]

No less crucial was her decision to restudy the lithics from Emireh cave, excavated by Turville-Petre in 1925. The assemblage of Layer F at El-Wad demonstrated mixed features that led her to recognize a transitional phase bridging the Middle and the Upper Paleolithic. She noted that the Emireh point (triangular in shape with bifacial retouch at the base) was, despite its rarity, the tool-type marking this transition. In her published paper she retracted her original dismissal of Turville-Petre's observations and established the notion of the Emiran culture as the first entity in the local sequence of the Upper Paleolithic. Her position gained support from Neuville's observations, although Stekelis suggested (on the basis of his renewed excavations at Kebara) that the Emireh point, as a type fossil, could also be found in the latest Mousterian.[80] Further support for Garrod's position came from the excavations of Boker Tachtit in the Negev. Level 1 (the earliest) and Level 2 contained Emireh points, and core refittings support the interpretation that these assemblages are the incipient Upper Paleolithic industry.[81]

Garrod also examined the Zuttiyeh assemblages, observing the similarity of the early ones to the industry of Tabun E. She now realized the implications of the various known human remains and concluded that the fragmentary skull from Zuttiyeh was older than those found in the Mousterian sites: it must therefore be "the most ancient human fossil from this region."[82] Her conclusion remains valid to this day.

While Garrod prepared her observations for publication, F. Bordes (a rising star in French Paleolithic studies and a former student of R. Vaufrey in the Institut de Paléontologie Humaine in Paris) studied Rust's collections from Yabrud and criticized Garrod for her field techniques and formulation of the archaeological assemblages. Bordes could not understand how one layer, such as Tabun E, could be seven meters thick and contain essentially the same industry. In a similar sequence at Yabrud rock shelter I, Rust identified more than one kind of lithic assemblage in his subdivision of fourteen layers (25–11). Responding to these comments, Garrod published a more detailed description of her excavation methods and a cross-section of Tabun indicating the thickness of her horizontal arbitrary units. She now called Tabun E "Acheulo-Yabrudian" and recognized the increasing presence of blades (including the backed items) in three horizons in layers Ea and Eb.[83] It should be noted that at that time she referred to this industry as "Pre-Aurignacian," following the term employed by Rust. The new term—*Amudian*—was only coined a few years later following her field seasons in Abri Zumoffen.[84] During his later reexcavation of Tabun, A. Jelinek identified one horizon of Amudian, which, like most early layers in this cave, was deformed into a basinlike deposit. This distorted stratigraphy explains why, digging horizontally, Garrod had divided it into three assemblages.[85]

On her way to Jerusalem, Garrod made a detour from Amman to Baghdad. Ralph S. Solecki, then excavating at Shanidar cave with its extraordinary Neanderthal cemetery, had written to tell her he had found unifacial points very like the "transitional" Emireh points in Shanidar Layer D, too deep in the Mousterian to be transitional. Garrod, who had never met him, hastened to see these for herself. Solecki, waiting at the airport, could only guess that she would look like "a female British archaeologist" and instantly recognized the woman in sensible jacket and skirt, close-fitting hat, and flat shoes.[86] To her relief the "Shanidar Emireh" points appeared significantly different from the Levantine, and out of this meeting grew another lasting friendship.

Garrod left her work in Jerusalem to spend ten days in Beirut, where the French Jesuit prehistorian Père Fleisch of the Université St. Joseph was pursuing the university's interest in the ancient raised shorelines of Lebanon. These seemed to Garrod most likely to provide the evidence she had long sought that would enable her to fit her Mount Carmel sequence into a wider geochronological framework. Her studies with E. W. Gardner in 1935 had shown that the Israeli coast and the Jordan valley formation could not do this. The potential of the Lebanese coastal sites may have been in her mind since her first years in the Near East—the earliest photographs she took of the Nahr el-Kelb, north of Beirut, are dated 1929.

Père Fleisch, who studied prehistory and geology while detained in France during the war, had sought advice on how to apply his knowledge to Lebanese Paleolithic chronology from Garrod's old friend Teilhard de Chardin. "Travaillez avec la mer," Teilhard had said, "Work with the sea."[87] Accordingly, Fleisch had continued his predecessor's exploration of the Lebanese coast and was now guardian of the flints found in a rock shelter on the Adlun promontory by Père Zumoffen some fifty years previously. When he showed these to his visitor, she noticed at once their similarity to the industries from Zuttiyeh and Tabun E, which she later named Amudian. Père Fleisch also took her to Zumoffen's rock shelter and the area of Ras Beirut to the north, where fossil dunes contained Levalloiso-Mousterian implements in the type of red loam similar to the *hamra* she had found with Gardner in the sandstone ridge near Mount Carmel. A few kilometers further north was Ras el-Kelb cave, also surveyed by Zumoffen and now studied by Fleisch. Wartime construction of a new railway line had partly destroyed it but exposed the deposits in a section that also contained Levalloiso-Mousterian flints. Convinced by her brief stay in Lebanon that here she could find answers to the questions raised in Palestine, she returned to Europe to begin planning a further major program of excavation and to write up her recent studies.

Garrod's life settled for a few years into a pattern of visits to England, summer seasons at the Angles-sur-l'Anglin site, and her own concentrated research. Her "armchair study" of Paleolithic spear-throwers demonstrates her enjoyment of this time, as well as her productivity.[88] She was disturbed only by an event that revived unhappy memories of the Glozel affair and put one of her oldest friendships under severe strain. Attending the 1956 Congrès Préhistorique de France, she heard the announcement that a new painted cave had been discovered. The Grotte de Miremont at Rouffignac is one of the largest in France. Its complex system of passages and galleries, stretching for several miles underground, had been explored and mapped since the nineteenth century by generations of speleologists and visited by prehistorians like Denis Peyrony and the Abbé Breuil. No one had reported paintings or engravings in the cave until, in 1948, drawings of rhinoceroses in black outline were seen in a place previously thought blank. Many more drawings and engravings, with mammoths predominating, were then noticed. Breuil visited again shortly before the 1956 announcement and unreservedly authenticated Rouffignac's art as truly Paleolithic. Irreconcilable opinions emerged as other expert visitors were asked to record their views. Suzanne de St. Mathurin and Germaine Henri-Martin dismissed the art as forgery. Garrod saw it for herself in 1958. She did not claim to be a specialist, and her careful account of the controversy for *Antiquity* avoided giving a personal opinion. However, she did not conceal her distress at the curious and contradictory sequence of events that put her closest friends in the country she loved on opposing sides. She had spent six months in 1957 compiling the Abbé's complete bibliography for his eightieth birthday, though she admitted to Miles Burkitt that these years "were clouded by differences of opinion." Garrod was a profoundly honest woman. Her doubts were as genuine as they had been over the Glozel affair thirty years before, and she would not compromise them even for the Abbé's sake.[89] They were reconciled before his death in 1961, she told Burkitt, and there is no mention of their disagreement in her generous obituary or her broadcast tribute to him.[90]

Rouffignac, though a cause of private pain, was peripheral to Garrod's interests at this time. Her main preoccupation was still the Paleolithic of the Near East and the clarification of its geochronology. She had not returned to the Epipaleolithic or to Natufian studies, but she followed the new projects and discoveries of Natufian house dwellings, art objects, and burials in Ain Mallaha (Eynan) by J. Perrot and in Nahal Oren by Stekelis, revising her opinions in their light. In 1957 the British Academy gave her an opportunity "to reconsider and tie together the knowledge that we already possess of this remarkable culture." No overall study had been attempted (apart from her student John Waechter's Ph.D. thesis) since she had discovered and named the Natufians at Shukbah cave almost thirty years earlier. This major lecture was both a celebration and, for Garrod, a valediction. She reviewed her own and later discoveries and theories, repeating her belief—based on the sickle blades and careful decoration of their hafts—"that the Lower Natufian people were probably the first agriculturalists." Typically, she ended with a call for new and more appropriate terminology for this critical period in cultural evolution, reinforced with secure dating.[91]

The Excavations in Lebanon

By 1958 Garrod's permits to excavate in Lebanon had been granted. She was now in her mid-sixties, and though she would work on for another five years, she had realized she could no longer carry the whole burden alone. A younger British woman, the archaeologist Diana Kirkbride, had heard

Garrod lecture on Tabun cave in Jerusalem and now agreed to work with her in Lebanon—at some cost to herself. Kirkbride was already a Neolithic specialist, cheerfully dismissive of the Paleolithic, but prepared to tolerate it for Garrod's sake.[92]

Work began at the rock shelter on the Adlun promontory, which Garrod named the Abri Zumoffen after its discoverer. During World War II, geologists had continued to trace the ancient shorelines of the area, and she decided to concentrate on the three most recent, at forty-five meters, fifteen meters, and six meters, corresponding to the three Tyrrhenian stages of the western Mediterranean. She hoped to find in the coastal caves and rock shelters "occupation layers in direct contact with ancient beaches, and so through the general shoreline chronology of the Mediterranean, to help in linking the Levantine industries with the glacial chronology of Europe."[93]

The Abri Zumoffen had formed in a limestone cliff on the fifteen-meter shoreline. To the south was a large cave, the Mugharet el-Bezez, which she decided to leave for the present. Two trenches (A and B) were opened in front of the Abri and a third (C) nearer to Bezez cave. In A and B she found the Amudian industry sandwiched between two beach layers, evidence, she thought, of human occupation when the sea was higher but starting to regress. A rather limited assemblage of Yabrudian industry capped the Amudian and seemed to date from a further stage in the sea's regression.

Garrod's plan to move the following year to the Bezez cave was changed by an urgent request from the Director of Antiquities, Emir Maurice Chehab, to go instead to Ras el-Kelb. The partial destruction of the front of the cave by the railway had been worsened by construction of a new road tunnel, which had removed the back part. The remaining deposits were now exposed as an eight-meter segment in the wall between road and rail. Garrod and her friends Suzanne de St. Mathurin and Germaine Henri-Martin endured seven weeks of excavation during the deafening drilling and blasting until the cracking roof became dangerous. The remaining brecciated deposits were removed in blocks for examination over the next three years in the peace of the National Museum of Beirut, though Garrod confessed to Ralph Solecki that it was dreary work.[94] Ras el-Kelb imposed a further strain on her health, which from this time on remained an anxiety. The full report did not appear until thirty years after her death, but Garrod's opinions are known from preliminary papers and her Huxley Lecture of 1962.[95] The Levalloiso-Mousterian industry, which occurred throughout the Ras el-Kelb deposits, corresponded to Tabun C, and, most important, the earliest level was directly in contact with the marine deposits of the six-meter ancient shoreline. The industries of the Abri Zumoffen were older;

thus the regression of the sea from the Adlun promontory must also be earlier. Radiocarbon dates became available for sites in Palestine, Syria, and Lebanon: burnt bone from hearths at Ras el-Kelb gave the oldest of these, more than 52,000 years B.P.

Bezez was a karstic cave, its floor collapsed into a deep sinkhole, a complication familiar to Garrod from Tabun and Shukbah. Five trenches were opened, and they found one unaffected by this feature. Three Paleolithic levels were identified: the fifteen-meter beach at the base was directly overlaid by the deepest Layer C containing an archaic Yabrudian industry similar to Tabun Ed; above it, Levalloiso-Mousterian (Layer B) corresponded approximately to Tabun D; what remained of the Upper Paleolithic (Layer A) seemed to resemble the Lebanese Ksar 'Akil Aurignacian layers more than those of the Palestine sites. In the state of knowledge of the time, still based on European terminology, Garrod concluded Layer C corresponded to the end of the Last (Riss-Würm) Interglacial.[96]

Garrod's position on chronological issues belonged to the era before Thermoluminescence (TL) and Electron Spin Resonance (ESR) dates, which lasted until the early 1980s. She and others used radiocarbon dates to argue about the age of various Mousterian assemblages and the available human remains. However, this is not the place to repeat the history of how our concepts of time depth in both human and cultural evolution have changed in the last fifteen years.[97]

The Last Years

Though a model of clarity in its published form, Garrod's Huxley Lecture of 1962 was difficult to write and delayed by further illness. Finally, she told Ralph Solecki, for nearly two months, "I buried myself in Cambridge in order to get it finished!" It was clear to Solecki that she now needed help in Lebanon: excavation at the Bezez was due to begin again in February 1963 after the Lebanese had investigated the recent upper layers in the cave. Solecki had offered his student, retired U.S. Army colonel James Skinner, for general duties. Garrod thankfully accepted. She found Skinner "a pillar of strength" who became, as always on her digs, a good friend.[98] Diana Kirkbride, again concealing her distaste for the Paleolithic for Garrod's sake, was co-leader of the party. Lorraine Copeland's participation as a novice volunteer determined her future career as a lithic analyst of Paleolithic industries.[99]

Garrod's health continued to deteriorate slowly. Her diaries of the Adlun dig record headaches and general malaise, and her colleagues remember periods of absence from the excavation—one especially serious absence caused by her now-weakening heart. Many lesser women would have given up. She did not. She realized that Adlun would be the last dig. Nevertheless, the following January she was writing to Solecki from Beirut. She had been in Damascus studying material that shed light on Yabrudian origins and intended further weeks of work in Beirut with her Adlun finds before the long task of writing up the report.[100]

In the summer of 1966 she broke her femur in a fall in her French garden. Extended periods in hospital in France and London now began. The frustrations she must have endured did not show. The nurses of St. Thomas' Hospital orthopedic center found her as much fun and good company as had her team at Mount Carmel and on all her excavations since.[101] Again she recovered. An interim report on the Bezez was completed,[102] and by 1968 she was in London working on the final report, with help from Lorraine Copeland and her former student John Waechter at the Institute of Archaeology. The Society of Antiquaries awarded her their Gold Medal that spring, presenting it in the rooms in Piccadilly where forty years before Dorothy Garrod had pleaded for new methods in Paleolithic archaeology. Accepting her medal, she now reminded the society that for its first two hundred years women could play no part in its active life. This situation had been rectified in 1920—"the long-awaited and by some, long-dreaded day, when the gates of the citadel were finally opened to the Amazons." Evidently deciding this was not the time to belabor the point, she noted many friends in the list of previous medallists without mentioning that she was the first woman to be thus honored. To Garrod's delighted surprise, Mary Kitson Clark was in the audience—their first meeting since the first season at Mount Carmel in 1929.[103]

In summer 1968 Garrod took a break from her work to stay with her cousin Madeleine Lovedy Smith at her Sussex home. On June 30, Miss Smith, who was a senior nurse at St. Thomas' Hospital, was concerned to observe a certain restlessness in her cousin's behavior. Later that day Garrod collapsed in the garden with a major stroke. Over the next months it became apparent that she would not recover.[104] She was moved to a Catholic nursing home in Cambridge, wanting the comfort of her faith and of her friends. She died there on December 18, 1968, aged seventy-six.

Conclusion

As an archaeologist Dorothy Garrod played a crucial role in the study of prehistory in Palestine and Lebanon. As a woman, she was not quite unique.

Flinders Petrie's student Gertrude Caton-Thompson, working in Egypt in the 1920s, had shown what women could achieve in such work in the Middle East and, in Iraq, Gertrude Bell, though not an archaeologist, profoundly influenced the study and preservation of antiquities there and elsewhere. In the British generation that followed, Dorothy Garrod, Kathleen Kenyon, and Joan Crowfoot-Payne had the advantage of both family status and tradition. Diana Kirkbride, in Jordan and Iraq, showed that it was possible to build a career in archaeology without such advantages. Garrod also saw a further group of women emerging locally (amid the constantly changing political situation from which the Arab-Israeli conflict developed) who would make significant contributions to the foundation of archaeology in the new state of Israel. Ruth Amiran and Olga Tufnell were two of these. But for her untimely death, Judith Marquet-Krause (archaeologist of the Early Bronze Age site of Ai) would also have been among them.

Dorothy Garrod herself belonged to the generation of European women whose lives were cruelly and irrevocably changed by the slaughter of World War I. The war robbed so many of their normal expectation of marriage and children. However, it also removed the painful choice between marriage and a career that gifted women of Garrod's time in Britain were usually obliged to make. Her intellectual powers and exceptional family background enabled her, instead, to follow a path that brought her another kind of joy. As a result, near the end of her career she could say of the ten great years (1925–35) of gradual revelation of the Near Eastern prehistoric succession in which she had played a unique role, "'Bliss was it in that dawn to be alive.'"[105] Joy was nevertheless hard-won. It was said in France, she once told her student Lorraine Copeland, that she had been lucky. "*Pas la chance,*" she had replied firmly, "not luck—*c'est courage et persévérance.*"[106]

WORKS BY DOROTHY ANNIE ELIZABETH GARROD
A SELECTED BIBLIOGRAPHY

Books, Monographs, and Articles

"Maglemose Harpoons." *Man* 24 (1924): 63.

"Le niveau inférieur de Kent's Cavern." *Revue Anthropologique* 34 (1924): 354–55.

"Le niveau inférieur de Kent's Hole: Une breche a ursus spelaeus avec outillage chelleen." *Bulletin de la Société Préhistorique Française* 22 (1925): 115–20.

"Solutrean Implements in England." *Man* 25 (1925): 84–85.

:ousin and god-daughter, for their family memories and loan of pho-
nd documents. We are grateful to Ralph S. Solecki for copies of Garrod's
eya D. Molleson for the loan of correspondence between Garrod and
)akley of the Natural History Museum, London; and Caroline Grigson
ıg our attention to Garrod's letters to Sir Arthur Keith. We should also
nk Christopher B. Stringer and Robert Kruszynski for advice on the dat-
obable age of the Gibraltar Neanderthal "Abel," and Paul G. Bahn and
. Lister for their current evaluation of the "Glozel affair" and the
: controversy.

:. Caton-Thompson, "Dorothy Annie Elizabeth Garrod, 1892–1968," *Pro-*
f the British Academy 55 (1969): 338–61.

. de St. Mathurin, "Dorothy Annie Elizabeth Garrod, 1892–1968 (Newn-
-1916)," *Newnham College Roll Letter,* 1969, 50–54.

1. A. Hamilton, *Newnham: An Informal Biography* (London, 1936).

:aton-Thompson "Garrod."

1rs. Mary Chitty (née Kitson Clark) represented Cambridge University
rrod's first season at Mount Carmel in 1929. She was aged ninety-two at
of writing, the only surviving member of the team (interview with
er and P.-J. Smith, October 26, 1996).

:. R. Marett, *A Jerseyman at Oxford* (Oxford, 1941), 185.

). Bar-Yosef and J. Callander, "A Forgotten Archaeologist: The Life of
ırville-Petre," *Palestine Exploration Quarterly* 129 (1997): 2–18.

). A. E. Garrod, "Henri Breuil: 1877–1961," *Man* 61 (1961): 206; contribu-
. Boyle et al., "Recollections of the Abbé Breuil," *Antiquity* 37 (1963): 14.

. de Chardin, *The Making of a Mind: Letters from a Soldier-Priest,*
(London, 1965), 305–6.

;. G. MacCurdy, "It Happened in My Time: The Autobiography of
rant MacCurdy," 1943, George Grant MacCurdy Papers, 995–3, Box 6,
Museum Archives, Harvard University.

.ater to become a national organization called the Prehistoric Society.

). A. E. Garrod, *The Upper Palaeolithic Age in Britain* (Oxford, 1926), 9.

MacCurdy, "My Time."

3reuil's disparaging comment is at last proved wrong: Paul Bahn, Paul Pet-
Sergio Ripoll, "Discovery of Cave Art in Britain," *Antiquity* 296 (2003):
Campbell, *The Upper Palaeolithic of Britain: A Study of Man and Nature*
:e Ice Age (Oxford, 1977).

). A. E. Garrod, L. H. Dudley Buxton, G. Elliot Smith, and Dorothea
te, "Excavation of a Mousterian Rock-Shelter at Devil's Tower, Gibral-
rnal of the Royal Anthropological Institute 58 (1928): 33–113.

H. Field, *The Track of Man* (New York, 1953), 4.

Garrod et al., "Mousterian Rock-Shelter"; Garrod's photograph albums
rved in the Fonds Suzanne Cassou de St. Mathurin, Bibliothèque de la
:s Antiquités Nationales, 78103 St. Germain-en-Laye, France; current age
n for "Abel," R. Kruszynski (personal communication); J-J. Hublin,
o Ruiz, P. Medira Lara, M. Fortugne S.F.-L. Reyss "The Mousterian Site
aya (Andalucía, Spain): Dating and Implications on the Palaeolithic Peo-

"Traits de silex sur phalanges de cheval paleolithiques." *Bulletin de la Société Préhistorique Française* 22 (1925): 295–96.

M. E. Pittard, coauthor. "Quelques pieces inedites de l'aurignacien superieur de la station Durand-Ruel (Dordogne)." *Revue Anthropologique* 36 (1926): 368–71.

M. R. Moir, coauthor. "Traces des differents glaciaires aux environs d'Ipswich (Angleterre)." In *Actes du Congrès,* 263–64. Paris, 1926.

Excavation of a Mousterian Rock Shelter at Devil's Tower, Gibraltar. Indianapolis, 1928?

L. H. Dudley Buxton, G. Elliot Smith, and Dorothea M. A. Bate, coauthors. "Excavation of a Mousterian Rock-Shelter at Devil's Tower, Gibraltar." *Journal of the Royal Anthropological Institute of Great Britain and Ireland* 58 (1928): 33–113.

"Notes on Some Mousterian Finds in Spain and Irak." In *Proceedings of the Prehistoric Society of East Anglia,* 268–72. Ipswich, 1928.

"Nova et Vetera: A Plea for a New Method in Palaeolithic Archaeology." In *Proceedings of the Prehistoric Society of East Anglia,* 260–67. Ipswich, 1928.

"Stone Age in Palestine." *Palacio* 26 (1929): 228–29.

"Fouilles paleolithiques en Palestine, 1928–1929." *Bulletin de la Société Préhistorique Française* 27 (1930): 151–60.

"Note on Three Objects of Mesolithic Age from a Cave in Palestine." *Man* 30 (1930): 77–78.

"The Palaeolithic of Southern Kurdistan: Excavations in the Caves of Zarzi and Hazar Merd." *Bulletin of the American School of Prehistoric Research* 6 (1930): 8–43.

"Excavations in the Caves of the Wady-el-Mughara, 1929–30." *Bulletin of the American School of Prehistoric Research* 7 (1931): 5–11.

"Mesolithic Burials from Caves in Palestine." *Man* 31 (1931): 145–46.

"Excavations in the Wady al-Mughara (Palestine), 1931." *Bulletin of the American School of Prehistoric Research* 8 (1932): 6–11.

A New Mesolithic Industry: The Natufian of Palestine. London, 1932.

A New Species of Fossil Man: Great Discoveries at Mt. Carmel. London, 1932.

"A New Mesolithic Industry: The Natufian of Palestine." *Journal of the Royal Anthropological Institute of Great Britain and Ireland* 62 (1932): 257–69.

Cave Dwellers in Palestine. Santa Fe, 1932.

"Fouilles préhistoriques au Mont Carmel, 1930–1931." In *Congrès Préhistorique de France. 10th, Nimes, Compte Rendu,* 60–65. Paris, 1933–34.

"Excavations at the Wady al-Mughara (Palestine), 1932–33." *Bulletin of the American School of Prehistoric Research* 10 (1934): 7–11.

"Excavations at the Wady al-Mughara 1932–3." *Palestine Exploration Fund, London, Quarterly Statement* 66 (1934): 85–89.

"Four or Five Thousand Years before the Children of Israel Came Seeking Their Promised Land, Palestine Had a Dry Climate and Was Mainly Desert." *Science* 79 suppl. (1934): 8.

"A New Mesolithic Industry: The Natufian of Palestine." In *Proceedings of International Congress for Prehistoric and Protohistoric Sciences,* 107–8. London, 1934.

"The Stone Age of Palestine." *Antiquity* 8 (1934): 133–50.

"Excavations in the Mugharet Et-Tabun (Palestine), 1934." *Bulletin of the American School of Prehistoric Research* 11 (1935): 54–58.

"A Summary of Seven Seasons' Work at the Wady el-Mughara." *Bulletin of the American School of Prehistoric Research* 12 (1936): 125–29.

"The Near East as a Gateway of Prehistoric Migration." *Bulletin of the American School of Prehistoric Research* 13 (1937): 17–21.

"The Near East as a Gateway of Prehistoric Migration." In *Early Man,* ed. G. G. MacCurdy, 33–40. Philadelphia, 1937.

The Stone Age of Mount Carmel, (Joint Expedition of the British School of Archaeology in Jerusalem and the American School of Prehistoric Research [1929–1934]). Oxford, 1937–39.

"The Upper Palaeolithic in the Light of Recent Discovery." In *Proceedings of the Prehistoric Society for 1938,* 1–26. Cambridge, 1938.

"Le burin dans le paleolithique inférieur et moyen du proche Orient." In *Melanges de Préhistoire et d'Anthropologie Offerts par ses Collègues, Amis et Disciples au Professeur Comte H. Bégouën.* Toulouse, 1939.

B. Howe, J. H. Gaul, and R. Popov, coauthors. "Excavations in the Cave of Bacho Kiro, Northeast Bulgaria." *Bulletin of the American School of Prehistoric Research* 15 (1939): 46–126 (2 pts.).

J. H. Gaul and B. Howe, coauthors. "Report on the A.S.P.R. Expedition to Anatolia, 1938." *Bulletin of the American School of Prehistoric Research* 15 (1939): 13–27.

"The Cave of Lascaux Near Montignac, Dordogne: Summary." *Man* 43 (1943): 42.

"Excavations at the Cave of Shukbah, Palestine, 1928." *Proceedings of the Prehistoric Society* 8 (1943): 1–20.

"The Upper Palaeolithic in the Light of Recent Discovery." In *Human Origins: An Introduction to Anthropology.* Chicago, 1945.

"The Magdalenian Rock-Shelter at Angles-sur-Anglin (Vienne): A Report." *Archaeological News Letter* 2 (1950): 196–97.

S. de Saint-Mathurin, coauthor. "La frise sculptée de l'abri du roc aux sorciers a Angles-sur-l'Anglin (Vienne)." *Anthropologie* 55 (1952): 413–24.

"A Transitional Industry from the Base of the Upper Palaeolithic in Palestine and Syria." *Journal of the Royal Anthropological Institute of Great Britain and Ireland* 81 (1952): 121–30.

"The Relations between South-West Asia and Europe in the Later Palaeolithic Age with Special Reference to the Origin of the Upper Palaeolithic Blade Cultures." *Journal of World History* 1 (1953): 13–37.

E. M. Clifford and H. S. Gracie, coauthors. "Flint Implements from Gloucestershire." *Antiquaries Journal* 34 (1954): 178–85.

"Excavations at the Mugharet Kebara, Mount Carmel, 1931: The Aurignacian Industries." *Proceedings of the Prehistoric Society* 20 (1955): 155–92.

"The Mugharet el-Emireh in Lower Galilee: Type-Station of the Emiran Industry." *Journal of the Royal Anthropological Institute of Great Britain and Ireland* 85 (1955): 141–62.

"Pierre Teilhard de Chardin, S.J.: 1881–1955." *Man* 55 (1955): 70.

"Acheuleo-Jabroudien et 'Pre-Aurignacien' de la grotte du Taboun (Mont Carmel): Etude stratigraphique et chronologique." *Quaternaria* 3 (1956): 39–59.

"Paleolithic Spear-Throwers." *Proceedings of the* 21–35.

S. de Saint-Mathurin, coauthor. "L'abri du Roc au Vienne)." In *Congrès Préhistorique de Fr Angoulème, 1956, Compte Rendu,* 89–94. Paris,

"Notes sur le Paleolithique superieur du Moyen *Préhistorique Française* 54 (1957): 439–46.

"Les rites funeraires des hommes fossiles du Mont 163–68. Brive, 1957.

"The Ancient Shore-Lines of the Lebanon, and the *Hundert Jahre Neanderthaler.* Düsseldorf, 1958.

"Rouffignac." *Antiquity* 32 (1958): 231–34.

"Excavation of a Palaeolithic Rock Shelter at Adl *tional Congress of Prehistoric and Protohistoric*

"Henri Breuil: 1877–1961 (Obituary)." *Man* 61 (196

"The Middle Palaeolithic of the Near East and t Man." *Journal of the Royal Anthropological In land* 92 (1962): 232–59.

"An Outline of Pleistocene Prehistory in Palestine- (1962): 541–46.

G. Henri-Martin, coauthor. "Fouilles au Ras El- *Préhistorique de France. XVIe, Monaco, 1959,* 1965.

Primitive Man in Egypt, Western Asia, and Europe

"A Pebble Industry of Early Würm Age from the A In *Studies in Prehistory,* ed. D. Sen and A. K. G

"Recollections of Glozel." *Antiquity* 42 (1968): 172-

"The Stone Age of Mount Carmel." In *Report of th School of Archaeology in Jerusalem and the Research, 1929–1934.* New York, 1980.

NOTES

The authors are grateful to the American School o Museum, Harvard University) for sponsoring the thèque du Musée des Antiquités Nationales (Saint Pitt Rivers Museum (University of Oxford), and t her knowledge of Dorothy Garrod's professorship at Saint Germain-en-Laye in the archives that cam We should also like to thank Lorraine Copeland, the late Diana Kirkbride, the late Joan Crowfoo Hawkes, all colleagues on Garrod's excavations, Peter Gathercole, Anne McBurney, Joan Oates, an ories of Garrod in Cambridge; and Madeleine Lov pling Processes of Western Europe," *Comptes rendus de l'Académie des Sciences de Paris,* ser. IIa, 321 (1995): 931–37.

18. O. Bar-Yosef, "The Date of Southwest Asia Neandertals," in *L'Homme de Néandertal,* ed. M. Otte, vol. 3 (Liège, 1988), 31–38.

19. D. A. E. Garrod, "Recollections of Glozel," *Antiquity* 42 (1968): 172–77; "L'Affaire Glozel," *Antiquity* 1 (1927): 181–88, is an entertaining account by *Antiquity*'s founder and first editor, O. G. S. Crawford. After visiting the site he concluded that the believers in the Glozel culture "have been the victims of a hoax"; the TL dating, recent "Glozelian" publications, and repetition of the allegations against Garrod have prompted a critical summary by a leading specialist in Palaeolithic art and the current holder of her former professorship of archaeology at Cambridge: P. G. Bahn and A. C. Renfrew, "Garrod and Glozel: The End of a Fiasco" in *Dorothy Garrod and the Progress of the Palaeolithic,* ed. W. Davies and R. Charles (Oxford, 1999), 76–83.

20. Bar-Yosef and Callander, "Turville-Petre."

21. MacCurdy, "My Time." MacCurdy was director of the American School of Prehistoric Research.

22. Bar-Yosef and Callander, "Turville-Petre."

23. British School of Archaeology in Jerusalem, Minute Book No. 1 (1918–60), entry for January 22, 1923.

24. Lady Mary Wortley Montagu (1689–1762) is chiefly remembered for introducing inoculation against smallpox from Constantinople, where her husband was British ambassador; Lady Hester Stanhope (1776–1839), eccentric and traveler, lived in the Levant from 1810, adopting local ways and intrigues but dying in destitution; Gertrude Bell (1868–1926), Arabist and traveler, was important in Arab politics and British intelligence during World War I, helped to establish Faisal I as ruler of Iraq under British mandate, and was instrumental in creating the Baghdad Museum and Antiquities Service, models used subsequently in all other British mandated territories.

25. D. A. E. Garrod, "Notes on Some Mousterian Finds in Spain and Irak: II. Mousterian Implements from Southern Kurdistan," *Proceedings of the Prehistoric Society of East Anglia* 5 (1928): 270–72.

26. Edna Woodbury died before Garrod's full report (n. 29 infra) on Shukbah was published; George Woodbury became a research associate at the Peabody Museum of Harvard University.

27. D. A. E. Garrod, "Excavation of a Palaeolithic Cave in Western Judea," *Palestine Exploration Fund Quarterly Statement* 60 (1928): 182–85; and D. A. E. Garrod, "Excavations at the Cave of Shukbah, Palestine, 1928," *Proceedings of the Prehistoric Society* 8 (1942): 1–20.

28. Capsian was an Epipaleolithic culture in North Africa, ca. 10,000–6,000 B.P. Garrod, "Palaeolithic Cave in Western Judea," 183.

29. D. A. E. Garrod, "A New Mesolithic Industry: The Natufian of Palestine," *Journal of the Royal Anthropological Institute* 62 (1932): 257–70.

30. D. A. E. Garrod and D. M. A. Bate, *The Stone Age of Mount Carmel,* vol. 1 (Oxford, 1937).

31. Garrod, "Palaeolithic Cave in Western Judea," 185.

32. D. A. E. Garrod, "Nova et Vetera: A Plea for a New Method in Palaeolithic Archaeology," presidential address, September 28, 1928, *Proceedings of the Prehistoric Society of East Anglia* 5 (1929): 260–67; J. R. Sackett, "From de Mortillet to Bordes: A Century of French Palaeolithic Research," in *Towards a History of Archaeology,* ed. G. E. Daniel (London, 1981), 85–99; G. E. Daniel, *A Hundred and Fifty Years of Archaeology* (London, 1975).

33. D. A. E. Garrod, "The Palaeolithic of Southern Kurdistan: Excavations in the Caves of Zarzi and Hazar Merd," *Bulletin of the American School of Prehistoric Research* 6 (1930): 9–43, 13; Field, *The Track of Man.*

34. Philip E. L. Smith, *Palaeolithic Archaeology in Iran* (Philadelphia, 1986).

35. G. Wahida, "The Re-excavation of Zarzi," *Proceedings of the Prehistoric Society* 47 (1981): 19–40.

36. Garrod, "Palaeolithic of Southern Kurdistan"; R. S. Solecki, *Shanidar: The Humanity of Neanderthal Man* (London, 1972), 124.

37. "Haifa Harbour Works," Colonial Office File CO733/149/4 31355, Public Record Office, London, 1928; E. T. Richmond's Report, "A Preliminary Note Describing the Investigations Made at the Antiquity Site at Wady al-Mughara in November, 1928" (incorporating Charles Lambert's excavation report) is preserved in the same file, Public Record Office, London, 1928.

38. Colonial Office File CO733/140/4, Public Record Office, London, 1928.

39. G. G. MacCurdy, foreword to Garrod and Bate, *Mount Carmel.*

40. Kitson Clark, interview.

41. A. Marshack, "Paleolithic Image Making and Symboling in Europe and the Middle East: A Comparative Review," in M. Conkey, O. Soffer, D. Stratmann, and N. G. Jablonski, *Beyond Art: Pleistocene Image and Symbol,* Memoirs of California Academy of Sciences 23 (San Francisco, 1997), 53–91.

42. D. A. E. Garrod, "Excavations in the Mugharet El-Wad, near Athlit. April–June, 1929," *Palestine Exploration Fund Quarterly Statement* 62 (1929): 220–22.

43. D. A. E. Garrod, "Athlit, Wady Mughara 1929–30," unpublished handwritten notes, April 3–June 18, box 58, inventory no. 33 428, in Fonds Suzanne Cassou de St. Mathurin, Bibliothèque de la Musée des Antiquités Nationales, 78103 St. Germain-en-Laye, France; M. Kitson Clark, unpublished notebook, April–June 1929, for Mount Carmel excavation, box 63, inventory no. 33 431 in the same archive. For procedure to access this archive see P-J. Smith, J. Callander, P. G. Bahn, and G. Pinçon "Dorothy Garrod in Words and Pictures," *Antiquity* 71 (1997): 265–70.

44. D. A. E. Garrod, "Notes sur le Paléolithique supérieur du Moyen Orient," *Bulletin de la Société Préhistorique Française* 54 (1957): 439–46; H. Breuil, *Les subdivision de Paléolithique supérieur et leur signification,* 2d ed. (Paris, 1937).

45. D. A. E. Garrod, "Excavations at the Mugharet El-Wad, 1930," *Palestine Exploration Fund Quarterly Statement* 64 (1931): 99–103.

46. Garrod, "Mugharet El-Wad, 1930," 103.

47. Garrod, "A New Mesolithic Industry," 267.

48. D. A. E. Garrod, "Excavations in the Wady El-Mughara, 1931," *Palestine Exploration Fund Quarterly Statement* 66 (1932): 46–51.

49. L. Copeland, "The Middle and Upper Palaeolithic of Lebanon and Syria in

"Traits de silex sur phalanges de cheval paleolithiques." *Bulletin de la Société Préhistorique Française* 22 (1925): 295–96.

M. E. Pittard, coauthor. "Quelques pieces inedites de l'aurignacien superieur de la station Durand-Ruel (Dordogne)." *Revue Anthropologique* 36 (1926): 368–71.

M. R. Moir, coauthor. "Traces des differents glaciaires aux environs d'Ipswich (Angleterre)." In *Actes du Congrès,* 263–64. Paris, 1926.

Excavation of a Mousterian Rock Shelter at Devil's Tower, Gibraltar. Indianapolis, 1928?

L. H. Dudley Buxton, G. Elliot Smith, and Dorothea M. A. Bate, coauthors. "Excavation of a Mousterian Rock-Shelter at Devil's Tower, Gibraltar." *Journal of the Royal Anthropological Institute of Great Britain and Ireland* 58 (1928): 33–113.

"Notes on Some Mousterian Finds in Spain and Irak." In *Proceedings of the Prehistoric Society of East Anglia,* 268–72. Ipswich, 1928.

"Nova et Vetera: A Plea for a New Method in Palaeolithic Archaeology." In *Proceedings of the Prehistoric Society of East Anglia,* 260–67. Ipswich, 1928.

"Stone Age in Palestine." *Palacio* 26 (1929): 228–29.

"Fouilles paleolithiques en Palestine, 1928–1929." *Bulletin de la Société Préhistorique Française* 27 (1930): 151–60.

"Note on Three Objects of Mesolithic Age from a Cave in Palestine." *Man* 30 (1930): 77–78.

"The Palaeolithic of Southern Kurdistan: Excavations in the Caves of Zarzi and Hazar Merd." *Bulletin of the American School of Prehistoric Research* 6 (1930): 8–43.

"Excavations in the Caves of the Wady-el-Mughara, 1929–30." *Bulletin of the American School of Prehistoric Research* 7 (1931): 5–11.

"Mesolithic Burials from Caves in Palestine." *Man* 31 (1931): 145–46.

"Excavations in the Wady al-Mughara (Palestine), 1931." *Bulletin of the American School of Prehistoric Research* 8 (1932): 6–11.

A New Mesolithic Industry: The Natufian of Palestine. London, 1932.

A New Species of Fossil Man: Great Discoveries at Mt. Carmel. London, 1932.

"A New Mesolithic Industry: The Natufian of Palestine." *Journal of the Royal Anthropological Institute of Great Britain and Ireland* 62 (1932): 257–69.

Cave Dwellers in Palestine. Santa Fe, 1932.

"Fouilles préhistoriques au Mont Carmel, 1930–1931." In *Congrès Préhistorique de France. 10th, Nimes, Compte Rendu,* 60–65. Paris, 1933–34.

"Excavations at the Wady al-Mughara (Palestine), 1932–33." *Bulletin of the American School of Prehistoric Research* 10 (1934): 7–11.

"Excavations at the Wady al-Mughara 1932–3." *Palestine Exploration Fund, London, Quarterly Statement* 66 (1934): 85–89.

"Four or Five Thousand Years before the Children of Israel Came Seeking Their Promised Land, Palestine Had a Dry Climate and Was Mainly Desert." *Science* 79 suppl. (1934): 8.

"A New Mesolithic Industry: The Natufian of Palestine." In *Proceedings of International Congress for Prehistoric and Protohistoric Sciences,* 107–8. London, 1934.

"The Stone Age of Palestine." *Antiquity* 8 (1934): 133–50.

"Excavations in the Mugharet Et-Tabun (Palestine), 1934." *Bulletin of the American School of Prehistoric Research* 11 (1935): 54–58.

"A Summary of Seven Seasons' Work at the Wady el-Mughara." *Bulletin of the American School of Prehistoric Research* 12 (1936): 125–29.

"The Near East as a Gateway of Prehistoric Migration." *Bulletin of the American School of Prehistoric Research* 13 (1937): 17–21.

"The Near East as a Gateway of Prehistoric Migration." In *Early Man,* ed. G. G. MacCurdy, 33–40. Philadelphia, 1937.

The Stone Age of Mount Carmel, (Joint Expedition of the British School of Archaeology in Jerusalem and the American School of Prehistoric Research [1929–1934]). Oxford, 1937–39.

"The Upper Palaeolithic in the Light of Recent Discovery." In *Proceedings of the Prehistoric Society for 1938,* 1–26. Cambridge, 1938.

"Le burin dans le paleolithique inférieur et moyen du proche Orient." In *Melanges de Préhistoire et d'Anthropologie Offerts par ses Collègues, Amis et Disciples au Professeur Comte H. Bégouën.* Toulouse, 1939.

B. Howe, J. H. Gaul, and R. Popov, coauthors. "Excavations in the Cave of Bacho Kiro, Northeast Bulgaria." *Bulletin of the American School of Prehistoric Research* 15 (1939): 46–126 (2 pts.).

J. H. Gaul and B. Howe, coauthors. "Report on the A.S.P.R. Expedition to Anatolia, 1938." *Bulletin of the American School of Prehistoric Research* 15 (1939): 13–27.

"The Cave of Lascaux Near Montignac, Dordogne: Summary." *Man* 43 (1943): 42.

"Excavations at the Cave of Shukbah, Palestine, 1928." *Proceedings of the Prehistoric Society* 8 (1943): 1–20.

"The Upper Palaeolithic in the Light of Recent Discovery." In *Human Origins: An Introduction to Anthropology.* Chicago, 1945.

"The Magdalenian Rock-Shelter at Angles-sur-Anglin (Vienne): A Report." *Archaeological News Letter* 2 (1950): 196–97.

S. de Saint-Mathurin, coauthor. "La frise sculptée de l'abri du roc aux sorciers a Angles-sur-l'Anglin (Vienne)." *Anthropologie* 55 (1952): 413–24.

"A Transitional Industry from the Base of the Upper Palaeolithic in Palestine and Syria." *Journal of the Royal Anthropological Institute of Great Britain and Ireland* 81 (1952): 121–30.

"The Relations between South-West Asia and Europe in the Later Palaeolithic Age with Special Reference to the Origin of the Upper Palaeolithic Blade Cultures." *Journal of World History* 1 (1953): 13–37.

E. M. Clifford and H. S. Gracie, coauthors. "Flint Implements from Gloucestershire." *Antiquaries Journal* 34 (1954): 178–85.

"Excavations at the Mugharet Kebara, Mount Carmel, 1931: The Aurignacian Industries." *Proceedings of the Prehistoric Society* 20 (1955): 155–92.

"The Mugharet el-Emireh in Lower Galilee: Type-Station of the Emiran Industry." *Journal of the Royal Anthropological Institute of Great Britain and Ireland* 85 (1955): 141–62.

"Pierre Teilhard de Chardin, S.J.: 1881–1955." *Man* 55 (1955): 70.

"Acheuleo-Jabroudien et 'Pre-Aurignacien' de la grotte du Taboun (Mont Carmel): Etude stratigraphique et chronologique." *Quaternaria* 3 (1956): 39–59.

"Paleolithic Spear-Throwers." *Proceedings of the Prehistoric Society* 21 (1956): 21–35.

S. de Saint-Mathurin, coauthor. "L'abri du Roc aux Sorciers (Angles-sur-l'Anglin, Vienne)." In *Congrès Préhistorique de France. 15th session, Poitiers-Angoulème, 1956, Compte Rendu,* 89–94. Paris, 1957.

"Notes sur le Paleolithique superieur du Moyen Orient." *Bulletin de la Société Préhistorique Française* 54 (1957): 439–46.

"Les rites funeraires des hommes fossiles du Mont Carmel." In *Melanges Pittard,* 163–68. Brive, 1957.

"The Ancient Shore-Lines of the Lebanon, and the Dating of Mt. Carmel Man." In *Hundert Jahre Neanderthaler.* Düsseldorf, 1958.

"Rouffignac." *Antiquity* 32 (1958): 231–34.

"Excavation of a Palaeolithic Rock Shelter at Adlun, Lebanon 1958." In *International Congress of Prehistoric and Protohistoric Sciences,* 313–20. Berlin, 1961.

"Henri Breuil: 1877–1961 (Obituary)." *Man* 61 (1961): 205–7.

"The Middle Palaeolithic of the Near East and the Problem of Mount Carmel Man." *Journal of the Royal Anthropological Institute of Great Britain and Ireland* 92 (1962): 232–59.

"An Outline of Pleistocene Prehistory in Palestine-Lebanon-Syria." *Quaternaria* 6 (1962): 541–46.

G. Henri-Martin, coauthor. "Fouilles au Ras El-Kelb-Liban 1959." In *Congrès Préhistorique de France. XVIe, Monaco, 1959, Compte Rendu,* 564–72. Paris, 1965.

Primitive Man in Egypt, Western Asia, and Europe. Cambridge, 1965.

"A Pebble Industry of Early Würm Age from the Abri Zumoffen, South Lebanon." In *Studies in Prehistory,* ed. D. Sen and A. K. Ghosh, 41–48. Calcutta, 1966.

"Recollections of Glozel." *Antiquity* 42 (1968): 172–77.

"The Stone Age of Mount Carmel." In *Report of the Joint Expedition of the British School of Archaeology in Jerusalem and the American School of Prehistoric Research, 1929–1934.* New York, 1980.

NOTES

The authors are grateful to the American School of Prehistoric Research (Peabody Museum, Harvard University) for sponsoring the archival research in the Bibliothèque du Musée des Antiquités Nationales (Saint Germain-en-Laye, Paris) and the Pitt Rivers Museum (University of Oxford), and to Pamela-Jane Smith for sharing her knowledge of Dorothy Garrod's professorship at Cambridge and early research at Saint Germain-en-Laye in the archives that came to light through her initiative. We should also like to thank Lorraine Copeland, Mary Chitty (née Kitson Clark), the late Diana Kirkbride, the late Joan Crowfoot-Payne, and the late Jacquetta Hawkes, all colleagues on Garrod's excavations, for oral interviews; Ruth Daniel, Peter Gathercole, Anne McBurney, Joan Oates, and Mary Thatcher for their memories of Garrod in Cambridge; and Madeleine Lovedy Smith and Antonia Benedek,

Garrod's cousin and god-daughter, for their family memories and loan of photographs and documents. We are grateful to Ralph S. Solecki for copies of Garrod's letters; Theya D. Molleson for the loan of correspondence between Garrod and Kenneth Oakley of the Natural History Museum, London; and Caroline Grigson for drawing our attention to Garrod's letters to Sir Arthur Keith. We should also like to thank Christopher B. Stringer and Robert Kruszynski for advice on the dating and probable age of the Gibraltar Neanderthal "Abel," and Paul G. Bahn and Adrian M. Lister for their current evaluation of the "Glozel affair" and the Rouffignac controversy.

1. G. Caton-Thompson, "Dorothy Annie Elizabeth Garrod, 1892–1968," *Proceedings of the British Academy* 55 (1969): 338–61.

2. S. de St. Mathurin, "Dorothy Annie Elizabeth Garrod, 1892–1968 (Newnham 1913–1916)," *Newnham College Roll Letter,* 1969, 50–54.

3. M. A. Hamilton, *Newnham: An Informal Biography* (London, 1936).

4. Caton-Thompson "Garrod."

5. Mrs. Mary Chitty (née Kitson Clark) represented Cambridge University during Garrod's first season at Mount Carmel in 1929. She was aged ninety-two at the time of writing, the only surviving member of the team (interview with J. Callander and P.-J. Smith, October 26, 1996).

6. R. R. Marett, *A Jerseyman at Oxford* (Oxford, 1941), 185.

7. O. Bar-Yosef and J. Callander, "A Forgotten Archaeologist: The Life of Francis Turville-Petre," *Palestine Exploration Quarterly* 129 (1997): 2–18.

8. D. A. E. Garrod, "Henri Breuil: 1877–1961," *Man* 61 (1961): 206; contribution to M. Boyle et al., "Recollections of the Abbé Breuil," *Antiquity* 37 (1963): 14.

9. T. de Chardin, *The Making of a Mind: Letters from a Soldier-Priest, 1914–1919* (London, 1965), 305–6.

10. G. G. MacCurdy, "It Happened in My Time: The Autobiography of George Grant MacCurdy," 1943, George Grant MacCurdy Papers, 995–3, Box 6, Peabody Museum Archives, Harvard University.

11. Later to become a national organization called the Prehistoric Society.

12. D. A. E. Garrod, *The Upper Palaeolithic Age in Britain* (Oxford, 1926), 9.

13. MacCurdy, "My Time."

14. Breuil's disparaging comment is at last proved wrong: Paul Bahn, Paul Pettitt, and Sergio Ripoll, "Discovery of Cave Art in Britain," *Antiquity* 296 (2003): 227–31. J. Campbell, *The Upper Palaeolithic of Britain: A Study of Man and Nature in the Late Ice Age* (Oxford, 1977).

15. D. A. E. Garrod, L. H. Dudley Buxton, G. Elliot Smith, and Dorothea M. A. Bate, "Excavation of a Mousterian Rock-Shelter at Devil's Tower, Gibraltar," *Journal of the Royal Anthropological Institute* 58 (1928): 33–113.

16. H. Field, *The Track of Man* (New York, 1953), 4.

17. Garrod et al., "Mousterian Rock-Shelter"; Garrod's photograph albums are preserved in the Fonds Suzanne Cassou de St. Mathurin, Bibliothèque de la Musée des Antiquités Nationales, 78103 St. Germain-en-Laye, France; current age estimation for "Abel," R. Kruszynski (personal communication); J-J. Hublin, C. Barroso Ruiz, P. Medira Lara, M. Fortugne S.F.-L. Reyss "The Mousterian Site of Zafarraya (Andalucía, Spain): Dating and Implications on the Palaeolithic Peo-

the Light of Recent Research," in *Problems in Prehistory: North Africa and the Levant,* ed. F. Wendorf and A. E. Marks (Dallas, 1975), 317–50; A. J. Jelinek, "The Middle Palaeolithic in the Southern Levant from the Perspective of the Tabun Cave," in *Préhistoire du Levant,* ed. J. Cauvin and P. Sanlaville (Paris, 1981), 265–80; A. J. Jelinek, "The Tabun Cave and Paleolithic Man in the Levant," *Science* 216, no. 4553 (1982): 1369–75; A. Ronen and A. Tsatskin, "New Interpretation of the Oldest Part of the Tabun Cave Sequence, Mount Carmel, Israel," in *Man and Environment in the Palaeolithic,* ed. H. Ullrich (Liège, 1995), 265–81; O. Bar-Yosef, "The Lower and Middle Palaeolithic in the Mediterranean Levant: Chronology and Cultural Entities," in Ullrich, *Man and Environment,* 247–63; O. Bar-Yosef, "The Chronology of the Middle Paleolithic of the Levant," in *Neandertals and Modern Humans in Western Asia,* ed. T. Akazawa, K. Aoki, and O. Bar-Yosef (New York, 1998), 39–56.

50. F. Turville-Petre, "Excavations in the Mugharet el-Kebarah," *Journal of the Royal Anthropological Institute* 62 (1932): 271–76.

51. D. A. E. Garrod, "Excavations at the Mugharet Kebara, Mount Carmel, 1931: The Aurignacian Industries," *Proceedings of the Prehistoric Society* 20 (1954): 155–92.

52. Bar-Yosef and Callander, "Turville-Petre."

53. J. Hawkes, interview with J. Callander, 1990.

54. Garrod and Bate, *Mount Carmel,* 64.

55. T. D. McCown, "The Oldest Complete Skeletons of Man." *Bulletin of the American School of Prehistoric Research* 10 (1934): 13–18; O. Bar-Yosef and J. Callander, "The Woman from Tabun: Garrod's Doubts in Historical Perspective," *Journal of Human Evolution* (1999): 879–85.

56. R. Vaufrey, "Paléolithique et Mésolithique palestiniens." *Revue scientifique* 79 (1939): 390–406.

57. Garrod and Bate, *Mount Carmel.*

58. See A. Rust, *Die Höhlenfunde von Jabrud (Syrien)* (Neumünster, 1950) and D. A. E. Garrod, "Acheuléo-Jabrudien et 'Pre-Aurignacien' de la grotte du Taboun (Mont Carmel): Etude stratigraphique et chronologique," *Quaternaria* 3 (1956): 39–59.

59. D. A .E. Garrod and E. W. Gardner, "Pleistocene Coastal Deposits in Palestine," *Nature* 135 (1935): 908–9.

60. Most authorities agree the *kurkar* ridges were formed from both beach and wind-blown sands and that the layers of *hamra* represent soil formation. There are diverse chronological interpretations, but the red loam containing Mousterian implements is often known as the "Mousterian *hamra.*" See W. R. Farrand and A. Ronen, "Observations on the Kurkar-Hamra Succession on the Carmel Coastal Plain," *Tel-Aviv* 1 (1974): 45–54; A. Tsatskin and A. Ronen, "Micromorphology of a Mousterian Paleosol in Aeolianites at the Site Habonim, Israel," *Catena* 34 (1999): 365–84. See also A. Ronen, "Mousterian Sites in Red Loam in the Coastal Plain of Mount Carmel," in *Eretz-Israel: Archaeological, Historical, and Geographical Studies,* vol. 13, *Moshe Stekelis Memorial Volume,* ed. B. Arensburg and O. Bar-Yosef (Jerusalem, 1977), 183–90.

61. Now Gesher Benot Ya'aqov.

62. D. A. E. Garrod, "The Middle Palaeolithic of the Near East and the Prob-

lem of Mount Carmel Man," *Journal of the Royal Anthropological Institute* 92 (1962): 232–51.

63. M. Stekelis, "The Palaeolithic Deposits of Jisr Banat Yaqub," *Bulletin of the Research Council of Israel* 9G, nos. 2–3 (1960): 61–90.

64. N. Goren-Inbar and I. Saragusti, "An Acheulian Biface Assemblage from Gesher Benot Ya'aqov, Israel: Indications of African Affinities," *Journal of Field Archaeology* 23 (1966): 15–30.

65. Garrod and Bate, *Mount Carmel,* 123.

66. F. Turville-Petre, *Researches in Prehistoric Galilee, 1925–1926* (London, 1927); G. Zumoffen, *La Phénicie avant des Phéniciens* (Beirut, 1900); P. Karge, *Rephaïm. Die vorgeschichtliche Kultur Palästinas und Phöniziens* (Münster, 1917).

67. D. A. E. Garrod et al., "Report on the A.S.P.R. Expedition to Anatolia, 1938," *Bulletin of the American School of Prehistoric Research* 15 (1939): 13–27.

68. D. A. E. Garrod, "Excavations in the Cave of Bacho Kiro, North-East Bulgaria," *Bulletin of the American School of Prehistoric Research* 15 (1939): 46–80.

69. J. Kozlowski, *Excavation in the Bacho Kiro Cave (Bulgaria): Final Report* (Warsaw, 1982); J. Kozlowski, "The Transition from the Middle to the Early Upper Palaeolithic in Central Europe and the Balkans," in *The Early Upper Palaeolithic: Evidence from Europe and the Near East,* ed. J. F. Hoffecker and C. A. Wolf, BAR International Series 437 (Oxford, 1988), 193–235.

70. G. E. Daniel, *Some Small Harvest* (London, 1986); R. Daniel, interview with J. Callander, 1997; P.-J. Smith, personal communication.

71. Caton-Thompson, "Garrod," 340.

72. P.-J. Smith, personal communication; Garrod, "Shukbah, Palestine, 1928."

73. Daniel, *Some Small Harvest,* 98.

74. Caton-Thompson, "Garrod," 339. Robin Kenward (née Place), interview with P.-J. Smith.

75. D. A. E. Garrod, letter to Sir Arthur Keith, January 21, 1954, Archives of the Royal College of Surgeons of England Library, London, box KLI, letters A–M.

76. J. G. D. Clark, *Prehistory at Cambridge and Beyond* (Cambridge, 1989); M. Thatcher, interview with J. Callander and P.-J. Smith, 1996. P.-J. Smith, "Dorothy Garrod First Woman Professor at Cambridge" *Antiquity* 74 (2000): 131–36.

77. Garrod, "Problem of Mount Carmel Man."

78. Garrod, "Finding the Earliest Realistic Portrait in the History of Man," *Illustrated London News,* July 16, 1949, 91; D. Garrod and S. de St. Mathurin, "The Master Sculptors of 12,000 Years Ago Revealed," *Illustrated London News,* March 15, 1952, 454; J. Crowfoot-Payne, interview with J. Callander, 1993.

79. Garrod, "Mugharet Kebara, Mount Carmel."

80. D. A. E. Garrod, "The Mugharet-el-Emireh in Lower Galilee, Type-Station of the Emiran Industry," *Journal of the Royal Anthropological Institute* 85 (1955): 141–62; F. Turville-Petre, "Excavation of Two Palaeolithic Caves in Galilee," *British School of Archaeology in Jerusalem, Bulletin* 7 (1925): 99–101; R. Neuville, "Le Paléolithique et le Mésolithique de Désert de Judée," *Archives de L'Institut de Paléontologie Humaine,* Memoir 24 (Paris, 1951).

81. A. E. Marks and D. Kaufman, "Boker Tachtit: The Artifacts," in *Prehistory and Paleoenvironments in the Central Negev, Israel,* ed. A. E. Marks, vol. 3

(Dallas, 1983): 69–126; P. Volkman, "Boker Tachtit: Core Reconstructions," in *Prehistory and Paleoenvironments in the Central Negev, Israel,* 3:127–90.

82. D. A. E. Garrod, letter to Sir Arthur Keith, January 21, 1954, Archives of the Royal College of Surgeons of England Library, London, box KLI, letters A–M.

83. Garrod, "Grotte du Taboun."

84. D. A. E. Garrod and D. Kirkbride, "The Excavations of the Abri Zumoffen, A Palaeolithic Rock-Shelter near Adlun, South Lebanon, 1958," *Bulletin du Musée de Beyrouth* 16 (1961): 8–46.

85. A. J. Jelinek, "The Amudian in the Context of the Mugharan Tradition at the Tabun Cave, Mt. Carmel, Israel," in *The Emergence of Modern Humans,* ed. P. Mellars (Edinburgh, 1990), 81–90.

86. Solecki, *Shanidar,* 126.

87. Garrod, "Problem of Mount Carmel Man," 237.

88. D. A. E. Garrod, "Palaeolithic Spear-Throwers," *Proceedings of the Prehistoric Society* 21 (1955): 21–35.

89. D. A. E. Garrod, "Rouffignac," *Antiquity* 32 (1958): 231–34; letter to Miles Burkitt, August 25, 1961. Current opinion is that the engravings and most drawings at Rouffignac are genuine; some are clumsy in execution, but the anatomical details of the mammoths are hard to explain other than by observation of the live animal. A few images remain doubtful, notably the rhinoceros frieze; P. G. Bahn and A. M. Lister, *Mammoths* (New York, 1994) and personal communication from both authors. Pigment analysis, as well as radiocarbon dating of any organic material thus obtained, would solve the mystery, but despite many pleas since the original discovery, no scientific techniques have yet been applied. P. G. Bahn, "The 'Dead Wood' Stage of Prehistoric Art Studies: Style Is Not Enough," in *Rock Art Studies: The Post-stylistic Era, or Where Do We Go from Here?* ed. M. Lorblanchet and P. G. Bahn, Oxbow Monograph 35 (Oxford, 1993), 51–59.

90. Garrod, "Henri Breuil."

91. D. A. E. Garrod, "The Natufian Culture: The Life and Economy of a Mesolithic People in the Near East," *Proceedings of the British Academy* 43 (1957): 211–27.

92. D. Kirkbride, interviews with J. Callander, 1994–95.

93. Garrod, "Problem of Mount Carmel Man," 232.

94. D. A. E. Garrod, letter to Ralph S. Solecki, November 3, 1960.

95. L. Copeland and N. M. Moloney, eds., *The Mousterian Cave Site at Ras el-Kelb, Lebanon* British Archaeological Reports. International Series 706 (Oxford, 1998). D. A. E. Garrod and D. Henri-Martin, "Rapport préliminaire sur la fouille d'une grotte au Ras el-Kelb," *Bulletin du Musée de Beyrouth* 16 (1961): 61–67; Garrod, "Problem of Mount Carmel Man."

96. D. Roe, ed., *Adlun in the Stone Age: The Excavations of D. A. E. Garrod in the Lebanon, 1958–63,* British Archaeological Reports International Series 159 (Oxford, 1983).

97. Garrod's interest in dating methods is demonstrated in her correspondence over many years with Dr. Kenneth Oakley, of the Natural History Museum, London. Some survives there; more is preserved in the Garrod Archive in France (supra n. 43). The earlier levels at her sites lay beyond the limit of radiocarbon dating, but since her death some have been dated by the scientific methods now available, e.g.,

H. Valladas, J.-L. Joron, G. Valladas, B. Arensburg, O. Bar-Yosef, A. Belfer-Cohen, P. Goldberg, H. Laville, L. Meignen, Y. Rak, E. Tchernov, A. M. Tillier, and B. Vandermeersch, "Thermoluminescence Dates for the Neanderthal Burial Site at Kebara in Israel," *Nature* 330 (1987): 159–60; H. Valladas, J.-L. Reyss, J.-L. Joron, G. Valladas, O. Bar-Yosef, and B. Vandermeersch, "Thermoluminescence Dating of Mousterian 'Proto-Cro-Magnon' Remains from Israel and the Origin of Modern Man," *Nature* 331 (1988): 614–15; R. Grün, C. B. Stringer, and H. P. Schwarcz, "ESR Dating of Teeth from Garrod's Tabun Cave Collection," *Journal of Human Evolution* 20 (1991): 231–48; N. Mercier, H. Valladas, G. Valladas, and J.-L. Reyss, "TL Dates of Burnt Flints from Jelinek's Excavations at Tabun and Their Implications," *Journal of Archaeological Science* 22 (1995): 495–508.

98. D. A. E. Garrod, letter to Ralph S. Solecki, August 11, 1962.

99. L. Copeland, interview with J. Callander, 1993.

100. D. A. E. Garrod, letter to Ralph S. Solecki, January 26, 1964.

101. D. A. E. Garrod, letter to Ralph S. Solecki, July 20, 1966; St. Mathurin, "Garrod."

102. D. A. E. Garrod, "Mugharet el-Bezez, Adlun (Lebanon): Interim Report, July 1965," *Bulletin du Musée de Beyrouth* 19 (1966): 5–10.

103. D. A. E. Garrod, unpublished acceptance speech to the Society of Antiquaries, London, April 23, 1968. Garrod's manuscript for her speech is preserved in box b1, inventory no. 33431, Fonds Suzanne Cassou de St. Mathurin, Bibliotheque de la Musée des Antiquités Nationales, 78103 St. Germain-en-Laye, France.

104. M. Lovedy Smith, interview with J. Callander, 1998.

105. Garrod was quoting William Wordsworth's poem *The Prelude,* book xi, 1, 108 (1805) in her Huxley Lecture, "Problem of Mount Carmel Man."

106. L. Copeland, personal communication.

Winifred Lamb

(1894–1963)

David W. J. Gill

WINIFRED LAMB IS HONORED among archaeologists for her pioneering fieldwork and her significant contribution to the study of Greek bronzes. She was involved with a series of excavations in Greece—at Mycenae, at Sparta and in Macedonia—before directing her own excavations at Thermi on Lesbos. She also excavated in Anatolia, at Kusura, and it was her interest in the prehistory of Anatolia that helped to establish the British Institute of Archaeology at Ankara after World War II. Her publication *Greek and Roman Bronzes* is considered one of the best general introductions on this subject. Throughout her years of active fieldwork she was Honorary Keeper of Greek Antiquities at the Fitzwilliam Museum in the University of Cambridge, a period that lasted nearly forty years.

Early Life and Education

Born in London on November 3, 1894, Winifred Lamb was the only child of Edmund George and Mabel Lamb, of Holly Lodge, Campden Hill. She was a Roman Catholic like her father. The family originally lived at Old Lodge, near Salisbury in Wiltshire, and then moved to Borden Wood in West Sussex.[1] Her father, who had been educated at Merton College, Oxford, was a landowner and, from 1906 to 1910, a Liberal Member of Parliament for North Herefordshire. Lamb received her education at home in company with girls of another family. Her subsequent success at Cambridge was in part due to her father's instruction. Lamb's mother, who had attended Newnham, a women's college, also took part in her education, and her contribution should not be underestimated. On April 22, 1921, during a tour of the Peloponnese, Lamb wrote: "Do you remember, Mother, my reading to you oracles about the 1st Messenian War, one day in Holly Lodge verandah."[2]

Lamb read classics at Cambridge. She was admitted to Newnham College in 1913. Newnham had by this time won "notable distinction" in classics, in part through the endeavors of Jane E. Harrison, Newnham College lecturer in classical archaeology (1899–1922), who was noted for her work in Greek archaeology and religion.[3] At this point women were not members of Cambridge University, and there was considerable opposition from some sectors to women being admitted to courses.[4] Indeed, Sir William Ridgeway, the Disney Professor of Archaeology, refused to let Lamb attend his classical archaeology lectures even though he had allowed women to attend in previous years.[5] This was no doubt in part due to his intense dislike of Jane Harrison: "It was said of Ridgeway that his friends found it difficult to recall exactly what his theories about drama and religion in ancient Greece comprised, save that they were all points the opposite of Jane Harrison's."[6]

While at Newnham, Lamb "found it difficult to acclimatize herself to the communal life of the college."[7] She seems to have made few friends, though an exception was apparently Muriel E. H. Lloyd, who also read classics.[8] However, her interest in classical archaeology at this stage of her life made itself quite apparent. She began to acquire Greek pottery. In 1916 she purchased a Late Cypriot oinochoe.[9] In 1917 she made further purchases of Greek pottery at the sale of the Hope heirlooms.[10]

The War Years: Naval Intelligence

Lamb completed the Classical Tripos at Cambridge in 1917 and then joined the Naval Intelligence Department (Room 40) at the Admiralty in London.[11] John Beazley, who was to become an eminent expert in Greek vases, was also a member of Room 40.[12] Perhaps it was this contact with Beazley that helped Lamb further her interest in Greek pottery. In 1918 Lamb published a study of seven Greek pots in the *Journal of Hellenic Studies.*[13] It is clear that Beazley had been in a position to help her with the study.[14] Lamb's writing shows that she sensed anonymous pot-painters at work: a painter of black-figured lekythoi could have "ingenuity and some dramatic instinct"; the style of a red-figured *kotyle* "generally points to the Brygos painter"; a red-figured column-krater belonged to "the Polygnotan circle."[15] This approach is in marked contrast to that adopted by E. M. W. Tillyard, who may have lectured to Lamb in her first year at Cambridge. Tillyard had started to write a catalog of the Hope vases (prior to the 1917 sale) in 1913 but was only able to complete it after the collection had been dispersed. This work followed the more traditional stylistic groupings rather than those of painters and workshops being adopted by Beazley.[16]

Lamb's interest in Greek painted pottery is also reflected in her review of Joseph Clark Hoppin's book *Euthymides and His Fellows,* which had been published in 1917.[17] It reveals her familiarity with the attempts to attribute unsigned Greek pots and the new "science of vases." Indeed, her review concludes with an anticipation of the future study of similar painters. Such interest in the decoration of Athenian pottery could well have come from her association with Beazley during the war years. Their work in deciphering enemy codes, in part through the identification of individual anonymous signalers, may have assisted with this approach.[18] Yet her interest was not confined to Greek pottery, as reflected in her review of the *Catalogue of the Arretine Pottery in the Museum of Fine Arts, Boston.*[19] She was clearly impressed with the layout and detail of the book, concluding that such "dainty and attractive [objects] cannot fail to be a source of enjoyment as well as of information."[20]

Excavations

As well as undertaking curatorial responsibilities at the Fitzwilliam Museum in Cambridge, Lamb joined a series of excavations in Greece under the auspices of the British School at Athens.[21] It is important to remember that these were early days for the involvement of women in such activities.[22] Indeed, it was only in the winter of 1920 that women were admitted as residents of the hostel of the British School.[23] Details of Lamb's frequent visits to Greece and the British School at Athens during the 1920s and 1930s are recorded in letters to her parents.[24]

Lamb first visited the School as an official student on Monday, October 18, 1920, the day she arrived in Athens, although she was staying at a hotel. She had tea with two individuals who were to influence her work in Greece: the British vice-consul F. B. Welch, who was to accompany her on many walks round Attica,[25] and Carl Blegen of the American School, with whom she was to excavate at Mycenae.[26] Lamb made several trips around Greece with two of the other women at the School, May Herford and Lilian Chandler (Mrs. Batey).[27] In a cartoon dating to 1920 and based on an Attic black-figured amphora, Lamb showed a group of five students (F. B. Welch, Mrs. Ashmole, Bernard Ashmole, May Herford, and Lilian Chandler) advancing on the housekeeper, Kalliope; friezes of tennis rackets and orthodox priests completed the scene.[28]

Lamb was soon introduced to the classical sites of Greece. Her first day in Athens was spent on the Acropolis; this was followed by an extended trip to Delphi and Boeotia. Clearly the site of Delphi captured her imagination:

> Delphi itself is very wonderful, with Parnassus towering above, and a deep gorge where rises the Castalian spring. Almost always there were a couple of eagles, or perhaps one, wheeling about and making queer cries, and sometimes a flight of birds as a gust of wind would come out of the gorge with a curious rushing sound. I don't wonder the Persians turned back in alarm when they went to Delphi.[29]

On her return to Athens she viewed the funeral of King Alexander of Greece, gaining admission through the good offices of Welch. On the following Monday, Lamb was proud to announce that she had started working in the Acropolis Museum, "a fascinating place."[30] During her stay in Athens she was able to join a number of British School walks to various sites in Attica. She was moved by her visit to Marathon, no doubt remembering the horrors of the Great War, so recently ended: "The battlefield of Marathon we saw rather early. It was a grey, rather cold day and the 'soros' was extraordinarily impressive. One wanted to be able to take off one's hat like a man."[31]

The sight of Lamb, Herford and Chandler walking the Greek countryside was clearly unusual. In November 1920 Lamb recalled meeting a peasant woman who "told us that girls like ourselves could never cross Hymettus and we had far better come back to Spata and stay with her."[32] Other school trips were arranged, like the one at the end of November 1920 to Aegina. Lamb returned home for Christmas but returned to Greece in the spring of 1921. In March she visited Corinth, Akrocorinth, and Isthmia, followed by a trip (with Herford and Chandler) to Crete in early April. Arthur Evans's excavation at Knossos impressed her. In a letter home she wrote:

> Yesterday (Sunday) we went to Knossos. The palace is more wonderful than that of Phaistos but less perfect and the situation is disappointing. But what pleases my childish soul in these Minoan palaces are the staircases and steps—think of running up and down a prehistoric staircase of 4 flights as at Knossos!

In late April there followed a tour of the Peloponnese. She then visited Nauplion and Thebes before leaving for the Mycenae excavations. The excavation was to begin officially on May 22, "though Miss Lamb and Miss Herford arrived two days before and occupied themselves in arranging the workroom and other preparations." The women found accommodation at the "La Belle Helène."[33]

Lamb does not seem to have been at the British School in the autumn of 1921 but returned in April 1922. After a trip to Argos and Sparta, she resumed work on the Mycenae finds at Nauplion, though frustrated by lack of access to the museum, which led to her commandeering the keys of both the museum and the cases.[34] During this study visit she was able to visit the Swedish excavations of Asine at Tolon with Wace and Miles Burkitt.[35] She recalled, "the finds are all very near the surface, almost in pockets of the rock which makes dull digging." In early May she took a voyage up the Euripus and was able to visit the prehistoric site of Dhimini. She was struck by this part of Greece: "Central Thessaly is the sort of country one might see in a dream, flat and desolate with weird shaped hills at intervals."

Additional trips into Thessaly were conducted in April 1925 after the Macedonian excavations. Lamb had been due to go on a walking holiday in Arcadia with Gertrude Caton-Thompson during April. They met at Piraeus and on Easter Sunday took the train to Mycenae, sleeping on the floor at La Belle Helène. Lamb developed a bad cough during the night, which turned into whooping cough, and the trip had to be abandoned.[36]

The British School also brought Lamb into contact with other excavators. For example, on November 20, 1920 she had tea at the school with "Seager, one of the Americans who digs in Crete, . . . told most amusing and scandalous stories about all the other archaeologists. Great fun."[37] Her fluency in German brought her into regular contact with members of the German School, including F. Studniczka and W. Dörpfeld.[38] Such connections were to be continued as she started her work in Anatolia. Lamb clearly loved the British School at Athens. In early June of 1924, after working at the Sparta excavation, she wrote home:

> Here I am back in the place which, next to B[orden] W[ood], I love most in the world—the familiar streets and the little green pine trees and the people playing Turkish airs on funny little concertinas . . . Borden Wood I love a degree too much to have the feeling of perfection; and I also love this place passionately here as I love Borden tenderly.[39]

Lamb was eventually granted a life studentship of the school in 1931 and served for many years on the managing committee.

Mycenae

In the spring of 1920 the British School at Athens began its first campaign at Mycenae under the directorship of Alan J. B. Wace and the codirectorship of C. W. Blegen of the American School.[40] Although Lamb had not been in Greece as a student of the British School during the season, Wace had allocated the publication of the frescoes to her, and she had been busy working on them over the winter.[41] As a student of the school, Lamb joined the second season of excavations, which were supported financially by her parents.[42] The excavations resumed in May 1921 and Lamb was in "principal charge" of the excavation of the Palace.[43] During the 1922 campaign, she was second-in-command to Wace during the excavations; she left "Athens for Mycenae on May 11, and began work the next day with six men."[44] In this season she was working on the tombs in the Kalkani cemetery.[45] One member of the excavation team was Miss Hilda L. Lorimer. Both Lamb and Lorimer, as well as other women on the team, stayed at the hotel La Belle Helène.[46] The 1923 season consisted of working through the finds at Athens and Nauplion.[47] Lamb was involved in both centers; at Athens with Miss Eldridge and Miss J. Pybus[48] and at Nauplion with Professor Droop,[49] Mr. and Mrs. A. W. Gomme (Miss Phyllis Emmerson), and Mr. W. A. Heurtley.[50] The excavations were terminated because of the committee's decision not to reappoint Wace as director of the School.[51]

Lamb herself seems to have been chiefly responsible for the publication of the frescoes found during the excavations—in particular, those from the Ramp House, which had been excavated by Schliemann in 1876 but completed by the British team in 1921.[52] She was able to demonstrate that fragments of fresco found by Schliemann (but without precise findspot) joined some of the fragments found during the later excavations.[53] The report also shows her associations with scholars, acknowledging Sir Arthur Evans and Stephanos Xanthoudides (the ephor on Crete).[54]

Lamb also coauthored the publication of various aspects of the Palace at Mycenae,[55] reporting on the Pithos area, the Court, the Shrine and adjoining areas, the Megaron, and the Ante-chamber to the domestic quarters. The Palace itself had been excavated by Christos Tsountas in 1886, been reexamined by G. Rodenwalt in 1914, and become the subject of the British excavations from 1920 to 1923. Lamb's publication of the frescoes included not only those discovered by the British School but also those excavated by Tsountas and was thus able to put the earlier work into context. In this way solid museum work enhanced Lamb's interpretation of her own excavated material. She was also sensitive to chronological issues, noting the related pottery.[56] The publication of the Court included a detailed discussion of the painted stucco floor.[57] It reappraised Rodenwalt's 1914 study, suggesting that his reconstruction was not entirely accurate. The study of the Shrine and adjoining chambers addressed the stucco altars and fragmentary wall paintings.[58] Careful excavation also uncovered traces of the clay roof still with the impression of reeds and brushwood.[59] The report on the Megaron discussed the wall decoration, and Lamb was able to draw parallels with those from the Ramp House.[60] She shows a degree of sophistication in trying to date the frescoes, dismissing earlier attempts to place them in Late Helladic I; in part she was considering the length of time that a fresco would have been viewed.[61] The final study, which again should be attributed to Lamb, examines the paintings from the antechamber to the domestic quarters. Interestingly, parallels are drawn between the painting and textile details, an area that was to interest Wace in future years.[62]

The reports also draw attention to environmental data, which was to become a feature of Lamb's own excavation reports. Such remains included oyster shells and the bones of sheep and swine.[63] The report of the chamber tombs, published by Wace, was accompanied by a detailed appendix on the skulls by Professor Carl M. Fürst.[64] The detailed studies of pottery, metalwork, engraved gems, and other material no doubt provided a model for Lamb's publication of her own excavations of Kusura, which appeared in *Archaeologia*.

Lamb managed to acquire a small number of finds from Mycenae, which were donated to the Fitzwilliam in 1922 by the British School at Athens, perhaps, in part, because her parents were among the benefactors of the excavations.[65] In the previous year she herself had given a number of spindle whorls from the site.[66] In 1923 an "anonymous friend" of Wace made a substantial donation of Mycenaean material, mostly replicas, to the Fitzwilliam.[67] In 1922 Lamb also donated sherds from Korakou in the Corinthia.[68]

Vardaroftsa and Sarátse, Macedonia

In early 1924 Lamb was working with W. A. Heurtley, assistant director of the British School, on the excavations of the mound at Vardaroftsa in Macedonia, thirty-five kilometers northwest of Salonika. This project was intended to consolidate earlier survey work by Heurtley and Cuttle in western Chalcidice and western Macedonia.[69] Lamb had taken an interest in the excavations in May 1922.[70] The team tested the mound to a depth of five meters and provided important information about the post-Mycenaean period in Macedonia. Lamb was responsible for the surveying, which she described as "really hard but great fun." In 1925 she also seems to have been responsible for a trench.

Unlike the excavations at Mycenae and Sparta, this excavation provided only basic accommodation for women; published photographs show the tents pitched alongside the mound. She wrote in a letter, "A good little tent, even though I did have to dress with one hand one morning and hold it down with the other."[71] In fact the only other woman on the team appears to have been Heurtley's wife, Eileen, who was present as "caterer and cook."[72] Lamb wrote home about the living conditions in early March 1924:

> It is not so cold at nights now and I sleep beautifully even if fully clad (I change clothes when dressing). An early cup of tea and biscuits at 7, work till 8.30. Breakfast till 9, work 9–12, lunch 12–1.30, work 1.30–4, tea at 4. Work ends at 6.

She enjoyed the excavation so much that she rejoined the team the following March, stoically putting up with the basic conditions: "I am no colder in bed than I have often been at Cambridge." By April Lamb was suffering from a form of bronchitis.[73] Such excavation experience will no doubt have prepared Lamb for later work in Anatolia. This excavation may also have started to raise questions in Lamb's mind about the links among the different regions bordering the Aegean: Macedonia, Thessaly, and western Anatolia. This is certainly true for the specific comparisons made with Troy and the Toumba of Protesilaos, both of which Lamb studied in later years.[74]

The Macedonian excavation also tried to place the site in its original environmental setting.[75]

The Macedonian work with Heurtley had set Lamb to thinking about excavating her own prehistoric "mound." She returned to Greece in mid-October 1927 and, after a short trip to Mycenae and Nauplion, set off for the Gulf of Corinth—including a visit to Thermon—in the first week of November to look for a suitable site.[76] On October 29, she wrote to her mother suggesting that the search for a suitable site would not be easy. Lamb expected to rejoin Heurtley in March 1928. She may have been in the region again in late 1928 as in that year she presented to the Fitzwilliam a range of sherds collected from Drama, Lembet, and Sedes.[77] In spring 1929 she rejoined Heurtley's team to work on the Bronze Age site of Sarátse before her own excavation at Thermi.[78]

Sparta

Renewed excavations by the British School started at Sparta in March 1924 under the directorship of A. M. Woodward and the codirectorship of Margaret Hobling.[79] This change in emphasis in part reflected the school's desire to work on a classical site. After her work at Mycenae through the early 1920s, Lamb was readmitted as a student of the British School during the 1923–24 session and then annually between 1927 and 1934.[80] Earlier in the year Lamb had been working with Heurtley in Macedonia and only joined the Sparta excavation a week after it had started. According to Woodward, she was given specific charge of "two trial trenches, which yielded valuable results."[81] Woodward later recalled "her careful technique helped materially to unravel the complicated stratification of the precinct of Athena Chalkioikos."[82] Lamb, however, gave a less sanguine view of her responsibilities in a letter to her mother:

> I am so penitent about my early dull letters from the dig, but it was not enlivening when I had only the Byzantine suburb and six of Cullen's men. Now I have nine in four trial pits (I had rarely done trial pits at Mycenae so am glad of the experience) . . . [In contrast,] Miss Hobling on the top of the hill has got some nice bronze objects and one topping ivory griffon's head two inches long.[83]

Lamb's confidence in her own techniques is reflected in her comment that "George the foreman regards anyone who has dug at Mycenae as privileged."[84]

Lamb found that the excavations tried her patience, especially with Woodward. She recounted her frustrations in a letter home, at the same time expressing concern for her father's failing health.

> [I] told the Director that as things were slack in my part of the dig I ought to go home on Thursday next. Whereupon he promised me the area on the Acropolis west of Miss Hobling's as well as what I am digging now and two more men. So I shall stay on and do it unless you write for me. The dig ends at the end of May anyway. The Acropolis region has (1) excellent archaic pottery (2) archaic bronzes and (sometimes) archaic pottery. Also I should like to finish the house with the mosaic which is very pretty.[85]

This letter also reveals Woodward's emphasis on recovering inscriptions from the excavation:

> The last bits behind the Byzantine wall (looking for inscriptions) are most formidable in depth and refuse to reach virgin soil. The men say that they are going down to the world below. I feel as if I was, when, aided by a rope and a precarious foothold, I descend.

Woodward, himself a rock climber, descended the hole unaided and "found it none too easy."

Lamb also was responsible for preparing the bronzes from the acropolis for publication.[86] In 1927 she recounted to her mother:

> Woodward paid me the compliment of asking me to publish the bronzes recently found at Sparta which include a plum. He said he had very much liked my article on Arcadian bronzes in the B.S.A. I accepted. It will mean three or four days at Sparta (no more) on the way to Heurtley's dig.[87]

Her subsequent study shows her familiarity with such collections as those in Athens and Berlin, as well as the literature relating to museum collections. She was also able to put in context Fitzwilliam holdings such as the small bronze helmeted head acquired by Col. W. M. Leake at Kaiapha in Elis.[88] Moreover, she took the opportunity to reassess the bronze finds from earlier excavations.[89]

Lamb seems to have enjoyed her time on the excavation, where conditions were more comfortable than in Macedonia. She recalled, "The four girls are in an inn, but it is not at all bad for Sparta and I have a room to myself." The day's program started at 6:15 and, after eating some bread and butter and tea, a little before 7:00, work began. There were breaks at 8:30 for breakfast, 12:00–2:00 for lunch, and 4:30 for a cup of tea, and the day ended at 6:00. Yet her disagreements with Woodward made her feel glad that "Sparta is over."[90] She did, however, make particular friends of Cuttle—with whom she had been working in Macedonia—and Piet de Jong. She wrote, "Cuttle, ambitious and anxious about careers and scholarships, looks on archaeology in a way remarkably like mine. But de Jong has more joy of life than almost anyone I know, and it was he who, unconsciously perhaps, made the party so merry and prevented undue despondency, when things were not going well, by his historic series of caricatures."[91]

Lamb used her time in Sparta to travel, enjoying a trip in late April to the Mani with Hobling.[92] It is possible that she acquired the bronze figure of an athlete for the Fitzwilliam at this time. She noted confidently that it came from Sparta; presumably she was given the opportunity to buy it.[93]

The Sparta excavations constituted a turning point in Lamb's career. In a reflective letter written on her way home from the excavations, she confided to her mother that "Archaeology is a wonderful life."[94] She had clearly been frustrated at having to work under Woodward and Hobling, in contrast to Mycenae, where she had been second-in-command under Wace. In the same letter she wrote, "I suppose it was really painful for your rather autocratic daughter not to have the same position as at Mycenae," and continued, "I've learned enough to run a dig of my own, in fact many sorts of digs including the kinds not illustrated at Mycenae. And I have enjoyed unearthing archaic objects of great charm and beauty."

Although much of the rest of her career was dedicated to prehistoric archaeology, she did excavate Archaic sites at Antissa and Kato Phana, as well as reviewing some books on Archaic sculpture and writing up her own studies of bronzes and pottery. In early June she took the opportunity to discuss her career with "the General"—Woodward—and it seems that her mind was fixed on her own excavation.

> First of all, we discussed my future (a most interesting topic!) and he suggested all sorts of attractive and practical schemes for my next year's dig, which will not be the school dig. I am not going to work under Wace again, which remark is made quite without bitterness and is merely a statement.[95]

She also clearly wished to avoid working under Woodward again.

As in the Mycenae excavations, the British School at Athens, with the cooperation of the Greek government, gave a generous donation of excavated material from Sparta to the Fitzwilliam. The British Museum and the Ashmolean Museum were also recipients.[96] These objects, acquired in 1923, complemented the earlier material from Amyklai acquired in 1907.

Methymna, Lesbos

In autumn 1928 Lamb undertook a fortnight's trial excavation to the northwest of the modern town of Methymna (Mólivo) on the island of Lesbos.[97] This site was located in the area known as the "Dabbia," a promontory within the line of the ancient city walls. The excavation discovered occupation from the seventh century B.C. (and possibly back to the ninth) through to the Roman period.[98] As the soil was quite shallow, there was little stratigraphy, and so "further excavation was considered inadvisable"; indeed Roman sherds were found on bedrock.[99] Lamb found one structure, a house, which can be dated by two pieces of Çandarlı ware of the first century B.C. and the first century A.D.[100] She recognized that the excavation "gave additional evidence of the longevity of bucchero wares, which, on this site, were either plain or decorated with stamped or incised patterns."[101] Some of this pottery was published in her study of gray wares from Lesbos.[102] Apart from a sherd of Corinthian and one piece of East Greek, the "chief find" was "a pretty bronze statuette of Eros," probably Hellenistic in date.[103] The Roman wares, which were published by F. N. Pryce at Lamb's request, included Eastern Sigillata A, a large amount of Çandarlı ware, and two sherds of Late Roman C ware, one of which can be dated to the early sixth century A.D.[104] Lamb's own verdict on the excavation was that "though it is not an epoch making excavation, it is a really useful one" as it shed light on Lesbian pottery.[105]

Thermi, Lesbos

Lamb's previous excavation experience had been mostly linked to the Bronze Age, notably at Mycenae and in Macedonia. Her work with Heurtley had suggested associations between Macedonia and western Anatolia, and Lesbos seemed to offer an opportunity to explore this link. She had already been looking for a prehistoric site in mainland Greece in late 1927, and in March 1928 she went to Lesbos looking for a suitable site.[106] Lamb made a preliminary survey in March and April, which led to her short exploratory excavation at Methymna in the autumn. In November she resumed her field walking with R. W. Hutchinson. Few sites offered themselves, and they decided to search a new corner of the island. Her letter home reveals the events that followed:

> Then the weather broke. Next day torrents of rain. We took the post bus to a place called Thermi, the last possible place, where there was a river, a great bay and other things associated with prehistoric settlements. The rain was clearing when we got out of the car. We looked at the coast, and I said it does look rather like a little mound, but perhaps it is natural, and the Squire [i.e., Hutchinson] said, "it isn't much smaller than the one at Myli." So we went to the place indicated. It was at the edge of the sea, and we walked at the water's edge because there was a section cut by the sea. Yes, a few pot sherds, indefinite. So it must have been inhabited . . . what about this sherd? Rather early surely? And that? Hand made. Then the plums began to show in the slice of cake: a sherd of "rippled ware" (very proto proto), a beautiful handle like Troy, first city, a rim like early Macedonian ware, a base like early Helladic . . . we just stood with our boots in the water and dug these out with pocket knives.[107]

Lamb was clearly anxious that another archaeologist might try to claim the site first: "I think we should lie fairly low about it, or rather sufficiently low to prevent any chance of anyone else bagging the site."[108] She need not have worried. Straight from Macedonia, Lamb started the first season of excavations at Thermi on April 5, 1929, working in conjunction with R. W. Hutchinson, with whom she had worked at Mycenae.[109] Attention was drawn to the fact that this was the first prehistoric site excavated on the island.[110] This work turned into a major undertaking, and excavations continued, largely at her own expense, until 1933.[111]

The reports reveal the careful planning Lamb undertook. She clearly favored area excavations that would work downward layer by layer, revealing the "superposed settlements."[112] Although she was able to adopt this method for the southern part of the site, the requirements of the owner in the northern section forced her to dig down to virgin soil during every season. She also proposed "to leave unexcavated samples representative of all five towns in case anyone should, at some future date, wish to check our conclusions."[113]

Lamb discovered a series of towns at Thermi. The houses are well built of stone, and the settlements were without protecting walls. She noticed that the use of houses in Town III differed markedly from that in Town II.

Only Town V was finally defended, but this town was destroyed by fire, and no Late Helladic IIIb or sub-Mycenaean pottery was found. This led Lamb to look to the Homeric tradition of Achilles' raid on Lesbos. As she stated eloquently, "our site, which starts in the obscurity of the prehistoric age, ends in a period when the feeble light of tradition is about to give place to the brighter illumination of history."[114]

The excavation report is marked by a careful record of the location of the finds, which is linked to the stratigraphy. For example, Lamb developed a scheme for relating the presence of pottery in different sections to the different strata.[115] Elsewhere the numbers of differently shaped bone tools were related in proportion to their appearance in different strata.[116] The report emphasized the ceramic sequence and fabrics, devoting four chapters to them, with comprehensive catalog, illustration, and profile drawings. This emphasis reflected Lamb's knowledge of the pottery from various sites in the region. Her Early Bronze Age Class A pottery was linked in shape to pottery from the Troad, although the decoration was linked to other regions in Anatolia; Class B pottery was linked to Yortan material; and Class C pottery was perceived as having more independence.[117]

This intensive treatment of the pottery is also reflected in two articles Lamb published in 1932: the first on gray wares from Lesbos and the second on pottery from Schliemann's excavations in the Troad, which she studied in Berlin.[118] The Lesbos review not only discussed her own finds from Antissa and Methymna on Lesbos, but it also considered material from Böhlau's excavations at Pyrrha on Lesbos and Larissa in Anatolia. Lamb also included material from Schliemann's excavation, expanding upon this in her second article, which reviewed the material from Calvert's excavations at Hanai Tepe as well as Schliemann's excavations at Besika Tepe and Bali Dagh. As with her study of Greek bronzes, she linked her fieldwork closely to museum studies,[119] allowing her to make chronological comparisons for Thermi. Thus, for example, Troy IIa coincided with Thermi IV and V.[120]

Lamb, apparently, was working in Athens in October 1929 on the Thermi finds and from there moved to Istanbul to work on material in the archaeological museum. Her own knowledge of Troy can be traced back to this period. She "visited Chanak (Çanakkale) and the site of Troy with a view to studying the relations between Troy and prehistoric Mytilene [sc. Lesbos]."[121] This seems to have given her the inspiration to investigate the relationship between Lesbos and Troy, as well as the Cyclades and the rest of Bronze Age Greece.[122] In 1932 she made a second visit to Troy and from there went to Ankara.[123]

Lamb recognized the value of the specialist study of what many considered minor objects in the excavations. The location of fragmentary carbonized remains was carefully recorded, and Helen Bancroft of the Imperial Forestry Institute in Oxford then studied them.[124] Thus oak remains were found from Town IV, vines from Town III, conifers from Towns IV or V, and possible olives from Towns IV or V. Further technical study on a bronze pin was undertaken by O. Davies, although Professor C. Desch supplied the main analyses of metal.[125] The stone implements were sent to Professor Ktenas of Athens University, who demonstrated that they were imported from Asia Minor and the Cyclades.[126] Other specialists studied seeds, shells, flints, and human and animal bones.[127] The study of the animal bones, which included nine or ten species, showed that goats, pigs, and deer were very common. The ox was rare, and there were two dog skulls. Other specialized studies, each presented in a chapter of its own, included terra-cotta, metal, stone, bone, and small finds. The collection of such "environmental" information began with the work of Sir Arthur Evans on Crete and J. P. Harland at Tsoungiza Hill at Nemea during the excavations of 1926–27.[128] Indeed such issues were being raised by Kenton F. Vickery's *Food in Early Greece,* which was published in 1936.[129]

The final excavation report won Lamb considerable praise, if only for the speed of its production. The illustrations were lauded and the excavation team "congratulated on a report that is a model both of lucidity and of circumspection."[130] Wace, who influenced Lamb's excavating and publishing approaches, was unstinting in his praise, describing it as "admirably objective and straightforward."[131] One reason she was able to produce the report so quickly was that she had spent part of each year working on the finds.[132]

In 1932 Lamb gave a lecture on Thermi to the Society of Antiquaries of London just a month prior to being elected a fellow.[133] Later in the same year she read a conference paper on Thermi to the First International Congress of Prehistoric and Protohistoric Sciences in London.[134] This paper reflected her interest in Troy and other Anatolian sites. The excavations themselves provided a representative selection of material from the Fitzwilliam, acquired from 1929 to 1933.[135] In 1936 she gave a lecture titled "The Background of Troy" as part of the exhibition at the Royal Academy of Arts, London, "British Archaeological Discoveries in Greece and Crete, 1886–1936."[136] The exhibition, which celebrated the fiftieth anniversary of the British School at Athens, included displays from Lamb's excavations at both Thermi and Antissa.[137]

Antissa, Lesbos

In 1931 Lamb conducted trial excavations at Antissa, sixteen kilometers southwest of Methymna; further excavations were carried out in 1932 and 1933.[138] She had first visited the site in 1928 when looking for a suitable prehistoric location.[139] Lamb accepted R. Koldeway's identification of Ovriokastro as the site.[140] Using most of the team from Thermi, she explored the Castro, the promontory, the Acropolis, and the cemetery.[141] One of the aims of the excavations was to obtain "Mycenaean" and Archaic material. In the first season there were three areas of excavation: the Acropolis, the Castro, and the Neck. Although the Castro could not be securely dated to the Late Bronze Age, the Acropolis did yield pottery of that period, as well as some relating to Troy VI, and later Archaic bucchero. The Neck was the most productive area, yielding material from the Bronze Age to the Byzantine period.

One of the key structures found was an early apsidal building, perhaps built in the tenth to ninth centuries B.C. and replaced by a successor in the eighth. Lamb considered the possibility that these were early temples.[142] A paved area and polygonal walls were dated to the Late Archaic period. One of the features of the classical site was a stoa more than 12.5 meters long that probably dated to the fourth century B.C.[143] Further work was carried out in the cemetery south of the Acropolis, where Protocorinthian, Rhodian, and bucchero pots were found, as well as fragments of two ceramic coffins.[144]

Detailed notes on the pottery gave particular prominence to the Lesbian Gray Ware.[145] Lamb recognized the importance of the imported wares, such as those from the Cyclades, Rhodes, Corinth, Laconia, and Attica. The discussion included references to material newly published in the Oxford fascicule of the *Corpus Vasorum Antiquorum,* a volume that Lamb clearly had with her on Lesbos, as her review gave her address as Mytilene.[146] Metal, bone, and stone artifacts were also highlighted.

In her report Lamb considered the possibility of coastal change since antiquity, especially as some of the earliest levels were below sea level.[147] A detailed section differentiated between the various soil colorations, ash, and sand.[148] It was clear that she pushed the excavation team hard. They rose at 5:00 A.M., though they had a midday break of three and a half hours. Lamb herself recognized that this site was not the most important.

> Our dig is very exciting—we have evidently struck the right spot—but they are very hard to disentangle, though it is fun. Not much to

describe. I feel we shall get into architectural textbooks, but that we shall not have much to talk about at tea parties. And one can't go as quickly as we did at Thermi.[149]

Chios

In 1932 Lamb "investigated" sites on Chios, which seems to have led to her direction of the British School excavation at Kato Phana in 1934. It was not an easy excavation, as one night there had been illicit digging, apparently by the workmen themselves. The site itself had been excavated from 1913 to 1915 by K. Kourouniotis, who had discovered the remains of the temple of Apollo mentioned by Strabo.[150] The decision to reexcavate was taken in light of the progress made in the area of East Greek art. Lamb recognized that Chios was one of the chief centers of this world and that a study of its contribution had "become a pressing need."[151] In a letter written June 9, 1934, she commented that "archaeology will be grateful to us for tidying up the problems of a site it has been curious about for twenty years even though there are no sensational finds, and we hope a short season will see us through."

It is perhaps characteristic of Lamb that she acknowledged the generosity of not only Kourouniotis but also a range of other people who had assisted with the excavation and the related study.[152] She was also ready to note the help of colleagues, especially that of Miss Nine Six and James Brock, who studied the architecture of the site.

Lamb perceived a continuation of the location's religious function from Geometric sanctuary through to Christian basilica. Her excavation showed sensitivity to the changing chronological sequence. A wall made of "irregular limestone blocks" was considered associated with finds of the Geometric period and was thus interpreted as the boundary of the *temenos*.[153] The Archaic *temenos* wall, which had been identified by Kourouniotis, was traced for some seventy-four meters. Its structure was carefully noted, including the use of red stone or marble in places. The sanctuary area seemed to have been accessed by two flights of stairs on the north side of the wall. Although Lamb was unable to date the wall from the foundations, which rested on bedrock, some of the deposits from behind the wall and associated with its construction "yielded a few Naukratite sherds of indefinite character . . . but [which] are definitely post-Geometric."[154] She also made careful sections through the deposits outside the walls. At the lowest level, which consisted of "dark earth," she discovered numerous sherds and small objects; the latest pottery was "Naukratite A." This she argued could not "antedate the wall, but must have been washed over or thrown down after the wall was finished."[155] The material itself she dated to circa 600–580. The next phase in the life of the sanctuary was associated with large deposits of stones and limestone chips, which were linked with pottery conventionally dated to the second half of the sixth century. The study also considered the remains of a Christian church and a basilica.

The report was supported by detailed studies of the various categories of finds accompanied by line drawings and plates. Lamb was extending Beazley's notion of anonymous artists to bronzes when she noted that a griffin cauldron protome might be by "the same artist" as one acquired by Kourioniotis, although she doubted that they were from the same cauldron.[156] Other parts of the report considered faience, amber, and pottery; Alan Shorter commented on the scarabs.

Lamb's familiarity with the East Greek world gave her the opportunity to review Ernst Buschor's three volumes on Archaic sculpture from the island of Samos.[157] Their publication raised questions in Lamb's mind about the nature and definition of Samian art and the previous attribution to Samos of other works of art. Although she criticized Buschor's essay style, she had special praise for the plates, "good photographs and excellent reproductions, which go far to prove the superiority of half-tone over collotype for objects like these."[158] Such words reflect the concern of an archaeologist keen to bring the results of her excavations to colleagues.

Kusura

With the Thermi excavations completed, Lamb's thoughts turned to work in mainland Anatolia and its relationship with prehistoric Greece. Such a move rightly places her in the "advance guard" of those who recognized the important link.[159]

> She was . . . one of the first classical archaeologists after Hogarth and Garstang to seek light on the problems of Greek archaeology from Anatolia, and this at a time when conditions of living and working in Turkey were hard and primitive, and particularly difficult for a woman.[160]

Four influences can perhaps be recognized in her decision. The first was the perceived link between the pottery found under the Bronze Age mounds in Macedonia and the material from Troy. The second were her visits to Hisarlık (Troy) in 1929 and 1932, as well as her work on Schliemann's material in Berlin.[161] The third influence was her familiarity with Böhlau's excavations at Pyrrha on Lesbos and Larissa in Anatolia,[162] and the fourth was no doubt the influence of Kurt Bittel, director of the German excavations at Bogazköy and a man Lamb saw as "the chief authority on prehistoric Anatolia."[163] She followed his definition of two main cultural areas—one in western and southwestern Anatolia, represented by Troy, Senirce, and Yortan; the other included Alişar, Kültepe, and Boğazköy in the central and eastern regions.[164] Lamb recognized that there was a gap in this picture in the western uplands of Anatolia; she thus looked for a site that would connect the Maeander valley (and thus the Aegean) with the region around Ankara and the route southeastward toward Syria. In the year that she started her excavation at Kusura she wrote a major review article of Bittel's *Prähistorische Forschung in Kleinasien* (1934), commenting that it provided "a sound basis" for work in the "most promising field" of Anatolian prehistory.[165] Bittel's work also discussed Lamb's own excavations at Thermi, which placed Lesbos in its regional context.[166] But she criticized Bittel's failure to take account of Heurtley's work in Macedonia, including the excavation of Sarátsı with which Lamb had been involved immediately prior to her work at Thermi.[167]

The site of Kusura was selected after exploration of the region around Afyon in April 1935.[168] Lamb had clearly researched material from this region and was familiar with objects like a jug in the Ashmolean Museum in Oxford that apparently came from a mound between Emet and Aezani.[169] Kusura, some fifty-five kilometers southwest of Afyon Karahisar, was seen as the "most promising [site], first because of its excellent position on one of the routes to the south, secondly by reason of the unusual potsherds with wide horizontal ribs which I picked up on the surface." The credit, as ever, was given to someone else, in this case the director of the Afyon Museum, Süleyman Göncer.[170]

Work started in 1935, when Lamb, with Miss E. W. Gardner, conducted a *sondage*. The 1936 season lasted ten weeks and was staffed by Mr. and Mrs. J. R. Stewart, Miss Rachel Clay (Mrs. Maxwell-Hyslop), and the site architect Mr. R. H. Macartney.[171] The site itself consisted of a cemetery, published by Stewart,[172] and the mound that formed the main urban settlement. The 1937 season, which lasted from June to August, saw renewed emphasis on the identification of the final Period C of the site and the extent to which it was linked to the Hittite culture of central Anatolia. Lamb included such members of her first team as Macartney and Clay, as well as her former colleague from Chios, Miss Six.[173]

In Lamb's view the site was first occupied in the "Chalcolithic Age," a period that seems to have been local (Period A). In the second phase (Period B) she detected cultural links with pottery of southwest Anatolia. At the end of this second period she noted the appearance of "red-cross bowls," a type found at Troy and at that time dated to circa 2000 B.C. The transition to the third period (Period C) was characterized by the introduction of wheel-made pottery, which to Lamb indicated links with the "Hittite interior." This third phase seems to have been marked by a settlement with stone foundations. She thought the final phase of the settlement belonged to the start of the Iron Age, partly because of the absence of Phrygian painted pottery.[174] Occasionally, Lamb noted evidence for cultic activity, such as the pile of *Fumaria* and heliotrope seeds as well as the skull of an ox, which seem to have been placed deliberately in front of a decorated column that was linked to a whitewashed "oblong structure like an altar."[175] She noted that this was located at the highest point of the mound and oriented toward the rising sun.

She clearly interpreted the finds in light of her previous experience. Pits in Period B were associated with "house-pits or *bothroi*" found at Thermi, and jugs enclosed in a wall found a parallel from a bastion at the same site.[176] The transition from Period B to C was marked by the presence of a coarse ware, "just as at Thermi it preceded the introduction of good wheel-made vases."[177]

The reports contained full discussion of the pottery and were accompanied by sectioned pottery drawings, forming the basis for her cultural links. These included the red-cross bowls of Period B, which were associated with Troy, as well as more defined links with Senirce and Punarbaşi Göl in southwestern Anatolia and Ahlatlibel near Ankara.[178] Further detailed studies of the various pottery appeared as a result of the 1937 excavations.[179] These parallels show the interest that Lamb took in previous and contemporary excavations of the region in which she was working.

Other specialized reports examined the terra-cotta (including figures), seals and beads, metal, and stone and bone objects.[180] Again each category of material was carefully illustrated in line drawings. Even the three glass beads from Period C were scrupulously listed.[181] A metals analysis by Professor Desch formed an appendix to the report.[182]

The object reports are careful to relate the pieces to their actual findspots. This interest in stratigraphic sequence is revealed in the second aim of the 1937 season. Lamb wished to relate the results from each of the areas to one another. In particular, she wanted to understand the link between the construction of the houses with the stone foundations and the previous Period B. As at Thermi, Lamb was also careful to retain environmental data. For example, beside a hearth of Period B were some seeds of *Triticum monococcum*, which was the type of wheat found at Troy.[183] The transitional Period B to C contained numerous seeds of *Fumaria* (fumitory), as well as processed lentils, *Lens esculenta*, which had apparently been stored in specially prepared pits.[184] Skeletal remains were also submitted for further examination to Dr. Şevket Aziz Kansu.[185] This interest in technical expertise is even revealed in her desire to have the stone "celts" from Period B analyzed in order to establish a source.[186] Lamb's report shows her enthusiasm for collaboration and willingness to acknowledge assistance. She incorporated J. R. Stewart's study of the cemetery, where fourteen graves were excavated. Each grave was carefully measured and its orientation noted, as well as the type of burial and associated pottery. Miss N. Six's help was acknowledged in the study of the metal objects and for "points in connection with the manufacture and use of the tools."[187]

Lamb's report concludes that Kusura was "a provincial town, mainly dependent on local resources but in touch with its eastern and western neighbours."[188] Its expansion was explained in terms of population movements from the west of Anatolia, with the reduced Period C settlement populated by people under the Hittite sphere of influence. Such theories of population movement, so popular in the 1930s, may no longer be accepted, but they show that Lamb was interpreting her finds alongside the theories of other contemporary archaeologists. The report itself ends rather inconclusively. Trained as a classicist, Lamb looked forward to the day when historical documents would interpret "the archaeological data more fully."[189] In particular, she was disappointed that she discovered no evidence for the rebellion in the Afyon area known from the Hittite document, the "Misdeed of Madduwatta." She concludes: "Here, as in other matters, we must resign ourselves to the fact that it is notoriously difficult to reconcile historical documents with what has been unearthed by the spade."[190] She continues with a further thought:

> quotations from ancient texts in classical authors . . . raise hopes of riches which are not fulfilled by the actual remains, archaeologists are accustomed to this form of disillusionment.[191]

This work in Anatolia led Lamb to reflect further on excavations and research by other colleagues. Her thoughts appeared in two reviews of Anatolian books. Her own humility and sense of inadequacy in the face of such a task comes through strongly.[192] She recognized the weaknesses in the excavated knowledge of Bronze Age Anatolia, in particular the coastal regions, and realized that such limitations could distort any interpretation. Yet in these years just before the outbreak of World War II she accepted Bittel's thesis of "the gradually increasing supremacy of the Indo-european ingredient in the population [of Boğazköy], which . . . may . . . be responsible for the individual characteristic in the major forms of art at Boğazköy."[193]

With her excavations at Kusura, Lamb became an authority on Anatolian prehistory. In 1937 she gave a lecture, "Recent Developments in the Prehistory of Anatolia," to the Society of Antiquaries in London.[194] Her additional interest in adjoining areas such as Cyprus and Syria was to continue after World War II, especially through the foundation of the British Institute of Archaeology at Ankara.[195]

The Fitzwilliam Museum

In 1919 Sydney Cockerell, director of the Fitzwilliam Museum in the University of Cambridge, invited Lamb to be the honorary keeper of Greek and Roman antiquities.[196] She accepted the position and held it until 1958.[197] This major task required her to order the collection, which had never before been properly curated. For example, in 1921 Lamb registered the material acquired from the Cyprus Exploration Fund excavations of 1890.[198]

Greek and Roman Bronzes

One area of research for Lamb during the 1920s was Greek and Roman bronzes. Her interest in this area of classical archaeology can perhaps be traced back to at least 1915, when she purchased a bronze Geometric bull.[199] She was admitted as a student of the British School at Rome for the session 1926–27 to work on ancient bronzes. In October 1927 she wrote to her mother from Athens:

> I am doing a surprising amount of work on the bronzes. Nowhere except at Rome and Athens does one live in the same house as a first-class library—let me correct this, Athens is first class, Rome second class. And the museum has all the material for filling in gaps. I go there every morning.

In 1929 she published bronzes found during excavations at Sparta, a site not only rich in seventh-century products, but also well stratified and carefully excavated. Therefore, whatever was found there during the excavations can be now dated with unusual accuracy, and throws valuable light on a period when all arts save pottery are comparatively obscure.[200]

She also published a study of bronzes from Arcadia researched during a series of trips to Greece.[201] She wrote that "reviewing the Arcadian industry, we are struck by its vitality and its independence, as well as by the determination with which the Arcadian people patronised home-made goods."[202]

These studies finally culminated in the book *Greek and Roman Bronzes,* which appeared in 1929 as part of the Methuen series Handbooks on Archaeology. This series was under the general editorship of A. B. Cook, who, at the time, was reader in classical archaeology at Cambridge. (Cook almost certainly lectured and tutored Lamb at Cambridge.)[203] The work clearly reflects Lamb's familiarity with the material she discussed on visits to some of the major collections in Europe.[204] Particular attention should be drawn to large numbers of Mycenaean and Greek bronzes that she was allowed to study in the National Museum in Athens through the good offices of Dr. P. Kastriotis[205] and Mlle. Pappaspiridou. E. J. Forsdyke of the British Museum lavishly praised the book for "provid[ing] an orderly conspectus of all the significant material, and a critical account of its history" and noted that it was "written with an appreciation of the beauty and humour of Greek art which is not the less attractive for sometimes being feminine."[206]

The Prehistoric and Archaic Displays

One of Lamb's initial projects in the Fitzwilliam was the creation of a prehistoric and Archaic Greek gallery in the former Coin Room.[207] One of the guiding hands behind the project, and certainly the donor of representative objects for the new gallery, was Lamb's former colleague from Mycenae, A. J. B. Wace. Wace and R. C. Bosanquet helped Lamb to develop the Cycladic collections. These had been denuded following the removal of Richard M. Dawkins's Early Cycladic loan material in 1920.[208] The National Museum in Athens generously presented a number of bowls and a jar from the excavated cemetery at Chalandriani on the island of Syros in 1923.[209]

In order to make the gallery representative of prehistoric Greece, Lamb acquired replicas of some key finds made at Mycenae and elsewhere. In this context she acquired the so-called Fitzwilliam Goddess in early 1926. The figure was known by early September 1925 according to correspondence between Charles Seltman and Sir Arthur Evans.[210] Lamb was clearly keen on what she thought was an early piece of sculpture that would make the Fitzwilliam "world famous."[211] Such an interest in Bronze Age art may well be linked to her earliest days of excavation at Mycenae, and it was to Wace, her colleague from the Mycenae excavations, that she offered the authorship of the specialized publication.[212] Indeed it was Wace who arranged for a notice to be placed in *The Times* and who was allowed to present a paper on the goddess in July 1926 to the Hellenic Society.[213]

The goddess had been acquired through Charles Seltman, a Fellow of Queens' College in Cambridge.[214] But when the director of the museum, Sydney Cockerell, planned a Mediterranean cruise that summer, Stephanos Xanthoudides, the ephor on Crete, contacted him to say that the goddess was a forgery.[215] Indeed, some rumors had already been circulating in Cambridge in the early summer of 1926.[216] On Cockerell's return, Forsdyke at the British Museum showed him photographs of apparent "sisters" to the goddess. In spite of this Wace pressed ahead with the monograph, and the goddess was used as the frontispiece for the first volume of plates for the *Cambridge Ancient History*.[217]

Lamb reacted badly to the hostile reviews of the monograph, especially to the suggestion that the goddess could be a forgery.[218] By 1947 she still recalled, in verse, the Cretan lady "with a tarnished reputation."[219] Lamb may have been trying to confirm the identification of the forger when she visited Crete to see Evans in April 1928.[220] Her own illness and the death of her father in 1925 can perhaps best explain Lamb's lack of judgment in this acquisition.[221] Lamb had been in hospital at Athens in April 1925 due to a bout of whooping cough and there are several references to Lamb's apparent ill health.[222]

Greek Vases

During the 1920s Lamb started to prepare two fascicules of the *Corpus Vasorum Antiquorum* for the Fitzwilliam Museum. This project was to mark the growth of the collection since the publication of Gardner's *Catalogue of Vases* in 1897,[223] especially in light of the acquisition of pots from the Hope sale in 1917 and duplicates from the British School at Athens. The first fascicule was to be published in 1930 and the second, containing pots from the collection of Charles Ricketts and Charles Shannon that had been on loan to the museum, in 1936.[224] Lamb's interests in the "science of vases" can be traced back as far as 1918, and her views on what constituted a useful catalog can be detected from that same period.[225]

Lamb clearly worked well with Beazley. When he published his *Attische Vasenmaler des Rotfigurigen Stils* in 1925, four pots from Lamb's private collection were listed and a painter, "Der Lambmaler," named in her honor.[226] Indeed Beazley praised Lamb in his review of the *Corpus Vasorum Antiquorum* for her "fine piece of work" and in particular her plates.[227] Even so he criticized the numbering of the two volumes, as well as the additional section on the Ricketts and Shannon collection.[228] This may reflect Beazley's hurt pride at Lamb's earlier criticisms of the second Ashmolean fascicule. She had lamented that "the plates are not given consecutive numbers which refer to the museum, but only those numbers which refer to Great Britain. This makes reference difficult."[229] T. B. L. Webster, of the University of Manchester, also praised the "high standard" of her volume, in particular for providing "photographs which can really be used for work." He noted that "Miss Lamb is abreast with the latest literature."[230] This last comment can be linked to the period when Lamb was writing on Greek pottery—a time when she was heavily involved with the excavations at Thermi—and can also be associated with a series of reviews of books on Attic pottery.

In 1930 Lamb reviewed Beazley's *Attic Black-Figure: A Sketch* (1928), first given as a lecture to the British Academy. She appreciated the opportunity "to admire the art with which a complex subject is developed and to enjoy the beautiful if sometimes too exotic English."[231] For Lamb this was a "perfect" introduction, which anticipated a larger work by Beazley. Despite the praise, her background as an archaeologist is reflected in her criticism of Beazley's "scarcity of dates."[232] Her review of H. R. W. Smith's *New Aspects of the Menon Painter,* written in the same year, also reflects the debates over defining anonymous painters and tensions over the final arbitrator. For Lamb, Beazley's eye was crucial: "Beazley agrees with the attribution of the aryballos and two of the four plates . . . but not, apparently, with that of the cups." She was also critical of the "very bad photographs" of some of the pots in the volume.[233]

In the following years she reviewed a number of Beazley's works. In 1931 she praised the "brilliantly written" *Der Berliner Maler* (1930).[234] A second review of the same volume appeared in the following year. She wrote, convinced of the intellectual validity of attributing unsigned pots to specific painters, "We shrink from imagining what we should have missed if one of the greatest of fifth-century artists had continued incognito."[235]

She had rather missed the point that Beazley had raised a humble craft to the height of art.[236] Her views on how to present archaeological information are again revealed in her praise of the "beautiful plates," though she regrets that a complete view of the stamnos in Castle Ashby was not reproduced. Her personal admiration for Beazley is also quite evident.[237]

Her preparation of the two fascicules of the *Corpus Vasorum Antiquorum* qualified her to review the second fascicule of the Ashmolean Museum, which was published in 1931.[238] Her humility is reflected in her praise of the first fascicule's "alarmingly high standard," a standard that Lamb probably thought she could not emulate. This second fascicule had contributions not only by Beazley but also by two other people she admired: Humfry Payne, director of the British School at Athens, on the Cretan and Corinthian pottery; and Miss E. R. Price on the East Greek. Such collaboration, as Lamb viewed it, resulted in "not only an excellent presentation . . . but a very precious contribution to our knowledge of Greek ceramics." Given Lamb's work on Lesbos at that time, she made special note of Price's "invaluable" classification of the East Greek material. Another review, of a catalog of the collection of Greek pottery in the Royal Ontario Museum, appeared in 1931.[239] Her critique provides an insight into what can only be her own preparation of the fascicules of the Fitzwilliam Museum:

> Few tasks are more exacting than that of writing the text of a catalogue. It is redeemed from drudgery by the need for careful elimination of what is unimportant and careful arrangement of what is essential: it may even be inspired by the hope of producing descriptions which are pleasant to read, like those in Professor Beazley's Corpus Vasorum. In short, the author, in the midst of his anxiety to give adequate and accurate information, must be careful not to exhaust himself or to risk exhausting his readers.[240]

Again she has an eye for the plates, and although she praises the catalog for illustrating every object, she is critical of "indistinct" plates and the small scale of reproduction.

This appears to have been one of Lamb's last reviews of Greek pottery. From this period onward problems surrounding the Bronze Age seem to have dominated her research interests, probably because of her involvement with the excavations at Thermi. Her interests were not confined, however, to the eastern Mediterranean. In 1931 Lamb reviewed Sir Themistocles Zammit's *Prehistoric Malta: The Tarxien Temples.* Zammit had been a benefactor of the Fitzwilliam, donating five lamps and other antiquities in 1924.[241]

Acquisitions and Research

Lamb's frequent visits to Athens allowed her to make a considerable number of acquisitions for the Fitzwilliam.[242] One of the main barriers to developing the collection had been lack of funds. As early as 1925 Sydney Cockerell, the director of the museum at that time, had started an antiquities fund to buy antiquities from the National Museum at Athens that were considered to be duplicates.[243] In 1929, seemingly at Cockerell's suggestion, Lamb went to examine some of these duplicates at the National Museum and "found a number of their choice small things which our museum needs, as well as one or two second-rate but quite useful larger things."[244] These she asked the museum to put to one side. In 1932 the Fitzwilliam was still waiting to acquire the objects that Lamb had identified.[245] In fact, this scheme came to nothing, and on January 2, 1935, Lamb wrote to Cockerell strongly advising him "to dip into that special fund for Greek antiquities, which you collected with a view to purchasing vases, etc., at Athens." Indeed she seems to have purchased an Attic stamnos for eighty pounds from Segredakis from this same fund on January 12, 1935.[246] Although most of the money was spent in 1935, primarily on Greek and Etruscan pottery, the fund continued to exist until 1946. The other main source of acquisitions during this period was through the Friends of the Fitzwilliam, a body that donated Greek antiquities on a virtually annual basis from 1923 to 1937.[247]

Lamb's contacts with Athenian society put her in the way of some attractive acquisitions for the Fitzwilliam.[248] She had tea with Sophia Schliemann on Easter Day (April 16) 1922. The visit coincided with a period of financial problems for Madame Schliemann, who in 1926 was forced to sell her house in Athens, Iliou Melathron, to the Greek government. This may have been the occasion for the acquisition of an Attic red-figured pyxis that had belonged to Heinrich Schliemann.[249] In 1933 and 1934 Lamb was to acquire objects at Athens through T. Zoumboulakis.

Lamb's work in Anatolia led her to research parts of the collection at the Fitzwilliam. In the paper published in honor of the seventieth birthday of Professor Sir John L. Myres, she considered a group of west Anatolian pots. She recognized that "lacking a pedigree, they still have, as it were, a passport; and any of them that belongs to a civilisation inadequately represented in this country deserves a welcome." Although the objects did not come from a stratified excavation, she felt they were still valuable, as Anatolian objects were underrepresented in Britain at that time.[250]

The objects had been acquired from two sources: the first, in 1908, from Alan Wace, who had visited Izmir in that year; the second from the 1926 bequest of Professor Ridgeway, which consisted of pots he had acquired in 1909 from Charles van Lennep in Izmir.[251] Although the findspots were perhaps unreliable, the publication reveals Lamb's familiarity with the Anatolian collections in London and Oxford.[252] The material was also interpreted in light of her excavations at Thermi and Kusura. Thus the decoration on a jug was linked to a style that ceased in Thermi Towns IV or V, and a collar-necked jar finds a parallel at Kusura.[253] The study itself led her to reflect further on the lack of stratified material from western Anatolia, and this turned her mind to further urgent excavation.[254]

The War Years

In the early war years Lamb lived at Liphook, no doubt looking after her now-frail mother. Gertrude Caton-Thompson also recalled her involvement with Polish refugees.[255] Lamb continued to correspond with Cockerell, even though he had now left the Fitzwilliam. In one letter she recounted the story of an air raid warden wandering around the country lanes in the local clergyman's surplice so that military vehicles would not run him down in the blackout. This had given rise to the story of a local ghost![256]

In 1940 Lamb's contribution to archaeology, and specifically her work at Thermi, was acknowledged by the University of Cambridge with the award of a Sc.D. The examiners were Professor Gordon Childe of Edinburgh and Carl Blegen. Alan Wace was technically Laurence Professor of Classical Archaeology in Cambridge, though he was in Greece preparing for the expected German invasion.

On September 23, 1941, Lamb was invited to volunteer for the position of Greek language supervisor at the BBC, a post deemed to be of "national importance." By September 30, 1941, she had decided to accept, as the post seemed very attractive. Her mother had died on August 21, 1941, and her eagerness to take up the position may have been linked to this loss.[257] The Lamb family's house, Borden Wood, was taken over by war-displaced nuns until 1946. In 1942 she joined the Turkish Section of the Near East Department of the BBC, where she was employed until 1946. Her responsibilities were audience reaction and information. During the final stages of the war her lodgings in north London were hit by a German V2 rocket. Her housemates were killed, and Lamb herself was buried in the rubble, "saved by a window frame hurled over her in the explosion."[258] She was left with numerous metal splinters in her body.

The Postwar Years

As honorary keeper, Lamb continued to make new acquisitions for the Fitzwilliam after the war. In 1946 she recommended that the museum should purchase two Etruscan bronzes from Sotheby's with the help of the National Arts-Collection Fund.[259] Etruscan material had played a small role in her interests, although she was struck by the publication of P. J. Riis's study of Etruscan sculpture, which she saw as marking "a turning-point in Etruscan studies."[260] Perhaps she felt that it was the right time to be purchasing Etruscan antiquities. Sadly these bronzes turned out to be fakes.

This experience, added to the Fitzwilliam Goddess episode, seems to have made her more cautious. In 1951 she advised Carl Winter against buying a marble head from Sotheby's because "if B[eazley] and A[shmole] like it and if we eventually got it, someone will pop up six months later and tell us that he knows the man whose great-grandfather made it in a back garden in Florence."[261] Likewise in 1953 she was reluctant to buy two Greek terra-cottas from Nigel Clive because "it has been my practice not to buy terracottas, owing to their being easy to forge."[262]

In 1947 Lamb requested permission from the director Carl Winter to change the cases in the "archaic room." The main gallery ("the long gallery") was also to have a new case in which she hoped to place "those horrible South Italian vases."[263] During this period she was also preparing a guide for the Fitzwilliam[264] when she wrote the following poem to Carl Winter:

The Greek Department has on show
Statues collected long ago
And rather bad. So turn from these
And view our small antiquities:
The cups that held Athenian wine
With dainty pictures, neat and fine;
Lady from Crete in adoration
(But with a tarnished reputation)
Bronzes superbly patinated
And each one accurately dated!

> Products of Rhodes and Thessaly
> And colonies across the sea.
> And when you're tired of Greece and Rome
> Buy picture cards, and study them at home.[265]

Her taste was also expressed when the museum was offered "an immense bronze nail reputed to have come from Caligula's barge." Her response to Winter was immediate: "I do NOT want an IMMENSE BRONZE NAIL." Winter himself pleaded with her, describing the nail as quite "lovely." It was in fact acquired.[266] In 1948 Lady D'Abernon donated a Roman marble head, which was a copy of a Greek athlete by Polykleitos. Winter wrote to the benefactor that Lamb found it "the kind of acquisition she has always dreamed of for the Fitzwilliam. She thinks it perfectly beautiful."[267]

Lamb started to lend her own objects to the Fitzwilliam, including some "rather nice Greek vases," to coincide with a meeting of classical archaeologists in Cambridge during 1951. This loan was to include some fourteen pots and three bronze jugs.[268] She also donated a bronze Etruscan tripod ornament in 1952.[269] In 1955 she decided to give the Fitzwilliam the Greek pots they had on loan from her.[270] Further items were offered in March 1957, including an Anatolian torque.[271] In 1955 Lamb was faced with a dilemma. Dr. Halet Çambel was due to visit the museum, and she realized that it would not be diplomatic for her to see the pots from Babaköy, which J. Stewart had probably smuggled out of Turkey without a permit.[272] A pot from Kusura (which had been restored from a single sherd) was withdrawn from exhibition and put "out of sight."[273]

Lamb made several attempts to resign as honorary keeper at the Fitzwilliam. As early as February 1944 she expressed the view to Louis C. G. Clarke, then director of the Fitzwilliam, that she ought to resign once the "hostilities" were over. Clarke called her view nonsense: "I don't want to hear any more about this." In January 1951 she wrote to the new director, Carl Winter, again requesting to retire. He replied immediately that he "should really be very much distressed and the Museum would be at a great loss." She responded with her view of being an honorary keeper.

> Honorary Keeperships are odd affairs. I regard their duties as follows:
>
> 1. They should NOT visit less than one day a month, and, if there is work to do, more often.
> 2. They should produce catalogues if asked. That I would no longer

wish to do, as I am concentrating on Anatolian prehistory and could not write a good catalogue on Classical Greek antiquities.

3. They should attend sales if necessary. I always hope that such a necessity will not arise . . .

   There is of course another view of Honorary Keeperships: that they are given to people who are a) eminent, b) well-off. There is an amateurish element about that . . . hon. Keepers are the oddest body theoretically, however nice individually.[274]

In spite of these protestations she was to continue in this capacity until 1958. A tribute to her appeared in the museum's annual report. Thanking her for thirty-eight years of service, she was called "an invaluable guide and counselor to three successive Directors." She took that as "a most charming, happy and unusual compliment."[275]

The British Institute of Archaeology at Ankara

Part of Lamb's postwar energies were dedicated to the founding of the British Institute of Archaeology at Ankara.[276] She was one of the group called together in September 1946 by Professor John Garstang to lay the foundations of the institute, and she subsequently served as its honorary secretary from 1948 to 1957, then as its vice president. She also acted as chair of the Policy Committee, which was intended to focus research in specific areas. Her interest in this area of study was reflected in a major review article, "New Developments in Early Anatolian Archaeology," published in *Iraq* in 1949. Although modest about her own achievements at Kusura, the article serves to review the excavations conducted during World War II in a field Lamb considered "one of the youngest branches of archaeology."[277] One of its aims was to make known material published in Turkish and German.[278] It covered issues about early prospectors and settlers, terminology, and reviews of northern and central Anatolia in the second millennium B.C.

In this period Lamb also wrote a number of reviews of excavation reports relating to the archaeology of prehistoric Anatolia. These include discussions of work at Alaca Höyük, Karahöyük, Karatepe, and Yümük Tepe (Mersin). She recognized that contemporary knowledge about the region had been "enlarged" due to such research.[279] Lamb also took an interest in later periods of Anatolian prehistory and, indeed, protohistory. She reviewed the excavation reports of Karahöyük and Karatepe, both in southeastern Turkey.[280]

In her review of Tahsin Özgüç's work on burial patterns in Anatolia, Lamb drew attention to the way that religious beliefs could be inferred.[281] This theme was to be developed in her paper on early Anatolian shrines, which was published in a volume of *Anatolian Studies* dedicated to the memory of Professor John Garstang, the excavator of Mersin whose book she reviewed in 1954.[282] She recalled how, back in 1936, "the news of the professor's arrival to dig in Cilicia quickly penetrated to a remote village [sc. Kusura] some 300 miles away."[283] Although she recognized the absence of specific temples in Anatolia, she drew attention to the appearance of shrines in private houses. Her starting point was Garstang's evidence from Mersin, which had occurred in Early (Level XX) to Middle Chalcolithic levels. She also returned to the "pillar-shrine" at Kusura with its offerings of seeds and the skull of an ox.[284] She finally considered evidence from Troy and Boğazköy. In 1951 Lamb returned to an issue that she had first considered when contemplating the link between Thermi and Troy, the spread of face-urns.[285]

This responsibility with the British Institute took her to Ankara in 1950 and 1952. Although she did not undertake any excavations, in June and July 1952 she traveled to the vilayets (provinces) of Erzerum and Trabzon "while studying the north-eastern cultures of the third millennium."[286] The results of this trip were written up for *Anatolian Studies.* One noticeable element of Lamb's study, including the title of the work, was the use of the word *culture,* for example in the South Caucasian or Kura-Araks culture.[287] This terminology almost certainly reflects the influence of Professor V. G. Childe, who had been one of the examiners for Lamb's Cambridge Sc.D. Indeed Lamb acknowledged Childe's "invaluable suggestions and criticisms" on her paper.[288] Moreover, she recognized a particular type of pottery with horned knobs, which she linked to Karaz, a mound fifteen to sixteen kilometers northwest of Erzerum and excavated by Dr. Hamit Koşay in 1942 and 1944.

Failing Health and Death

Lamb's health failed, and she was seriously ill from 1958 to 1963. Her biographer, Gertrude Caton-Thompson, felt that Lamb never recovered from the injuries she sustained during the war.[289] She spent her last years at Borden Wood and died on September 16, 1963, at age sixty-eight. Her funeral was at the Roman Catholic church in Midhurst, where she had been a major benefactor. She was buried in the local cemetery. Many of her books and pamphlets were bequeathed to the British School at Athens, and the

East Aegean and Anatolian antiquities remaining in her home at Borden Wood were offered to the Fitzwilliam.[290] Her own view of her work was that "all [her] archaeological material, notebooks, maps, drawings, photographs, can be burnt; the cupboard in the gun-room passage is full of stuff that can be burnt including the archaeological specimens." Her cousin, Mildred, was reluctant to carry out these instructions until she had taken advice.[291] She did in fact leave a number of objects to the Fitzwilliam, including seven items that belonged to her great-grandfather, Joseph Lamb of Cumbria.[292]

Conclusion

> Winifred Lamb was a sensitive woman, easily hurt by criticism. A tribute to her goes on to describe her character: . . . naturally shy and reserved though her excellent manners concealed these traits from the casual observer . . . She was extremely sympathetic not only to her friends but to any employee whether English, Greek or Turk and very fond of animals especially dogs and horses. At Borden Wood she used to ride in her earlier years but in Greece and Turkey where the animals were mules or donkeys and the saddles wooden she preferred to walk . . . Her consideration for her workmen produced general loyalty and affection for her among them, and various people in need in Lesbos and in Turkey benefited from her secret generosity.[293]

In the *Annual Report of the British Institute of Archaeology at Ankara* she was described as "diffident in manner but unswerving in purpose, always careful to undertake nothing that could not be performed."[294] *The Times* wrote, "Her kindness, modesty, generosity and encouragement of younger people were a pattern to others. Such traits were typical of her character, which will long cause her memory to be loved."[295] And the British School at Athens recorded "her unfailing kindness and modesty, her sympathy and encouragement of younger people, her friendship, fairness and generosity."[296]

She was an able linguist, with a mastery of German, Greek, and Turkish. She set high standards for herself, and her excavation reports appeared with remarkable speed. Her frequent comments in reviews reveal her desire to present information that could be used and understood by others. This standard was set not only for her fieldwork but also for the publication of museum objects. Although not always widely acknowledged by subsequent archaeologists, she was clearly recognized by her own generation.

Although Lamb is often associated with the Greek islands and Anatolia, her love of Greece is reflected in her review of H. D. F. Kitto's *In the Mountains of Greece.*[297] She, like Kitto, found mainland Greece "irresistible," and it clearly made her feel nostalgic. Indeed Woodward, in response to the Anatolian emphasis in her *Times* obituary, wrote: "While Anatolia claimed more of her interest and activities in her later years those who knew her well realized that Greece still occupied first place in her heart."[298] Her love of Greece is perhaps best summarized in her poem, "Greece from England," dedicated to her mother.[299]

If I should ever see the "Hills of Heaven"
They would be all bare rocks and olive trees
And upland pastures full of travelling bees
And sound of sheep bells, when the sheep are driven

To seek some shelter in the hot spring weather;
For Heaven would be the hills of Greece in spring.
To this be added but one other thing:
That you and I should walk those hills together.

WORKS BY WINIFRED LAMB
A SELECTED BIBLIOGRAPHY

Books, Monographs, and Articles

"Some Vases from the Hope Collection." *Journal of Hellenic Studies* 38 (1918): 27–36.

"Excavations at Mycenae III. Frescoes from the Ramp House." *Annual of the British School at Athens* 24 (1919–21): 189–99, plates 7–10.

A. J. B. Wace, coauthor. "Excavations at Mycenae VIII. The Palace 3. The Pithos Area." 25 (1921–23): 160–79.

A. J. B. Wace, coauthor. "Excavations at Mycenae VIII. The Palace 6. The Court." *Annual of the British School at Athens* 25 (1921–23): 188–204.

A. J. B. Wace, coauthor. "Excavations at Mycenae VIII. The Palace 13. The Shrine and Adjoining Areas." *Annual of the British School at Athens* 25 (1921–23): 223–32.

A. J. B. Wace, coauthor. "Excavations at Mycenae VIII. The Palace 14. The Megaron." *Annual of the British School at Athens* 25 (1921–23): 232–57.

A. J. B. Wace, coauthor. "Excavations at Mycenae VIII. The Palace 15. The Antechamber to Domestic Quarters." *Annual of the British School at Athens* 25 (1921–23): 257–63.

"Byways in Attica." *Newnham College Roll Letter* (1922): 70–73.

"Stamped Pithoi Fragments in the Collection of the British School." *Annual of the British School at Athens* 26 (1923–25): 72–77, plates 11–12.
"Arcadian Bronze Statuettes." *Annual of the British School at Athens* 27 (1925–26): 133–48, plates 24–25.
"Excavations at Sparta, 1906–1910: 6. Notes on Some Bronzes from the Orthia Site." *Annual of the British School at Athens* 28 (1926–27): 96–106, plates 11–12.
"Excavations at Sparta, 1927: 5. Bronzes from the Acropolis, 1924–1927." *Annual of the British School at Athens* 28 (1926–27): 82–95, plates 8–10.
Δοκιμαστικὴ Σκαφὴ εἰς (Μόλυβον) τῆς Λέσβου. *Archaiologikon Deltion* 11 (1928): suppl. 41–42.
R. W. Hutchinson, coauthor. "Excavations at Thermi on Lesbos." *Annual of the British School at Athens* 30 (1928–29, 1929–30): 1–52, plates 1–10.
Greek and Roman Bronzes. London: Methuen, 1929.
Corpus Vasorum Antiquorum. Fitzwilliam Museum 1 (1930).
J. K. Brock, coauthor. "Excavations at Thermi." *Annual of the British School at Athens* 31 (1930–31): 148–65, plates 24–25.
"Antissa." *Annual of the British School at Athens* 31 (1930–31): 166–78, plates 27–28.
"'Finds' in a Prehistoric Town: Thermi, on Mytilene (Lesbos)." *Illustrated London News,* February 14, 1931, 266.
"Troy and Kindred Settlements in the Early Bronze Age." *Proceedings of the Classical Association* (1931): 20–21.
"Antissa." *Annual of the British School at Athens* 32 (1931–32): 41–67, plates 17–25.
"Grey Wares from Lesbos." *Journal of Hellenic Studies* 52 (1932): 1–12, plate 1.
"Schliemann's Prehistoric Sites in the Troad." *Prähistorische Zeitschrift* 23 (1932): 111–31.
"The Site of Troy." *Antiquity* 21, no. 6 (1932): 71–81, plates 1–2.
"Ausgrabungen in Thermi auf Lesbos." *Archäologischer Anzeiger* 48 (1933): 363–69.
"The Development of the Troad Civilization in the Early Bronze Age, Illustrated by Thermi in Lesbos." In *Proceedings of the First International Congress of Prehistoric and Protohistoric Sciences, London, August 1–6, 1932* (London, 1934), 185–86.
"Excavations at Kato Phana in Chios." *Annual of the British School at Athens* 35 (1934–35): 138–64, plates 27–37.
Corpus Vasorum Antiquorum. Fitzwilliam Museum 2 (1936).
"Excavations at Kusura near Afyon Karahisar." *Archaeologia* 86 (1936): 1–64, plates 1–8.
"Excavations at Kusura near Sandikli, Vilayet Afyon-Karahisar." *Archäologischer Anzeiger* 51 (1936): 406–11.
Excavations at Thermi in Lesbos. Cambridge: Cambridge University Press, 1936.
"Some West Anatolian Vases at Cambridge." *Annual of the British School at Athens* 37 (1936–37): 166–71, plates 23–24.
"Excavations at Kusura near Afyon Karahisar: II." *Archaeologia* 87 (1937): 217–73, plates 78–84.
"The Priest Who Played Dominoes." *Time and Tide,* January 29, 1938, 131–32.
H. Bancroft, coauthor. "Report on the Lesbos Charcoals." *Annual of the British School at Athens* 39 (1938–39): 88–89.

"Some Recent Developments in Anatolian Archaeology." In *Anatolian Studies Presented to W. H. Buckler,* ed. W. M. Calder and J. Keil, 129–50. Manchester: Manchester University Press, 1939.

F. N. Pryce, coauthor. "Sigillata from Lesbos." *Journal of Hellenic Studies* 60 (1940): 96–98.

"New Developments in Early Anatolian Archaeology." *Iraq* 11 (1949): 188–203.

"Face-Urns and Kindred Types in Anatolia." *Annual of the British School at Athens* 46 (1951): 75–80, plate 12.

"The Culture of North-east Anatolia and Its Neighbours." *Anatolian Studies* 4 (1954): 21–32.

"Prof. John Garstang." *The Times* (Sept. 20, 1956): 14.

"Some Early Anatolian Shrines." *Anatolian Studies* 6 (1956): 87–94.

Reviews

Euthymides and His Fellows, by J. C. Hoppin. *Classical Review* 33 (1919): 73–74.

Catalogue of Arretine Pottery in the Museum of Fine Arts, Boston, by G. H. Chase. *Classical Review* 33 (1919): 78–79.

Attic Black-Figure: A Sketch, by J. D. Beazley. *Classical Review* 44 (1930): 40.

New Aspects of the Menon Painter, by H. R. W. Smith. *Classical Review* 44 (1930): 196.

Der Berliner Maler, by J. D. Beazley. *Classical Review* 45 (1931): 176–77.

A Catalogue of the Greek Vases in the Royal Ontario Museum of Archaeology, Toronto, by D. M. Robinson, C. G. Harcum, and J. H. Iliffe. *Classical Review* 45 (1931): 229–31.

Who Were the Greeks? by J. L. Myres. *Journal of Hellenic Studies* 51 (1931): 291–92.

Prehistoric Malta: The Tarxien Temples, by Sir Themistocles Zammit. *Journal of Hellenic Studies* 51 (1931): 292–93.

Bilder Griechischer Vasen: Der Berliner Maler, by J. D. Beazley. *Classical Review* 46 (1932): 87–88.

Corpus Vasorum Antiquorum, by J. D. Beazley, H. G. G. Payne, and E. R. Price. *Classical Review* 46 (1932): 160–61.

In the Mountains of Greece, by H. D. F. Kitto. *Journal of Hellenic Studies* 53 (1933): 305–6.

Altsamische Standbilder, vol. 1, by E. Buschor. *Journal of Hellenic Studies* 54 (1934): 214–15.

Altsamische Standbilder, vol. 2, by E. Buschor. *Journal of Hellenic Studies* 55 (1935): 244.

Prähistorische Forschung in Kleinasien, by K. Bittel. *Gnomon* 11 (1935): 649–52.

Altsamische Standbilder, vol. 3, by E. Buschor. *Journal of Hellenic Studies* 57 (1937): 90–91.

Frühe Griechische Sagenbilder, by R. Hampe. *Journal of Hellenic Studies* 57 (1937): 89–90.

Die Ruinen von Bogazköy and *Bogazköy: Die Kleinfunde der Grabungen 1906–1912,* vol. 1, by K. Bittel. *Journal of Hellenic Studies* 57 (1937): 258–59.
The Excavations at Erimi, 1933–5, by P. Dikaios. *Antiquaries Journal* 18 (1938): 426–28.
Die Metallindustrie Anatoliens in der Zeit von 1500–700 vor Chr., by S. Przeworski. *Journal of Hellenic Studies* 59 (1939): 291–92.
Prehistoric Macedonia, by W. A. Heurtley. *Man* 40, no. 33 (1940): 28–29.
Ugaritica, études relatives aux découvertes de Ras Shamra, vol. 1, by C. Schaeffer. *Antiquaries Journal* 20 (1940): 392–94.
Tyrrhenika: An Archaeological Study of the Etruscan Sculpture in the Archaic and Classical Periods, by P. J. Riis. *Journal of Hellenic Studies* 65 (1945): 123.
Ausgrabungen von Alaca Höyük: Ein Vorbericht über die im Auftrage der türkischen Geschichts Kommission im Sommer 1936 durchgeführten Forschungen und Entdeckungen, by H. Z. Koşay. *Journal of Hellenic Studies* 66 (1946): 130.
Die Bestattungsbraeuche im vorgeschichtlichen Anatolien, by T. Özgüç and *Türk Tarih Kurumu Tarafindan Karahöyük Hafriyati Rapouru, 1947: Ausgrabungen in Karahöyük,* by T. and N. Özgüç. *Journal of Hellenic Studies* 70 (1950): 83–84.
Karatepe Kazilari (Birinci Ön-Rapor). Die Ausgrabungen auf dem Karatepe (Erster-Vorbericht) by H. Th. Bossert, V. B. Alkim, N. Çambel, N. Ongunsu, and I. Süzen. *Journal of Hellenic Studies* 71 (1951): 263–64.
Prehistoric Mersin: Yümük Tepe in Southern Turkey, by J. Garstang. *Antiquaries Journal* 74 (1954): 82–83.
The Coming of Iron to Greece, by T. Burton Brown. *Journal of Hellenic Studies* 76 (1956): 122–23.
Early Anatolia. A Description of Early Civilisation in Asia Minor, as Recorded by the Last Half-Century of Excavating and Exploration, by Seton Lloyd. *Journal of Hellenic Studies* 77 (1957): 365.

NOTES

I would like to acknowledge the help of Ian Begg, Anne Bull (Newnham College Archives), Kevin Butcher, (the late) Robert Cook, Gina Coulthard (British Institute of Archaeology at Ankara), John Donaldson (Museum of Classical Archaeology, Cambridge), Margaret Drower, Bryan Feuer, Lesley Fitton (British Museum), C. M. Güthenke, Donald Haggis, Amalia Kakissis (British School at Athens), Brian Kenney, Kenneth Lapatin, Don Lateiner, N. Momigliano, Paul Naiditch, Daniel Pullen, Valerie Scott (British School at Rome), Andrew Sherratt, Michael Simpson, Pamela Jane Smith, Christopher Stray, Frank Stubbings, Nancy and Sarantis Symeonoglou, David Traill, Michael Vickers, (the late) Helen Waterhouse, Hector Williams, Penny Wilson (British School at Athens), Paul Woudhuysen (Fitzwilliam Museum, Cambridge), James Wright, John Younger, as well as other contributors to Aegeanet. The late Richard Lamb, Winifred Lamb's cousin, most generously granted me access to papers still in the possession of the family. Special thanks must go to Deborah Hedgecock, who listed the Lamb papers as a volunteer at the Fitzwilliam Museum and has drawn my attention to other details.

Lamb's correspondence can be found in the Department of Manuscripts and Printed Books, the Department of Antiquities at the Fitzwilliam Museum, and the Department of Western Manuscripts at the British Library. Further correspondence and photographic albums are in the archive of the British School at Athens. Her collection of antiquities is now mostly at the Fitzwilliam Museum, though some items were given to the Museum of Classical Archaeology.

The main obituaries are Gertrude Caton-Thompson, "Winifred Lamb, 1894–1963 (Newnham, 1913–17)," Newnham College, *Roll Letter* (1964), 50–52; R. D. B[arnett], "Winifred Lamb," *British School at Athens Annual Report, 1962–63,* 16–18; *The Times* (London), September 18, 1963; an illustrated essay on her life appears in Rachel Hood, *Faces of Archaeology in Greece: Caricatures by Piet de Jong* (Oxford, 1998), 70–75, no. 12. A basic summary can be found in D. Ridgway, "Lamb, Winifred (1894–1963)," in *An Encyclopedia of the History of Classical Archaeology,* ed. N. Thomson de Grummond (London: Fitzroy Dearborn, 1996), 657. For Lamb's friendship with Gertrude Caton-Thompson see Gertrude Caton-Thompson, *Mixed Memoirs* (London: Paradigm Press, 1983), esp. 87, 98–99, 152, 156, 164, 202, 214, 226, and 316; cf. Margaret Drower, "Gertrude Caton-Thompson," in this volume. I am grateful to Margaret Drower for information about their association.

1. Holly Lodge was the residence of Lamb's maternal grandparents, Mr. and Mrs. Stephen Winkworth (*Newnham Register,* 1:v). Lamb's birth certificate records that she was born at Holly Lodge. Edmund Lamb's occupation is recorded as "Gentleman of Independent Means" Lamb recalled some of her childhood experiences in an unpublished essay, "Tails that wag for us. A sketch." (Lamb family archive).

2. Cf. *Newnham Register,* 1:248 for Lamb's education at home. Lamb's mother, Mabel Winkworth Lamb, had gone up to Newnham in 1880. Mabel's parents had been early benefactors of Newnham; Mrs. Winkworth was on the Council of Newnham College from 1880 to 1905. For earlier history of the Winkworth family: *Letters and Memorials of Catherine Winkworth Edited by her Sister* (Clifton, 1883). I am grateful to the late Richard Lamb for granting me access to Mabel Winkworth's copy, dated April 15, 1883.

3. C. N. L. Brooke, *A History of the University of Cambridge,* vol. 4, *1870–1990* (Cambridge, 1993), 319–20; *Newnham Register,* 1:8–9. See J. Stewart, *Jane Ellen Harrison: a Portrait from Letters* (London, 1959); Sandra J. Peacock, *Jane Ellen Harrison: the Mask and the Self* (New Haven, 1988); Mary Beard, *The Invention of Jane Harrison* (Revealing Antiquity vol. 14; Cambridge [Mass.]: Harvard University Press, 2000). For a list of Harrison's published works see Shelley Arlen, *The Cambridge Ritualists: An Annotated Bibliography of the Works by and about Jane Ellen Harrison, Gilbert Murray, Francis M. Cornford, and Arthur Bernard Cook* (Metuchen, N.J., Scarecrow Press 1990), 18–79.

4. For a view of Cambridge before the First World War and some of the opposition to women being admitted as members of the university see Gordon Johnson, *University Politics: F. M. Cornford's Cambridge and His Advice to the Young Academic Politician* (Cambridge, 1994). Although a supporter of archaeology and anthropology at Cambridge, Ridgeway was one of the leaders of the cam-

paign opposing the admission of women to Cambridge University (Johnson, *University Politics,* 205, 320). For classical archaeology in Cambridge see the inaugural lecture by A. B. Cook, the first Laurence Professor of Classical Archaeology: A. B. Cook, *The Rise and Progress of Classical Archaeology with Special Reference to the University of Cambridge: An Inaugural Lecture* (Cambridge, 1931).

5. Lamb was refused access to Ridgeway's lectures. The reason for exclusion was because of her membership of the Union of Democratic Control; see A. Robinson, *The Life and Work of Jane Ellen Harrison* (Oxford: Oxford University Press, 2002), 280.

6. Brooke, *Cambridge,* 320.

7. R. W. Hutchinson, in the unpublished "Winifred Lamb: A Tribute." (Lamb family archive).

8. *Newnham Register,* 1:249. Lloyd was the daughter of Dr. Albert H. Lloyd of Christ's College. The Lloyds were generous benefactors of the Fitzwilliam, helping to establish the Prehistoric Room within the Department of Greek and Roman Antiquities.

9. R. V. Nicholls, "Recent Additions by the Fitzwilliam Museum, Cambridge," *Archaeological Reports* 12 (1965–66): 45, no. 3.

10. Winifred Lamb, "Some Vases from the Hope Collection," *Journal of Hellenic Studies* (hereafter *JHS*) 38 (1918): 27–36. The collection was sold at Christie's, July 23, 1917. The Fitzwilliam purchased several pots, partly through the good offices of Otto Beit and John Charrington, and an Attic red-figured pelike attributed to "the Pig painter" was given by the National Arts-Collection Fund: D. W. J. Gill in *Treasures from the Fitzwilliam: "The Increase of Learning and Other Great Objects of That Noble Foundation"* (Cambridge, 1989), 5, no. 4. The pottery listed in Nicholls, "Recent Additions" (44–51) indicates Lamb made purchases of Corinthian aryballoi in 1917 (nos. 4–5), a Campanian red-figure bell-krater in 1918 (no. 17), an Attic red-figured askos in 1919 (no. 10), an Attic red-figured hydria in 1920 (no. 12). To the Hope "vases" can be added an Attic black-figured lekythos (Nicholls, "Recent Additions," no. 9). Bronzes include a sub-Mycenaean horse purchased in 1922 (no. 24) and a Peloponnesian lion in 1928 (no. 29).

11. The classical tripos was the scheme of study that for men would lead to the qualification of a bachelor of arts degree. At this time women could not receive a Cambridge degree. Lamb obtained a first-class degree but did not formally receive it until 1925: R. D. Barnett, *British School at Athens Annual Report, 1962–63,* 17. For the role of women in Room 40 in the final stages of the war see P. Fitzgerald, *The Knox Brothers* (London, 1977), 145–46. *Newnham Register,* 1:248, records her position as clerk. She would have been involved in the intelligence campaign against German submarines, which included the deciphering of codes: see P. Beesly, *Room 40: British Naval Intelligence, 1914–18* (San Diego, 1982); A. J. Marder, *From the Dreadnought to Scapa Flow: The Royal Navy in the Fisher Era, 1904–1919,* vol. 4, *1917: Year of Crisis* (London, 1969), 265.

12. B. Ashmole, "Sir John Beazley, 1885–1970," *PBA* 56 (1970): 443–61. Beazley had the rank of lieutenant in the Royal Naval Volunteer Reserve (RNVR). He became University Lecturer in Greek Vases at Oxford in 1920 and, in 1925, he was elected to the Lincoln Chair of Classical Archaeology at Oxford. Hutchinson, "Winifred Lamb," noted the "happy relationships with her companions at the

Admiralty." Other classicists connected with naval intelligence included Frank E. Adcock, in Room 40, and (Sir) John L. Myres and Richard M. Dawkins, both serving in the Mediterranean.

13. These pots, from the Hope sale (Christie's, July 23, 1917, lots 19, 32, 53, 93 [four]), were in her private collection. Lamb presented a black-figured amphora to the Ashmolean Museum, Oxford, in 1918 (AN 1918.64): M. Vickers, *Ancient Greek Pottery* (Oxford, 1999), 23, no. 12.

14. Lamb, "Vases from Hope Collection," 27 n. 1. Elsewhere (34 n. 19) she acknowledged a link between the red-figured cup in the British Museum, which she had associated with her example, and Beazley's further attribution "by the same hand" of a cup in the C. W. Lunsingh Scheurleer collection at The Hague.

15. See Lamb, "Vases from Hope Collection," 30, 31, 34. See also the section on "The Brygos Painter" in J. D. Beazley, *Attic Red-Figured Vases in American Museums* (Cambridge, Mass., 1918), 89–93, and the section on "Polygnotos" in Beazley, *American Museums,* 171–72.

16. E. M. W. Tillyard, *The Hope Vases: A Catalogue and a Discussion of the Hope Collection of Greek Vases with an Introduction on the History of the Collection and on Late Attic and South Italian Vases* (Cambridge, 1923). It should be noted that William Ridgeway was specifically mentioned for his "constant interest and quickening sympathy." Lamb was also mentioned as one of the present owners of Hope material.

17. Lamb, review of *Euthymides and His Fellows,* by J. C. Hoppin, *Classical Review* (hereafter *CR*) 33 (1919): 73–74. For Hoppin: S. L. Dyson, *Ancient Marbles to American Shores: Classical Archaeology in the United States* (Philadelphia, 1998), 83 ("one of the first artifact specialists in American classical archaeology").

18. I am grateful to Dr. C. A. Stray for first discussing this possibility with me.

19. Lamb, review of *Catalogue of Arretine Pottery in the Museum of Fine Arts, Boston,* by G. H. Chase, *CR* 33 (1919): 78–79.

20. Ibid., 79.

21. Caton-Thompson, "Lamb," also mentions Lamb's activity on Ithaca; this appears to be a mistake. See H. Waterhouse, *The British School at Athens: The First Hundred Years* (London, 1986), 32.

22. See, for example, J. P. Droop, *Archaeological Excavation* (Cambridge, 1915), 63–64. The first woman holder of a British School studentship was Margaret M. Hardie of Newnham College in 1910: Waterhouse, *British School,* 134. Lamb was not a subscriber to the British School at Athens until she joined the Mycenae excavations.

23. This was caused by the changing political situation in Athens and the absence of Alan J. B. Wace, the director.

24. These are preserved in the Lamb archive at the British School at Athens.

25. Lamb was to write to her parents that Welch was "the best company in the world" (quoted in Waterhouse, *British School,* 135) and "delightful, rather soldierly and a broad-minded Tory" (letter of November 1, 1920). The political comment was no doubt for the benefit of her liberal father. For a photograph of Winifred Lamb and F. B. Welch: Hood, *Faces of Archaeology,* 74.

26. Hood, *Faces of Archaeology,* 154–60.

27. Waterhouse, *British School,* 26.

28. Waterhouse, *British School,* 136 fig. Lamb was one of four women at the British School in this year. Herford was working on architectural terra-cottas and prehistoric pottery, Chandler on the Attic frontier and its fortresses. The fourth, Mrs. Hondius, was working on Greek flora. See the report of the Annual Meeting 1920–21 in *BSA* 24 (1919–20, 1920–21): 234. J. D. Beazley did similar doodles: see M. Robertson, "Beazley and After," *Müncher Jahrbuch der bildenden Kunst,* 3d ser., 27 (1976): 32, fig. 4. A black-figure amphora was used to illustrate the cover of a folder containing a series of papers in the family archive. Herford's unpublished letters home contain much material about Lamb.

29. Letter of October 28, 1920. The Delphi trip was made with Herford.

30. Letter of November 1, 1920.

31. The visit was particularly poignant for Herford, who had lost her brother Siegfried, the celebrated climber, during the First World War. The visit virtually coincided with Armistice Day, marking the end of the First World War on the eleventh hour, of the eleventh day, of the eleventh month.

32. For the dangers see "English Ladies Robbed on Mt Pentelikon," *The Times,* April 16, 1923. The women were Grace Chapman and Hilda Maybury.

33. She traveled with Leonard Woolley ("an interesting talker and a man of the world and nice appreciative eyes") as far as Corinth on May 9. She arrived at Mycenae with Herford on May 20, 1921. A. J. B. Wace, "Excavations at Mycenae I. The Campaign of 1920," *BSA* 24 (1919–20, 1920–21): 185.

34. Letter of April 25, 1922.

35. For Burkitt's interest in the prehistory of Greece see Miles C. Burkitt, "A Visit to Crete," *Proceedings of the Prehistoric Society of East Anglia* 3, no. 3 (1920–21): 580–86. I am grateful to Pamela Jane Smith for this reference.

36. See Caton-Thompson, *Mixed Memoirs,* 98–99.

37. Richard Seager (1882–1925) had excavated at Vasilike, Pseira, and Mochlos: Dyson, *Ancient Marbles,* 90. This mention fills a small gap in Seager's biography: Marshall J. Becker and Philip P. Betancourt, *Richard Berry Seager: Pioneer Archaeologist and Proper Gentleman* (Philadelphia, 1997), esp. 157–58.

38. She wrote about hearing Dörpfeld lecture on the Acropolis in Athens on April 15, 1922. For the background to this period: Suzanne L. Marchand, *Down from Olympus: Archaeology and Philhellenism in Germany, 1750–1970* (Princeton, 1996).

39. In a letter of June 2, 1924.

40. Waterhouse, *British School,* 26. The excavation ran from April 23 to July 9, 1920: Wace, "Excavations at Mycenae I," 185. Other members of the team were Mr. Casson, Mr. Collingham, Mr. Lawrence, Mr. Tierney, and Mr. Hutton, along with Mr. R. S. Cole and Mr. and Mrs. A. W. Gomme. Mrs. Schliemann visited the excavation during June. For Wace: Hood, *Faces of Archaeology,* 40–46.

41. Letter of March 9, 1921: "The frescoes found last year are quite enough to write a nice paper on and interesting—I have been working at all the Mycenaean frescoes in the museum for the last few days." On May 17, 1921, she hoped to look at the frescoes in the museum at Thebes. Wace was clearly putting pressure on her to complete her study as on May 5, 1921, she wrote, "What I have to fear is that I mayn't do the frescoes properly now Mr Wace has left me so little time and I have refused to come out in the autumn." Lamb's trips to Crete and Nauplion in April

and May 1921 were probably linked to the study of the frescoes. The study was published in the *BSA:* W. Lamb, "Excavations at Mycenae III. Frescoes from the Ramp House," *BSA* 24 (1919–20, 1920–21): 189–99, plates 7–10.

42. Lamb's parents also contributed fifty pounds and thirty pounds to the Mycenae excavation fund for 1920–21 and 1921–22 respectively: *BSA* 24 (1919–20, 1920–21): 243; 25 (1921–22, 1922–23): 446. These were not insubstantial contributions; the total support in 1920–21 was a little over £428. The donation was apparently made directly to Wace (letter of April 28, 1921). Lamb's father was a subscriber to the British School at Athens from 1920–21 until his death. Mabel, Lamb's mother, was later to help fund the excavations in the Fayoum of Lamb's friend Gertrude Caton-Thompson: *Annual Report of the Fitzwilliam Museum, Cambridge* (1927): 2.

43. A. J. B. Wace, "Excavations at Mycenae II. The Campaign of 1921," *BSA* 24 (1919–20, 1920–21): 188; Wace, "Excavations at Mycenae VIII. The Palace. 1 Introduction," *BSA* 25 (1921–22, 1922–23): 148 n. 1. Wace, "Excavations at Mycenae II. The Campaign of 1921," *BSA* 24 (1919–20, 1920–21): 187 recorded that the 1921 "excavation began on May 22nd, though Miss Lamb and Miss Herford arrived two days before and occupied themselves in arranging the workroom and other preparations."

44. A. J. B. Wace, "Excavations at Mycenae V. The Campaign of 1922," *BSA* 25 (1921–22, 1922–23): 3.

45. Wace, "The Campaign of 1922," 4. See A. J. B. Wace, "Chamber Tombs at Mycenae," *Archaeologia* 82 (1932): 1; apart from Lamb the team consisted of Dr. C. A. Boethius, W. A. Heurtley, R. W. Hutchinson, and Miss H. L. Lorimer.

46. Wace, "Excavations at Mycenae V," 3. Lorimer's work at the British School at Athens is discussed in D. W. J. Gill, "'The Passion of Hazard': Women at the British School at Athens before the First World War," *BSA* 97 (2002): 491–510.

47. She was to return to Nauplion in 1925: *BSA* 26 (1923–24, 1924–25): 338.

48. Pybus overlapped with Lamb at Newnham, where she took the classical tripos from 1910 to 1914. At the time of the Mycenae excavations she was an assistant mistress at the Central High School in Newcastle upon Tyne (1919–25). In October 1925 she married A. M. Woodward, the excavator of Sparta. *Newnham Register,* 1:225.

49. Hood, *Faces of Archaeology,* 128–31. The caricature was drawn at Sparta in 1927. Droop had written *Archaeological Excavation,* Cambridge Archaeological and Ethnological Series (Cambridge, 1915).

50. A. J. B. Wace, "Mycenae V. The Campaign of 1923," *BSA* 25 (1921–22, 1922–23): 5. Lamb apparently "was only in Greece for a short time" (*BSA* 25 (1921–22, 1922—23) 453).

51. Waterhouse, *British School,* 27. For further details of Wace in this period: D. W. J. Gill, "Alan J. B. Wace," in *The Dictionary of National Biography* (Oxford, due in 2004).

52. Lamb, "Ramp House," 189, noted that the work was conducted "by ourselves."

53. Ibid., 190.

54. Ibid., 191 n. 5 (an association with Knossos), and 197 n. 4 (an association with Tylissos). Lamb had studied the Knossos frescoes in the spring.

55. A. J. B. Wace and W. Lamb, "Excavations at Mycenae VIII. 3. The Pithos Area," "6. The Court," "13. The Shrine and Adjoining Chambers," "14. The Megaron," "15. The Ante-chamber to Domestic Quarters," *BSA* 25 (1921–22, 1922–23): 160–79, 188–204, 223–63.

56. E.g., Lamb and Wace, "The Pithos Area," 172.

57. Wace and Lamb, "The Court," 193–95.

58. Wace and Lamb, "Shrine and Adjoining Chambers," 224–26.

59. Ibid., 232.

60. Wace and Lamb, "The Megaron," 235–37, 249–55.

61. Ibid., 254–55.

62. Wace and Lamb, "Ante-chamber to Domestic Quarters," 258–59; Waterhouse, *British School,* 23. For Wace's publications on textiles: Helen Waterhouse, "Bibliography, 1903–1950," *BSA* 46 (1951): 232–43; Waterhouse, "A. J. B. Wace: Supplementary Bibliography," *BSA* 63 (1968): 327–29.

63. E.g., Lamb and Wace, "The Pithos Area," 173, 174.

64. C. M. Fürst, "Appendix: The Skulls," *Archaeologia* 82 (1932): 225–32. This study was apparently conducted in part at Lamb's instigation.

65. FM GR.5a–h.1922. Wace, "The Campaign of 1922," 4.

66. FM GR.37a–d.1921. She retained one in her collection: FM GR.60.1963.

67. They form the series FM GR.12.1923. This donor was almost certainly Lamb.

68. FM GR.2.1922. This had been excavated by the Americans under Carl Blegen, who had worked at Mycenae with Wace. For the site: Carl W. Blegen, *Korakou: A Prehistoric Settlement Near Corinth* (New York: American School of Classical Studies at Athens, 1921).

69. Annual report for 1924–25 in *BSA* 26 (1923–24, 1924–25): 338, 343–45; W. A. Heurtley and R. W. Hutchinson, "Report on Excavations at the Toumba and Tables of Vardaróftsa, Macedonia, 1925, 1926. Part I. The Toumba," *BSA* 27 (1925–26): 1–66. This report noted that apart from this work "and except for a short journey in Thessaly and a visit to Nauplion, [Lamb] spent the remainder of her time at Athens, where she worked on the subject of Greek Bronzes. She returned early in May to England, after about nine weeks in Greece." Other members of the team included Mr. W. L. Cuttle (who had worked with Lamb at Sparta) and Mr. H. H. Keen. Both Lamb and Keen came out specifically for the purpose of working on the excavation. She worked on the High and Low Tables. See also Waterhouse, *British School,* 30–31, and W. A. Heurtley, "Pottery from Macedonian Mounds," *BSA* 26 (1923–24, 1924–25): 30–37. Winifred Lamb captured the experience of life on such an excavation in her unpublished short story, "The Treasure Hunters," now in the Lamb family archive

70. Letter of May 4, 1922.

71. Letter of April 3, 1925.

72. Heurtley and Hutchinson, "Vardaróftsa," 4. For Eileen Heurtley: Hood, *Faces of Archaeology,* 144–49. The caricature is dated 1925. Like Winifred Lamb, both Eileen and Walter Heurtley were Roman Catholics.

73. Letter of March 17, 1925.

74. For the association, Heurtley and Hutchinson, "Vardaróftsa," 52.

75. Ibid., 64–65.

76. Details of Lamb's Aetolian tour in May 1928 are provided in her typescript "North-west Passage," sub-titled in her own hand, "Diary of a trip to Aetolia & Epirus." A copy is kept in the archive of the British School at Athens.

77. FM GR.14.1928. Three sherds are now in the Museum of Classical Archaeology, Cambridge (SD 60–62).

78. Details in *BSA* 30 (1928–29, 1929–30): 260, 264–65 ("Prehistoric Sites in Macedonia"). The excavation lasted from March 11 to April 13, although Lamb only spent a "short time" there before starting her own excavation at Thermi on April 5. The team consisted of Mr. and Mrs. Heurtley, Mr. C. A. Ralegh Radford (later Director of the British School at Rome), Mr. O. Davies, Miss Sylvia Benton, and Mr. G. A. D. Tait. For further comments, including parallels with Thermi, see W. A. Heurtley, "Prehistoric Macedonia," in *Proceedings of the First International Congress of Prehistoric and Protohistoric Sciences, London, August 1–6, 1932* (London, 1934), 186–88; Heurtley, *Prehistoric Macedonia* (Cambridge, 1939).

79. Waterhouse, *British School,* 27, 105. The official dates for the excavations were April 7 to May 31, 1924, and April 13 to May 30, 1925. See A. M. Woodward, "Excavations at Sparta, 1924–25. I. Introductory," *BSA* 26 (1923–24, 1924–25): 116–18; A. M. Woodward and M. B. Hobling, "Excavations at Sparta, 1924–25. 4. The Acropolis. 1. The Site," *BSA* 26 (1923–24, 1924–25): 240–52. For Woodward and Hobling: Hood, *Faces of Archaeology,* 60–64, 76–79. Other members of the team included Mr. Cuttle (who was later to excavate with Lamb at Thermi) and the architect Piet de Jong. Lamb's parents contributed £50 (out of a total of £803) toward the Sparta excavations; Lamb herself donated £10 to the Sparta excavations in 1925 although she was working in Macedonia; during the session 1927–28 Lamb's mother donated £10. Woodward added his own tribute to Lamb after her death in a letter to *The Times,* September 21, 1963.

80. She published an account of Melian stamped pithos fragments in the British School at Athens in the *BSA* for 1923–25. We should note that this break was in part due to her father's death on January 3, 1925, which was followed in 1926 by the saga of the Fitzwilliam Goddess. During the session 1927–28 Lamb spent time "both in Athens and Sparta preparing for the *Annual* a study of the chief bronze finds from the [Sparta] excavations on the Acropolis and at the Orthia Sanctuary": *BSA* 29 (1927–28): 304.

81. Woodward and Hobling, "Excavations at Sparta, 1924–25," 240. Lamb's activity was specifically dated to May 1924. One of her duties was to log results. The annual report for 1923–24 in *BSA* 26 (1923–24, 1924–25): 314 recorded that Lamb was at Sparta for the "second half of April and May."

82. Woodward, *The Times,* September 21, 1963.

83. Letter of May 2, 1924.

84. George Alexopoulos, a native of Charvati (Mycenae), had excavated with Wace at Mycenae and also at Prosymna with Blegen: Hood, *Faces of Archaeology,* 94–97.

85. Letter of Monday, May 10, 1924.

86. W. Lamb, "Excavations at Sparta, 1927: 5. Bronzes from the Acropolis,

1924–1927," *BSA* 28 (1926–27): 82–95, plates 8–10. Note Waterhouse, *British School,* 105–6.

87. Letter of November 23, 1927. Her article "Arcadian Bronze Statuettes" had appeared in *BSA* 27 (1925–26): 133–48, plates 24–25. Heurtley's dig refers to the excavation in Macedonia.

88. Cambridge FM GR.15.1864. Lamb, "Bronzes from the Acropolis," 92, under no. 23.

89. W. Lamb, "Excavations at Sparta, 1906–1910: 6. Notes on Some Bronzes from the Orthia Site," *BSA* 28 (1926–27): 96–106, plates 11–12.

90. In a letter written in the train to Athens on May 29, 1924.

91. Letter of May 29, 1924. The de Jong comment is quoted by Waterhouse, *British School,* 137. De Jong had also been involved with Wace's work at Mycenae. Woodward (*The Times,* September 21, 1963) described Lamb as "an active and congenial member of the team." The caricatures appear in Hood, *Faces of Archaeology,* nos. 10–17 (1924), 18–21 (1925), 22–23 (1926), and 24 (1927), and p. 272 (Gladys Parkin).

92. She wrote an account of the trip for her parents, "A Thirsty Pilgrimage."

93. Lamb, "Bronzes from the Acropolis," 84, fig. 1, 85. The inventory number is in fact GR. 11.1928, not 28.10.

94. Letter of May 29, 1924.

95. Letter of June 2, 1924.

96. In a letter of April 24, 1922 Lamb wrote home, "I believe [Wace] has been summoned to Sparta to choose duplicates of the finds from the excavations which will go to Oxford and Cambridge." This would suggest that the finds came from the earlier British excavations.

97. A. M. Woodward, "Archaeology in Greece, 1928–1929," *JHS* 49 (1929): 223; W. Lamb and F. N. Pryce, "Sigillata from Lesbos," *JHS* 60 (1940): 96–98; also Lamb, "Excavations in Lesbos," *BSA* 30 (1928–29, 1929–30): 266.

98. Lamb later noted (*Excavations at Thermi in Lesbos* [Cambridge, 1936], 1) that there was "nothing earlier than the Late Bronze Age." Apart from Methymna she also considered Arisba.

99. Lamb and Pryce, "Sigillata from Lesbos," 96.

100. Ibid., 96–97, fig. 1, nos. 5–6. The sherds are now in the Museum of Classical Archaeology in Cambridge: MZ103, MZ109. The identification of the fabric was made by Dr. John Hayes.

101. Lamb, "Excavations in Lesbos," 265.

102. Lamb, "Grey Wares from Lesbos," *JHS* 52 (1932): 4–11.

103. Lamb, "Excavations in Lesbos," 265.

104. Lamb and Pryce, "Sigillata from Lesbos." All the sherds are in the Museum of Classical Archaeology in Cambridge. The fabrics were identified by Dr. John Hayes in 1992.

105. Letter of November 13, 1928.

106. In a letter of March 30, 1928, she clearly had little expectation of finding a suitable site: "I don't believe I shall find a prehistoric site here, all the same, it will surprise me if I do. But it will have been worth while trying." In a letter of April 4, 1928, she was finding it difficult to identify prehistoric sites because of the longevity of pottery styles: "Have I found a site to dig? I can't say if what I've found will do

till I've seen Blegen or someone like him. The ancient Lesbians made a lot of black wall that looked prehistoric and isn't."

107. Letter of November 13, 1928.

108. Ibid.

109. The excavation lasted until June 1, 1929. The 1930 season lasted from March 31 to June 30; the 1931 season from March 21 to June 11; in 1932 Lamb was on Lesbos from March 22 to July 5 (May 29 to July 3 at Antissa). For Hutchinson, see Wace, "The Campaign of 1922," 3.

110. Woodward, "Archaeology in Greece," 223.

111. In March and early April, Lamb had been excavating with Heurtley at Sarátsi in Macedonia. The year 1929 was when Humfry Payne became director of the British School: Waterhouse, *British School,* 30. Lamb recorded her experience at Thermi in three unpublished essays: "The Conversion of Andoni," "A Woman as a Woman Should Be," and "First Aid." Hutchinson, "Winifred Lamb," noted Lamb's "consideration for her workmen" and "her secret generosity" to "various people in need in Lesbos and in Turkey." All papers are in the Lamb family archive.

112. W. Lamb and R. W. Hutchinson, "Excavations at Thermi," *BSA* 30 (1928–29, 1929–30): 3. This is described as "the ideal way of excavating."

113. Ibid.

114. Hom. *Il.* 9.129–30. Lamb, *Thermi,* 72, 213. Lamb was clearly influenced by Myres's book, *Who Were the Greeks?* (p. 116), which she reviewed for the *Journal of Hellenic Studies* in 1931.

115. Lamb, *Thermi,* 74, fig. 25.

116. Ibid., 198, fig. 60.

117. Ibid., 86–90.

118. Lamb, "Grey Wares from Lesbos"; "Schliemann's Prehistoric Sites in the Troad," *Prähistorische Zeitschrift* 23 (1932): 111–31.

119. She studied Schliemann's material in the Museum für Völkerkunde in Berlin through the good offices of its director, Dr. Wilhelm Unversagt, who had been appointed in 1926. Unversagt was still director in 1945 when he handed over the Trojan antiquities to the victorious Russian troops. See C. Moorehead, *The Lost Treasures of Troy* (London, 1994), 258, 278. Lamb also studied material from Mytilene in the British Museum: "Grey Wares from Lesbos," 11. This included the sherd inv. 1932.2–18.1, which had been given by Charles T. Newton. Presumably Lamb had been studying unaccessioned material in early 1932 and had asked for an inventory number to be assigned. I am grateful to Lesley Fitton for identifying the link with Newton.

120. Lamb, "Schliemann's Prehistoric Sites," 112.

121. Annual Report in *BSA* 30 (1928–29, 1929–30): 284.

122. She reflected on this in her "The Site of Troy," *Antiquity* 6 (1932): 71–81. The obituary in *The Times* also emphasizes her visit to Troy. In her first report, published in the annual report, she commented that the "civilisation [of Thermi] was already allied to that of Troy and Yortan: whether it was a colony of Troy is uncertain owing to the absence of the characteristically Trojan face-urns": Annual Report in *BSA* 30 (1928–29, 1929–30): 265.

123. Annual Report in *BSA* 32 (1931–32): 257.

124. W. Lamb and H. Bancroft, "Report on the Lesbos Charcoals," *BSA* 39 (1938–39): 88–89.

125. O. Davies, "The Chemical Composition of Archaic Greek Bronze," *BSA* 35 (1934–35): 132, w ("given to me by the kindness of Miss Lamb"). Lamb had earlier excavated with Davies at Sarátsi in Macedonia. See further Lamb and Brock, "Excavations at Thermi," 4, 39–40; Lamb, *Thermi,* 214–15. These analyses included material from each of the towns.

126. Lamb and Brock, "Excavations at Thermi," 4, 46; H. G. G. Payne, "Archaeology in Greece, 1930–1931," *JHS* 51 (1931): 202; Lamb, *Thermi,* 195–96. We should note that the excavations themselves were reported in *The Times* on March 13, 1930, 12; cf. *Antiquity* 4 (1930): 243.

127. Lamb, *Thermi,* 216–18. The seed study was conducted by Mrs. Reid. Corn was noted as being absent. Other identified seeds included remains of leguminous seeds, poppy seeds, and a possible crab apple. The shell study, by Mr. Robson and Mr. Tomlin, concluded that shellfish was an important part of the local diet. Professor Koumares of the University of Athens studied human bones, and the animal bone study was conducted by Miss D. Bate at the South Kensington Museum (now the Natural History Museum).

128. A reference I owe to Daniel Pullen. Harland collected examples of grain and acorns.

129. K. F. Vickery, *Food in Early Greece,* Illinois Studies in the Social Sciences 20.3 (Urbana, 1936), esp. 40 and 44 (references to Thermi). I owe this reference to Ian Begg.

130. D. B. Harden in *CR* 50 (1936): 233.

131. A. J. B. Wace in *Antiquaries Journal* (hereafter *AntJ*) 19 (1939): 98–99. He also described the illustrations as "excellent." Other reviews include *Times Literary Supplement,* September 5, 1936, 710; H. Philippart, *L'Antiquité Classique* 5 (1936): 440–41; V. G. Childe, *JHS* 57 (1937): 84–86; S. Casson, *Antiquity* 11 (1937): 123–24; C. W. Blegen, *American Journal of Archaeology* 42 (1938): 593–94; K. Bittel, *Germania* 21 (1937): 278–81.

132. E.g., Lamb went to Athens in October 1929 specifically to work on the Thermi finds; after the 1930 season she had two weeks in Athens before leaving; in the autumn of 1930 she spent two months working on the finds "and prepared a report for publication" (Annual Report in *BSA* 31 [1930–31]: 184); in 1933 Lamb was in Greece from January to the end of July (with the exception of March and April) to work in Athens on the Lesbos material (Annual Report in *BSA* 33 [1932–33]: 211). In a letter of January 27, 1933, she wrote, "I'm getting a lot of work done and I've had to draw all but small vases and lids myself."

133. The paper was read on Thursday, January 28, 1932 (reported in *AntJ* 12 [1932]: 341), and she was elected on Thursday, February 25.

134. August 1–6, 1932. W. Lamb, "The Development of the Troad Civilization in the Early Bronze Age, Illustrated by Thermi in Lesbos," *Proceedings of the First International Congress of Prehistoric and Protohistoric Sciences, London, August 1–6, 1932* (London, 1934), 185–86.

135. D. W. J. Gill, *Findspots of Greek and Roman Antiquities in the Fitzwilliam Museum, Cambridge* (Cambridge: Fitzwilliam Museum, 1992), 51–53.

136. Exhib. cat. Royal Academy of Arts, London, *British Archaeological Discoveries in Greece and Crete, 1886–1936* (London, 1936), v. The lecture was given on Wednesday, November 11.

137. Ibid., 67–68.

138. Payne, "Archaeology in Greece, 1930–1931," 202–3; Payne, "Archaeology in Greece, 1931–2," *JHS* 52 (1932): 251; Annual Report in *BSA* 31 (1930–31): 184, 189; W. Lamb, "Mytilene (Thermi and Antissa)," *BSA* 32 (1931–32): 264–65; W. Lamb, "Mytilene," *BSA* 33 (1932–33): 215–16. See also W. Lamb, "Antissa," *BSA* 31 (1930–31): 166–78, plates 27–28; W. Lamb, "Antissa," *BSA* 32 (1931–32): 41–67, plates 17–25 (hereafter cited as "Antissa II"). The dates of the excavation were June 15 to June 27, 1931; May 29 to July 3, 1932. The excavation was conducted immediately after the Thermi season. Lamb, Brock, and Six took photographs; Lamb did much of the surveying for the plans. A range of material from Antissa is now in the Museum of Classical Archaeology, Cambridge (A 1–10). This includes Aeolian bucchero, East Greek pottery, and a scarab.

139. The first visit by caique was in March 1928. In a letter of November 13, 1928, she wrote of a second visit to Antissa with Hutchinson: "though 'the Squire' had picked up one valuable imported Mycenaean fragment at Antissa (a very jolly trip this time) it did not tell us anything about the prehistoric Lesbians themselves."

140. R. Koldewey, *Die antiken Baureste der Insel Lesbos* (Berlin, 1890), 19.

141. In a characteristic way she acknowledged the collaboration of Mr. E. Paraskevaïdes, ephor of antiquities for the northeastern Aegean: "Antissa," 167.

142. Lamb, "Antissa II," 42–45.

143. J. J. Coulton, *The Architectural Development of the Greek Stoa* (Oxford, 1976), 215.

144. This work was carried out by Six and Cook: Lamb, "Antissa II," 63–66. In 1933 further cremations and inhumations were found: W. Lamb, "Mytilene," *BSA* 33 (1932–33): 215–16. Cook joined the end of the dig.

145. Lamb, "Antissa," 177–78; Lamb, "Antissa II," 51–62.

146. Lamb, review of *Corpus Vasorum Antiquorum,* by J. D. Beazley, H. G. G. Payne, and E. R. Price, *CR* 46 (1932): 160–61. See "Antissa II," 60, with reference to *Corpus Vasorum Antiquorum* Oxford II, plate lxv.3.

147. Lamb, "Antissa," 167; Annual Report in *BSA* 31 (1930–31): 189.

148. Lamb, "Antissa," 168, fig. 1.

149. Letter of June 19, 1933.

150. K. Kourioniotis, "Ἀνασκαφαὶ καὶ ἔρεύαι ἐν Χίῳ," *Archaiologikon Deltion* 1 (1915): 64–93; K. Kourioniotis, "Ἀνασκαφαὶ καὶ ἔρεύαι ἐν Χίῳ: 2," *Archaiologikon Deltion* 2 (1916): 190–215. See Strabo 14.1.35: "then to Phanai, a deep harbour, and to a temple of Apollo and a grove of palm trees" (based on Loeb trans.).

151. W. Lamb, "Excavations at Kato Phana in Chios," *BSA* 35 (1934–35): 138. We should note Lamb's interest in Archaic East Greek pottery in her review of "Vases at Oxford," in *CR* 46 (1932): 160–61. For further notes on her excavation: Waterhouse, *British School,* 113.

152. See Lamb, "Kato Phana," 139 n. 1, where she notes the assistance of Madias, Argenti, and Choremes, as well as Pappaiannoudes, in connection with the museum.

153. Ibid., 139.

154. Ibid., 140. Naukratite sherds are now known as Chiot.

155. Ibid.

156. Ibid., 148.

157. Lamb, reviews of *Altsamische Standbilder,* by E. Buschor, vols. 1, 2, and 3, *JHS* 54 (1934): 214–15; 55 (1935): 244; 57 (1937): 90–91.

158. Lamb, review of *Altsamische Standbilder,* vol. 2. Lamb's interest in archaeological photography is reflected in her gift of "a Ross whole-plate camera with lens and dark-slides, the whole in a hide leather carrying case" to the Institute of Archaeology, London: *University of London, Institute of Archaeology, Sixteenth Annual Report, August 1, 1958–July 31, 1959* (1960), 11.

159. Caton-Thompson, "Lamb," 51.

160. Winifred Lamb's obituary in *The Times,* September 21, 1963. We should also note that Margaret Hardie (later Hasluck), also of Newnham College, had worked in Turkey with Sir William Ramsey before World War I: Waterhouse, *British School,* 134; see also M. M. Hardie, "The Shrine of Mên Askaenos at Pisidian Antioch," *JHS* 32 (1912): 111–50.

161. Lamb in fact deposited a number of sherds from Troy at the Fitzwilliam Museum: FM GR.8a–f.1929; many of these are now in the Museum of Classical Archaeology (TY 13–29, 43–80). The sherds can be assigned to Troy 2–6. See also her "The Site of Troy." She visited Troy again on May 26, 1932 (mentioned in a letter of May 28, 1932). She noted that Blegen and Dörpfeld, among others, were there and that she was shown round the excavations. Lamb was particularly critical of their excavation strategy: "They take 1½ hours over lunch, and work at low pressure for ten hours a day, which I think a bad plan." Her visit to Troy was followed on the Friday by a tour of "the mounds of the Troad in a car driven by a marvellous Turkish chauffeur called Ramsey . . . We are all in love with Turkey—and we like the Turks." From Çanakkale Lamb left for Ankara (Angora) "because Myres and Childe said I must see the Anatolian stuff there. And we shall leave Angora as soon as possible to save expense and get back to Mytilene, on the 9th June at the latest. The Angora stuff is going to be discussed in this year's prehistoric congress, and I want to wipe Burton Brown's eye." Burton Brown excavated in Azerbaijan and held a diffusionist view. I am grateful to Andrew Sherratt for drawing my attention to this.

162. Lamb, "Grey Wares from Lesbos," 2.

163. Lamb, review of *Die Ruinen von Bogazköy and Bogazköy: Die Kleinfunde der Grabungen 1906–1912,* vol. 1, by K. Bittel, *JHS* 57 (1937): 258. See also Lamb, review of *Prähistorische Forschung in Kleinasien,* by K. Bittel, *Gnomon* 11 (1935): 649–52. There are references in Lamb's correspondence to meetings with Bittel in Istanbul.

164. Lamb, review of *Prähistorische Forschung in Kleinasien,* 650.

165. Ibid., 649.

166. Ibid., 650–51.

167. Ibid., 652.

168. Lamb (ibid., 651) commented: "I have recently picked up a quantity of sherds that seem to be eastern, as well as others of the Yortan class on mounds near Afyon." See also a letter of April 14, 1935: "The day after tomorrow we drive (carriage) to a village with a mound." This expedition was described in her "Adventures

in Anatolia" (copy in the Lamb family archive); this is discussed by D. W. J. Gill, "'A Rich and Promising Site': Winifred Lamb (1894–1963), Kusura and Anatolian Archaeology," *Anatolian Studies* 50 (2000): 1–10.

169. W. Lamb, "Excavations at Kusura near Afyon Karahisar," *Archaeologia* 86 (1936): 1–2 (hereafter cited as "Kusura"). Michael Vickers has kindly identified the jug in the Ashmolean Museum, Oxford as AN 1895.64, found at Emit near the headwaters of the Rhyndakos: Myres, "Pot-Fabrics of Asia Minor," *Journal of the Anthropological Institute* 33 (1903): 373. Elsewhere Lamb doubted the provenance of this jug, as "exploration of this district has since proved that no early settlement exists there": review of *Prähistorische Forschung in Kleinasien,* 649.

170. "Kusura," 2; W. Lamb, "Excavations at Kusura near Afyon Karahisar: II," *Archaeologia* 87 (1937): 219 (hereafter cited as "Kusura II"). She also acknowledged other members of the department of antiquities. Gönçer is described in Lamb's unpublished account of her search for a prehistoric site, "Adventures in Anatolia."

171. The excavation was the setting for a short unpublished murder mystery, "The Inspector Interferes," by Winifred Lamb in the Lamb family archive. The excavator is Miss Nancy Wood from Cambridge, assisted by Mr. John and Mrs. Lucy Buchannan (a spelling used in her address book for William B. C. Buchannan [Hood, *Faces of Archaeology,* 90–93], a colleague from the Sparta excavations), Mr. Mcleod (the architect), Miss Olivia Stone (University of London), and the Turkish museum director, Mustafa Demir.

172. J. R. Stewart, "The Cemetery," in "Kusura," 54–64.

173. "Kusura II," 219, gives a list of the team. It should be noted that one of the sponsors of the excavations was Mr. A. L. Reckitt, himself a benefactor of the Department of Antiquities at the Fitzwilliam Museum.

174. A useful summary can be found in "Kusura," 4. For the endpoint: "Kusura," 24.

175. Ibid., 12. Lamb returned to this in "Some Early Anatolian Shrines," *Anatolian Studies* 6 (1956): 89.

176. "Kusura," 5.

177. Ibid., 11.

178. Ibid., 17, 21.

179. "Kusura II," 235–51.

180. "Kusura," 28–54; "Kusura II," 251–72.

181. "Kusura," 54; "Kusura II," 273.

182. "Kusura," 64.

183. Ibid., 10. The seeds, and others from elsewhere on the site, were identified by Mrs. Reid. Wood was identified by Helen Bancroft ("Kusura II," 219 n. 3), who had worked on the Thermi material.

184. "Kusura," 11.

185. "Kusura II," 228.

186. Ibid., 260 n. 2.

187. Ibid., 257.

188. Ibid., 273.

189. Ibid.

190. Ibid.

191. Lamb, review of *Die Metallindustrie Anatoliens in der Zeit von 1500–700 vor Chr.,* by S. Przeworski, *JHS* 59 (1939): 292.

192. Lamb, review of *Die Ruinen von Bogazköy,* 258–59; and review of *Die Metallindustrie Anatoliens,* 291.

193. Lamb, review of *Die Ruinen von Bogazköy,* 259.

194. Reported in the *AntJ* 17 (1937): 359. It was given on February 18.

195. Lamb, review of *The Excavations at Erimi,* by P. Dikaios, *AntJ* 18 (1938): 426–28; Lamb, review of *Ugaritica, etudes relatives aux decouvertes de Ras Shamra,* by C. Schaeffer *AntJ* 20 (1940): 392–94.

196. Lamb succeeded Frederick Henry Marshall, Fellow of Emmanuel College, Cambridge, who had been appointed honorary keeper of Greek and Roman antiquities in 1913 (see his obituary in *Emmanuel College Magazine* 38, 1955–56). For a full discussion of this period, D. W. J. Gill, "Winifred Lamb and the Fitzwilliam Museum," in *Classics in Cambridge,* ed. C. A. Stray, *Proceedings of the Cambridge Philological Society,* suppl. 24 (Cambridge, 1999): 135–56. Even today honorary keepers at the Fitzwilliam are "appointed" by the director and syndicate without any reference to the university. There were no keepers at the Fitzwilliam until 1947–48.

197. Lamb is connected with the acquisition of two objects in this period: a bowl (GR.4.1916) and a hydria (GR.4.1919).

198. *Corpus Vasorum Antiquorum,* 2:15. For Cyprus Exploration Fund material see D. W. J. Gill, *Donors and Former Owners of Greek and Roman Antiquities in the Fitzwilliam Museum, Cambridge* (Cambridge, 1992), 49–57.

199. Nicholls, "Recent Additions," 49–50, no. 26. This coincided with the publication of G. M. A. Richter, *The Metropolitan Museum of Art: Greek, Etruscan, and Roman Bronzes* (New York, 1915).

200. Lamb, "Bronzes from the Acropolis." Cf. W. Lamb, *Greek and Roman Bronzes* (London, 1929), 78. She was working on this material in 1927–28: *BSA* 29 (1927–28): 304.

201. During this period she also acquired a wide selection of small bronze votives from the important site of Pherae (Velestino). The series of objects: FM GR3.1926, GR.6.1927, GR.6.1928. Lamb illustrates some in *Greek and Roman Bronzes,* plate 13, b–c, and elsewhere (37 n. 13), noting that they "were purchased at Athens and said to come from Velestino." See also Lamb, "Excavations at Sparta, 1906–1910," 99. She also noted a small votive, which she purchased "in the bazaar" at Athens in 1921 and which was then in Cambridge. Lamb had traveled through Thessaly in 1925 after her excavation in Macedonia: *BSA* 26 (1923–24, 1924–25): 338.

202. Lamb, "Arcadian Bronze Statuettes." Cf. Lamb, *Greek and Roman Bronzes,* 96: The article in the *BSA* was mostly based on a study of material in Athens and Berlin.

203. In reports of her work in Greece in 1925, she wrote that she spent time at Athens "work[ing] on the subject of Greek Bronzes": *BSA* 26 (1923–24, 1924–25): 338. During the session 1927–28 Lamb "spent two short periods in Greece working on her book of ancient bronze statuettes": *BSA* 29 (1927–28): 304.

204. Lamb, *Greek and Roman Bronzes,* viii–ix. She lists help at the following

museums: the British Museum, the National Museum at Athens; Berlin; the Louvre; the Bibliothèque Nationale; Munich; Vienna; Florence; Naples; Candia; and New York. During the academic session 1926–27, Lamb was an associate at the British School at Rome working on ancient bronzes (*British School at Rome, Annual Report to the Subscribers* 27 [1926–27]: 3). It seems unlikely that Lamb visited the Metropolitan Museum of Art in New York. I am grateful to Brian Kenney and Dr Dietrich von Bothmer for information about Lamb's correspondence with Gisela Richter.

205. Lamb's contacts with the National Museum provided an entrée for Cockerell when he visited Athens in 1927: K. Butcher and D. W. J. Gill, "The Director, the Dealer, the Goddess, and Her Champions: The Acquisition of the Fitzwilliam Goddess," *American Journal of Archaeology* 97 (1993): 392.

206. E. J. Forsdyke in *JHS* 49 (1929): 283–84.

207. For full details, including benefactors of the project: Gill, "Lamb and the Fitzwilliam." The gallery now displays Cypriot antiquities (1999).

208. Dawkins had been a benefactor of the Fitzwilliam in 1906 and 1909: Gill, *Donors,* 57–58. Removal of the loan material took place when Dawkins was appointed Bywater and Sotheby Professor of Byzantine and Modern Greek Language and Literature in Oxford.

209. FM GR.7a–g.1923. These will receive a full discussion in R. G. Arnott and D. W. J. Gill, *Cycladica in Cambridge* (Cambridge, in preparation). For the material in Oxford: S. Sherratt, *Catalogue of Cycladic Antiquities in the Ashmolean Museum: The Captive Spirit* (Oxford, 2000).

210. The goddess is discussed in K. Lapatin, *Mysteries of the Snake Goddess. Art, Desire, and the Forging of History* (New York: Houghton Mifflin, 2002), 96–98.

211. In a letter on January 13, 1926, to Cockerell, Lamb inadvertently wrote about "my" galleries—and crossed it out. See Butcher and Gill, "The Director," 383–401.

212. A. J. B. Wace, *A Cretan Statuette in the Fitzwilliam Museum: A Study in Minoan Costume* (Cambridge, 1927). It was Wace who arranged for publicity in the *Illustrated London News* on February 13, 1926.

213. Butcher and Gill, "The Director," 388, 389–90. Lamb had by this time some reservations about the wisdom of allowing Wace such access: Butcher and Gill, "The Director," 390.

214. In early April 1924 Lamb had tea with Charles and Isabel Seltman in Athens. His association with the classical collections at the museum included the acquisition in 1924 of a sauceboat and two bowls from Asine, a site being excavated at the time (FM GR.24, 25,27.1924). In October 1928 he waived the fee of forty pounds for a seventh-century B.C. lebes; see Butcher and Gill, "The Director," 400.

215. Butcher and Gill, "The Director," 390–91. Xanthoudides had previously helped Lamb during her publication of the frescoes from the Ramp House at Mycenae.

216. Butcher and Gill, "The Director," 390. These were being spread by "the queer red-headed man," possibly Charles Bicknell, curator of the Lewis Collection at Corpus Christi College, Cambridge.

217. Butcher and Gill, "The Director," 391 and 393 (for reviews). It is significant

that Wace had a guiding hand in the *Cambridge Ancient History* rather than Evans. For this rivalry see Gill, "Alan J. B. Wace."

218. Butcher and Gill, "The Director," 396. Letter of January 26, 1928. It is perhaps significant that P. J. Dixon, Craven Student at the British School at Athens (1927–28) should write a favorable review of the monograph: "A Cretan Statuette in the Fitzwilliam Museum," *CR* 43 (1929): 18–19.

219. Butcher and Gill, "The Director," 399.

220. Although the identity of the forger is not absolutely clear, a craftsman who had been working on the reconstructions on Knossos possibly created the piece. Indeed E. Gilliéron *fils* may have been associated with the deed; he had formerly worked with Lamb during the Mycenae and Sparta excavations. Wace, "The Campaign of 1923," 5; A. M. Woodward, "Excavations at Sparta," *BSA* 26 (1923–24, 1924–25): 266. For Woolley's view see his autobiographical *As I Seem to Remember* (London, 1962), 21–23.

221. Edmund George Lamb died on January 3, 1925. Lamb received an inheritance, part of which she clearly wished to give to the Fitzwilliam.

222. Many of her letters were written from a sanatorium: Butcher and Gill, "The Director," 387–88; Caton-Thompson, *Mixed Memoirs,* 98–99.

223. E. A. Gardner, *Catalogue of Vases* (Cambridge, 1897). See also D. W. J. Gill, *A Concordance to E.A. Gardner, "Catalogue of Vases"* (Cambridge, 1992). Lamb wrote a short story, "The Satyr," about a black-figure amphora, formerly in the possession of "the Lord Delamere who had collected him in Italy in 1795" and which was to be acquired by the Fitzwilliam. In Lamb family archive.

224. For Ricketts and Shannon and their collection: Joseph Darracott, *All for Art: The Ricketts and Shannon Collection* (Cambridge, 1979); Darracott, *The World of Charles Ricketts* (London, 1980); P. Delaney, *Charles Ricketts: A Biography* (Oxford, 1990).

225. Lamb, "Vases from Hope Collection." For example, in her review of the *Catalogue of the Arretine Pottery in the Museum of Fine Arts, Boston,* in *CR* 53 (1919): 78–79.

226. J. D. Beazley, *Attische Vasenmaler des rotfigurigen Stils* (Tübingen, 1925), 151.29, 181.71, 381.4, 407.1 (column-krater attributed to "Der Lambmaler"). Beazley later considered works attributed to this painter to have been the late work of his "painter of the Louvre Centauromachy." See J. D. Beazley, *Attic Red-Figure Vase Painters* (Oxford, 1942), 710.30. This volume included seven of Lamb's pots. Beazley's *Attic Black-Figure Vase Painters* was to include four pots; although they were listed under Borden Wood, Beazley noted that Lamb had given her "vases" to Cambridge.

227. J. D. Beazley, review of W. Lamb, *Corpus Vasorum Antiquorum: Great Britain 11 = Cambridge 2* (Oxford, 1936), in *JHS* 59 (1939): 302. We should note that Lamb and Beazley were working at the British School at Athens at the same time: e.g., "Annual Meeting of Subscribers," *BSA* 25 (1921–22, 1922–23): 439, "Mr Beazley examined red-figured vases in the Museums at Athens, Eleusis and Myconos." Beazley read the manuscripts of both the Cambridge fascicules and the proofs of the first; e.g. *Corpus Vasorum Antiquorum,* vol. 1: "I cannot sufficiently emphasize my gratitude and my book's obligation to him [sc. Beazley] for his suggestions and

emendations." E. Haspels and N. Six, both collaborators with Lamb on her excavations, assisted with the second fascicule. Other reviews of the two fascicules include A. S. F. Gow, *CR* 44 (1930): 195; J. D. Beazley, *JHS* 51 (1931): 120; C. Dugas, *Revue d'Études Anciennes* 33 (1931): 87–88; anon., *Times Literary Supplement,* January 30, 1937, 77.

228. J. D. Beazley in *JHS* 59 (1939): 302.

229. Lamb in *CR* 46 (1932): 161.

230. T. B. L. Webster, review of W. Lamb, *Corpus Vasorum Antiquorum: Great Britain 11 = Cambridge 2* (Oxford, 1936), in *CR* 51 (1937): 87.

231. Lamb in *CR* 44 (1930): 40.

232. Webster in his review praised Lamb for always providing an approximate date in the *Corpus Vasorum Antiquorum.*

233. Lamb, review of *New Aspects of the Menon Painter,* by H. R. W. Smith, *CR* 44 (1930): 196. Her address is given as Mytilene.

234. Lamb, review of *Der Berliner Maler,* by J. D. Beazley, *CR* 45 (1931): 176–77. Her address is given as Athens.

235. Lamb, review of *Bilder Griechischer Vasen: Der Berliner Maler,* by J. D. Beazley, *CR* 46 (1932): 87–88.

236. On this see M. Vickers and D. Gill, *Artful Crafts: Ancient Greek Silverware and Pottery* (Oxford, 1994).

237. Lamb, review of *Der Berliner Maler,* 177: "Lovers of Professor Beazley's style will notice with pleasure and admiration."

238. Lamb in *CR* 46 (1932): 160–61. This was written at Mytilene.

239. Lamb, review of *A Catalogue of the Greek Vases in the Royal Ontario Museum of Archaeology, Toronto,* by D. M. Robinson, C. G. Harcum, and J. H. Iliffe, *CR* 45 (1931): 229–31.

240. Ibid., 230.

241. FM GR.28a–h.1924: Gill, *Donors,* 163.

242. For Lamb's role in the acquisition policy: Gill, "Lamb and the Fitzwilliam."

243. W. A. L. Reckitt in a letter to Cockerell of September 5, 1927, mentioned that he would be "very pleased to contribute up to one hundred pounds towards the Purchase Fund," especially "if you are able to allocate my contribution to a particular purchase."

244. Letter from Lamb to Cockerell, December 4, 1929. Cokerell had met Kastriotis at the National Museum in September 1927: Butcher and Gill, "The Director," 392.

245. Lamb wrote to Cockerell on July 28, 1932, informing him that the National Museum had said it was "going to sell in December." One of Lamb's more informal touches was added to this letter: "Postman half an hour too early. Report [on objects] follows next post."

246. FM GR.2.1935.

247. For full details: Gill, "Lamb and the Fitzwilliam."

248. Waterhouse, *British School,* 79.

249. FM GR.1.1922. See D. A. Traill, *Schliemann of Troy: Treasure and Deceit* (London, 1995), 300.

250. Lamb, "Some West Anatolian Vases at Cambridge," *BSA* 37 (1936–37):

166–71, plates 23–24. She even noted that "Professor Myres has examined these vases and discussed them with me, and their publication is a small token of my gratitude."

251. For van Lennep: S. Heuck Allen, *Finding the Walls of Troy: Frank Calvert and Heinrich Schliemann at Hisarlik* (Berkeley, 1999), 294 n. 8, 304 n. 144. See also review by D. W. J. Gill, in *Antiquity* 73 (1999): 968.

252. E.g., Lamb, "West Anatolian Vases," 167, 168.

253. Ibid., 168–69.

254. Lamb, "West Anatolian Vases," 170–71. This paper was published in 1940, and such excavations would be impossible for many years.

255. Caton-Thompson, *Mixed Memoirs,* 202.

256. The letter is in the files of the Department of Antiquities at the Fitzwilliam Museum.

257. I have been unable to discover any references to Lamb in the BBC archives. Caton-Thompson, *Mixed Memoirs,* 226.

258. Caton-Thompson, "Lamb," 51; Caton-Thompson, *Mixed Memoirs,* 226. The rocket attack was on October 5, 1944.

259. Butcher and Gill, "The Director," 400. They had apparently raised "no suspicions in Beazley or Ashmole."

260. Lamb, review of *Tyrrhenika: An Archaeological Study of the Etruscan Sculpture in the Archaic and Classical Periods,* by P. J. Riis, *JHS* 65 (1945): 123.

261. In a note to Carl Winter, April 25, 1951.

262. Note to Jack Goodison, November 14, 1953.

263. In a note to Carl Winter, July 15, 1947. The case itself was authorized in October 1947. During the later redesign of the galleries under Lamb's successor, Richard Nicholls, the South Italian collection was removed from the long gallery and placed in the smaller of the two rooms.

264. *Handbook to the Fitzwilliam Museum, Cambridge* (Cambridge, 1952).

265. Quoted in Butcher and Gill, "The Director," 399.

266. FM GR.11.1947. The nail was offered by a Mrs. Tharp.

267. FM GR.3.1948. See L. Budde and R. Nicholls, *A Catalogue of the Greek and Roman Sculpture in the Fitzwilliam Museum, Cambridge* (Cambridge, 1967), no. 42.

268. Listed in a memorandum of February 9, 1951.

269. FM GR.1.1952. In this year the classical collections had received a transfer of material from the University Museum of Archaeology and Anthropology.

270. In a note to Carl Winter, April 24, 1955. The Museum Syndicate (April 29, 1955) expressed its thanks for "the most generous act" and acknowledged the "tremendous amount" she had done to help the Fitzwilliam. A total of nineteen objects arrived in that year.

271. FM GR.10.1957. This had been acquired at Iomile in Turkey from Haydal Bey.

272. Stewart had been Lamb's collaborator from Kusura. Çambel collaborated with Robert J. Braidwood on the major prehistoric site at Çayönü. I am grateful to Andrew Sherratt for pointing out this link.

273. The bowl in question is FM GR.9.1938.

274. She expressed this view in a letter to Carl Winter in August 1958.

275. In a letter to Carl Winter, September 25, 1959, in response to the *Annual Report of the Fitzwilliam Museum Syndicate for the Year 1958,* 1. Lamb was in fact quite unhappy with subsequent developments at the Fitzwilliam and wrote several letters to the former director, Sir Sydney Cockerell, on the subject; these are now in the Department of Western Manuscripts at the British Museum.

276. Details are given in the *Annual Report of the British Institute of Archaeology at Ankara* 15 (1963): 2–3. The state of the institute was attributed "to the quiet and patient work of Winifred Lamb."

277. W. Lamb, "New Developments in Early Anatolian Archaeology," *Iraq* 11 (1949): 188. Lamb's modesty is also reflected in her conclusion: "Perhaps the foregoing pages have, after all, been over loaded with accounts of things found, without sufficient interpretation. But it is better to be dry than to be misleading" (202).

278. "Therefore a person whose opportunities and obligations have led to the study of both Turkish and German periodicals should try to make the results available: hence this paper" (ibid., 188)

279. Lamb, review of *Ausgrabungen von Alaca Höyük: Ein Vorbericht über die im Auftrage der türkischen Geschichts Kommission im Sommer 1936 durchgeführten Forschungen und Entdeckungen,* by H. Z. Koşay, *JHS* 66 (1946): 130.

280. Lamb, review of *Die Bestattungsbraeuche im vorgeschichtlichen Anatolien,* by T. Özgüç and *Türk Tarih Kurumu Tarafindan Karahöyük Hafriyati Rapouru, 1947: Ausgrabungen in Karahöyük,* by T. and N. Özgüç, *JHS* 70 (1950): 83–84; Lamb, review of *Karatepe Kazilari (Birinci Ön-Rapor). Die Ausgrabungen auf dem Karatepe (Erster-Vorbericht)* by H. Th. Bossert, V. B. Alkim, N. Çambel, N. Ongunsu, and I. Süzen, *JHS* 71 (1951): 263–64.

281. Lamb, review of *Die Bestattungsbraeuche.*

282. Lamb, "Some Early Anatolian Shrines." Also see Lamb, review of *Prehistoric Mersin: Yümük Tepe in Southern Turkey,* by J. Garstang, *JHS* 74 (1954): 82–83. Lamb's assistance was noted in Garstang's volume (Oxford, 1953).

283. "Prof. John Garstang," *The Times,* September 20, 1956, 14.

284. Lamb, "Some Early Anatolian Shrines," 89.

285. W. Lamb, "Face-Urns and Kindred Types in Anatolia," *BSA* 46 (1951): 75–80, plate 12—a volume dedicated to Wace.

286. *Annual Report of the British Institute of Archaeology at Ankara* 4 (1952): 5 = *Anatolian Studies* 3 (1953): 3.

287. Now defined as the Kura-Araxes culture, Eastern Anatolian Bronze Age, or Transcaucasian Early Bronze Age; see P. Bahn, ed., *Collins Dictionary of Archaeology* (Glasgow, 1992), 272–73.

288. W. Lamb, "The Culture of North-east Anatolia and Its Neighbours," *Anatolian Studies* 4 (1954): 22 n. 1. Lamb also used the word in relation to the "chalcolithic culture" at Alaca Hüyük: review of *Ausgrabungen von Alaca Höyük,* 130. In her review of *Prähistorische Forschung in Kleinasien,* 650, she used the term "cultural areas." At the time, Childe was director of the Institute of Archaeology, University of London.

289. Caton-Thompson, *Mixed Memoirs,* 87.

290. Waterhouse, *British School,* 70. A summary of her will appeared in *The Times,* October 22, 1963: "Dr. Winifred Lamb, of Chithurst, Sussex, the classical archaeologist, left £492,366 gross, £481,500 net (duty paid, £308,099). After personal

bequests she left £500 for the benefit of the Roman Catholic parish church of Midhurst." Lamb was a Roman Catholic, attending Mass on Thera (noted in a letter of July 31, 1933). Richard Lamb informed me that Lamb was largely responsible for the construction of the Roman Catholic church at Midhurst.

291. In a letter to Carl Winter, December 11, 1963.

292. Nicholls, "Recent Additions," 44. Some items were also given to the Museum of Classical Archaeology in Cambridge.

293. Hutchinson, "Winifred Lamb."

294. *Annual Report* 15 (1963): 3 = *Anatolian Studies* 14 (1964): 3–4.

295. A. M. Woodward, *The Times,* September 21, 1963.

296. R. D. Barnett, *British School at Athens Annual Report,* 1962–63, 18.

297. Lamb, review of *In the Mountains of Greece,* by H. D. F. Kitto, *JHS* 53 (1933): 305–6.

298. *The Times,* September 21, 1963.

299. The poem is one of several in the Lamb archive. This is dated 1924 and subtitled: "To M.L. from Sparta."

Theresa B. Goell

(1901–1985)

Donald H. Sanders
with David W. J. Gill

AS A WOMAN OF FORTITUDE and perseverance Theresa Goell carved out a lasting place in the annals of archaeology. Her pioneering work included the use of new geophysical techniques for her excavation at Nemrud Dagi in Turkey and a fresh approach in interpreting the finds. The period of time covered by Goell's career in archaeology exhibits many characteristics of a bygone era. The travel anxieties, the slow communication, and the hardships of excavation in remote places, especially for a woman, are described in her long and detailed letters. Recognizing those difficulties may help us better understand the type of archaeology practiced then and help us better interpret the findings of those days, especially if we appreciate under what conditions the finds were excavated. Just as we endeavor to understand artifacts within the cultural context that produced them, so, too, the work of our field's pioneers is best understood in its original social and professional context.

Early Life and Education

Theresa Bathsheba Goell was born in Manhattan on July 17, 1901, to Jacob Goell and Mary Samowitz Goell. Soon after, the family moved to Brooklyn, where Goell was raised and educated. After graduating from Erasmus High School, she attended Syracuse University (1919–21) before transferring to Radcliffe College, where she graduated Phi Beta Kappa in 1923 with a Bachelor of Arts degree. Her studies included philosophy, social ethics, and housing. Of her education she said: "I think what I learned at Radcliffe was motivation. I might just as well have gone the other way. I might have settled down, gardened, and painted and played Piano."[1]

Two turning points in her life occurred while she was still at Radcliffe. The first was a hearing loss, eventually diagnosed as otosclerosis. Her increasing deafness was initially overcome by learning lip-reading and later by using hearing aids. The second was her marriage to Cyrus Levinthal. After graduating, they had a son, Jay, who remained their only child. They enrolled together at Cambridge University, England, in 1926. However, the marriage did not last very long and, by 1932, they were divorced. Goell assumed the responsibility for her son's upbringing. When she went to live in Palestine from 1932 to 1934, Jay lived with her sister in the United States. After that Goell and Jay lived together in New York, and he was sent to boarding school in 1939. Goell didn't live abroad again until 1946–50 when she went to Tarsus. By then her son was in his twenties.[2]

Goell studied art history, architecture, and archaeology at Newnham College, Cambridge. She received the equivalent of a Bachelor of Arts degree in architecture upon graduation. Her interest in archaeology, especially the ancient history of Palestine and other eastern Mediterranean countries, was sparked by her studies under Dr. Theodore Fyfe, who, at that time, was working as the architect for the Knossos, Crete, excavations.[3] It is also likely that Cambridge archaeologists Gertrude Caton-Thompson and Winifred Lamb influenced her as well. According to Goell herself, the roots of her interest may be traced back to childhood. As she explained during an interview for the *Radcliffe Quarterly:*

> I think I've been interested in archaeology—or something like it—since I was a child. We had a big farmhouse in the Catskills [at

> Hunter, New York] with fields and woods, and my parents used to get mad when I didn't come back for meals. I was always taking things apart, and my love of working things out with my hands has never left me.[4]

In the spring of 1933, Goell went to Jerusalem and worked under the auspices of the American Schools of Oriental Research (ASOR) there. She took on simple archaeological tasks in the city, at Jerash and in Trans-Jordan. She did general drawing for Dr. William Stinespring, then of Duke University, and drawing pottery for Dr. Aage Schmidt of the Danish Expedition in Palestine. She also drew pottery for Prof. William F. Albright (who resumed the office of Director of the Schools on his return from America) and his Tel El Ful material, a site he had started to reexcavate in September 1933.[5] Her friendship with Prof. Albright proved lasting and mutually supportive. She also spent times cataloging and describing the photographic plates from the Jerash churches being excavated by Dr. Clarence Fisher and Mr. John Crowfoot, then director of the British School in Jerusalem, and assisted with preparation of the photographic records of the joint American Schools and Yale University Jerash campaign.[6] Goell stayed on in Palestine through 1934 and continued to work with ASOR. She took on more work for the Jerash excavations—reconstructions of figurines, lamps, and small finds—and later that year worked as architectural assistant with the joint American Schools–Yale University Jerash expedition, producing measured drawings and plans of buildings from the Hellenistic and Byzantine periods.

Return to North America

Goell returned to New York in 1935 and began instruction at the New York University School of Fine and Applied Arts to improve her mechanical drafting and life-drawing skills, which she saw as essential to her continuation in archaeology. In 1936, a traveling fellowship she won from Newnham College, Cambridge, had to be postponed due to the political turmoil in the Middle East. Not able to obtain further archaeological work, Goell worked for two and a half years as architectural and window display designer for Hearns Department Stores in New York City, the Bronx, and Newark, New Jersey.[7]

Goell returned to archaeology in September 1938, when she enrolled in the Institute of Fine Arts, New York University. She was to study with Prof. Karl Lehmann and Dr. Walter Cook, then director of the institute.[8] She planned, at that time, to go into teaching and possibly museum work in archaeology, and realized that extra class time would be needed. She intended to write her master's thesis on Palmyrene sculpture and its relation to the sculpture of the Roman provinces in the Near East. Prof. Lehmann was her advisor. However, neither her teaching career nor her work on Palmyrene sculpture would develop, as Lehmann suggested new possibilities. Goell was to recall:

> The wish to explore the tomb-sanctuary of Antiochus had become almost compulsive in 1939 when I first became acquainted with Nemrud Dagi while a graduate student in Classical archaeology at the New York University Institute of Fine Arts. My professor there, the late Karl Lehmann, suggested that I might profitably take an interest in the obscure monument since I had already done fieldwork in the eastern Mediterranean. Professor Lehmann thought that I might bring a fresh approach to the evaluation of the complex through a study of its architecture and sculpture in the light of our augmented knowledge of the ancient Near East . . . The more I delved into the complicated problems which the plan, style, and construction presented, the more dissatisfied I became to experience the monument only vicariously through literature. I wanted to explore Nemrud Dagi myself . . . I was anxious to find someone who had been to the site. I inquired among the Near Eastern archaeologists who were working in America during the war years but without success. During the war years when the East was inaccessible, Antiochus and Nemrud Dagi remained a frustrating mirage.[9]

Both of her early mentors, Profs. Albright and Lehmann, had told her that because of her sex and deafness, she probably could not count on an academic career; thus they dissuaded her from pursuing a doctorate degree. Goell apparently heartily accepted their advice, as she really wanted to excavate, not teach.[10] The archaeological explorations at Nemrud Dagh were to become her life's work.[11]

Although Goell continued to take courses at the Institute of Fine Arts and Columbia University from 1939 to 1945, she also began to work as her contribution to the war effort, causing her to take incompletes in a number of courses. She undertook drafting and tracing for several engineering firms in the Red Hook District of the Brooklyn harbor that were under contract to the U.S. Navy.[12] When she started work, she was the only woman among twelve hundred men; soon other women began drafting as well.[13]

Tarsus and a Return to Archaeology

With the Second World War drawing to a close Goell was able to realize her hope to go out to Turkey to investigate Nemrud Dagi. She was helped by an invitation from Professor Hetty Goldman of the Institute for Advanced Study in Princeton to join the American excavations at Tarsus in Cilicia.[14] Goldman had been excavating at Tarsus before the outbreak of war. She was well known for encouraging women, such as Dorothy Cox, Virginia Grace, and Frances Follin Jones, to participate in her excavations.[15]

Goell arrived at Tarsus at the very end of 1946, and for the next few months she was completely involved in the excavations. One of her first tasks was to travel to Ankara in order to reestablish contact with the Department of Antiquities, and while she was there she met Professor H. G. Güterbock of the University of Ankara. At Goell's request, Albright enrolled Güterbock, in February 1947, as an associate member of ASOR. The enrollment was to be fruitful for ASOR, as Güterbock assisted with the editorship of the *Journal of Cuneiform Studies*. Goell considered the season at Tarsus to have been "satisfactory." "There is quite a difference working with masonry of Palestine and the unburned mud brick walls of Anatolia," she wrote.[16]

The First Visit to Nemrud Dagi

Goell's arrival at Tarsus gave her the springboard she needed to travel to Nemrud Dagi. However, the site itself was not well documented. She was to recall:

> Even though I had no inkling where Nemrud Dagi was or how to get there, as it did not appear on the maps available to me, I still felt that I was coming closer to my dream, although the reality itself still lay many days away hidden in a mysterious no-man's land. To deepen the mystery, no amount of questioning on my part in Istanbul, Ankara, Tarsus or on trains and buses brought forth one man or woman who had ever seen Nemrud Dagi. It seemed to lie in one of the most isolated and deserted regions, without railway, motor roads or convenient means of communication. It was hidden away and shut off.[17]

Her lead came from Dr. Ramiç Erdim, eye and ear specialist and director of the Tarsus hospital. Erdim had formerly worked at the Trachoma

Clinic at Adiyaman, not far from Nemrud Dagi, and was able to supply further information, though he tried to discourage Goell, a single woman, from making such a journey. Nevertheless, her mind was made up, and when the Tarsus excavations closed, she started her expedition, leaving by overnight train on July 19, 1947.

> Nemrud Dagi is snowcapped and practically inaccessible for about eight months of the year, I was told. But I had no choice; I made preparations to go. When the fieldwork at Tarsus closed for the summer, in July 1947, I was able to start off at last into the no-man's land of ancient Commagene. As I was leaving our expedition house, my good friend and carpenter, Isa Usta (Jesus the Craftsman), who did not want me to go alone, "gave" me his son to help with camping equipment. As I began to depart Isa restrained me and carefully directed my steps to make certain that I crossed the threshold with my right foot first, to ensure good luck on our journey.

She goes on to describe the sixteen-hour train journey in detail.

> The train traversed what surely must have been the footsteps of St. Paul and Alexander the Great. The yellow, parched eroded landscape seemed scarcely capable of supporting its historical past and the traditions with which the region vibrated. During the night the route turned sharply northward and the next morning found us ascending higher and higher up a series of picturesque mountain passes with refreshing leaping streams, until we reached Gölbasi (the Head of the Lake). It was one of those isolated tankstops where the puffing engine was filled with water. A huge crowd waited on the platform; they piled into the train and we continued.
>
> The mountains began to give way and finally the plain of Akça Dagi opened up, one of the most fertile areas of Turkey. Malatya was a surprising contrast to the almost depopulated region we had left behind us. It is a bustling market and caravan city, and the terminus for the main northern crossing of the Euphrates. Modern concrete and stone buildings stand cheek by jowl with medieval half-timbered and mudbrick houses with high-pitched tiled roofs. I checked in with the police and paid my respects to the Department of Education, called on the vali (governor) and explained my mission. I received clearance to proceed on to Adiyaman, a caravan city in the center of Commagenian plain. Returning by train to Gölbasi,

I wondered how we would get to Adiyaman, but then a shout arose from the throng that there would be a truck leaving immediately. The trucks in this region, where there are no railways going toward the Euphrates settlements, carry both freight and passengers with sheep and chickens in their arms.

As we left for the East, we were entering the heart of Commagene. The truck ride was hair-raising because the road was not much more that a cattle track. Later on I observed to one of the inhabitants of the region that this was a very dangerous road. He disagreed with me. When we had become more friendly, I learned that his father was dead. As my friend was still a young man, I commented that his father must have been very young when he died, and I asked what disease he had had. My friend replied, no disease, he was killed in an automobile accident. Thereupon, I asked where, and my friend answered casually, on this road from Gölbasi to Adiyaman, near the hairpin turn; the car went over the cliff. My rejoinder, but you told me that the road isn't dangerous, brought the reply, no, the road is not dangerous, the brakes didn't hold.

It took four hours to cover about twenty-four miles. Weary, I was quite unprepared for the tumultuous midnight turmoil which greeted the arrival of the first Western woman in the town within the memory of the oldest citizen. The crowds were also celebrating the feast of Ramazan, fasting by day and feasting by night.

The next days in Adiyaman were passed in a round of entertainment by the officials, the mayor, the district commissioner, and all local dignitaries to whom I explained my mission and answered questions about how democracy works. All was accompanied, of course, by drinking gallons of thick sweet Turkish coffee and consuming large quantities of Turkish delight. During my visit to the head official in Government House, I was carefully questioned about my intentions and what I was doing in Adiyaman. I explained that Nemrud Dagi was my goal. Apparently, he was convinced, because he got up from his desk, walked to the balcony facing open country, and pointed up toward the distant horizon. Following the direction of his finger, I saw Nemrud Dagi for the first time, gleaming brazenly like a mirage in the vibrating shifting heatwaves. The photographs and all my reading had not prepared me for the stupendous sight. Yet, Nemrud Dagi, the landmark dominating the whole countryside, remained out of reach and elusive.

In the nighttime a policeman came to me to take me to wives of the officials, who were foregathered on the roof of a house. There in the dusk stood two of the largest wooden beds I had ever seen; the women sat in one and the children squatted on the other. None of them had ever met an American woman before and like females all over the world, they were most interested in my clothes; they considered my anxiety to go to Nemrud Dagi in such hot weather, when I could be sitting in the shade, eccentric and a mental aberration. They seemed rather disgusted to find that everything I wore was cotton and not nylon. They became even more deflated, because I had no personal friends among the Hollywood stars and could not give them any gossip about their "pets" Clark Gable and Betty Grable.

About midnight the policemen returned to announce that a truck was leaving immediately for Yeni Kâhta. We all piled in and were off over an even worse track than before to cover the forty-five miles to that village. It would be the last place where there would be supplies and conveyance available before attempting the climb to Nemrud Dagi.

Around three in the morning we came to a halt in the midst of nowhere; I was numb. In sign language the driver instructed me to wait, and then he disappeared, as did all the other passengers. There I stood alone in the dark, buffeted by a howling dust storm, with a dazed boy by my side. The driver returned with the village watchman who motioned me to follow. We entered a building; his flashlight revealed a dusty concrete floor in a large empty room. The man pointed to the floor and disappeared. I crawled into my sleeping bag and settled down for the night. Looking up I noticed two of the largest and heaviest picture frames I have ever seen, or so it seemed to me in my distorted view at three in the morning. One frame enclosed a portrait of Atatürk (Kemal Pasha), the Father of the Turkish Republic, the other held a portrait of Inönü, the President of the Republic. Not wanting to be decapitated by these two great leaders of the nation, in the event of an earthquake during the night, I moved my sleeping bag to a safer position.

The next morning I was welcomed by Ömer Khan, the chief of the gendarmerie of the district, and by a reception of the local dignitaries including the mayor, judge, a lawyer, a tax director, and other heads of the village bureaucracy. The School Director, Bedri Özbey, greeted me like an old friend and acted as Master of Ceremonies. He was a very devout Moslem; and he was respected as a sage and local historian. It was said of him that "from his tongue Turkish, Kurdish,

Persian, and Arabic flowed like a river." I was very excited when he informed me that Nemrud Dagi was well-known in Persian and Arabic literature. However, to this day, I have never been able to find one reference in Eastern literature which would fill the gap from which we suffer in Western literature regarding the sanctuary.

I was raring to start for Nemrud Dagi the next day, but no move was made to expedite my departure. There it was, always in view, beckoning me, but I seemed to have become rooted in Yeni Kâhta. For the next few days, Ömer Bey was checking my credentials with Malatya and was politely stalling until he had a reply from them. I was also kept busy taking pictures, immortalizing personalities, and telling them the history of Commagene and Antiochus. During this time, I did not meet one woman and only had glimpses of beautifully draped figures through open courtyard doors. However, the officials' wives prepared remarkable "feasts of Petronius" in their kitchens and took turns sending them to Ömer Bey's house. Here a circle of men sat and chatted happily from sunrise to late at night. They shared the feast round a huge table in the hall by day or in the garden by night, accompanied by pipe, horn, and drum. Time was passing and nothing was happening. Suddenly, as if by magic, everything fell into shape, and I was alerted one night that early the next morning, my fifth day in Yeni Kâhta, we would start out for Nemrud Dagi.

The next morning I was surprised to discover that I was to be honored by an entourage of my "Swiss Guards" of the past few days. I was given the seat of honor next to the driver of the truck which had been pressed into service for the twenty-mile journey to Eski Kâhta, where the ascent to Nemrud Dagi by foot and animal begins. My companions piled into the open-topped back to be roasted in the blazing sun which beat down like a blast furnace. A scout clung to the outside of the truck; his function was to hop off and clear away any obstructions that might lie in our path. Passing through grain fields on the edge of the village presented no thrills, but soon the landscape changed and we were on the wild eroded heights overlooking the valley of the Kâhta Çay, the ancient River Nymphaios. About an hour after our departure there rose before us, like a mirage, the tumulus of Karakus, the sepulchral monument of the women of the dynasty of Antiochus I. Bedri Bey kept up a running description of the landscape and the local history. Nemrud Dagi was always coming closer and seemed to be guiding our path.

After it seemed that the roads could not become worse, we were confronted by a pleasant surprise—a remarkably well-preserved Roman arched bridge flanked originally at each end by two columns, one of which is now missing. The bridge is called the Cendere Köprüsü (the Bridge of Alexander), and I was informed quite earnestly that Alexander the Great had passed here. The bridge spans the rocky cliff banks of the Cendere Çay, which flows into the Kâhta Çay a short distance away. The Latin inscription on the bridge informs us that it was built on the site of an older bridge by the four cities of Commagene in honor of the Roman Emperor Septimius Severus.

One may question why this magnificent structure should have been placed in such an isolated spot. Actually, it is very strategically placed and stands at what is even today the junction of the routes which lead over the high passes of the Anti-Taurus Mountains to the Cappadocian steppes. Scholars have usually taken it for granted that, when the ancients marched from East to West and North to South on military campaigns or caravan or trade routes, they passed the Euphrates and the mountain barriers either to the north, at Malatya, or to the south, at Birbeck, east of Gaziantep. This is not the case at all. This bridge of Septimius Severus is only one of the witnesses to a complicated network of routes that traversed the region of Commagene connecting western Turkey and the East to the regions of Amida (modern Diyarbakir) and Lake Van.

We reached the bridge, my gentlemen companions, who were certainly not accustomed to the rigors of such travel, were almost sunstruck and the cold gushing waters of the Cendere Çay could not be resisted. Refreshed, we moved on, and after some even worse hurdles than before, which we overcame with life and limb intact, the truck came to a steaming halt under a rare tree near the mosque of Eski Kâhta. We had stopped at the foot of one of the most picturesque castles in the Middle East. We must recall that this was Ramazan (Ramadan) and most of the men were fasting and were by now faint; some of them remained in the shade of the mosque courtyard.

After a short halt, we left Eski Kâhta following the rough notch with its perpendicular overhanging cliffs toward Horik Köy. The shepherd settlement of Horik lay half-way up Nemrud Dagi. It was there that I had my closest and most thrilling glimpse of the tumulus tomb of Antiochus, crowning Nemrud Dagi like a snowcap against the enameled blue sky.

The news of our excursion had spread like wildfire through the villages, and what had started as a lone scientific expedition, turned out to be a cavalcade of pilgrims going up to the sanctuary. Whilst I, on the one hand, was clinging to my balking horse for safety, the young boys were scampering around in Dionysiac frenzy dancing up the mountain or doing acrobatics on their animals. During this trip, I was never really able to convince these worried Turks that I was not completely insane in coming here, and that for me it was the culmination of nine years of studying, working, planning, and dreaming of Nemrud Dagi and the riddles of the civilization that remained buried under its forbidding slopes, now, for me, only a few miles away.

Late that night we reached the *yayla* [alpine summer retreat] where in the hot summer months several villagers from the northern slopes of the mountain congregate at its spring. Here, we all assembled in one large room with a huge fire blazing at one side; we were now about 7,000 feet above sea level and nearly at the top of Nemrud Dagi where the nights turn very cold. Sixteen of us slept on the clay-stamped floor with our heads against the walls and our feet facing the center of the room. At daybreak we were fed a shepherd's meal of fresh-baked bread, high cones of cheese, and ayran, a combination of curdled milk of goats and sheep mixed with water.

The younger generation rushed on ahead of us, but I, not accustomed to this high altitude, had become rather heavy footed and could feel the too sudden change of altitude from the plain of Kâhta to the heights of Nemrud Dagi in one day. I, therefore, brought up the rear, following the path which our later excavations proved to be the ancient Processional Way up to the East Terrace. Reaching the court of the East Terrace, I was stunned by the stupendous and glorious sculptures depicting Antiochus and his guards. As a foil behind them reared the great mass of the mound of chipped stones which had been heaped up to protect the remains of Antiochus in his last resting place. I had made it at last.

After seeing the site, I was convinced that the nineteenth-century publications, the only other first-hand records of the site, had not said the last word about Antiochus' outdoor temple-tomb. I found the site in an extremely chaotic state. However, since Nemrud Dagi is located in one of the most remote parts of Turkey, far from the beaten path or villages, the site had escaped the fate of most lowland ancient monuments, where stone is scarce. That is, the site had not

> been used as a quarry for building stones or lime kilns. I firmly believed that by systematically excavating the site one would be able to augment the knowledge which the early investigators had brought to light during their brief surface explorations. As it turned out, we were able to clarify important and previously incorrect aspects and to uncover unsuspected features of the site's architecture, sculpture, and inscriptions.[18]

Surviving the trek, Goell returned to Tarsus to wrap up the season's work.

The Nemrud Dagi Years

Having finally reached the site that seemed for so long but a legend, Theresa Goell began planning a way to fulfill her dream of many years—to excavate the tomb of Antiochus I of Commagene, atop Nemrud Dagi. The Hellenistic sanctuary, relatively unknown at this time, had preoccupied her ever since her trip in 1947. Circumstances now appeared ready for her attempt to unlock its secrets and to change scholarly perception of its purpose, its builder, and its place in the artistic, religious, and historical development of the first century B.C. Returning to New York in the autumn of 1950, she went to see Lehmann to discuss the possibility of excavating the site.

She visited Nemrud Dagh again in 1951 and reiterated her beliefs that the monument deserved to be better appreciated by ancient art and architectural historians. During that visit, both she and Dr. Friedrich Karl Dörner of Münster, another Commagenian scholar who had visited the site in 1938, visited the site within days of each other without meeting or knowing of the other's visit. Dörner had also been a student of Professor Karl Lehmann but in Germany before the war. He had hoped to excavate the site with Dr. Rudolf Naumann. Goell had returned to Commagene with Dr. Albrecht Goetze and made interim arrangements with the local gentry and peasants for a preliminary survey and excavation of Nemrud Dagi.[19] Separately, both she and Dörner returned to the Department of Antiquities in Ankara to request a permit or priority to excavate the tomb of Antiochus in the near future. It became clear that the two of them had the same goal in mind. After protracted and often strenuous negotiation over nearly two years, they decided to join forces with the consent of each of their sponsors, sharing enthusiasm, experience, equipment, and personnel.

In 1952, Goell began the arduous task of raising funds for the distant and difficult excavation site, set seven thousand feet (2,150 m) above sea level on one of the highest peaks of the Anti-Taurus Mountains, days from the nearest supply stores and over an hour from the nearest water source. She also needed to arrange a field team and complete her obligations at Tarsus. With Albright's encouragement things started to move in the winter of 1952.

> At the winter luncheon of ASOR in 1952 at the Jewish Theological Seminary [in New York] I spoke with Professor [Carl] Krealing [sic] about the project and sponsoring it and he was most enthusiastic as a listener, and told me to tell Goetze about it as I could not present it in person to your committee and Trustees . . . Professor Lehmann approached Miss Goldman at the same time in Princeton at the Archaeological Institute of American meeting and asked whether she would recommend me as director. She did most enthusiastically.[20]

Planning and fund-raising continued. In July 1952, at the suggestion of Karl Lehmann, Goell and Carl Kraeling went to the Bollingen Foundation together "where we received a most friendly welcome. Miss Vaun Gilmor seemed fascinated, especially because of the religious angle and urged us to send the memorandum to reach them on October 1st [1952]."[21] In the meanwhile, Mr. Barrett of the Bollingen Foundation visited Lehmann's dig at Samothrace that was being sponsored by the foundation. Although Goell had been reassured by Lehmann that this project was coming to a close, he was given funds for the following season that might have been allotted to Nemrud Dagi.

Finally, by summer 1953, everything was falling into place. Goell and Dr. Dörner came to terms; a survey team was arranged; permits were secured; and sponsorship by the American Philosophical Society and funding from the Bollingen Foundation came through.[22] The Bollingen grant was for two thousand dollars, and this was supplemented by a financial contribution from Goell's sister and brother-in-law, Eva and Philip Godfrey, who supported her for much of her career. An ad hoc Nemrud Dagh committee had been formed under the chairmanship of Professor George G. Cameron.[23] Members would include Professor Hetty Goldman, Professor Karl Lehmann, Professor Carl H. Kraeling, then president of ASOR and director of the Oriental Institute in Chicago, Professor A. Henry Detweiler, as well as Albright and Goell as consultants. In late April, Goell started to make applications to the Turkish Department of Antiquities and Museums for a permit to make a survey of the mound and to travel and make observations of the region of Commagene.[24] She planned to apply for grants for publication and for the 1954 excavation season.[25]

The unique working arrangement that Theresa Goell and Friedrich Karl Dörner had agreed upon allowed her to excavate atop Nemrud Dagi with Dörner as her epigrapher (the site was already well known for its lengthy and important Greek ritual and genealogical inscriptions). At the same time, Dörner was given a permit to excavate the settlement site of Antiochus's father, Mithradates Callinicus, set at the foot of Nemrud Dagi at Arsameia-on-the-Nymphaios, where Goell would serve as field architect. The deal worked well and each participated under the other's directorship through the full excavations of both sites. However, the preparations, seasonal grind, and subsequent publication schedules eventually strained their relationship. To this mix was added the postwar psychological stress of Goell's ardent Zionism and Dörner's nationality—they were Jew and German forced to depend on each other's expertise and assistance in relatively close quarters under harsh living conditions.

Goell planned to leave for Turkey in mid-June, though the start was delayed due to problems with the permit. Unfortunately, the direct ship to Istanbul with the project equipment was canceled and she found herself accompanying the material on the *Liberté* to France, then taking the Orient Express from Paris to Istanbul.[26]

> I am looking forward to several months of concentrated work on the mountaintop far away from telephones, formalities, officials, and eternal signatures on stamps. All went so well and quickly (not too quick for me as the precious time and money dwindle as officials are engaged in looking up laws) because the ground was so well prepared by us in America—especially that wonder-working document with the gold medallion and blue and red ribbons. I clipped my photograph to it and the preliminary permit to dig . . . and took equipment baggage out of luggage van and customs and sent it out east direct by train in record time of one and a half weeks from Istanbul . . . I had to talk for days to expedite all this, but did not have to pay any duty on the strange unfeminine luggage like gasoline motors, plastic, rubber etc. that I had with me . . . But the paper work is over and after presenting credentials to the governor of Malatya Vilayet and drinking coffee with *kaimakams* [head official, as of a district], school directors, landowners, and exchanging the wit and wisdom of the sages, I shall insallah find myself with Antiochus and the Gods on Nemrud Dagh.[27]

It was not unusual for Goell to spend months traveling to and from the site, carrying, at times, several thousand pounds of equipment for her remote excavation and campsite. Despite all the provisions, life atop Nemrud Dagi was not easy. It was an isolated spot where not many Westerners had traveled, let alone an unaccompanied female. She was a Western woman in charge of, often, over one hundred Turkish and Kurdish workers, as well as her international crew of colleagues. Furthermore, her leadership position caused her to deal quite strictly with other women who were not up to the high standards she had set for herself. In a letter to Albright she expressed the awareness she felt as a woman in the field and explained her views in detail.

> When I was younger I used to think that you imposed difficult conditions on women in archaeology, but I have become perhaps even stricter than you—because I can allow myself the luxury of discriminating against my sisters. I have made a rule that no wives can come along and make a nuisance of themselves and no young girls well-recommended who have not yet proven that they will remain in archaeology. One wastes too much energy with the disrupting idle wives and the dilettante young ladies. I warned Dörner that I am not running a training school and no one but the active staff can be present. Any visitors with the strength to ascend the heights of Antiochus will of course be a welcome sight—even the wives . . . Dr. Dörner replied that he was relieved to hear my attitude about the staff. I attribute it to the rigid discipline that I was subjected to in the American School in Jerusalem during your tenure there, and I can admit now that it was decisive in keeping me in archaeology and learning how to concentrate on what was on hand.[28]

During the summer days, temperatures could reach 130° F. in the sun and then plummet to near freezing at night. There were also windstorms that could be devastating, forcing Goell's team to construct two-meter-high stone walls around each tent to protect them and the campsite, which soon resembled a small, fortified settlement.[29] In vivid style, Goell recorded her harrowing experiences at the site.

> [In late October, nearing the end of the 1953 season], we seized the advent of a rainless and cloudless day to return to the summit of Nemrud Dagh. We slept overnight halfway up at Horik . . . [In the] morning we were awakened by an uproar of the wind as though wild

> animals had been let loose . . . Despite being considered *bir tahta eksit* ["having a board loose"], which we already were considered in August [at the outset of this our first, survey, season], we set out with our mules and drivers . . . We were taken by a shortcut which turned out to mean that we, the humans and animals, climbed up a practically vertical face of sharp rock of the west side of Nemrud Dagh. To say that I "climbed" is wishful thinking. Actually it was a scramble on all fours . . . [When we finally reached the tomb] the sockets for the orthostats were filled with thick ice; the wind nearly lifted us off our feet. Our shelter had lost its roof . . . and our men were suggesting that we would die if we remained. Our wet wood fire smoked until we were blind. Reminiscing about the deep snow that Hamdy Bey reported and the hardships of Humann and Puchstein [in their late-nineteenth-century investigations] . . . we set to work. I am certain that we would have survived the night in our sleeping bags, but even our old-faithfuls refused to subject their beloved mules to such a speculation.[30]

The complexity and difficulty of excavating such a site was recalled in an interview for the *Radcliffe Quarterly* in 1967:

> There's no water on top of Nemrud Dagh. It has to be brought from a spring at the base of the mountain, an hour-and-a-half away by mule. Our mule train goes back and forth, all day long, no matter what the weather. Our postman travels two days by foot and mule to the nearest post office, and also for supplies such as sugar, macaroni, kerosene, and other staples. For vegetables and meat, we have men who go about from settlement to settlement on the Euphrates side of the mountain base.
>
> People ask me how I stand living on a stony, treeless, waterless mountain . . . But I like it . . . It was not only archaeological work in Commagene . . . As soon as we set up our camp, workers and neighbors from far and near bring their families for medical aid . . . What a variety of diseases the people bring to me for aid. Sometimes . . . falling from rocks while tending their flocks or being kicked in the face by a mule. Then, half-dead, they take the long hazardous walk up the mountain. I ask them, Why don't you go to the doctor—there is one a two-day trip away? . . . They [reply by saying that] they trust me, I will not let them die . . . I'm not a trained doctor, but I had two first-aid courses during the war, and that prepared me for emergen-

> cies. My colleague would warn me that I would be imprisoned for illegal practice of medicine, but I would tell him, first let me save them—then I'll worry about prison.[31]

A full excavation season followed in 1954. Most of her time, prior to leaving for Turkey, was spent gathering up a staff, including tunnel engineers who were to begin burrowing into the rubble tumulus that is the focal point of the Nemrud Dagi site. During the same season, she and Prof. Dörner excavated at Arsameia, and Goell also continued to work on drawings for Tarsus. Goell spent from June until October in Turkey before going on to Münster, where she fell ill and had to go the hospital.

During 1955, Goell was in Münster recuperating and then in London working, before returning only briefly to New York City. She was then off for London, Istanbul, and Ankara, battling customs, as usual, to allow her to bring in her thousands of pounds of camp equipment. Once, the rental van carrying her equipment arrived at the Orient Express train station with its roof crushed under the weight of the crates piled high on top. The new season again stretched from July to October. Dörner, however, had developed a repeat case of malaria and remained in Germany. Adding to her difficulties, political tensions had been mounting in Turkey due to the Cyprus crisis. Goell recognized signs of "overzealous nationalism in Istanbul."

> The destroyed shops of foreigners and boarded-up fronts made a dampening impression after the heavenly thrones of Antiochus. All was not bliss on Nemrud Dagh as the same currents that finally burst out as a flood simultaneously in Izmir and Istanbul, already began to make themselves felt early in the summer on Nemrud Dagh, through the person of our Turkish commissar who hated our Kurdish workers and let them know it, and through labor troubles stirred up by what I consider agent provocateurs, among our noble savage workers.[32]

Goell planned to be home for the meeting of the ASOR committee on November 26. After the excavations, avoiding a trip to Münster, she took the *Queen Elizabeth* across the Atlantic, arriving in New York on November 8. She had not yet located the tomb of Antiochus, her ultimate goal, but the accomplishments at Nemrud Dagi thus far kept her optimistic about future seasons. She had found "enough evidence to clear up problems relating to the tomb-complex," and the Bollingen Foundation had promised ten thousand dollars for the following season.[33]

With her return to America, Goell was able to work on a preliminary report for the year, and started to think about the cultural context for her finds. In a letter to Albright she rehearsed her approaches.

> I realize that there is some exception taken to some of my views regarding the connections or comparisons I have given in interpreting the monument. But I believe it is mainly a difference in terminology. It is necessary to get together with the experts and exchange views and see, for instance, whether Central Anatolia (which really describes nothing historically or stylistically), or North Syrian-Late Hittite, or some other term can be used as a substitute for my "Hittite." My remarks are not for eternity and are subject to change . . . But I still believe that vestiges of Old Anatolian did persist into Hellenistic times, and also might have been revived in the revivalistic-archaistic tendencies at the time of Antiochus.[34]

One of the lighter touches of the winter was the receipt of a letter from the kaimakam of the Kahta region. Fearing that she had caused some great offence, Goell discovered that it contained a request for a green or black Shaeffer fountain pen.[35] A fountain pen was the least of the items she would bring to Turkey. Much of the bulk of the material that Goell transported to Nemrud Dagi and Samosata, throughout her work there from the 1950s into the 1970s, was clothing and medicine. These items she would distribute to the local population of Commagene in times of need, such as a family illness or death. She took it upon herself to take care of her workers, most of whom were Kurdish, often to the dismay of her Turkish staff.

Plans were made for the 1956 season. Goell had hoped to conclude the fieldwork at Nemrud Dagi in 1955, but it was clear that more could be done to find the tomb. A ten-thousand-dollar grant was offered from the Bollingen Foundation for the 1956 season.[36] Goell also hoped to extend her research to Samosata and Arsameia and to be joined by Dörner, George R. H. Wright (the architect from the earlier season), as well as the tunnel-men from the 1955 excavations. The international team was to consist of ten coworkers and over one hundred local laborers. Goell expected the tunnelers to be "of great help in all phases of the spraying and lifting reliefs, statues, inscriptions, excavations, time keeping, transportation, camp maintenance, etc., etc., and will give us all more time to concentrate on the archaeological work of final recording." She also looked forward to Prof. John Young, from Johns Hopkins University, joining them later in the season after spending time in Greece.[37]

Even by 1956, the last year of excavation, Nemrud Dagi was a whole day's journey removed by motor and animal transport from Yeni Kâhta, the nearest modern village with shops, post office, school, bank, and gendarmerie. Plane connections existed between the outside world and Malatya, but from there to Nemrud Dagi was still a strenuous two-day's journey by train or bus, then jeep, and, finally, horse or donkey carrying camp equipment, food, clothing, and excavation supplies. In late May, the site was still covered with snow, and so Goell spent the first month excavating with Dörner at Arsameia on what appeared to be an outdoor sanctuary.[38] Goell wrote to Young in Athens, "the snow on the west terrace still is up to the foreheads of the colossal heads on the terrace level . . . about two meters high. The tent site is also covered with snow but will be melted soon."[39] Goell advised Young to travel via Adiyaman, where she advised him to collect his residence permit. She continued:

> There is still snow on the mountain but between the 15th or 23rd of June or thereabouts we shall be expecting you . . . Just do not kill yourself on the way and be sure to protect yourself against the sun. I am sending your mosquitoe net to Adiyaman to the director of the Yeni Hotel . . . really a Han for camions . . . There is now a daily bus from Adiyaman to Yeni Kâhta which is a great savings and also the post-jeep if you can find it and camions. Insist on sitting with the drivers . . . I still see snow on the Malatya mountain. In Malatya go to the Kanta Palas Hotel, if you stay overnight . . . There is a train every afternoon at 4PM to Gölbasi and perhaps you can find a camion or someone going to Adiyaman. It arrives at Gölbasi at 8PM and costs only a few liras. In Adiyaman the hotel people will take you in. I shall write to them to expect you. I am afraid that the rough mountain road on a mule would be too much for you and you would be tired for weeks. The Gölbasi-Adiyaman way will be much easier though longer.[40]

Young finally arrived at Nemrud Dagi on June 25 to be greeted by a terrible storm.

In spite of the weather, she reported that they had "brought to light some additional fine and instructive sculpture to add to the repertoire of Hellenistic sculpture and culture."[41] However, her troubles continued when she encountered great difficulty in dispatching the Nemrud Dagh and Arsameia equipment to Istanbul by train, as a limit of thirty kilograms had been imposed.[42]

From Turkey she traveled to Germany and Münster, and by January she was in London, where she had to wait for the completion of the drawings before she could return to America.[43] She finally arrived home at the end of March on the *Queen Mary*.[44] On Thursday, April 15 the Nemrud Dagi ad hoc committee met in Hetty Goldman's office, at which time Goell presented a report on the 1956 season:

> Miss Goell had been concerned with the problem of the preservation of the monument prior to 1947, during and subsequent to the time of excavating the site. She informed the members that she had taken steps with the Department of Antiquities and Museums of the Ministry of Education of Turkey, the Governor of the Vilayet at Adiyaman . . . and with the local officials to persuade them to maintain, preserve, and possibly restore the tomb as a national monument. In 1956, she succeeded in having a watchman appointed by the government . . . He was responsible for guarding the Arsameia and Nemrud Dagh excavations against vandalism . . . Since the distance between the two monuments can only be covered on foot or by animal and takes about three and a half hours, the services of one man were naturally insufficient. But Miss Goell continued requesting the government to appoint separate men for each palace [*sic*], with the result that Nemrud Dagh now has its own watchman . . . [He] is on year-round duty, except at the monument in the months when Nemrud Dagh is inaccessible due to heavy snows.
>
> Miss Goell also reported that she had negotiated with the Ministry of Public Works and the Governor of Adiyaman, the Mayor and Kaimakam of Kâhta, and members of Parliament concerning the repair of roads and the construction of new roads to make Eski Kâhta, at the base of Nemrud Dagh, more accessible to jeeps and trucks, and also suggested improving the path to Nemrud Dagh to make the monument itself more accessible for the transport of passengers and equipment. She was informed in the autumn of 1956 that the Department of Public Works had voted a sum of 200,000 liras for the improvement and construction of roads leading to Nemrud Dagh.[45]

It is rare for women, and Western women at that, to address the Turkish Ministry directly, and also to get results. The roads that Goell had requested were indeed built and maintained. A guard still watches the site. A pathway was constructed to lead visitors from the road up to the terraces, and a tourist shop with refreshments and meals was erected at the end of the road leading up to the site. Even today, hotels continue to be built nearby and access roads are being added.

In 1957, Goell was at home concentrating on tracking down and editing interim reports from her coworkers. She also began to assemble the material necessary for the final publication, especially for the sculpture and inscriptions, among the most important evidence from the site. She was becoming increasingly concerned about the state of funds, in part caused by an extended stay in London earlier in the year. She asked Albright if she might be eligible for some sort of fellowship while she was preparing the final publication of Nemrud Dagi. She also wondered if her contribution to the Tarsus volumes as well as her work on Nemrud Dagi would qualify her for a doctorate. Albright did not hold out much hope for a fellowship, but suggested that she apply for a grant.[46]

In early October, Dörner arrived to work at the Institute for Advanced Study in Princeton. This encouraged Goell, who wrote to Young that she expected the publication of Nemrud Dagi "to be complete in our lifetime" (unfortunately, this expectation was never realized. The Nemrud Dagi publication did not make it to press in Goell's, Dörner's, or Young's lifetime).[47] By December, the plates for the Arsameia volume had been completed and work was expected on the Nemrud Dagi volume.[48]

Another issue of concern for Goell was the storage of the latex rubber squeezes that she had taken in Turkey. These had been made by Goell and her brother Kermit Goell at Nemrud Dagi, Arsameia, and Gerger, as well as at the Bridge of Septimius Severus. In 1954 Kraeling had arranged for them to be moved from the Institute for Advanced Study at Princeton to the Department of Classics at Yale, but Professor Frank E. Brown and Professor C. Bradford Welles had informed Goell that they no longer wished to be responsible for them. They were, however, open to an outright gift. Albright was able to negotiate the arrangement so that they could be transferred to Yale before Goell's departure at the end of May.[49]

Goell was also hard at work on raising funds for the final publication of the Nemrud Dagi volume. She was encouraged to learn that the East Berlin Museum had created a Commagene room to exhibit the material brought back from the late-nineteenth-century German expedition to the site. Also noteworthy was the publication of a substantial interim report of her seasons at Nemrud Dagi.[50]

Excavations resumed at Nemrud Dagi at the end of July 1958, but again the team faced severe storms, and they were restricted to what Goell described as "tent-work."[51] They hoped to conclude their work by late August before moving for a week's work at Arsameia. During the season they had acquired the services of a young Turkish architect-surveyor from Ankara.[52] They had also been restricted by the lack of technical men for hire.[53] This had, in part, been caused by the construction of a new road to the site:

> The other excitement is still going on—the construction of a road to Nemrud Dagh, which is expected to reach Horik this season. There probably will be a few murders also as the paymasters keep no workers lists and take off a percentage, and men who have worked, say, 20 days receive two days pay. The men, accustomed now to the Nemrud Dagh system expect full pay for all time put in, and they all marched, 150 strong to Alut where Aziz telephoned the vali [governor] and complained. He promised to come in three days and asked them to return to work.[54]

In letters to Albright and Young, Goell noted and described the finds of new pieces of inscription that she and the watchman, Mehmet Yetkin of Horik, had discovered. She also hoped to visit a "Late Hittite" site at Ancus where there were both inscriptions—one on basalt—and a sculpture showing "a seated queen holding a spindle."[55] She writes of making rubber squeezes and of seeing limestone molding fragments apparently from some colossal building. The fragments bore inscriptions indicating an attribution to Antiochus I of Commagene. *Ancus* is not a local word, but it could be a corruption of *Antiochus,* and basalt, commonly used by the Hittites and later peoples, is not native to this area, but provided Goell with evidence of possible Hittite and then later Hellenistic reuse of the same site. Such connections between the Hellenistic period of Antiochus and the great civilizations of Anatolia's past strengthened her belief in similar ritual and architectural connections between Nemrud Dagi and Hittite and Syro-Hittite sites of the region.[56] Such steadfast beliefs stood Goell apart from archaeologists and ancient art historians of the past and of her own day; yet she never wavered in her contentions.

A new difficulty presented itself to Goell when U.S. Marines landed in the Lebanon, in July 1958, to support the government in its pro-Western stance. Obviously, there were concerns about security in the area of Nemrud Dagi. In the face of potential trouble, Goell had been requested to send some of the reliefs to the Bedestan Museum for a Commagenian section.[57]

There was also a further complication with the Nemrud Dagi watchman that forced her to move the expedition supplies from Dörner's villa-storehouse on the Kâhta Chai. Apparently, the "watchman made off with the second married woman, and the community was threatening to stone him and the house, or at least, burn it down."[58]

For a week in September the team moved to Arsameia, where Goell worked with the architect. She then returned to a particularly stormy Nemrud Dagi, where "it was no longer possible to keep the tents down—we were using huge boulders to anchor the guy ropes, in addition to stone walls around the tents . . . it became apparent that it was time to leave Nemrud Dagi to the elements."[59] Before leaving the site special care was taken to protect the excavation and the finds. "All heads and animals and reliefs were surrounded or covered by walls of rubble-stone and suffered practically no damage. Some objects were buried, although in this case we sometimes found that they were dug up during our absence. The fragments which could be transported such as Darius of the East-Terrace . . . were removed to the watchman's house in Horik, where we photographed them."[60]

Goell then moved to the headman's house at Eski Kâhta but was delayed by the death of his daughter from malaria-pneumonia. Held up by rain and falls of snow, she was still working there in December and attempting to meet the medical needs of the community.[61] She planned to go on to Ankara, but first waited for the architect to complete the Nemrud Dagi drawings and to encourage those working on Arsameia to prepare their reports.[62] She was particularly pleased with the report by David Stronach on the metal finds, mostly arrowheads, from both Arsameia and Nemrud Dagi.[63]

In mid-December Goell eventually arrived in Ankara, where the winter months took their toll.

> At present I have la grippe, finally. Something had to happen. I was keeping on like an automaton and wondered how long I could survive the artificial respiration I had to administer to get the others moving. It is practically impossible to work with anyone here. They have no sense of time or obligation or hearts . . . It has been severely cold and it has snowed on and off for several weeks. Motor access to the museum . . . is shut off, and I was walking up every day. The place is freezing, the cubbyhole offices blazing hot from a belly stove. Going in and out from office to sandboxes where I was taking pictures finally finished me.[64]

To her frustration she discovered that a complete set of photographs of the site were completely out of focus. She also attempted to have some of the materials analyzed, but as they could not leave Turkey, she had to ask the American Overseas Petroleum Company if they could assist.[65]

At last Goell left Ankara for Athens. She stayed at the Acropole Palas Hotel, where she had stayed on her way to Tarsus in 1946. John Young was away in southern Attica near Sounion, and so she planned to visit the museums and the Acropolis. She also planned a trip to the Peloponnese to see Corinth, Mycenae, and Olympia. Most importantly, Goell could at last relax after the pressures of Ankara.

After a short stay in Athens, she was on the move again, taking a ship up the Adriatic to Venice before moving to Münster to work on the Nemrud Dagi manuscript with Dörner.[66] However, Dörner had other plans, and Goell found that the Arsameia publication had become the priority.[67] During August, Goell traveled to London to work on Islamic pottery to obtain comparanda for Arsameia and other Commagenian sites.[68] She returned to Münster for further work on the Arsameia publication before leaving for New York in early September. Although she felt that progress had been made, Dörner's taking "several" vacations, as well as the site architect suffering from a series of heart attacks, had frustrated her.[69]

Interim Nemrud Dagi reports continued to filter in as work on the Arsameia material continued apace. Some dissension in the ranks of her team surfaced, regarding procedure, timeliness of completion, and personal issues, all of which caused distractions and burdens that in some instances were to last for two decades more. It was at this time that the Johns Hopkins Press initiated conversations with Goell about publishing the Nemrud Dagi excavation report.[70] Goell raised questions about the slow progress of some of the important chapters of the publication, and who would come up with the funds to pay for the publication, whether done by Johns Hopkins, Augustin, or some other press.[71]

> It seems a chronic disease in these United States, everyone far too busy. I can well understand it. Geÿmis, olsun! [Wishing you a speedy recovery!] But we would like to finish the Nemrud Dagh publication, particularly since we have so much good-will and friendly and practical support behind us. Besides, I would like to get back into the field with new work, and that is impossible when we do not finish what we began.[72]

In March the Nemrud Dagi committee, at Detweiler's suggestion, requested a short report on the preparation of the publication. Goell had realized that Dörner was now concentrating on the Arsameia publication and that until it was complete, he would not consider Nemrud Dagi. At the end of March she dispatched a copy of a tentative table of contents for the Nemrud Dagi publication. Parts were already ready or nearly so: the geology report by Dr. H.-G. Bachmann of Göttingen University and Goell; a report on the iron arrowheads and other small objects by David Stronach of Cambridge University and the Nippur excavations. Goell was also completing the report on the architecture. She envisaged a volume of texts and a second volume of about two hundred plates and plans.[73] By June Goell had prepared a set of prints to show to sponsors and publishers for the volume.[74]

Goell traveled extensively in 1960, from July through December. Her travels included Münster, Helsinki, Moscow, Berlin, Rome, and London. Interim Nemrud Dagi reports filtered in, but only after she prodded her colleagues in person—her own version of "shuttle diplomacy." Dörner continued to frustrate her, as he was postponing the work on the Nemrud Dagi publication in favor of an excavation in Bithynia with Arif Mansel. However, his plans were frustrated by a military coup in Turkey and he had been advised not to pursue his fieldwork. At the end of July she left by train for Moscow, via Copenhagen, Stockholm, Helsinki and Leningrad, to give a paper on the Nemrud Dagi excavations at the Congress for Orientalists.[75] She returned via East Berlin, where she was able to study the Nemrud Dagi and other relevant Western Asiatic material.[76] Goell returned to America with the Arsameia volume partially in press, and looking forward to concentrating on the Nemrud Dagi volume.[77] However, on the home front, her nephew had died, and her sister, Mrs. Godfrey, had suffered a nervous breakdown.[78]

Goell continued throughout 1961 to push coworkers toward finalizing their Nemrud Dagi manuscripts. She also tried to revise her master's thesis on Nemrud Dagi at the suggestion of Professor Craig H. Smyth, director of the Institute of Fine Arts, New York University.[79] As it turns out, Goell did not manage to complete the manuscript for her master's degree either this year or at any time during her life (an annotated typescript from 1961 is the latest version she attempted).[80] Nevertheless, in recognition of her years of research into Commagenian history and her efforts to complete the Nemrud Dagi thesis, she was posthumously awarded the degree in 1990. One encouragement was the publication of a survey of her work in the *National Geographic*.[81]

In late July Goell left by ship for Münster, where she found Dörner at a clinic receiving treatment for a liver complaint, though he was still expecting to make his postponed trip to Bithynia to study Greek inscriptions. From Münster, Goell planned to travel to Turkey, partly by car, where she hoped to rephotograph the Nomos inscriptions as well as study the reliefs in the Ankara Museum.[82] Due to the government coup in 1960 and continuing political upheavals in Turkey during 1961, when Goell arrived there she found the country quite changed. A new governmental regime was in place, along with new attitudes. She arrived in Turkey on August 12, via Salonika. She then waited for a permit to go into the military zone of Commagene. At the end of August she finally arrived at Nemrud Dagi, for what she hoped would be a two-week season of study.[83] In fact she was to stay for a much longer period, planning to return to Ankara in early November.[84] In October, the site was visited by a group of photographers, models, and interpreters from *Harper's Bazaar.* Goell was to recount the incident to Albright:

> If you have seen or heard about a Nemrud Dagh article in *Harpers Bazaar* [January 1962] by one of their staff—the unexpected visitation was under the aegis of the Turkish Information Office in New York. When I had something to say about the Turkish technique to the public relations officer of the United States Embassy, he replied that "after all, the monument belongs to the Turks." The Embassy, the Turkish Dept. of Antiquities, the Propaganda, Press and Tourist Departments of the Turkish Republic and just about everyone else—except myself and some friends and colleagues—were delighted with it. The group of seven photographers, models, and interpreters were brought up at sunset in October when we were just about struggling for survival. They came with the aid and abetting of the government. I could not send them down to Horik to be eaten up by bears at night on the way—and made room for them overnight. I received no prior notification and they certainly were surprised to find me in October—but had heard in Adiyaman that I might still be there. The officials have even allowed European photographers to spend days on Nemrud Dagh in our absence—uncovering all the monuments, taking complete sets of pictures, wrecking the place and publishing them all over the world without communicating with us. The Turks expect us to observe all the regulations, and more, but they feel free to do as they please, as well as the government watchman for whom the bakshish from the tourists is a gold-mine, and he allows them to

> run amuck over the place, as I have notified the government more than once.[85]

U.S. Air Force personnel, from Adana, also regularly visited the site, and Goell was bound by protocol to be their guide.

> The visitation of journalists, photographers, models, and interpreters, in addition to other travelers and practically the whole US Air Force stationed in Adana added to the complications, as the role of being an unexpected hostess, charming through thick and thin, was not counted on . . . Had I not been there in October when [the tourists] appeared they would have taken apart the place with the help of the government watchman who has allowed all nationalities of journalists and photographers to record the place. They stay for days, I was informed, and have flooded Europe and Turkey with articles about Nemrud Dagh, so I am told, and I have not seen the articles, nor do I know the authors. The Turks think it wonderful and no amount of complaints or notices to the local and national authorities, that they as well as we have some obligations, make any difference. They are hungry for tourists and to give Turkey good cultural propaganda and Nemrud Dagh is their chief target now . . . I would have been happier if I had never been forced to be their hostess.[86]

Goell was also becoming increasingly concerned about damage to the site, not least because of problems with the new site watchman. In November she reported to Albright, "I was shocked at the considerable damage to the sculptures by the constant opening of the walls we had built around them for protection. Some tourists spend days on Nemrud Dagi taking photographs with the bekÿi's [watchman's] help; he became rich collecting baksis. I have reported the damage and the carelessness of the bekÿi to the Department of Antiquities." She continued describing how the watchman had been exploiting his position "having become rich on the $20 a month salary, enlarged his house and placed our boxes in a magara [pit] in the depths of his cellar, causing damage to the boxes and labels. I spent considerable time and effort repairing the damage."[87]

Because of these personnel problems, Goell arranged for some of the stone fragments from Nemrud Dagi to be removed to the house of Aziz Sahin, the site foreman, at Eski Kâhta. She then hoped to travel to Ankara and then to Münster, where she hoped "to finish with Dr. Dörner once and for all time . . . It has been too costly in health and budget to keep on going to Muenster to administer artificial respiration to get some Nemrud Dagh reaction out of him."[88]

At the same time, demands persisted to get the Arsameia publication finished. To complicate matters, Prof. John Young announced in 1961 that he had re-identified key figures at Nemrud Dagi. This re-identification, when accepted and published, would completely alter their understanding of the site. It would also rectify iconographical and stylistic misinterpretations that had persisted in the literature for nearly one hundred years.[89] She learned that Young was to give a paper on re-identifying the Nemrud Dagi material at the AIA annual meeting in Detroit.[90]

In late March 1962 Goell was preparing to visit London to check the footnotes for the Arsameia volume.[91] While there, she gave a lecture on her work for the Institute of Archaeology at the University of London, then under the directorship of Professor William ("Peter") Grimes. In April, Goell had been hoping to get the architect Johannes Glozaga, who had served in the 1954 season, to travel to America to complete the drawings, as she discovered that he was to be free for four months.[92] In the end she worked with him in Münster, preparing a final version of the general plan of the tumulus with its courts and processional ways.[93]

Goell became discouraged by the news that Young would be unable to deliver a manuscript before October 1963.[94] However, she returned to Münster and finally saw the Arsameia volume go to press as the first archaeological report to be published by the German Institute of Archaeology in Istanbul.[95] Professor Kurt Bittel also informed her that, in recognition of her work in archaeological science in Commagene, she had been elected corresponding member of the Deutsches Archäologisches Institut in Berlin, an honor she greatly cherished.

Geophysical Testing and the Samsat Excavations

After nearly two years abroad, Goell returned home in March 1963. But she did not remain still for long. She began a new phase in her efforts to locate the tomb chamber of King Antiochus. While on one of her trips, Goell had seen and learned about new geophysical techniques being applied to the remote exploration of Etruscan chamber tombs.[96] She immediately recognized the potential. Since the discovery of Antiochus's tomb remained elusive, the new possibilities presented undeniable attractions. By bringing many different leading-edge techniques to Turkey for archaeological exploration, Goell became a pioneer in yet another facet of her profession.

Two seasons of geophysical probing of the tumulus, the terraces, and the area all around the monument ensued. The project was supported with a grant of $10,780 by the National Geographic Society.[97] Goell left in mid-July for Rome, where she was to discuss plans with the Lerici Foundation, and then on to Nemrud Dagi. She was to be assisted by two engineers from the Lerici foundation, a photographer from the National Geographic Society, and a mining engineer, Heinrich Bürger of Marl-Westphalia.[98] Numerous new techniques were brought to bear on the problem. However, no tomb chamber was discovered, nor any hint of its whereabouts.

This new chapter in the exploration of Nemrud Dagi lasted from August into September. Many seismic and electrical resistivity soundings were made with the assistance of between ten and thirty local workers. As was her routine, Goell also rephotographed and rechecked measurements of key elements of the site. At the beginning of October she reported to Albright:

> The reports of our experiments—circulated by the local gossip and trouble-makers—that we were blowing up Nemrud Dagh created a running sensation, and we were visited frequently by gendarmes, muhtars [headmen], and local officials. Finally, I was summoned to Yeni Kahta and Adiyaman to explain what we were blowing up. It was quite a trip in the midst of our work, but my descriptions and the photographs of the sound-waves allayed all suspicions about what we were doing with dynamite in a restricted military zone. They finally were convinced that I had received clean permission for the work and after six days of running around I was on Nemrud Dagh again—rather weather-beaten but safe and sound.[99]

During 1964, Goell spent the first six months at home in New York. In February she received the Arsameia volume.[100] The geophysical report from the 1963 season arrived from Milan, and it encouraged her to make plans for the 1964 season, first at Nemrud Dagi, and then at Samsat.[101] In March Goell wrote to Albright:

> I am now waiting for additional information from Dr. Lerici about saws for cutting the crystalline limestone on the East Terrace of Nemrud Dagh should the anomaly probe give positive results . . . We do not want one with a high vibration for fear of shaking down the statues still in situ . . . As soon as the National Geographic Society Research Committee votes to allocate funds for the continuation of

the 1963 sounding on Nemrud Dagh in 1964, I shall wind up the plans for the project. We shall try to be on Nemrud Dagh in June to avoid the heavy winds. It was almost impossible to work there last summer—the vibrations of the wind being stronger than the vibrations of the dynamite explosions.

The Department of Antiquities and Museums of the Turkish Republic has already sent me a permit to continue in 1964 on Nemrud Dagh, and a separate permit to make a sondage at Samosata (Samsat) to study the pottery sequence. We are not allowed to use even a pick to gather sherds during a field-trip. I therefore requested the permit in order to be able to survey the site and collect sherds without being harassed by the local police and school authorities who do their duty (representing the Department of Antiquities) by keeping us drinking lemonade and coffee instead of gathering sherds and taking pictures.[102]

The Lerici Foundation was concerned with developing suitable equipment that would penetrate the chamber-tomb of Antiochus, one of the prime objectives of the geophysical survey. The expedition was to be joined by Jeremy Hutt, then at the University of Oregon, as the geophysicist.[103] That summer Goell embarked on another series of geophysical probes on Nemrud Dagi, initially investigating an anomaly discovered in 1963 on the East Terrace. For six weeks, her team engaged in seismic, gravity, and magnetometric surveys around the terraces and tumulus of Nemrud Dagi. Ultimately, the results proved either negative or inconclusive, due primarily to the friable nature of the local rock, making detection of artificial cavities nearly impossible.[104] Not to be discouraged, Goell continued to search for more advanced techniques of subsurface exploration. She applied for additional funding when new methods appeared, but was not granted further assistance and did not attempt any other geophysical expeditions.

Goell stayed on at Nemrud Dagi into the autumn, when her attention turned to directing a series of sondages into the eastern rim of the mound at Samsat, ancient Samosata (the administrative center of ancient Commagene). Located along the west bank of the Euphrates River, strategically situated at one of the few natural crossings of the river, it thus had commercial and military importance. One of her main aims was to clarify the stratigraphic sequence. The sixty-meter-high mound of Samsat contains stratigraphy from the Chalcolithic Period (from about 5000 B.C.) through the Seljuk period, when the Mongols destroyed the city in the mid–thirteenth century. This initial season at Samsat was the first of three seasons (1964, 1967, and 1970) during which she was able to uncover only a very small portion of the site or its stratigraphy, especially of the Roman, Byzantine, Arab, and Seljuk Turk periods. She was not able to explore the Commagenian period.[105] Among her finds were abundant ceramic remains testifying to the very long history of the site.

She returned from the excavations via Ankara where she worked in the Archaeological Museum.[106] She then traveled to Münster to work with Dörner on the Nemrud Dagi report, but learned instead that he was leaving for a holiday in Sicily and that on his return at the end of April he planned to leave for Turkey.[107] She realized that little progress would be made and traveled to London before sailing back to New York, arriving in late April.

Goell planned to complete the Nemrud Dagi publication that summer. She wrote to Hutt requesting all his prints and negatives, as well as any field notes.[108] During the summer of 1965, she traveled to Washington, D.C., to narrate a National Geographic Society film (shot in 1964 and 1965 atop Nemrud Dagi) about Nemrud Dagi.[109] For the rest of the year, she was concerned with trying to complete all or part of the Nemrud Dagi manuscript. Things were not helped when Young was hit by a car, which resulted in a two-month hospital stay. Albright encouraged Goell to be ruthless in trying to bypass Dörner, who was perceived as the main block to publication:

> So I beg of you to forget about any contribution which Doerner [Dörner] has not made and just include whatever you have from him, and if you have to fill up material, do it on your own or get John [Young] to help you. I mean this very seriously, since I know that one of the situations which distresses John more than anything else is the fact that his work on the sculptures, etc. is just lying fallow while you wait for Doerner. All you have to do is to go ahead as you are. If you haven't completed your own part, I suggest that you condense what you were going to say and leave out, as much as possible, any historical discussions. If you leave them out as much as possible, you will remove any remotely justifiable complaint from Doerner.[110]

Goell remained at home in New York for the most of 1966, in order to work on revising Nemrud Dagi reports, updating drawings, and working on Samsat material. Yet again, circumstances seemed determined to thwart her progress. She wrote:

> There was far too much to prepare and not enough time to do so, hence did not arrange for an expedition to Turkey this summer. The geophysicist-geologist . . . who was my consultant in New York was killed in an automobile accident in Libya; the professor [Erwin Reifler, University of Washington, Seattle] who was working on the system of measurements of Nemrud Dagh died of a heart attack; the Turk who was drawing sections of the Arsameia ceramics was killed in a bus accident in Ankara; Professor John Young who is working on the Nemrud Dagh sculpture for the final publication was knocked down by an automobile in Baltimore and had his knee broken, and he has been in the hospital for many months now. And other distressing accidents to friends and colleagues—I therefore decided to wait until the climate settles before making plans for this year. All is well with me personally, but with so many losses . . . one begins to feel very sad indeed.[111]

Goell planned to leave for the excavations at Samosata in June 1967, with plans to travel to Iran to look for comparative material.[112] She started on the excavations in August with "a large group of workers."[113] The aim was to reveal more of the architectural history of the mound and refine the stratigraphic sequence of the settlements there in order to determine their relationship with the contemporaneous cultures of the Near East. The excavations closed in early September, and she was able to move to Nemrud Dagi to check details for the final report.[114] After her late summer–early fall season there, she spent the rest of the year in Ankara working on both the Samsat finds and the Nemrud Dagi reports.

Dörner contacted Albright over the problems with the Nemrud Dagi publication. Albright gave the verdict that Dörner's contribution was "in good shape" and that there was no need to translate it from German into English.[115] He encouraged Goell to write a preface and send volume 1 to press. Still in Turkey in 1968, she resisted Albright's call for immediate publication of the Nemrud Dagi material, as she insisted that both Young's and Dörner's contributions were incomplete.

In January 1968 she was still in Adiyaman, where she was "marooned for ages by rain, snow, floods, mud, broken down bridges, bitter cold, hurricanes, etc. etc. etc." She joked that "it is easy to imagine why Antiochus worshipped and placated such a pantheon of weather and nature gods."[116] One of the things to delay her was the arrival of a competent topographer who would map the details of the remains at Samsat.[117] While still in the East, Goell traveled to Iran during June to work on Samsat comparisons and to visit Persepolis; but no excavation seems to have been undertaken this year.[118] She finally returned home in September, where she planned to bring together Young's and Dörner's contributions for the final report of the Nemrud Dagi publication.[119] During 1970, work continued on her various projects, and Nemrud Dagi reports continued to trickle in from colleagues. In February, Professor Ernest C. Wright had informed Goell that ASOR had set a one-year time limit for the completion of the Nemrud Dagi publication, and that the Nemrud Dagi ad hoc committee, now some twenty years old, should be wound up.[120]

During the summer and early fall months, Goell returned to Turkey to resume excavations at Samsat. Her season at Samsat in 1970 exemplified her entire archaeological tenure in Turkey. There were the normal long waits in Ankara for permits and various local clearances to use equipment; the season stretched again into early fall. As was usual for Goell's digs, she accompanied the fieldwork with the construction of a small camp for her staff and workers, which, down near the Euphrates River, consisted of small adobe huts (instead of the tents surrounded by high stone walls erected atop Nemrud Dagi). The region around Samsat even in the 1970s resembled the medieval period in social and political structure. Wealthy Turkish landowners tended to be in charge of poorer Kurdish workers, who were treated like serfs and property. Numerous arguments between Goell and the landowners over who owned the rights to have Kurds work for them disrupted the fieldwork. There were even local beatings of workers and the smuggling of arms, drugs, and antiquities. Goell did her best as peacemaker and intercessor, demonstrating over and over again her skill in dealing with landowners, even though she was woman. Among the constraints of excavations at Samsat was the mere two hours of electric power each night. During that time daily record keeping had to take place and the photographs taken of trench progress had to be developed, inventoried, and mounted on index cards on which Goell would describe the image.[121]

Excavations Cease and Final Struggles to Publish Begin

Goell remained in Turkey into early 1971 and then returned home to New York City to try to move forward on the Nemrud Dagi manuscript. For a variety of reasons, including unrest in the Middle East, she decided not to excavate. In September, William F. Albright, her confidant and advisor, died. During 1972 Goell continued to amass revised reports from Nemrud Dagi coworkers. More of her close friends and colleagues, including

Albrecht Goetze, passed away.[122] In July she sustained a fall, which injured her back; and she may have been developing an ulcer.

Goell eventually decided that she needed to return to Turkey (via research stops in London and Münster) and spent most of 1973 there, mainly working at the museum in Ankara. She also began to arrange, with the Department of Antiquities, a season of restoration work at Nemrud Dagi to stabilize some of the monuments against the weather and the increasing onslaught of tourists.[123] She was granted permission to restore some key aspects of Nemrud Dagi. She returned to America for a few months to apply for funding from the National Geographic Foundation. She wanted money for a new geophysical probing to continue the search for the tomb of Antiochus and to determine the true nature of the spiral feature winding up to the summit of Nemrud Dagi, discovered during the 1964 tests.[124] Not being able to locate the tomb chamber was considered by Goell to have been a major gap in her archaeological contributions, more so than the publication of the other Nemrud Dagi excavation results. From July until mid-September 1973, Goell and a small staff restored the Step Pyramid and the northern colossal steps on the East Terrace of Nemrud Dagi.

The fiftieth-anniversary celebration of the founding of the Turkish Republic was held in 1973, and the Ministry of Culture awarded Goell a citation in recognition of her contributions to Anatolian history, culture, and art. She was the only American and only female archaeologist to be invited to attend the festivities.[125] Work on the Nemrud Dagi manuscript continued to be her main concern for 1973 and 1974, though very little work was actually accomplished these two years, despite another trip to London and Münster in May. Hutt suggested new radar techniques for remote sensing of archaeological material and negotiations began between Goell and members of the Stanford Research Institute, in particular with Lambert Dolphin, who had successfully used such methods in Egypt.[126] A planned trip to Turkey was disrupted by the Turkish invasion of northern Cyprus.[127]

During 1975 Young and Dörner met in Germany to coordinate their joint chapter on sculpture and inscriptions for the Nemrud Dagi publication. Goell hoped to have a further project in the summer using underground radar to locate Antiochus's tomb, but the grants did not appear in time.[128] In the end the unsettled political situation made it impossible for Goell to visit Nemrud Dagi to make further notes.[129] She was invited to present a paper, "Apollo-Mithra: A Tutelary Deity of Antiochus I of Commagene at His Hierothesion on Nemrud Dagi in Southeastern Turkey," at the Second International Congress of Mithraic Studies in Teheran that September.[130]

In 1976, Goell received Nemrud Dagi reports about the sculpture and inscriptions, the metal finds, and the geography and geology from coworkers. Much was still not to her liking, being incomplete or not up to date in some fashion. She hoped to make a further exploration of Nemrud Dagi in July 1976 with Lambert Dolphin of the Stanford Research Institute.[131] During a visit to Germany, her legs become paralyzed and she was diagnosed as having a tumor on her spine, necessitating immediate surgery and a lengthy recuperation there. Goell spent several months of early 1977 in the hospital in Münster recovering from her operation and then some recuperating at her sister's house in Florida.[132] Later in the year she felt well enough to return to New York, where she prepared a report on the Samsat excavations for the National Geographic Society, while planning new geophysical expeditions to Nemrud Dagi. Her recovery continued, and by October she was thinking of a possible season of work at Nemrud Dagi with Lambert Dolphin in 1978.[133] Goell remained at home for the first half of 1978, moving forward on her Nemrud Dagi final report. However, she was hit hard once again by the death of her colleague, John Young. While he had not yet completed his analysis of the Nemrud Dagi sculpture, he had, before his death, nearly completed his portion of the joint manuscript with Dörner.

By April, Goell was given permission by her doctors to work at Samsat. She left America in June 1978 and spent the second half of the year back in Turkey. She worked on Samsat material in Ankara. She had earlier expressed concern about the flooding of the Euphrates valley as a result of the Keban Dam project, now under way.[134] She had good reason to be concerned because the series of dams eventually flooded the entire plain and submerged the whole mound of Samsat as well as numerous other ancient sites. At this time she also heard about a new find in the town of Horik (about five kilometers southwest of Nemrud Dagi) that began to confirm her theories about large-scale series of processional ways designed by King Antiochus to lead his subjects up to Nemrud Dagi from the surrounding communities. Unfortunately, and unhappily, the negotiations, the travel, and the cajoling all ended with a whimper. Upon her death in 1985, the Nemrud Dagi final excavation report remained unfinished, the final season of excavations at Samsat were never published, and Goell did not locate the tomb chamber of King Antiochus. Despite these gaps in her work, she showed heroic perseverance in the face of daunting situations. She thought with originality, and her lifetime achievements were many.

Conclusion

Theresa Goell clearly refused to abide by the rules society had laid out for the women of her day. She chose a profession dominated by men and ventured into territories where Western women were rarely, if ever, seen. Added to those challenges, she suffered from a hearing loss that her academic advisors considered a severe handicap. She, however, did not let these outside forces stop her. She went against conventional wisdom regarding her career in respect to the location of her fieldwork and with regard to her interpretation of the finds. She was a pioneer in the use of newly developed scientific equipment. She traveled alone, with thousands of pounds of supplies and equipment, speaking the local language with proficiency and authority. She nearly single-handedly opened up ancient Commagene to the world, leading the way for the preservation of ancient sites and the paving of local access roads. And for her many accomplishments, Theresa Goell earned an honored place in the archaeology of Anatolia, and was officially recognized by the government of the Republic of Turkey.

So much detail of Goell's life can be reconstructed because she was a prodigious letter-writer. Her correspondents included family members, friends, colleagues and sponsors. She always took time for pleasantries, remembering to ask about family and health while, in serious tones, detailing work schedules, deadlines, season activities, and the business at hand. Her descriptions of places and people were so vivid that, even today, all her experiences come alive for the reader. Nevertheless, her tone could be caustic and sharp, if answers to questions were not as forthcoming as hers to others always were.

Theresa Goell's place in the annals of archaeology rests not only on her personal accomplishments and discoveries in Commagene, but also in her unwavering belief that King Antiochus I of Commagene (and his art, architecture, religious proclivities, and uncanny historical knowledge) deserved more respected recognition than history had provided for him. She set out to put the record straight, expose numerous inaccuracies, and right untruths about his reign and sanctuaries. All this she did—amid harrowing extremes of weather and relatively primitive communication and transportation conditions—to reach the heavenly thrones.

WORKS BY THERESA B. GOELL
A SELECTED BIBLIOGRAPHY

Books, Monographs, and Articles

"Nemrud Dagh: The Tomb of Antiochus I, King of Commagene." *Archaeology* 5, no. 3 (1952): 136–44.

Dörner, Friedrich Karl, coauthor. "The Last Resting-Place of Antiochus I, King of Kommagene: the colossal statuary of a fantastic mountain-top burial monument." *Illustrated London News*, June 18, 1955, 1094–97.

"Report of the Preliminary Survey of the Tomb of Antiochus I, King of Commagene Conducted by the American Schools of Oriental Research in 1953." *Türk Arkeoloji Dergisi* 6, no. 1 (1956): 3–6.

The Tomb of Antiochus I." *Scientific American* 195, no. 1 (1956): 38–44.

"Ancient Wealth of Turkey." *American-Turkish Topics* (July 1957): 6–7.

"The Excavation of the Hierothesion of Antiochus I of Commagene on Nemrud Dagh (1953–1956)." *Bulletin of the American Schools of Oriental Research* 147 (1957): 4–22.

"Archaeological Work at Nemrud Dag, Turkey." *Yearbook of the American Philosophical Society* (1958): 366–72.

"Das Grabmal Antiochus I in Kommagene." In *Deutsch-Türkische Gesellschaft E.V. 30*, 1–5. Bonn: Mitteilungen, 1959.

"Throne above the Euphrates." *National Geographic*, 119, no. 3 (1961): 390–405.

"Hierothesion des Mithradates Kallinikos von 1953–1956." In *Deutsches Archäologisches Institut, Istanbuler Forschungen 23*. Berlin: Gebruder Mann, 1963.

Dörner, Friedrich Karl, coauthor. "Arsameia am Nymphaios: Die Ausgrabungen im Hierothesion des Mithradates Kallinikos von 1953–1956." In *Deutsches Archäologisches Institut, Istanbuler Forschungen 23*. Berlin: Gebruder Mann, 1963.

"Samosata." *Archaeological Society of Staten Island News Notes* 1, no. 2 (1967): 1–3.

"Geophysical Survey of the Hierothesion and Tomb of Antiochus I of Commagene, Turkey." *National Geographic Society Research Reports, 1963 Projects* (1968): 83–102.

"The Nemrud Dagh (Turkey) Geophysical Surveys of 1964." *National Geographic Society Research Reports, 1964 Projects* (1969): 61–81.

"Samosata Archaeological Excavations, Turkey, 1967." *National Geographic Society Research Reports, 1967 Projects* (1974): 83–109.

Suggested Readings about Theresa B. Goell

Cronin, Paula Budlong. "A Jack-of-All-Trades." *Radcliffe Quarterly* (1967): 5–9.

Moseley, Eva S. "Goell, Theresa Bathsheba." *American National Biography*, vol. 9. New York: Oxford University Press, 1999.

"Virtual Reality Model of Site of Nemrud Dagi." *Learning Sites, Inc.* http//www.learningsites.com/NemrudDagi/nemdagi-2.htm.

Selected Archival Material

The Theresa B. Goell archives are housed at the Arthur and Elizabeth Schlesinger Library on the History of Women in America, Radcliffe College (about thirty-five boxes containing her personal papers) and at the Semitic Museum, Harvard University (about forty boxes of papers, photographs, drawings, and squeezes of her professional material). Included in the archives are unpublished articles dealing with Commagene and Nemrud Dagh dating from 1952 to circa 1977. Some squeezes are also located at Yale University. The Columbia University Oral History Office holds an interview with Goell taken in 1965 (although in a letter to Sanders, the Oral History Office acknowledged that they could no longer find the original transcript of that interview). The Goell family also holds some material pertaining to her life and work.

NOTES

We are grateful to the Goell family for generously and graciously granting Sanders access to the family papers. Sanders met and talked with Theresa Goell before her death on December 18, 1985; he was then gathering information for the final publication of the Nemrud Dagi site. See Donald H. Sanders, ed., *Nemrud Dagi: The "Hierothesion" of Antiochus I of Commagene* (Eisenbrauns: Winona Lake, 1996). Correspondence has been cited from the Theresa Goell archives: letters to/from Prof. John Young (Johns Hopkins University), who studied the sculpture from Nemrud Dagi; to/from Gladys Walton, American Schools of Oriental Research, Yale University; to/from editors at the John Hopkins Press; to/from staff of the National Geographic Society; to/from Mr. Jeremy Hutt, geophysicist; to/from Prof. William F. Albright (Johns Hopkins University), member and then chair of the Nemrud Dagi ad hoc committee.

1. Paula Budlong Cronin, "A Jack-of-All-Trades," *Radcliffe Quarterly* 51, no. 2: (1967): 5–9.

2. Interview with Martha Goell Lubell, Theresa Goell's niece.

3. Radcliffe archives summary: a typescript, unpublished summary of the holdings at Radcliffe at the Goell Archive boxes that includes a two-page biography; the summary was prepared in Nov. 1990 by Mary Ide, for more information contact the Schlesinger Library, Radcliffe. See also Eva S. Moseley, "Goell, Theresa Bathsheba," *American National Biography,* vol. 9 (New York: Oxford University Press, 1999), 160–62.

4. Cronin, "Jack-of-All-Trades," 5.

5. Kevin E. Stilley, "Albright, William Foxwell," *American National Biography,* vol. 1 (New York: Oxford University Press, 1999). For the Tel El Ful excavation see Leona Glidden Running and David Noel Freedman, *William Foxwell Albright: A Twentieth-Century Genius* (New York: Two Continents Publishing Group, 1975).

6. For Fisher at the school in this period, see Running and Freedman, *William Foxwell Albright,* 181. For the Jerash project see Philip J. King, *American Archaeol-*

ogy in the Mideast: A History of the American Schools of Oriental Research (Philadelphia: The American Schools of Oriental Research, 1983), 87–89.

7. Goell 1939, "Letters to Committee of Fellowship" Radcliffe College, Feb. 24, 1939 (from the Goell Archive collection). Radcliffe archives summary.

8. Lehmann had been appointed in 1935, following his dismissal from his post at Münster in 1933. Cook is reported as saying, "Hitler is my best friend; he shakes the tree and I collect the apples." Stephen L. Dyson, *Ancient Marbles to American Shores* (Philadelphia: University of Pennsylvania Press, 1998), 226.

9. Goell c.1952, "The Tumulus Tomb of Antiochus I, King of Commagene (69–34 BC): an analysis of its Neo-Classical and Neo-Hittite features" (unpublished manuscript pages). Goell 1961a, "The Hierothesion or Tomb-Sanctuary of Antiochus I of Commagene" (latest version of her unfinished master's thesis, prepared for the Institute of Fine Arts, NYU, written in May 1961 and not revised. For further details: letter of June 27, 1953, to Albright, where Nemrud Dagi was described as "a strange monument."

10. Moseley, "Goell, Theresa Bathsheba," 2.

11. Sanders and his company, Learning Sites, Inc., have created an interactive 3D computer model of the site of Nemrud Dagi based on the Goell excavation data; this virtual reality model shows how the site might originally have appeared at the time of King Antiochus I (images can be found on the company's website: http://www.learningsites.com/NemrudDagi/nemdagi-2.htm).

12. During World War II, Theresa's son, Jay Levinthal, served in the U.S. Navy. The correspondence between mother and son, at the time, was extremely warm. Interview with Martha Goell Lubell.

13. Cronin, "Jack-of-All-Trades," 7.

14. Details of the invitation are recalled by Goell in a letter of June 27, 1953, to Albright that suggests that he had recommended, in Jerusalem, that she contact Goldman.

15. See Dyson, *Ancient Marbles,* 94; Louis E. Lord, *A History of the American School of Classical Studies at Athens, 1882–1942: An Intercollegiate Project.* (Cambridge: Harvard University Press, 1947); Rachel Hood, *Faces of Archaeology in Greece: Caricatures by Piet de Jong* (Oxford: Leopard's Head Press, 1998).

16. Letter of November 5, 1947, to Albright.

17. Letter of February 18, 1963, to Albright.

18. Goell's notes from the Nemrud Dagi archives.

19. Running and Freedman, *William Foxwell Albright,* 185–86. Goetze, a German Gentile, had been a professor at Marburg University, but he had been dismissed from his post in the 1930s. He then became director of the Baghdad School. He then came to the United States and was the Sterling Professor of Assyriology and Babylonian Literature at Yale University. Writing to Albright in June 1953, Goell recalled that Albrecht Goetze had been supportive of her proposal: "My first reaction was toward the American Schools since I was in close touch with Goetze who had come to us to be rescued when he fled from Baghdad, and with whom I had kept in touch, as well as with other members toward whom I always cherished the warmest feelings of friendship from by-gone days in Jerusalem."

20. Letter of June 27, 1953, from Goell in Princeton to Albright.

21. Ibid.

22. Correspondence between Goell and Albright in April, May, and June 1953.

23. Details of the committee (first formed in March 15, 1952) are given in a letter of April 23, 1953, sent from Princeton to Albright.

24. Letter of April 25, 1953, from Goell in Princeton to Albright. Goell requested a supporting letter from the Nemrud Dagi committee.

25. Letter of February 27, 1953, from Goell in Princeton to Albright.

26. Letter of July 1, 1953, from Goell in New York City to Albright.

27. Letter of August 9, 1953, from Goell in Ankara to Albright.

28. Letter of May 21, 1953, to Albright.

29. Cronin, "Jack-of-All-Trades," 8.

30. Written in 1953 from Kâhta, Turkey, to Carl Kraeling, president of ASOR. See also Carl H. Kraeling, *Gerasa, City of the Decapolis* (New Haven: American Schools of Oriental Research, 1938).

31. Cronin, "Jack-of-All-Trades," 8–9.

32. Letter of November 11, 1955, to Albright. For a recounting of one such incident between the commissar and Miss Goell's workers, see Donald H. Sanders, ed., *Nemrud Dagi: The "Hierothesion" of Antiochus I of Commagene* (Eisenbrauns: Winona Lake, 1996), xxxix–xliv.

33. Letter of November 11, 1955, to Albright. Eventually, that lead proved false. The tomb chamber was never located.

34. Letter of November 16, 1955.

35. Letter of December 4, 1955 to Albright.

36. Receipt of the grant was noted in a letter of March 5, 1956, to Albright. The grant was to include "Dr. Dörner, the architect, myself and other members of the staff, technicians, the Turkish Commissar, laborers and other expenses necessary to make it possible to have a final season this year."

37. Letter of February 25, 1956, to Prof. John Young, who was studying the Nemrud Dagi sculpture. See John H. Young, "Commagenian Tiaras: Royal and Divine," *American Journal of Archaeology* 68 (1964): 29–34.

38. Letter of July 1, 1956, to Albright.

39. Letter of May 24, 1956.

40. Letter of June 1, 1956.

41. Letter of August 26, 1956, from Goell in Kâhta to Albright.

42. Detail in a letter of January 22, 1957, from Goell in London to Young.

43. Letter of February 17, 1957, from Goell in London to Young.

44. Letter of March 28, 1957, from Goell in New York to Young.

45. Minutes of the Nemrud Dagi ad hoc committee meeting, April 25, 1956, a copy of which was sent to Albright.

46. Letter of August 13, 1957, from Goell in New York City to Albright and Albright's letter of reply dated August 19, 1957.

47. Letter of October 20, 1957, from Goell in New York City to Young.

48. Letter of December 2, 1957, from Goell in New York City to Albright.

49. Letters of April 26, 1958, and May 15, 1958, from Goell to Albright.

50. Goell, "The Excavation of the Hierothesion of Antiochus I of Commagene Nemrud Dagi (1953–1956)" *Bulletin of the American Schools of Oriental Research* 147 (1957): 4–22.

51. Letter of August 24, 1958, from Goell at the American Embassy, Ankara, to Albright.

52. Goell recorded in a letter of October 14, 1958, to Young that the architect "was overwhelmed by the wind and was depressed most of the time."

53. Goell mentioned in a letter of August 24, 1958, to Albright that such qualified men now expected three thousand liras a month; "Everything is sky-high and I wonder how any foreigners can work here."

54. Letter of October 14, 1958, to Young from the home of Aziz Sahin, Goell's right-hand man and muhtar of Eski Kâhta.

55. Letter of August 24, 1958, from Goell in Ankara to Albright.

56. Sanders, *Nemrud Dagi.*

57. Letter of August 24, 1958, to Albright from Goell at the American Embassy, Ankara. "I am in the midst of the military area . . . I have special permission to stay here and to travel in the region, but can not cross over to Siverek which lies below us on the other side of the Euphrates."

58. Letter of October 1, 1958, to Albright from Goell in Eski Kâhta.

59. Letter of November 4, 1958, to Albright from Goell in Ankara.

60. Letter of July 21, 1959, to Albright from Goell in Münster.

61. Letter of December 5, 1958, from Goell at Eski Kâhta to Young.

62. Letter of January 17, 1959, to Young from Goell in Ankara.

63. Letter of February 5, 1959, to Albright from Goell in Ankara.

64. Letter of February 28, 1959, to Young from Goell in Ankara.

65. Ibid.

66. Letter of April 30, 1959, from Goell in Münster to Young Goell had unfortunately been booked into steerage class on the ship.

67. Letter of June 8, 1959, to Albright from Goell in Münster.

68. Letter of August 15, 1959, from Goell in London to Young. Goell acknowledged the receipt of Young's contribution on Arsameia that was being translated into German.

69. Letter of August 24, 1959, to Albright from Goell in Münster.

70. Letter of September 28, 1959, to Young, mentioning Mr. Kyle of the Johns Hopkins University Press.

71. In December the Bollingen Foundation authorized a one-thousand-dollar grant toward the preparation of the Nemrud Dagi manuscript (letter of December 1, 1959, from Goell to Albright).

72. Letter of November 15, 1959, to Young from Goell in New York.

73. Letters of March 24 and 25, 1960, to Albright from Goell in New York.

74. Letter of June 18, 1960, from Goell in New York to Young.

75. Details of her plans appear in a letter of June 29, 1960, to Albright.

76. Letter of September [?] 1960 from Goell in Münster to Young.

77. Letter of November 27, 1960, from Goell in New York to Albright.

78. Letter of December 1, 1960, from Goell in New York to Young.

79. Letter of March 30, 1961, from Goell in New York to Albright.

80. Goell, "Tumulus Tomb of Antiochus I."

81. Goell, "Throne above the Euphrates," *National Geographic* 119.3 (1961b): 390–405.

82. Letter of August 3, 1961, from Goell in Münster to John Kyle, Johns Hopkins Press.

83. Letter of August 30, 1961, from Goell in Eski Kâhta to Albright.

84. Letter of November 6, 1961, from Goell in Eski Kâhta to Young.

85. Letter of March 8, 1962.

86. Letter of March 15, 1962, to Young from Münster. Goell was later asked to lecture to the Adana personnel as part of the University of Maryland extension scheme.

87. Letter of November 17, 1961, from Goell in Eski Kâhta.

88. Ibid.

89. Young, "Commagenian Tiaras."

90. Letter of February 28, 1962, from Goell in Münster to Young.

91. Letter of March 26, 1962, from Goell in Münster to Albright. Goell mentioned that the library in Münster had been "bombed out."

92. Letter of April 5, 1962, from Goell in Münster to Gladys Walton.

93. Letter of August 15, 1962, to Albright from Goell in Münster.

94. Letter of January 7, 1963, to Albright from Goell in London.

95. Letter of February 18, 1963, to Albright from Goell in Münster.

96. Carlo Lerici used both aerial photography and soil resistivity to identify the location of Etruscan tombs during the 1950s. Although these techniques were untested in archaeological contexts at that time, they are used widely today. See Colin Renfrew and Paul Bahn, *Archaeology: Theory, Methods, and Practice,* 2d ed. (London: Thames and Hudson, 1996), 85.

97. Letter of June 25, 1963, to Albright from Goell in New York City. In another letter (April 26, 1963, to Albright) Goell also mentioned the support of Dennis Flanagan, editor of *Scientific American.* Goell's sister and her husband, Mr. and Mrs. Philip Godfrey, were to pay for Goell's private expenses as they had done on previous expeditions.

98. Letter of June 25, 1963, to Albright from Goell in New York City.

99. Letter of October 1, 1963, to Albright from Goell in Eski Kâhta.

100. Theresa B. Goell and Friedrich Karl Dörner, "Arsameia am Nymphaios: Die Ausgrabungen im Hierothesion des Mithradates Kallinikos von 1953–1956," in *Deutsches Archäologisches Institut,* Istanbuler Forschungen 23 (Berlin: Gebruder Mann, 1963).

101. Letters of February 15, 1964, from Goell in New York City to Young and Albright.

102. Letter of March 10, 1964, from Goell in New York City to Albright.

103. Letter of June 3, 1964, from Goell in New York City to Hutt.

104. A complete recounting of the 1963 and 1964 tests and their conclusions can be found in Sanders, *Nemrud Dagi,* 52–85.

105. See Moseley, "Goell, Theresa Bathsheba," 160–62. Subsequent excavations, prior to the submerging of the site beneath a reservoir, have brought to light material from large buildings attributed to that dynasty; see, for example, the interim reports by Nimet Ozgüç in *Kazi Sonuclari Toplantisi* and *Belleten.*

106. Letter of October 20, 1964, from Goell in Ankara to Albright.

107. Letter of April 8, 1965, from Goell in Münster to Albright.

108. Letter of June 28, 1965.

109. *Nemrud Dagh: The Mystery Mountain,* narrated by Theresa Goell, photographed by David S. Boyer, edited by Gerald L. Wiley.

110. Letter of November 22, 1965, to Goell from Albright.

111. Letter of July 12, 1966, from Goell in New York City to Hutt.

112. Letter of June 8, 1967, to Hutt from Goell in New York City. Goell had also planned to travel to Baghdad and Damascus, but in Iraq, Kurdish fighting erupted sporadically and the government was battling a series of attempted and successful coups.

113. Letter of August 8, 1967, from Goell in Samsat to Hutt.

114. Letter of September 12, 1967, from Goell at Adiyaman, Turkey to Edwin W. Snider, secretary, Committee for Research and Exploration, the National Geographic Society.

115. Letter of December 12, 1967, from Albright.

116. Letters of January 19, 1968, from Goell in Adiyaman to Albright and Hutt.

117. Letter of January 24, 1968, from Goell in Adiyaman to Hutt.

118. Letter of June 4, 1968, from Ankara to National Geographic Society, Melvin M. Payne, president.

119. Her hopes are revealed in a letter of January 22, 1968, to Young.

120. Letter of February 11, 1970, from Goell in New York City to Albright.

121. Personal communication with Mr. Jon Goell, nephew of Theresa Goell, 1998.

122. In a letter of February 14, 1972, from Goell in New York City to Young, she mentions the death of her brother Milton Goell, as well as that of Albright, Albrecht Goetze, and Young's wife, Sue.

123. Letter of November 6, 1972, from Goell in Ankara to Hutt. The restoration was planned for the spring of 1973.

124. According to a letter to Hutt (February 1, 1973) she planned to leave Ankara in early February for Germany and America. By mid-February she was in London making enquiries about a drill (letter of February 15, 1973 from Goell in London to Hutt).

125. Moseley, "Goell, Theresa Bathsheba," 160–62.

126. Letter of April 10, 1974, from Goell in New York City to Hutt regarding the use of new electromagnetic sounders. See also letter of May 15, 1974 from Goell in New York City to Hutt.

127. Letter of November 5, 1974, from Goell in New York City to Hutt.

128. Letter of March 15, 1975, from Goell in New York City to Hutt. Goell was still in communication with Lambert Dolphin. The decision to drop the geophysical survey was made in May. See letter of May 12, 1975, from Goell in New York City to Hutt.

129. Letter of June 3, 1975, from Goell in New York City to Hutt.

130. Her paper did not appear in the published conference proceedings, *Etudes Mithriaques: Actes du 2e Congrès International, Téhéran, du Ier au 8 Septembre 1975,* Acta Iranica 17 (Leiden: Brill, 1978). Goell had been invited to the conference by the queen of Iran (letter of April 1, 1975, from Goell in New York City to Hutt).

131. Letter of January 29, 1976, from Goell in New York City to Hutt.

132. Letter of May 23, 1977, from Goell in Florida to Melvin Payne, chairman, Committee for Research and Exploration, National Geographic Society. Goell noted that she was in hospital in Germany for nine months. Further details were given in a letter of September 2, 1977, from Goell in New York City to Young.

133. Letter of October 3, 1977, from Goell in New York City to Hutt.

134. Letter of April 25, 1978, from Goell in New York City to Hutt.

Kathleen Kenyon

(1906–1978)

William G. Dever

IT IS BOTH AN HONOR AND A CHALLENGE to write a brief summary of the life and career of Kathleen Kenyon and to assess her role as one of the first women in Near Eastern archaeology. Despite formidable obstacles, her pioneering efforts and achievements placed her at the forefront of her field. Kenyon needed neither imagined competition with men nor feminist rhetoric to reinforce her in reaching her goals. She was so focused on her career that she, I would argue, simply intended to excel in her chosen profession; and with her talent, single-mindedness, and considerable energy she did just that. Kenyon achieved larger-than-life stature as an archaeologist, and for that we celebrate a career that spanned almost fifty years.

Early Life and Education

Kathleen Mary Kenyon was born in London on January 5, 1906. Her father, Sir Frederick Kenyon, an eminent biblical scholar and expert in ancient manuscripts, was soon to become director of the British Museum (1909–30) and later president of the British Academy (1917–21). Sir Frederick was also a prime mover in the establishment of the British School of Archaeology in Jerusalem in 1901 and subsequently was chairman of that institute, which his daughter was later to direct with such distinction.[1]

Because of the privileged circumstances of her birth and early childhood, Kenyon was brought up in daily contact with the archaeological establishment of the late Victorian era in England and must have been familiar with many of the prominent antiquarians of the time. I once asked her, over before-dinner drinks (she was very fond of Gordon's gin), whether her noted father's interests in archaeology and the Bible had had anything to do with her becoming an archaeologist in the Holy Land. She drew herself up rather stiffly and harrumphed, "Absolutely not!" That was probably true, because her own early career was devoted to Romano-British archaeology, although her work in that field was later overshadowed by her brilliant exploits in the Middle East.[2] Many today are unaware of her earlier achievements in Britain. Kay Prag, however, one of her foremost protégés, has observed how many of Kenyon's ("K.," as her closest associates called her) own traits of personality were uncannily like those of her father. In an obituary of her father, who died in 1952 (the year after Kenyon's election as honorary director of the British School of Archaeology in Jerusalem), H. E. Bell noted Sir Frederick's shrewd intelligence, which enabled him as an administrator to cut right to the heart of the matter. Other characteristics noted included his practical opportunism; his great dignity and strength of character; his single-minded devotion to duty; his lofty conception of the demands of profession; his flair for simplification with a popular audience; and the fact that he was rather shy but kind and not a born conversationalist. These same characteristics could have been used, quite easily, to describe Sir Frederick's daughter. Many were virtues instilled in childhood and youth that fitted Kenyon well for her later career.

It was also fortuitous that Kenyon's circumstances assured her of appropriate social class, family connections, and a modest private income. Later, Wheeler acknowledged how useful these assets had been when Kenyon became director of the British School of Archaeology and began work at Jericho in the 1950s.[3] Nearly all the British women pioneers (and many men) in Near Eastern archaeology had come from such circles. But to her credit, Kenyon always devoted herself to training young people of more modest means to make a profession of archaeology and to compete on their own. Noblesse oblige or not, it was noble.

Young Kenyon went off to St. Paul's and then to Somerville College at Oxford, where she finished her baccalaureate degree in 1929 in medieval studies. She did not go on for graduate work, however, and never obtained the Ph.D. degree, which she later was to confer on others at London and Oxford. As she once remarked to me when we were comparing the British and American educational systems, in her day the Ph.D. was considered "an American affectation." (Indeed, Oxford never offered the Ph.D. in archaeology until the late 1950s.)[4] Kenyon never had much use for things American, since she was a colonialist at heart. She once confessed that she never really understood George Ernest Wright, who taught at Harvard. He had come from a Midwestern Presbyterian manse—rather too "low church," she thought.[5]

Already in early school days, Kenyon had manifested that physical stamina which was to serve her so well later in the hot and dusty Jordan Valley at Jericho, for she was the captain of her hockey team. At Oxford, she also became the first woman president of the Oxford University Archaeology Society.[6]

Iron Age and Romano-British Archaeology

Kenyon later noted that the two great influences on her career in archaeology were her teachers, the legendary and eccentric Vere Gordon Childe, the foremost European archaeologist of his day; and R. E. M. ("Rik") Wheeler, later Sir Mortimer, one of the most innovative and colorful field archaeologists of the time.[7] While she never envied, much less imitated, the flamboyance of her mentors, she learned the importance of synthesis from Childe and the rigors of stratigraphic fieldwork from Wheeler. Her own widely read manual, *Beginning in Archaeology* (1952), her first book, actually preceded Wheeler's classic *Archaeology from the Earth* (1954) by two years, her work less elegant than his but more practical. This early concentration on fieldwork—her insistence on the careful observation of stratification in section drawings and the recording of the raw data—was to become the defining characteristic of her later work in Palestine and the substance of her major contributions to the discipline.

This then-distinctive approach to excavation came, in fact, to be called by others in the 1960s and 1970s the "Wheeler-Kenyon" method—a term that she herself disliked.[8] Perhaps this was a reflection of Kenyon's innate modesty and sense of propriety, but it was also due to the fact that in later life she wished to be thought of independently of Wheeler.[9] Her gruff manner often obscured her gentler personal qualities, and she showed obvious impatience with excavators who did not possess an immediate and intuitive grasp of stratigraphic complexities, in which she reveled and excelled. I recall the day in 1967 when she visited our excavations in Israel, for the first time accessible to her after the Six-Day War. We thought to give her a polite tour of the various fields, since it was midmorning and predictably hot. In Field I, she listened briefly to my explanation of the stratigraphy, then leapt into the trench. She drew her Marshalltown trowel out of her handbag, and proceeded to slash away at our section (or "balk" in her terminology)[10] with great verve, pointing out the foundation trench for the great Middle Bronze Age city wall. In five minutes, she had instinctively seized upon the fundamental problem and had forwarded a solution (she never merely "suggested"). And Kenyon turned out to be absolutely right. I never forgot that astonishing on-the-spot demonstration of the natural talent for dirt archaeology and acute sense of observation that made Kenyon a brilliant field archaeologist. There was none her equal at this, not even Wheeler himself, I think.

Kenyon's prowess was first demonstrated in 1930–39, when in her midtwenties she began fieldwork under Wheeler's tutelage at Verulamium near St. Alban's, a complex site that would have tested the mettle of the most experienced archaeologist.[11] Kenyon, twenty-four at the time, had been in the field only one short season before that, in 1929. She had accompanied the great archaeologist Gertrude Caton-Thompson to Zimbabwe (then Southern Rhodesia) as a neophyte photographer. At Verulamium, Kenyon was assigned to excavate the Roman theater on her own, which she did with precision and dispatch in a little over one season, publishing it the following year (1935). She adopted, of course, Wheeler's grid-and-balk system, which he had already popularized but which Kenyon now refined considerably.

When Wheeler moved on to his famous excavations at Maiden Castle near Dorchester, Kenyon began work on her own on two major cities of Roman Britain, Wroxeter (Viroconium) near Shrewsbury and Leicester (Raatae) in the East Midlands. At the former site she excavated in 1936–37, at the latter in 1936–39. They were published respectively in 1940 and 1942, during World War II, when Kenyon was confined to the Institute of Archaeology at the University of London. Meanwhile, in 1935, Wheeler had nominated her as secretary of the Palestine Exploration Fund (PEF) in London, in effect the ranking executive officer, a post in which she continued until 1954. (She also served as honorary treasurer, 1948–59; and on the executive committee until her death).

Kenyon continued her work in Iron Age and Romano-British archaeology until 1953: at Breedon-on-the Hill in 1946; at Southwark in 1945–45; at Sutton Walls in 1948–51; and again at Verulamium in 1952–53. She prepared and published several final reports of these sites between 1948 and 1959, in all of which she demonstrated the close attention to stratigraphic detail that characterized her work throughout. It should also be noted that Kenyon, while contributing enormously to the popularization of the so-called Wheeler-Kenyon stratigraphic methods, had increasingly departed from her mentor in the application of these methods. Lacking Wheeler's legendary flair, which made his publication of Verulamium in 1936 the object of considerable criticism, in her own published work Kenyon was more cautious and balanced. She also distanced herself from the heated controversy provoked by Wheeler's publication of Verulamium. Even from the outset, in the early 1930s, Kenyon's close associates had observed that a good deal of meticulous recording and attention to section drawings—her trademark—was derived from Wheeler's much-beloved wife Tessa. Tessa played a vital role at Verulamium until her untimely death in 1936 and supervised much of the day-to-day work, while Wheeler himself was increasingly becoming a public figure (an "adventurer in archaeology," as his biographer Jacquetta Hawkes called him).

Doyenne of Palestinian Archaeology

By the early 1950s, with the end of the war, Kenyon's long service to the Palestine Exploration Society in London and her concentration on the archaeology of Britain were also coming to an end. She left the secretaryship of the PEF in 1954, having held that office for nearly two decades under the most trying circumstances: combining publication of her fieldwork during the war and burdensome administration both at the PEF and on behalf of the reopening of the British School in Jerusalem.

Kenyon had already begun the PEF-sponsored excavations at Jericho in 1952. In 1956 she was appointed resident director of the newly resurrected British School of Archaeology in Jerusalem, a post that she was to hold until 1967. Wheeler, then chairman of the British Council, had supported her nomination. Later he noted that Kenyon's role in the reopening of the Jerusalem School was pivotal and that the School's growing reputation by the 1960s was "essentially due, not to the modest generosity of H. M. Treasurer, but to the fortunate availability of a scholar of first-class quality, fortified by a small but useful domestic bank-balance and other accessible outside resources."[12]

Jericho and Jerusalem in the 1950s and 1960s did not constitute either Kenyon's first exposure or her earliest significant contributions to Palestinian archaeology. In 1931 to 1935, thanks to John Crowfoot's recognition of her abilities in the field in Britain, she had been invited at the age of thirty-two to become a senior member of the staff of the "Joint Expedition to Samaria" in Palestine.[13] There Kenyon had worked with two young Jewish archaeologists who were part of the *yishuv,* or Jewish resettlement of Palestine, later to become prominent Israeli archaeologists: Nahman Avigad and Eliezer Sukenik.[14] Fieldwork, at that time, had to be combined with her continuing obligations at home, so she spent summers digging in Palestine, the rest of the year excavating and writing in Britain.

Samaria, the capital of the northern kingdom of Israel in the ninth and eighth centuries B.C., is a small but imposing hilltop site some fifty miles north of Jerusalem. It has not only Iron Age monumental architecture but also an imposing temple, theater, fortifications, and a colonnaded lower city and off-site hippodrome, all dating to the time of Septimius Severus, circa A.D. 200. Early excavations at Samaria had been undertaken by the noted Egyptian archaeologist, George Andrew Reisner of Harvard University, in 1908–10, but they remained unpublished until 1924.

Samaria was once again to prove a notoriously challenging site, largely because it was not a typical multilayered tell, or mound. The Iron Age levels consisted of large stone-built structures that had many phases of reuse and alteration, with much robbing of early masonry and few sealed deposits on living surfaces. Young Kenyon attacked the remains with her characteristic confidence and the full use of the methods that she had learned and refined with Wheeler in Britain. Here the problem, however, was that there was left very little of the debris, that is, the soil layers, upon which Kenyon's stratigraphic approach had largely depended. (Later archaeologists were to describe hers as the "balk-debris layer" method.) Instead, she encountered stone foundations resting on bedrock, robber trenches and "ghost walls," and exceedingly complex architecture—much of it compressed within about three centuries. There was also the difficulty of working with a large team, something rather new to Kenyon.

Kenyon's early work in Samaria did not win much attraction at first, not even when it resulted in her first article on methodology in 1939. This article, in the *Palestine Exploration Quarterly,* did not credit Reisner much for what later came to be recognized as remarkably progressive methods for

1908–10.[15] Kenyon's own minute stratigraphic analysis of the Iron Age structures on the Israelite acropolis was published promptly in 1942, as part of *The Buildings at Samaria. Samaria-Sebaste 1,* with J. W. Crowfoot and E. L. Sukenik. Her major contribution at Samaria, however, was not evident until the belated publication of *Samaria-Sebaste 3. The Objects,* with J. W. and G. M. Crowfoot in 1957, which had been delayed by the war years. Here she extended her earlier coverage of the architecture to include her first detailed analysis of Palestinian pottery, from the few Early Bronze Age deposits to the Hellenistic and Roman periods. The principle that Kenyon applied here was that buildings should be dated by the latest pottery in the "makeup," or subfloor fills, together with that in the foundation trenches and other constructional features. Although she took this to be proper British method, its presuppositions ran counter to those of American and Israeli archaeologists, as well as some Europeans.

The leading French authority, Père Roland de Vaux, had already anticipated later criticisms in 1955 when he compared Kenyon's Iron Age pottery on the basis of visual inspection with his excavations at Tell el-Far^{c}ah north (biblical Tirzeh) and suggested that her "Building Periods" and "Pottery Periods" were not contemporary. In early reviews of *Samaria 3,* the most prominent American archaeologist, W. F. Albright (1958), hinted at the same conclusion, argued in much more detail the next year by his protégé G. E. Wright (1959).[16] Wright firmly separated her "Building Periods" I–VIII from her "Pottery Periods" I–VIII, moving the latter one phase later and correlating it with the next stratum up, in essence dating all Kenyon's building a full stratum earlier. Two leading Israeli archaeologists, Yohanan Aharoni and Ruth Amiran (1958), also criticized her ceramic and stratigraphic arguments.[17] Thus the most preeminent Palestinian archaeologists of Kenyon's time took immediate exception to the results of her application of British methods to a key site in Palestine.

Although Kenyon herself remained characteristically aloof, the controversy that she provoked at Samaria was so fundamental for archaeological method—and indeed for biblical studies—that it still affects the discipline. In the early 1990s renewed examinations of the Samaria stratigraphy and chronology prompted a heated debate over that site and its correlation with three other key Iron Age sites in Israel: Hazor, Megiddo, and Gezer. It also resulted in a two-volume Harvard dissertation by R. E. Tappy, published as *The Archaeology of Israelite Samaria,* volume I, *Early Iron Age through the Ninth Century* BCE (1992); volume II, *The Eighth Century BCE* (2001).[18]

Samaria had certainly proven a testing ground for Kenyon's methods; but, as we have seen, her work in the 1930s did not have much impact on

Palestinian archaeology until its publication in 1952 and especially in 1957. By that time, she was resident director of the British School in Jerusalem (1956–67). More importantly, she had launched what was to become her major field project in Palestine, at another famous biblical site, Jericho, where she directed large-scale excavation from 1952 to 1958. The spectacular discoveries, especially of the long Neolithic period (ca. 9000–4000 B.C.), plus the reputation of Jericho itself, soon made Kenyon an internationally acclaimed figure, easily the foremost British Palestinian archaeologist. In fact, she was to dominate British archaeology for the next twenty years, until her death. Her only peers in the larger field were W. F. Albright and G. E. Wright in America; Père Roland de Vaux at the École Biblique et Archéologique in Jerusalem; and Yigael Yadin in Israel. Kenyon was the only woman in this group of international celebrities.[19]

One reason for Kenyon's fame, as well as her lasting influence on the discipline, was the fact that Jericho became the training ground for a whole generation of younger archaeologists, thus diffusing her methods. The list of the names of more than 150 trench supervisors in the Jericho and Jerusalem volumes reads like a *Who's Who* of later British archaeologists. Jericho was for British archaeology in Palestine what Shechem and Gezer were for the Americans and Hazor for the Israelis. These excavation projects in the 1950s and 1960s established the "national schools," often rivals, that have shaped the modern discipline. One might also add the burgeoning Jordanian school, also influenced by Kenyon and her successor at the new British school in Amman, Crystal-M. Bennett. Not only was Kenyon, now in her mature years, self-consciously applying her methods on a large scale on her own, but she was attracting a circle of disciples whom she seemed almost to mesmerize. Kay Prag writes of the excitement of working with Kenyon at Jericho, "Working with K. we strove to reach her standards, flowered her with praise, felt her warmth; where she led, we followed."[20] For many, it was their first dig in the Holy Land, "a personal revelation on the road to Damascus."[21]

Stories of the camaraderie of life in the dig camp at Jericho are legion, all of them dominated by the imposing figure of "K," who inspired a mixture of awe and affection in those around her, apprentices learning their trade from an acknowledged master. Yet this enduring sense of personal loyalty to their teacher did not prevent Kenyon's students and protégés from seeing her faults, for like all larger-than-life personages she did things on a grand scale, and not all of her efforts succeeded. That Kenyon did not overpower and nearly paralyze her students (as Albright often did) is a great tribute to her.

Notably her Canadian associate director, A. Douglas Tushingham, has published several candid vignettes of life on the Jericho dig. He reminisces about K's sixteen-hour working days; her driving the students to test out every idea and interpretation; even after-hours amusements like the famous "lowest Boat Race on record," rowed in punts on the Dead Sea and timed to coincide with the Oxford-Cambridge event back home. As Tushingham concludes:

> Her knowledge, experience, diligence and enthusiasm, her high standards and the patience and skill with which she inculcated them, her modesty, friendliness, sense of humour and tolerance—all these qualities have entitled her to the honours she has received, and the love and respect which she has engendered in all those who have been privileged to know and work with her.[22]

Kay Prag, however, no less loyal to Kenyon, observed that "she could be devastating, when she felt the situation merited it."[23] I can attest to that, for on one occasion when I was taking her around Israel to visit digs, we stopped at an excavation that was, in fact, being directed by a student of hers. She stood on the balk and listened patiently while down in the trench he gave an elaborate interpretation of a nicely cut and tagged section—obviously prepared in anticipation of her visit. When he concluded and looked up for her approval, she simply said, "Nonsense!" She then opened her purse and took out her trowel, hopped down into the trench and began chopping away at the section, as she had done at Gezer, pointing out with obvious delight missed pits and foundation trenches (which she insisted must always exist). One never forgot a lesson like that.

The Jericho excavations, as Roger Moorey of the Ashmolean Museum has noted, were a turning point in methodology in the archaeology of Palestine and also constituted Kenyon's greatest claim to an enduring reputation in the discipline.[24] The discoveries in themselves were dramatic enough and completely overturned earlier interpretations based on erroneous field techniques. But it was Kenyon's revolutionary approach to field techniques that galvanized attention: the apparent triumph of new methods of excavating and recording at a large, complex Palestinian mound. The impact on American excavators working in Jordan was profound, and it led directly to the extension of these methods in the reexcavation of major sites like Shechem, under G. E. Wright (1957–); Ta^canach, under Paul W. Lapp (1963–68); and ^cAi, under J. A. Callaway (1964–72). At all these sites, Jericho-trained American staff members and Arab "technical men" played a major role in excavation strategy and methodology. Later, Kenyon's methods were introduced in Israel at Gezer (1964–73).[25]

It is to be regretted that Kenyon's methods were not seen in action earlier in Israel because of the partition of Palestine in 1948. It would have been fascinating to see, for instance, what she and Yadin, who was excavating at Hazor about the same time (1955–58), would have made of each other. Unfortunately, by the time Kenyon's methods were finally taken seriously by Israeli excavators, in the 1970s, Kenyon was an infrequent visitor. In the meanwhile, the Israeli follow-up to her excavations in Jerusalem (1961–67) had revealed some of the inherent problems of her deep, narrow trenches. One must also admit that Arab-Israeli politics tended to stigmatize foreign excavators who chose to work in Jordan.[26]

It was always intended that Kenyon's effort to record the entire three-dimensional context of every object in each locus and phase and stratum in a mound would be finally realized in full publication. There, all the plans, especially the sections on which so much of her interpretation depended, would be presented in detail as the basis for the final synthesis. As Kenyon herself once said in a review of the first Gezer volume: "The proof of the pudding is in the eating."[27] Hers was, undoubtedly, the most ambitious, multistage excavation project ever undertaken in Palestine, but the grand design could not be carried through to publication. Two large volumes on the tombs appeared promptly in 1960 and 1965. These, however, presented discrete units of material, much of it not representative of domestic deposits, and certainly not a demonstration of the potential results of Kenyon's stratigraphic work on the tell. The remaining three Jericho volumes appeared only in 1981–83, after her death. They included her text as far as it was along, but they lacked the final integration that she alone could have provided, which might have vindicated her methods.[28] The sad fact is these final volumes contain such a mass of undigested information that they have proven almost impossible to use and have not even been widely reviewed. Part of the difficulty in publishing the Jericho tell was that nearly all of even Kenyon's prodigious energies were absorbed by continuing academic and administrative duties in Britain and the launching of new excavations in Jerusalem. But, as several of her colleagues have pointed out, the difficulty was also due to the sheer quantity of detail that her methods produced, as well as to her own inability to delegate responsibilities.[29]

Fresh from her exploits at Jericho, Kenyon turned her attention to Jerusalem. There she began excavations in 1962 and concluded with the planned final season in 1967, despite the Six-Day War. Now for the only time in her life, Kenyon dug in Israeli-held territories. The Jerusalem project was to prove too much, however, even for one of Kenyon's legendary stamina, for when she began she was fifty-five and had ahead of her the vast unpublished Jericho material.[30] Even less of Kenyon's own work in Jerusalem was ever published; *Jerusalem* I (1985), *Jerusalem* II (1990), and *Jerusalem* IV (1995) are almost entirely the work of others.[31] Meanwhile, it must be conceded that extensive Israeli excavations all over old Jerusalem since 1967 have made the results of her small and scattered soundings—all she was allowed to do under the Jordanian authorities—largely obsolete. Once again the exposures were too small, as several critics pointed out (sometimes unfairly) and as Kenyon herself finally seemed to recognize.[32] The real problem, however, lay deeper: her emphasis on sections may have been well suited to deep soundings on a typical tell like Jericho, which had previously been dug, but this approach did not prove satisfactory in dealing with monumental architecture, or even residential areas, when exposures were so limited. Furthermore, scattered sections and architectural plans could not easily be harmonized. Prag has noted that the archives of Kenyon's work in Jerusalem, as at Jericho, reveal a certain lack of coordination between the surveyors who drew the plans and Kenyon's drawings of the sections, which she always insisted on doing herself. The same weakness is seen in her work at Sabratha in North Africa in 1948–51, where the main objective seems to have been the production of detailed section drawings. In the Forum and East Forum Temple, the 115 trenches in her field report are illustrated by no fewer than forty-four sections; but plans are in short supply, and there is no plan at all of a complete pre-Roman building.[33]

Kenyon in the Academic World

Kenyon's active participation in the administration of archaeological institutes was a major part of her professional life. She first had an administrative position at the PEF (1935–55); then she served as acting director at the Institute of Archaeology at London University, when Wheeler was absent during the war; and, finally, she became director of the British School of Archaeology in Jerusalem (1956–67). These duties, by which she supported her career, represent a continuous record of administrative responsibility that spans more than thirty years—all the while she was carrying out major field excavations in three countries. When one is tempted to criticize Kenyon for not publishing her Jericho and Jerusalem excavations fully (a failing hardly unique to her), it may be worth recalling how many obligations she willingly took on in the service of her profession. Again, one sees her characteristic sense of duty, even when costly.

Kenyon resigned as director of the British School in Jerusalem in 1967, just before the British were readjusting their strategy after the Israeli takeover of the Old City and were beginning to transfer most of their fieldwork to Jordan. She stayed on, however, as chairman of the British School, and she remained vitally interested in work in "Palestine." She was herself a prime mover in launching the British Institute for History and Archaeology in Amman, which finally opened in 1978 just after her death. Now, however, she began the final phase of her career, continuing full-time as principal of St. Hugh's College at Oxford, her alma mater, where she had been appointed in 1962 and where she taught and ably administered until her retirement in 1973.

This was not, of course, Kenyon's first academic appointment, for she had been lecturer at the Institute of Archaeology of London University (begun by Wheeler in 1936) from 1948 to 1962. She had also long had an interest both in teaching archaeological method to students and in disseminating to a wider audience the results of archaeological excavation that she found so exciting. There is no doubt that Kenyon was an effective lecturer, given her eminent standing in the discipline, her energy and enthusiasm, and her long-standing commitment to teaching field archaeology, not to mention her close involvement with sites like Jericho and Jerusalem. Earlier she had conducted what we would now call "field schools," for the University of Birmingham at Breedon-on-the-Hill and Sutton Walls in 1948–51. And, of course, both the Jericho and Jerusalem excavations had been "teaching digs" par excellence. Her own first book, in 1952, *Beginning in Archaeology,* intended as a handbook, had set forth clearly the methodological principles that she spent her life advocating and that she now taught.

As early as 1943, while acting director of the Institute of Archaeology in London, Kenyon had addressed a congress at Oxford on "The Future of Archaeology" and had expressed her view of the proper training of students in Palestinian archaeology. In sharp contrast to J. D. Beazley (Lincoln Professor of Classical Art and Archaeology at Oxford), who stressed a broad knowledge of language, literature, history, and culture in his preceding lecture, Kenyon declared that "training in the history and cultural background of the region" should only be of a general nature but that "the techniques of excavation and the necessary adjuncts" must be the student's "primary concern." She, however, did not feel that knowledge of biblical Hebrew was necessary. Instead, the excavator could simply consult a biblical expert when needed.[34] These views were expressed with Kenyon's usual self-confidence, and they are indeed representative of her expertise as a technician.

During the final Oxford years, Kenyon continued her publications and her excavations in Jerusalem. *Jericho* II appeared during these years (1965), as did her chapters on Palestine for the third revision of the *Cambridge Ancient History* (1965–73). She also published two popular books: *Jerusalem—Excavating 3000 Years of History* (1967) and *Royal Cities of the Old Testament* (1971); her 1963 Schweich Lectures at the British Academy, *Amorites and Canaanites* (1966); and the second and third editions of her textbook *Archaeology of the Holy Land* (1965, 1970). An essay for the *Harvard Theological Review* volume in memory of Paul W. Lapp (1971), one of the few Americans she admired, was devoted to a defense of her methods, including the workup of pottery for publication, which she recognized had come under increasing attack. A number of reviews also appeared, of the excavations at Hazor, Gezer, and Beersheba, as well as a fond obituary of her longtime friend and associate, Père Roland de Vaux, who had been associated with her in the Jerusalem excavations at the beginning (1961–63).

Kenyon was not a principal at Oxford in name only, appointed simply for her fame; she was actively involved in the affairs of the university and was a colorful teacher who attracted a wide following. Indeed, the best and most charming account of Kenyon as a person during these years comes, as Prag has pointed out, from her successor as principal at Oxford, Rachel Tricket.[35] Finally, as a measure of her success as an academic, one might note that she was instrumental in placing well over a dozen graduates of London and Oxford in various positions—some of them in posts at the Jerusalem and Amman schools that she herself had helped to create. A number of the graduates she produced in the field and in the classroom were women. Kenyon was self-confessedly not "a dyed-in-the-wool academic," either by temperament or training; but her sense of duty, her love of students, and above all the fact that she provided a remarkable role model, made her effective, if somewhat unconventional, in the academy.

In the matter of scholarship in the narrower sense, one must evaluate Kenyon's publications. They were numerous enough, especially considering the enormous responsibilities that she took on in field excavation, teaching, administration and fund-raising, and the popularization of archaeology. She published sixteen books and monographs (plus considerable parts of the Jericho and Jerusalem volumes that appeared after her death), more than eighty articles and chapters, and a number of reviews and notices.[36]

Breaking Ground

Kathleen Kenyon in Perspective

It is difficult, if not somewhat presumptuous, to attempt to place an archaeologist of Kenyon's stature in critical perspective. Yet no biography of her would be complete without such an attempt. I am encouraged in the effort by the fact that several of Kenyon's closest associates in Britain have provided us with remarkably candid assessments—a refreshing change from the effusive and obsequious praise that is offered in so many obituaries of leading figures. Kenyon's students and colleagues admired her enormously, but they had learned from her to be critical of all archaeological endeavors, including her own. Here I will group my comments under several headings, largely because Kenyon's lifelong work was so multifaceted.

Promotion, Publicity, and Politics

At first, such a topic may seem strange, or at least peripheral. But the profession of archaeology is unlike many others in that the excavators of prominent sites do tend to become celebrities, and they must often play on that simply to raise funds for their projects. Certainly Kenyon's mentor Sir Mortimer Wheeler understood these facts of life well and promoted his sites and himself brilliantly. He even became a national television celebrity when he hosted shows such as *Buried Treasure* and *Animal, Vegetable, or Mineral?* in the 1950s (which Kenyon later said distanced him from his professional colleagues). Furthermore, if one worked in the Middle East, as both Wheeler and Kenyon had done, it was virtually impossible to separate archaeology from national politics.[37] In Kenyon's case, her earlier work at Samaria was done in what was then British Mandatory Palestine. When she returned in the 1950s and 1960s, Jericho and Jerusalem were part of the "West Bank" of the Hashemite Kingdom of Jordan, with the recently established State of Israel across the border and inaccessible. Then, in her final season at Jerusalem in the summer of 1967, Kenyon found herself working under Israeli administration.

The simple fact is that all foreign Palestinian archaeologists excavating after 1948 have been forced by artificial borders and by the hostile modern political situation to "choose sides." And no matter how hard archaeologists tried to separate archaeology and politics, to remain neutral as it were, they were likely to become identified with one "side" or the other. Kenyon's choice was in effect made for her when she went to Jericho in 1952—one could say in 1948, after the Arab-Israeli War divided Jerusalem and left the British School of Archaeology in the Arab sector along with the Old City. The same events resulted in the American School of Oriental Research, the German School of Archaeology, and the French École Biblique et Archéologique being under Jordanian administration after 1948. Thus it happened that nearly all the other foreign excavators ended up also working in Jordan in the 1950s and 1960s.[38] It is noteworthy that none of the other foreign excavators was labeled "pro-Arab," as Kenyon was on several occasions, particularly after the 1967 war.

When Kenyon ended her directorship of the British School in 1967, she had hoped to be appointed chair of the Council for the British School of Archaeology in Jerusalem, the sponsoring institution in London. Wheeler, however, sought to block Kenyon's appointment on the grounds that she was "too pro-Arab" for the post-1967 situation. She was furious with her onetime mentor, protesting that she knew many Israelis and could work with them. Wheeler was saddened by the whole affair, and although he was adamant, Kenyon became chair and remained so until her death.[39] It was perhaps unfortunate that Kenyon was a signatory of a supposedly "secret" UNESCO report shortly after the war, condemning the Israeli excavations around the Western Wall and Temple Mount, then being carried out on a large scale by the grand old man of Israeli archaeology, Benyamin Mazar. The report was leaked to Israelis and used to support their charges against Kenyon. She was vindicated, however, in my opinion, when some years later it became obvious that Mazar's continuing Temple Mount excavations were not simply politically insensitive but were indeed being done too hastily and with inadequate methods.[40]

Was Kenyon "pro-Arab"? I doubt it, although she was, like many other foreign excavators in Jordan and the West Bank, an Arab sympathizer. Awni Dajani, the director of the Jordanian Department of Antiquities, was one of her Ph.D.'s, and she had many Arab and Palestinian friends. Yet I believe it is fair to say that Kenyon's quarrels with some Israeli archaeologists were almost entirely about their radically differing methods: she could be very outspoken about what she saw as inferior excavation techniques. Part of the standoff was simply that Kenyon had not had any contact with Israelis until after 1967, had not even been able to visit Israel because it would have jeopardized her good relations with the Jordanian authorities. After the 1967 war, however, she carried out the planned final season in Israeli-held Jerusalem, and thereafter she came regularly to visit Israel. It was my privilege to guide her around the sites on many occasions, and we had long conversations while driving. She could be very blunt about work that she considered substandard; but I never heard a word during our candid talks that was not thoroughly professional. When I hosted large public receptions for Kenyon at the American School in Jerusalem during her summer visits in the early 1970s, she was delighted to meet and converse with virtually the entire Israeli archaeological establishment. I do not think that Kenyon was any more "pro-Arab" than Israeli archaeologists have been "anti-Jordanian." Happily, the peace accords now in place, although far from a permanent settlement, may soon obviate the need for foreign archaeologists working in Israel and Jordan—the "two halves" of ancient Palestine—to choose sides.

Archaeological Method

Clearly Kenyon's major claim to fame in Palestinian archaeology was the fact that she so boldly and vigorously championed new stratigraphical methods, considered at the time revolutionary, and deliberately employed these methods at three famous biblical sites. Yet controversy had surrounded Kenyon's methods as early as the publication of *Samaria-Sebaste 3* in 1957, as we have seen. And as time has passed, there has been a widespread recognition of the limitations of Kenyon's methods, despite their salutary stress at the time (and still today) on better stratigraphy.

First, Kenyon's system of unconnected, deep narrow trenches, which had served her so well at Verulamium (and possibly even at Samaria), when applied to Palestinian mounds provided too limited exposures and entailed great difficulties in coordinating the various fields. Those flaws were already evident at Jericho in the 1950s, where Kenyon's major Trench I became so narrow as it went down that the basal Neolithic levels were barely exposed (even though, by chance, they contained significant finds). Scarcely a single complete building was cleared and planned anywhere on the mound. Photography was also impeded in such deep *sondages*. Several critics, not just Israelis, have pointed out the problems, as I had done in 1973.[41] Kenyon tacitly acknowledged these limitations later, and it was said that she even thought of going back to Jericho to remedy them. But, at the time, she was reluctant to expand any of her trenches laterally. She even declared:

> It is therefore an absolute principle of excavations, which allows of no exceptions at all, that the whole area must not be cleared simultaneously. Standing sections (i.e. baulks) must be left at frequent intervals from the surface down.[42]

It turned out later that the same flaws were to be seen in Kenyon's excavations at Sabratha in North Africa (1948–51) when these were being prepared for publication in 1986. As Kenrick, who published the material, put it: "The sections were drawn almost entirely by her, and this is clearly where the emphasis of her excavation strategy lay. Accurate plans of the trenches are in contrastingly short supply: there is rarely more than a measured plan of each trench, made either at the end of the excavation, or at a stage which it had reached when the architect responsible happened to be working in that area."[43] Prag has noted that there are similar problems with the Jerusalem archives, and furthermore Kenyon's small exposures originally at Samaria in the 1930s meant that no single "Building" or "Pottery Period" there was represented by a sample of more than fifty sherds.[44] Moorey accepts the criticism of Kenyon that I had offered in 1973, stating that "the truth of Dever's comment is there for all to see in her work."

Both Prag and Moorey have insisted that it is not necessarily the "balk-debris layer" approach that is at fault, however, but rather Kenyon's logistics in employing it, and I would strongly concur. The method *can* be adapted for very large exposures, if balks are periodically removed after being drawn and carefully reestablished on the same grid, as we proved in Field VI at Gezer, where twenty-six five-meter by five-meter squares were opened in this manner, fully recorded, and carried down all the way to bedrock.[45] Yet Kenyon herself was not as single-mindedly devoted to section drawings as some of her critics charged. She obviously saw sections not only as basic but also as a means toward the end of complete contextual recording.

Misunderstandings have arisen largely, it seems to me, because of the irony that the great innovator of the use of balks in Palestinian archaeology did not live to publish a single, fully interpreted section drawing of her own. As Moorey observes astutely, one has the impression "that this aspect of the Wheeler-Kenyon method daunts those who never worked with her, or were never able to observe her closely in action, much more than those who did."[46] We at Gezer had observed her, and we did not hesitate to imitate her, with some modifications. Israeli archaeologists often came to visit us in 1964–67 to see the "British-American" method in use, at one remove, as it were. They expressed their misgivings openly; but it is significant that by the 1980s many Israeli archaeologists were drawing some sections.[47]

The latter is something of an irony because meanwhile back in Britain many archaeologists had quietly abandoned the rather rigid grid system for an excavation technique that has come to be called the "open field" or "rolling balk" method. This still entails the drawing of frequent sections, but it eschews a regular grid for arbitrary and flexible section lines that can be shifted according to the features being revealed. This approach, now widely seen in Britain, is often associated with the so-called Harris matrix system of modeling and phasing the three-dimensional relationships of the vast number of loci that are recorded on any modern stratigraphic system. These modifications of Wheeler-Kenyon method are now found on a few American excavations in Israel, but the majority of digs in both Israel and Jordan employ a version of the Gezer-modified "balk-debris layer" system.[48] In any case, it is important to state clearly that without Kenyon's bold efforts to grapple with the problems of the three-dimensional recording of tells, the still newer methods would not have been possible. Regrettably, pioneers are often unappreciated.

A second aspect of Kenyon's method that has come under criticism is that her ambitious goal of "total retrieval" produces too much data. Even if these data could be synthesized and published (which many doubted), so much detail was superfluous; one could not see the forest for the trees. Again, we are deprived by the lack of her final publications of Jericho and Jerusalem from seeing how Kenyon would ideally have addressed this problem. She was undoubtedly aware of the difficulty—"the enormity of the task defeated her . . . if indeed it was capable of realization at all"—as Kenrick later observed of her work in 1948–51 at Sabratha in North Africa.[49]

Moorey has also sensed that the real problem in Kenyon's fieldwork was that it produced so much data that it could not be assimilated, much less published in full. As he says: "On Jericho she laboured long and to the end, through endless distractions, wanted and unwanted. Her failure in this will only serve to endorse already voiced doubts about the publication of material so meticulously recorded as hers was." Moorey goes on to say that "to apply the Wheeler-Kenyon method properly and to publish the results on anything but the smallest scale is a task, as the Americans have realized, for carefully balanced and integrated teams, not for one person, even with the remarkable determination and capacity for hard work that Kathleen Kenyon conspicuously had."[50]

In retrospect, it seems clear that Kenyon's methods, featuring the minute examination of small areas in deep soundings, may have been suited to the reexcavation of tells that had been previously excavated with inadequate methods, where little material remained. But they were less than ideal for the excavation of virgin sites or one-period sites where lateral exposure was necessary. Thus Kenyon's methods were borrowed with considerable success on American digs at Shechem, Ta^{c}anach, ^{c}Ai, Gezer, and several sites in Transjordan, and even at Israeli-dug Lachish. They would, however, have proven less suitable at sites like Hazor, Dan, Dor, Massada, Beersheba, Arad, and elsewhere in Israel, which were being dug for the first time. The difference in sites may explain much of the controversy over Kenyon's methods. As Kenyon demonstrated, there is no "right" way to dig a mound, but there are many wrong ways; and about that, she was adamant.

Scholarship

It is obvious that the real test of any archaeological method (or theory) is whether or not it helps to achieve the overall goal of archaeology, which, to put it simply, is an explanation of culture, of cultural contact, and of cultural change over time. It is at this level—integration, synthesis, and publication—that Kenyon's scholarship must finally be judged. Clearly she was able to synthesize effectively at the popular level, both in lectures and in several books for the general public. She also published a number of more detailed excavation reports, although mostly preliminary. Yet in all candor, her colleagues admired her mostly as a technician, not a scholar; and I daresay that she probably thought of herself in the same way. Certainly she was never happier than when she was in the field, analyzing her own and others' sections. She seemed ill at ease in purely academic settings, the need for formality inhibiting her natural enthusiasm and confidence. When I last saw her at a symposium in Tübingen, Germany, in 1977, I found her looking distinctly uncomfortable at the reception following her lecture. As we stepped aside, sipping sherry and chatting, she was amused by the honorary doctorate in theology that the five-hundred-year-old university had just conferred on her and was impatient to talk instead of the forthcoming Jericho tell volumes.

I have already spoken of the difficulties Kenyon encountered in applying her stratigraphic methods at Jericho and Jerusalem, which in the end hindered, and certainly delayed, her scholarly interpretation of the excavated material. In addition to stratigraphy, the other basic tool of Palestinian archaeology has traditionally been comparative ceramic typology and chronology. Here, too, Kenyon's early analyses were never carried through to publication, but today her typological methods are seen to have had several fundamental flaws. For one thing, many of Kenyon's basic ceramic groups were derived from the several hundred tombs excavated at Jericho. But, as is well known, tomb groups may contain many atypical forms and assemblages of vessels. Furthermore, tomb deposits with several sequential burials will inevitably be mixed, no matter how skillful the excavator. In addition, Kenyon categorized the tomb pottery on the basis of whole forms, but the tell pottery on the basis of rim profiles. Both procedures are defensible; but, as Prag has pointed out, the resultant typologies at Jericho cannot in fact be correlated.[51]

Furthermore, once Kenyon had sorted the pottery into phases based on her reading of the stratigraphy, then classified the pottery into her types and recorded the number of examples of each type in a given stratigraphic phase, she discarded most of the material. Thus the irony is that Kenyon's entire system—designed to insure that every sherd and object could be traced back to its exact context—breaks down in the only instances where she employed it. Franken and Steiner, in trying to use Kenyon's "type-series" in publishing *Jerusalem* II after her death, discovered that they could not go back to the material to reassess her original phasing of the pottery, since she had in effect "covered her tracks."[52] Similarly, Kenrick found her type-series and the treatment of pottery the chief barrier to the completion of the Sabratha report, as we have seen. Again, the inherent shortcomings of the system are largely responsible for Kenyon's inability to complete the final publication of her major sites.

The tragedy is that the shortcomings of *any* system are unlikely to be realized until workup of the material for publication begins; and if that commences only after many seasons of fieldwork are over, it is too late. I suspect that many an excavator in Palestinian archaeology has gone back to the field indefinitely simply because he or she sensed that the task is interminable. It is easier to excavate additional material, hoping that more data will resolve the dilemma, than it is to revise basic methodology that is at fault. Nevertheless, Kenyon's basic system, as modified at other sites, can be made to work, and both the detailed stratigraphic and ceramic analyses can be fully published, as several American excavations have demonstrated.[53] Whether so much detail is desirable, or whether these final reports should be taken as model publications, is, of course, another matter.

In the absence of final excavation reports, Kenyon's scholarly accomplishments will have to be judged from her other publications. A number of her books, to be sure, were popular works, including nontechnical accounts of her work at Jericho and Jerusalem; but her four larger works on Samaria and Jericho are part of the basic literature of the discipline (see the evaluations above). Her articles are mostly reports of her fieldwork in Britain and Palestine, along with brief standard treatments in dictionaries and biblical commentaries, and finally a number of popular accounts in the *London Illustrated News* and elsewhere. Her three chapters in the third edition of the *Cambridge Ancient History* (1971–73) were largely technical analyses of the stratigraphy of the few sites she knew firsthand, and they certainly suffer by comparison with the masterly chapters on other periods in Palestine by Albright and de Vaux.[54] It is, however, difficult even in retrospect to suggest a British specialist in Bronze Age Palestine who could have done a better job at the time. Of her many articles, only a few addressed broader issues and could be considered original scholarly contributions: articles on method (1935, 1971); and on stratigraphic problems at Tell el-ᶜAjjûl, Hazor, Megiddo, and Samaria.[55] Her several reviews were provocative but somewhat idiosyncratic. She addressed the controversial relationship between archaeology and biblical studies only rarely and never very critically. It must be acknowledged that Kenyon's strengths were always those of a field archaeologist, not of a research scholar or one capable of producing broad historical or cultural syntheses. Moorey points out that Kenyon was "neither an intellectual by temperament nor a scholar by training."[56] She is thus not seen to advantage in many of her publications, which were descriptive and based largely on her own fieldwork, the few attempts at historical and cultural explanations being rather simplistic.

One of Kenyon's few original and creative concepts was her characterization of the Late Chalcolithic–Early Bronze I horizon as a "Proto-Urban" stage of development. Her designation of Albright's "Middle Bronze I," my "Early Bronze IV," as an "Intermediate Early-Middle Bronze" horizon also has merit, but it has won less acceptance.[57] Perhaps the greatest weakness of Kenyon's scholarship was that her preoccupation with other matters, and perhaps her own personal inclinations, did not incline her to read widely. Her spare citations, particularly of non-British works, show that after the resumption of her fieldwork in Palestine in 1952 Kenyon increasingly lost touch with the literature. Even on issues of field methodology, her first love, she did not engage in much published dialogue. As for the burgeoning literature on archaeological theory, ethno-archaeology, and the "new archaeology" of the 1970s, Kenyon was oblivious (as many others were). In any case, these developments came too late to have had any impact on her work.[58] Kenyon was a superb technician, but she was not a theorist, nor did she claim to be an anthropologist or cultural historian. In this, she was a product of her own time, as we all are.

Many of Kenyon's limitations in both fieldwork and publication, obvious in retrospect, seem to have been due to her propensity for working alone. She insisted on drawing her own sections, often without the input of the area supervisor or critical discussions with other staff members about interpretation. She read her pottery on her own, and in fact she did not have on her staff any ceramic specialists who could have supplemented and corrected her, as would have been found, for instance, on most American excavations.[59] She recruited many students on her digs, of course, but they were usually quite junior, only square supervisors. The "teamwork concept" that came to characterize those American excavations in Jordan and Israel that adopted Kenyon's methods was inconceivable to her. As Moorey put it:

> Kathleen Kenyon was a natural autocrat for whom systematic delegation was virtually impossible. It gave her the strengths of a great general in the field, singularity of purpose, firm control of strategy and decisive tactics; but with the large, young supervisory teams she used, particularly at Jerusalem (1961–1967), it came to place almost inhuman demands on her powers of concentration, assimilation and attention to detail.[60]

Conclusion

It remains only to comment on Kathleen Kenyon's career as a woman in the field of Near Eastern archaeology, which until recently has been dominated by men. She herself would have scoffed at the question, and no doubt would have resented it, for it is clear that from the beginning she thought of herself as an archaeologist, not a "woman archaeologist." One might speculate, of course, on how much advantage she had in a man's world because of the strong traits of leadership she inherited from her father or because of her own rather formidable appearance and manner. Her supreme self-confidence was, of course, a great asset, because she wasted no time or energy comparing herself with others, men or women.

It is true that Kenyon became a role model for a number of younger British women in archaeology, but from all the evidence that was not what she had intended. One could say that Kathleen Kenyon was born a "liberated woman" before it became an issue. The best proof of that is the fact that for all her admiration of her mentor Sir Mortimer Wheeler—one of the most dominant archaeological personalities imaginable—she showed her independence from the beginning, and later she withstood him on a number of occasions.[61]

These observations are not meant to suggest that Kenyon did not face obstacles in Britain and the Middle East in her rise to prominence in archaeology, for she did. As we have noted, British Palestinian archaeology had never suffered from the domination of male clerics, as American archaeology did. In the 1930s–1950s, however, there were relatively few women in British archaeology and even fewer in Near Eastern archaeology. Furthermore, it was difficult for a woman to be accepted as a dig director in the Arab countries where Kenyon chose to work. But she overcame these obstacles, as all others. Jacquetta Hawkes, Wheeler's biographer, said of Kenyon:

> Lacking in grace in her appearance and writing of English, she became a good administrator and a great excavator by sheer weight of character. She could command her work-force, whether of British laborers or [Arab] felaheen, with complete authority.[62]

Finally, it may be helpful to place Kenyon in the larger context of British women in Near Eastern archaeology. Preceding her in Palestine were a few other distinguished women, such as Joan Crowfoot, Dorothy Garrod, and Olga Tufnell; there was also her near-contemporary Diana Kirkbride, then her own student Crystal Bennett.[63] In Mesopotamia, there were Rachel Maxwell-Hyslop and Barbara Parker (later Lady Mallowan), both of whom had been among the first students enrolled in the London Institute of Archaeology when it opened in 1934, the year before Kenyon became the secretary.[64] Most of these British female archaeologists came from privileged circles, as Kenyon herself did. But that fact should not minimize our appreciation of their achievement of stature in the discipline of archaeology, for that generation still had formidable obstacles to overcome. None did so more spectacularly than Kathleen Kenyon.

WORKS BY KATHLEEN KENYON
A SELECTED BIBLIOGRAPHY

Books, Monographs, and Articles

Beginning in Archaeology. London: Phoenix House, 1952.

"Tombs of the Intermediate Early Bronze-Middle Bronze Age at Tel el-Ajjul." *Annual of the Department of Antiquities in Jordan* 3 (1956): 41–55.

Digging Up Jericho. London: Ernst Benn, 1957.

J. W. Crowfoot and G. M. Crowfoot, coauthors. *Samaria-Sebaste*. vol. 3, *The Objects*. London: Palestine Exploration Fund, 1957.

"Some Notes on the Early and Middle Bronze Age Strata of Megiddo." *Eretz-Israel* 5 (1958): 51–60.

Archaeology in the Holy Land. London: Ernst Benn, 1960.
Excavations at Jericho: Tombs Excavated in 1952–4. Vol. 1. London: British School of Archaeology in Jerusalem, 1960.
"Megiddo, Hazor, Samaria, and Chronology." *London Institute of Archaeology Bulletin* 4 (1964): 143–57.
Excavations at Jericho: Tombs Excavated in 1955–8. Vol. 2. London: British School of Archaeology in Jerusalem, 1965.
Amorites and Canaanites. London: Oxford University Press, 1966.
Jerusalem—Excavating 3000 Years of History. London: Thames and Hudson, 1967.
"Middle and Late Bronze Age Strata at Megiddo." *Levant* 1 (1969): 25–60.
"An Essay on Archaeological Technique: The Publication of Results from the Excavation of a Tell." *Harvard Theological Review* 64 (1971): 241–79.
Royal Cities of the Old Testament. London: Barrie and Jenkins, 1971.
"Syria and Palestine, c. 2160–1780 B.C." *Cambridge Ancient History.* 3d ed. Vol. 1, pt. 2, 1971.
"Palestine in the Middle Bronze Age." *Cambridge Ancient History.* 3d ed. Vol. 2, pt. 1, 1973.
"Palestine in the Time of the 18th Dynasty." *Cambridge Ancient History.* 3d ed. Vol. 2, pt. 1, 1973.
Digging Up Jerusalem. London: Ernst Benn, 1974.

Suggested Readings about Kathleen Kenyon

Moorey, P. R. S. "British Women in Near Eastern Archaeology: Kathleen Kenyon and the Pioneers." *Palestine Exploration Quarterly* 124 (1992): 91–100.
Moorey, P. R. S. and P. J. Parr, eds. *Archaeology in the Levant: Essays for Kathleen Kenyon.* Warminster: Aris and Phillips, 1985.
Prag, K. "Kathleen Kenyon and Archaeology in the Holy Land." *Palestine Exploration Quarterly* 124 (1992): 109–23.
Wilkes, J. "Kathleen Kenyon in Roman Britain." *Palestine Exploration Quarterly* 124 (1992): 101–8.

NOTES

This biography is based largely on Kenyon's own published works, but it also depends on several perceptive obituaries and on lectures given later in her memory at St. Hugh's College, Oxford, in 1991. I base some remarks on my own acquaintance with her from 1964 onward, when I had many opportunities to exchange visits with her in the field at Jerusalem and Gezer, as well as many stimulating hours spent with her on field trips and social occasions while I was director of the American schools (the Nelson Glueck School of Biblical Archaeology and the W. F. Albright Institute of Archaeological Research) in Jerusalem. The bibliography gives references to her major publications in Syro-Palestinian archaeology and to some other sources of information. For obituaries, see P. R. S. Moorey, "Kathleen

Kenyon and Palestinian Archaeology," *Palestine Exploration Quarterly* 111 (1979): 3–10; W. G. Dever, "Kathleen Kenyon (1906–1978): A Tribute," *Bulletin of the American Schools of Oriental Research* 232 (1978): 3, 4; A. D. Tushingham, "Kathleen Mary Kenyon 1906–1978," *Proceedings of the British Academy* 71 (1985): 555–82. For her *festschrift,* with complete biography and a personal appreciation by M. M. and A. D. Tushingham (pp. ix–x), see P. R. S. Moorey and P. J. Parr, eds., *Archaeology in the Levant: Essays for Kathleen Kenyon* (Warminster: Aris and Phillips, 1985).

1. P. R. S. Moorey and P. J. Parr, eds., *Archaeology in the Levant: Essays for Kathleen Kenyon* (Warminster: Aris and Phillips, 1985).

2. J. Wilkes, "Kathleen Kenyon in Roman Britain," *Palestine Exploration Quarterly* 124 (1992): 101–8.

3. Cited in P. R. S. Moorey, "British Women in Near Eastern Archaeology: Kathleen Kenyon and the Pioneers," *Palestine Exploration Quarterly* 124 (1992): 99.

4. Oxford did not offer an undergraduate course in archaeology until 1992.

5. Kenyon's opinion was expressed in a conversation with me about Wright, who was my teacher at Harvard.

6. Moorey, "British Women," 91.

7. For Wheeler, see his autobiography, *Still Digging* (London: Michael Joseph, 1955); and the critical biography by Jacquetta Hawkes, *Mortimer Wheeler: Adventurer in Archaeology* (London: Weidenfeld and Nicolson, 1982). Both Wheeler and Hawkes comment on several aspects of Kenyon's career in passing.

8. Her dislike was partly, I think, innate modesty; but it was also due to the fact that in later life she wished to be thought of independently of Wheeler.

9. For my own characterization, now rather widely used, of her approach as the "balk-debris layer method," see W. G. Dever, "Two Approaches to Archaeological Method: The Architectural and the Stratigraphic," *Eretz-Israel* 11 (1973): 1*–8*.

10. A *balk* is the one-meter-wide "wall" of earth separating one trench from another. In a "grid and balk system" the site looks like a chessboard, wherein every ten meters or so a balk separates one trench from another.

11. For a more detailed account of the following, see Wilkes, "Kenyon in Roman Britain."

12. Moorey, "British Women," 99.

13. There Kenyon worked with two young Jewish archaeologists who were part of the *yishuv,* or Jewish resettlement of Palestine, later to become prominent Israeli archaeologists: Nahman Avigad and Eliezer Sukenik (Yadin's father), who was codirector for the Hebrew University of Jerusalem.

14. Sukenik, the father of eminent archaeologist Yigael Yadin, was codirector for the Hebrew University of Jerusalem.

15. See G. E. Wright, "Archaeological Method in Palestine—an American Interpretation," *Eretz-Israel* 9 (1969): 125–29; and cf. Moorey, "Kenyon and Palestinian Archaeology," 4.

16. See W. F. Albright, "Recent Progress in Palestinian Archaeology: Samaria-Sebaste III and Hazor I," *Bulletin of the American Schools of Oriental Research* 150 (1958): 21–25; G. E. Wright, "Israelite Samaria and Iron Age Chronology," *Bulletin of the American Schools of Oriental Research* 155 (1959): 13–29.

17. Y. Aharoni and R. Amiran, "A New Scheme for the Sub-division of the Iron Age in Palestine," *Israel Exploration Journal* 8 (1958): 171–84.

18. Cf. *Bulletin of the American Schools of Oriental Research* 277–78 (1990): 1–130; R. E. Tappy, *The Archaeology of Israelite Samaria,* vol. 1, *Early Iron Age through the Ninth Century* BCE (Atlanta: Scholars Press, 1992); volume 2, *The Eighth Century BCE* (Atlanta: Scholars Press, 2001).

19. One might, however, add two noted Israeli women archaeologists, Ruth Amiran and Trude Dothan, although neither had international reputations until later.

20. Prag, "Kenyon and Archaeology," 113.

21. Ibid.

22. A. D. Tushingham, in Moorey and Parr, *Archaeology in the Levant,* x.

23. Prag, "Kenyon and Archaeology," 118.

24. Moorey, "Kenyon and Palestinian Archaeology," 6, 7.

25. This methodology was supervised by Dever and others trained at Shechem by staff who had worked with Kenyon at Jericho.

26. This situation led some Israelis to conclude that Kenyon was "pro-Arab"—a charge that I believe was unfounded. There is a fuller discussion of this issue below. For Israeli criticisms of Kenyon's methods, see Y. Aharoni, "Remarks on the 'Israeli' Method of Excavation," *Eretz-Israel* 11 (1973): 48–53 (English summary, 23*). See also n. 49 below.

27. Review of W. G. Dever, H. Darrell Lance, and G. E. Wright, *Gezer I. Report of the 1964–66 Seasons* (1970), *Palestine Exploration Quarterly* 105 (1973): 170.

28. See bibliography.

29. See especially Moorey, "Kenyon and Palestinian Archaeology," 7; Prag, "Kenyon and Archaeology," 114. Already in 1982 I had pointed out the difficulties in publishing the mass of detail that is now routinely recorded; see W. G. Dever, "Retrospects and Prospects in Biblical and Syro-Palestinian Archaeology," *Biblical Archaeologist* 45 (1982): 103–7.

30. Prag, "Kenyon and Archaeology," 114.

31. She published only two popular books on Jerusalem, in 1967 and 1974; for these and the final reports by others, see bibliography.

32. For criticisms of Jerusalem, see A. Mazar, "Israel Archaeology," in *Benchmarks in Time and Culture: An Introduction to Palestinian Archaeology,* ed. J. F. Drinkard Jr., G. L. Mattingly, and J. M. Miller (Atlanta: Scholars Press, 1988), 120, 121. For Kenyon's tacit recognition that her exposures at Jericho had been too small, see Moorey, "Kenyon and Palestinian Archaeology," 7. I do not think that she ever deigned to reply to the same criticism of Jerusalem.

33. P. M. Kenrick, the publisher of the final Sabratha report, as quoted in Prag, "Kenyon and Archaeology," 114, 115.

34. Quoted in Wilkes, "Kenyon in Roman Britain," 102.

35. See Prag, "Kenyon and Archaeology," 120, referring to R. Trickett, "Kathleen Kenyon," *St. Hugh's College Chronicle* (1978–79), 35–40 (a copy of which I have through the courtesy of Kay Prag). Among other vignettes are those of Kenyon and her long succession of disreputable mongrel dogs, to whom she was devoted.

36. For Kenyon's bibliography through 1975, see Moorey and Parr, *Archaeol-*

ogy in the Levant, xi–xiv. I have abridged this in the bibliography here, eliminating the publications on Britain and the many minor or popular pieces on Palestine. For the final Jericho volumes, in which much of the text is hers, see bibliography.

37. Wheeler had worked in India and Pakistan, where he was director of the Department of Antiquities and of very important excavations in the Indus Valley.

38. These were G. E. Wright at Shechem, J. B. Pritchard at Gibeon, P. W. Lapp at Ta^{c}anach and elsewhere, J. A. Callaway at ^{c}Ai, and Père Roland de Vaux at Tell el-Farcah (the Germans were largely inactive).

39. Related in Hawkes, *Mortimer Wheeler,* 350–52.

40. As director of the Nelson Glueck School of Biblical Archaeology in Jerusalem and one of the few other ranking foreign archaeologists, I also contributed a statement to UNESCO, criticizing Mazar's excavations as substandard. It is now generally acknowledged, even by Mazar's own students and colleagues, that the Temple Mount excavations, while a current tourist attraction (and political statement?), are a disaster and will never be published.

41. See references in n. 16 above.

42. Kenyon, *Beginning in Archaeology* (London: Phoenix House, 1952), 77. As Moorey, however, points out, this rather dogmatic statement of principle was meant to be applied pragmatically, according to the type of site, as Kenyon went on to say; see Moorey, "Kenyon and Palestinian Archaeology," 7; and cf. Prag, "Kenyon and Archaeology," 114.

43. Kenrick, *Sabratha,* 4, quoted in Prag, "Kenyon and Archaeology," 115.

44. Prag, "Kenyon and Archaeology," 7.

45. See Dever, "Two Approaches"; and Dever et al., *Gezer IV. The 1967–71 Seasons in Field VI, The Acropolis, Field VI* (Jerusalem: Hebrew Union College, 1987).

46. Moorey, "Kenyon and Palestinian Archaeology," 7. I had made a similar observation in 1973 in Dever, "Two Approaches," pointing out that frequent section drawing was not all that difficult and that in any case its many advantages far outweighed any logistical difficulties involved. I suspect that some excavators in Israel do not draw many sections largely because they are undisciplined, not because they have tried the method and found good reasons for rejecting it.

47. There has been little open recognition of the derivation of this improved technique in the Israeli literature; but see D. Ussishkin, "Excavations at Tel Lachish—1973–1977—Preliminary Report," *Tel Aviv* 5 (1978): 3–6.

48. See, with direct criticisms of Wheeler and Kenyon, P. Barker, *Techniques of Archaeological Excavation* (London: B. T. Batsford, 1977), 15–26; E. C. Harris, *Principles of Archaeological Stratigraphy* (New York: Academic Press, 1979), 19; 49, 81–86, 121. Despite these criticisms, which are based on current British techniques and which regard regular balks as unnecessary, I think that Kenyon's grid system is, or can be, better suited to typical multilayered Middle Eastern mounds. The Harvard excavations at Ashkelon under Lawrence Stager, trained at Gezer, use the "open-field" system; but no publications of results have yet been seen, so in my judgment the question of this system's worth is still open.

49. Kenrick, *Sabratha,* quoted in Prag, "Kenyon and Archaeology," 117. Kenrick was speaking largely about trying to apply her type-system of pottery across an entire site, but the complexity of Kenyon's system as a whole exhibits the same

difficulties. There was an early euphoria among American excavators in Israel concerning Kenyon's method, sparked by our own introduction of them at Gezer in 1964–73. But as one of the few who had actually had experience in publishing material dug this way, I pointed out in 1980 the formidable tasks of integration that were involved. See "Archaeological Method in Israel: A Continuing Revolution," *Biblical Archaeologist* 43 (1980): 41–48. The truth of my prediction that few digs using this system would ever publish final reports is unfortunately clear today. Among American excavations, only Gezer I–V and ᶜAi I–II (the latter by J. A. Callaway, trained partly at Jericho) can claim to have carried the method in its full application through to publication. Yet the crisis of how best to publish a truly stratigraphically dug Palestinian site has only deepened; cf. H. Shanks, ed., *Archaeology's Publication Problem* (Washington, D.C.: Biblical Archaeology Society, 1996).

50. Moorey, "Kenyon and Palestinian Archaeology," 8, citing American modifications to Kenyon's method, pioneered at Gezer and later elsewhere in Israel.

51. Prag, "Kenyon and Archaeology," 116, 117.

52. H. J. Frankin and M. L. Steiner, *Excavations in Jerusalem, 1961–1967,* vol. 2 (Jerusalem: British School of Archaeology in Jerusalem, 1990), 62ff., quoted in Prag, "Kenyon and Archaeology," 117. That she similarly "covered her tracks" at Samaria in the 1930s has now been shown by Tappy's definitive study *Israelite Samaria,* based in part on a reexamination of her original field notes; see Tappy, v.

53. See n. 49 above.

54. This criticism is also voiced by Moorey, "Kenyon and Palestinian Archaeology," 8, 9.

55. See the appended bibliography.

56. Moorey, "Kenyon and Palestinian Archaeology," 8; cf. Prag, "Kenyon and Archaeology," 119.

57. W. G. Dever, "Social Structure in the Early Bronze IV Period in Palestine," in *The Archaeology of Society in the Holy Land,* ed. T. E. Levy (Leicester: Leicester University Press, 1993), 283–96. On the "Proto-Urban" era, see now the work of my student Alexander H. Joffe, *Settlement and Society in the Early Bronze I and II Southern Levant* (Sheffield: Sheffield Academic Press, 1993).

58. For a candid assessment of Kenyon and the concept of "archaeology as a science," see Prag, "Kenyon and Archaeology," 117, 118. On the advent of the "New Archaeology" in Palestinian archaeology, see W. G. Dever, "The Impact of the 'New Archaeology' on Syro-Palestinian Archaeology," *Bulletin of the American Schools of Oriental Research* 242 (1981): 15–29.

59. It was at the point of pottery analysis that G. E. Wright entered his most telling criticism of Kenyon's methods, which otherwise he admired and attempted to adopt at Shechem; see "Archaeological Method in Palestine," 132, 133. Most would acknowledge that the attempt to blend the Albrightian-American method with that of Kenyon was not realized at Shechem but only by his students at Gezer in 1964–73; cf. n. 49 above. For Kenyon's defense of her handling of the pottery, see "An Essay on Archaeological Technique: The Publication of Results from the Excavation of a Tell," *Harvard Theological Review* 64 (1971): 241–79.

60. Moorey, "Kenyon and Palestinian Archaeology," 7.

61. See Wilkes, "Kenyon in Roman Britain," 104; cf. Hawkes, *Mortimer Wheeler,* 350–52.

62. Hawkes, *Mortimer Wheeler,* 132.

63. In British archaeology today in Israel and Jordan, there are as many women as men, many of them second-generation Kenyon students. On Kenyon's creating positions and opportunities in archaeology for both men and women, see further Prag, "Kenyon and Archaeology," 120. For the broader context within British archaeology, see especially Moorey, "British Women."

64. Moorey, "British Women," 98.

Conclusion

OVER THE YEARS, THE WOMEN we call "pioneers" have been recognized, individually, for their outstanding contributions to the field of archaeology. They have enjoyed respect for their fieldwork, innovative technological methods, and published research. Some have been recognized with honorary degrees from distinguished institutions, while others received recognition from learned societies or from the governments where they lived or worked.[1] Although these women led modest, hardworking lives, they each had an identity that was vivid and compelling and were lifted out of the ordinary by their extraordinary gifts for research, learning, and teaching. Now their stories have been told.

Early in their careers these women were fortunate to meet and be taught by the foremost scholars and teachers of their day. They also had the good fortune to have the support of a mentor-advocate, who welcomed and respected them as if they were already members of the archaeological establishment. Mentoring, in fact, is a way of professional life in archaeology today, and so it was in previous generations. As each of these women established herself in her profession, she, in turn, mentored the next generation. In some cases, there was a strong bond with a single individual, and in others, the influence extended to legions of students.

Not surprisingly, therefore, we find many links between the pioneer women. Margaret Murray taught Gertrude Caton-Thompson. In turn, Gertrude Caton-Thompson took Kathleen Kenyon to excavate in Zimbabwe. Edith Hall Dohan worked at Gournia under Harriet Boyd Hawes; Esther Van Deman was helpful to Gertrude Bell; and, while at Cambridge,

Theresa Goell was probably influenced by both Gertrude Caton-Thompson and Winifred Lamb and, later in her career, was advised by Hetty Goldman.

In the early twentieth century archaeologists—women among them—were offered teaching positions at universities. Dorothy Garrod held a chair at Cambridge; Margaret Murray taught for years at University College London (but she had to wait until she was sixty-four to be promoted to assistant professor!); Harriet Boyd Hawes taught at Wellesley College; Edith Hall Dohan taught at Mount Holyoke and at Bryn Mawr; and Hetty Goldman taught at Johns Hopkins and was then the first female appointed to a permanent position at the Institute for Advanced Study in Princeton. Women filled curatorship positions as well. Winifred Lamb held the position of Honorary Keeper of Greek Antiquities at the Fitzwilliam Museum at Cambridge; and Edith Hall Dohan was the curator of the Classical Collections at the University of Pennsylvania Museum.

The majority of these pioneers were productive scholars, although two of them failed to complete the final publication of their respective excavations.[2] Think of the publications by Dieulafoy of Susa and the Hassan Mosque; of Esther Van Deman's publications of Roman construction techniques and aqueducts—still important and still used today; of Margaret Murray's Egyptological tomes; of Gertrude Bell's *The Thousand and One Churches* or *The Desert and the Sown;* of Harriet Boyd Hawes's *Gournia;* of Edith Hall Dohan's studies of Italic tomb groups; of Hetty Goldman's *Tarsus,* Gertrude Caton-Thompson's *Hammamiya;* of Dorothy Garrod's volumes devoted to her Natufian discoveries at Shukbah, Wadi el-Mughara, or El Wad; of Winifred Lamb's pivotal and speedy publication of her excavations at Thermi and Kusura as well as her many catalogs.

Beyond the excavation site, the classroom and the library these women committed themselves to caring for the well-being of those who worked for them. For years Theresa Goell served her Turkish and Kurdish workmen by giving them and their families medicines, food, and clothing. Kathleen Kenyon personally underwrote financial aid for her students, and Gertrude Caton-Thompson left a generous legacy to University College London to enable students and staff to continue their research in Egyptology.

Their volunteerism saw them engaged in pressing issues of the day, and, to be sure, they made a difference. They took active roles when war broke out around them. Jane Dieulafoy worked at a clinic and saw ambulance service as a soldier; Margaret Murray devoted herself to the Serbian cause; Gertrude Bell served the Red Cross; Harriet Boyd Hawes worked as a nurse in three wars and organized a feeding camp in Corfu; Gertrude Caton-

Thompson raised money for refugee organizations, and Winifred Lamb worked in the British Naval Intelligence Service Department. In addition, both Hetty Goldman and Theresa Goell took active measures to help the war effort in World War II. Goldman sponsored academic refugees who were fleeing from the Nazis and worked as a member of the Red Cross Commission to Greece; and Theresa Goell used her drafting abilities to work for engineering firms under contract to the U.S. Navy.

Many took part and played a role in the political and social controversies of the day. In true individualistic fashion, they resolutely followed their own paths. Jane Dieulafoy defied the mores of French society by exclusively adopting male clothing as a mode of dress. Gertrude Caton-Thompson had strong feminist sympathies, while Gertrude Bell was a supporter of the anti-suffrage movement.

Many of them pursued interests separate from their archaeological careers. Erudite in a wide range of subjects, Margaret Murray taught languages, history, religion, and arts and crafts of the early Egyptians while simultaneously devising a grammar of ancient Egyptian and another one of Coptic. She was also interested in witchcraft and lectured and published on the subject. Or we have the legacy of Esther Van Deman's much-admired photographs. Her portraits of Italian peasant women in the Campagna as well as her numerous pictures of every site she visited are not only recognized as an invaluable record of a life and time now lost but are also considered an outstanding artistic endeavor. Her artistry has been recognized publicly by exhibitions of her work in both Italy and the United States. Also in pursuit of a creative outlet, Winifred Lamb wrote short stories and a murder mystery, and Jane Dieulafoy was a published novelist who even had one of her stories turned into an opera with music by Camille Saint-Saëns.

There were difficult moments in the lives of many of these women. They were romantics, but in some of their lives there is a sense of melancholia. Gertrude Bell, the eccentric with irrepressible vitality, was respected and viewed as an exceptional woman (but not a colleague); despite being both accomplished and enjoying great renown, she took a fatal dose of barbiturates. Or think of Kathleen Kenyon's frustration with Mortimer Wheeler, who tried to block her appointment to the Council for the British School of Archaeology in Jerusalem by accusing her of being "too pro-Arab"; and the anguish felt by Theresa Goell when she was ignored by Friedrich Karl Dörner, who for years blocked her publication of Commagene.

Replacing a traditional lifestyle based on marriage and the "contained" roles of wife and mother, the pioneer women explored new ways to live using the discipline of archaeology as a foundation. Serious academic pursuit and, in many cases, employment were part of the fabric of this lifestyle. Only in a few cases did these archaeologists marry. Of the twelve women discussed in this volume only three—Jane Dieulafoy, Harriet Boyd Hawes, and Edith Hall Dohan—were married, and only the latter two had children. Theresa Goell did marry early in life and had a son. But she did not take her husband's name and within a few years she was divorced.

One wonders if some of the others minded not being married or if they found their independence and freedom through female companionship. Many of these women led all-female or very nearly all-female expeditions. Why was this so? Would no man (or very few men) of that time join a team led by a women? Or was it that these particular women felt more comfortable working with other women? It is difficult to give a definitive answer to these questions. In this connection we might consider the views of J. R. Droop, who taught at the University of Liverpool and was long associated with the British School at Athens. In 1915 he wrote:

> By way of epilogue I may perhaps venture a short word on the question much discussed in certain quarters, whether in the work of excavation it is a good thing to have co-operation between men and women. I have no intention of discussing whether or no women possess the qualities best suited for such work; opinions, I believe, vary on the point, but I have never seen a trained lady excavator at work, so that my view if expressed would be valueless.
>
> Of a mixed dig, however, I have seen something, and it is an experiment that I would be reluctant to try again; I would grant if need be that women are admirably fitted for the work, yet I would uphold that they should undertake it by themselves.
>
> My reasons are two-fold and chiefly personal. In the first place there are the proprieties; I have never had a very reverent care for these abstractions, but I think it is not everywhere sufficiently realised that the proprieties that have to be considered are not only those that rule in England or America, but those of the lands where it is proposed to dig; the view to be considered is the view of the inhabitants, Greek, Turk, or Egyptian. My chief reasons, I said, were personal, but I hasten to add that they have nothing to do with the particular ladies with whom I was associated; should these lines meet their eyes I hope they will believe me when I say that before and after the excavations I thought them charming; during it however because they, or we, were in the wrong place their charm was not seen. My

> objections lie in this, that the work of excavation on the dig and off it lays on those who share in it a bond of closer daily intercourse than is conceivable, except perhaps in the Navy where privacy is said to be unobtainable except for a captain; with the right men that is one of the charms of life, but between men and women, except in chance cases, I do not believe that such close and unavoidable companionship can ever be other than a source of irritation; at any rate I believe that, however it affects women, the ordinary male at least cannot stand it. It is true that it might also be a source of matrimony, but as that would mean a temporary end to serious work of two members of the expedition, it can hardly be used as an argument for co-operation. Marriage apart, and I can imagine a man conducting a small excavation very happily with this wife, mixed digging I think means a loss of easiness in the atmosphere and consequent loss of efficiency.
>
> A minor, and yet to my mind weighty, objection lies in one particular form of constraint entailed by the presence of ladies, it must add to all the strains of an excavation, and they are many, the further strain of politeness and self-restraint in moments of stress, moments that will occur on the best regulated dig, when you want to say just what you think without translation, which before ladies, whatever their feelings about it, cannot be done.[3]

This passage is illuminating. We quote it not to criticize Droop but because we believe it provides a vivid picture of the professional environment in which many of these women archaeologists lived. By reading and considering Droop's opinions one can better understand and better appreciate the opportunities and challenges facing many of the women profiled in this volume. And one can thereby appreciate all the more the magnitude of their accomplishments.

NOTES

1. For example, Dorothy Garrod was presented with a gold medal from the Society of Antiquaries; Gertrude Bell was made a Commander of the British Empire; and, in France, Jane Dieulafoy received the cross of the Legion of Honor.

2. Theresa Goell and Kathleen Kenyon did not publish their major excavations, although Kenyon did publish popular books on archaeology, *Digging Up Jericho*

and *Archaeology in the Holy Land;* and Goell lectured on her work and wrote a number of excavation reports and magazine articles.

3. *Archaeological Excavation* (Cambridge, 1915), 63–64. We are grateful to Nico Momogliano for calling attention to this passage.

Glossary

Albright, William F. (1891–1971). American orientalist and archaeologist. Excavated in Palestine at Tell Beit Mirsim, Bethel, and Beth Zur. Director of the American School of Oriental Research in Jerusalem, 1920–29, 1933–36.

Ashby, Thomas (1874–1931). British archaeologist. Director of the British School at Rome, 1906–25.

Beazley, John D. (1885–1970). British archaeologist and art historian. Specialized in Attic vase painting.

Bieber, Margarete (1879–1978). German-American art historian. Specialized in Greek and Roman theater, Hellenistic sculpture, and ancient dress.

Blegen, Carl (1887–1971). American archaeologist. Excavated at many sites, in particular Troy and Pylos.

Botta, Paul-Émile (1802–1870). French diplomat at Mosul in Iraq, Jerusalem, and Tripoli in Libya. Excavated at Khorsabad.

Buck, Carl D. (1866–1955). American classicist. Specialized in Greek and Latin philology.

Caskey, Elizabeth G. (1910–1994). American classicist and archaeologist. Excavated at Lerna and Kea.

Caskey, John L. (1908–1981). American archaeologist. Excavated at Troy, Lerna, and Kea. Director of the American School of Classical Studies at Athens, 1949–59.

Caskey, Lacey D. (1880–1944). American art historian. Specialized in Greek art.

Childe, V. Gordon (1892–1957). British prehistorian.

de Jong, Piet (1887–1967). British artist, caricaturist, and architectural draftsman. Worked in Greece.

de Morgan, Jacques (1857–1924). French prehistorian and orientalist.

de Sarzec, Ernest (1837–1901). French diplomat at Basra and Baghdad in Iraq. Excavated at Tello.

Dinsmoor, William B. (1886–1973). American archaeologist. Historian of Greek architecture.

Dörpfeld, Wilhelm (1853–1940). German architect and archaeologist. Excavated at, among other sites, Olympia, Troy, and on Ithaca. Director of the German Archaeological Institute at Athens, 1887–1912.

Dussaud, René (1868–1958). French historian of the ancient Near East.

Evans, Arthur (1851–1941). British archaeologist. Excavated at Knossos on Crete.

Ghirshman, Roman (1895–1979). French archaeologist. Excavated at Susa and numerous other sites in Iran.

Goetze, Albrecht (1897–1971). German-American Assyriologist. Director of the American School of Oriental Research in Baghdad, 1947–56.

Herzfeld, Ernst (1879–1948). German-American archaeologist. Excavated at, among other sites, Persepolis, Samarra, and Tall-I bakun.

Heuzey, Leon (1831–1922). French archaeologist and art historian. Excavated in Macedonia.

Hogarth, David G. (1862–1927). British archaeologist. Director of the British School at Athens, 1897–1900.

Hülsen, Christian (1858–1935). German archaeologist. An authority on Roman topography.

Layard, Austen Henry (1817–1894). British archaeologist. Excavated at Nineveh, Khorsabad, and Nimrud.

Lehmann, Karl (1894–1960). German-American art historian and archaeologist. Excavated at Samothrace.

Loftus, William Kenneth (1821–1858). British archaeologist. Excavated in the Near East.

Mallowan, Max (1904–1978). British archaeologist. Excavated at Ur, Halaf, Tell Brak, and Nimrud in Mesopotamia. Director of the British School of Archaeology in Iraq, 1947–61. Husband of Agatha Christie.

Meritt, Benjamin D. (1899–1989). American historian. Specialized in Attic epigraphy.

Petrie, W. M. Flinders (1853–1942). British archaeologist. Excavated at many sites in Egypt and Palestine.

Ramsay, William M. (1851–1939). British historian. Specialized in Graeco-Roman Anatolia.

Randall-MacIver, David (1873–1945). British archaeologist. Specialized in late Italian prehistory.

Reinach, Salomon (1858–1932). French archaeologist and historian.

Richter, Gisela M. A. (1882–1979). German-American art historian. Specialized in Greek art.

Sarre, Friedrich (1865–1945). German art historian and archaeologist. Specialized in the ancient Near East.

Strong, Eugénie Sellers (1860–1943). British archaeologist and art historian. An authority on Roman sculpture.

Swindler, Mary Hamilton (1884–1967). American archaeologist and art historian. An authority on ancient painting. Editor of the *American Journal of Archaeology*, 1932–46.

van Berchem, Max (1863–1921). Historian and epigrapher. Specialized in Islamic archaeology.

Walker, Alice Leslie (Kosmopoulos) (1885–1954). American archaeologist. Worked in Greece.

Ward, William Hayes (1835–1916). American archaeologist. Specialized in the ancient Near East.

Wheeler, Mortimer (1890–1976). British archaeologist. Excavated at Verulamium and Maiden Castle in Britain as well as Taxila and other Indus cities.

Woolley, C. Leonard (1880–1960). British archaeologist. Excavated at Carchemish and Alalakh in Syria, Amarna in Egypt, and Ur in Mesopotamia.

Contributors

Julia M. Asher-Greve is the author of the first scholarly book on women in ancient Mesopotamia, *Frauen in altsumerischer Zeit* (1985) and has worked and published on Mesopotamian art, women, and gender. She is editor of *NIN—Journal of Gender Studies in Antiquity.*

Ofer Bar-Yosef is the MacCurdy Professor of Prehistoric Archaeology, Peabody Museum, Harvard University. His field projects and publications concern Lower, Middle, Upper Paleolithic, and Epi-Paleolithic sites and prehistoric entities mostly in Western Asia. He is currently interested in the origins of agriculture in the Near East and China.

Ann Brown studied modern history at Trinity College, Dublin. She was assistant in the Department of Antiquities, Ashmolean Museum, Oxford, for thirty-five years. She has published many articles and books on Arthur Evans's life, travels in Crete, and excavations at Knossos.

Jane Callander specialized in archaeology as a staff researcher for BBC Television's Science Department. Since leaving the BBC in 1993 she has combined academic study with research into the early prehistoric archaeological work in the Levant under the British Mandatory government. In 2002 she received a master's degree in archaeology at University College London.

William G. Dever is Professor Emeritus of Near Eastern Archaeology and Anthropology at the University of Arizona. A specialist in the archaeology of ancient Palestine, he has directed more than thirty excavations in Israel and has published numerous books and articles on the subject.

Margaret S. Drower was a Reader in Ancient History at University College, London. She is a Visiting Professor at the Institute of Archaeology in University College London and a Fellow of the Society of Antiquaries.

Vasso Fotou studied archaeology at the Sorbonne and architecture at the École des Beaux-Arts, Paris. She was assistant in the Department of Archaeology, University of Ioannina, Greece, and is now an independent scholar living in England. She has excavated and carried out research at many sites in Crete and has published a monograph on Harriet Boyd's excavation archive.

David W. J. Gill is Sub-Dean of the Faculty of Arts and Social Studies and Senior Lecturer in Ancient History at the University of Wales Swansea. He was a member of the Methana field survey in Greece and is currently working on the publication of the excavations of the Greek city of Euesperides in Cyrenaica (Libya). He is coauthor (with Michael Vickers) of *Artful Crafts: Ancient Greek Silverware and Pottery.*

Eve Gran-Aymerich is a teacher and researcher in Paris. Her work focuses on the history of French archaeology within an international and comparative perspective. The author of numerous scholarly articles and a biography of Jane Dieulafoy, she has also published two books in the series Éditions du CNRS: *Naissance de l'archéologie moderne,* 1798–1945, and a *Dictionnaire biographique d'archéologie, 1798–1945.*

Machteld J. Mellink is Leslie Clark Professor Emerita of Classics at Bryn Mawr College. A recipient of the Gold Medal of the Archaeological Institute of America, she was cited as "'Dean' of American excavators in Turkey, preeminent scholar of Anatolian cultures, tireless defender of 'the Record of the Past' and of ethics in archaeology." Prof. Mellink has excavated and published material from numerous sites in Anatolia.

Katherine Dohan Morrow is the granddaughter of Edith Hall Dohan. She graduated from Smith College in 1976 and received her Ph.D. in classical archaeology in 1982 from Bryn Mawr College. She is the author of *Greek Footwear and the Dating of Sculpture.*

Kathleen M. Quinn is a Ph.D. candidate in Classical archaeology at the University of Cincinnati. She has excavated at sites in the United States, Turkey, and Greece. Currently she is writing the first comprehensive study of the Byzantine period at Troy.

Margaret Cool Root received her B.A. and Ph.D. from Bryn Mawr College. Since 1978 she has been a member of the faculty of the University of Michigan's Department of the History of Art and its Interdepartmental Program in Classical Art and Archaeology as well as a curator at the Kelsey Museum of Archaeology. Her special area of interest is the art and archaeology of the Achaemenid Persian Empire.

Donald H. Sanders was trained and educated as an architect (B.Arch., Western Reserve University) and an archaeologist (Ph.D., Columbia University). His special interest is the application of nontraditional methods (including advanced computer graphics, virtual reality, and behavioral science techniques) to the study and presentation of architecture of the past. He is the founder and president of Learning Sites, Inc.

Katherine Welch is Associate Professor of Fine Arts at New York University's Institute of Fine Arts. She is an art historian with a particular interest in the art and archaeology of ancient Rome and Italy and is the author of *The Roman Amphitheater from Its Origins to the Colosseum*. She also has excavated in Cyprus, south Italy, and Greece, as well as in Turkey.

Index

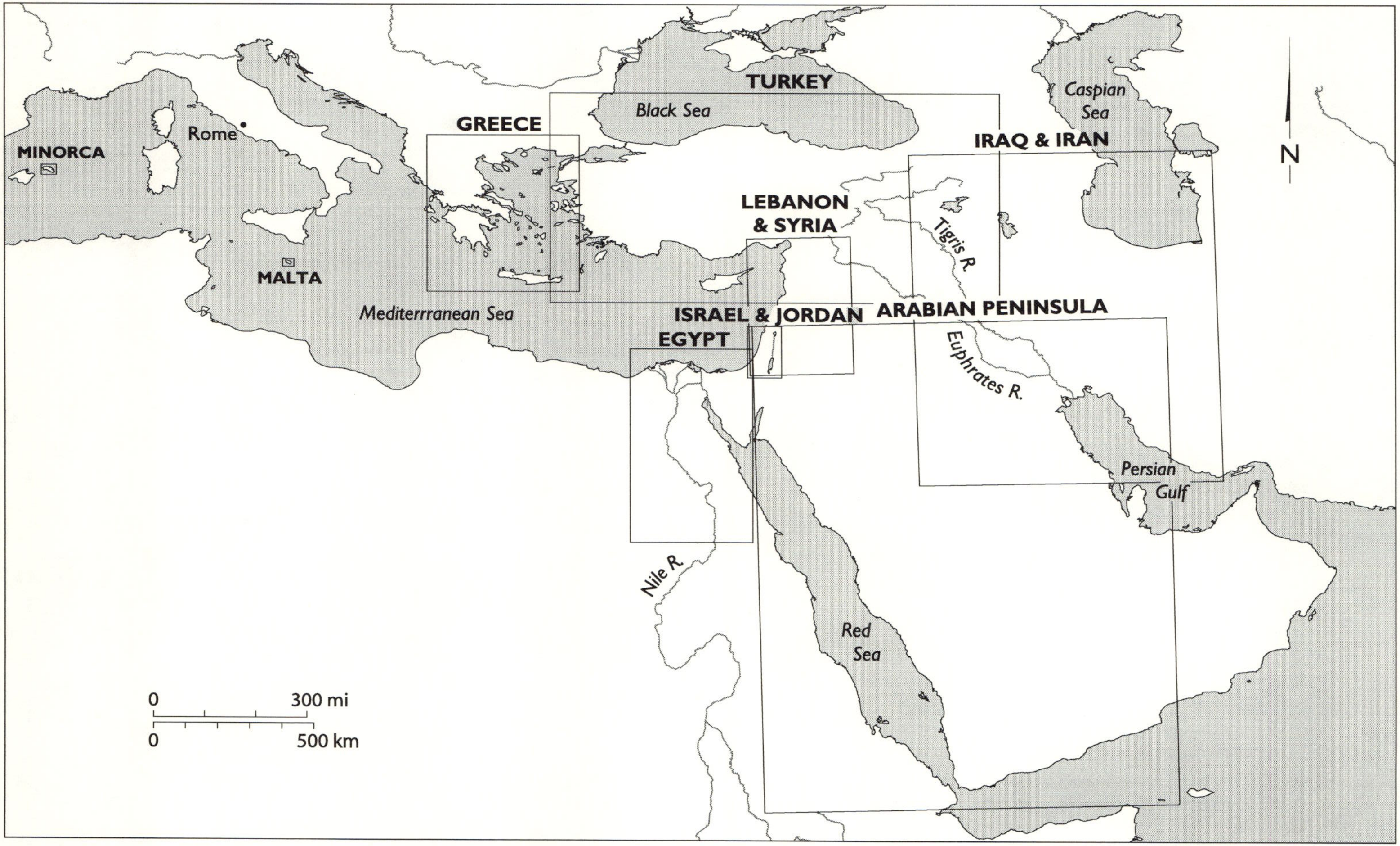

The Mediterranean Region and the Middle East

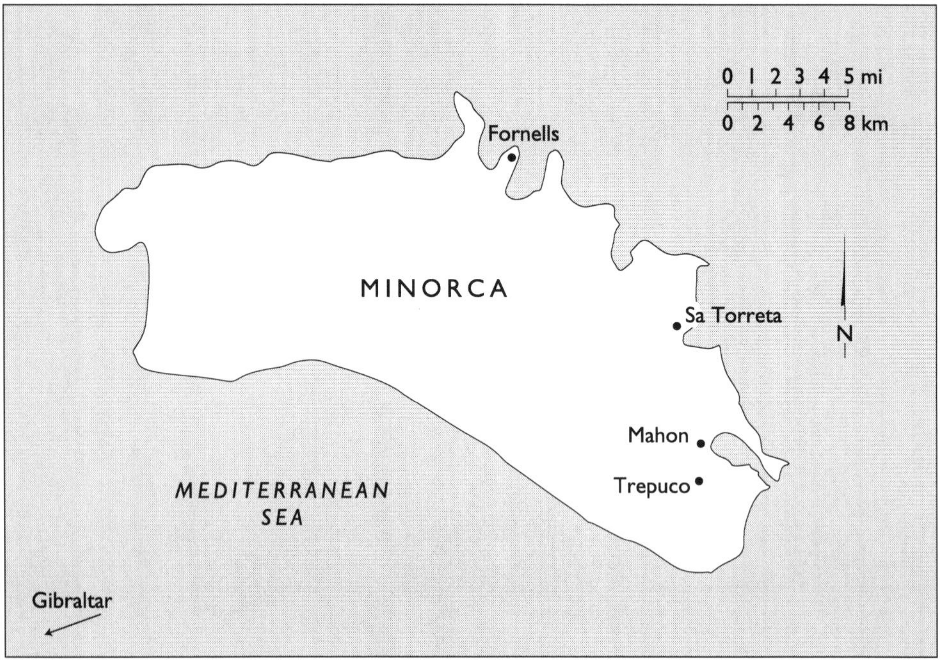

Minorca

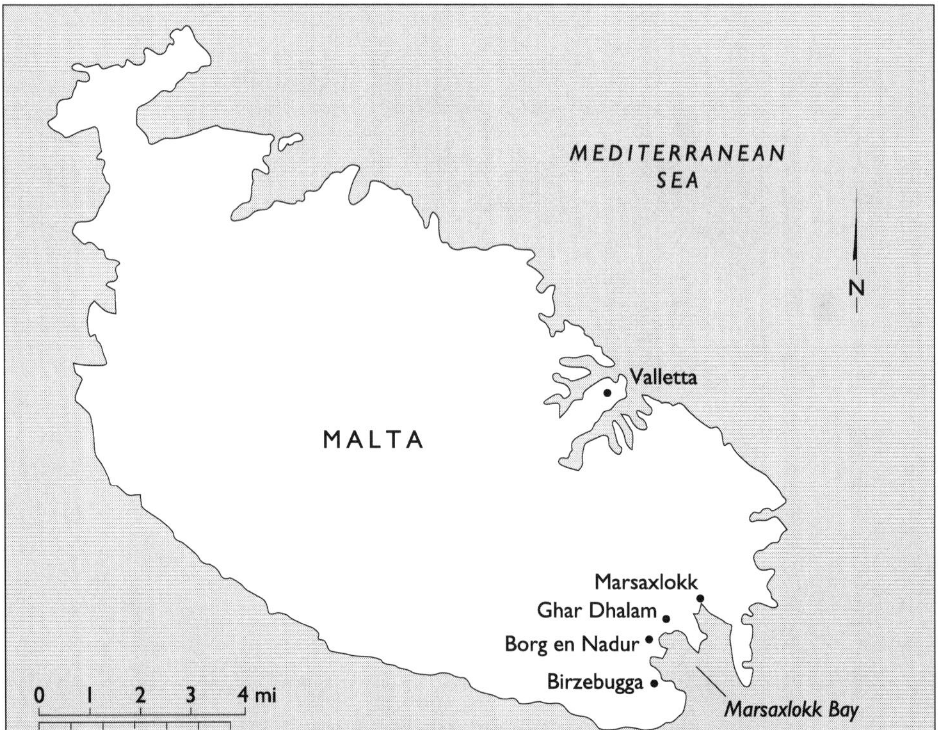

Malta

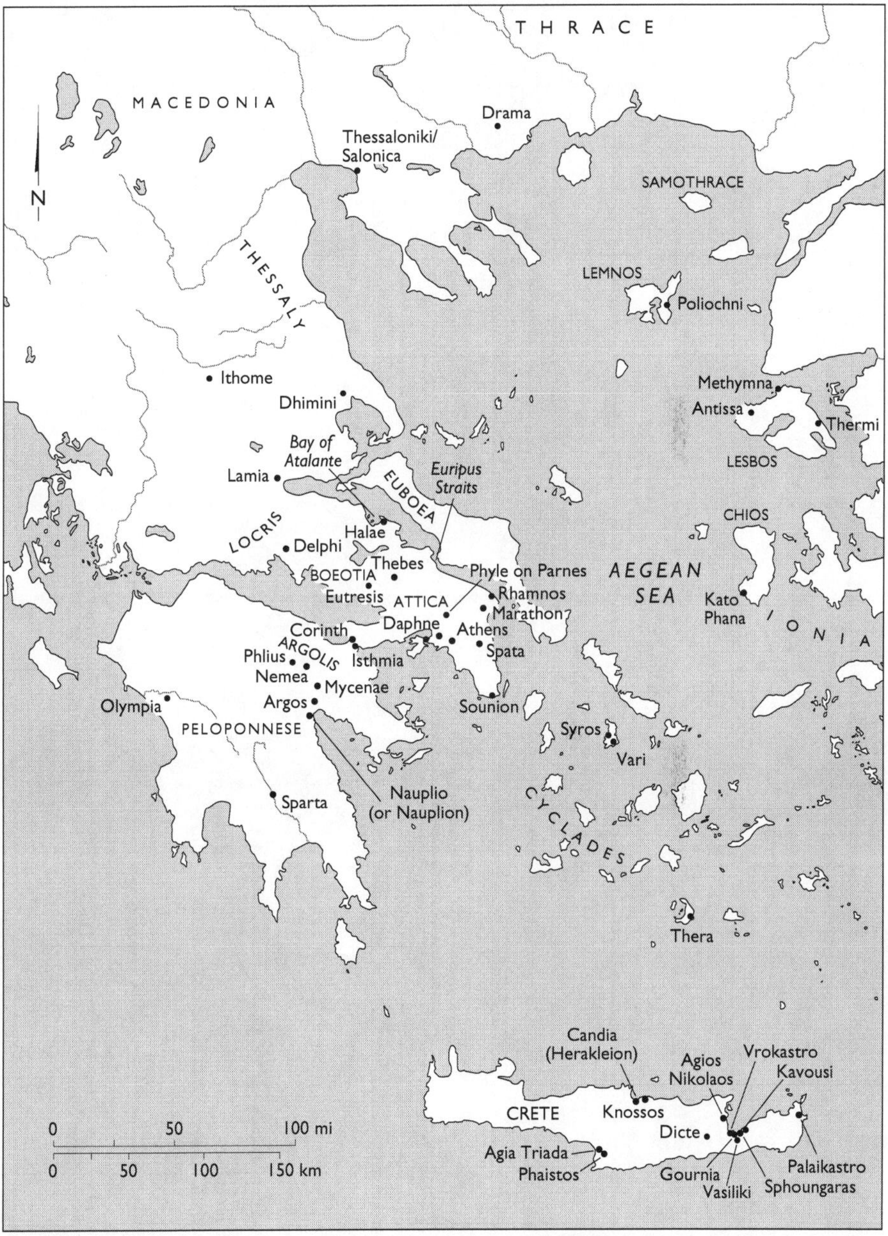
THRACE
MACEDONIA
N
Drama
Thessaloniki/
Salonica
SAMOTHRACE
THESSALY
LEMNOS
Poliochni
Ithome
Dhimini
Methymna
Antissa
Thermi
LESBOS
Bay of
Atalante
Lamia
EUBOEA
Euripus
Straits
CHIOS
LOCRIS
Halae
Delphi
Thebes
BOEOTIA
Phyle on Parnes
AEGEAN
SEA
Eutresis
ATTICA
Rhamnos
Marathon
Kato
Phana
IONIA
Daphne
Corinth
Athens
ARGOLIS
Spata
Phlius
Isthmia
Nemea
Mycenae
Argos
Sounion
Olympia
PELOPONNESE
Syros
Vari
Sparta
Nauplio
(or Nauplion)
CYCLADES
Thera
Candia
(Herakleion)
Agios
Nikolaos
Vrokastro
Kavousi
Knossos
CRETE
Dicte
0
50
100 mi
0
50
100
150 km
Agia Triada
Phaistos
Gournia
Vasiliki
Sphoungaras
Palaikastro

Greece

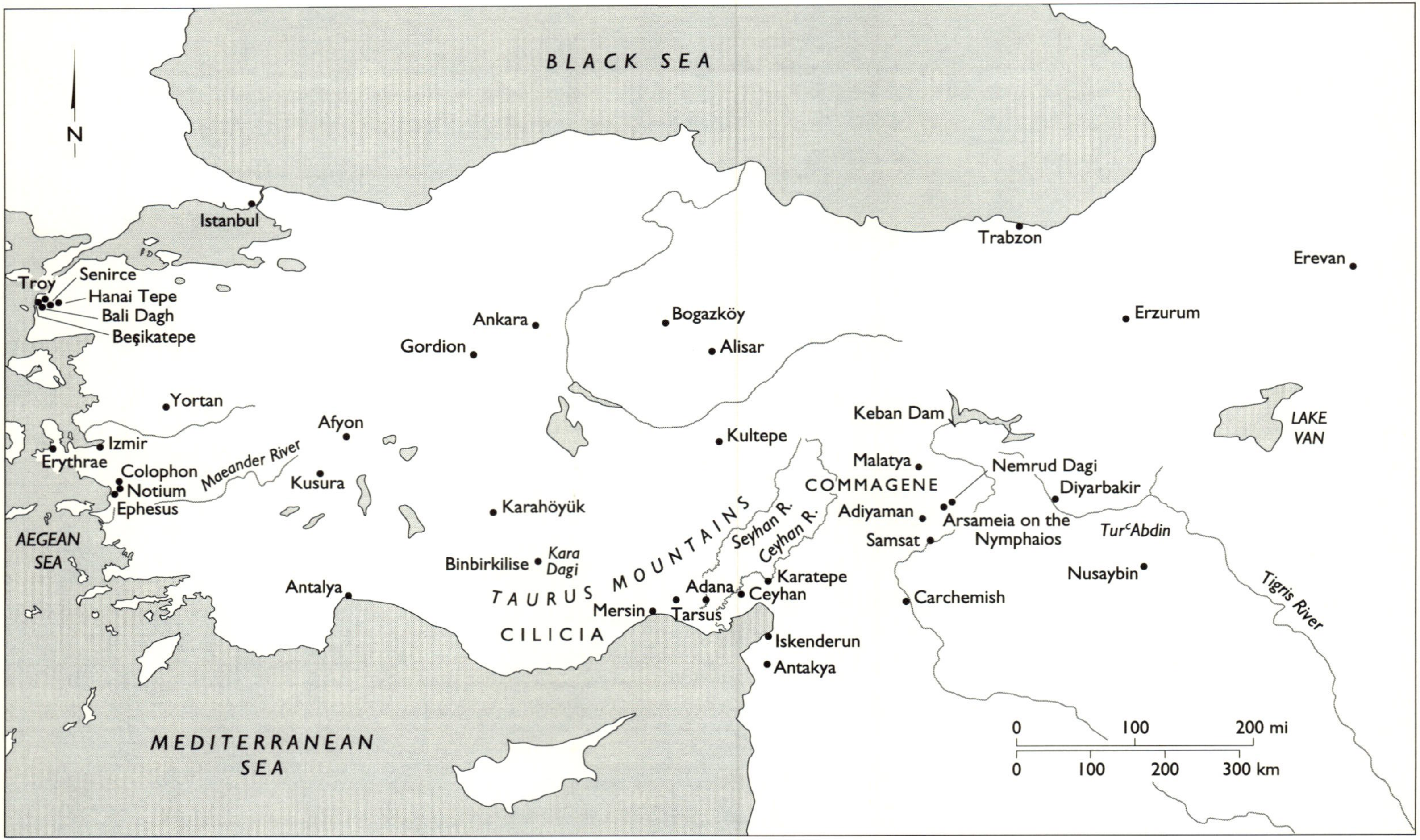
N
BLACK SEA
Istanbul
Trabzon
Erevan
Troy
Senirce
Hanai Tepe
Bali Dagh
Beşikatepe
Ankara
Gordion
Bogazköy
Alisar
Erzurum
Yortan
Afyon
Izmir
Erythrae
Colophon
Notium
Ephesus
Maeander River
Kusura
Karahöyük
Kultepe
Keban Dam
LAKE VAN
Malatya
Nemrud Dagi
COMMAGENE
Diyarbakir
Adiyaman
Arsameia on the Nymphaios
Samsat
Tur^cAbdin
Nusaybin
AEGEAN SEA
Binbirkilise
Kara Dagi
TAURUS MOUNTAINS
Seyhan R.
Ceyhan R.
Karatepe
Adana
Ceyhan
Antalya
Mersin
Tarsus
Carchemish
Tigris River
CILICIA
Iskenderun
Antakya
MEDITERRANEAN SEA
0 100 200 mi
0 100 200 300 km

Turkey

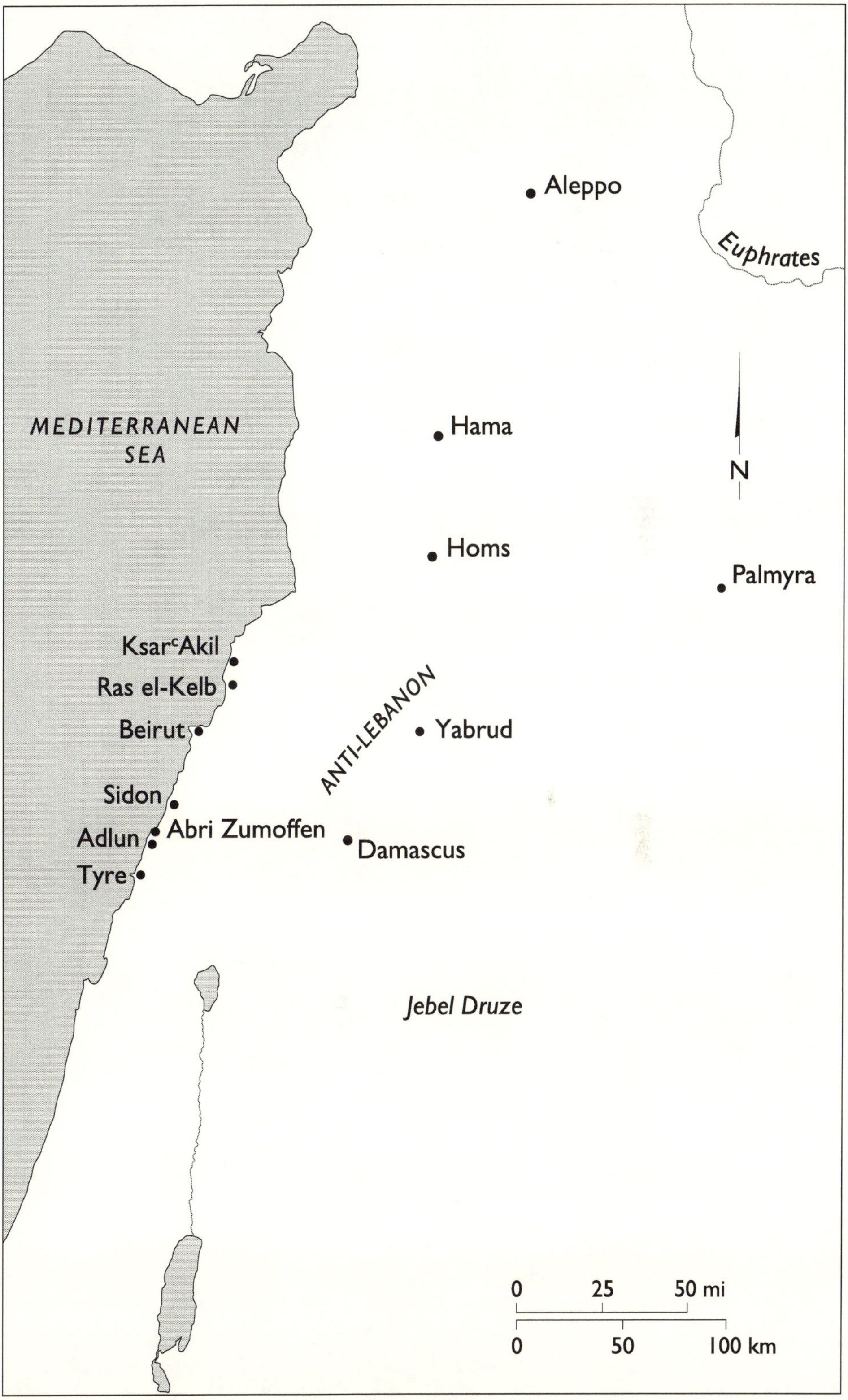

Lebanon and Syria

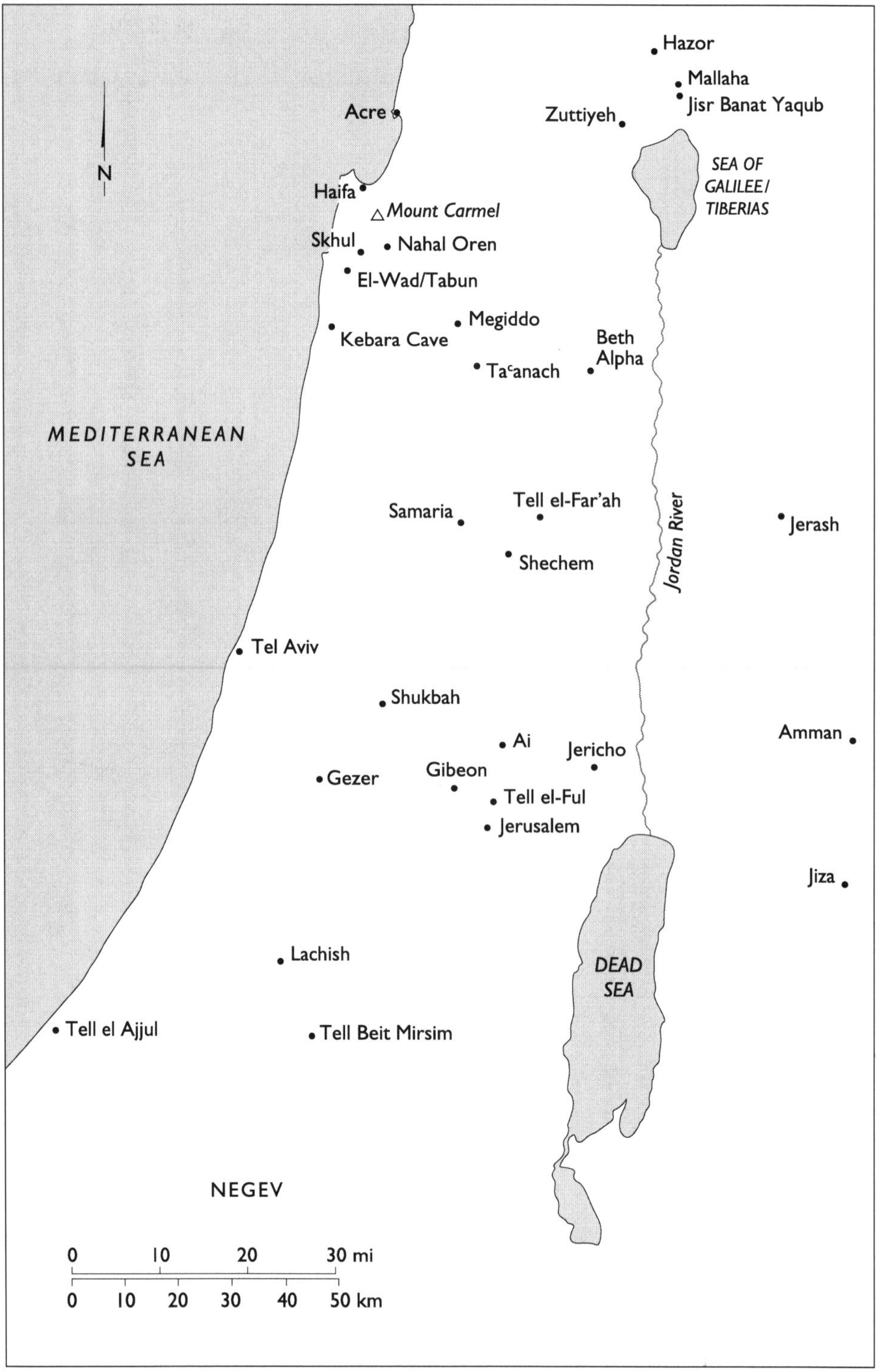

Israel and Jordan

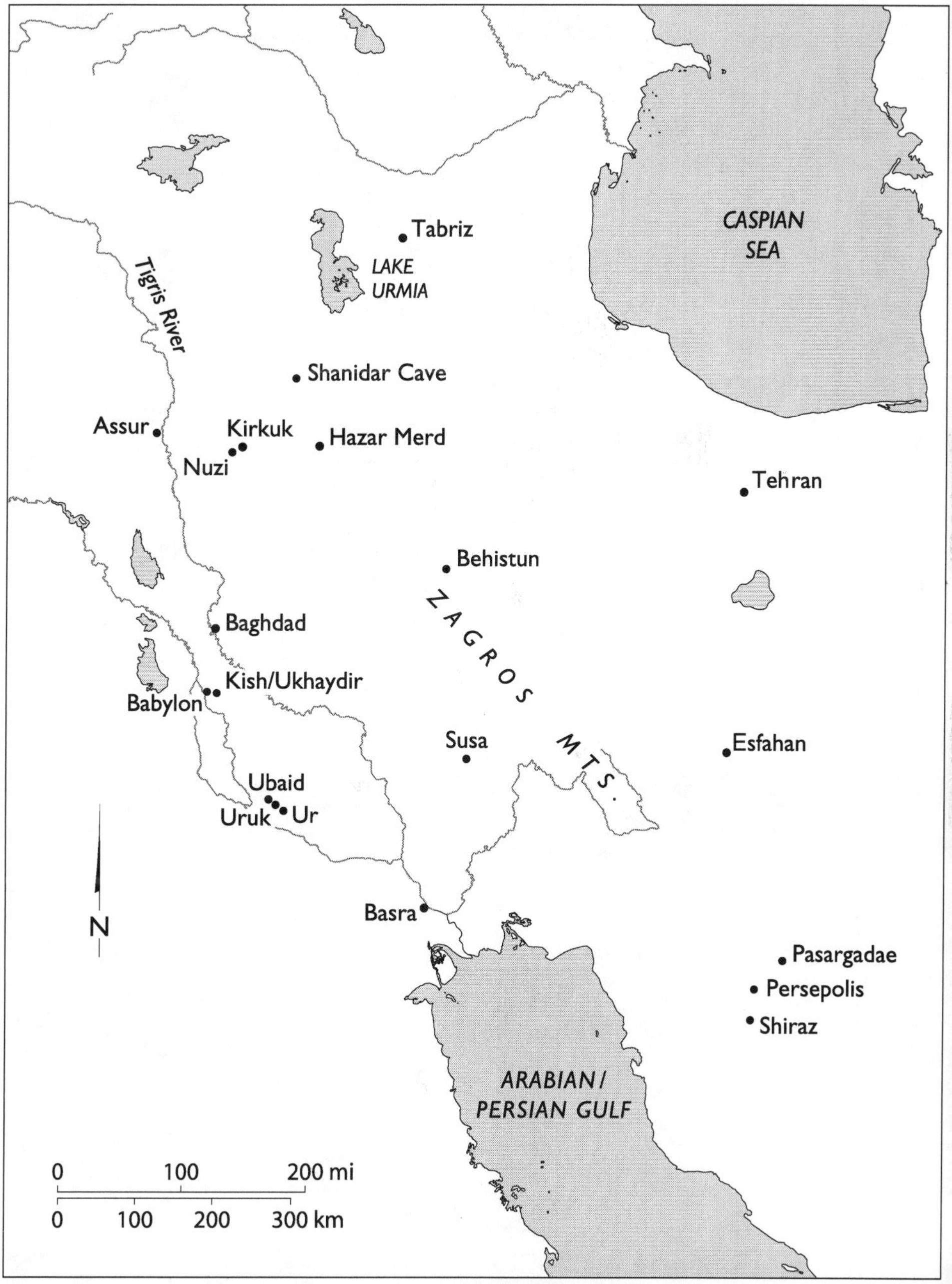

Iraq and Iran

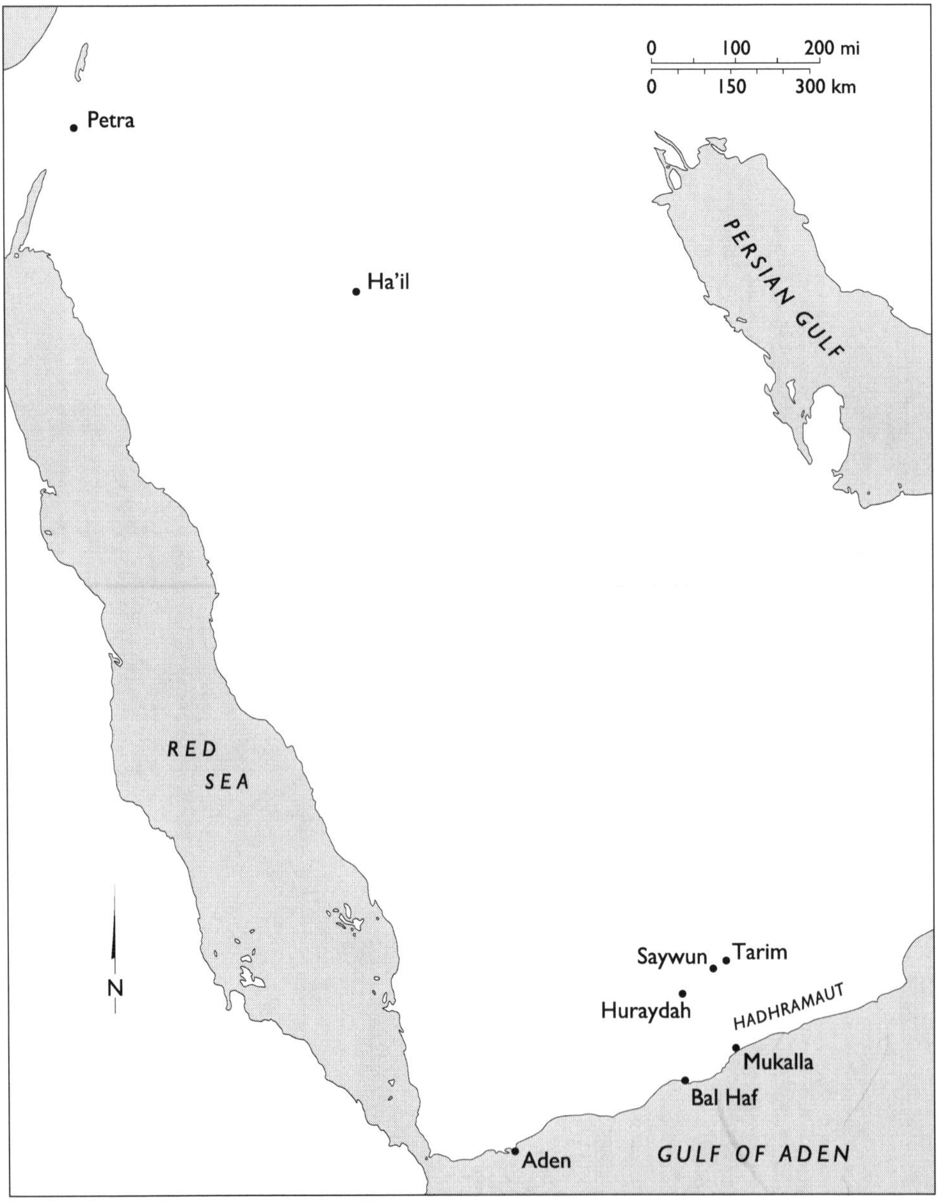

Arabian Peninsula

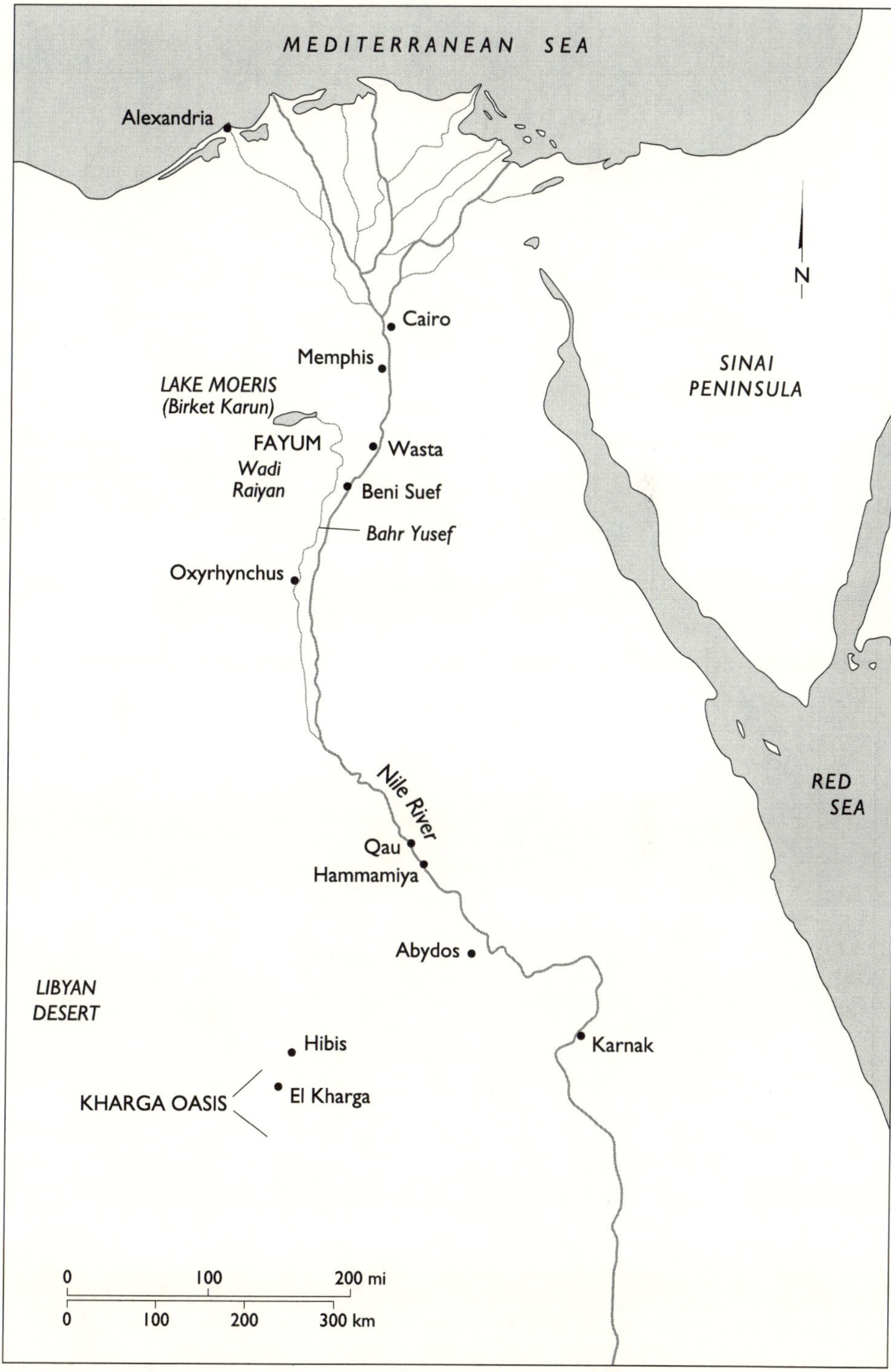
MEDITERRANEAN SEA
Alexandria
N
Cairo
Memphis
SINAI
PENINSULA
LAKE MOERIS
(Birket Karun)
FAYUM
Wasta
Wadi
Raiyan
Beni Suef
Bahr Yusef
Oxyrhynchus
Nile River
RED
SEA
Qau
Hammamiya
Abydos
LIBYAN
DESERT
Hibis
Karnak
KHARGA OASIS
El Kharga
0
100
200 mi
0
100
200
300 km

Egypt